The Life and Times of
General Andrew Pickens

The Life and Times of

GENERAL
ANDREW
PICKENS

Revolutionary War Hero,
American Founder

Rod Andrew Jr.

THE UNIVERSITY OF NORTH CAROLINA PRESS

Chapel Hill

Published with the assistance of the Fred W. Morrison
Fund of the University of North Carolina Press.

Cover illustration: portrait of Andrew Pickens courtesy of the Portrait
Collection of Historic Properties, Clemson University.

The University of North Carolina Press has been a member
of the Green Press Initiative since 2003.

LIBRARY OF CONGRESS CATALOGING-IN-PUBLICATION DATA
Names: Andrew, Rod, Jr.
Title: The life and times of General Andrew Pickens : Revolutionary
War hero, American founder / Rod Andrew Jr.
Description: Chapel Hill : University of North Carolina Press, [2017] |
Includes bibliographical references and index.
Identifiers: LCCN 2016036179 | ISBN 9781469631530 (cloth : alk. paper) |
ISBN 9781469672151 (pbk : alk. paper) | ISBN 9781469631547 (ebook)
Subjects: LCSH: Pickens, Andrew, 1739–1817. | Generals—
United States—Biography. | Legislators—United States—Biography. |
United States—History—Revolution, 1775–1783—Biography. |
United States—History—1783–1865—Biography.
Classification: LCC E207.P63 A63 2017 | DDC 975.7/03092 [B] —dc23
LC record available at https://lccn.loc.gov/2016036179

Contents

Figures & Maps

Preface

The old gentleman rode straight and stiff in the saddle into the village of Pendleton, South Carolina, one day in the late 1790s. He was about five feet ten inches tall, "quite lean & slender—quite ugly," one man remembered.[1] He was dressed simply and neatly, wearing a wide beaver hat. Virtually every person who noticed him would have immediately recognized him as General Andrew Pickens—hero of the Revolution, successful merchant and planter, respected judge, legislator, and Indian treaty commissioner. The general dismounted and conducted his business quietly and modestly. "He conversed but little," the observer noted, "and by no means freely; except with particular friends, and of these he was remarkably choice. And even with them, he was slow and guarded." Even on the few occasions when Pickens addressed other citizens publicly (and this was not one of them), his words were few, simple, and direct. There was no soaring oratory, no classical references, no rhetorical flourishes.

Pendleton itself was little more than a glorified crossroads, with a courthouse and a few stores and cabins around the town square and a Presbyterian church about three miles away. Located in the far northwest corner of the state, Pendleton was on the outer edge of white settlement in the area. Only fifteen years before, it had been Cherokee country, a place where, in time of war, no white man, woman, or child could have safely dwelled. Many of the white inhabitants of the area were veterans of the brutal, merciless, and seemingly never-ending war that had driven those Indians away. It was the same war that, in their view, had defeated the bloodthirsty, treasonous Tories and the red-coated brutish soldiers of a distant, hated king. Already they had forgotten the treachery and butchery that they themselves had inflicted on their Indian and Tory neighbors, but they did remember the courage and fortitude it had taken to prevail, and no man had exhibited more valor, honesty of purpose, and implacable will than the old general himself.

He was one of them. Like Pickens, many of his neighbors were ethnically Scotch-Irish, nearly all of them Presbyterians or members of other dissenting, non-Anglican sects. Many of their parents and grandparents had come from the north of Ireland and the wild, lawless borderlands between northern England and southwestern Scotland. For generations their ancestors had fought English kings, lords, and bishops, as well as rival countrymen, for survival, for vengeance, and for the right to worship as they chose. Many later migrated to Pennsylvania, where their quarrelsome ways quickly exhausted the patience of the peace-loving Quakers. From there they moved south and southwest into the sparsely occupied mountain valleys and foothills of Virginia and the Carolinas, attempting to tame the frontier as they carved out their own place with frequently hostile Indians on one side and condescending, neglectful colonial assemblies on the other.

Also like the people around him, the general had not started life with vast lands, wealth, or slaves. He enjoyed few educational advantages; he was functionally literate but not much more. Then, either by God's favor or his own merit, it seemed, he had prospered, accumulating wealth and profiting by the spread of slavery into the western portions of the state. Even as slavery was growing and making some in their region richer, however, there was debate and soul-searching within their churches as to what God's will might be when it came to owning other human beings.

Religion was important to these Calvinists and evangelicals, formerly "dissenters" to the established church. Many, like the general, had been born or come of age while the fires of the Great Awakening were still smoldering in the American colonies, and the new nation was on the verge of a second national revival that would have an even greater impact than the first. They still believed in a God who would hold them accountable for their conduct, both as individuals and as a people, but who also offered forgiveness and new life through repentance and faith. The general himself had been a devout Presbyterian all his life—sober, upright, and pious. In every new place he settled, as he helped push the frontier westward, he had been a founding member and elected elder of the local congregation, just as he was at the church on the outskirts of town.

While the recent struggle had inflicted all the horrors of civil war on the South Carolina backcountry, there had been much of the heroic in the general's and the people's fight for republican liberty. At one point, by the summer of 1780, South Carolina was essentially conquered by men loyal to the king. Many of those on the Whig side were arrested, hounded from their homes, or forced to take oaths of allegiance. When the British occupation proved to be more onerous than promised, when their oaths of allegiance did not protect them from oppression, they had renounced their assurances to the king's officers and risen up again. All over the province, but especially in the backcountry, small farmers and frontiersmen turned out in large numbers to avenge the attacks of the Tories and the British soldiers and their Indian allies. Battle by battle, ambush by raid, led by fierce, determined men like the general, they had retaken the state and joined in the fight to liberate their neighboring states of Georgia and North Carolina. Their determination was decisive in the ultimate outcome of the American Revolution. Pickens had made a name for himself as a militia officer during the first five years of the conflict. After the British overwhelmed Whig resistance in the spring of 1780, Pickens had accepted parole like most others. In fact, when patriot resistance sprang back to life that summer, Pickens had been slow to renounce his oath to the British authorities, strictly observing his parole until his own family and plantation were attacked by marauding Tories. Then he had rejoined the cause and become one of the most important militia leaders on the southern frontier, playing a leading role in victories at Cowpens, Augusta, Eutaw, and dozens of smaller actions.

Among themselves, the people of the backcountry enjoyed a form of rough equality. But even among this proud, egalitarian lot, the old general enjoyed universal respect. On this day, as was his habit, he moved slowly about the village square, "with as much solemnity as if at church . . . every one giving way & addressing him respectfully, and he once in a while, touching his [hat]—occasionally meeting with, and taking by the hand, an old friend, with a little commonplace conversation, & then pass[ing] on. Thus would he spend two or three hours," his fellow citizen remembered, "and then mount & away." The observer continued, "Gen. Pickens was a rare instance of merit receiving its full and just reward."[2]

William Martin recorded his admiring description of Andrew Pickens, including the general's occasional visits to downtown Pendleton, in 1843. One senses that while Martin idolized Pickens as a hero of the new Republic, he wished that he had known him better. In fact, Andrew Pickens was a man whom few knew well. He spoke little and wrote little, and when he did he disclosed little about his inner self. More than two centuries later, it is no less difficult to get into the heart and mind of this hero of the Revolution. Even Pickens's contemporaries recognized that he was a man whose actions spoke louder than his words. Therefore, I have tried to identify persistent themes and courses of action in Pickens's life and use them to better understand who he was. The challenge is a difficult one, but the potential rewards are great. Pickens's life can tell us a great deal about the times in which he lived and what he and his contemporaries most valued. It reveals or clarifies much about the settlement and growth of the southern backcountry; the bloody civil war conducted there in the struggle for independence; how the people who won that war passionately embraced their newfound freedom while simultaneously profiting from slavery; the virtues they hoped to see in their leaders and fellow citizens; and how they viewed their Indian neighbors who were often enemies, often trading partners, and occasionally—as in Pickens's case—friends.

In this book's first chapters covering Pickens's early life, I introduce three themes—liberty, order, and virtue—that are fundamental to the rest of the narrative. "Liberty" meant the freedom to pursue economic gain and to worship and speak as one chose with minimal interference. Early eighteenth-century Americans, including the large Scotch-Irish population to which Pickens belonged, were at first a bit more likely to think of that freedom as it applied to families. These recent Presbyterian emigrants from Ireland worshipped in family groups, and they also made their migrations with a mind to establish the prosperity of their families and to ensure that there would be enough land to support all their sons' families as they came of age. They did not move south and west simply to escape English authority but to claim and clear productive land, build mills and stores, and establish trading enterprises. Within Pickens's own lifetime, this pattern of family migrations began to break down, and more and more Americans moved to new lands without necessarily accompanying their parents, siblings, or cousins. In other words, they began to pursue economic gain more as individuals rather than exclusively as families. Throughout the period, though, a fundamental component of liberty was the right to pursue economic gain without undue hindrance.

"Order" meant the wise and efficient enforcement of just laws. Earlier scholarship on the American frontier in general (and on the Scotch-Irish in particular) has made much of its lawlessness. Perhaps, as more recent scholarship has shown, this was largely because the leading citizens of that frontier so frequently complained of it. They continually petitioned the colonial assemblies and royal authorities for courts, sheriffs, and military forces to protect them from the ruffians, bandits, and Indians who made frontier life so dangerous. Without order, families were not safe, and neither were the crops, mills, stores, and commerce that liberty made possible.

The emphasis on the enforcement of just laws did not mean, however, that colonial white settlers on the frontier understood order in purely secular, legalistic ways. Americans, particularly those raised in the Calvinist tradition, such as Congregationalists and Presbyterians, also understood order and even the law itself in moral terms. An orderly and moral congregation—and society—depended upon the collective and individual morality of its members. Thus, both liberty and order depended on the private and public virtue of the people. Without virtue, the search for liberty became destructive of the public order. Immoral men, in search of their own happiness, committed adultery and robbery; they oppressed the freedom of other men in order to expand their own autonomy and power. Society thus descended into anarchy and no one was safe. Liberty, order, and virtue were fully interdependent.

Despite the fact that Pickens wrote no religious tracts, religion plays a critical role in this biography. I believe this approach is justified by the facts of Pickens's life and by his contemporaries' comments about his piety and devotion to the Presbyterian church. Wherever Pickens moved in his adult life—Long Cane, Pendleton, and then Tamassee, South Carolina—he helped organize a new congregation, became one of its main financial supports, and assumed the formal role of church elder. Contemporaries usually noted his prominence as a lay leader when they mentioned his church or Pickens himself. Those who knew him particularly well and stayed as guests at his house recorded that he was strict in holding daily family devotions and reading scripture, so it seems clear that Pickens took his faith very seriously. Some of Pickens's pastors made their political opinions obvious by their vocal support of the Whig cause in the American Revolution and by actually shouldering arms in the ranks of the patriot militia. Others clearly enunciated their outlook on republicanism, virtue, social and moral order, citizenship, and slavery, and their opinions were fairly uniform with that of other American Presbyterians, except perhaps on the divisive issue of slavery. None of Pickens's political or economic behavior or any of his sparse political commentary suggests that he disagreed with these clergymen, so it is possible to reach reasonable conclusions about Pickens's own beliefs. As a devout Presbyterian, Pickens shared his coreligionists' assumption that Christian worship and doctrine was vital for public and private virtue and therefore to liberty and order. Accordingly, the Scotch-Irish established churches wherever more than a few families settled, and Pickens himself was a church elder and founder for most of his adult life.

Protestant Reformed doctrine stressed that man's inborn propensity for sin was the primary threat to virtue, order, and liberty; human nature ensured that the world was generally a chaotic, dangerous, and sinful place. Real life reflected doctrine for Pickens himself, for he came of age in a turbulent world. He witnessed violent death at an early age and spent a great deal of his life fighting bandits, plunderers, Tories, British soldiers, and Indians. And he learned early that even those who fought alongside him were prone to tyranny, cruelty, and inhumanity, whether they were members of the Regulator movement in the pre-Revolutionary backcountry, patriot militiamen exacting vengeance on their Tory neighbors, or other white men as they murdered Indians and violated treaties—honest agreements that he himself had negotiated with Native American tribes. And, in the latter half of his life, many Americans, including Presbyterians in the South, began to question whether it was virtuous to suppress the liberty of Africans in order to more fully enjoy one's own.

During Pickens's lifetime, English-speaking Americans were attempting to create a new type of society. The entire project of overthrowing monarchy and replacing it with a republic revolved around the question of how to protect liberty, order, and virtue without kings and the principle of hereditary authority. Pickens and his contemporaries did not reject the principle of authority itself but rather sought to construct new bases for it. As Americans of the Revolutionary era extended citizenship and genteel status to more white men—some of whom, like Pickens, were originally from the middling ranks—they did not do the same for women, blacks, or Indians. As they asserted their right to lead, both established and emerging elites benefited from existing assumptions about gender and race, and they also perpetuated them. The disorder and violence of the Revolutionary War itself often prevented women from exercising agency and resulted in their victimization and dependence on male protection. And some white Americans began emphasizing the racial differences between themselves and blacks and Indians even more in order to justify slavery and western expansion. As social historians of the period have reminded us, investing white men with citizenship and elite status meant denying those advantages to others.

America's new republican elites based their claims to authority not just on their race and gender, however, but also on their claims to virtue. Calvinist doctrine merged with Enlightenment ideals—which on the surface were more secular—to create the political philosophy of republicanism. As American elites of the 1780s solidified their own authority, they were also trying to construct an entirely new political order in which liberty and order were protected by men selected to lead because of their "virtue" rather than their lineage. They had no illusions about the difficulty of their task. The evangelical tradition told them that men were naturally prone to sin and to violate the rights of their fellow men. Yet the Revolutionary generation had also inherited a classical republican tradition that said that republics were impossible, and therefore so was liberty, unless at least some men could be counted on to rise above their own selfish interests. The state must find virtuous men who devoted themselves to the welfare and liberties of their fellow citizens.[3] Many devout Americans hoped the gospel of Christ would help restrain vice, but they also looked to the vigilance and courage of human beings. Men had to be ready to take up arms to fight Indians, frontier bandits, or the hireling soldiers of a tyrant king. Leaders had to announce a course of action, enlist recruits, pursue the enemy, and fight. Times of disorder and rampant vice required the services of those who were, in Pickens's words, "brave and active" or men of "courage and action."[4] Pickens's success in rising from frontier obscurity to a hero of the new Republic resulted from his contemporaries' consensus that he was virtuous and that he could be counted on to defend liberty and fight disorder. This was the selfless public virtue of the new model republican citizen—a new ideal for political and social leadership in the public sphere.

Closely intertwined with the term "virtue" is "honor." The two words were related in Pickens's day as well, though not in exactly the same ways as now. Cultural historians have paid careful attention to the ethical system of "honor" in eighteenth- and nineteenth-century America. Honor provided an ethical code that profoundly influenced the behavior and self-image of Americans, especially white men, who hoped to enjoy respect and social status among their peers and dependents. According to some scholars, honor was external—in other words, honor was public reputation; it was the status and respect that one's neighbors and peers accorded to an individual based on perception of his courage, integrity, independence of will, patriotism, and physical and social power. The public also considered an "honorable" man to be someone who was willing and able to defend his and his family's reputations, as well as their persons. "Private" morality had nothing to do with one's honor unless private virtues and vices were publicly known. Indeed, it was virtually impossible for men to look inside themselves and persuade themselves of their own moral self-worth if the community refused to accord it to them. Faced with insult and disgrace, their only options were violent expressions of vindication, such as duels or other forms of combat, or self-exile from the community. In his influential study *Southern Honor: Ethics and Behavior in the Old South*, Bertram Wyatt-Brown defines "honor" by contrasting it with "dignity," a new, competing ethic that recognized the intrinsic moral worth of every human being. Wyatt-Brown asserts that "dignity" had its roots in evangelical religion and began to transform the antebellum North long before it affected the values and customs of southerners. In dignity, a man could persuade himself of his own moral self-worth rather than be measured by public approval or disgrace.[5]

Other historians have been less willing to emphasize the dichotomy between "private" morality and public reputation. Joanne B. Freeman's study of honor in the new Republic, for example, concedes that "reputation . . . an identity as determined by others . . . was not unlike honor." However, honor was "reputation with a moral dimension." Partly it consisted of social rank, but it also included "character . . . personality with a moral dimension, referring to the mixture of traits, vices, and virtues that determined a person's social worth." And the standards of behavior to which a man of honor must adhere were not purely external; they could also come from religious or moral conviction, or "higher" law. An honorable gentleman, explains Freeman, was someone "whose strength of character ensured that his word was his pledge; it was not the civil law, but the higher, *self-imposed* law of honor that governed his actions and made him a trustworthy and reliable man among equals" (emphasis added).[6] Indeed, a man who allowed his actions to be entirely governed by public approval rather than by inner moral conviction was not independent at all and therefore not honorable.

I have chosen to rely mainly on the term "virtue" rather than "honor" in this book. Partly this is because of the increasingly complicated use of the latter term in modern scholarship, and partly it is because Pickens never participated in the type of behavior still most commonly associated with Revolutionary era or antebellum southern "honor"—that is, fighting duels or giving and receiving "challenges." And finally it is because I suspect that Andrew Pickens was a man who was driven to a large extent by his inner convictions. Like most human beings, Pickens certainly did care about his public reputation, and undoubtedly he was influenced by his own generation's perceptions of what constituted ethical and admirable behavior. But it seems to me that his deep religious convictions also equipped—or at least allowed—him to assess his own moral worth independent of public

Preface

opinion. In one of his rare introspective comments about his own life, Pickens wrote to Henry Lee in 1814, "I leave it to my Country to say, whether in my public transactions, I have discharged the duties assigned me with honesty & fidelity & whether I have been an humble instrument in the hand of Providence, to its advantage—But whatever the *public* sentiment may be I have a *witness within myself* that my public life & conduct have been moved & actuated by an ardent zeal for the welfare & happiness of my beloved Country" (emphasis added).[7] And in the most detailed description of Pickens by a man who knew him well, William Martin suggested that people admired him for his private virtue as well as for his public service. The old general, Martin claimed, was "mild" in his domestic relations and was someone who lived a "long and well spent life in public and private employment; so that he became proverbial for honesty & fidelity."[8]

I try to illuminate these themes of liberty, order, and virtue as the narrative proceeds through each chronological phase of Pickens's life, beginning with his family's migrations to America and through the southern backcountry before he came of age. Pickens's rise as a backcountry merchant, planter, church elder, and justice of the peace in Ninety Six District in the 1760s and early 1770s occurred against the backdrop of a search for order in the late colonial southern backcountry. Richard N. Brown and Rachel Klein have each ably described the rise of a backcountry elite of "leading men" who acquired larger than average landholdings, built mills and stores, and even obtained small numbers of slaves. Brown and Klein show that these men were anxious to suppress crime (robbery, arson, kidnapping, theft, and prostitution) and near-anarchy in the wake of the Cherokee War (1760–61) by lobbying the provincial capital in Charleston for sheriffs, courts, and military protection and by forming extralegal paramilitary units of "Regulators."[9] Both authors emphasize the economic interests of these leading men of the backcountry. Ultimately, the establishment of courts and lawful order was designed to safeguard their economic concerns. I agree that this was part of their motivation but suggest that Pickens's story shows that they were driven by moral and religious sensibility as well, not to mention by a natural concern for the safety of their families.[10]

In their coverage of Pickens's role in the American Revolution, previous biographies have understandably celebrated his battlefield achievements and noted his leadership ability. At the "Ring Fight" of 1776 and the battles of Kettle Creek, Cowpens, Eutaw, and Augusta; during his numerous forays into Cherokee country; and in his leadership of the loosely organized but resilient frontier militia, Pickens stood out for his tactical skill, logistical sense, and sometimes just plain good luck. He also seemed to have a quiet confidence and implacable determination that influenced other men to follow him, including militiamen and unpaid partisans. Pickens's achievements also demonstrate the military importance of the backcountry militia in denying resources and recruits to British and Tory forces, something noted half a century ago in Clyde Ferguson's massive dissertation on Pickens.[11]

There are many more important things to say, however, about Andrew Pickens and the American Revolution. The first question that must be addressed is why Pickens joined the Whig cause, early and enthusiastically. If Pickens valued order, why did he participate in a revolution? I have tried to answer this question in several ways. First, I have pointed out, as have others, the widespread preference for the Whig cause among Presbyterians during the American Revolution. In South Carolina, this tendency for Presbyterians to support the new Whig regime in Charleston rather than the ousted royal authorities was noticeable by 1775 and unmistakable by the summer of 1780. Most historians are convinced by anecdotal evidence from both American and British sources that Presbyterians and their Congregationalist coreligionists in New England were near the forefront of the American Revolution. Indeed, for more than a century, there had been little love lost between Scottish and Irish Presbyterians and English Puritans on the one hand and Anglican British monarchs on the other. These Calvinist groups readily absorbed portrayals of the monarchy and royal court as corrupt and prone to tyranny. John Calvin himself had left little room for rebellion against secular authorities in his sixteenth-century writings. By the time of the Revolution, however, the Calvinist emphasis on the depravity of man inspired a great distrust for monarchical government and a corresponding embrace of republicanism. Indeed, some historians point out that there was so much overlap between Calvinist doctrine and eighteenth-century republicanism that it was "difficult to discern where one left off and the other began."[12] The pervasiveness of anti-monarchical, republican sentiment in American Presbyterianism makes it unsurprising that Pickens embraced it as well. Moreover, there is abundant anecdotal evidence of Presbyterians in the Ninety Six and Long Cane area, including Pickens's kinsmen and local clergymen, joining the patriot cause and taking up arms.[13]

Another way to explain Pickens's Whig sympathies is to recognize that many Whigs saw support for the patriot cause as a way of defending public order and the physical security of the frontier, not as a rebellion against legitimate authority. The American Revolution came early to South Carolina. By 1774, royal government was no longer functioning in the province. With Whig revolutionaries controlling the machinery of government, it was loyalists who had to prove they were not "disaffected" with good government by supporting a boycott of British goods and signing a Revolutionary document called the "Association." The final straw for many Whig-leaning backcountry residents was the surprise attacks launched by Cherokee Indians on South Carolina's western settlements in 1776. Some white men had defected to the Cherokees and actually participated in the attacks; all were identified as loyalists. In the eyes of Pickens and many others, the king himself had unleashed terror and anarchy against his own subjects rather than providing protection and order. For all of these reasons, many backcountry leaders saw support for the Revolutionary cause as a bid for order and good government, not as rebellion.

What is lacking in previous Pickens biographies, I believe, is a holistic understanding of the war in the backcountry, a civil war in which militia and partisan forces were the key elements in the larger project of defending and restoring civil order and security. Modern counterinsurgency operations have generally shown that victory in such a war usually goes to the side that can provide security to the population. This is something that Pickens, as a resident of the area in which he primarily fought, intuitively understood. Pickens fought well in several pitched battles against British regulars, but his more frequent and arguably more important enemies were local Tories and nearby Cherokees and Creeks who could appear suddenly to steal, rob, kidnap, murder, scalp, and burn, as well as disrupt the gathering of crops and local trade. In fact, this study will be attuned to what recent studies have shown—that the Indian tribes were not peripheral to the American Revolution in the South but rather central to it, and that the more pressing concern for Whigs in interior districts was usually not the British army but their Tory neighbors, whom they saw not as defenders of order but rather as threats to it. Consequently, long after Nathanael Greene's and George Washington's Continental forces ceased sparring with British regulars in 1781, Pickens's war in the backcountry continued. For him and his neighbors, the war was not over until the Indian threat was crushed, backcountry Tory bandits were killed or driven away, courts were reopened, and civil order was restored.

One element of Pickens's military leadership that has gone relatively unnoticed was his rare ability as a militia officer to work well with

Continental army officers such as Daniel Morgan, Nathanael Greene, and Henry Lee. Unlike the majority of militia officers, especially the resilient but fractious Thomas Sumter, Pickens had little difficulty cooperating with Continental officers and rarely felt the need to assert his autonomy against them. At Cowpens, in the North Carolina campaign of early 1781, and during the siege of Augusta, the siege of Ninety Six, and the Eutaw campaign, Pickens proved not only that his troops were effective in the militia's counterinsurgency role but also that he could lead them well in conventional-style battles alongside Continental regulars.

Even during the height of the chaotic, murderous war on the southern frontier, Pickens, a partisan leader, often appeared as a force of order and restraint rather than as one of lawlessness. When South Carolina appeared conquered after the British capture of Charleston in May 1780, Pickens, like many other patriot leaders, laid down his arms and signed a parole rather than continued with guerrilla warfare. He was one of the last important partisan leaders to break his parole and did so only when it was obvious, first, that the British had violated the parole agreement by making additional demands on former Whig-minded subjects and, second, that pillaging, plunder, oppression, and disorder only increased under British and Tory rule. Later, he objected strongly to killings of captured Tories, despite the torture and murder of one of his own brothers who had served in the patriot militia.

After the war, Pickens participated in the restoration of civil order at the local, state, and national levels and promoted the establishment of counties, townships, courts, schools, and churches in the previously Cherokee-dominated northwestern portion of South Carolina. He was a justice of the peace, church elder and delegate to the Presbyterian Synod of the Carolinas, rising planter and merchant, state legislator, and congressman. As the ranking militia officer in the backcountry, he commanded all the state militia in the western portion of the state. Most notably, he served as a federal Indian treaty commissioner and boundary commissioner many times between 1785 and 1802 and was continuously involved in Indian-white relations on the southern frontier throughout that period.

Thus much of the book emphasizes the process by which Pickens was accepted into the ranks of South Carolina's political elite. To cross the line into gentility in the late colonial and early Republic periods, men from the yeoman and tradesman ranks had to amass a certain measure of wealth, enough to be free from manual labor and from the caprice of others. Several historians have explained, however, that just as important was the acquisition of urbane tastes, literary knowledge, and polished manners. Especially admired was the ability to display wit and to engage in repartee mingled with modesty and prudence in conversation. Other signs of gentility were one's dress and the architecture and furnishings of one's house.

Pickens emerged from his previous non-elite status at the end of the Revolutionary War as a respected gentleman entrusted with many of the public offices associated with that rank—general, judge, state legislator, congressman, and diplomat. In doing so, he managed to acquire several attributes of gentility but not others. Pickens appreciated the value of books and education, for example, but possessed little of either. By his own admission, he lacked literary knowledge. His "Hopewell" house, built in the 1780s, was not ostentatious but did have some of the marks of a "genteel" house—a "double cell" floor plan instead of one large room per floor, as well as a broad porch. The same was true of his dress as a legislator and justice of the peace: knee breeches and white stockings, frilled shirt, tricornered hat, and a brace of pistols—neat but not flamboyant. He was not eloquent in writing nor sophisticated in speech. His bearing and demeanor suggested taciturn, grim self-confidence but never aristocratic grace.[14]

Yet he had other qualities that white Americans admired. In an age in which aristocratic gentility had to accommodate growing egalitarianism and the search for republican virtue, Pickens was an example of how to mediate between the two.[15] Pickens's contemporaries believed he possessed the private morality, self-control, and public-minded selflessness that were supposed to define republican leadership. Also, during the Revolutionary War, a time in which military skill and valor became almost the sine qua non of the patriot, Pickens had proved himself as an excellent military officer who was respected by friends and foes alike. His status as an up-and-coming slaveholder and landholder also aided his acceptance among South Carolina's slaveholding elite. Rachel Klein has shown how wealthy planters from South Carolina's lowcountry were eager to form political and economic alliances with backcountry leaders like Pickens, despite their plebeian origins. Thus, it was not only wealth but also the converging interests of lowcountry aristocrats and emerging backcountry planters that could aid the latter in achieving the social status and political power reserved for gentlemen.

As a state legislator, Pickens did not directly challenge the leadership of lowcountry slaveholding elites. His goals, in fact, aligned closely with theirs. Pickens supported internal improvements such as ferries, roads, and bridges; promoted law and order through upholding the authority of sheriffs and tax collectors; and favored state support of educational and religious organizations. Klein has documented the alliance between lowcountry Federalists and backcountry Republicans like Pickens, though she does not make it clear that Pickens was more closely identified with the Federalists themselves, not the Republicans, until 1799 or 1800.[16]

As a congressman between 1793 and 1795, Pickens was relatively rare in being a southerner from an interior district who voted more often with the Federalists. He appreciated the need for active government that could establish legal and moral order in the new Republic—violence and vice had to be restrained. Only decisive leadership at the national level could provide a measure of justice for the Indians and thereby preserve order on the frontier. Treaties had to be obeyed, and Indians and whites who murdered each other had to be punished, not by acts of private vengeance but by the "strong hand of government."[17] The assumptions that brought Pickens to this viewpoint, however, did not necessarily match those of other Federalists. As a frontier fighter of yeoman origins, he had less use for the strands of Federalism that emphasized hierarchy and deference to one's social betters. And while he thought lawful authority must be obeyed, it did not have the right to restrict freedom of speech and conscience. When Federalism moved further in this direction at the end of the 1790s with the Alien and Sedition Acts, Pickens broke with it.

An updated analysis of Pickens's dealings with the Native American tribes in the South is long overdue. Much of the post–Revolutionary War section of this book studies Pickens's dealings with the Cherokees, Creeks, Chickasaws, and Choctaws. Previous generations of southerners, and biographers writing over half a century ago, recognized Pickens's important role as a peacemaker. Pickens was involved in numerous treaties, would-be treaties in which the negotiations failed, boundary-marking expeditions, correspondence with Cherokee and Creek leaders that aimed to avert war, and the mobilization of white militia units—not only in response to Creek attacks but also to protect delegations of Cherokee leaders traveling from the national capital in Philadelphia back to their villages.

At the time that Clyde Ferguson and Alice Noble Waring were completing their Pickens biographies in the early 1960s, a new wave of scholarship indicated that historians, and later the general public, were more aware than ever of the injustice inflicted on the Indians in the early history of the United States. Government officials, soldiers, and ordinary white settlers were all implicated in the campaign of fraud and violence that nearly destroyed Native American culture east of the Mississippi by the time of the Jacksonian period. More recently, some historians have noted that white

Americans were far from united in their approach to dealing with Indians. It is true that many, particularly in frontier areas, saw the very presence of Indians as a threat to liberty, order, and prosperity. Indians' claim to land they did not cultivate (according to white definitions) endangered the freedom of white Americans to become landowners and thereby stake their claim to full citizenship. This viewpoint, however, was not unanimous. A number of federal officials and a few elites in eastern states thought the greed and lawlessness of some states and western settlers threatened not only order and peace on the frontier but also the nation's honor—its claims to being a virtuous republic dedicated to law, humanity, and justice. This latter group consisted mostly of Federalists such as George Washington, Henry Knox, Benjamin Hawkins, and, most decidedly, Pickens himself. These men certainly had racial prejudices and generally believed that the Indians could not survive unless they adopted white ways. Many like Pickens, however, worked tirelessly to conclude treaties and mark boundaries that would protect Indian claims, impose order on the frontier, and prevent war. They bitterly complained about the aggressive policies of state governments and lawless frontier citizens—Pickens and others called them the "disorderly people"—who violated federal treaties, murdered inoffensive Indians, and attacked undefended villages.[18]

Though Pickens shared these federal and eastern leaders' views on Indian-white relations, he was unique among this faction in several ways. First, he was a westerner who leaned toward the Federalists rather than toward the Republicans until the late 1790s. Second, few of them were as exclusively identified with the frontier as was Pickens. And third, hardly any of the white leaders who fought hard for just treatment of the Indians had originally achieved fame and prominence as Indian fighters. Pickens's reputation as a scourge to the Cherokees was well established before he seemingly transformed into a peacemaker. Before he was a large landowner, legislator, or diplomat, Pickens had been a warrior who had participated in and personally led devastating campaigns against the Cherokees. By the mid-1780s, however, Indian leaders had already come to see him as an honest negotiator who was truly interested in peace. It is in Indian relations, in fact, that Pickens's acute moral sense is most evident from his own words. In many letters to state governors and fellow federal officials, he bitterly condemned other frontiersmen who massacred Indians, trespassed on their lands, and violated treaties. On one occasion in 1788, he reacted furiously to the killing of several Cherokee chiefs, including his friend The Tassel, by Tennessee militiamen carrying a white flag of truce. Pickens's protests over this incident helped lead to the arrest of Tennessee militia leader John Sevier several months later.

Pickens's Indian dealings were often complex, but I hope that my coverage of them illuminates two key ideas. The first theme is the extent to which some white leaders saw just treatment of the Indians as a moral problem. Second, Pickens's experience illustrates the recognition in several recent works that the conflict on the frontier was not just between whites and Indians; rather, it was also a complicated interaction between the conflicting goals of Indians, federal leaders, and white settlers and state governments such as North Carolina, Georgia, and Tennessee. Thus, racial hatred and the rapacious land hunger of whites was not the full story of Indian-white relations after the Revolution. Many elite Americans, including Pickens, believed that national honor and a morally defined political order required just and humane treatment of the Indians. Ultimately, of course, the United States as a whole failed to do justice to the native tribes, but there was a cohort of political leaders in the early Republic who hoped to conform Indian policy to principles of justice and humanity, not simply of self-interest, and who believed that only federal control of Indian policy could make that possible.[19]

This book also gives more careful attention to Pickens's involvement with slavery than previous biographies have. Older works rightly emphasize Pickens's strict piety but neglect critical analysis of how his Christian convictions coexisted with his acceptance of slavery and his emergence as a large slaveholder by backcountry standards. The most they offer are claims that he was a "kind" master, a statement for which there is some evidence. There is much more that can be said, however, for southern Presbyterians within Pickens's own presbytery and synod were wrestling with the question of slavery during the very period in which Pickens was becoming established as a slaveholder and, it seems, contemplating the manumission of his slaves. As an elder in his congregation and an occasional delegate to his presbytery and to the Synod of the Carolinas, Pickens undoubtedly participated in the debate, though he left no writings on the subject other than his will. This book examines these debates as closely as possible through church minutes and arguments of pro- and antislavery ministers, some of whom served Pickens's own congregation.

Pickens's rise to prominence coincided with his becoming a slaveholder and the growth of his holdings. Pickens had acquired his first two slaves by 1773. He probably obtained more during the war and, on a limited scale, followed Thomas Sumter's policy of distributing slaves seized from loyalists to his troops in lieu of currency for their pay. Thus he was fully capable of perceiving African Americans primarily as economic assets. At the time, Pickens's white contemporaries saw his actions as ethical and proper. This was not because Pickens demonstrated concern for the confiscated slaves' well-being but because he scrupulously disposed of them as directed by law and did not attempt to profit personally. Evidence suggests, though, that wartime experiences led him to a greater recognition of at least some enslaved people as individuals who merited a degree of respect. One of the first slaves Pickens had acquired was "Old Dick," a man who accompanied Pickens on many of his military campaigns. Pickens related some of Old Dick's feats to his children and told them that he was "as brave a man as ever faced battle." After the war, Pickens allowed Old Dick to carry a large knife anywhere on the plantation and allowed no one, including his own sons, to speak harshly to him.[20]

By 1790, Pickens owned thirty-three slaves and was the largest slave-holder in the up-country county of Pendleton. About that time, several Presbyterian ministers in the Carolinas challenged the morality of slavery, and the issue roiled the denomination at the national level. I surmise that it was at this time that Pickens, as well as other southern Presbyterians, began to give serious thought to the question of slavery's morality. Evangelical Christianity inspired much of the attack on slavery, as well as much of its defense. Minutes from synod meetings and other ecclesiastical and local sources show that the morality of slavery was an open question in the Synod of the Carolinas from the late 1780s until around 1810. Pickens apparently opposed abolitionism but seems to have supported several conclusions that southern Presbyterian leaders settled on by 1810: first, gradual emancipation in the abstract was a good idea, but rapid abolition would threaten the social order, so the church should refrain from pressuring the state on that policy. Second, masters had a religious duty to treat their slaves humanely and see that they received spiritual instruction, including learning to read the scriptures. Pendleton court records and wills from the 1790s indicate that Pickens and other local magistrates were beginning to adopt this paternalistic approach. Pickens was among the local elites who often intervened to see that blacks were treated humanely, that black families were kept together, that slaves were taught to read the Bible, and in some cases that slaves were manumitted.

The main written evidence from Pickens himself that reveals his attitude toward slavery is his will. Pickens instructed his heirs that as his slaves had been a means by which God, in his inscrutable will, had allowed his family to enjoy comfort and prosperity, he desired "that they may be used with justice, and humanity," and asked that a "humain and careful" overseer be employed. He also stipulated that if his youngest son, Joseph, died before he did, his slaves were to be freed and were to receive a tract of land along with all the tools and livestock necessary to support themselves.[21] Pickens's will was not an antislavery statement, but it was somewhat unusual for its time and place. His son Joseph did not die young, and it is unlikely that his enslaved people were ever freed. But it is further evidence that Pickens was striving to reconcile slavery with religion and morality.

There are some things this book does not or cannot do. The sources do not allow a traditional biography of Andrew Pickens to provide a very sophisticated analysis of his views on gender conventions, slave experiences, Revolutionary era economic thought, or Native American society without going far beyond the evidence and entering the realm of conjecture. Pickens wrote and said almost nothing on these topics. On the subject of gender, for example, there are no surviving letters between him and his wife, Becky, or with other female relatives, nor did Becky leave any writings of her own. Becky is a fascinating character, and I include her in the narrative whenever the sources allow, but the only surviving descriptions of her were written decades or even centuries after her death by people who did not know her. Thus, there are a few things we can conclude about Andrew and Becky's partnership and her role as mistress of the household, but not much.

There is also little that can be done to help Pickens's slaves emerge as multidimensional characters with their own thoughts and motivations. Except for Old Dick, we know little about them except some of their names, and even the information about Dick comes from Pickens's descendants, not from Dick himself. Even secondary sources give only limited help in this regard. While several studies over the last few decades have shed light on the experiences of African Americans during the Revolutionary period, the majority of the sources and information comes either from north of the Carolinas or from the cities and the lowcountry; relatively little comes from the backcountry of the Carolinas and Georgia. Even then individual names and stories are rare.[22]

Other readers may be hoping for deep analysis of how Pickens and his contemporaries viewed issues of currency, credit, debt, and government economic policy—"political economy" in the parlance of their day. While I give some attention to Pickens's views on these matters, he wrote and said very little on them publicly, and certainly not with the sophistication of men like Thomas Jefferson, Alexander Hamilton, James Madison,

Benjamin Franklin, Patrick Henry, George Mason, or the Pinckneys of South Carolina.[23]

Likewise, I cannot hope to add to the excellent work that Theda Perdue, Gregory Evans Dowd, Colin Calloway, Claudio Saunt, Cynthia Cumfer, Angela Pulley Hudson, Daniel J. Tortora, Robbie Ethridge, and several others have done in giving us a multidimensional understanding of the southern Indians during this time, including the transformations and internal factions occurring in their societies as a result of contact with whites. In the latter half of his life Pickens was intensely interested in the project of preserving peace with the Indians, but he rarely concerned himself with the changes that the historians listed above have described so well. I have chosen therefore to focus on Pickens's own actions, motivations, and perceptions and to avoid assumptions that are unsupported by the evidence.[24]

What I have worked especially hard to do is bring Pickens himself to life. One of my strategies has been to maximize my use of a few special contemporary sources whenever possible. These include two autobiographical letters that Pickens wrote to his former comrade in arms Henry Lee in 1811, the lengthy portrait of him penned by William Martin long after Pickens's death, and a handful of other letters in which Pickens seems temporarily to drop his mask of stern reserve and reveal just a little more of himself. I quote from those sources often and use excerpts from them to introduce new chapters. Still, even on those rare occasions in which we are allowed to see something of Pickens's inner self, what often appears is a man who is capable of great compassion, who nevertheless rarely allows himself the luxury of sentimentality, and who holds himself to a high standard of duty, courage, and what he considers upright behavior.

We have a great deal of scholarship on eighteenth- and early nineteenth-century America that studies the transformations of that era in the light of social power and the success of white male elites in manipulating it. What is sometimes missing is the recognition that white Americans of the period were profoundly interested in their conceptions of virtue as they forged a new society in the fires and ashes of the Revolution. When Americans of the late colonial period worked hard to impose order on chaos, particularly in the backcountry, they appealed not only to government institutions but also to morality, especially as the latter was defined by evangelical Christianity. They then replaced a monarchical government with a republican one, substituting some aristocratic rulers with non-elites. In doing so, they constructed a new leadership ethic based on the selflessness of republican virtue. Then, as they attempted to build a republic that could protect liberty and promote economic gain, many of them believed that this could not be done properly without a "morally defined political order," again drawing much of their inspiration from religion.[25] Even when dealing with pagan "savages," white elites strove to present themselves as honest, just, and magnanimous. Though convinced of their cultural superiority over Indians, many of them nevertheless regarded treaty violations and massacres of Indians as blights on the nation's honor. Andrew Pickens's life is particularly useful for demonstrating this moral sensibility—first, because his own contemporaries almost unanimously saw him as virtuous and respectable by the standards of their day, and second, because of his apparently deep religious convictions.

Accepting that questions of morality and virtue were just as important to eighteenth-century Americans as those of social power involving race, class, and gender does not mean we have to concede they were always virtuous by our standards, or even by their own. Obviously, they failed badly in doing justice to Native Americans and did not extend the blessings of liberty to African Americans or to women. These are facts that cannot be disputed. I stress that Pickens found himself trying to chart a moral course in a chaotic, sinful—Christians would say "fallen"—world. Indeed, Pickens himself, as a devout Calvinist, would probably have agreed that even the noblest actions of sinful man are tainted to some degree by selfish motives.

I hope that a study of this military hero, civic leader, and "self-made man" will provide a better understanding of who he was and of the times in which he lived. He was a product—and a shaper—of the frontier Revolutionary ethic of his day. That ethic's combination of courage, faith, and violence; the desire for order and freedom; and the growth of opportunity alongside racism and inequality defined the new American Republic and was formed during the seven decades in which Pickens lived.

ONE

Family Pilgrimage

I was born in Pennsylvania. . . . [M]y father removed with his
family when I was very young, to Virginia and settled for a few
Years, and in the year 1752 or 3 removed to the Waxhaws . . . of
South Carolina—My Father & Mother came from Ireland; my
Father's progenitors emigrated from France after the revocation
of the Edict of Nantes.

Andrew Pickens to Henry Lee, August 28, 1811

Andrew Pickens was thirteen years old by the time his family settled near
the border of North and South Carolina. His family's arrival in the Waxhaws district along the Catawba River was only the latest stop in the Pickens
clan's migrations, a journey of three-quarters of a century that had included
sojourns in France, Scotland, Ireland, Pennsylvania, and Virginia. It was
a journey filled with several generations' worth of religious persecution,
economic hardship and opportunity, and ever-present threats from external
enemies. The long pilgrimage shaped the Pickenses and their kinsmen, who
have become known in American history as the Scotch-Irish. The mythol-
ogy surrounding them imagines the people of Ireland and the British borderlands as having a mystical, unbreakable connection to home, yet the
experience of the Scotch-Irish who eventually arrived in America was one
defined by migration. And as often as we think of them as stubborn, bellig-
erent people spoiling for a fight, the Pickenses, like many others, were more
often than not fleeing persecution in search of order and peace.

Religion was the cause of many of these persecutions and migrations, particularly in the seventeenth and early eighteenth centuries, and it is one of the defining themes of the ancestral history of the Scotch-Irish. As the Protestant Reformation swept over Europe, Scotland was deeply influenced by the teachings of John Calvin and his protégé John Knox and became the home of Presbyterianism, a form of worship and church governance inspired by Calvinist and Reformed doctrine. By the mid-seventeenth century, Presbyterianism was so firmly entrenched in Scotland that it became a marker of Scottish identity despite—and perhaps because of—intense opposition from English monarchs determined to force Presbyterians into the Anglican fold. The persecution intensified after the restoration of Charles II in 1660. It was probably in 1661 that Andrew Picken (or Picon), a Scotch Presbyterian, fled Scotland for France, where one family tradition asserts he found a position in the French court. Though France was officially Catholic, French-Scottish relations were generally good at the time. Andrew Picken's son Robert married within the Protestant Calvinist faith with his union to a young Huguenot widow, Jean (or Jane) Bonneau.[1]

Eventually France, too, became an unsuitable home for Calvinists such as Huguenots or Presbyterians. In 1685, King Louis XIV announced the Edict of Fontainebleau, which revoked all legal protections that the Protestant minority had enjoyed in France. Huguenot churches and towns were destroyed, thousands were butchered, and Huguenot children were taken from their parents and put into Catholic homes. The Huguenots fled by the hundreds of thousands. Pickens family tradition asserts that Robert Picken had "every inducement" to remain in France, suggesting that he had the opportunity to keep his position in the French court if he would convert to Catholicism.[2] If true, his decision to take his family back to Scotland was a bold one, for the situation of Scottish Presbyterians in the 1680s was nearly as desperate as that of other Protestants in France. Even today in Scotland, the years 1680 to 1688 are known as the "Killing Time." Charles II and James II slaughtered thousands of Presbyterians in England and Scotland who refused to renounce their faith, while others faced prison, torture, and banishment. Indeed, at the very time that Robert Picken and his family returned to Scotland, other Scottish Presbyterians were fleeing to Ulster Province in Ireland and to the New World.[3]

Robert Picken's family joined the tide of Scottish immigrants to Ireland, but there the persecution continued. In 1703 the Test Act required all religious dissenters to conduct their marriages and funerals in the rites of the royally sanctioned Church of England or Church of Ireland, and dozens of public officials in Ulster lost their positions when they refused to take communion in the established church. After the end of Queen Anne's War in 1713, Presbyterians and other dissenters began leaving Scotland and Ireland for America in large numbers; this migration spiked around 1718 and continued for over half a century. By the eve of the American Revolution, some 200,000–250,000 Ulster and Lowland Scots had left their homes for the New World.[4]

The Pickenses (who began adding an "s" to their surname shortly after their arrival in America) became part of this migration trend as well. At least one of Robert Picken's sons, William, and probably a brother, Israel, arrived in Bucks County, Pennsylvania, north of Philadelphia, along with their wives and children as early as 1719, but certainly by 1722. Along with many other Scotch-Irish immigrants in that region, they joined the local Dutch Reformed Church, a likeminded Calvinist sect, where William was soon elected an elder. From there several of William's children joined other Scotch-Irish families in moving some eighty miles west to Paxton Township, Lancaster County, near present-day Harrisburg. One of these sons was Andrew, whose wife, Ann, gave birth to a son, also christened Andrew, on September 19, 1739.[5]

Andrew Jr. was an infant when his family moved once again. His father, Andrew, along with the elder Andrew's brothers Israel, John, Gabriel, and William and sister Lucy along with her second husband, John Kerr, began arriving in Augusta County, Virginia, in the Shenandoah Valley, in 1740. Again the Pickenses were part of a larger trend, this time of Scotch-Irish settlers moving south into the backcountry frontiers of Virginia and the Carolinas. Like the migration from the British Isles, it was a migration of families and clans. At least one of the inducements this time was free land. Virginia, like other southern colonies, was eager to attract white Protestant settlers to its backcountry and offered land to freeholders who brought family members or servants into the colony at their own expense. Little Andrew Pickens's father and uncles prospered in Virginia. Andrew Sr. and John were among the first justices of the Augusta County Court when it was formally organized in 1745. By that year, Andrew Sr. had acquired more than 600 acres and was considering yet another move, to Anson County, North Carolina, along the North Carolina–South Carolina border. The Pickens brothers and their families worshipped at Tinkling Springs Church, the first Presbyterian church in western Virginia, led by a colorful, redoubtable pastor named John Craig—the first permanent Presbyterian pastor in western Virginia—who ministered in Augusta County from 1740 to 1774.[6]

There were other reasons besides religious persecution for the Pickens's early migrations: rising rents and greedy landlords in Ireland, government trade restrictions on the Ulster linen industry, and famine—and of course the religious oppression they faced also translated into political and legal discrimination. Later the prospects of cheap or free land from Pennsylvania and from southern colonies provided a clear economic incentive. But the stubborn adherence to the Presbyterian faith and the sacrifices endured profoundly shaped Scotch-Irish identity, and they were indelibly stamped in popular memory. As early as the Scots Confession of 1560, says one scholar, a foundation was laid for a "national, antityrannical religious ethos that established deep, pervasive roots" in the culture of the Scots who migrated to Ireland and to America.[7] The centuries-long conflict between Scottish Presbyterianism and royal authority became a source of ethnic identity and family pride and would profoundly shape the worldview and politics of the descendants of the survivors of the "Killing Time."[8]

This biography is not a religious history, but because religion was so central to Andrew Pickens's life and family legacy, it is worthwhile to understand what made Presbyterianism distinctive. In the case of the Scotch-Irish Calvinists and their descendants who came to America, Presbyterianism strengthened social solidarity, provided a way of understanding the world, offered emotional support and ways to comprehend human suffering, and provided ethical standards as a guide to living in their dangerous, chaotic, and often violent world.[9]

The Calvinist theology that informed Presbyterianism first and foremost emphasized the absolute sovereignty of God, as well as his ultimate goodness. The passionate belief that God was working out his purposes in human history could translate into great personal courage, resistance to tyranny, and an impulse for social and political reform among its adherents. God was sovereign and he was good; thus his followers could, and must, fight for the right, trusting in his favor and protection. Yet that same sense that God had ordained all things could also lead to an unfortunate acceptance of the status quo and acceptance of social inequalities, particularly in the southern colonies where slavery was spreading.

Calvinist theology, though, had a built-in explanation for how its doctrines could lead to sin and human error. The problem was not in God's word or in true Christian doctrine but in man himself. This was the second of the great pillars in Calvinist thought—the insistence on human depravity. Man was inherently sinful. While all men and women justly deserved God's wrath and punishment, the Almighty had, in his inscrutable wisdom and for reasons known only to him, mercifully predestined some of these undeserving wretches for repentance and salvation. Others, including many who enjoyed positions of wealth and authority, were in rebellion against God and destined for damnation. This doctrine led to suspicion or fear of concentrations of power and often fostered heroic resistance to magistrates and kings. "At the same time," notes one religious historian, "the sense of being numbered among God's elect . . . often pushed in the opposite direction—toward an arrogant confidence that they were on the side of right and that any who opposed their political visions were opposing God."[10]

Man's propensity for sin, his desires of the flesh and quest for self-aggrandizement, meant that the church had to be a force for moral and community order—not just among its own members but *especially* among them. Man's brute passions were dangerous not only to himself but to the entire community. It was probably no surprise to Andrew Pickens that, after each great struggle in which he fought—the defeat of the Cherokees, victories over backcountry outlaws in the Regulator movement and then over British tyrants and Tory marauders—what followed was no Eden of human virtue. After each triumph, it seemed, those who had fought on the "right side" succumbed to greed, selfishness, and loss of virtue. What was needed was more of God's word, more sound preaching, more law and order, and close attendance to the principles of true religion.

Finally, Presbyterianism, like other Calvinist sects including Puritanism, was deeply influenced by the idea that God dealt with communities and bodies of believers as a corporate whole, not just as individuals. God's word contained explicit instructions for the moral life of the individual and the community. Christians and Christian communities that obediently and humbly sought God's will and his forgiveness when they departed from it could be sure of his favor and protection, even in the midst of hardship. He would work out his purposes through them and prosper them, and they would honor him. In the words of Jeremiah 32:38, "They shall be my people, and I will be their God" (King James Version).

These doctrines found expression in religious customs that emphasized both egalitarianism and a stern moral code. Presbyterian congregations, in America at least, were led and disciplined by elders they themselves elected, not by appointed priests and bishops. Pastors were "called" by a congregation, not simply assigned to them without the flock's approval. When taking communion, worshippers sat together and were served by the elders rather than knelt before a priest. The elders, in turn, were responsible for church discipline. Members (as well as elders and pastors) could be publicly rebuked or expelled from the congregation for immoral behavior until they repented. Elders also were responsible for "fencing the table"—excluding from communion those who were openly leading sinful lives. Such policing was important, because open rebellion against God's commands was not simply a matter of individual morality; it also jeopardized God's approval of the community as a whole if it was not corrected. Elders could not preach, however. Respect for the purity of God's word required that a man be licensed to preach or ordained as a minister only after attending seminary and being examined by the presbytery, the ruling body overseeing a number of congregations. In colonial America, then, there was a chronic shortage of licensed preachers throughout the rapidly expanding American frontier, so that the most common pattern was for a minister to serve more than one congregation, preaching and administering sacraments to one on one Sunday and to another the next. It was not uncommon for Presbyterian congregations in the southern backcountry to go for several years without a formal pastor, in which cases they continued to sing and pray in their churches and in private homes under the leadership of the elders.[11]

When the Pickens family arrived in Augusta County, Virginia, around 1740, they came under the pastorate of John Craig, minister at Tinkling Spring Church. Contemporary and nineteenth-century sources make it clear that what was valued in a minister was doctrinally sound but "affective," or emotional, heartfelt sermons, a pious lifestyle, and firmness of conviction to the point of stubbornness and militancy. In the time of the Revolution, stories would abound of Presbyterian ministers preaching on Sunday morning with a musket literally by their side, proclaiming the justice of the patriot cause and joining, if not leading, their male congregants in the field against the British.[12] John Craig was one of those figures who fit exactly the stereotype of the hard-shell man of God, and he was certainly the first minister young Andrew Pickens Jr. would have remembered. Reverend Craig typically walked five miles every Sunday morning to the place of worship, carrying a Bible in one hand and usually a rifle over his shoulder in case of an Indian attack. The men of his congregation also brought rifles and powder horns to worship. The course of the Lord's Day at Tinkling Spring Church differed little from that in other Presbyterian congregations in America or the old country. Craig preached until noon, though there were breaks for hymns and prayers. The people then ate dinner, after which the preaching began again and continued until sunset.[13]

In church history and lore, Craig appears as a kind man with a tough exterior: "although the look of severity sometimes came over the face of this minister," says one sentimental account, "his heart was always full of tenderness."[14] As in other like communities, the people in Augusta County were governed partly by the king's law and partly by the Ten Commandments. Congregants were publicly punished for drunkenness, lying, and violating the Sabbath with long journeys or "profane songs."[15] Craig's hardness, or stubbornness, revealed itself in numerous ways. He may have riled some of his congregation with his inflexibility when the first permanent church building was completed in 1745. There was a dispute over whether the new structure would be located next to Tinkling Spring or another location preferred by Craig. Apparently a majority of members voted for the Tinkling Spring location, and the irate Craig vowed never to drink from the spring, declaring, "Well, I am resolved that not one drop of that water shall tinkle down my throat."[16] Of course he kept the oath. On another occasion, however, it was Craig's fierce resolve that epitomized what later generations of Scotch-Irish Americans admired about their ancestors. In 1755, General Edward Braddock's force of British regulars and colonial militia met a stunning defeat in western Pennsylvania at the hands of the French and their Indian allies, leaving the colonial frontier fearful and exposed to the enemy. Many settlers fled eastward, to Craig's disgust. Craig recorded his own exhortations to his flock thus: "I opposed that scheme [flight and resettlement] as a scandal to our nation, falling below our brave ancestors, making ourselves a reproach among Virginians, a dishonor to our friends at home, an evidence of cowardice, want of faith and noble Christian dependence on God as able to save and deliver from the heathen; and withal, a lasting blot forever on all our posterity." With such an implied rebuke ringing in their ears, a large portion of the congregation stayed and followed Craig's leadership in building small stone forts for defense.[17]

This combination of religious faith, strict morality, and stern determination formed the social context and background of young Andrew Pickens's upbringing. Some two or three years before Braddock's defeat and John Craig's mobilization of his flock, however, the Pickens family had already left Augusta County for yet another new frontier settlement. They were near the leading edge of the tide of Scotch-Irish settlers pushing beyond Virginia into the backcountry of the Carolinas.

Their next journey southward serves as a reminder that after the Scotch-Irish removal to America, religion was no longer a significant factor in their migrations; it had been replaced by economic motives. One problem for the Pickenses was that so many of their former countrymen were leaving Ulster for America. As thousands poured into Pennsylvania every year, what was once cheap land became more expensive. Though Scotch-Irish farmers were flourishing, they foresaw increasing difficulty in acquiring substantial farms for their sons. Meanwhile, colonial governments in Virginia and the two Carolinas beckoned them with offers of free land, hoping to increase their populations and build a buffer of white Protestant settlement against Indian and French threats.

Andrew Pickens Sr. and his brothers had been church elders in Bucks County, Pennsylvania, a marker of social respectability and status at the time. But they left for Lancaster County, and then left there for the valley of Virginia, where Andrew and his brother John became justices of the peace. Andrew owned 600 acres of land in Augusta County by 1745. By that time he had three sons—Joseph, born 1737, Andrew, born 1739, and John, born 1745. There were also two daughters—Jane (or Jean) born around 1740, and Catherine. There was enough land to survive on, but Andrew Sr. may have felt he needed more to ensure future prosperity for his growing brood, and cheap land in the Shenandoah Valley was rapidly disappearing. A pattern soon emerged that favored large land speculators over smaller landholders in western Virginia. Colonial elites and wealthy speculators typically received preference over middling farmers like the Pickenses when applying for land patents. Over time, the latter were squeezed out in the scramble for land.[18] Meanwhile, the colony of North Carolina was granting tracts of land to thousands of Scotch-Irish and German settlers moving south from Pennsylvania and Virginia, with the acreage dependent on the household's "condition to cultivate and improve it."[19] The Pickenses were now fleeing neither religious persecution nor economic distress but simply seeking more opportunity and making hardheaded calculations about the prospects for their children. Tinkling Springs and other like churches provided social discipline, community, and spiritual sustenance, but these benefits were not enough to override the desire for greater wealth and economic security. In his adult years, Andrew Pickens Jr. would continue this pattern of leaving an established home where his status and reputation were secure in search of greater opportunity.[20]

In October 1751 Andrew Pickens Sr. received a grant of 800 acres in Anson County from the provincial government of North Carolina.[21] He moved his family there in 1752 or 1753 after receiving another grant of 551 acres situated along Waxhaw Creek, which flowed into the Catawba River between modern-day Lancaster, South Carolina, and Charlotte, North

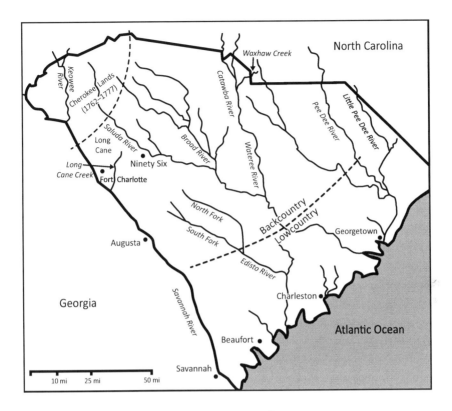

South Carolina in the 1760s *(Map by Chris Cartledge)*

Carolina. During the next several years, he would become one of the earliest pillars of the Waxhaws community, a rapidly growing settlement of Scotch-Irish farmers, some of them moving up the Catawba River from the South Carolina lowcountry but more usually arriving like himself via the Great Wagon Road from Pennsylvania and Virginia. Soon after thirteen-year-old Andrew's arrival in the area, his father was named as a justice for Anson County and later became captain of the local militia. Young Andrew and his older brother Joseph and uncle William served in the ranks. Andrew Sr. purchased five acres that he donated for the establishment of a courthouse; he was also one of five trustees appointed for the care of the property that became the site of the Waxhaws Presbyterian meetinghouse. When itinerant preachers visited the area, they often stayed at the house of Justice Pickens. His son could not help but notice that his father was a man his neighbors looked to for the establishment of security and social order.[22]

The Waxhaws community was one where "kinship mattered most," in the words of Peter N. Moore's careful study. Families and kin migrated together and settled near each other; kinship also influenced marriage patterns and "lubricated the exchange economy." Within two years of Andrew Pickens Sr.'s move to the Waxhaws, Martha Pickens, the widow of his brother Israel, obtained land in Anson County as well, as did his brother William.[23] It was a world of small independent farmers, where almost every white man owned land and almost no one owned slaves. Agriculture served the purposes of home consumption and local trade, not far-flung commercial networks. It was also, Moore explains, a "deeply religious world." The Waxhaws congregation had a permanent minister at least by 1756, an impressive accomplishment in a frontier community, given the shortage of trained Presbyterian clergymen. Weekly church attendance was high. Moreover, argues Moore, "the people of the Waxhaws thought of themselves in religious terms. Their identity was bound as tightly to Presbyterianism as it was to their local kin group, their race consciousness, their ethnic heritage, and their status as a class of independent small farmers."[24]

As strong as these community ties were, and as much as the people of the Waxhaws may have looked to men like Andrew Pickens Sr. to maintain order, they knew that the world was neither a safe nor a virtuous and orderly place. Sinful man was too often driven by his own folly and greed. One threat to order and safety in the Waxhaws (though probably the least serious one) was the "savages"—the Catawba Indians—living just beyond the northern and western boundaries of the community. On the one hand, the Catawbas had proven themselves decades earlier as useful allies to the South Carolina provincial government when compared with the more frequent opposition of the Waxhaws band. They also served as a buffer against the Cherokee and Iroquois tribes who raided from farther north. On the other hand, there was friction between the Catawbas and the rapidly expanding white community, especially once settlers began pouring into the area after 1750, settling along or even within the bounds of Catawba territory. The Catawbas sometimes responded by burning settlers' fences, killing their cattle and stealing their horses, and burgling their homes. Whites unscrupulously traded liquor to the Catawbas for deerskins and encroached on their land, and one white man murdered a Catawba woman. As loss of territory, disease, and alcohol weakened the tribe in the late 1750s, their decline only magnified the threat of the Cherokees. It was no wonder that Waxhaws settlers turned to seemingly reliable men like Andrew Pickens Sr. to command the militia.[25]

While the people of the Waxhaws could never ignore the danger of Indian attacks, often it was internal strife and individual greed that seemed more of a threat to the peace of the community. One anomaly of the Waxhaws settlement was that the area in which it lay was claimed by both North and South Carolina. Most of the settlers, including the Pickenses, received their land by grant from the northern province, and the Anson County court in North Carolina was where they paid their taxes and conducted their legal business. Andrew Pickens Sr., of course, held his judgeship and militia rank in that colony. The boundary between the two colonies, however, had not been surveyed as far west as the Waxhaws. Later it would be determined that the original settlement, including the Pickens land, was actually south of the border. Moreover, a few settlers held headrights to their land by virtue of the colony of South Carolina. In 1754, Justice Pickens found himself trying to settle a quarrel between a Captain William Moore, who had been granted a parcel of land by North Carolina, and John Douglas, who simultaneously gained title to the same tract through South Carolina. Pickens reported that the two men "strove each with the other which should enjoy the Premises which occasioned much Contentions Quarrelings and Fightings between them, and Moore plows up the others Turnips and one turned Cattle into the others Wheat."[26] Pickens was powerless to resolve this particular case and, as backcountry authorities often did, submitted it to the two men's neighbors. The community ultimately referred the case back to the colonial authorities of North Carolina. North Carolina governor Arthur Dobbs noted that there were "perpetual Quarrels" among settlers living close to the colonial boundary, "sometimes end[ing] in Death."[27] The moral might seem to be that too often the wisdom of men and human institutions was simply inadequate to resolve "Quarrels" resulting from other men's sinful pride. In a secular sense, though, the lesson might be that what was needed was stronger and better government. Sometimes local judges, church elders, and community leaders needed help from higher authority, not independence from it.[28]

Another source of community disorder was sins of the flesh. In 1756, members of the Waxhaws congregation believed they had been blessed with their first permanent pastor. A schoolmaster named Robert Miller, originally from Scotland, was licensed to preach on February 7 and appointed to serve the Waxhaws settlement as soon as possible. Miller, "a man of popular talents and a lively preacher," arrived in the spring and began his ministry.[29] He met and married Andrew Pickens Jr.'s younger sister Jane who would have been sixteen in 1756—relatively young for marriage, but not unusually so. Miller had not served the congregation long, however, before he was deposed for adultery. The exact order of events is difficult to ascertain. He had previously been deposed by a presbytery in Scotland for the same crime, and it seems that the people of the Waxhaws did not yet know that when they called him to ministry. It is possible that he committed the same offense again after coming to South Carolina, either before or after his marriage to young Jane Pickens. In any event, he was officially deposed as minister for the Waxhaws congregation in June 1758. In March 1758, he and Jane sold his "plantation," donating four and a half acres to the congregation for a church and cemetery. One of the citizens attesting the deed was Andrew Pickens Jr. The elder Andrew Pickens was dead, and it is notable that the younger son, Andrew, was the attester and not his older brother, Joseph.[30]

Reverend Miller's donation of land may have been an act of penance, and an authoritative source on Presbyterian history in South Carolina reports that "it is believed that Mr. Miller repented sincerely of this his sin, and lived afterwards a virtuous life as a private Christian."[31] Future events would seem to indicate this was the case. After Jane and Robert moved to a newer settlement in the Long Cane region, the people there appealed to the presbytery for Miller's reinstatement, testifying to his repentance and upright life, but had no success. Interestingly, some of the other Long Cane settlers at that time were Andrew Jr. and Jane's other brothers. During the Revolutionary War, Miller served as a military chaplain while his brother-in-law Andrew was an officer of high rank in the patriot militia. Despite Miller's later repentance, his sins temporarily had brought heartbreak and havoc to the Pickens family and the Waxhaws community. Besides the embarrassment to a respected family, his lack of self-control had left the Waxhaws congregation once again without a pastor and probably served as a warning to young Andrew Pickens.[32]

Thus far, it has been possible to describe only the historical events that brought young Andrew Pickens and his clan to the Waxhaws and the social, religious, and economic context in which he came of age. It is difficult to learn much about the boy himself. Sometime in 1757, however, when Andrew was seventeen years old, his father died. This pivotal event in the lives of the Pickenses soon revealed a great deal about Andrew Pickens Jr.—not so much about his inner self but about what his neighbors and family members thought of him. For whatever reasons, others seemed to be confident in the young man's competence, judgment, and ability to lead.

The first clue to this fact comes from the will of Andrew Pickens Sr., written in November 1756 and probated in 1757. The will made it clear that the patriarch entrusted leadership of the family to his second son, Andrew, not Joseph, who was a year and a half older. The elder Pickens divided his 551-acre plantation (no mention is made of the 800-acre grant he received from the colony of North Carolina, and it is unclear whether he still retained it at his death) between Andrew and Joseph. Andrew was to receive 300 acres surveyed "off ye upper end" of the plantation, and Joseph the remaining 251 acres. This may have been an equitable division, with Joseph's "lower" tract adjoining Waxhaw Creek and thus as valuable as Andrew's 300 acres. In other ways, though, Andrew Sr. clearly showed that he expected his second son to assume the mantle of leadership. Andrew was to be left a "ten-pound piece," which he was to use within five years to buy a tract of 200 acres for the youngest child, John, then still a boy. All the "moveables" on the plantation were left to the children's mother, Ann, and after her death they would become Andrew's. The daughters, Catherine and Jane, were already married and received no significant share.[33]

Others in the Waxhaws community looked to young Andrew to represent the Pickens clan. When Andrew's sister Jane and her husband, Robert Miller, donated their four-and-a-half-acre lot to the local congregation, it was Andrew who was one of the attesters to the deed. A few years later, at the age of only twenty-one, Andrew was made a lieutenant in his militia company as it marched off to fight the Cherokees. The status and respect enjoyed by the elder Andrew Pickens is not enough to explain the confidence that other Waxhaws residents expressed in his son Andrew, for Joseph, the eldest, was not entrusted with these leadership roles. As long as Andrew's brothers lived, in fact, he continued to lead them.[34]

Possibly others admired Pickens's physical vitality. For most of his adult life, other men recognized Pickens as a sturdy horseman, outdoorsman, and soldier. It may be that he acquired that reputation early on. Many years later, Pickens wrote tersely to Henry "Light Horse Harry" Lee, "I was young, fond of a gun and an active life and was much out in [the Cherokee] war, was intrusted for some time with a small detachment of men on the frontiers."[35]

Later in life, Pickens would appear to others as a reserved, stern man of few words. He may have been more outgoing, though, when he was younger. In fact, nothing that has been said here about stern Calvinist morality should disguise the fact that frontier life was often rowdy. The land in the southern backcountry yielded enough that one could prosper from a reasonable amount of labor and still have ample time for hunting, fishing, and the "vigorous athleticism of frontier sports."[36] Reminiscences of pioneers refer to wrestling, racing, and competitive shooting among the men. Community events included cornhuskings, house raisings, "strenuous dancing," and, yes, whiskey.[37] Religion and social mores frowned on habitual drunkenness but had not yet insisted on abstaining—there was as yet no temperance movement in America. Even clergymen owned stills, and so did respectable citizens like Andrew Pickens Sr. Weddings, in particular, were boisterous events to which the entire community was invited by word of mouth. As historian James G. Leyburn explains, "The occasion generally began with the young men racing for a bottle of whisky, the winner having the right to be the first to kiss the bride; and it ended with the 'bedding' of the couple, accompanied by ribald good wishes for the beginning of a large family and finally by a . . . raucous serenade on pots and pans."[38] Many people remembered Pickens's wedding to Rebecca Calhoun in 1765, in fact, as one of the most exuberant celebrations on the old frontier.[39] Young Andrew Pickens knew how to have a good time.

Still, one cannot escape the impression that it was reliability, not revelry, that made others trust Pickens at a very young age. When the tensions between white men and Cherokee Indians burst forth into savagery and horror in 1760, when the grim realities of warfare and terror struck hard on the Carolina frontier and the men of the Waxhaws marched off to fight, one of the officers they chose to follow was the twenty-one-year-old Andrew Pickens.

TWO

Family, War, and Order

I was young, fond of a gun and an active life
and was much out in [the Cherokee] war.

Andrew Pickens to Henry Lee, August 28, 1811

War, or the threat of war, was an ever-present reality in the world of young Andrew Pickens. His ancestors had faced the threats of brutal royal troops in Scotland and the retaliations of native Irish Catholics in Ulster and of Indians in Pennsylvania. His own family had left the Shenandoah Valley in Virginia before the French and Indian War brought the threat of Indian attacks there, but dozens of families who were their former neighbors fled the Shenandoah after Braddock's Defeat and joined the Pickenses in the Waxhaws a few years later. In the Waxhaws region itself, the neighboring Catawbas were only a weak and sporadic threat, but the Cherokees were another matter. Tension between the Cherokees and the South Carolina colony increased as white settlers pushed deeper into the Carolina piedmont and unscrupulous traders cheated the Cherokees. A series of Indian attacks took place throughout South Carolina in 1751; in 1754, Cherokee warriors murdered sixteen or seventeen whites near Buffalo Creek along the North Carolina–South Carolina border, not far from the Waxhaws.[1] Officially, there was a fragile Anglo-Cherokee alliance during much of the 1750s, but depredations and atrocities by both sides mounted from 1756 to 1759.[2] In 1759, South Carolina royal governor William Henry Lyttelton foolishly declared war on the Cherokees, launching a punitive expedition that cost the colony dearly in lives and treasure, and forced a treaty that was so humiliating to the Cherokees that it virtually ensured future bloodshed.[3]

Thus, the threat of violet encounters with Indians was a fact of life on the Carolina frontier, even if most whites rarely saw an Indian in the flesh. People like the Pickenses know that brutality and bloodshed could emerge from the forest at any time. And yet, without a doubt, the wave of Cherokee attacks that struck the Carolina frontier in the winter of 1760 was a horrible and terrifying shock. The hardest blow fell upon the fledgling Long Cane settlement, about one hundred miles southwest of the Waxhaws.

The Long Cane settlement was just northwest of Ninety Six, a trading post where white traders and Cherokees had met for decades. In 1747, the "Lower Towns" Cherokees had sold the area between Ninety Six Creek and Long Cane Creek to the South Carolina provincial government, and dozens of white families moved into the area, many of them Scotch-Irish families coming down the Great Wagon Road from Virginia. One of these families was the Calhouns, who had lived in Lancaster County, Pennsylvania, at the same time as the Pickenses and whose stay in Augusta County, Virginia, also overlapped with the Pickenses'. In 1756, four Calhoun brothers—James, Ezekiel, William, and Patrick—began acquiring tracts in the Long Cane area from the South Carolina government. They moved there with their wives and children; their widowed sister, Mary Noble; and their elderly mother, Catherine. At least some of the land settled on by the Calhouns was beyond the boundary of Long Cane Creek, but the Calhoun family and other settlers claimed that the Cherokees had approved of their settlement and that they had gotten along well with them for several years.[4]

When the first reports of Indian attacks reached the Long Cane community, most of the settlers, about 150 to 250 of them, decided to load their wagons on February 1, 1760, and dash to safety in Augusta, Georgia, some sixty miles away. Once on the road, they were easy prey for approximately 100 Cherokee warriors who ambushed and decimated the party before most of the white men could even fire their rifles. After a short skirmish, the Cherokees withdrew, leaving twenty-three settlers killed, including Catherine, the matriarch of the Calhoun clan. William Calhoun, a father of four, lost his six-year-old daughter (killed), his four-year-old daughter (taken and held captive for fourteen years), and his two-year-old daughter (taken and never seen again). When his brother Patrick Calhoun and others returned to the scene of the massacre days later, they found nine children still alive, some of whom had been scalped and left for dead, as well as some twenty mangled corpses. One terrified child who was rescued was Rebecca Calhoun, the daughter of Ezekiel Calhoun. She had hidden in the canebrakes and watched as her grandmother Catherine had been tomahawked and scalped.[5]

Family, War, and Order

Throughout February, Cherokee bands attacked other settlements in the South Carolina backcountry, killing or abducting scores of white settlers. Reports of the massacres, particularly that of the Long Cane settlers, sent shock waves throughout the colony. Terrified settlers crowded into makeshift forts where disease and hunger prevailed.[6] Presbyterian pastor Archibald Simpson recorded that frightened refugees he ministered to seemed "stupefied with horror and amazement."[7] The Calhouns sought refuge with friends in the Waxhaws. It was then that Andrew Pickens, twenty, met or was reacquainted with Rebecca Calhoun, fifteen. Tradition records that "Becky" had blue eyes and black hair and was vivacious and lovely. In contrast to the more serious Andrew, she had a "girlish playfulness that never deserted her, even in old age."[8]

That spring a British force of 1,200 regulars under Colonel Archibald Montgomery, along with seven troops of colonial "Rangers" and forty Catawba Indians, marched into the frontier. Montgomery burned Cherokee villages and corn, fought one pitched battle, and returned to Charleston by the end of the summer declaring success and fooling no one. His campaign left scores of British and American losses and the Cherokees confident of their ability to withstand another white expedition. Some sources claim that Pickens participated in this campaign, but that is not certain.[9]

In 1761, the colony raised a provincial regiment to serve alongside Lieutenant Colonel James Grant's regiment of British regulars as it launched another campaign against the Cherokees. Pickens became a lieutenant in the provincial regiment and served under several young officers who, like him, would later become leaders in South Carolina's Revolutionary War: Henry Laurens, William Moultrie, Francis Marion (later known as the "Swamp Fox"), and Isaac Huger. Twenty-one-year-old Lieutenant Pickens got his first taste of war that summer at Etchohih, near the Cherokee town of Estatoe, where the Cherokees had inflicted a heavy blow on Montgomery the previous year. This time the British troops and American provincials came off better, and in fact the provincials, in the rear of the column and cut off from the British regulars, bore the brunt of the Cherokee attack and drove the enemy away. Afterward Grant blazed a trail of devastation through the "Middle Towns" of the Cherokees, burning fifteen villages to the ground, slaughtering cattle, and destroying 1,500 acres of corn and beans.[10] This work of desolation, though later dubbed wholly inadequate by some colonial officers and by civilian public opinion, seemed tragic enough to many provincial soldiers who were present. Henry Laurens, the lieutenant colonel of the provincial regiment, wrote, "This work tho necessary often makes my heart bleed. The Cherokees has totally abandoned these Towns & fled with their wretched Women & Children across the Mountains. . . . They have already suffer'd greatly & will be reduced to extreme misery as the Winter advances."[11] The destruction affected young Andrew Pickens as well. Fifty years later the memory stayed with him, even after witnessing the horrors of the Revolutionary War in the backcountry. After describing his service in Grant's expedition in his letter to Henry Lee, he recalled, "I learned something of brittish cruelty which I always abhorred."[12] By the end of Grant's expedition, the Cherokees had suffered even more from the cruel war than the white colonists had and soon came to terms.

Pickens went home to the Waxhaws, but he may have already decided to move to the Long Cane area. His decision to do so was probably based on a combination of personal ambition, affection for Becky Calhoun, and family strategy. He had marched through the area during the Cherokee war and seen it firsthand.[13] He had also come to know the Calhouns better, including Becky, and that family clearly intended to return to their homes once the Cherokees were defeated. His aged mother, Ann (called Nancy by his father), was still in the Waxhaws, and that fact may have delayed his departure. Ann needed her sons and in fact had suffered a devastating blow in 1761 (perhaps while Pickens was away at war) when a tornado had thoroughly demolished her house. Miraculously, Mrs. Pickens and the several other women with her in the house at the time were unhurt, but the event must have been unsettling to say the least and made the old widow even more dependent on her sons.[14] From December 1762 to July 1763, Pickens had grants of 250 acres, 300 acres, 100 acres, and 200 acres certified along Long Cane Creek, close to the Calhouns.[15] The man who surveyed the tracts was Patrick Calhoun, Becky's uncle. Patrick also surveyed a 300-acre tract nearby for an Ann Pickens, possibly Andrew Pickens's mother, on November 2, 1762.[16] By 1763, Pickens's mother had passed away and there was little to hold him in the Waxhaws. He and his older brother, Joseph, sold the family homestead and made their move to the Long Cane area.

By the 1760s, the search for individual opportunity and personal profit was becoming more important to backcountry settlers in America. Yet the family was still very important as an economic unit, and often when land was bought and sold it was done so among family members. Even when it was sold to strangers, the transaction could still be part of a family economic strategy.[17] This was certainly true in the Pickenses' case. When Andrew Pickens sold his share of the land in the Waxhaws and moved to the Long Cane settlement, brother Joseph and his wife, Eleanor, apparently moved with him, though there is no record of Joseph purchasing land on his own until 1765, again suggesting Andrew was the business leader within the family.[18] Younger brother John, aged twenty or twenty-one, acquired 200 acres nearby in 1765, probably with the help of Andrew and Joseph and in keeping with their deceased father's wishes.[19] Their sister Jane and her husband, Robert Miller, moved there about the same time, acquiring 100 acres of land adjacent to one of Andrew's tracts. The survey was done by cousin John Pickens Jr. (who was the brother of Joseph's wife, Eleanor, meaning that Joseph married his first cousin).[20] Pickens's uncles John Pickens Sr. and Gabriel Pickens also came to the area.[21] Just like the prior moves of the Pickenses, the one to the Long Cane area (by now called Granville County, a part of Ninety Six District) was the migration of a clan, not individuals. Still, the apparent consensus of all these Pickens men that Long Cane was the place to be probably indicates that all of them perceived, individually, economic benefit in the move.

Andrew Pickens's move to Long Cane, in fact, was the first step in his becoming part of a rising backcountry elite interested more than ever in order and peace and in safeguarding its own opportunities for increasing wealth. It would be strange to think that when twenty-three-year-old Andrew, already a militia officer and war veteran, moved to the Ninety Six District, he did not intend to become a man of importance and responsibility—a justice of the peace, a church elder, a respected military figure should war return, and a substantial landowner. That is exactly what his father had been and is exactly what he himself would soon become, and in fact he began accumulating hundreds of acres in the area right away, even before he emigrated from the Waxhaws.

Nothing whatsoever guaranteed that he would be successful. The area he was moving to had been physically, economically, and socially devastated by the Cherokee War. Though the war had left the Waxhaws community mostly intact, it had destroyed law, order, and civilized society elsewhere along the South Carolina frontier, including the Congarees and Wateree areas, Saxe-Gotha Township, and of course Long Cane and throughout the Ninety Six District. Hundreds of families had abandoned their lands and fled to frontier forts, where disease, starvation, crime, and prostitution flourished. Houses, farms, and mills were destroyed, livestock ran wild, and there had been no local courts or jails on the frontier even before the war. In May 1761, the provincial government had raised "Rangers," mounted troops who were intended to fight the Cherokees; instead they had plundered the white inhabitants.[22]

The new and returning settlers in the backcountry depended on the distant provincial government in Charleston to provide courts and jails. Churches, however, they could establish on their own, and many continued to look to their local congregation and to religion to provide spiritual sustenance and at least some measure of moral order in the larger community. Despite the lack of ordained clergymen, the Presbyterians, like other dissenting sects including Baptists and Methodists, wasted no time before organizing congregations in the wilderness. The Calhouns had begun doing so in Long Cane in 1760, but their efforts had been disrupted by the Cherokee attacks. After the Cherokee War, these efforts resumed, and Pickens, young as he was, took a leading role.[23] In 1764, one of the Presbyterian ministers who visited the area for several weeks to encourage the flock was William Richardson, the pastor of Pickens's recent home in the Waxhaws who had replaced Robert Miller.[24] Around the year 1769 or shortly afterward, Pickens was part of a five-man committee chosen to divide and organize the growing Long Cane flock into five distinct congregations. Visiting ministers or local elders conducted worship services under a large chestnut tree on Pickens's property. Later a meetinghouse was built nearby. Meanwhile, in 1768, Pickens had built a log fort with a stone foundation near his home, in what is now the town of Abbeville, primarily for protection.[25] This sturdy structure often doubled as a church during the Revolution, indicating that the Pickens home remained a gathering place for worshippers. Within a few years of the post–Cherokee War resettlement of the area, a congregation of 500 families had formed in the Long Cane area, despite the absence of a full-time minister. There were some twenty other Presbyterian congregations in the backcountry.[26]

The local Presbyterian church, like those of other dissenting sects, had played a significant, if not the primary, role in regulating community mores in communities in Augusta County and the Waxhaws, where it had few rivals. In the Waxhaws, for instance, there was no other church for many years, and the local congregation was the central institution around which the community was organized. Society in the Ninety Six area, though, was more diverse and dynamic. Settlers were pouring in rapidly, and many of them were rival Baptists and Methodists or even recently arrived French-speaking Huguenots.[27] Other settlers were indifferent or openly hostile to religion of any kind. Some openly flouted strictures against drunkenness, gambling, fornication, and idleness and lived free of the discipline of church elders and deacons. Their behavior, or even their very presence, underscored the need for moral order and discipline, which the Presbyterian church could not provide in the same way it had in older, less diverse settlements.

The bulk of those who settled, or resettled, the frontier after the defeat of the Cherokees were yeomen farmers or small planters who owned their own land. Despite his late father's relative prominence, it is probably within this class that Pickens should be grouped while still a young man in his twenties. Pickens had a good name among his neighbors but no more wealth than could be extracted from a few hundred acres of land, a holding that was average to slightly above average in size.

Within this large class of small planters, however, there was "a core of what would become a backcountry elite," men who were prospering as farmers, storekeepers, merchants, and millers, striving to increase their landholdings and to acquire slaves to make their land more profitable.[28] Due to their initiative, abilities, and wealth, their neighbors came to recognize them as leaders and to turn to them for the maintenance of order. As backcountry society developed more settled institutions, they became the church leaders, justices of the peace, and militia officers. Historian Richard M. Brown refers to them in his work as the "leading men"; Rachel Klein calls them "backcountry elites" or, in deference to a term used by people at the time, "men of influence."[29] They were not wholly a new type. Anglo-American colonists had regularly reserved the positions of sheriff, justice of the peace, and church vestryman to the more established members of the yeoman class; Scottish feudal and Scotch-Irish culture had long accorded a certain deference to local lairds, chieftains, and elders. Perhaps what was new was that the rapid expansion of the South Carolina backcountry after the Cherokee War, the availability of land, and the dangers of the frontier made family origins less important. At the same time, these changes rewarded an individual's own boldness, initiative, physical courage, and acquisitiveness more than ever.[30]

With the shortage of labor and inadequate transportation for getting cash crops to market, farming alone could not provide the wealth these "leading men" sought. Though they always considered themselves "planters" first and foremost, they also owned mills and ferries. Some, like Pickens, went into trade, owning stores or becoming middlemen between lowcountry merchants and the Cherokee and Creek Indians. They were also beginning to acquire a small number of slaves. Slaves made up no more than one-tenth of the population of the backcountry, but obtaining them was emerging as a strategy for backcountry elites to gain wealth. And for the men of this nascent pseudo-merchant class to succeed, they would need to tame the state of near-anarchy into which the region seemed to be descending.[31]

For the moment, the main threat to order and peace was not the Cherokees but a third class of whites sometimes called the "hunters," "Crackers," or "lower people."[32] These were unsettled frontiersmen who lived by hunting, by trading with and cheating the Indians, and, increasingly, by stealing from settled white farmers. Their ranks consisted of debtors, gamblers, displaced settlers who had not recovered from the destruction of the Cherokee War, deserters, and sometimes escaped slaves or interracially mixed people outside the fringes of respectable society. During and immediately after the chaos of the war, many of them turned to full-time banditry and lived in "outlaw settlements" away from white farming communities.[33]

By the summer of 1766, a full-fledged crime wave was sweeping over the backcountry. The outlaws committed dozens of robberies, assaults, and kidnappings among the more settled, respectable yeomen and planters—stealing horses and money, burning houses, beating and flogging respected citizens and "leading men" who refused to reveal the location of their valuables, and raping and abducting their daughters. Store owners and tavern keepers who resisted the robbers might find themselves tortured or their buildings burned to the ground with them still inside. Those settlers who prospered most were the most likely to become victims, one settler complaining that "the lowest state of poverty [was] to be preferred to riches and affluence."[34] Anyone who was rumored to have saved as much as fifty pounds "jeopardized his own life. No man was safe who was rumored to have such a sum."[35]

What made the crime wave even more intolerable was that the provincial government of South Carolina provided virtually no protection to its frontier settlers. The low-country rice and indigo planters and the aristocratic "placemen" from England who monopolized the colonial government back in Charleston came from a different social and economic world from that of the frontier. The differences between lowcountry and backcountry were dramatic. While backcountry yeomen and small planters supported themselves with a variety of crops and economic activities and relatively few blacks lived among them, the wealth of the lowcountry rested solidly on rice and slaves. By the 1760s, the nineteen coastal parishes contained less than one-quarter of the white population but 86 percent of its taxable wealth and more than 90 percent of its slaves. The size of the colonial assembly was limited to forty-eight members, forty-six of them from the lowcountry. The backcountry, holding three-fourths of the white population, was represented only by the two delegates from the parish of St. Mark, which had been created specifically so that the inland population would have a voice, however weak.[36]

The leading planters of the lowcountry and rich Charleston merchants did value the backcountry settlements, in a way. The frontier was a useful buffer against the Indians, and the white inhabitants of the coastal parishes, heavily outnumbered by the black people all around them, saw the white men of the backcountry as vital resources in case of a large-scale slave rebellion. Backcountrymen, likewise, did not desire such a rebellion, as it would leave them with a hostile black population on one side and Indians on the other.[37]

But the coastal elites did virtually nothing to help the backcountry maintain law and order. To begin with, the absence of local courts and magistrates was extremely inconvenient and expensive for inland settlers. Criminal cases and all civil suits involving an amount more than twenty pounds sterling required the backcountry settler to make a trip to Charleston, a journey of several days at least. This hardship made it difficult to prosecute criminals and collect debts and impeded commercial development by increasing the risk to lenders. Likewise, a small planter who wished to swear headrights and thereby solidify his claim to a land grant had to make the same trek. As Walter Edgar has noted, "If a person wanted to register a deed, prove a will, swear out a warrant, or file a lawsuit, a trip to Charleston was necessary. Estimates on travel times to the provincial capital . . . ranged from ten days to two weeks from Long Cane to a week or so from Ninety Six or Camden. Travel by wagon took more than twice as long."[38]

Without local courts, justices, and jails, it was hard for backcountry leaders to fight crime. Their efforts received a further rebuff in March 1767 due to Governor Lord Charles Montagu's leniency. The provincial government in Charleston that month managed to achieve only six convictions of backcountry bandits. Five of the culprits, guilty of robbing houses or stealing horses and sentenced to hang, received a pardon from the governor. After another wave of outrages washed over the region that summer, the "leading men" and other established farmers had had enough. This time they took the law into their own hands.[39]

Throughout the backcountry, communities organized bands of men to retaliate against the outlaws. With local "leading men" such as James Mayson, Moses Kirkland, Robert Cunningham, and William Wofford at their head, these bands attacked the outlaw communities, burned houses belonging to men suspected of harboring horse thieves, and flogged the criminals they captured. On October 6, Governor Montagu, alarmed at the illegality of these proceedings but still insensitive to the problems that caused them, denounced the vigilantes' "riots and disturbances" and ordered them to disperse.[40] Montagu's proclamation did no good, and two days later the outlaws counterattacked against the landholding vigilantes with a new wave of house burnings. James Mayson, a major in the militia and the vigilantes' leader in the Ninety Six area, was abducted from his home, bound, and "dragg'd, and insulted all the way" for a distance of eighty miles before being released.[41]

Meanwhile, the vigilantes organized themselves more formally. Now calling themselves "Regulators," they swore to support each other and "to execute the Laws against all Villains and Harbourers of Villains."[42] Some of their leaders also sent a petition to the colonial assembly, in which they explained that their only goal was to establish lawful order in their communities. They demanded that the provincial government provide schools, jails, courts, and courthouses. They insisted also on "Coercive Laws fram'd for the Punishment of Idleness and Vice, and for the lessening the Number of Vagrant and Indigent Persons, who now pray on the Industrious."[43] They wanted stricter regulations of taverns, restrictions on "hunters," and the creation of parishes in the backcountry so that they might gain more representation in the assembly. By the time the petition was presented, Charlestonians and other lowcountry Carolinians were beginning to understand the nature of the struggle—the *South Carolina Gazette* reported in late October that "the peaceful inhabitants . . . in a kind of desperation . . . have formed associations, to expel the villains from wherever they can get at them, and to do themselves justice in a summary way."[44]

It is impossible to determine exactly what role Andrew Pickens played in the Regulator movement. Certainly he represented the type of settler who would have supported and might have participated in it, even if he was still relatively young and not established enough to help lead it. As the Regulators began to succeed in suppressing the bandits, Pickens's uncle-by-marriage Patrick Calhoun was one of the handful of men who emerged from the more orderly environment to take his place in the colonial assembly, and Pickens himself would soon become a justice of the peace. Rachel Klein has argued that the Regulators did not wish simply to restore order but rather a certain kind of order, one that would protect their own ambitions as merchants, planters, and rising or aspiring slaveholders. Probably her argument is correct, as far as it goes, but there is no need to dismiss the Regulators' goals as primarily cynical and economic. The threat to the settlers and to their families' safety was real and terrifying. Neighbors, friends, and fellow churchgoers were being robbed, vandalized, and abducted. As a young husband and father, Pickens would have needed no

Family, War, and Order

economic motive at all to ride with the Regulators, or at least to support them in the early stages. By the time of the 1766 crime wave, he had been married to Becky for fourteen months and had an infant daughter, Mary, to protect and provide for.[45]

The problem was that just as the Regulators gained victory over the outlaws, they themselves became a threat to the peace of the community. On November 19, 1767, the assembly provided for two companies of mounted Rangers to be raised to take on the outlaws. The officers commissioned to lead this officially sanctioned force were leaders of the Regulators, and the rank and file also consisted of the most determined and active Regulators. During the winter of 1767–68, the Regulators chased outlaws into North Carolina, recovered 100 stolen horses and thirty-five abducted girls, and captured, shot, or summarily hung a number of outlaws. Having defeated the outlaw gangs, they now turned their attention to the marginal elements of backcountry society—vagrants, gamblers, and the poorest of farmers who pilfered from established landowners. They sometimes cruelly punished "infamous women" and men who were too lazy to provide for their families. They usurped the power of justices and constables, harassing those they believed to be cooperating with the outlaws or those who attempted to prosecute them for their excesses. Even those who supported the Regulators admitted that they were going too far, and a backlash appeared in the form of another organization, perhaps less principled and more opportunistic, whose participants called themselves the "Moderators." Their appearance and the Regulators' excesses made it even more difficult to determine who were the real villains. In March 1769, colonial authorities and a few prominent backcountry leaders narrowly prevented a pitched battle between the Regulators and the Moderators. The Moderators, having helped check the Regulators, disbanded. Soon the level of violence subsided. Fortunately, the king's subsequent approval of the assembly's Circuit Court Act in November satisfied nearly all of the grievances of the Regulators and the backcountry as a whole.[46]

Again, while there is no proof that Pickens actually rode with the Regulators, it is not difficult to guess his general views. As a man who strived for the rest of his life for the establishment of public order and community virtue, he almost certainly supported the Regulators' original goals but attempted to stand aloof from their later excesses. This was certainly the attitude of his prominent in-laws, Patrick and William Calhoun, who would have been also his neighbors and patrons. On July 4, 1769, a few months after the Regulator-Moderator truce, four leading men of the Ninety Six–Long Cane area joined in a pro-Regulator petition. Patrick and William were two of them; a third was Andrew Williamson, who would later serve as Pickens's immediate superior in the Revolutionary War. Seeing that the Regulators had lost a good deal of the approbation they had briefly enjoyed from the colonial government, and perhaps anticipating that properly appointed officials were soon to reestablish authority in the backcountry, the signers of the petition positioned themselves as the real defenders of order—as those who supported the Regulators' initial aims but who stood above the fray enough to see that the Regulators, too, had misbehaved. Calling for a vagrancy law, the petitioners stated the lack of such a statute "hath been in a great measure the occasion of the Regulators laying themselves open to the Law, and to a set of people called Moderators, who, we hear behave themselves worse than even the Regulators."[47]

Although Pickens apparently was not a leader in the Regulator movement, he certainly benefited from the results of it, including local courts and more backcountry representation in the assembly. His kinsman Patrick Calhoun served in the legislature, and Pickens himself became a justice of the peace in one of the newly established courts in 1769. Besides, he was emerging as one of the lay leaders of the Presbyterian church. In addition to his farming activities, he was beginning to establish a thriving business trading with the Indians, though he still referred to himself as a "planter." In fact, he sold some of his land in 1773 in order to build up his investments in his merchant activities.

By that same year, Pickens had also turned to the other economic strategy that was beginning to work for the backcountry elite—owning slaves. As indicated earlier, slavery was not yet a mainstay of the backcountry's economy. In 1773, however, Pickens borrowed £1,560 from a Charleston lawyer and put up two slaves, Dick and July, as security for the loan. (He obviously paid the loan back, as both slaves were mentioned in his 1809 will.)[48] At this time, there was virtually no opposition in the churches to slavery, though it would emerge later. White Americans, as a rule, simply had not come around to questioning the institution or thinking about it as a moral issue. Pickens, it seems, acquired slaves just as soon as it was economically feasible to do so.

By late 1774, Pickens had established himself as a rising member of the "backcountry elite," or a leading man. At the age of thirty-five, he was a slave owner, merchant, justice of the peace, church leader, and moderately large landowner. He was also the father of four—Mary, Ezekiel, Ann, and Jane Bonneau.[49] Pickens knew that he lived in a disorderly, chaotic, and "sinful" world—both experience and Calvinist doctrine made it clear. To confront evil and anarchy, to protect their families and their own interests, good men had to step forward. They had to impose law and order, attend to the duties of religion, organize, and often fight. Yet even when mortal threats were confronted, even when the "good guys" won, they themselves could become oppressors. Royal troops sent to check Indian barbarity could resort to cruelty; Regulators organized to crush outlaws could themselves become tyrants. As a rising merchant and family man, Pickens had every reason to long for, and every reason to pursue, more security and peace in the backcountry. Instead, he, his family, and his neighbors, survivors of the Cherokee and Regulator wars, would soon witness more upheaval, violence, and destruction than they had ever imagined.

THREE

The Backcountry Militia

There was much hard service ... of which I had a full share.

Andrew Pickens to Henry Lee, August 28, 1811

On November 19, 1775, Captain Andrew Pickens found himself, along with 559 other armed men, defending a stockade in Ninety Six. With him were relatives, friends, neighbors, and an older, more prominent neighbor, Major Andrew Williamson, who commanded the garrison. Pickens and his "Whig" or "patriot" comrades claimed to represent the new, Revolutionary Provincial Congress of South Carolina and to be defending good government and "Liberty." Their equally determined opponents were other Americans—backcountry men who were "loyal" or "loyalist" subjects— known as "Tories." They were convinced that the real threat to safety, order, and freedom was not the king and his ministers but the allegedly self-serving colonial leaders who opposed him. For both sides, passions were already inflamed and the stakes were already high. But few had any idea that their communities and all of South Carolina were soon to descend into unprecedented depths of pillage, plunder, savagery, and social collapse.

The story of South Carolina's revolution is long and complicated, and figuring the backcountry into the narrative adds even more complexity. The object here is not to retell that entire story but to situate Andrew Pickens in the midst of it and to understand how and why he emerged as an early leader, if initially one of middling rank, in the "patriot" cause. The original leaders of that cause, who were overwhelmingly wealthy planters and merchants from the lowcountry, found that they had to depend more than ever on the local leaders of the backcountry if they wanted their cause to succeed. What should also be understood is that the frontier patriot militia in South Carolina was not simply a band of "rebels" wishing to overthrow all governmental restraint. One might think of them, instead, as the volunteer constabulary upholding the new Whig government in Charleston. By the time of the siege of Ninety Six, these Whig or "patriot" authorities considered the militia the most tangible force for law and order in the backcountry. And it was those authorities, not the crown's ministers, who had been pulling the strings in South Carolina for well over a year.

While the South Carolina backcountry had struggled to build an orderly society in the 1760s, the elites of the lowcountry had different concerns. They had seen bandits, Regulators, and the establishment of circuit courts in the interior districts as distractions at worst, or at best as smaller parts of a larger issue. Coastal planters and merchants were more apt to focus their attention on London and the royal appointees arriving from the metropolis than on the frontier to their west. While the frontiersmen were preoccupied with Indians and bandits, the lowcountry reacted vehemently against the Stamp Act, inept appointees of the crown, and other irritations coming from London. By 1771, cooperation between the provincial Commons and crown-appointed governors in Charleston had broken down so thoroughly that one could argue that royal government was no longer operational in South Carolina; this was the last year that the colonial government actually passed any legislation. After that time, the Tea Act of 1773 and the Coercive Acts of 1774 further inflamed colonial opposition. By 1774, royal government no longer existed at all in South Carolina, and the colonial assembly and a "General Committee" attempted to direct events; beginning in 1775, a "Provincial Congress" claimed to govern from Charleston.[1]

Before the spring of 1775, most of the outrage against the British authorities was confined to the coast. On the one hand, many people of the backcountry had no affection for the lowcountry elites leading the American protest, the same aristocrats who had for decades so callously spurned their pleas for more representation and better local government. Indeed, most German settlers in the Orangeburg and Dutch Fork settlements felt they owed their status as landowners to the German-born king of Britain, George II, and were generally loyal to the crown. Loyalist or "Tory" sentiment was also strong in what was still considered the northern part of the vast Ninety Six District— the land between the Broad and Saluda Rivers. In other communities such as Long Cane, west of the Saluda, a majority of residents took the Whig side of the question. Much in the backcountry depended on the attitudes of

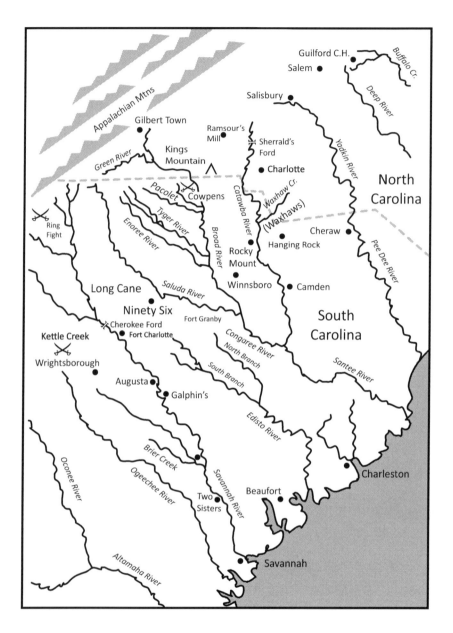

Western Carolinas during the Revolution *(Map by Chris Cartledge)*

"leading men" in each community who could bring scores or even hundreds of neighbors with them in the cause they chose. Some of them, such as Thomas Fletchall of the Fairforest community in the region between the Saluda and Broad Rivers and Thomas Brown of Augusta, Georgia, just across the Savannah River, were steadfast loyalists throughout the conflict. Other influential figures such as Moses Kirkland and Robert and Patrick Cunningham were willing enough, or might have been willing enough, to serve the patriot cause until personal slights and jealousies or calculating self-interest drove them into the king's camp. Still other backcountry settlers remained steadfastly neutral until one side or the other, Whigs or Tories, mistreated them, after which they angrily retaliated by joining the side that had not.[2]

And yet there were several reasons why a backcountry settler might oppose the king and join the Whig leaders, and most of them applied in Andrew Pickens's case. Some local leading men in the backcountry, after the approval of the Circuit Court Act in 1769 and the suppression of banditry, embraced new hopes of profitable relations with the lowcountry. Business contacts between the two Carolina regions were becoming more important, as suggested by Pickens's own dealings with Charleston merchants. And the coastal nabobs governing from Charleston had actually shown more respect for the backcountry's needs of late. Soon after the Regulator movement, they had respectfully heard Pickens's kinsman Patrick Calhoun and other backcountry leaders and passed the Circuit Court Act. It was the king who had initially vetoed the legislation in 1768 and had also vetoed the legislature's attempt to create two new parishes, giving the backcountry more representation—thus it was London, not Charleston, that appeared more hostile to the backcountry's interests.[3] Moreover, all of Pickens's relatives, and many of his most prominent neighbors in Long Cane, were firmly in the patriot camp. Patrick Calhoun, in fact, soon became a member of the Provincial Congress and thus one of the backcountry's most prominent representatives in the Revolutionary government. William Calhoun and Andrew Williamson also took the Whig side.

Sensitivity to Pickens's family and religious background also reminds us that in the experience of Scotch-Irish Presbyterianism, tyranny and vice seemed inherent to royal government. It might be unwise to assume that Scotch-Irish Presbyterians of Pickens's generation still nursed grudges for what had been done to their grandparents and older ancestors in Ulster. On the other hand, unlike the German settlers in South Carolina, they also had no particular reason to favor English rule; the English crown had never done anything for them.[4]

Pickens, like most Americans of his generation and educational background, left no written musings on religious doctrine or political philosophy. Yet he was intensely active as a church elder and church founder throughout his life, and as the most prominent historian of the Scotch-Irish has pointed out, the Presbyterian church had been for much of his life "the one effective social institution" in Scotch-Irish frontier communities.[5] The Calvinist-Presbyterian tradition in which Pickens was raised and in which he worshipped contained vital underpinnings for eighteenth-century American republicanism. Calvinist emphasis on the fallen state of man and his inherent sinfulness led to at least two conclusions concerning human authority—first, the existence of law and authority were vital to maintaining moral and social order; and second, authority could not be safely entrusted to any one man or body of men. Thus, the power of monarchs, bishops, and parliaments had to be limited and counterbalanced. Calvinist thinking from the sixteenth through the eighteenth centuries also included a strong preference for representative government, both in the church and in secular government. Finally, Calvinist thought from Calvin himself to the leaders of French Huguenots, Scottish Presbyterians, English Puritans, and American Congregationalists and Presbyterians included emphasis on "covenant theology." One tenet of covenant theology was that there was a compact between people and their government and that, in severe cases of abuse by the latter, the people were justified in overthrowing it. Calvin himself had been very reluctant to sanction rebellion against civil magistrates, though some of his later writings seemed to leave the door open. His later followers, including Huguenots, Puritans, and, most saliently, Scottish Presbyterians, left ample room in their doctrines for popular rebellion; some of the greatest threats to the absolute claims of royal authority in Europe from the late sixteenth to the late eighteenth centuries came from those Calvinist traditions.[6]

During and immediately after the war, both sides in the Revolutionary War regarded Presbyterians—and their Congregationalist coreligionists of Puritan extraction—as unanimous supporters of American independence. Assuming that religious dissent against Anglicanism was synonymous with treason, the king himself had reportedly condemned the American Revolution as a "Presbyterian rebellion." A Hessian officer had written in 1778, "Call this war by whatever name you may, only call it not an American rebellion. It is nothing more or less than a Scotch Irish Presbyterian rebellion."[7] American loyalists also frequently blamed Presbyterianism and Congregationalism; one reported to London that "Presbyterianism is really at the Bottom of this whole conspiracy."[8]

There was a decided tendency for Congregationalists and Presbyterians to favor the Whig cause, especially from North Carolina northward. Several historians of religion have pointed out that Whig political ideology and the doctrine of Calvinist Reformed churches in America were wholly compatible, to the extent that "it was increasingly difficult to discern where one left off and the other began."[9] In South Carolina, there was initially some ambivalence among Presbyterian congregations, though there is ample evidence of Presbyterian clergymen supporting the cause of American liberty. Some later historians have doubted contemporary claims that American Presbyterians overwhelmingly supported the Whig cause, particularly in the Carolinas, as there is no surviving evidence that could provide statistical proof of those claims. Anecdotal evidence, however, certainly suggests it and proves at least that a number of Presbyterian clergymen of the backcountry were vehement and militant in their support of the patriot cause, literally leading the men of their congregations into the ranks.[10] One of the most important Whig voices in the South Carolina backcountry in 1776 had been the Presbyterian minister William Tennent. In the Long Cane community, Pickens sometimes had his troops muster near the home of the local Presbyterian minister and fiery revolutionary John Harris, who preached adamantly in favor of republicanism. At least once, Harris preached at the stone blockhouse Pickens had built near his own home.[11] As we shall see, the passion and vehemence of those Presbyterian clergymen and their flocks who did support the Revolutionary cause was undeniable.

Many historians note the backcountry's concern for "order" and how support for the Revolutionary cause often seemed the most effective way to safeguard it. For example, Rachel Klein emphasizes the merging interests of lowcountry and frontier elites—both desired stability that would allow commercial activity and the expansion of plantation agriculture. There were two threats to order that most concerned white South Carolinians—the lowcountry feared slave rebellions, and the backcountry dreaded Indian attacks. Either of these events promised not only the breakdown of lawful order but also the destruction of white men's property and prosperity, not to mention their families and their lives. Whichever side hoped to claim the allegiance of most white South Carolinians would have to prove its devotion to preventing either of these calamities. During 1775 and 1776, much of the white population grew convinced that the British government was actually scheming to instigate these events, not prevent them—to harm its subjects, not protect them.[12] Thus, it would be wrong to regard Revolutionary leaders in the backcountry simply as "rebels" who were impatient of authority for its own sake. It was no accident that the men who led the Regulator movement in the name of law and order overwhelmingly supported the patriot cause in the Revolution.[13]

To be sure, by the time of the siege of Ninety Six, other South Carolinians had either remained ambivalent or come to opposite conclusions on the relative merits of Whig versus royal authority. But such was not the case with Andrew Pickens. The devout Scotch-Irish Presbyterian frontiersman, family man, church elder, rising planter, and frontier merchant saw nothing incompatible between service in the patriot cause and the demands of private interest, civic duty, and indeed religious duty and family loyalty.

Between 1774 and 1776, Revolutionary leaders in South Carolina established themselves as the authorities in the province; even as they did so, their actions had a polarizing effect on public opinion in the backcountry. From December 1773 through 1775, a succession of "committees" and "congresses" had supplanted the royally sanctioned government and effectively ran the colony. The "Mass Meeting," formed on December 3, 1773, to make a stand against the Tea Act, in turn formed the General Committee. In the summer of 1774, the General Committee called for a General Meeting, which sent five delegates to the First Continental Congress meeting in Philadelphia. Present at the General Meeting was a respectable contingent of delegates from the backcountry.[14]

When the Continental Congress delegates returned from Philadelphia to Charleston in November, they reported on the Congress's establishment of a Continental Association, a nearly complete embargo of trade with Great Britain. The General Committee therefore formed an "Association" to enforce the embargo and boycott in every community. The General Committee also formed a "Secret Committee" with the mission of acquiring arms and ammunition and finally called for the election of a provincial congress that would meet in January 1775. Though still looking out for their own interests first, the lowcountry leaders made a bid for the support of the backcountry—55 of the Congress's 187 delegates would be from the backcountry settlements. Those selected from the Ninety Six District included Patrick and William Calhoun; Colonel James Mayson; Pickens's business associate John Lewis Gervais; Pickens's future military commander Major Andrew Williamson; and his future subordinate Le Roy Hammond.[15]

Over the course of the next nine to twelve months, the Provincial Congress and Secret Committee moved aggressively to solidify their control. Several events came to a head in the spring. The Secret Committee intercepted government mail from British officials to those in the colonies, including letters indicating that the British planned to use military force against the "rebels." Shortly thereafter, in April, the Secret Committee seized 1,600 pounds of gunpowder, 800 muskets, and 200 swords from the colony's official stores.

Despite all the turmoil in the lowcountry, most backcountry South Carolinians had been able to avoid taking sides in 1774 and the winter of 1775. Several events in the spring and summer of 1775 changed this. The first was the growing suspicion that the British were willing to unleash Indian attacks on the frontier as a means of punishing the colonies and forcing them to remain under the crown's authority. On May 3, a letter arrived from Arthur Lee, a Virginian in London, warning that British authorities planned to incite Cherokee attacks on the frontier and slave rebellions in the lowcountry. The charges were untrue but widely believed. This coincided with rumors that Captain John Stuart, Britain's Indian superintendent in the South, had betrayed a white frontier garrison in 1763 and subsequently encouraged a Cherokee attack later that year. Moreover, a leading patriot in Georgia, James Habersham, saw a letter to Stuart from Stuart's deputy, Alexander Cameron, that seemed to suggest that the two Indian agents were plotting to incite an attack on the frontier. Cameron was actually in Long Cane when he wrote the letter, in which he promised Stuart that he could lead down "any number [of Cherokees] that [Stuart] thought proper, whenever called up in support of his Majesty and Government."[16] Actually the two officials were endeavoring to prevent hostilities with the Indians, but the ambiguous wording of the letter convinced many Georgians and Carolinians otherwise. When the scandal erupted, Stuart promptly and wisely fled to the British fort at St. Augustine, Florida, and Cameron withdrew into Cherokee territory. Thus many South Carolinians suspected the British of attempting to incite slave rebellions and Indian attacks. In the words of one author, "two better accusations could not have been found to rally the population of South Carolina behind the patriot cause."[17]

Moreover, news arrived in May 1775 that seemed to confirm the rumors that Britain planned to crush American colonial protests with armed force. On April 19, a large body of British redcoats marched on the towns of Lexington and Concord, Massachusetts, and blood was shed. A "Committee of Intelligence" reported this event to the backcountry, declaring that the king's troops had "commenced hostilities against this continent," seized and destroyed property, "slaughtered the unarmed," and "massacred our fellow-subjects in Massachusetts Bay." The people of America, however, had fought back with courage and virtue, and God had blessed them and punished the wicked on the day of the British attacks: "the Divine vengeance pursued the guilty, even from the rising up of the sun until the going down of the same—the King's troops were discomfited—they fled before our injured friends—the night saved them from total destruction."[18]

Amid news of fighting at Lexington and Concord and swirling rumors of impending slave revolts and Indian attacks, the Provincial Congress convened again hastily on June 1, and Patrick Calhoun was a delegate. One of the urgent tasks of the Congress was a military mobilization. The revolutionaries created two new "regiments of foot" of 750 men each and appointed its officers. For the backcountry, the Provincial Congress authorized a regiment of "Rangers" to consist of 450 men and appointed its officers from the commander, a lieutenant colonel, down to the rank of first lieutenant. This was part of a deliberate attempt to win the support of backcountry leaders by appointing them officers in a regiment that would do most of its service in their area. There was significant competition for the positions of lieutenant colonel and major in the Rangers, though no one seemed particularly surprised when William Thomson was named lieutenant colonel. The three leading candidates for the post of major—James Mayson, Robert Cunningham, and Moses Kirkland—were all men who had military experience and lived not far from Ninety Six. Pickens believed that Cunningham "would have made the best officer." The position went to Mayson, however, "which so exasperated the others," remembered Pickens, "that they immediately took the other side of the question." Both Kirkland and Cunningham were influential men, and Pickens believed that if Cunningham had been elected major, there "would not have [been] so violent an opposition to our cause."[19]

The three new provincial regiments, however, were only part of South Carolina's military establishment. The colony already had an existing militia organization of twelve loosely organized regiments. The senior officers of these existing organizations were, of course, among the most influential men of their communities, and much depended on which "side of the question" they would take. Whigs fervently hoped that all of them would abandon support of the crown and declare themselves willing to defend the "liberties of America." Meanwhile, a "Council of Safety" would exercise immediate control over the three provincial regiments and the militia regiments.

Besides organizing the military force of the province, the Provincial Congress showed that it was more determined than ever to suppress dissent against the Revolutionary movement. The delegates adopted and signed a new "Association." This document did not concern itself merely with embargoes and boycotts but instead called for every South Carolinian to declare his commitment to defend the constitutional rights of Americans against imperial authority. Denouncing the "commencement of hostilities" against their fellow subjects in Massachusetts, the recent actions of a "wicked and despotic ministry," and the threat of "insurrections" instigated by British officials, the Provincial Congress declared that the people of South Carolina had been driven to take up arms:

> We therefore, the subscribers, inhabitants of *South-Carolina*, holding ourselves bound, by that most sacred of all obligations, the duty of good citizens towards an injured country, and thoroughly convinced, that, under our present circumstances, we shall be justified before God and man, resisting force by force; DO UNITE ourselves, under every tie of religion and of honour, and associate, as a band in her defence, against every foe: Hereby solemnly engaging that, whenever our Continental or Provincial Councils shall decree it necessary, we will go forth, and be ready to sacrifice our lives and fortunes to secure her freedom and safety.

The kicker was the last sentence, in which the Congress indicated that it would tolerate no dissent from those who were reluctant to go along: "And we will hold all those persons inimical to the liberty of the colonies, who shall refuse to subscribe this association."[20] "Leading men" in every town and crossroads were appointed to enforce the "Association." Those who refused to sign it were stigmatized and harassed, especially in the lowcountry where the authority of the Provincial Congress was more secure. Clearly the Whig leaders were flexing their muscles; implicitly, "rebels" were defined as those who opposed their authority. There was probably little soul-searching for Andrew Pickens. Local enforcers of the Association in Ninety Six District were his relatives and most prominent neighbors—including the Calhouns, Andrew Williamson, and Le Roy Hammond.[21]

While it may have been rather natural for Pickens to side with the Association, other backcountry residents objected angrily to the high-handed tactics of "congresses," "secret committees," "associations," and the like. In some areas, a few of the very men who were counted on to uphold the Association were its most stubborn opponents. One of them was Colonel Thomas Fletchall, who resided in the Fairforest Creek area between the Broad and Saluda Rivers. Fletchall still held his militia colonel's commission from the king and still commanded one of the twelve original regiments that the Provincial Congress hoped would come over to the Whig side. He also held positions as coroner and justice of the peace, as well as some 1,650 acres, making him the most important "leading man" between the Broad and Saluda.[22] When Fletchall mustered his militia regiment on July 13 to present the new Association to his troops and ask who wanted to sign it, he did so in a way that indicated his disapproval. Not a single man stepped forward to sign; instead, they would later bind themselves into a rival "association" that opposed the Whig authorities. Even as Fletchall was mustering his men, a nervous Council of Safety was writing to pressure him to declare for the patriot cause. Fletchall was corpulent, slow-moving, and often overly cautious but was nevertheless not a man to be bullied at this early stage. He defiantly informed the Council of Safety that "not one man in fifty" in his district had ever given his assent to the authority of the Provincial Congress or the Council of Safety. "I am resolved," he concluded, "and do utterly refuse to take up arms against my King."[23]

Fletchall was not the only "leading man" of the backcountry who disapproved of the machinations of the Whig revolutionaries. Major Joseph Robinson, a militia officer in the New Acquisition District (modern York County), was actually more energetic in the loyalist cause than Fletchall. It was he who actually drafted the "Counter-Association" signed by his men and by Fletchall's. The counter-associators, or "nonassociators," expressed a desire to live in peace with their neighbors but adamantly refused to obey any laws other than those passed by His Majesty's government or by the original, duly constituted General Assembly. Other prominent loyalists included the brothers Robert and Patrick Cunningham. Robert was a planter and justice of the peace with military talent who lived on the eastern bank of the Saluda, just six miles from Ninety Six. His brother Patrick, also influential, lived farther upstream. Their cousin William Cunningham lived west of Ninety Six and thus very close to Pickens. Later known as "Bloody Bill," he would become one of the most vicious and hated Tory leaders in South Carolina. From just across the Savannah River in Augusta, the young, fiery, and capable Thomas Brown came to Fletchall's followers and offered his support. Brown had arrived in America in 1774 with seventy-four indentured servants and established himself as a large planter on 5,600 acres of land north of Augusta. In the summer of 1775 he refused the demand of Georgia patriots to sign their Association. Their response was to drag him from his house, tie him to a tree five miles away, and roast the soles of his feet with burning torches. By doing so, they created an even more adamant and dangerous enemy. Shrewdly monitoring events and nursing his own grudges was the backcountry merchant and planter Moses Kirkland, for the time being a Whig. Angry that the Provincial Congress had given him only a captain's commission rather than a major's in the new backcountry provincial Rangers, Kirkland would soon switch sides and become a loyalist.[24]

Thus while the Provincial Congress had gone far toward asserting its authority in the coastal parishes in the first half of 1775, the backcountry— populous and militarily important—was still in play. Both sides worried about which way the frontier settlements would go. If they adhered to the king, the Whig rebellion in South Carolina might ultimately fail after all. And while the authority of the royal governor, Lord William Campbell, was virtually ignored in Charleston, Lord Campbell had extensive contact with Fletchall, Robinson, and other loyalists of the backcountry.

In an attempt to gain the decisive support of the frontier districts, the Council of Safety dispatched a delegation to travel throughout the region, explain the nature of the dispute between the colonies and Britain, and encourage expressions of loyalty to the cause of America. The key delegates were a fiery young revolutionary and member of the Council of Safety from the lowcountry, Judge William Drayton, and a Presbyterian minister and member of the Provincial Congress from Charleston, William Tennent. Tennent believed that Parliament was attempting to fix the shackles of "the most Abject Slavery" upon the American colonies.[25] He was also outraged by actions of some Anglican clergy in Massachusetts and by what he saw as an "Anglican plot" to install bishops in America and crush religious freedom. Recalling that in the past bishops had led the effort to stamp out Puritanism and Presbyterianism and that any current bishop would be a member of the House of Lords, Tennent charged that the "design was to . . . obtain bishops with civil powers." He claimed that Americans' ancestors, including Anglicans in South Carolina, had "fled from the hand of Episcopal tyranny in the intemperate days of [Archbishop William] Laud. They brought with them, they have handed down, a spirit of independency and a resolution to think for themselves."[26] At various locations, Drayton and Tennent were joined by others, including Baptist minister Oliver Hart and backcountry planter Colonel Richard Richardson of the Congarees area.

Drayton and Tennent set out on July 31, 1775, and had mixed success. The German settlers in the Saxe-Gotha District (on the south bank of the Congaree River near modern Columbia) were neutral at best and hostile at worst to the Whigs' arguments. In the New Acquisition, Tennent was able to win over substantial support of Presbyterians despite the influence of

Joseph Robinson. The Baptists in the Upper Dutch Fork region along the Broad River were generally unreceptive, as were many in the entire area between the Broad and Saluda where Fletchall held much sway. Tennent and Drayton had great success, however, in the Ninety Six District between the Saluda and Savannah Rivers, including the neighborhoods of Ninety Six and Long Cane. This was the territory of leading Whigs like the Calhouns, James Mayson, and Andrew Williamson, along with the up-and-coming Andrew Pickens, James McCall, and Robert Anderson.[27] Tennent reported some divided sentiment in Pickens's neighborhood, Long Cane, but the support "of some of our worthy members" had influenced a majority to sign the Association.[28] Tennent spoke on August 30 in the Long Cane community and received the support of Presbyterian minister John Harris and the respected Jewish patriot Francis Salvador. Later that evening he personally visited the Calhouns and other prominent men, one of them almost certainly Pickens. On September 1, Tennent reported to the Council of Safety that already three militia companies were formed, commanded by Major Terry, Captain Andrew Pickens, and Captain James McCall. It is likely that these companies had formed before Tennent's arrival, for local leaders greeted Tennent with their concern about a lack of ammunition. Tennent promised that the Council of Safety would supply them.[29]

By the end of August 1775, then, Pickens had irrevocably committed himself to the patriot cause, and he had done so at a time when nothing was certain. Everyone was operating in an environment of confusion and uncertainty. Tennent's and Drayton's journals and reports to the Council of Safety are full of rumors and alarms: the Cherokees were gathering for an attack; this or that band of loyalists was preparing to seize a fort or a supply of gunpowder; Moses Kirkland had deserted to the Tories; this or that person had joined or rejected the Association. Rather than sit on the sidelines and wait for the dust to settle or for Tories or Indians to strike first, Pickens took charge of several dozen men and asked for gunpowder.

The two sides narrowly avoided shedding each other's blood in September. Various bodies of militia were recruiting, forming, gathering supplies, and marching. On the Whig side, Andrew Pickens was actively leading one of them. By mid-September, Drayton had assembled around 1,000 men and four swivel guns less than a mile from the Ninety Six courthouse.[30] His principal forces consisted of the provincial Rangers under Colonel William Thomson and a number of militia companies under Major Andrew Williamson, one of them commanded by Pickens. Just across the

Saluda River, Fletchall, Brown, and Robert and Patrick Cunningham had assembled a larger number of loyalists. The latter, however, were poorly armed, badly supplied with powder, and poorly led, with Brown and the Cunninghams rebelling against Fletchall's timid leadership and reluctance to attack.[31] After an exchange of messages between the two sides, the fearful Fletchall and a few other loyalist officers rode into Drayton's camp on September 16 and signed the Treaty of Ninety Six. The treaty, on the one hand, was conciliatory. It stated that those who had opposed the Provincial Congress had done so out of "misunderstandings" and were interested only in living in peace with their neighbors. At the same time, however, the treaty was a victory declaration by Drayton. The loyalists were free to return home without harassment or penalty so long as they swore not to assist any British troops who might come into the province or speak against the authority of the Provincial Congress. Any loyalists who considered themselves unbound by the treaty would have to "abide by the consequences."[32]

Drayton was jubilant, but the Treaty of Ninety Six began to break down almost immediately. Brown and the Cunningham brothers had angrily refused the parley with Drayton and did not consider themselves bound by the treaty. And Drayton never intended to extend its protections to the traitor Kirkland, who had already fled to Charleston and joined the royal governor Campbell on board his ship. At least Kirkland was temporarily out of the way, and the Whigs were able to arrest Robert Cunningham and imprison him in Charleston.

Robert Cunningham's younger brother Patrick, however, soon got his revenge. The Whig authorities were anxious to keep the Cherokees on their side or at least neutral. Besides the rumors that British agents Stuart and Cameron had been attempting to instigate an Indian attack, some Cherokee chiefs themselves expressed their displeasure at not receiving their customary supply of ammunition that enabled them to hunt and supply deerskins to the white people, disrupting the normal flow of trade that was so vital to Cherokee prosperity. The Council of Safety therefore sent a shipment of 1,000 pounds of powder and 1,000 pounds of lead, guarded by a small escort of Rangers.[33] Patrick Cunningham and his men ambushed the convoy and captured the ammunition.[34]

Patrick Cunningham had allowed the guards of the ammunition convoy to escape with their lives, but his action undoubtedly raised the enmity between Whig and Tory to new levels of mistrust. First, it jeopardized the uneasy peace between the Cherokees and the Whig government. Second, backcountry loyalists were persuaded that the Council of Safety was supplying ammunition to the Cherokees so that the latter would attack *them*. Already Whigs had accused the British of such nefarious schemes; now South Carolinians themselves were so suspicious of their neighbors that they suspected each other of the ultimate treason on the frontier—bringing the Indian's tomahawk and the scalping knife to a fellow white man's family.

The Whigs reacted immediately in an effort to punish Patrick Cunningham. Major Andrew Williamson's Ninety Six regiment was still embodied and went in search of Cunningham. The loyalist forces under Cunningham and Joseph Robinson, however, were reassembling in large numbers due to the Cherokee rumors, and Williamson decided against an attack.

Williamson's force was a conglomeration of small bands of men—no fewer than twenty-five militia companies making a total of 523 men, for an average of 21 men per company, along with 37 Rangers under the command of Major James Mayson. The largest two companies were led by James McCall (54 men) and Andrew Pickens (40 men). Approaching their position at Ninety Six was Cunningham and Robinson's force of well over 1,500. In consultation with his twenty-five company commanders, Williamson decided to occupy a large open area belonging to Colonel John Savage and create a stockade out of existing outbuildings and a perimeter of vertical fence rails. The open ground would allow the patriots to employ their few small cannons effectively. Before the stockade was quite complete on November 19, the Tories arrived in force and surrounded it. They also captured a small brick jailhouse nearby. After a parley in which the Tories demanded an immediate surrender, the two sides began firing. The siege continued for three days and three nights. The patriots were expecting reinforcements, but in the meantime their situation was growing desperate. They were low on powder, had no water supply for much of the time, and suffered terribly from thirst. On the twenty-first, they made plans for a midnight raid led by five captains with twenty picked men from each of their companies. One of the captains was Pickens. Before darkness fell, however, the Tories requested another parley. Unknown to the Whigs, the loyalists had learned that the Whigs' Colonel Richard Richardson was approaching with a force of several thousand men and were eager to break off the action. The two sides agreed the next morning to a twenty-day truce, and the stockade was to be destroyed. Pickens was one of the men chosen from the Whig side to help negotiate the treaty. If victory could be claimed by either side, it went to the Whigs. They had lost twelve men wounded and one killed, while the Tory losses were probably twice that number. With Richardson closing fast, the loyalists then withdrew across the Saluda to the northeast, with their numbers and their morale shrinking as they went.[35]

Richardson, with more than 3,000 men, including militia and Continentals from North Carolina, pursued the Tories deep into their stronghold in the land between the Broad and Saluda Rivers. After the truce expired, Williamson joined Richardson with his entire force, almost certainly including Pickens. The massive, confidently advancing Whig army demoralized the Tories. Richardson's men captured Thomas Fletchall and sent him back to Charleston with at least 135 other prisoners. It seems there were hundreds more whom Richardson simply disarmed, spoke to kindly, and sent home with their promises not to oppose the patriot cause in the future. Most expressed their regret, claiming they had been misled by rumors that the Whig government intended to have them slaughtered by the Cherokees. On December 22, a part of Richardson's force surprised Patrick Cunningham in his camp at the Cane Brakes, in Cherokee territory. Cunningham barely escaped, but his force was routed and much of it captured. The next day, a rare winter storm struck the South Carolina backcountry, leaving one and a half to two feet of snow on the ground. It was followed two days later by rain, sleet, and flooding. The poorly clad troops attempted to sleep on frozen or soggy ground with no tents; many suffered from severe frostbite. Ever afterward, Richardson's expedition was remembered in South Carolina Revolutionary lore as the "Snow Campaign." Having captured hundreds of Tories and their ammunition and smashing what was left of the resistance, Richardson dismissed his militia regiments and companies to their home regions and declared victory.[36]

With the Tories seemingly defeated and royal governor Campbell out of the colony, the patriot authorities resumed the search at the beginning of 1776 for stability and order. As always there was the concern with external security: among other military measures, the Provincial Congress appointed Williamson, Pickens, and three other men to inspect a fort on the Savannah River eighteen miles above Fort Charlotte and report what repairs would be necessary to make it useful in resisting an Indian attack.[37] In March it adopted a constitution as a temporary means of ensuring lawful government until "a reconciliation with Great Britain upon just and constitutional principles" occurred.[38] The Provincial Congress then dissolved and reconstituted itself as a "General Assembly" with the relatively moderate John Rutledge selected as "President and Commander in Chief."[39] Pickens and his friends Robert Anderson and William Henderson were appointed as justices of the peace for Ninety Six in April. The formerly "treasonous" district between the Broad and Saluda Rivers was split into three districts: the Lower, the Little River, and the Spartan Districts.[40]

In the summer of 1776, there were new attacks on the province, and the Ninety Six militia regiment, along with Captain Andrew Pickens, was once again called to action. The British attempted a major sea-land attack against Charleston on June 28, and the patriots repulsed it. The British attack, however, nearly coincided with a series of Indian attacks all along the American frontier. Several of the eastern tribes—Delawares, Shawnees, and the Iroquois confederation—had convinced the Cherokees that the time was right to defend what was left of their own hunting grounds by attacking the whites who were rebelling against the great king across the ocean. For his part, British Indian agent John Stuart thought that a war would be disastrous for the Cherokees and unwise policy for the British. However, when he saw that the Cherokees had decided to join the campaign anyway, he tried to convince them that at the very least they should time their attacks to coincide with the British attack on Charleston.[41]

Some South Carolina Tories were so embittered at this point that they committed the unthinkable act of joining forces with the Cherokees against their fellow white settlers. White patriots believed that the Tories' actions were premeditated. Reverend James Creswell of Ninety Six asserted to William Drayton that these white traitors were "elated with the prospect" of an Indian attack and "made no secret of their expectations of safety." There was a "compact" between the Tories and the Indians, and when the frontier militia companies began to muster, the Tories refused to turn out to fight.[42] The extent of this prior Tory-Indian collusion is uncertain, but it is certain that when the patriot militia fought the Cherokees, some of their foes turned out to be white men—South Carolinians—dressed and painted as Indians. More important in the long run was the further demonization of Tories in the minds of Whigs—white men who would join with the Cherokees in their attacks were no better than the "savages" themselves.

The Cherokees struck in many places across the South Carolina frontier in early and mid-July. Just as in 1760, horrific tales of families being butchered and children kidnapped spread like wildfire. At least sixty white settlers were killed. Major Andrew Williamson once again mobilized the Ninety Six regiment with some 700 men, while Colonel Thomas Neel of the Catawba River area assembled another large force. A contingent of Virginia troops under Colonel William Christian and a North Carolina regiment under Brigadier General Griffith Rutherford were to cooperate with the South Carolina forces against the Cherokees.[43]

The crisis, as usual, brought to the fore the men who had already proven most active and most reliable when under arms. Williamson, now the commander of the regiment, had proven himself in the troubled times of the previous year. Though still officially a major, most contemporary accounts of the ensuing campaign refer to him as either "Colonel" or "General" Williamson, and he was probably officially promoted during the course of the campaign.[44] Williamson was a planter, well off by backcountry standards, and an emigrant from Scotland. One of his former soldiers described him as "a middle aged, bald, keen appearing man—a fine officer, who had great regard for the comfort of his men."[45] Williamson, the man of the hour in the Ninety Six District, in turn summoned the most reliable captains as company commanders, including Andrew Pickens and Pickens's friend Robert Anderson, as well as Pickens's brother Joseph. Also serving with the force was the wealthy and popular Jewish planter from England, Francis Salvador.

For all his leadership ability, Williamson was not experienced in fighting Indians. The same soldier—Andrew Pickens, a younger cousin of Captain Andrew Pickens—who praised Williamson as an officer also claimed that he "seemed to have little or no knowledge of Indian warfare."[46] Allegedly, every morning Williamson would have a small swivel gun in front of his tent fire a single round and would then have reveille sounded, making it easy for the Cherokees to track his position on a daily basis. The criticism may not have been completely unfair. Pickens and a number of other militia officers had served in the Cherokee War of 1760–61; Williamson, as a more recent immigrant to the colony, had not.

Pickens and other soon-to-be-accomplished Indian fighters would quickly demonstrate their knowledge of the rules of successful Indian warfare. First, beware of ambushes. Second, when attacked, officers must respond immediately, aggressively, and decisively. Timidity and indecision were guarantees of failure. Third, whenever possible, burn the Indians' unoccupied villages and their corn to make the victory a lasting one. With their shelter and food supply destroyed, the Indians would need years to recover and mount a counterattack. As William Drayton advised Salvador, "It is expected [that] . . . you cut up every Indian corn-field, and burn every Indian town—and that every Indian taken shall be the slave and property of the taker; that the nation be extirpated, and the lands become the property of the public. For my part, I shall never give my voice for a peace with the Cherokee Nation upon any other terms than their removal beyond the mountains."[47] Drayton was now a chief justice and had no formal military authority, but his attitude was typical of white Americans by the time of the Revolution. A younger Lieutenant Andrew Pickens had witnessed this policy of destruction during the 1761 expedition and, like other white officers, had been appalled at what he called "brittish cruelty."[48] Fifteen years later, Pickens and his comrades showed little compunction in carrying out the same policy.

These tactics—avoiding ambush, responding to one aggressively, and destroying Indian villages and food reserves—made sense because of the peculiar nature of frontier warfare between whites and native tribes and the relative strengths and weaknesses of the opposing sides. Most of the fighting was in forested areas and on territory where the Cherokees or other Indians enjoyed superior knowledge of the terrain and of the white soldiers' movements. Usually the Indians could pick the time and place of the battle. Once the fighting began, however, the whites generally enjoyed superior firepower and unit cohesion, even among the militiamen who had minimal knowledge of European drill. If they could employ these to their advantage and respond aggressively, they could often overwhelm and drive off the Indians. Finally, because the Indians were so elusive and avoided pitched battles except when fighting from ambush, the whites employed a "reconnaissance in force" approach when invading Indian territory. With scouts and allied Indians guiding their march, large bodies of white militiamen marched on their enemies' villages. This forced the Indians either to stand and fight against superior white firepower or to abandon their settlements and food reserves. This approach violated accepted rules of warfare among Europeans. On the American frontier, however, racial hatred made it acceptable; military considerations made it absolutely necessary.[49]

On July 31, the Ninety Six regiment was located at Twenty Three Mile Creek, southeast of the modern town of Pendleton, South Carolina. Here Williamson received word that the British Indian agent Alexander Cameron was about thirty miles away at Oconee Creek with about 12 white men and 150 Cherokees. Williamson decided to pounce on this enemy force and departed that night with 330 men on horseback. He crossed the Keowee River and approached the Indian village of Esseneca (or Seneca) around 1:00 A.M.[50]

Williamson believed reports that the village had been abandoned and approached boldly, but he was about to march right into an ambush. Both he and Francis Salvador were near the front of the column. Pickens's company was closer to the rear. The Cherokees were fully aware of his approach and had posted some men in the houses at the edge of town. Others waited behind a long fence that ran alongside the road. The Cherokees let the advance guard reach the first houses of the village itself, with the main body fully exposed along the length of the fence.

Suddenly the Cherokees and the Tories with them began firing. Salvador fell wounded almost immediately, Williamson's horse was killed beneath him, and at least a dozen other militiamen were wounded in the first minute or two of the fight. The patriots struggled to hold their own in the darkness, chaos, and deafening noise. The fight was taking place at point-blank range; men could make out silhouettes without recognizing faces, and patriot militiamen were intermixed with Cherokees and Tories. Some patriots fired at the muzzle blasts behind the fence. One Captain Smith saw a figure near Salvador and assumed it was the latter's servant attempting to tend to his wounds. He watched in horror as the "servant" turned out to be a Cherokee who scalped Salvador alive. The patriots recovered Salvador's body but he died, obviously in great agony, about forty-five minutes later.[51]

In the confusion, Pickens responded aggressively. He and his men rode forward to join the fight. After ordering them to dismount, he had his men hitch their horses to trees if they could do so quickly; if not, they were to leave their horses unhitched and join the fight. Pickens's arrival seems to have helped the patriots achieve fire superiority and stabilize the situation—the younger Andrew Pickens claimed that the captain's arrival "soon restored order."[52]

"Cousin" Andrew may have given Pickens too much credit, for more men were wounded before the Indians retired, including Cousin Andrew himself. It seems true, though, that prompt action and superior firepower eventually allowed the white militia to claim a victory. After the Indians withdrew, Williamson's men found large quantities of blood behind tree stumps and blood trails leading into the woods, as well as abandoned tomahawks and bloody blankets. Enemy losses were evidently significant. The patriots themselves lost almost twenty killed and wounded. The next morning they scalped the wounded Cherokee warriors they found on the field and burned Seneca to the ground. They destroyed hundreds of bushels of corn and peas as well as the Indians' livestock, leaving them no winter food supply. Cameron and the Indians had sprung a clever ambush but had little to show for it but dead warriors, a destroyed village, and the prospect of starvation.[53]

Williamson moved on to the village of Sugar Town, where he met Neel's force. With no Cherokee warriors in their way, the militiamen destroyed the village as well the towns of Estatoe, Quaratchie, Toxaway, and Oconee. Meanwhile, Williamson sent Pickens and Robert Anderson to scout toward the Tugaloo River, which now forms part of the mountainous border between South Carolina and Georgia. They returned to Williamson on August 9 and reported that there were enemy warriors in the hills on both sides of the river, which was about forty yards wide. Williamson marched his entire force to the Tugaloo the next day and found the Indians and some white men on some commanding high ground on the other side ready to contest his crossing. Williamson ordered a detachment of men under Pickens and Anderson upstream to find another crossing and encircle the enemy from behind. Once again Pickens displayed a penchant for prompt and bold action. As he and his men moved upstream, they observed Indians moving parallel to them on the opposite bank and could not find an unopposed crossing site. Finally, Pickens found a "shoaly place" and ordered the men to cross. Anderson objected, pointing out that the bushes on the opposite bank were "full of Indians." Pickens replied that even if they marched all the way to the head of the river, there would be Indians there as well. Shouting "Come boys, follow me!" Pickens and his horse plunged into the river, with a "shower" of bullets landing around him. Pickens lifted his feet to keep them dry, and as he did so, a ball penetrated his saddle skirt and struck his horse exactly where his thigh would have been. Despite the heavy fire, the entire detachment reached the opposite bank with no casualties. The patriot militia was then able to flank the enemy forces out of their position on the knob, and the Indians and Tories fled.[54]

The campaign continued in its course of destruction, with Williamson burning more villages and corn as he advanced through the Cherokee "Lower Towns" in what is now the mountainous, extreme northwest corner of South Carolina. On August 12 the column reached the village of Tamassee. With his main body remaining in the village, Williamson dispatched groups of men to patrol the surrounding hills, including a detachment of sixty men under Pickens. Later in the day Pickens's force divided, with Anderson taking twenty-five men and Pickens taking thirty-five and a scout of mixed Indian-white descent named Branan.

Around 3:00 P.M. Pickens committed the mistake of walking into an ambush. His men saw an Indian "spy" and began pursuing him. Within minutes they found themselves in grave danger. They were in the middle of a grassy field, and all around them, to their horror, were Cherokee warriors rising out of the grass. Pickens was surrounded by a force several times the size of his, perhaps 180 or 200 Indians. The Cherokees began closing in as

Pickens's men formed themselves into a circle. Branan understood Cherokee and overheard the warriors shouting to each other to save their ammunition and close in on the whites and use their tomahawks. Branan advised Pickens to have his men lie down—to load their rifles from a prone position and rise to a squatting or kneeling position to fire. Pickens shouted some orders, and the white men began firing in relays once the Indians came to within about twenty-five yards of their perimeter. Their rifle fire took a heavy toll. Branan was soon wounded, after which Pickens discarded his own jammed rifle, took up Branan's, and resumed firing. Much of the fighting was done at tomahawk range, as Pickens's men killed three Indians with "corn knives and Tomahawks."[55] At times the Cherokee assault lost momentum as the Indians paused to drag their wounded away to prevent them from being scalped. Pickens's small band was holding its own but had taken heavy casualties and was still in a desperate situation. At least a third of his men were wounded, and every man was "covered litterally with blood & smoke."[56]

Meanwhile, Williamson and the other reconnoitering companies heard the gunfire about two miles away and went as quickly as they could to Pickens's assistance. The first to arrive was Pickens's brother, located with Williamson's main body at the village. Joseph Pickens had called for volunteers to join him; when some hesitated, he angrily departed with those who responded immediately. His arrival was followed shortly by small contingents under Anderson, Major Jonathan Downs, and finally 150 men with Williamson himself. The reinforcements added their firepower to the fight, and the Indians withdrew after a struggle that lasted at least an hour and a quarter. By every account, enemy losses were severe. Williamson counted sixteen enemy bodies within a space of 150 yards and guessed that total Indian losses could not have been fewer than sixty killed and wounded. As usual, the white troops took scalps from the Indian corpses. Williamson's force lost one man killed and fifteen wounded, three of whom later died. Probably all of these losses were from Pickens's small detachment of thirty-five. Some accounts claim that when the fighting was over, Joseph Pickens angrily cursed those who had refused to come with him immediately to rescue his brother. Pickens, in turn, calmly rebuked Joseph for his language.[57]

The "Ring Fight," as it came to be known, added greatly to Pickens's fighting reputation. He was certainly not the first white officer to walk into an Indian ambush, and he clearly displayed the knack for keeping his men steady when their initial reaction might have been terror and flight. More than that, Pickens began acquiring an aura of invincibility—he and his men should not have survived. Some white sources claim that it was as a result of

Andrew Pickens
(Portrait Collection of Historic Properties, Clemson University)

this battle that the Indians began calling Pickens "Sky-a-gun-sta" or "Great Warrior."[58] For his part, Williamson wrote twelve days later to Thomas Sumter, who was marching to reinforce him, to bring a major's commission for Pickens when he came.

Williamson paused at Seneca for several weeks to reprovision his forces and await Sumter's arrival. In mid-September, having destroyed the Cherokee Lower Towns, he advanced into present-day North Carolina, where Major Pickens made contact with Rutherford's force. The combined white army destroyed the Cherokee "Middle Towns" in the North Carolina mountains. By October 11, Williamson's regiment had devastated a total of thirty-six Indian towns, returned to South Carolina, and disbanded.[59]

Characteristically, Pickens recorded little of his service in the Revolutionary cause in 1775–76. His autobiographical letter to Henry Lee mentioned nothing about the battles of Ninety Six, Seneca, or the Tugaloo River or about the Ring Fight. His only comment about the entire period was that "there was much hard service with the disaffected white people as also with the Indians during the years before the fall of Charleston, of which I had a full share."[60] There are hints, though, that he related some stories to his family and that much of that oral tradition survived. Francis W. Pickens, his grandson, recalled that "my father has often told me that his father considered [the Ring Fight] the greatest danger he ever encountered, and that he was determined to live or die on the spot."[61]

The Cherokee campaign of 1776 dealt a devastating blow to the Cherokees. Early the following year, they negotiated a treaty with the South Carolina government relinquishing what are now the counties of Anderson, Greenville, most of Oconee, and Pickens, essentially filling out the boundaries of modern South Carolina.[62] The strategic threat from the Cherokees was greatly reduced. The campaign also permanently established Pickens's reputation as a successful Indian fighter, both among white Americans and among the Indians themselves.

Finally, it concluded the first phase of intense fighting in South Carolina's revolution. By the end of 1776, South Carolina had ratified the Declaration of Independence, and its new state government seemed secure. Farther north, George Washington's ragged band was retreating through New York and New Jersey and suffering one setback after another, but South Carolina patriots had achieved major victories over all three of their enemies—the Tories within, the British in Charleston Harbor, and the Indians to the west. In achieving this, the great planters and merchants of the lowcountry had to rely on the rougher-hewn "leading men" of the backcountry more than ever before. Not only had they astutely allowed the frontiersmen to participate in congresses and assemblies, but they also had found their military services indispensable. The backcountry militia, untrained as it was in European-style tactics, had effectively suppressed Tory opposition and crushed the Cherokees. Its services had been vital in achieving the order, security, and "liberty" so craved by the leading white men of the province.[63] And its officers were already shaping what the new republican leader should look like. The lowcountry aristocrats were still in a dominant position. But Revolutionary South Carolina had also had to turn to men with less wealth and no pedigrees, to men who often lacked polished manners, smooth speech, and sometimes even a formal education—men like Andrew Pickens.

FOUR

Defending the New Order, 1777–1779

I believe it was the severest check & chastisement the tories
ever received in South Carolina or Georgia.

Andrew Pickens to Henry Lee, August 28, 1811

The repulse of the British attack on Charleston and the crushing defeat inflicted on the Cherokees in 1776 led to a three-year period of relative peace in South Carolina. The Cherokee population in what is now the northwestern corner of the state was decimated. The South Carolina militia had played the primary role in suppressing and demoralizing the Tories and inflicting irreparable damage on the Indians—two groups whose strength and eagerness the British would need if they ever hoped to reconquer Georgia and the Carolinas.[1]

Whig authorities in South Carolina seized the opportunity to celebrate the Declaration of Independence ratified by the Continental Congress in Philadelphia, write a new state constitution, and attempt to strengthen civil society and the citizens' loyalty to the state. The project of building a stable republican society, though, was inextricably tied to military organization and defense. Thus, in time of war, the state as a whole turned to a different type of leader, though these new leaders had long been important in the backcountry. Faced with multiple internal and external threats and the need for an effective and rapidly deployable militia, South Carolina more than ever needed men who not only commanded respect in their local communities but also could inspire other men to rally to the colors and enlist, make decisions in the midst of war's uncertainties, and lead in combat. The rising prominence of Andrew Pickens as a civil and military leader illustrated how expectations of leaders were changing. Pickens had few of the traditional prerequisites for leadership under the old aristocratic system. He did not have a good education, great wealth, or even average speaking ability. He was, however, seen as honest, steady in times of uncertainty, and adept at leading other men in war. He was humane toward his enemies whenever possible but unflinching in applying violence when military necessity required it. He was exactly the kind of man that the fledgling republican state of South Carolina needed in its attempts to shore up liberty and order.

Pickens himself spent part of 1776 and all of 1777 in peaceful pursuits. He had been elected a justice of the peace for Ninety Six District early in 1776 and presumably resumed his duties in that role after the conclusion of the Cherokee campaign. He was also one of the district's ten representatives in South Carolina's Second General Assembly, which sat from late 1776 to 1778. The election took place in the autumn of 1776, and voters of the Ninety Six District chose men who, like Pickens, had served as Whig militia officers: James Moore, Le Roy Hammond, Robert Anderson, Andrew Williamson, and James Mayson. Other prominent Whig leaders of Ninety Six who were Pickens's kinsmen were elected as well, including Patrick Calhoun and Pickens's brother-in-law, John Ewing Colhoun.[2]

The Second General Assembly soon took up the task of drafting a state constitution to replace the temporary document that had hastily been drawn up in March. The final product ratified in 1777 reflected a mixture of Revolutionary ideology and the continued dominance of the lowcountry aristocracy. The backcountry was allotted only 64 of the 202 seats in the house of representatives, only slightly higher proportionally than the 40 out of 184 seats allotted in 1769.[3] Each district or parish in the state had one seat in the senate, except for Charleston, which got two. The property qualifications for governor and lieutenant governor were so high that they virtually excluded even prosperous men of the backcountry.[4]

On the other hand, the new constitution fully embraced ideals of personal liberty. The Anglican Church was disestablished in the name of religious freedom, to the great satisfaction of "dissenting sects" such as Presbyterians, Baptists, and Methodists. The constitution reduced the power of the chief executive and decreed that "liberty of the press" would be "inviolably preserved." Moreover, no person was to be "deprived of his life, liberty, or property, but by the judgment of his peers, or by the law of the land."[5] White South Carolinians of both the Tory and Whig factions were destined to deprive each other of these basic rights continually in the years to come, but neither Andrew Pickens nor the vast majority of his neighbors could have found any fault with these explicit promises of individual liberty as they appeared on paper.

South Carolinians also took advantage of the relative peace to establish educational institutions. The Mount Zion Society formed in February 1777 to organize education in the inland districts, beginning in the district of Camden. Lowcountry Episcopalians, Huguenots, Lutherans from Orangeburg, and Scotch-Irish Presbyterians from the backcountry came together for this venture and clearly perceived public education as intertwined with religious and moral improvement. Pickens formally joined the association a year later. For the rest of his public career, Pickens would be an enthusiastic supporter of education, clearly placing great value on opportunities he personally had never enjoyed.[6]

With a new state constitution in place, the General Assembly passed several acts in March 1778 intended to enforce civil order, as well as to mobilize the entire state on a military footing. These laws gave extraordinary authority to the state's military officers, including local captains such as Pickens. The three laws ratified on March 28, 1778, clearly envisioned the military organization of the state and the establishment of an orderly, civil society as part of the same project. Civil-military leaders were entrusted with both. In "An Act Enforcing An Assurance of Allegiance and Fidelity to the State," the General Assembly required every free male over the age of sixteen to swear allegiance to the state of South Carolina and to defend it from King George III, as well as from his successors and "abettors."[7] The legislature entrusted the administration of this oath to the regimental commanders of the militia, assisted by the other officers. The penalties for refusing to take the oath were severe.

A second law passed on March 28 was "An Act For completing the quota of Troops to be raised by this State for the Continental service; and for other purposes therein mentioned." Captains of militia companies were to make report to the local justice of the peace of all "idle, lewd, disorderly men, who have no habitations or settled place of abode . . . all sturdy beggars, and all strolling or straggling persons" within their district.[8] Such vagrants would be enlisted in a South Carolina regiment of the Continental army, subject to all the regulations, pay, and benefits as men who had volunteered. Also, men who engaged in the dangerous and disruptive practice of "fire hunting" would be considered "vagrants" and likewise enlisted in the Continental army.[9] Other provisions established penalties for selling alcohol to the soldiers, concealing deserters, or buying or acquiring the arms, equipment, or clothing of a soldier. Obviously, in practice, military officers would be the primary enforcers of these laws as well. Finally, the law attempted to ensure orderly settlement of the area in the northwestern corner of the state recently acquired from the Indians in the 1777 treaty. The General Assembly reserved the land between the Tugaloo and Keowee Rivers for veterans—no one could settle it until the conclusion of the war and until veterans had the opportunity to claim a bounty of 200 acres. Noting that some vagrants had already illegally occupied some of the land, the assembly placed the new territory under the jurisdiction of Ninety Six District and its magistrates.[10]

Finally, the Militia Law passed on the same day reorganized the state militia and gave its officers yet more authority and responsibility. The state's militia was divided into three brigades, each commanded by a brigadier general. Regiments with more than 1,200 men would be broken up, and each regiment remaining would have at least 600 men. The regimental colonel, lieutenant colonel, major, and adjutant would be "nominated by a majority of the field officers" and then commissioned by the governor.[11] Captains would ensure that their companies mustered and drilled once a month, and regimental commanders were required to muster the entire regiment once every six months. Every able-bodied man was required to join the nearest militia company and to report to musters with arms in good condition. It was up to captains of companies to punish those who did not.[12]

The Militia Act of 1778 stipulated that no regiment could be ordered to deploy more than three-fourths of its men outside its home state. For the lowcountry districts, this was clearly intended as a safeguard against a slave insurrection while the able-bodied men were away. The backcountry, meanwhile, had all too often suffered from the depredations of raiding Indians and "disorderly stragglers" to feel safe with its entire militia force sent away.[13] The state's leadership desired a docile, orderly slave population at home but also authorized the enlistment of enslaved men in the militia as hatchet men or pioneers or for fatigue duty, so long as they made up no more than one-third of their respective companies. In case of general alarm, the governor and privy council were to make the decision on whether this step would be taken but, again, the burden of enforcing the policy would fall on the militia captains. They would decide which slaves were fit and useful and would require slave owners to provide lists of their able slaves. Slave owners would receive reimbursement for their slaves' services, wounds, or death, but if they refused to provide slaves that were asked for, a "majority of the officers of the said [militia] company" were to seize fifty pounds of currency from the recalcitrant owners and turn the fine over to the state treasury.[14]

Defending the New Order, 1777–1779

Thus, as a militia captain, Pickens was to exercise not only military authority but great civil authority as well. The line between civil and military authority was blurred; meanwhile, the General Assembly had legitimized the social prestige and political authority of military officers, including middling sorts from the backcountry such as Pickens. By the end of that year, Pickens would have even more authority—Williamson would become one of the three brigade commanders and Pickens would be appointed colonel of Williamson's old regiment from the Ninety Six District.

Williamson, Pickens, and several other militia officers who also served in the legislature scarcely had time to vote on these new bills in late March before they had to mobilize their troops and embark on another campaign. Though there was relatively little military action within the state in 1778, some South Carolinians armed and spent much time in the field and some time fighting outside the state's borders. For them and Major Andrew Pickens, it was "a year of much service and little glory."[15] The main threat was Tory forces operating from the area around the St. Marys River in northern Florida, from which they had launched a series of raids into Georgia and South Carolina. The most important enemy force was the East Florida Rangers, led by Colonel Thomas Brown, the capable Tory officer who had endured torture from Whig militiamen but refused to abandon the king's cause. Brown's raids had captured Whig farmers' cattle and strongly encouraged Tory resistance and recruiting efforts in Georgia and South Carolina. Several hundred loyalists in the backcountry left their homes seeking safety with Brown and with British forces in Florida, and some joined the British army. Meanwhile, another force of 500 to 800 men, mostly plunderers and thieves, assembled in early April in Ninety Six District. Led by the notorious and hated brigand John Scovel (also frequently spelled "Scophol" or "Coffel"), they had moved southward in an effort to join Brown.

To eliminate these threats, Major General Robert Howe of the Continental army launched an expedition in May 1778 with 1,100 Continental soldiers from Georgia and South Carolina. South Carolina president Rawlins Lowndes ordered Colonel Andrew Williamson to call out his militia and join Howe, and Georgia governor John Houstoun of Georgia led a contingent of Georgia militia as well.

The campaign was little short of being a fiasco. Campaigning in late spring and summer in the lowlands of southern Georgia, Howe's Continentals suffered from inadequate supplies, brutal heat and humidity, insects, and disease. Similar difficulties faced the backcountry militia led by Colonel Williamson. Pickens was one of the subordinate commanders on this mission, although five other men with the rank of colonel were present and leading local contingents as well. It took Williamson's force of 1,200 militiamen weeks to make the long journey down the Savannah to join Howe, and throughout the campaign Williamson seemed reluctant to cooperate with the Continental army commander.[16] Moreover, and somewhat understandably, the militia seemed far more intent on locating John Scovel, the hated enemy of the backcountry, and bringing him to battle than on attacking the British fort on the St. Marys. This caused more delays in Williamson reaching Howe. On July 11, Williamson finally joined Howe on the St. Marys. By that time, Howe had reached Fort Tonyn only to find that the British had simply destroyed the fort and withdrawn, content to let "season and climate" do their work for them against the Whig forces.[17] Howe decided to withdraw his Continentals to South Carolina.

Pickens and Georgia militia leader Elijah Clarke, however, led large patrols into Alligator Swamp in search of Brown; one participant said that Pickens's patrol consisted of 500 men.[18] By the time Pickens reached the spot where Brown had emplaced a battery on a nearby creek, Brown had once again withdrawn. Witnesses said "there were no engagements," though one man who served under Pickens remembered that there was a "small skirmish" in which one man was wounded and "a horse shot."[19] Clarke's force, meanwhile, was ambushed and suffered twelve casualties. On July 25, Pickens's and the other contingents belonging to Williamson's exhausted and discouraged militia force were ordered to return home. Though the campaign accomplished little, it may offer more evidence of the growing confidence other officers placed in Pickens. The fact that Williamson would entrust 500 weary, frustrated militiamen of his 1,200-man force to Pickens when at least five more senior officers—colonels—were present suggests a high level of trust in his abilities. It is also possible that the experience affected Pickens's thinking on combined Regular-militia operations. Later in his career Pickens would stand out as a militia leader who was willing and able to cooperate with Regular state or Continental forces. Here he witnessed an example of what happened when that cooperation did not occur.[20]

Pickens had scarcely returned to Long Cane after the St. Marys expedition before he had to resume the field. Encouraged by the British, Indians were attacking the Georgia frontier and forcing the inhabitants to flee to small forts and blockhouses. Pickens led several of the companies under his command as they went to Georgia's aid. As usual when the backcountry militia assembled, the mobilization resembled a gathering of the clans. One company was led by Alexander Noble, husband of Catherine Calhoun, sister of Pickens's wife, Becky. One young man serving under Noble was John Harris, who would later become Pickens's son-in-law. Another junior officer who reported to Pickens was his older brother, Joseph, whose company was embodied for three months to serve in Georgia. On August 29, Pickens ordered another company under John Irvine to assemble on September 4 "where the Long Cane road crosses Little River" near the house of Reverend John Harris, a fiery Presbyterian, pro-Revolution minister who served several congregations in Ninety Six District.[21]

It is not clear exactly how long Pickens was in the field, but the campaign lasted at least through the end of November, and probably longer. Again, there were no dramatic results, but by the end of the year Pickens had solidified his reputation as a soldier and as a "leading man" of the backcountry in time of war. As a previous biographer has noted, he had become "almost a clan leader among a clannish people and had proved himself a capable fighter."[22] Sometime near the end of the year 1778 he was promoted to colonel, having risen rapidly from the rank of lieutenant since 1775. No evidence survives of Pickens angling, seeking, or "pulling wires" in an effort to be promoted, or even seeking glory or praise.[23] Instead, as Clyde Ferguson points out, he had become a possessor of "the prestige element, the inexplicable quality that makes undisciplined soldiers follow a leader."[24] Of course he was related to the prominent Calhouns, but it appears that Pickens was already gaining a reputation as a dependable and unflappable leader—one who combined a quiet firmness and confidence with boldness and decisiveness when the guns began to shoot. At the battle of Kettle Creek in the following year, Pickens would solidify that reputation once and for all.

Even as Whig governments in the South were working to solidify their control in 1778, the British high command was planning a renewed effort to return the southern colonies to the crown's authority. The British war effort in the New England and middle colonies had seen only mixed success after three years of fighting, and the British placed great confidence in the level of loyalist support in Georgia, the Carolinas, and Virginia. In March 1778, Lord George Germain, the king's secretary of state for the colonies, announced Britain's new strategy of focusing on the South in a letter to Sir Henry Clinton, commander of British forces in North America. Clinton's plans for an invasion of the South were delayed until November, however, by the presence of a French fleet off the southern American coast. But even as the South Carolina and Georgia Whigs struggled to dislodge a few hundred Tories from the St. Marys River area in Florida, Clinton was making plans that would result in bringing a force of more than 3,000 British soldiers to Savannah, Georgia. The British hoped and believed that this would encourage thousands of "loyal" Georgians and Carolinians, now cowed by the Revolutionary governments, to rally to the king's colors and crush the American rebellion.

British plans met with immediate success. Clinton's invasion force of 3,000 to 3,500 Scotch Highlanders, Hessians, and New York loyalists was commanded by Lieutenant Colonel Archibald Campbell, widely respected on both sides as an excellent soldier. Campbell landed near Savannah on December 23, 1778. General Robert Howe's 1,100 Continentals held a strong position apparently blocking the British route into the city. On the twenty-ninth, however, aided by information from a local slave and perhaps by Howe's carelessness, the British found a route into the rear of Howe's position and outflanked him. Howe escaped with less than half of his force. In losing Savannah, he also lost scores of artillery pieces and a virtual mountain of supplies. It was one of the most damaging American defeats of the Revolutionary War. Campbell was soon joined, as planned, by Major General Augustine Prevost's British-Tory force of 900 men from east Florida. This allowed Campbell to push north with a large proportion of the British force into the interior of Georgia, meeting almost uninterrupted success in skirmish after skirmish. By January 29, 1779, he had captured Augusta with a force of 1,500 men. The British issued a proclamation calling on all loyalists to rise up and free themselves from "slavery," offered ten guineas to anyone who provided information leading to the arrest of leading rebels, and recruited Tories to their ranks. Many Georgians took the oath of allegiance to the king, while those who did not fled with their families and livestock to South Carolina. Campbell reported later that he had recruited more than 1,100 Georgia men to his colors and organized them into twenty militia companies. This was far fewer than the 6,000 that the British had hoped to recruit, but it was clear that the British had the momentum. In little over a month, they had reconquered Georgia.[25]

By late January 1779, the only patriot force in any position to check Campbell's progress was the South Carolina militia under newly promoted Brigadier General Andrew Williamson. Williamson had been on the Georgia side of the Savannah River near Augusta with about 700 men. When Campbell had advanced on Augusta, Williamson had withdrawn into South Carolina. One of Williamson's principal subordinates was Andrew Pickens, promoted to colonel when Williamson was promoted to brigadier and given command of Williamson's old regiment. Pickens's regiment was

Defending the New Order, 1777–1779

the one element of Williamson's brigade that was not located with the rest of the brigade; most of it was dispersed at various posts between the Saluda and Savannah Rivers in upper South Carolina to guard against Indian incursions.

Over the next several weeks, Pickens would emerge as the principal leader in a combined effort by South Carolina and Georgia militia to drive the British and Tories out of upper Georgia. The process began with Pickens's determination to help a band of Georgia militia reverse the tactical situation in the local area about thirty miles upstream of Augusta. Around the end of January, a 100-man remnant of Georgia militia under Colonel John Dooly and Lieutenant Colonel Elijah Clarke had retreated into South Carolina. They attempted to recross the Savannah a few days later in early February but were driven back into South Carolina by Lieutenant Colonel John Hamilton's Tory cavalry. Dooly informed Pickens of Hamilton's presence on the Savannah, and the Whig militia noted that Hamilton appeared to be preparing to cross the river into South Carolina.[26]

During the ensuing campaign Pickens emerged as a man of decisive action more clearly than ever before. Away from Williamson's immediate control, he made decisions quickly, attacked aggressively, and demanded and received cooperation from the men around him. Upon hearing from Dooly, Pickens sprang into action, immediately gathering the 250 men he "could hastily collect," he recalled, and marched down to the river to join Dooly and Clarke.[27] He ordered all the rafts and boats to be moved to the Carolina side of the river to prevent Hamilton's crossing. With a combined force of 350 men, Pickens and Dooly decided to attack the Tories. As Pickens related, "We maneuvered opposite each other for two days up & down the River for ten miles—on the evening of the second day he disappeared—I immediately sent two men to reconnoitre to know whether it was a feint or whether he was gone some distance."[28] Pickens's scouts informed him that Hamilton had occupied a small fort about ten miles from the river. Even though it was dark, Pickens immediately ordered the entire force to cross into Georgia at Cowen's Ferry. With only one flatboat available, the crossing was not complete until it was nearly daylight.[29]

Pickens then acted decisively to ensure unity of command and bolster his own authority. As long as the combined Georgia-Carolina force was in South Carolina, Pickens, whose colonel's commission came from the latter state, was clearly in command. Once they were in Georgia, however, Dooly rightfully should have commanded the force. Pickens apparently decided that he would not take the responsibility for the outcome of a campaign in which he did not give the orders, particularly since two-thirds of the unit were originally from his command. Immediately after crossing the river, Pickens paraded the entire force and approached Dooly personally. Pickens told Dooly that unless the Georgia officer acknowledged him as the commander, he would go no further. Dooly readily agreed. Pickens then addressed the entire formation and "told them I was determined to pursue the enemy & attack him wherever I found him." Anyone who did not wish to follow him could go home, he said, but among those who stayed to fight, Pickens was "determined to be obeyed." In response to this show of confidence and determination, the troops "all heartily agreed." It was now "clear light," Pickens remembered, and the entire force began the ten-mile march to the fort where Hamilton had been located.[30]

Upon arriving at the fort, Pickens learned that Hamilton's Tories had already moved farther west toward Carr's (or Kerr's) Fort, an old stockade occupied by eight or nine old men (Whigs) and some women and children. Reckoning that his column could not reach Carr's Fort before Hamilton, Pickens planned a trap. He sent two men ahead to enter the fort, close the gate, and tell the small garrison to delay Hamilton's entry. Then Pickens would appear and trap the Tories between his own men and the fort. The two advance scouts arrived just before Hamilton but failed in their mission. According to Pickens, the two men "were so neglectful or stupid as not to mention their business until Hamilton stepped in after them."[31] Thus, Pickens's main force arrived just in time to see Hamilton entering the fort through the open gates.[32]

Pickens's men were able to fire some shots at the last of Hamilton's men as they entered the fort and captured their horses and baggage. A brisk fire ensued in which a few of Pickens's men were wounded. However, Pickens's men surrounded the fort and then captured a small log cabin nearby that commanded a spring—the fort's water supply—and provided an excellent means of firing into the fort itself.[33] The capture of the stockade appeared imminent, but Pickens did not wish to waste any time. He sent a flag of truce asking the Tories to surrender to avoid further bloodshed, but Hamilton refused. Pickens then considered a plan to burn the fort. Pickens intended to wait for dark and then load lightwood onto an old wagon, set it on fire, and roll the wagon down a slope to the side of the fort. The presence of women and children in the fort, however, caused Pickens and his officers to reconsider. As Pickens reported later, the fort was "full of little old cabbins and very dry," and burning the fort risked inflicting a horrid death on noncombatants.[34] With this in mind, he asked Hamilton to release the

Defending the New Order, 1777–1779

women and children, but Hamilton again refused. It seems that Pickens had decided not to follow through with firing the fort when, just before dark, he received a message that changed his plan entirely.[35]

The courier had been sent by Captain Joseph Pickens, Pickens's older brother and leader of some of Colonel Pickens's men still in South Carolina. With Joseph were small bands of men led by Captains Robert Anderson, William Baskins, and John Miller, making a total contingent of some 80 militia. The report concerned a new and more ominous threat. It was a Tory force of more than 700 men recruited from western North Carolina and northern South Carolina—the region between the Catawba and Saluda Rivers—under the command of Colonel James Boyd.[36]

Colonel Boyd appears in the narrative as a somewhat mysterious figure. There is little to no mention of him prior to the 1779 campaign, and only one contemporary source references his first name.[37] Clearly, though, neither side considered him to be a negligible character. Lieutenant Colonel Archibald Campbell, and perhaps even Sir Henry Clinton himself, had made Boyd part of British plans to secure upper Georgia. Boyd had probably been with the British at Savannah. Several accounts, including Pickens's, claim that Boyd had then traveled to New York to confer with Clinton before returning to the Carolina backcountry to recruit his force. Whether this meeting actually occurred is uncertain, but Campbell had certainly enlisted Boyd's aid in raising a large loyalist force. With the help of Lieutenant Colonel John Moore of North Carolina, Boyd was to organize a Tory force recruited from western North Carolina and northern South Carolina above the Saluda and then assist in the pacification of the frontier.[38]

The Whigs, too, were interested in Boyd. If postwar accounts of the battle of Kettle Creek can be believed, Pickens knew Boyd before the battle. Pickens himself later described Boyd as "a man of courage and action."[39] In late January and early February, the Tory force began gathering in North Carolina and marched to South Carolina and then into Pickens's own upper Ninety Six District and the Long Cane settlement itself. Bands of Whigs attempted to attack Boyd and disperse his Tories but found them to be too strong. Boyd picked up more recruits as he went and moved so rapidly that he was difficult to track.[40]

Upon hearing of Boyd's presence, Pickens immediately abandoned the siege of Carr's Fort, leaving a line of fires burning through the night so that Hamilton would be unaware of his departure. He recrossed the Savannah River on February 11 and marched the twelve miles to Long Cane in hopes of finding the Tory leader. He had difficulty locating him, however, and sent out several scouts to find him. On the twelfth, Boyd was actually crossing farther upstream, beyond the range of Pickens's scouts, at Cherokee Ford. However, Pickens's detachment of eighty men under Anderson, Baskins, Miller, and Joseph Pickens was on the Georgia side of the river. When they discovered Boyd's crossing site, they attacked aggressively, despite being heavily outnumbered. About half of the Tories were on the Georgia side when the attack began, and the Whigs had some success before they were driven off. Casualties were heavy. The Whigs lost 16 men killed and 16 taken prisoner, including Baskins and Miller. Boyd lost 100, most of them having drowned in a panic in the river or deserted. The remainder of Anderson's force joined Pickens, increasing the size of his force to around 400.[41]

Pickens continued the pursuit despite the fact that he was chasing a force of 600 with one of 400. He crossed the Savannah at Cedar Shoal, sent out more scouts, and began moving up the Broad River on February 13. By this time Pickens was convinced that Boyd intended to join Campbell to the south in Augusta and was determined to prevent that union. Pickens's scouts, or "spies," as he called them, informed him on the thirteenth that Boyd had just crossed to the western side of the Broad River at Webb's Ferry, about eight or ten miles upstream from Pickens. Pickens crossed at a slightly more southerly point, Fish Dam Ford, and continued west with scouts keeping him informed of Boyd's location. That night his men slept on their arms. At that point the two forces were merely four miles apart, and "spies" from both sides exchanged a few shots with each other before nightfall. Pickens's men rose early the next morning, February 14, and soon passed through Boyd's campsite of the night before. Pickens continued the pursuit with scouts ahead of him, "as fast & with as much caution as possible," he wrote.[42] Around 10 A.M. the Tory force began beating its drums and hoisted its colors. Pickens, only about a mile away, prepared for action.[43]

Pickens clearly felt that he led inexperienced troops, necessitating that he give detailed instructions to his men. He told those who had a little food to divide it with their comrades and then had all the guns quickly inspected and primed. Pickens's principal scout, Captain James McCall, informed him that the Tories seemed unaware of his presence. They had crossed to the west side of Kettle Creek where they had found a few cattle and had stopped to butcher them and prepare a breakfast. Pickens quickly devised his attack plan. He took care to prevent losing the element of surprise, ordering that any man who spotted the enemy was not to fire but instead to let him know. Colonel Dooly would advance on the right with 100 men and attempt to overwhelm Boyd's flank; Lieutenant Colonel Clarke would advance on the left with another 100 and attempt to do the same on that side. Pickens, with the remaining 200, would advance in the center directly onto the rear of Boyd's column as the latter retreated to the west. Preceding Pickens would be an advance guard, about 150 yards in front of his main body of troops. In Pickens's line of march lay a hill, which he would descend before crossing Kettle Creek. Beyond the creek was a large field where the Tories were butchering the cattle. All three of Pickens's columns would have to negotiate thick stands of cane and swampy ground on either side of the creek itself. Still, had Pickens's double envelopment plan been executed properly, he should have been able to surround Boyd on three sides and annihilate the unsuspecting Tory force.[44]

Once again, however, the inexperience or lack of discipline of Pickens's militiamen became a factor. The advance guard spotted the Tories and, according to Pickens, "being too eager & not attending to their orders they imprudently fired on them." Pickens lost the advantage of surprise, and Boyd, as "a man of courage and action," quickly recrossed the creek with a body of men.[45] Before Pickens's main body had arrived, Boyd and the Tories with him had taken a position on top of the hill on Pickens's side of the creek. They lay down and concealed themselves beneath a fence and some fallen trees. As Pickens came within thirty yards of the fence, Boyd surprised him with a deadly volley, killing and wounding several of his men. Boyd and his men then began running back to their main body, and the patriots were able to return fire. "Fortunately for us," Pickens related, "when Boyd had run about 100 yards, three balls passed through him." Boyd was mortally wounded but still alive.[46]

The fighting then became intense. For about twenty minutes, Pickens's men endured a galling fire coming from Tories in the canes alongside the creek. On his left and right, Pickens's flank divisions under Dooly and Clarke either could not or would not force their crossing of Kettle Creek as quickly as Pickens desired. Undoubtedly they were slowed by enemy fire and the marshy terrain, but Pickens's assessment was that their slowness "was not for want of courage but for want of experience & a knowledge of the necessity of obeying orders."[47] By the time most of Pickens's force reached the creek, the majority of the Tories had fled to the other side. The loyalist Major William Spurgin was bravely trying to reorganize the enemy force and form on the open hill beyond the creek. Clarke, having now found a better crossing point over the creek, ordered his men to charge and promptly had a horse shot from underneath him. Still he and his men charged across the creek and attacked Spurgin's right flank. At this point, Clarke was undoubtedly out-numbered by the Tory force on the hill, and the Whigs could have still lost the battle. Pickens and Dooly, however, doggedly pushed on, crossed the creek, and reinforced Clarke's fire with their own from another direction. Spurgin was now receiving fire from at least two sides. The firing continued for another half hour, and then the Tories broke and ran or surrendered. Altogether the battle had lasted two hours.[48]

Casualty reports on both sides varied considerably, though it was clear to both that the Whigs had won a decisive victory. Total losses on the Tory side (killed, wounded, and missing) may have totaled 70; 22 were captured on the actual battlefield. However, more stragglers from Boyd's force were rounded up over the next few days until the total number of cap-tured Tories surpassed 100. What was most important was that the force largely disintegrated. By the time its remnants finally reached Campbell's main British-Tory army, its strength was down from an original 700 to 270. Additionally, Pickens captured several hundred horses and a great deal of baggage. As many as 20 of Pickens's men were killed, though his superior, Andrew Williamson, reported that Pickens lost 4 men killed, 3 mortally wounded, and 15 wounded. Pickens's comment in his 1811 letter to Henry Lee was that "our loss was inconsiderable, though some brave men fell & some died of their wounds."[49] Finally, Pickens was able to recapture his men that had fallen into enemy hands days earlier at Cherokee Ford on the Savannah.

After the battle, several stories circulated about Pickens that portrayed him as an honorable and gracious victor. Some were undoubtedly true, including Pickens's own claim that he allowed some of the captured Tories to stay and bury their dead. Afterward these prisoners were paroled to visit their families as long as they promised to return to Whig captivity; all did so.[50]

The more romantic stories revolve around a conversation that allegedly took place between Pickens and the dying Colonel Boyd shortly after the battle. Indeed, there are so many such stories that it seems probable that the two commanders did speak before Boyd died. All of them highlight magnanimity on the part of Pickens and either stubbornness, courage, or excessive pride on the part of Boyd. One story simply asserts that when Pickens approached Boyd, the latter asked who had won the battle. When Pickens reported that he had, Boyd claimed that he had fought in a glorious cause and that the outcome would have been a Tory victory if he had not fallen.[51] Another story recounted by Andrew Lee Pickens in 1934 is that Pickens saw the severity of Boyd's wounds and immediately concluded he should help the Tory officer prepare for death: "With that militant type of religion that carried Presbyterians to victory, from Oliver Cromwell to Stonewall Jackson, Pickens asked if he should pray with the dying man. Perverted patriotism may have colored the answer that tradition has preserved in some accounts, which state that Boyd was an infidel and spurned the offer with the remark, 'I want none of a damned rebel's prayers.'"[52]

The account that is most romantic of all comes from an 1847 letter by Francis W. Pickens, Andrew Pickens's grandson. This one states that Pickens personally knew Boyd well before the battle and that the latter was a "brave, gallant, high-toned man." When Pickens approached Boyd, he told him, "Boyd, I am pained to see you in such suffering, and in such a cause." Interrupting him, Boyd raised himself on one elbow and replied, "Sir, I glory in the cause; I die for my King and Country." Pickens asked Boyd what he could do for him, and Boyd asked Pickens to write to his wife, living in the vicinity of Newberry, South Carolina, and to deliver a brooch he had for her. Later, when Pickens faithfully delivered the brooch, Mrs. Boyd did not receive it well. Pickens told the widow that her husband "died like a man." Mrs. Boyd, described by Francis Pickens as a "large, masculine woman," then "turned on her heel and exclaimed 'It's a lie! No damned rebel ever killed my husband!'"[53]

These latter two stories, besides presenting one of either the Tory characters in an unfavorable light, portrayed Pickens as a sentimental, gallant hero. Interestingly, Pickens himself related none of them in his detailed account of the battle to Henry Lee. Perhaps Francis Pickens had projected nineteenth-century ideals of romance and chivalry onto the character of his grandfather, who fought not in a time of medieval gallantry but in the brutal, hard-bitten world of the southern frontier in the American Revolution. Undoubtedly Pickens intended to treat prisoners humanely, and evidently there was some civil conversation between him and Boyd as the latter lay dying. He may have even made an effort to deliver items to Boyd's widow. But the stories imply that Pickens was somebody he was not. Pickens was a man of decency but not sentimentality—not when it came to war. God demanded basic decency and merciful treatment of defeated foes, but war demanded a hardheaded and fierce pragmatism. Boyd may have been a brave man who deserved an honorable death, but that only made it more "fortunate" for the patriot side when "three balls passed through him."

The battle of Kettle Creek had important results for Pickens personally and for the war in Georgia and South Carolina. Pickens himself considered it "the severest conflict I ever had" with Tory forces.[54] His detailed coverage of it in his long autobiographical letter to Henry Lee suggests his pride in the battle as one of his most important contributions to the patriot cause. Indeed, his first time in independent command of a large force was a major test of his leadership and again bolstered his reputation as a commander.[55] He had responded decisively to two enemy threats—first from Hamilton and then from Boyd—quickly assembled the bulk of his regiment, and successfully led a joint force of militia from not one but two states. Skillfully using reconnaissance and local intelligence, he had pursued and surprised a larger force and devised a logical plan of attack that took into account the element of surprise and the strength of the center of the enemy's position. When surprise was lost and the battle did not go initially as planned, his determined leadership, along with that of Elijah Clarke and others, kept his men in the fight and resulted in victory.

Pickens wrote to Henry Lee that he had been "particular in my account of the affair at Kettle Creek because . . . I believe it was the severest check & chastisement the tories ever received in South Carolina or Georgia."[56] Historians have concurred with Pickens that Kettle Creek was a devastating blow to the Tory cause. Clyde Ferguson points out that after Kettle Creek, never again would large Tory uprisings occur in Georgia and the Carolinas unless large British occupying forces were present. From 1775 to early 1779, loyalists such as Moses Kirkland, Thomas Fletchall, and Thomas Brown had raised large Tory bands with little more than moral encouragement from the king's army. Boyd, after a meeting with Campbell in Savannah, had been able to raise several hundred loyalists from as far away as the Catawba River valley in North Carolina. But the results this time had been disastrous for Tory hopes in the southern backcountry. Many were now arrested, tried for treason, and harassed by their Whig neighbors and authorities. From then on they would be more cautious. Would-be Tory recruits would stay at home unless they could be sure of the long-term presence of British troops in their area, an assurance they rarely had. Patrick Ferguson would recruit a significant Tory force in the Carolina backcountry in 1780, but only when a large British army was then occupying South Carolina and the Whig cause appeared to be defeated. Usually, however, Tories gathered only in "small parties . . . for plunder and the redress of individual grievances."[57]

In the short term, Pickens's victory at Kettle Creek was the key event in reversing British gains in upper Georgia. In combination with a smaller, earlier patriot success at Beaufort, it led to a swelling of the ranks of the Whig militia. Williamson's force opposite Augusta doubled to 1,400 men. On the day of the battle at Kettle Creek, Campbell had already begun withdrawing his Tory force from Augusta, and now he was pursued and harassed by cavalrymen under Colonel Le Roy Hammond of Williamson's brigade. Near Brier Creek, about forty miles south of Augusta, Hammond surprised a small Tory force and captured four officers and twenty-one privates. Meanwhile Pickens had briefly departed Georgia. He had reentered his home state on the day after the Kettle Creek battle, February 15, turned over his prisoners, made arrangements for his wounded, and "refreshed" his force, as he recalled.[58]

A resounding British victory in the first week of March temporarily stemmed the tide of patriot success in Georgia, until Pickens struck again. Brigadier General John Ashe occupied a position on Brier Creek with nearly 1,300 North Carolina militia, Georgia Continentals, and South Carolina light cavalry. There, on March 3, Ashe's force was outflanked, surprised, and routed by a British force of 900 redcoats and loyalists under Lieutenant Colonel Mark Prevost. More than 150 patriots were killed and nearly 200 captured in a defeat that was so embarrassing that Ashe asked for a court of inquiry to clear his name.[59] The British victory had little long-term effect, however; Tories were still reluctant to join the ranks after their debacle at Kettle Creek, and patriot recruits continued to pour in.[60] Thus the British did not have enough manpower to hold territory in upper Georgia, a problem they attempted to alleviate by assembling a strong force of pro-British Indians. At the time of the Brier Creek fiasco, Pickens was probably still in South Carolina. By March 14, Williamson had ordered him to return to the Savannah River, specifically Cowen's Ferry. There Pickens assembled his companies and crossed the river in response to reports of a large force of Tories farther upstream on Brier Creek, about thirty-five miles south of Augusta. Reinforced by Le Roy Hammond's cavalry and John Dooly's Georgia troops, he now commanded a force of roughly 500 men and two small field pieces. When Pickens reached the village of Wrightsborough, west of Augusta, he learned that 700 Creek Indians, some Tories, and a band of some 40 Cherokees who refused to honor the 1777 treaty had gathered about twenty-five miles to the southwest at Fulsom's Fort on the Ogeechee River. They had been assembled by David Taitt, the British agent to the Creeks. Pickens set out for the enemy camp, but before he could get there, a local Tory informed the Indians of his approach. By the time Pickens arrived at the enemy camp, the Indians and Tories had burned the fort, abandoned some of their supplies, divided into three groups, and fled. One group returned to the Creek nation; another fled farther up the Ogeechee to attack white settlements; and a third attempted to join the British in

Savannah. Pickens divided his men and pursued the latter two bands, over-taking and scattering both of them while killing eight Indians and capturing three. More patriot successes followed until late summer, when the British presence in Georgia was confined to the immediate environs of Savannah. Seventy of those captured by Pickens's men in the Kettle Creek area were tried in Charleston for treason; other Georgia and South Carolina loyalists ceased joining the British ranks. Pickens proudly stated that "the defeat of Coln Boyd with the dispersion of the Indians, with Tate [sic] completely disappointed the designs of the British at that time."[61]

By mid-April the situation in upper Georgia was well enough in hand that the patriot authorities began using the backcountry militia to assist in the ongoing war of maneuver and skirmish in the lowcountry between Savannah and Charleston. Continental army major general Benjamin Lincoln, with a growing American force, was attempting to defend Charleston and recapture Savannah from the wily British lieutenant colonel Mark Prevost, under the command of his older brother Major General Augustine Prevost. Though Lincoln had showed ability earlier in the war in the North, increasingly he seemed beyond his depth in his jousts with the Prevosts.

In late April, Lincoln and Williamson's militia brigade (including Pickens) crossed into Georgia to seal off any more supplies of that state's backcountry from British forces in Savannah. At least one careful historian has criticized this move, since the recent militia victories in Georgia rendered it almost wholly unnecessary.[62] Lincoln also intended, however, to protect a meeting of the Georgia legislature, which was scheduled to meet in Augusta on May 1. Major General Prevost responded to Lincoln's move by threatening Charleston, inducing Lincoln to leave Augusta and march in that direction. These movements eventually resulted in a sharp action at Stono Ferry, near Charleston. On June 20, Lincoln's 3,000-man army attacked a veteran force of 800 redcoats, Hessians, and Carolina loyalists in a fairly well fortified position commanded by Lieutenant Colonel John Maitland. Though the patriot militia initially drove back the Hessians on the British left, Lincoln failed to take advantage of the opportunity, and Maitland shifted men from the Seventy-First Highlander Regiment to save his endangered left. For more than an hour firing continued all along the front, with unequal results due to the British being protected by redoubts. As American casualties mounted and a small number of British reinforcements began to arrive on the field, Lincoln withdrew.[63]

Lincoln ordered Pickens to take charge of the rear guard and cover the retreat. Leading Colonel David Mason's Virginia Militia Brigade and fifty cavalrymen of Lieutenant Colonel David Horry's South Carolina Light Horse, Pickens was able to stop the British pursuit and evacuate several wounded American officers. While doing so, his horse was killed underneath him. Lincoln reported that "the retreat was conducted in an orderly and regular manner, our platoons frequently facing about and firing by the word of command upon their pursuers."[64]

Stono Ferry was a stinging tactical defeat, but it, too, brought no lasting operational or strategic benefit to the British. Maitland withdrew from the area three days later, and soon all British forces were back in Savannah, except for an unimportant British post on Port Royal Island, South Carolina. Once again Pickens himself had justified the growing confidence placed in him by other officers. With Continental troops present, it was notable that Lincoln entrusted the difficult task of covering the retreat from Stono Ferry to a militia officer, Andrew Pickens.

At this point in the year 1779, the South Carolina militia under Williamson and Pickens was losing manpower. Men had been slipping away from the ranks individually for some time. By mid-June, much of Pickens's regiment had been in the field continuously for at least five months, considered to be a long tour of duty for the militia. Almost certainly some of Pickens's men had been on duty longer than the law allowed.[65] Moreover, as they campaigned on the coast, rumors reached them from Ninety Six District of another large Indian-Tory force allegedly ready to pounce on the backcountry settlements. Whereas Pickens's regiment had consisted of more than 250 men in February, Williamson's entire brigade, including Pickens's regiment, amounted to just 417 by the time of the battle of Stono's Ferry in June. By July 5, most of Pickens's men were gone. Later that month, Williamson convinced the commander of South Carolina's state forces, Major General William Moultrie, to have Governor John Rutledge dismiss the entire brigade.[66]

Pickens was home no longer than a couple of weeks before he had to muster his regiment again. The disturbing rumors of another large Indian and Tory force about to attack the frontier, ridiculed by Moultrie and other lowcountry leaders, were true. While members of the Ninety Six militia brigade were helping to defend the coastal parishes, threats to their own homes and families had reemerged. Some Cherokee chieftains and bands still refused to honor the treaty of 1777 and spent the summer attacking white frontier settlements. Instigating the attacks was Alexander Cameron, who had replaced John Stuart as the British superintendent of Indian affairs in the South. When Williamson received reports of an Indian raid in South

Carolina in which the Cherokees killed several settlers and carried off some women, he remobilized parts of his brigade. Pickens mustered his regiment on August 10. Williamson's goal was to punish the disaffected Cherokees and capture Cameron.

The expedition left Beaver Dam Creek, Georgia, on August 20. On the twenty-fifth, aided by intelligence provided by an Indian ally named Man Killer, Captain Joseph Pickens and twenty horsemen were able to capture "The Terrapin" and his nephew, who were enemy Cherokee leaders. The next day Williamson's men burned the Indian village of Saraquoe and destroyed the Indians' corn there, the villagers' main food supply. Williamson then dispatched Colonel Andrew Pickens with 160 men to capture two white traders who had encouraged the Indians' raids, as well as Cameron. The white troublemakers escaped into the mountains, and Pickens returned to the main body of Williamson's brigade. Advancing into northern Georgia and the mountains of North Carolina, the brigade destroyed six more Cherokee towns, including the one where Cameron had resided, as well as the corn. Within days, "The Wolf" and Good Warrior, leaders of the disaffected Cherokees, approached Williamson and begged him to end the campaign in exchange for them moving to the "settled" Cherokee towns and abandoning their attacks.[67]

Once again, it appears that Andrew Pickens had not shrunk from the implications of waging all-out war and dispensing the white frontiersman's revenge on the Indians. When the campaign was over, the *South Carolina Gazette* estimated that the militia had destroyed at least 50,000 bushels of corn, "which is the severest chastisement that can be given to Indians."[68] Because of the actions of Indian enemies, cynical British agents, and the rough justice of the frontier meted out by the Ninety Six militia, it is virtually certain that some "innocent" Indians suffered in the August–September 1779 campaign. Yet every white patriot on the frontier, including Pickens, would have been more relieved by the results of the campaign than concerned over the suffering of the peaceful Indians.

At the conclusion of the Cherokee campaign, a large portion of Williamson's brigade, minus Pickens's regiment, marched south to assist Continental troops in their siege of Savannah. Pickens and at least some of his men were on active duty until mid-October but remained in the upcountry as a shield against further Indian attacks.[69] The final Franco-American assault on the British works on Savannah on October 9 failed. As was the case at Stono Ferry and the St. Marys River, the use of the militia as a supplementary source of manpower to reinforce a conventional army and defeat British regulars had not brought excellent results. The men of the militia had proved far more useful, and indeed indispensable, in fighting and suppressing their Tory neighbors and nearby Indians. Indeed, the undisciplined but tough and hardy backcountry militia was the reason that the southern interior was still under the control of the new United States and the patriot state governments. Though the militiamen had been effective in fighting their type of warfare, they could be unreliable unless led by men who had proved they were confident, decisive, and just as hardy as the frontier farmers who followed them. By the end of the year 1779, Andrew Pickens had emerged as one of their most respected leaders.[70]

FIVE

Liberty and Virtue in a Conquered Land

They considered themselves bound by conscience and honor.

Hugh McCall, History of Georgia

By the autumn of 1779, it seemed the tide of the war was beginning to turn against the patriot forces in the South. Revolutionary leaders had controlled the machinery of state government in Charleston for at least three years, and the pro-Revolution leading men of the frontier such as Andrew Pickens had firmer control over the Georgia and South Carolina backcountry than ever before. And yet, from both the statewide and national perspective, the outlook appeared grim. Although George Washington's army in New Jersey was still intact and in fact better trained than ever before, the economy of the fledgling United States had collapsed. The official currency was worthless and the Continental army suffered from lack of supplies and clothing.

Congress had provided little support to the Deep South states of South Carolina and Georgia. Patriots in those two states felt that while they had contributed much to the defense of New England and the nation as a whole, Congress had abandoned them. This conviction, wrote one of South Carolina's early historians, "took deep possession of the public mind and pervaded all classes."[1] What Continental forces had arrived had seen little success under American generals Robert Howe and Benjamin Lincoln. The southern state governments were still intact due partly to the exertions of the militia in suppressing the Tories and the Indians and partly to the fact that the British had concentrated their efforts farther north. Now that was about to change—the British, having had limited success in the New England and middle states, were bringing massive combat power to the South.

A large British army under General Sir Henry Clinton arrived near Charleston in February 1780; in March he began a siege of the city with more than 12,600 troops. By that time Congress had finally reinforced Lincoln with Continental troops from Virginia and North Carolina, and he would eventually command about 5,700 men. Unfortunately, he took no advantage of the swampy terrain and saltwater creeks around the city. Lincoln unwisely allowed civilian leaders to convince him to keep his force in the city itself and thus stranded on the peninsula known as Charleston Neck.[2]

South Carolina had regular state troops and militiamen from Charleston with Lincoln, but the militia from the backcountry districts responded to the Charleston crisis reluctantly. In February, Governor John Rutledge had ordered all the state's militia to Charleston, but the backcountry contingents hesitated due to rumors of smallpox in the capital. Also, the resources and the military energy of the backcountry were wearing thin. Complaints had been pouring into the General Assembly for at least a year about the lack of salt, the scarcity of money, the need for courts, and the lack of protection for citizens when the militia was deployed. Brigadier General Andrew Williamson was accused of slowness in raising troops in the current emergency, but the truth was that it was hard to recruit. Militia organizations from Ninety Six and other regions of the state refused or delayed coming to Charleston, to the disgust of Governor Rutledge.[3]

Nevertheless, Williamson and Pickens had, in fact, managed to put men in the field. Williamson convinced Lincoln and apparently Rutledge that the militia could do more good as a diversion and in maintaining security along the frontier than in attempting to relieve the siege of Charleston with only a few hundred men. In January and February Pickens operated in the Augusta area, patrolling along the Savannah River to prevent incursions by Indians or Georgia Tories. On March 6, Williamson ordered him and 122 men to Wurth's Ferry on the Edisto to clear the area of "Banditti who have lately committed many outrages and robberies upon the inhabitants."[4]

Around March 20, Pickens joined forces with some Georgia militia under Colonel John Twiggs and proceeded down the Ogeechee River toward Savannah in hopes of capturing the Tory leader Daniel McGirth. McGirth had been raiding Whig inhabitants in the region. Pickens and Twiggs defeated him in a small skirmish and recaptured some slaves that had been stolen from South Carolina. Soon after, a group of armed black men attacked Pickens. With them were some white men, including two overseers formerly employed by Georgia royal governor Sir James Wright. Pickens routed this force, killing about sixty. Finally, on April 4, the Whig forces defeated a British attack on their position on the south side of the Ogeechee. Pickens and Twiggs then marched to Augusta and reported all that had happened. The Georgia governor, with the consent of the council, issued an order to Pickens and Twiggs authorizing them to sell all the slaves belonging to Tories and to allow the captors to keep the proceeds. Obviously, patriot forces were not willing to accept black men as partners in the struggle for liberty—they regarded them either as property or as enemies, and sometimes both.[5]

Early in May, Williamson ordered Pickens to take his force toward Charleston. It is unclear what Williamson hoped Pickens could accomplish for the relief of Lincoln's surrounded garrison. Pickens, however, joined Colonel James Williams's regiment, forming a total force of 300 militiamen at the "Ridge" between Augusta and the Saluda River, and the force then began moving toward Charleston. Before it reached the capital, however, the militiamen received devastating news: Charleston had surrendered on May 12, and Lincoln's entire garrison was captured.[6]

The fall of Charleston was the worst blow to American arms in the entire Revolutionary War. Lincoln surrendered more than 5,500 men, the largest surrender of any American force until the capitulation of Douglas MacArthur's army in the Philippines in 1942. The Charleston disaster sent shock waves throughout the state, thoroughly demoralizing the patriot militia. Williams and Pickens immediately split up. Williams's regiment moved to Camden, where it surrendered, while Pickens moved back toward Ninety Six. Meanwhile, Governor Rutledge and a few members of the privy council had escaped from Charleston and were in flight. Most leading citizens of Charleston, including those who had been active revolutionaries, swore loyalty to the crown. State and local government collapsed.[7]

British forces consisting of regular army regiments and loyal provincial troops recruited in the northern states quickly penetrated the South Carolina interior over the next several weeks and attempted to recruit and organize a local Tory militia. General Charles Earl Cornwallis himself retired to Charleston while elements of his army began establishing fortified outposts in June and July. Colonel Lord Francis Rawdon garrisoned Camden with three regiments: one regiment held Rocky Mount, just south of the Waxhaws region along the Catawba River; Colonel Thomas Brown's

Liberty and Virtue in a Conquered Land

Florida Rangers garrisoned Augusta; and Colonel Nisbet Balfour set up another British base at Ninety Six with a mixed force of regulars and loyalist provincials from New York and New Jersey. In early August, Balfour was replaced by Lieutenant Colonel John Harris Cruger, who commanded about 300 men consisting principally of the First Battalion, DeLancey's Brigade (New York loyalists), and the Third Battalion, New Jersey Volunteers. From time to time regular army and Tory detachments would temporarily reinforce the British post at Ninety Six.[8]

Meanwhile, patriot militia units submitted, one by one, to the same generous terms of parole given to the troops who had surrendered in Charleston. As long as they laid down their arms and promised not to take them up again, they would be pardoned and not disturbed. For those who simply wanted to be left alone and to salvage some stability and security in the wake of the British triumph, it was an offer they could not refuse.

Andrew Williamson would later be charged with treason by Pickens and other patriot leaders. Immediately after the fall of Charleston, however, he seemed to be casting about for some way to continue the resistance. When the fateful news reached him on May 16, Williamson had just canceled plans for a new attack on Savannah due to the failure of the militia to enlist. He then conferred with Georgia governor Richard Howley and other Georgia authorities, but the Whig leadership could not agree on what to do next. Unable to do anything meaningful in Georgia and lacking support and guidance from his own state's civil authorities, Williamson called for a meeting at White Hall, his plantation, of all his field officers and the leading men of Ninety Six. Pickens did not attend; he was just returning to the vicinity of Ninety Six from his aborted march on Charleston and was still in the field. At the council, Williamson proposed retreating rapidly to North Carolina and continuing the fight. Still, Williamson's leadership was too vacillating to be effective. He conceded the danger to the men's families and said that he would adopt whatever course was voted upon by a majority of the council. Only a handful of officers voted to keep fighting. Williamson requested that the council delay its decision until he could consult with Pickens, and the entire council then rode over to Pickens's camp. Williamson spoke to Pickens privately and then made an impassioned plea, this time in front of the officers and Pickens's assembled troops. He concluded by asking every man who intended to follow him into North Carolina to continue the fight to raise his hand. To the disgust of Captain Samuel Hammond, one of the diehards, only five or six men raised their hands. Andrew Pickens was not one of them.[9]

The turnaround in South Carolina was rapid and stunning to the inhabitants. For years war and insecurity had taken their toll on those who were pro-Whig or neutral, but at least the Tories were suppressed. Now the Tories were in control. Within a matter of days, detachments of loyalists appeared in the backcountry to accept the surrender and parole of Whig units. The old Tory foe Richard Pearis took his men to Ninety Six and accepted the surrender of the two companies with Williamson at White Hall on or about June 12. Three days later Pickens and his 300 men marched out and laid down their arms as well. They could only hope that the British would be true to their word to leave them alone in exchange for laying down their arms. By the middle of June, South Carolina was conquered—virtually no organized resistance remained.

Apparently at this point Pickens's desire for peace and order temporarily overcame his commitment to American independence, as it did for most of his fellow citizens. It seemed clear that the Revolutionary cause was beaten. It was not the case that Pickens had "no choice" but to sign his parole. He certainly could have still chosen to continue the fight in the name of American patriotism. However, that would have meant the seizure of his property, the flight of his family, and his reduction to the status of a bandit—a fighter without a home of his own, forced to pillage and steal. The desire for order and security trumped liberty.

Almost as soon as British mastery of South Carolina seemed secure, however, the conquerors began to overplay their hand. The rapid collapse of Whig resistance after the fall of Charleston convinced General Clinton that British assumptions about the mass of public opinion in the southern colonies had been correct all along. Throughout the war, British officers and ministers believed that most residents in the South favored royal authority. They thought that a ruling clique, with the help of dissenting clergymen, had managed to seize power, but that a determined show of force would bring the South firmly back under royal authority. Thus, Clinton decided he could afford to demand more than neutrality from South Carolinians. He reneged on the parole agreement. Those former Continental soldiers and the bulk of those militiamen who had been paroled now had to take an oath of loyalty to the crown and actually take up arms for the British whenever called upon. Those who took the oath were promised protection; those who refused were to be treated as "rebels and enemies to their country" and potentially have their estates confiscated.[10] Two days after issuing this second proclamation, Clinton confidently departed South Carolina for New York, leaving the results of this disastrous policy decision in the lap of General Cornwallis.[11]

Liberty and Virtue in a Conquered Land

Clinton's new demands imparted a breath of new life to the resistance. Colonel Rawdon informed Cornwallis that the "unfortunate Proclamation of 3d. of June has had very unfavorable consequences. The majority of the Inhabitants of the Frontier Districts, tho' ill disposed to us . . . were not actually in arms against us . . . and nine out of ten of them are now embodied on the part of the Rebels."[12] Rawdon probably exaggerated the numbers of men in the "Rebels'" ranks, but another officer essentially agreed, commenting on the large number of South Carolinians who had hoped "to live quietly upon their estates, as prisoners upon parole, and enjoying a kind of neutrality." Now they were "disgusted" by Clinton's proclamation, "which, without their consent, abrogated the paroles that had been granted, and, in one instant, converted them either into loyal subjects or rebels."[13]

It is possible that, before Pickens took his oath and accepted "the protection," he had made a failed attempt to escape British control and rejoin one of the few small patriot bands that had still not submitted.[14] By mid-July, however, he had taken an oath to support British government in exchange for protection, and senior British officers began expressing hope that his support would eventually be open and active.[15] Cornwallis, left in charge after Clinton's departure, had decided that it was better to have popular former rebels like Pickens alive and neutralized rather than martyred or driven back into the rebel ranks. Instead of confiscating the estates of or hanging Revolutionary leaders, whom he dubbed the "notoriously disaffected," Cornwallis decreed that they were to remain at home and supply "moderate contributions of provisions, wagons, horses, &c, towards carrying on the war."[16]

The prospect of peace and security under British rule vanished immediately as stories of British atrocities and brutal retaliations by Whigs washed over the state. One of the first outrages reported was the burning of the home of Thomas Sumter. Sumter, a native of Virginia, had come to South Carolina as a young man, an escapee from debtors' prison with no prospects. Through ambition, determination, and a fortunate marriage, he had acquired a plantation at Nelson's Ferry on the Santee River, about halfway between Charleston and modern-day Columbia. He had also obtained a commission, leaving the Continental army as a colonel in 1778 due to ill health. In late May, only weeks after the fall of Charleston, Lieutenant Colonel Banastre Tarleton led a mobile strike force of the king's forces into the Nelson's Ferry area. Tarleton commanded the British Legion, a mixed force of British dragoons and loyalist infantrymen recruited largely in New York. A veteran of the fighting in the northern states, Tarleton had welded his command into a tightly disciplined, aggressive force that reflected his own persona. Energetic and fierce, he regarded American provincials as a rebellious population to be cowed into submission, not befriended. Thus, despite his talents as a fighter, Tarleton was not the best fit for the British counterinsurgency mission among a people who were not easily cowed. Nor did Cornwallis take many measures to restrain him. As one modern historian asks rhetorically, "Did [Tarleton] think to daunt, by such measures, a people who had endured a wilderness trek from Pennsylvania or Virginia and perhaps the savagery of frontier warfare along the way?"[17]

Tarleton's legion reached Sumter's plantation on May 28. Only hours before, Sumter's eleven-year-old son had warned his father that British troops were nearby, and Sumter had fled northward. When Tarleton arrived and found Sumter absent, his troops stole what they wanted and then physically carried Mrs. Sumter out of the house. As she watched, they burned it to the ground. Sumter's house was not the only abode to suffer such a fate; numerous reports of wanton destruction and plundering emerged at this time. Over the next several months, the king's men rampaged from the Pee Dee River to the Saluda, burning homes, roughing up women and children, stealing food and livestock, and murdering captured Whigs or even inoffensive citizens. The blow inflicted on the Sumter family was particularly important, if only because it earned the implacable enmity of Sumter himself. It was not that Sumter was a particularly talented officer; in fact he would often prove to be a vain and uncooperative subordinate. He did, however, become a rallying point for the resistance and a symbol of American defiance. He obtained a brigadier general's commission from Governor-in-exile Rutledge and united thousands of angry backcountry settlers in the cause.[18]

The atrocities continued as British forces advanced upward along the Santee, the Wateree, and the Broad Rivers. The day after burning Sumter's home and riding hard day and night, Tarleton's dragoons fell upon a column of Virginia Continentals under Colonel Abraham Buford as it was withdrawing through the Waxhaws region toward North Carolina.[19] Allegedly, as some of Buford's men raised their hands and asked for quarter, Tarleton's men mercilessly hacked them down with their sabers. Though some of Buford's wounded men were treated humanely, the phrase "Tarleton's quarter" immediately spread among the population, serving as both a bitter reminder of defeat and an inspiration for vengeance.[20]

British and Tory brutality turned vast swaths of the backcountry into a "giant hornet's nest that had been poked."[21] While the British maintained

Liberty and Virtue in a Conquered Land

firm control of their main bases at Rocky Mount, Cheraw, Camden, and Ninety Six, bands of angry men gathered throughout the countryside determined to ambush British columns and wreak vengeance on their Tory neighbors. The British could leave their bases to rampage and pillage, but that behavior only stimulated enlistments in the patriot bands, not in the loyalist militia. Ninety Six District, situated between the Saluda and Savannah Rivers, remained relatively calm, but along the Enoree, the Broad, the Catawba-Wateree, and the upper Santee, British depredations and equally cruel Whig retaliations brought misery and tragedy. In several Whig victories, the lopsided casualty count along with the small number of British or Tory troops reported captured indicated that the patriot side was revisiting "Tarleton's quarter" on its foes. Meanwhile, in the coastal plain north of Charleston, the daring and elusive Francis Marion, the "Swamp Fox," terrorized British outposts and supply columns and showed little mercy to captured Tories. No family, Tory or Whig, was safe. South Carolina descended into a Hobbesian state of crime and anarchy.

Some destructive acts stemmed from the British conviction that Presbyterianism in the middle and southern colonies and the influence of Puritanism in New England was at the heart of the American rebellion. As previously related, King George himself had reportedly condemned the American Revolution as a "Presbyterian rebellion." Even up to the end of the war, the British were convinced that the Calvinist sects were at the heart of the American rebellion. When the British government finally concluded that the American war was lost, the elder statesman and literary figure Horace Walpole told Parliament, "There is no use crying about it. Cousin America has run off with a Presbyterian parson, and that is the end of it."[22]

This hostility to Presbyterianism manifested itself in 1780 and 1781 as British and Tory officers equated the destruction of Presbyterianism with enforcing submission to the crown. Major James Wemyss made it a policy to burn Presbyterian churches in South Carolina, calling all such churches "sedition shops."[23] In July, Captain Christian Huck, a loyalist officer from Philadelphia, summoned a number of old men to "make peace with them." When the elderly subjects assembled, he began to "harrangue" them instead, swearing that even if "God almighty had become a Rebel . . . if there were 20 Gods on that side, they would all be conquered." If Christ himself were to lead the rebels, Huck boasted, he would still defeat them. Whig colonel William Hill claimed that this "impious blasphemy" convinced many men in his ranks that they would become "instruments in the hand of Heaven to punish this enemy for his wickedness and blasphemy."

Major Joseph McJunkin's recollection was very similar—"Huck's cruelty and profane boasts" so angered the "Irish Presbyterians" of the Catawba River region "that they demanded to be led against him."[24]

If South Carolina Presbyterians as a whole exhibited a mild preference for the Whig cause in the early stages of the war, by the summer of 1780 those leanings had transformed into fierce and implacable determination. For some, the fight was no longer a political dispute but rather a holy war. The minister John Harris, Pickens's neighbor, preached the gospel and the cause of republican liberty from the pulpit with a musket by his side and an ammunition pouch suspended from his neck.[25] Near Pickens's former home in the Waxhaws, Reverend John Simpson fiercely exhorted his two congregations to defy British tyranny in the summer of 1780. Simpson took up a musket himself and joined partisan bands commanded by two of his flock, John McClure and William Bratton, serving as both chaplain and private. Days later, enemy troops evicted his wife and children from their home and burned his house and his books. (After the war, Simpson would minister near Pickens's new home in Pendleton District.)[26] In neighboring North Carolina, Presbyterian pastors such as Samuel Doak, David Caldwell, and James Hall would play similar militant roles.[27]

Thus, in most of the state, British rule quickly became the calamity that only the most extreme Whigs had predicted five years before. By unleashing Tory vandalism (much of which was retaliation for previous Whig excesses); by committing murder; by burning churches, prayer books, and hymnals; and by leaving women and children homeless, the British and their Tory cohorts had proven themselves the archenemies of liberty, order, and virtue. Despite Whig retaliations against their Tory neighbors, there was probably little doubt in Pickens's mind as to which side represented good and which represented evil. Still, deciding on his own course was more complicated. He had sworn allegiance to the king in exchange for protection; reenlisting on the side of good would ironically mean committing the evil act of oath breaking. Moreover, his own Ninety Six area had so far escaped the worst of the punishments inflicted on other areas of the state. In Ninety Six, Colonel Nisbet Balfour and his replacement, Lieutenant Colonel John Harris Cruger, attempted to secure the loyalty or at least the neutrality of the most respected former rebels in the district. Cruger, a New York loyalist and an able officer, worked hard to maintain order and prevent plundering, retaining some respect among South Carolina Whigs.[28] One of Cruger's officers was a Captain George Ker in the First Battalion, DeLancey's Brigade, who even formed a friendship with Pickens.[29]

Liberty and Virtue in a Conquered Land

Balfour himself had arrived at Ninety Six on June 22. Only two days later, he informed Cornwallis that the British had far fewer "friends" in the district than he had expected and that "things are by no means, in any sort of settled state." Though presently overawed by the presence of British troops, "the smallest change" could bring them back to rebellion. As for the rebels being disarmed, "it is a joke; they have given in only useless arms and keep their good ones." Balfour believed there were two possible courses of action. The first was to march into the country, violate the parole agreements administered by the Tory commanders Richard Pearis and Thomas Brown, seize former rebel leaders such as Pickens, disarm any "suspicious persons," and recruit and arm only those who were totally loyal. The second was to bring the "leading men" over to the British side, "trust them to a certain degree . . . and give them a part in the defence of the country."[30] Balfour preferred the latter course.

Thus, senior British officers from Cornwallis himself to Balfour, Cruger, Ker, and others were particularly eager to win over Williamson and Pickens.[31] With Williamson they were successful. Balfour told Cornwallis that he thought Williamson could be trusted and that the latter was working on Pickens to bring him over to the British side as well. Williamson told Balfour that if the British could win the support of Pickens and Colonel Le Roy Hammond, their influence along with Williamson's would be enough to win over the entire Ninety Six region.[32] Williamson never actually took up arms against his Whig neighbors, but he willingly made his resources and his plantation available to the British and tried to woo his former Whig comrades, including Pickens, to the crown's support.[33]

Andrew Pickens was another story. Traditional accounts paint him as someone whose sentiments were with the patriot cause but who steadfastly and adamantly honored his oath to the British until they violated theirs to him. This interpretation is generally correct, but the story is complicated. Unlike Williamson, Pickens stayed in contact not only with former Whigs but also with partisan leaders who were still actively fighting the British. It is not always clear what those communications were about, but they certainly did not consist of Pickens trying to convince those men to lay down their arms; largely they consisted instead of those men trying to persuade Pickens to retake the field for the cause of American liberty.

Meanwhile, the prospect of recruiting Pickens to their side seemed a tantalizing prize to the British as well. He was the most influential man in the Long Cane neighborhood. The British base at Ninety Six itself was secure, and in the late summer and early fall of 1780, the Whig insurrection across the district as a whole was not as serious as it was in areas to the north and east. But the British considered the Long Cane community a powder keg on the verge of exploding at any time and never felt their authority was secure there.[34] If Pickens could be won over, they could secure the western part of the district and probably recruit most of his old regiment into the loyalist ranks. He had a reputation as an excellent soldier, and, according to Lieutenant Colonel Isaac Allen—also in the Ninety Six area and Cruger's second-in-command and commander of the Third Battalion, New Jersey (loyalist) Volunteers—Pickens's regiment "was always esteemed the best in the rebel service."[35] Moreover, Williamson repeatedly assured Balfour and Cruger that Pickens could be trusted, and Cruger was inclined to believe him.[36] In mid-November, Williamson and Pickens indicated that they were willing to travel with Cruger to Charleston to consult with Balfour, though they never did.[37] By late November, though, Cruger wrote Cornwallis that he thought it "more than a possibility" that Pickens would accept a command of loyalist troops. If that came to pass, he thought, it would force "every man in the country . . . to declare and act for His Majesty or quit."[38]

Cornwallis was convinced of Pickens's value but not as sure of his trustworthiness as Cruger was. On August 27 he wrote, "By what I hear of Pickens I should think him worth getting. However, it may not be safe to enter into any treaty with him without the approbation of General Williamson."[39] A month later, Cornwallis further warned Balfour, "In regard to Pickens, I have great doubts. I have been told that there is a correspondence between him and Sumter, and the former is to have 500 men ready, and that when I advance they are to form a junction. You may perhaps get to the bottom of this business. If any means can be fallen upon to secure the neutrality, if not the friendship of [Pickens], I shall think it very good economy."[40] By the end of November, though, Cornwallis seemed to take on Cruger's hopes that Pickens could be persuaded to lead troops in the king's service: "I should be very glad to hear that [Pickens] would take a command."[41]

British hopes for securing Pickens and thereby the Long Cane region fluctuated in response to events. Pickens, too, though clearly seeking to do what seemed right and honorable to him, was reacting to events largely beyond his control. When Balfour arrived at Ninety Six on June 22, it is possible that Pickens was still in Tory custody and was turned over to him. (Pickens surrendered sometime in mid-June, and Andrew Hamilton's recollection years later was that the two of them were in British custody for "a month." Hamilton remembered being under the custody of an officer named Allen, almost certainly Lieutenant Colonel Isaac Allen.)[42] As soon as Balfour arrived, however, he began consulting with Williamson, who informed him that Pickens was one of the most influential men in the area and that the British should try to secure his cooperation.[43] Thus, Pickens and Hamilton were treated well and released, no doubt with their promises of good behavior. On the twenty-seventh Balfour heard rumors that there was a Whig uprising in Long Cane, but, he reported, Williamson immediately brought some of the leading subjects of the neighborhood to Balfour "and shewed clearly it was a falsity."[44] On July 19, Major Patrick Ferguson informed a subordinate that he had heard news of "a concerted uprising of the Rebels of Long Cane under Pickings."[45] Ferguson was actually north of the Saluda River when he wrote this, and misinformed, but his letter is another indication of British wariness of the Long Cane area and its highest-ranking former "rebel."

In September Pickens passed up a clear opportunity to rejoin the patriot ranks and instead cooperated with the British. Near the beginning of the month, his neighbor and former subordinate James McCall sought out Pickens to persuade him to abandon his neutrality and rejoin the fight. McCall's visit to Pickens was actually part of a much larger plan to recapture Augusta and then Ninety Six District. At that time, Elijah Clarke was recruiting in upper Georgia, and McCall's mission was to win over Pickens and recruit some 500 men from the western portion of South Carolina's Ninety Six District, which he was confident about doing if he could persuade Pickens. Thomas Sumter had reinforced these efforts by writing to Pickens himself.[46] Thus, Cornwallis's suspicion that there was some communication between Pickens and Sumter was correct. According to McCall's son Hugh, Pickens and other former officers of his regiment refused to take the field, stating that they were "bound by conscience and honor" to uphold their oaths until the British violated their own promise of protection.[47] Without Pickens's support, McCall could recruit no more than 80 men. With this much smaller force, McCall joined Clarke as the latter besieged Thomas Brown's loyalist garrison at Augusta.

Cruger at first was at a loss on how to respond to the threat to Augusta and Long Cane, given the small size of his garrison at Ninety Six. More than any other area in Ninety Six District, the British considered Long Cane to be, in Cornwallis's words, "much inclined to rebellion."[48] Pickens may have felt ample temptation to violate his parole and rejoin the Whigs. He certainly would not have endangered his reputation among most of his neighbors if he had done so; largely they were looking to him. Indeed, the key leaders on both sides—Cornwallis, Cruger, Balfour, Allen, Williamson,

McCall, Sumter, and Clarke—seemed convinced that his example almost alone determined which way the Long Cane region would go. Cruger consulted Williamson, who advised him to march immediately to Long Cane and meet with the leading men there to head off an uprising. Cruger did so and took Williamson with him. Williamson went to Pickens's house to secure his cooperation and called a meeting of the leading citizens. Cruger then went on to Augusta sixty miles to the south and raised the siege, routing Clarke in the process and enabling Brown to execute a number of captured Whigs in Augusta. Cruger reported that while pursuing Clarke, he made American rebels pay the "price of their treachery" by burning houses, driving off cattle, and seizing other property.[49] Meanwhile, Williamson could report to Balfour that the "principal people" in Long Cane had prevented an insurrection and that only a handful had gone off to join Clarke.[50] Pickens's reaction to the chaos and suffering from this event was that if the Whigs wished to make any future incursions into his area, they should do so in enough force to protect the people and maintain order. He traveled to Gilbert Town, North Carolina, where several bands of militia were gathering, and spoke to the officers there. According to Colonel William Campbell, Pickens advised that no more "small" parties of militia be sent to the Augusta–Long Cane area, "as it answered no other purpose than to draw upon our Friends in that Quarter the Resentment of our Enemies."[51]

By mid-October, there was another inducement for Pickens to rejoin the patriot ranks if his sole consideration was ending up on the winning side. On October 7, patriot militia bands from across the western Carolinas and what would become Tennessee wiped out a strong British-Tory force at Kings Mountain, near the North Carolina–South Carolina border west of Charlotte. These were the same men Pickens had visited days before in Gilbert Town. The British commander, Patrick Ferguson, was killed. Ferguson had previously threatened to destroy the settlements of the "over-mountain men" with "fire and sword" if they did not submit. The frontiersmen had shown what they thought of Ferguson's threats by not only banding together and defeating him but also by urinating on his corpse. Once again Tories in the Carolinas were demoralized and Revolutionary forces rejuvenated. By the end of the month, patriot forces completely controlled large swaths of northern South Carolina. Closer to home in Ninety Six, the British had been able to raise no more than 200 local militia, many of whom were unarmed. They were so dispirited now that Cruger and Cornwallis had no faith in their loyalty or usefulness. Still, Pickens did not declare for the Whig cause.

Another result of Kings Mountain was that Pickens's neighbors, and perhaps Cruger, asked for Pickens's help. Reports reached Ninety Six of the patriot militia brutally treating their Tory prisoners from the battle. As the "over-mountain men" withdrew north and west into the mountains, the British and Tory prisoners with them suffered from lack of clothing and blankets. Nine Tories were executed. Some of the suffering men were the sons of Pickens's neighbors; a few had previously served under him in the Whig ranks; perhaps he had once worshipped with their families at the Long Cane meetinghouse. Pickens therefore agreed to lead a three-man delegation to investigate the situation, returning on October 21.[52] Pickens's two visits to the Kings Mountain force (one before the battle and this one on October 21) suggest that he was either serving as a humanitarian or trying to act as a friend to both sides.

Pickens returned from his mission to North Carolina on October 21 perhaps distressed at what he had found. In November, one of two things occurred. Either Pickens thoroughly misled Cruger in order to more safely betray him, or else he seriously considered accepting a British commission until events near the end of the month abruptly changed his mind. As previously mentioned, it was in mid-November that he indicated willingness to travel with Cruger and Williamson to Charleston to consult with Balfour. It was also about this time that Cruger thought it probable that Pickens would accept command of a loyalist unit. Around November 26, Pickens and another former Whig officer, John Bowie, made plans to visit the British lieutenant colonel Isaac Allen. Malcolm Brown, a close confidant of Williamson, believed that Pickens and Bowie's purpose was to make "observations" to Allen that would help maintain order. Brown agreed that "every good man should do all in his power to reestablish tranquility in our Country which is at present so torn by different factions."[53]

Thus, Cruger's hopes for recruiting Pickens may have had some foundation in October and much of November. But what happened instead is that somewhere between the last days of November and December 8, Pickens decided once and for all to fight for American liberty. The military situation in the Ninety Six–Long Cane area was fluctuating almost on a daily basis. Around November 21 or 22, just days before Pickens planned for an interview with Allen, a band of forty or fifty patriot partisans came into Long Cane and plundered and disarmed local Tories, killing three. The local Tory militia was thoroughly intimidated, to Cruger's disgust. He sent a column of British regulars and provincial militia under Allen from Ninety Six to patrol throughout the Long Cane district; these troops returned in a few days without finding any "rebels." On December 4, patriot militia entered the Long Cane area again, this time in force. Colonel Elijah Clarke, Colonel John Twiggs, Colonel Benjamin Few, and Major James McCall arrived with some 500 men. They summoned both Williamson and Pickens to meet with them. Curiously, virtually all the sources treat this summons both as a polite request and as a friendly abduction. Samuel Hammond and a detachment were sent to White Hall on the fifth to retrieve Williamson and James McCall and his men were sent for Pickens "to bring them by force if necessary."[54] Both men went along, with Pickens asserting for the record that he did not go willingly, as he was still under parole. An earlier biographer was probably close to the mark with the comment, "The humor of the situation evidently appealed to both men and they accompanied their captors without resistance. Pickens declared that he came involuntarily."[55]

If Pickens claimed that he came against his will on December 5, he probably dissembled, either for the sake of his own reputation or to deceive Williamson and the British. That is because, in the last week of November, when Cruger sent a force to stop the Whig incursion of November 21–22, an event occurred that every American source cites as the cause of Pickens's renouncing his parole: British-Tory forces plundered his plantation and mistreated his family. The main source for this story was Hugh McCall, son of the James McCall who was Pickens's neighbor and the principal person entrusted with bringing Pickens back to the patriot cause. According to McCall,

> Colonel Pickens's house was plundered of moveable property, and the remainder wantonly destroyed. [In addition] M'Call's family was left without a change of clothing or bedding, and a halter put round the neck of one of his sons, by order of Dunlop [sic], with threats of execution, to extort secrets of which the youth was ignorant. The conditions of protection were now broken on the part of the British, and colonel Pickens with many of his officers and men, determined to resume their arms in the defence of their property and the rights of their country.[56]

In addition to robbing Pickens, the loyalist troops had burned his outbuildings and insulted and taunted his family.[57]

American sources blame the pillaging on Major James Dunlap, a hated Tory with the reputation of a scoundrel. British correspondence suggests that Dunlap himself was actually in Charleston for all or most of the period between November 24 until sometime in January, supposedly as part of a British effort to raise a troop of loyalist dragoons.[58] It is possible, of course, that

Liberty and Virtue in a Conquered Land

Tories who had previously ridden with Dunlap carried out the deed, or perhaps even that Dunlap briefly returned for long enough to commit it himself. What is incontrovertible is that the event occurred. Hugh McCall, the most important source for the event, was well placed to report on it. As the son of James McCall, thirteen years old at the time of the raid, he was quite possibly the lad who was tied up and threatened with execution. He certainly would have known what the Pickens family suffered as well. And British correspondence confirms that Cruger did send a large force under Allen on a weeklong expedition to scour the countryside after the band of forty to fifty "rebels" had mistreated a large number of Tories days before. Allen had returned to the base at Ninety Six on December 2. Indeed, the dating of events suggests that at the very time Pickens was away from home seeking to meet with Allen to discuss ways to secure peace and order in the area, Allen's forces were conducting the raid in which they attacked his home.[59] Whig sources assert that this was a punitive raid and that many citizens suffered from it.

Thus, when Pickens's former comrades returned to Long Cane in force on December 4, he already had ample justification in his own mind for renouncing his parole. When "summoned" or "abducted" by the Whig officers, Williamson refused to abandon his neutrality. It is unclear what Pickens said at the conference, but he seemingly deceived Williamson, Cruger's confidant, into believing he would take the same course.

After learning of this latest Whig intrusion (December 4) into the Long Cane district, Cruger sent another expedition under Allen to defeat it. In a pitched battle on December 11, the Whigs were defeated and driven away and Clarke and McCall were wounded.[60] Pickens, though, had already made his decision. Three days before the battle, with patriot forces still in control of Long Cane, Pickens had written a letter to American major general Nathanael Greene in Charlotte. Pickens was interceding for a man named Robert Hutton, currently imprisoned in Hillsborough, North Carolina, for allegedly impressing wagons for the use of British troops. A number of poor people "who had taken [the king's] protection, and yet were Friends to their country," had asked Hutton to gather food for them, and he had tried to comply. Pickens informed Greene that Hutton was "a real and sincere friend to the United States." Pickens was making a defense for those who had taken royal protection but whose motives had been to protect their own people from chaos and suffering. Undoubtedly he wished to portray his own actions in the same light. Thus, while Pickens still sought peace through Allen as late as November 26, by December 8 he was writing to Greene indicating he was preparing to rejoin the patriot cause. Next to his signature he wrote his rank of "Colonel," a sign that he had decided to renounce British protection. Another indicator that was the case was that the letter was also signed by Whigs A. Rapley, John Bowie, James McCall, and Robert Anderson, the last three of whom had all served in Pickens's regiment and who would serve under him again. McCall, of course, was actively serving in the Whig ranks at the time the letter was written. The British would have regarded Pickens as guilty of treason if they had intercepted this message.[61]

Pickens, then, had decided to rejoin the patriot ranks by December 8 and had informed other Whig leaders. He had cleverly hidden his intentions from both Williamson and Cruger. The latter was blissfully unaware of Pickens's defection when he wrote to Cornwallis on December 15. Cruger reported that on the fifth he had heard of an enemy party under Elijah Clarke and others "crossing the Saluda into Long Cane settlement. . . . They order'd Williamson, Pickens, and the principal men of the country who were on parole to attend them, alleging that we had violated the capitulation. They used both soothing and threatening arguments to those gentlemen, who, I have the pleasure to inform your Lordship, behaved like men of honor and persisted in a different opinion."[62] Cruger did not report that his troops had raided Pickens's home; in fact he probably still did not know about it himself. Neither Allen nor Cruger reported acts of plunder, pillage, or brutality by their men in the last week of November, but British officers often omitted this information when communicating with their superiors. Besides, announcing that their troops had mistreated Pickens, a man whom the British had courted for months, would have been an admission of incompetence and would have angered Cornwallis. But since Cruger still seemed confident of Pickens's loyalty on December 15, it seems likely he himself did not yet know of the foolish act.

The weeklong incursion into the Long Cane district by patriot forces on December 4 gave Pickens time to prepare for his big move. Sometime in mid-December, probably just before or after the patriot defeat on December 11, he sent his family northward to the settlements near the present border between North Carolina and Tennessee. One can imagine Pickens's wife, children, and a handful of slaves piled in wagons along with Clarke's defeated and wounded men. It would not have been Becky Pickens's first experience as a refugee. Pickens also had time to reveal his intentions to trusted former subordinates and extended family members such as the Calhouns. He then rode northward out of Long Cane to join the small army under Daniel Morgan near the Pacolet River. With him were his brother-in-law Major Alexander Noble; trusted subordinate and friend Captain Robert Anderson; a neighbor, Major David Boyce;

Liberty and Virtue in a Conquered Land

eighteen-year-old John Harris, Pickens's future son-in-law; and a total of some sixty to seventy men.[63]

One cannot explain the timing of Pickens's decision to rejoin the patriot ranks as crafty opportunism alone. Not a single Revolutionary officer ever did so, including those who had carried on the fight between June and November while Pickens was still at home enjoying the benefits of neutrality. When Pickens did rejoin the Whig cause and was promoted over those who had begged him for months to do so, none of them seemed to resent his tardiness or question his motives. Moreover, if Pickens had been simply waiting for a convenient moment to break his oath, he could have done this on several earlier occasions. In the wake of the collapse of the Whig government in late May and early June, there had been numerous victories by the patriot militia—Williamson's Plantation and Cedar Springs (July 12), Hanging Rock (August 6), Musgrove's Mill (August 19), and of course the astounding victory at Kings Mountain. Balfour and other officers had reported strong anti-British sentiment in Ninety Six District and particularly around Long Cane from the beginning. There had been British victories, as well, including Cornwallis's rout of Horatio Gates's army at Camden on August 16. The insurgency, however, had been gaining strength and territory long before Pickens made his move, and he could have safely allowed himself to be "kidnapped" by partisan leaders long before he did.[64] It had been a seesaw struggle, and there had been plenty of opportunity for Pickens to denounce his oath as one made under duress, as hundreds of other South Carolinians were doing. On the other hand, once Pickens did make his decision, he carefully hid it from Williamson and the British until the last minute. By the time senior British officers were aware of Pickens's departure, he had been able to get his family away from the area and confirm that a large number of men would join him when he left.

Pickens, then, was back in the fight. Just before he departed Long Cane, however, he performed one other task to satisfy the demands of honor and virtue—Pickens personally informed a British officer that he considered himself released from his parole and was rejoining the fight. Some older secondary accounts simply state that Pickens politely informed Cruger in writing of his decision.[65] But a persistent and widely accepted version that is both more colorful and more probable asserts that Pickens walked right into a British camp. The advantage of this version is that it is based on the account of young Hugh McCall, the lad described above who knew the Pickens family well. Pickens was not foolhardy enough to go directly to the main British base at Ninety Six, where Cruger was temporarily absent and Allen was in charge. Instead, he went to Williamson's home at White Hall. Here was a small detachment of loyalist troops under Captain George Ker, with whom Pickens had struck up a friendship. Pickens strode up to Ker and told him calmly but firmly that because of the damage done to his plantation, he was no longer bound by his parole agreement—he was rejoining the American ranks. Ker pled earnestly with Pickens to reconsider, reminding him that if he were captured, he would be executed. Pickens would be fighting, Ker warned, "with a halter around his neck."[66] But Pickens was adamant and spoke again with "cool determination."[67] According to several accounts, his exact words were "I have honorably and conscientiously adhered to the rules laid down in the protection I took, but now I consider myself completely absolved by the wanton plunder and waste, and the indignities that have been offered my family."[68] He also asked Ker to relay this message to Cruger and to "thank him for his civilities while I was under British protection."[69] Sadly, Ker finally expressed the hope Pickens would never be captured. As Pickens walked out and rode away, Ker made no effort to arrest him.[70]

Pickens's defection profoundly frustrated the British, who thought they were so close to bringing him over to their side.[71] Cruger probably did not hear of Pickens's decision right away, as Cornwallis had allowed him to go to Charleston for a few weeks. And quite possibly Ker neglected to mention to his superiors that Pickens had delivered his message to the captain's face—surely he knew they would be angry to learn that Ker had let Pickens get away. Allen did not report Pickens's defection to Cornwallis until December 29. He was convinced, however, that it was a serious setback to the British cause in the area. Allen gauged that Pickens's decision would require the presence of an additional 500 militia to maintain the British position in Ninety Six. "Williamson," Allen reported, "is at home, much distressed with the perfidious behavior of his friend Pickens."[72]

Pickens had finally decided that the demands of liberty, honor, and patriotism demanded an irrevocable choice. In making it, he sacrificed the last shreds of security that he had left. It was not just that he had left his home and the property he had built up over the last fifteen years in enemy hands; by renouncing his parole he was also, as Ker warned, fighting with a "halter around his neck." Cornwallis reacted by instructing Cruger and Allen that if Pickens had left any "Negroes, Cattle or other property" they must be seized and used for the supply of the king's troops. "I desire," Cornwallis stated, "that his house may be burnt, and his Plantations totally destroyed, & himself, if captured, instantly hanged."[73]

Liberty and Virtue in a Conquered Land

SIX

The "Brave and Valuable" Colonel Pickens

THE COWPENS CAMPAIGN

The Cool and determined Bravery repeatedly
displayed by Brigadier Pickens.

*Governor John Rutledge to the South Carolina
General Assembly, January 18, 1782*

Andrew Pickens's decision to rejoin the patriot cause was an act of choosing liberty and virtue over order, at least in his own mind. In a sense, wartime events had made the decision for him. The war had descended into barbarism. Both sides had murdered opposing soldiers attempting to surrender, butchered prisoners of war, pillaged, plundered, looted, and left the women and children of their enemies homeless and destitute. Whig officers had warned Pickens just before he rejoined them that neutrality was no longer an option; every man had to choose a side. They were right, and Pickens knew it. He had clung to order and security—the British "protection" as it was called—as long as he could. He had hoped that such a course was consistent with the virtue of keeping his oath and that it preserved at least a measure of personal liberty. But when the king's men ravaged the Long Cane community and raided his own plantation, there was little order or security left to preserve, and his choice was clear.

The fate of the Pickens family in the winter of 1780–81 illustrates the breakdown of order and security. One of the most prominent traditions surrounding Pickens is that a stone blockhouse he had built often served as a refuge for his family and neighbors when Indians or Tories threatened or controlled the Long Cane district. Pickens's grandson Francis Pickens asserted that at one point in the war, the family hid in the woods near their home while Pickens's slaves, led by Old Dick, kept them concealed and supplied. Some of the children at the time were sick with smallpox, and one of the boys died.[1]

Francis Pickens's claim that the family's slaves had been loyal was an indirect reminder of the chaos and tragedy in the dark days of the Revolution, but it glossed over the experiences and dilemmas faced by African Americans themselves. By the end of the Revolutionary War, there were 30,000 fewer black people living in South Carolina than there had been when the fighting began. Some 5,000 departed when their Tory masters fled the state near the end of the war. The rest were either seized by British troops or escaped to British lines on their own accord. Many of those were able to better their condition or even obtain their freedom, while others were personally confiscated by British officers and sold for the profit of the latter. Some were so dissatisfied by their treatment that they voluntarily returned to their masters. The vast majority of enslaved people who escaped to the British, of course, came from the lowcountry. However, there was ample opportunity for slaves who belonged to backcountry masters like Pickens to escape during the British occupation of the interior in 1780–81. Old Dick and Pickens's other slaves probably had the very real option of escaping. They may have heard stories of other African Americans who had done so and found themselves in equally bad conditions with the British. Perhaps some of Pickens's slaves took their chances anyway. If so, Francis Pickens chose not to record that fact while asserting the loyalty of the others.[2]

In December 1780, Pickens's wife and children were not just hiding near their home (and perhaps relying on their slaves' assistance) but also temporarily abandoning that home as refugees as Pickens sent them off into the mountains. Becky had long ago learned how to manage in her husband's absence. As her column of refugee wagons creaked northward, she was responsible both for any enslaved people who were with her and for her six children: Mary, fourteen; Ezekiel, twelve; Ann, ten; Jane Bonneau, six; Margaret, three; and Andrew, one.[3]

Pickens and his band of men departed Long Cane as a loosely organized militia formation of neighbors and kinsmen. As they moved north to join the Continental army forces under Brigadier General Daniel Morgan and then under Major General Nathanael Greene, however, Pickens the militia officer was beginning the period of his closest and most successful cooperation with regular army forces. The companies he led out of the Long Cane settlement at the end of 1780 differed from the Continental forces in many ways. Pickens was used to leading men who served no more than three months at a time, who felt their obligation to stay and fight diminished the farther they got from home, and among whom drill and discipline were looser. They were inferior soldiers when it came to standing in fixed ranks and exchanging volleys with professionally trained infantry. But they were excellent at laying ambushes and at conducting fast marches and quick raids followed by rapid retreats—"Indian fighting," or what was later called "guerrilla" warfare. They were armed typically with rifles rather than muskets, which had several tactical implications that will be discussed later. They usually brought their own horses from home and rode to their points of operation, dismounting before battle and leaving their horses in the care of a few selected men. Thus, they made up a sort of mounted infantry. Since they were not typically armed with traditional cavalry weapons such as sabers, they rarely fought from horseback, though this would begin to change around the time of the battle of Cowpens in January 1781.[4] Another important point is that after the collapse of South Carolina's Whig government in May 1780, the men of the patriot militia were not formally paid. For a time at least, they were true volunteers. Even more than before, militia officers such as Pickens had to lead their men by force of personality and persuasion.

Before the end of 1781, Pickens would prove himself to be among the most willing and adept militiamen when it came to operating with the Continental army. Unlike other militia officers, Pickens himself showed absolutely no reluctance to cooperate with and subordinate himself to higher-ranking Continental officers, never once attempting to go his own way by appealing to state autonomy. They in turn came to trust his reliability and judgment implicitly. Pickens and Continental army officers such as the New Englander Nathanael Greene, the frontier-savvy Daniel Morgan, and the aristocratic Virginian Henry "Light Horse Harry" Lee showed that the regular-militia partnership could be close and could bring victory.

After the fall of Charleston, Congress's attempt to continue the fight for the South with Continental forces had met with disaster when Major General Horatio Gates's force was crushed at Camden in August 1780. With Gates thoroughly discredited, General George Washington recommended that Major General Nathanael Greene take charge of the Southern Department. Greene the Rhode Islander and Pickens the southern partisan differed greatly in their backgrounds and personality yet ultimately shared much in their moral sense and in their strategic outlook. Greene was three years younger than Pickens and had grown up in settled New England, not

Nathanael Greene by Charles Willson Peale, from life, 1783
(*Courtesy Independence National Historical Park, Philadelphia, Pa.*)

in the southern backcountry. His family owned a successful iron forge and he had invested in commerce and shipping, while Pickens's hardscrabble story was one of migrations, farming, and establishing himself as a frontier merchant. Pickens's life had been periodically interrupted by the brutality of frontier warfare, and he was already a veteran when hostilities began with Britain in 1775. Greene, by contrast, had always been deeply interested in military affairs but had not seen combat prior to the Revolution. Pickens

The "Brave and Valuable" Colonel Pickens

was a devout Old Light Presbyterian with firm Calvinist convictions, while Greene had been raised as a Quaker. Both men greatly valued education, but Greene had obtained one despite the objections of his father, who was suspicious of book learning, while Pickens's lifelong regret was that the death of his father prevented him from obtaining, in his words, "even a good english education."[5] The two men also differed in their outward appearance and personality. While both of them at five feet ten inches were relatively tall for their day, Greene had a rather florid expression and a full face; his disposition was generally lighthearted and cheerful. Pickens, with his narrower face, prominent nose, and grim countenance, was severe and taciturn.

And yet the two of them were destined to form a fruitful partnership. Greene had left the Quaker fellowship in 1775 and was not devout, but he had deeply admired the piety and upright, sober lifestyle of his father. In a letter to his close friend Sammy Ward in 1772, Greene had written that "Plainness and Simplicity of Manners, stript of all the pain and Ornament of Policy, is what I ever admired, it wins the Affections by the force of its Persuasion."[6] It is easy to see Greene being drawn, then, to the plainspoken and unpretentious Andrew Pickens. Even as military commanders, the two seemed to have shared a similar moral sense, though they were used to serving in different environments. Pickens had a deep Calvinist conviction of man's depravity, and he fought on the frontier where brutality was commonplace, but he often registered his disgust with unnecessary killings and unwarranted savagery. In his earlier service in the more settled areas of the northern states, Greene had striven to prevent soldiers from stealing, swearing, or even swimming naked near civilian farmhouses. He was shocked at the savage nature of civil warfare when he came to the South and often relied on Pickens to punish American troops for committing atrocities. "How can we hope to have the blessings of heaven in our aims," he once asked his northern troops, "if we insult it with impunity?"[7] It seems that, like Presbyterians, Greene the lapsed Quaker shared the conviction that men were answerable individually and collectively to a God who intervened in the affairs of nations.[8]

Most important to Greene and Pickens's relationship, Greene arrived in the Carolinas with the conviction that his success in the South would depend largely on the militia. Earlier in the war he had expressed distrust of militia, but he knew he would have to utilize it well if he were to win in the South. For one thing, his own Continental forces were simply too weak to take on Cornwallis without the militia's help. When he arrived in the backcountry village of Charlotte on December 2, he found a ragged, dispirited force of 1,000 Continentals and perhaps 1,200 militiamen. A large number were unarmed and unfit for duty—the Virginia troops were literally naked except for breechcloths, and most of the men were living in makeshift huts due to the lack of tents. Facing this pitiful force were Cornwallis's 4,000 well-equipped men sixty miles to the south in Winnsboro, and by the end of the month Cornwallis would have some 9,000 troops in the southern theater.[9] Greene also could not ignore the fact that it was the militia and its style of warfare that had been most successful in the South so far. In the nearly four months between the Continentals' defeat at Camden and Greene's arrival in Charlotte, it had been the militia that had kept the Revolution alive in South Carolina and Georgia and won the signal victory at Kings Mountain in October. Conversely, when the Americans had pinned their hopes in the South on set-piece battles led by Continental officers, they had suffered their most serious defeats: Savannah, Charleston, and Camden. It was the militia commanders who were the most familiar with the terrain and adept at securing supplies and intelligence. Even before his arrival in Charlotte, Greene wrote Washington that he planned to supplement his force with militia and to utilize mobility and partisan tactics whenever necessary. "I see but little prospect of getting a force to contend with the enemy upon equal grounds, and must make the most of a kind of partizan war," Greene informed the commander in chief.[10]

Greene was soon fortunate to have the full cooperation of one of the most experienced "partizans," Andrew Pickens. When Pickens resumed his fight for American independence in December, surviving correspondence indicates that he first informed Greene of the Continental army, not Thomas Sumter, South Carolina's senior militia officer. Pickens moved immediately to join the closest American army, which happened to be Daniel Morgan's force of Continentals and militiamen on the Pacolet River. He also did not mind serving outside of South Carolina if it would help the larger cause. Of South Carolina's three most important militia commanders in 1781 and 1782—Sumter, Francis Marion, and Pickens—Pickens was the only one who campaigned extensively outside the state.

Greene did receive some small but welcome additions of Continental troops to his command in December and early January. He was joined by Lieutenant Colonel Light Horse Harry Lee of Virginia and his elite legion of dragoons and infantrymen, 300 strong. Another helpful addition was Lieutenant Colonel William Washington's 100 dragoons.[11] One of Greene's subordinates in Charlotte was Brigadier General Daniel Morgan, an "up-from-the-bootstraps brawler" and a grizzled veteran of the French

The "Brave and Valuable" Colonel Pickens

and Indian War.[12] A larger-than-life, charismatic figure, Morgan would be Pickens's immediate superior at the beginning of the 1781 campaign.

Greene made his first brilliant maneuver when he took the unorthodox step of dividing his army before Cornwallis's stronger force. He took the bulk of his force southeast from Charlotte toward Cheraw on the Pee Dee River. Meanwhile he sent Morgan with 320 Maryland and Delaware Continentals, 200 Virginia riflemen, and William Washington's 100 dragoons west toward the Pacolet River. Greene had no intention of fighting a general engagement at this time against Cornwallis. He reasoned, however, that if Cornwallis moved toward him on the Pee Dee, the British commander left his bases at Ninety Six and Augusta vulnerable to Morgan; if Cornwallis came after Morgan instead, he allowed Greene to threaten Georgetown and Charleston.[13] If Cornwallis did neither and remained at Winnsboro, he halted the momentum of his invasion and allowed American patriot forces to encourage the Whig population and continue to draw supplies from the Pee Dee and upper Broad River areas. Splitting the American force would also ease Greene's own supply difficulties. Meanwhile, Greene also sent reinforcements and encouragement to Francis Marion as the latter caused more trouble for the British in the lowcountry. Marion's forays could be useful as Morgan moved toward the Pacolet and as William Washington inflicted a stinging defeat on some Georgia Tories at Hammond's Store just north of the Saluda.[14]

Pickens joined Morgan at Grindal Shoals on the Pacolet sometime between December 25 and 29. Morgan reported to Greene that Pickens had sixty men with him; however, thirty or forty of them had temporarily gone to North Carolina to "secure their Effects" and would immediately return to Morgan.[15] Presumably many of these men were not only removing their property but also seeing to the temporary lodging of their families. Meanwhile, more troops were pouring into Morgan's camp. About the same time Pickens arrived, so did 120 North Carolina militiamen serving under Brigadier General William Davidson. Over the next three weeks, other contingents of South Carolina partisan militia similar to Pickens's and also more formally organized South Carolina State Troops came in. Morgan put all the South Carolina militia units under Pickens, and by January 17 he had given him formal command of those from North Carolina and Virginia as well. Meanwhile, some of the men who had come with Pickens from Long Cane, including his brother Captain Joseph Pickens and Major Samuel Hammond, were attached to the South Carolina State Troops. At the ensuing battle of Cowpens, Joseph Pickens would command the infantry portions of the South Carolina State Troops. Pickens's neighbor James McCall, now promoted to lieutenant colonel, would be given command of a body of South Carolina state dragoons that was placed under Colonel William Washington.[16]

Cornwallis responded to Greene's moves at the beginning of January by sending the hard-driving Lieutenant Colonel Banastre Tarleton after Washington and then after Morgan himself. Tarleton had 750 men, soon reinforced to just over 1,000. His column was a mixture of British regular army units and his veteran British Legion.[17] Eventually Cornwallis would move northward from Winnsboro in the area between the Broad and Wateree Rivers to cut off any survivors from what he expected would be Tarleton's thrashing of Morgan. By December 31, Morgan was contemplating retreat. He wrote Greene that his rapidly increasing numbers were making it impossible to continue to feed his army if he remained in the area. Morgan had already asked Pickens and Davidson if he could safely retreat "should we be pushed by a Superior Force." The two militia officers assured him that it could be easily done by "passing up the Savannah, and crossing over the Heads of the Rivers Along the Indian Line." Morgan asked Greene for permission to follow this course.[18]

While Davidson and Pickens had told Morgan what he needed to do if he retreated, it seems unlikely that they favored that option. Morgan himself was unsure if that were the correct course when he wrote Greene again on January 4. He was still concerned about his inability to supply himself unless he retreated, but he also mentioned other considerations that may have resulted from his consultations with his militia officers. Retreat, Morgan now recognized, would destroy "the Spirit which now begins to pervade the People and call them into the Field." A withdrawal could also cause the "Militia who have already Joined" to desert and possibly even join the enemy for their own safety.[19]

As a temporary solution to his dilemma, Morgan turned to the militia. He sent Pickens's militia and the South Carolina State Troops to the Fairforest Creek area near Union, ten to fifteen miles to the south of Morgan's own position at Grindal Shoals and about forty-five miles northwest of Cornwallis's main base at Winnsboro. Pickens's men could act as a screen and early warning of the enemy's approach. His removal there could also relieve Morgan's supply problem. As Pickens's men subsisted on flour from the mill belonging to the loyalist Thomas Fletchall, they also denied those provisions to the enemy.[20] And, as always, the presence of patriot militia in the area encouraged Whigs to enlist and Tories to lie low. By this time,

The "Brave and Valuable" Colonel Pickens

Morgan was already gaining confidence in the man to whom he entrusted this mission. "Colonel Pickens," he wrote Greene, "is a valuable, discreet, and attentive officer, and has the confidence of the militia."[21]

On January 12, Pickens sent word to Morgan that Tarleton, formerly close to Ninety Six, was moving rapidly north. Morgan used the next few days to continue to gather supplies, begin a withdrawal north to the Broad River, send out detachments to cover his flanks, and integrate into his army the numerous small bands of militia that continued to pour into his position. Meanwhile, Pickens's regiments also withdrew in the face of Tarleton's advance. On the morning of January 14, Pickens and Morgan conferred in person at Grindal Shoals. After a brief meeting, Pickens moved west up the Pacolet River into some hills and began assembling all his militia into one body—indicating that the time for gathering supplies was over and that a fight was expected soon.[22] Morgan spent the fourteenth and fifteenth retreating north to Thickety Creek and then following the creek upstream (north) toward the banks of the Broad River. On the fifteenth, less than forty-eight hours before the battle of Cowpens, Daniel Morgan was once again convinced that he should retreat. His letter to Greene of that day again tried to persuade his commander. Morgan asked Greene to order him back to Greene's main army and leave the militia to operate in northwestern South Carolina. The militia, he argued, would be less of a target for Tarleton or Cornwallis and could continue to "serve as a check on the disaffected [the Tories]."[23]

On January 16, however, Morgan reconsidered. He was now near the North Carolina border just five miles south of the Broad River, close to some fields known as the "Cowpens." That afternoon Morgan reconnoitered the area around the Cowpens and seems at least to have considered making a stand. He made jocular comments to several militiamen indicating that there would soon be a fight. This pleased some of the men, who had been disgusted at his earlier decision to retreat from Tarleton.[24]

Several considerations influenced Morgan's change of heart by the evening of the sixteenth. Another letter from Greene had recently arrived, and Greene still urged him to fight rather than withdraw.[25] Meanwhile, Tarleton continued to pursue and was gaining fast. The British officer had only a few days' worth of supplies for his legion, and as he advanced, he found that food was scarce in the area where Pickens's men had operated. The lack of food probably only added to Tarleton's usual sense of urgency (which in turn ensured that his men were badly fatigued by the time they finally caught up with Morgan).[26] Then, that evening (perhaps beginning in the daylight hours), Pickens and his individual regiments entered Morgan's camp, clearly eager to make a stand. Pickens informed Morgan that if he made a stand south of the Broad, he could guarantee that his men would fight. If he crossed to the North Carolina side of the river, however, they might well go home.[27] Thus, Morgan knew that he would probably have more men with him if he fought now than if he retreated farther and fought later. And he would certainly have to fight at some point, as Tarleton was very near and closing fast. Fighting the enemy on ground that he had already carefully reconnoitered would be better than being struck suddenly while on the march.

Morgan made his decision and then called a council among his senior officers and found them in a determined mood as well. Supposedly William Washington announced, "No burning, no flying: but face about and give battle to the enemy, and acquit ourselves like men."[28] Colonel John Eager Howard of the Maryland Continentals reported that more detachments of militiamen and state troops entered the camp throughout the night, "calling on Morgan for ammunition, and to know the state of affairs."[29] Howard recalled that "all the militia officers were anxious to fight. . . . Many of them had suffered much, their houses burnt & their families turned out of doors."[30] According to Howard, the high spirits of the militia helped convince Morgan "that he might well calculate on victory."[31]

Morgan settled on a general concept for how he would fight the battle early in the evening, but the details of each unit's role and their initial defensive positions evolved throughout the night. Modern tacticians would call Morgan's approach a "defense-in-depth," and he trusted the militia with an important role. As the British advanced northward toward Morgan's army, they would first encounter rifle fire from scattered pickets, or videttes. This fire would give the American army warning of Tarleton's approach and force the British to deploy from column into line. After the British passed through the pickets, they would receive more rifle fire from selected militiamen deployed in a thin line of skirmishers. Those skirmishers would fire a few rounds and then retire to a solid line of militia commanded by Pickens. Behind the militia line would be the "main line," with Morgan's veteran Continentals in the center. On the flanks of the main line were some Virginia and North Carolina militiamen, many of whom had seen much service with Morgan and the Continental regiments.

The ground would be rising slightly for Tarleton as he advanced. The highest ground on the field was near its northern end, where Morgan placed his main, or rearmost, line of defense. However, there were small folds of ground as well as trees that would conceal parts of Morgan's army as the British advanced. At first Tarleton would be able to see only part of the line

The "Brave and Valuable" Colonel Pickens

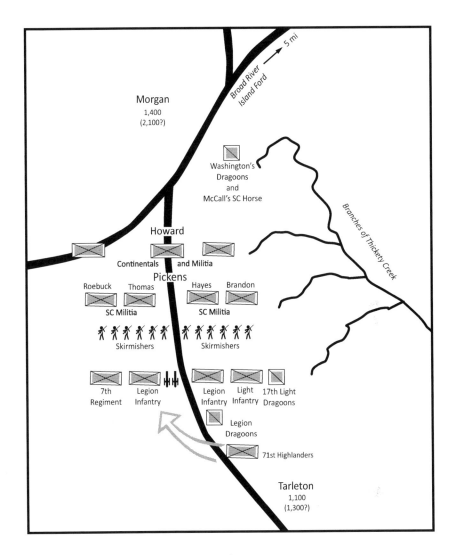

Battle of Cowpens *(Map by Chris Cartledge)*

of Pickens's militia deployed behind the skirmishers. He would have some visibility of the left of Pickens's line (opposite Tarleton's right) but not the rest of it. Nor would he see the main American line behind Pickens. On either side of Tarleton were deep creek beds, or ravines, giving some protection to Morgan's flanks.[32]

After firing a few rounds, the skirmishers would withdraw to the militia line commanded by Pickens fewer than 150 yards behind them. The militia would then fire one, two, maybe even three volleys and then withdraw behind the main line of Continentals, fewer than 150 yards in their rear. This plan took the strengths and weaknesses of the militia into account. Armed mainly with rifles, which were more far more accurate than muskets at medium or long range, the militiamen could seriously attrite the enemy's ranks. What they were not expected to do was withstand a charge against British bayonets. Rifles had greater range, but they took longer to reload than muskets did. Hence, Tarleton's officers knew that the proper response to a volley of militiamen's rifle fire was to charge before their enemy could reload. Due both to temperament and armament, those in the patriot militia would have little chance of standing their ground. Their rifles would be unloaded, and there was no way to affix bayonets to rifles. Therefore, they would not be properly armed for close combat against the bayonets of British infantry, the sabers of British dragoons, and the superb close-order discipline of British regulars. Morgan therefore wanted the militia to withdraw behind the protection of the Continental line before the issue came to that. Perhaps, he hoped, they could even re-form behind the Continentals and then reenter the fight. Then, as the British were somewhat disorganized from their losses by rifle fire and their attempt to pursue the militia, they would be stunned as they suddenly came face to face with a solid line of Continental infantry. Meanwhile William Washington's dragoons, reinforced by South Carolina state dragoons under James McCall, would serve as a mobile reserve capable of swooping down upon an exposed British flank or upon retreating enemy troops. Fortunately for Morgan, this was very similar to how the battle would actually unfold.[33]

Morgan took care to see that the militiamen understood their role and were mentally prepared for the fight. Before dawn, he and Pickens walked from "mess to mess of the militia." The jocular, charismatic Morgan did the talking—Joseph McJunkin recalled him saying, "Boys, get up, Benny is coming! You that have sweethearts, wives, children, or parents, must fight for them; and *above all, fight for liberty and for your country*!"[34] Morgan delighted the men with jokes on how badly they would whip "Ben," or "Benny," Tarleton. Militiaman Thomas Young recalled how Morgan explained their role in delivering a few volleys and then withdrawing: "Just hold your head up boys, three fires and you are free! And when you return to your homes, how the folks will bless you and the girls will kiss you for your gallant conduct."[35] McJunkin recalled that other militia officers such as James Jackson of Georgia, Pickens's "major of brigade," spoke to the militia as well. It seems that most men on this occasion remembered the folksy and jocular style of men like Morgan and Jackson better than the stern reserve of Pickens.[36]

The "Brave and Valuable" Colonel Pickens

Pickens's line consisted of four regiments, or battalions. On the far left was Colonel Thomas Brandon's Fairforest regiment. To its right was Colonel Joseph Hayes's Little River regiment. On its right, on the other side of the road that bisected the battlefield, was Lieutenant Colonel John Thomas's Spartan regiment, with another battalion of men from the Spartan District under Lieutenant Colonel Benjamin Roebuck on the far right. Many of Pickens's own Long Cane men were not in this line throughout the battle. Some served temporarily with James McCall's formation in Washington's dragoons, while others came under Samuel Hammond's command in the South Carolina State Troops. The Long Cane men temporarily under Hammond deployed first as skirmishers, then on the left flank of Pickens's militia line, and finally on the left flank of the main line.[37]

Tarleton's army arrived on the field at around first light, fatigued from five hours of solid marching and short rations. The day would be partly sunny, but the air was damp, misty, and very cold. Morgan's men, comparatively more rested and well fed, were likely chilled, having abandoned their campfires some time before and then deploying into line.[38]

As the British came onto the field, the advance pickets and then the line of skirmishers played their roles, causing some British casualties, delaying the enemy advance, and then withdrawing as planned. Pickens's line received the skirmishers back into its ranks. Pickens ordered his men not to fire until the enemy was within forty to fifty yards, an order that was "executed with great firmness." One reason for this order may have been that the militiamen were actually "well behind the crest" over which the British would advance before they reached them.[39] A premature volley would have Pickens's men firing at targets that were not yet fully exposed.

With several discharges of cannons and some cheers, the British then advanced rapidly and confidently against Pickens, with Tarleton personally leading the advance. A few of Pickens's men fired individually. Then, at a range of between thirty-five and fifty yards, the militia fired a volley. Each regiment fired separately, beginning with Brandon's men on the far left and followed by Thomas's, Hayes's, and then Roebuck's. The effect on the British line was devastating. One British lieutenant estimated that two-thirds of the infantry officers fell and nearly as many of the privates. After the battle, American soldiers were struck by the appearance of scores of British corpses lying in straight lines where they collided with the militia's rifle fire. The shock of receiving well-aimed rifle fire at point-blank range created "something like a recoil" in the British line.[40]

Some British units attempted a volley, but their fire was weak, ineffective, and too high. The British Light Infantry opposite Brandon's regiment did not fire but instead attempted to regroup and charge. By the time they charged, Brandon's men had reloaded and poured another volley into them, once again stopping them in their tracks. Yet British valor and discipline did not falter. None of the other militia regiments besides Brandon's got off a second volley before the British line regrouped and charged with fixed bayonets. With little other choice, Hayes's men in the center-left of the line took off toward the main line. This created a gap in the line, and Pickens shouted orders for the rest of the line to withdraw as well; there was probably no need for him to do so. The militiamen retreated through the ranks of the Continentals in their rear. Both a lieutenant and a sergeant major serving with the Delaware Continentals reported that the retreating militiamen in their front were nevertheless "in very good order, and not in the least confused."[41]

The British veterans cheered as they advanced through the militia's previous position, confident that the battle was won—once again, as at Camden and elsewhere, the ragtag rebels had succumbed to British discipline and valor. Then, however, they collided with the Continentals and other Americans on the main line. In the rear of the main line, Pickens and other militia officers began reorganizing their units. Some men apparently were already mounting their horses and trying to ride away, and others were wandering about attempting to find their messmates and officers, who in turn were trying to re-form their companies and battalions. Reports indicate, however, that overall there was minimal panic. That ended in a moment. Tarleton ordered a mounted charge of the Seventeenth Light Dragoons at and through the extreme left of the main line. Samuel Hammond and Joseph Pickens's South Carolina State Troops offered brief resistance but were smashed. Within seconds the dragoons were bearing down upon Andrew Pickens's militia just a few hundred feet away. Some men fled; others responded as their officers called to them to stand fast. In fact, the high casualty rate among South Carolina militia officers at Cowpens indicates that many of those officers chose to lead from the front on this occasion.[42] One example was Lieutenant Joseph Hughes of the Fair Forest regiment. Already wounded by a saber stroke on his right hand, Hughes outran his men to the rear with his sword drawn, then faced about and yelled at them to halt. Striking all around him to enforce obedience, he repeatedly called, "You d—d cowards, halt and fight—there is more danger in running than in fighting . . . !" Some of the militiamen were able to re-form and fire a volley at the dragoons pursuing them.[43]

The "Brave and Valuable" Colonel Pickens

Fortunately, William Washington's dragoons arrived just in time. Out-numbering Tarleton's dragoons, they collided with them and drove them away. Morgan, too, came on the scene and helped reorganize the militia. Soon Pickens began leading Hammond's re-formed South Carolina State Troops and the Spartan regiment back toward the front, just behind the right of the American main line. Meanwhile, contingents of militia from the Fair Forest and Littler River regiments returned to the front as well, but on the American left.[44]

The British and the Americans in the main line exchanged volleys for several minutes. At that point, a misunderstood order caused a withdrawal along the entire right of the American line. The British, especially the Seventy-First Regiment of Highlanders, believed the Americans were finally beaten and pursued aggressively. Morgan and other officers such as Colonel John Eager Howard, however, regained control over the situation. Howard's men faced about and poured a devastating volley into the Highlanders at the range of ten to fifteen yards. Howard then ordered a bayonet charge, just as Washington's dragoons charged into the Highlanders' left flank. It was also about that time that Pickens's men appeared at the front and joined the dragoons and Howard's infantry in attacking the British left. Devastated by a point-blank volley, a bayonet charge, a mounted charge against their left, and the fury of Pickens's resurgent militia, the Seventy-First attempted to withdraw and then disintegrated. Virtually surrounded and broken up into small bands, the regiment's proud officers began surrendering their swords to American officers, including Howard and Pickens. The rest of the British line surrendered or fled the field as Tarleton vainly attempted to rally them as the Americans pursued.[45]

The surrender of the Seventy-First made an impression on Pickens and stood out in his memory. Pickens recalled that Major Archibald McArthur, commander of the Seventy-First Highlanders, surrendered his sword to him "some distance from the battle ground."[46] In his autobiographical letter to Henry Lee in August 1811, the laconic Pickens gave few details about the battles he fought except for Kettle Creek. Exceptions to the rule were cases in which Pickens assumed that Lee knew little of what had transpired or in which he believed previous reports were inaccurate. Pickens therefore related little to Lee about the Cowpens battle, except for the very end of the fight. Pickens had just read a biography of the deceased James Jackson, his brigade major at Cowpens, which claimed that Jackson had captured the person and sword of Major McArthur. Years before, Jackson had claimed to others (not to Pickens) that he had been the one to capture McArthur and that due partially to Pickens's neglect he had not been properly mentioned in Morgan's official report to Congress. In 1797, Jackson's political enemies in Georgia were minimizing Jackson's wartime service, and Jackson complained to Morgan. Pickens heard of the criticism directed at Jackson, wrote a letter in Jackson's support, and asked Morgan to vouch for Jackson's services. However, he never conceded that Jackson was the one who captured McArthur. In 1811 he wrote to Lee,

> That part of the 71st which was there surrendered to me & I believe every officer of that Regiment delivered his sword into my hand—I see in a publication, the life of the late Genl Jackson of Georgia, by a Judge Carlton of Savannah, that Major McCarthur [sic] of the 71st Regiment delivered his sword to him—I think Jackson never told him so—Major McCarthur surrendered to me, some distance from the battleground & delivered his sword to me—Jackson acted with me at that time as Brigade Major—I sent back to Genl Morgan, by Major Jackson, Major McCarthur, with the sword—.[47]

Due probably to the confusion, Pickens's statement was not completely correct, either, for Howard reportedly delivered seven officers' swords to Morgan. In the chaos of the moment, some officers of the Seventy-First, including its commander, were surrendering to Pickens while others were surrendering to Howard with Pickens unaware of the fact.[48] The point is that the capitulation of the Seventy-First was a notable event in Pickens's mind, as well as it should have been. Pickens, commanding militia who supposedly could not stand up to British regulars, had taken at least a part in receiving the surrender of an elite unit of His Majesty's Royal Army.

In any event, the battle was not yet over and Pickens and Howard had no time to compare notes on who captured which swords. As British survivors were fleeing, Pickens encountered William Washington, whose dragoons were pursuing Tarleton. Pickens ordered Jackson, who, he told Lee, was "brave and active"—Pickens's highest compliment for an officer—to round up as many of the mounted militia as he could find and join the pursuit. Washington's and Pickens's mounted men pursued Tarleton for some twenty miles, capturing several more prisoners but failing to capture Tarleton or bring the remnants of his army to battle.[49]

Besides pursuit, the Whig militia also took time to plunder, relieving their prisoners and the British dead of clothing, equipment, officers' supplies of wine, and money. Pickens's slave Old Dick got into the action as well, perhaps partly for his own benefit but also definitely for his master's. Dick

The "Brave and Valuable" Colonel Pickens

found a badly wounded young British officer who was elegantly dressed, including a "fine pair of top boots." According to Francis W. Pickens, the officer was lying with his head leaning on the root of a tree when

> Dick stood up by him & placed his foot & knee out in the attitude to draw his boots, and the officer said to him, "Surely, my boy, you will not take them before I die." Dick [replied,] "Look mighty nice, and Massa need 'em so bad." The officer then said, "I am so thirsty; bring me a little water before I die, & then take the boots." Dick went & filled his own hat with water & brought it, & the officer drank freely, & did die, & Dick brought the boots to the tent of Gen. Pickens, and told it to all around.[50]

There was plenty to keep Pickens busy after the battle besides replacing his boots. Once again Morgan chose to use the militia as a rear guard and security element. Pickens and Washington returned to the site of the battle on January 18. Morgan, apprehending a determined and rapid pursuit by Cornwallis's main army, had already retreated to the north. Pickens's militia had been assigned to protect and make arrangements for the wounded and to keep charge of the prisoners. Overwhelmed by the number of casualties, the Whigs were able to find houses for their own wounded. At least eighty-seven British wounded, however, could not be moved. Pickens left them on the field under the care of British surgeons.[51] On the nineteenth, two days after the battle, Pickens caught up with Morgan at Gilbert Town, North Carolina. From there, Morgan marched east directly for Sherrald's Ford on the Catawba, hoping to cross it before Cornwallis could intercept him and prevent his reunion with Greene. Meanwhile the American commander sent Pickens on a more northerly route through a spur of the North Carolina mountains; he gave Pickens charge of some 500 prisoners and probably thirty-five wagons and 100 captured dragoon horses. The Virginia militia, whose enlistments were expiring, eventually escorted the prisoners north as they returned home. Some of Pickens's men, meanwhile, did not withdraw into North Carolina but stayed in South Carolina to protect the local Whig population from Tory reprisals in Morgan's absence.[52]

On a tactical level, Cowpens was one of the most devastating defeats inflicted on the British in the entire war. Tarleton's total loss in killed, wounded, and captured was well over 800, or approaching 80 percent of his force. His infantry units were wiped out and his mounted ones badly cut up. Morgan's loss by comparison (including the militia) was somewhere between 127 and 148 killed and wounded.[53] News of Tarleton's rout electrified the new American nation. On the larger stage, however, it did not immediately alter the strategic balance in the Carolinas, as Greene and Morgan were still forced to retreat before the more powerful Cornwallis.

The battle was also significant as the most successful combination yet of patriot militia and Continental forces on the battlefield. The militia had been useful, of course, in their usual roles of reconnaissance, intelligence, foraging, and suppression of local Tories. But for the first time they also had played a key role in a major battlefield victory against British regulars. Indeed it was previously unheard of for militia units to offer resistance, retreat, and then re-form and reenter the battle. Among the many things Morgan did well at Cowpens was effectively utilize the militia and recognize the talents of Andrew Pickens. Ironically he paid little attention to this success in his initial report to Greene, in which he seemed far more interested in recounting the actions of his Continentals, who had already served with him for some time. The only notable mention of a militia officer in his report was a reference to the "brave and valuable Colonel Pickens."[54]

It would not be long, however, until Continental officers, especially Greene, as well as politicians, came to a fuller appreciation of how important the militia's contribution had been. On January 25, Governor Rutledge promoted Pickens to brigadier general. Congress attempted to recognize the most important American leaders in the victory. The senior Continental officers received special medals—gold for Morgan and silver medals for William Washington and John Eager Howard. Congress also took the unusual step of rewarding an officer who did not come under its authority by awarding a sword to the state militia officer, Pickens. The militia received so much publicity that Greene felt the need to remind outsiders that his own Continentals were still in dire need of reinforcements and supplies; it would be "the greatest folly in the world" to trust the fate of American liberty to the militia alone. And yet Greene, too, praised Pickens's performance and admitted that "there is a great spirit of enterprise prevailing among the Militia of these Southern States; especially with the volunteers."[55] What was more telling is that he began to consult Pickens regularly for advice and support, just as he was already cultivating a relationship with Sumter and Marion.[56]

The victory indeed owed much to Morgan's leadership, to the determination of the men under his command, and to Andrew Pickens. The leading man of the Long Cane settlement, by the force of his reputation, had organized his men in enemy-held territory, united a disparate collection of militia bands to serve under him, and helped bring about seamless

The "Brave and Valuable" Colonel Pickens

cooperation between regulars and militia.[57] Most would argue, indeed, that without the presence and eagerness of Pickens and the militia, Morgan would have never decided to fight at Cowpens. For the rest of 1781 and 1782, Pickens would readily submit to and cooperate with Continental army officers. He knew that to win liberty and secure order—even to reclaim his own home—a war would have to be won, and to win that war the Continental army and the state militia needed each other. Nathanael Greene understood that as well.

SEVEN

The North Carolina Campaign

Altho I would serve my Country in any part,
I again repeat I had rather return.

Andrew Pickens to Nathanael Greene, March 5, 1781

Andrew Pickens had proven that his militia could fight effectively against British regulars in a conventional battle when properly led. Yet the militiamen were still ideally suited for other purposes. Covering the vast hinterlands between the two armies, their very presence ensured that a given region's food, supplies, and horses were gathered into the American army rather than into the British. Their activities also hindered the recruitment and conscription of men into the Tory ranks, bringing them instead into the patriots'; and sending the militia into the countryside was the best way to gain intelligence of the enemy's whereabouts, numbers, and intentions. Because of the militia's flexibility and usefulness, Morgan and Greene often vacillated on how best to employ it. When not pressed by Cornwallis and not anxious to gather every available fighting man at one place, they dispatched small parties into contested or British-held territory and contemplated sending Pickens's entire force deep into the enemy's rear. When a battle seemed imminent, however, they needed Pickens's prestige and skill as a leader of militia to assemble various units into a cohesive force. In fact, they even relied on him to recruit and assemble militia formations among men who did not know him. Pickens had some success in this task, but it was a challenge due to the local nature of military leadership on the frontier. None of the North Carolina and Virginia men had grievances against Pickens, but he was not one of their own and could never command the same degree of loyalty among them as he could of his own neighbors. And nearly all militiamen balked at serving far away from home. Men from Mecklenburg County in the southern piedmont of North Carolina began deserting when marched toward the northern border of their own state or into Virginia, as did Virginians when serving too far south. Even a majority of the South Carolina men who had served under Pickens at Cowpens began to drift back home once the army retreated into North Carolina, as Pickens had predicted they would.

With Tarleton defeated, Morgan predicted that Cornwallis would now take his own formidable combat power directly against him. Morgan thus sought to return to Greene and needed to put the Catawba River between him and Cornwallis to hinder the British pursuit. Hoping to confuse Cornwallis, he decided on a circuitous path, marching not east but north toward Gilbert Town, North Carolina.

On the morning of January 18, Pickens's men had returned to the Cowpens battlefield after a twenty-two-mile pursuit of Tarleton. Immediately they began another hard ride of forty miles to catch up with Morgan by nightfall at Gilbert Town. The next morning, Morgan put Pickens in charge of his 500 prisoners and his wagons. Morgan then marched eighty miles due east toward Sherrald's Ford on the Catawba, via Ramsour's Mill. To prevent recapture of the prisoners, he sent Pickens on a more northerly route into the mountains, toward Island Ford, seventeen miles upstream from Sherrald's Ford. Then Pickens marched back downstream to rejoin Morgan at Sherrald's, safe on the east side of the Catawba. Pickens's much longer march, slowed by prisoners and the wagon train, took him four days, and thirty years later he still remembered it as "fatiguing."[1]

Besides escorting prisoners, the militia served other purposes as well. A dozen men under Major Samuel Hammond, operating south of Morgan, kept him and Pickens informed of Cornwallis's movements and contributed to the safe withdrawal.[2] Morgan had been considering other missions for Pickens, including sabotage of enemy resources, seizure of supplies, and diversions. He had already sent one of Pickens's captains with a handful of men to kill a number of horses that the British had gathered on the Congaree. He hoped to have others seize a shipment of cloth. Moreover, he thought, a large militia formation could be sent back into western South Carolina or even Georgia to "draw the attention of the enemy that way, and much disconceart [Cornwallis's] plan." Morgan advised Greene that Pickens was the right officer for that mission, as he "is an enterprising man and a very judicious one."[3] Such a diversion could "keep up a show of opposition, and . . . cut of[f] small parties that may be sent out for the purpose of destroying the country, as I expect that will be their aim to prevent us from geting supplies in that back country."[4]

During the last week of January 1781, however, Cornwallis's rapid pursuit apparently delayed plans to send Pickens southward. On the twenty-fifth, Morgan reported to Greene that Cornwallis had reached Ramsour's Mill, just a day's march west of Morgan's position on the Catawba, and had been moving fast. Morgan picketed the fords of the Catawba—Sherrald's, Beattie's, Cowan's, and Tuckasegee—and began filling them in to make them impassable. He was aided by several days of miserable winter rains that swelled the Catawba, making it even more of an obstacle.

Greene, however, aware of Cornwallis's strength, soon abandoned any plans to make a determined stand on the Catawba. Pickens's force was rapidly dwindling, as most of his South Carolinians had returned home. Partially offsetting this loss, several hundred local men of Mecklenburg County, North Carolina had turned out to serve under North Carolina militia general William Davidson. Still, Greene decided to withdraw the wagon trains of his main army, the prisoners, and Morgan's Continentals northeastward to the Yadkin, in the vicinity of Salisbury. The militia would act as a rearguard to delay Cornwallis's crossing of the Catawba.[5]

Before dawn on February 1, there was a break in the rain, and Cornwallis attempted a crossing of Cowan's Ford with regular infantry and some remnants of Tarleton's dragoons. The earl himself plunged his horse into the river, and the disciplined British regulars waded through the ice-cold torrent. As they struggled through chest-deep water with sixty-pound packs, a few North Carolinians poured rifle fire into them; some were swept downstream. A local man reported "the river was full of 'em, a-snortin' and a-hollerin' and a-drownin'."[6] Still, the dogged British infantrymen gained the eastern bank. The gallant General Davidson appeared on the scene and formed a new line of defense but was soon shot in the heart and fell dead from his horse. After his fall, the North Carolina militia fled from all the fords toward Salisbury. Pickens and the small band of men still with him had been at one of the other fords, and they withdrew as well, slogging through the cold rain until they overtook Morgan at Salisbury.[7]

Greene now began the famous long winter retreat of 1781 that would ultimately lead to Cornwallis's failure in North Carolina. Greene was trying to prevent Cornwallis from reaching his goal of Virginia but wished to gather far more men, Continentals and militia, before bringing him

The North Carolina Campaign

to battle—hopefully another decisive battle such as Cowpens. Besides, as Cornwallis's columns pursued Greene, they could be vulnerable to ambushes by the militia.

Rallying the militia, though, was a problem. Greene had been disappointed with the turnout of the North Carolina militia even while the respected Davidson had been alive and had challenged the patriotism of the men from Salisbury County when they were slow to join Morgan on the Catawba.[8] Even Pickens may have had no more than forty South Carolina and Georgia men still with him now that they were serving outside their home states.[9]

Moreover, with Davidson now dead, something of a leadership vacuum was developing in Greene's army. A number of North Carolina militia officers wrote Greene and asked to be placed under the command of Daniel Morgan. Though a Continental officer, the rough-hewn, charismatic Morgan was a natural leader of militiamen. Morgan, however, was going home. He had been suffering in agony from sciatica for weeks and on many days was unable to walk or ride. Since January 24 he had been begging Greene to relieve him of command, and he would leave the army by February 9.[10] The next senior man available was Brigadier General Thomas Sumter, who said that he was still unable to take the field due to his previous wounds. Besides, Greene so far had been unable to secure close cooperation and coordination with Sumter and found him difficult to work with. Greene therefore informed the Salisbury men on the ninth that Morgan was unavailable and suggested that they accept Andrew Pickens as their commander, as Pickens was a "sensible Man and a great Officer."[11] The problem with Pickens was that he, like Sumter, was a South Carolinian. However, he did have rank; on January 25, South Carolina governor-in-exile John Rutledge had promoted Pickens to brigadier general in honor of his services at Cowpens. At least colonels and brigadier generals from North Carolina and Virginia would not have to complain about serving under a South Carolina colonel. Around February 11, the field officers of the Salisbury Brigade gathered and voted to follow Pickens.[12]

Greene had already decided to rely on Pickens anyway. On February 3, he had sent written orders to Pickens directing him to recruit and operate in the "rear of the enemy," meaning west of the Catawba. He was to gather "as large a force as possible" and harass the British in their march, which would "[prevent] their parties from being sent out on forage" and allow Pickens to provide Greene with intelligence. His men were to travel light, so that if Greene suddenly needed his manpower he could "move with expedition to join this army."[13] If he operated with North Carolina militia and there was no North Carolina officer of equal rank present, he was to assume overall command. Thus, Pickens was to carry out the primary tasks of the militia, but he was to do it with men who did not know him.

Pickens poured himself into his task. Over the next two weeks, he and a handful of men completed a long recruiting tour through western North Carolina. Beginning near Salisbury on February 3, he went as far west as modern-day Wilkes County and north to current Surry County, just below the Virginia line. He spoke with several militia commanders and sent dispatches to Virginia militia officers William Preston, William Campbell, and Isaac Shelby, as well as Colonel John Sevier, who led men from the "over-mountain" region of present-day Tennessee. Colonels Richard Allen and William Lenoir, with other detachments of North Carolina militia, joined Pickens on the Mitchell River in Surry County. Colonel Francis Locke of the Salisbury Brigade put his contingent under Pickens's command, as did several other officers. Pickens then began moving this assortment of men eastward in an effort to rejoin Greene. By the time he reached Guilford Court House on February 18, he had roughly 700 men with him and was about fifty miles to the rear of Cornwallis's army near Hillsborough. Greene was nearly eighty miles away, having withdrawn all the way to Boyd's Ferry, Virginia, on the Dan River.[14]

By retreating all the way to the Dan, Greene had temporarily conceded all of North Carolina to the British, who had hoped to catch him before he crossed that river. But he had protected his ragtag army from a general engagement with Cornwallis for which it was not yet ready. Greene had not simply been running, however; he had also been looking for an opportunity to fight elements of Cornwallis's force, if he could do so on favorable terms. In Virginia he was able to gather reinforcements and supplies while Cornwallis's army was exhausted, worn out, and poorly supplied from the long pursuit in miserable weather. When Greene saw that Cornwallis was falling back on Hillsborough, he mistakenly assumed that His Lordship intended to abandon all of North Carolina. He therefore recrossed the Dan and sent several letters to Pickens ordering him to pursue Cornwallis aggressively and "harass the rear of the enemy."[15]

Pickens was already doing what Greene wished before he received those orders. Perceiving Cornwallis's move to Hillsborough as Greene did—as a withdrawal—Pickens began moving east down the upper reaches of the Haw River, camping at places like High Rock Ford, Wetzell's Mill, Stony Creek, and Hycootie Creek just north of Hillsborough. The savvy Indian fighter mingled aggressiveness with wariness, however. He moved his men by detachments along different routes, camping a few miles from each other but close enough to come to each other's support if necessary. This dispersion made gathering provisions simpler. It also kept the enemy guessing as to his whereabouts and made it seem to local Tories as if their enemies were swarming over the entire countryside.[16]

Pickens also sent reconnaissance parties out at night to return in the morning, preventing surprise and keeping him advised of enemy movements. On February 21, he sent forty North Carolina mounted militiamen under his trusted friend James McCall to probe a reported enemy position near Hart's Mill, fewer than three miles from Hillsborough. Pickens's orders were to approach carefully and first determine the size of any enemy unit they might encounter. If the unit was larger than theirs, they were to avoid contact; if smaller, they should attack them but return quickly to him, "for as soon as an alarm should be given, it might be expected that the Cavalry and light troops of the enemy would be at our heels."[17] The Whig militia encountered a British lieutenant and twenty-seven men who formed to meet their attack.[18] Advised by Major Micajah Lewis, a Continental officer accompanying the expedition as a volunteer, McCall and the North Carolinians with him struck the enemy force in front and flank and overwhelmed it. When pursued by what they thought was British cavalry, the raiding party split up and evaded the pursuers. The raiding party returned to Pickens with nineteen British and Tory prisoners, having left eight dead and wounded enemy soldiers on the field. As Pickens reported to Greene, "We had not a man hurt."[19]

Later that day, after Pickens moved a short distance up Stony Creek and halted, the rear guard reported that "Tarleton was coming." Pickens quickly deployed riflemen behind a fence line and waited to ambush his old foe from Cowpens. In a few minutes, he discovered that the approaching horsemen were wearing not the green jackets of Tarleton's Legion but rather the green jackets of Lee's legion—American Continental dragoons under the command of Lieutenant Colonel Henry "Light Horse Harry" Lee of Virginia. They were perhaps the same mounted column that McCall's column had evaded, thinking it was British. This was the first time that Pickens and Lee had met, and the partnership between the Scotch-Irish frontiersman and the tidewater aristocrat quickly became a fruitful one. Apparently no friction developed between the Virginia Continental officer and Pickens. Like all officers whom Pickens respected, Lee was "brave and active," though with something of a chivalric, romantic flair.[20]

The North Carolina campaign, for Pickens, continued to exhibit all the typical features of the Revolutionary War in the South—the local nature of military leadership and military obligations among the militia; the tentative nature of the men's enlistment as campaigns took them farther away from home; and of course the sickening brutality of what was truly a civil war. Having recruited a force of 700 men, Pickens strove constantly to keep it together. He had the most difficulty with the men from the Salisbury Brigade. "They are constantly deserting and no persuasions can prevail with them," he reported to Greene. Pickens considered the Salisbury troops "among the worst Men" he had ever commanded, with the exception of "a few particular companies."[21] But even men whom Pickens knew better—those from northern South Carolina and Georgia—grew impatient serving so far from home. The Georgia officers, Pickens reported, "seem to hang back and the Georgians are daily scattering."[22] Major James Jackson of Georgia asked to be sent home to recruit more men. Partly this was because another Whig officer, Captain James McKay, was operating in Georgia and plundering friends as well as foes. Clearly Jackson and other Georgia men feared for the safety of their own homes. Meanwhile, Major Henry Dickson's men from "south of Catawba" wanted to make an expedition into South Carolina.[23] Those Salisbury Brigade men who did stay were badly supplied; some of Colonel Francis Locke's North Carolina men had no more than one musket ball.[24] Pickens told Greene he would be "infinitely obliged" if Greene could send him ammunition.[25]

As Pickens's columns traversed central North Carolina, he, like all Revolutionary era leaders, was generally unable to prevent plunder and mistreatment of the local population. One of his companies under Captain Joseph Graham experienced this challenge when marching through the "Moravian towns" around Salem on the way to Guilford Court House. The Moravian settlers, of German descent, generally leaned toward loyalism but were inoffensive and peaceful in their conduct. The "village superintendent" in Salem helped Graham's men obtain provisions and then asked for protection against another band of men who had come to plunder. When Graham confronted the ringleader, the man retorted that the Moravians were Tories, that his men had previously been robbed by Tories, and that they therefore "had a right to make themselves whole." It was not just that a cycle of retaliation governed the conduct of the war. As Graham explained, both sides in a war resort to the services of "the meanest of mankind (even Indians)." Therefore, "without regular discipline there will be marauding, devastation, and extravagances continually committed." Besides, war brought out the worst even in decent men. Men who were serving while not being supplied by their government thought they had a right to take "from friend or foe." Others, he said, would accuse a wealthy man "of toryism (sometimes without foundation) as a pretext to justify their conduct."[26]

Graham's description of the problem fit perfectly into Pickens's Calvinist worldview: men were naturally selfish and depraved. Even so-called good men—those who were on the right side and who had some virtues—were prone to sin. Pickens described the men under Captain James McKay, for example, as "very brave" but "bent chiefly to plunder and no doubt but at times Friends as well as foes suffer."[27] As Graham said, the Revolution "was not only a time that tried men's souls, but tried their honesty also, when they found themselves freed from legal restraints."[28] The breakdown of order made it more difficult for virtue to survive, in turn threatening the security of friend and foe alike.

The North Carolina campaign also had its share of lurid stories of bloodshed. A thin line, it seemed, distinguished courage from savagery, fighting élan from murder. Pickens was partially involved in at least one of these events. On February 25, reconnaissance parties reported to Pickens and Lee that Tarleton had left Haw's Fields near Hillsborough and was advancing toward them in the Haw River area. Tarleton's column, however, was smaller than the patriots' if Pickens and Lee combined forces. The two commanders therefore set out after Tarleton, hopeful that they could surprise him with superior numbers and crush him. Later in the afternoon, they reached a point where they expected to find him but were disappointed to discover that their prey had left. However, they had also received intelligence of a large body of Tories who had just formed in the area. (Tarleton was actually advancing to form a junction with this band of 300 men who had just assembled under Colonel John Pyle.) The two American commanders continued on, as part of their mission was to prevent loyalist units from joining Cornwallis's army. Sometime after 5:00 P.M., Lee's men, at the head of the column, came upon two Tories on horseback. The two young men mistook the green uniforms of Lee's legion for the green uniforms of Tarleton's and welcomed Lee enthusiastically, assuming he was Tarleton. Lee made the most of the mistake. Behind him were Captain Graham's mounted militia and behind that the rest of Pickens's troops. The Virginian rode alongside Pyles's men as they were formed along the road, smiling and complimenting the appearance of the Tory ranks. When he reached the end of the Tory line, there was Pyle himself. Lee claimed that he greeted Pyle, offered his hand, and was about to reveal his true identity when the situation suddenly changed.[29]

Graham's militia, directly behind Lee's column, thought initially that they had found friendly troops belonging to Major Henry Dickson, whose unit had got separated from the main column during the march. Graham, however, rode up and noticed that the strangers were wearing clean clothes (a strange sight among the mud-soaked Whig troops at this point) and that they displayed red strips in their hats, a practice of loyalist militia in the area. Graham told Captain Joseph Eggleston that the men only twenty steps from them were Tories and asked why they were still armed. Eggleston then asked one man, "To whom do you belong?" The Tory innocently replied, "A friend to his Majesty."[30] Eggleston responded by striking the man over the head. The Whig militia began slashing among the Tories near them, and shots were fired. Lee heard the shots and, seeing that the game was up, wheeled his men to the right, and they began attacking Pyle's hapless Tories with their sabers. Pyle's men had their arms slung and could not defend themselves. Some continued to believe they were facing Tarleton and protested that they belonged to the king, even as they were hacked down. As the fighting became more confused, some of Lee's men paused to ask their opponents whose side they were on. Having recently arrived from Virginia, they did not yet understand the local custom of loyalist troops wearing red bands in their hats and patriots wearing green twigs in theirs. Those belonging to Pyle readily volunteered that they were loyal to the king and were then slain. Even after the battle, some continued to believe that Tarleton had mistakenly attacked them. Nearly 100 of Pyle's men were killed, and most of the other 200 were left wounded or were dragged away by their friends. The patriot forces lost one horse.[31]

The immediate emotion for Pickens and Lee was not elation but concern and frustration. In victory, their men were thoroughly disorganized. Tarleton was only a few miles away, and if he arrived at that moment in good order the patriots would be routed. The two commanders "exhibited great perturbation," Graham remembered.[32] As darkness fell on the battlefield, however, they finally reorganized their men and withdrew, leaving nearly 300 dead or suffering Tories on the field. Nor was the macabre scene finished. A party of Catawba Indians (all of whom had taken the patriot side) came on the battlefield and thrust spears into seven or eight wounded men, killing them. Another account states that some of Lee's men hacked six prisoners to death with broadswords in retaliation for Tarleton's massacre of Colonel Abraham Buford's men at the Waxhaws.[33]

Later, the affair came to be known as "Pyle's Massacre," and Lee would feel compelled to justify his conduct. At the time, though, both Lee and

Pickens saw it simply as a victory that had brought excellent military results. It was thoroughly demoralizing to local Tories; as Pickens said, "It has knocked up Toryism altogether in this part." On the other hand, Pickens was disappointed that the collision with Pyle's Tories had ruined the opportunity to surprise and overwhelm Tarleton himself.[34] The Tories, for their part, were so traumatized by the event that it led directly to another tragedy. Less than two weeks after Pyle's rout, Tarleton came upon another body of Tory militia and asked that the men identify themselves. Unwilling to make the same mistake as Pyle in case the green-jacketed men were really Lee's, the Tories hesitated. Tarleton therefore charged and scattered them. Thus, in Pyle's Massacre, mistaken identity had led to Tories being killed by patriots; in this one, it led to Tories being killed by Tarleton. These two events, along with news that Greene had recrossed the Dan, completely destroyed loyalist morale in the North Carolina piedmont. Cornwallis was on his own, robbed of any meaningful support from the population.[35]

Over the next few days Pickens and Lee played a cat-and-mouse game of advance and retreat with Cornwallis's cavalry under Tarleton. After February 26, the scene of operations shifted some twenty miles to the west. Cornwallis, now bereft of loyalist support in the Hillsborough area on the Eno, moved west across the Haw in the area where Alamance Creek and Stinking Quarter emptied into that river. Greene moved as well, occupying the Reedy Fork area some ten or fifteen miles to the north. The patriot cavalry, consisting largely of Lee's dragoons and Pickens's mounted militia (now operating separately but in close coordination), served as a screen behind which Greene could conceal his movements and continue to gather strength before taking on Cornwallis himself. Their constant movements also frustrated efforts to assemble would-be Tory units. With Cornwallis's entire army on the move rather than just Tarleton's cavalry, Pickens knew he faced not only the danger of being surprised by the crafty Tarleton but also colliding with the superior strength of the British main force. Thus, he continued to be cagey in his movements. Decades later, Captain Joseph Graham remembered them well:

> His rule was to have his men formed and moving by 10:00 o'clock
> in the morning, to halt once or twice during the day for feeding,
> to move slowly and in different directions. . . . Whatever course
> he might be going, at sunset he never failed to turn nearly at right
> angles to it, either to the right or the left, for two or three miles
> before he halted for the night. He never camped two nights in

succession within some miles of the same place, and some days did not march more than eight or ten miles in all. By these movements it was impossible for the enemy, by any preconcerted plan, to strike at him with a detachment; for before they could arrive at the place where their information directed, he would be elsewhere. Thus he ran no risk of being obliged to fight against his will unless he should meet them by accident, which was hardly probable.[36]

By the end of the month, Pickens and Lee were also cooperating with Continental army colonel Otho Williams, who had taken over command of Greene's light troops and cavalry in Daniel Morgan's absence. While the militia had performed well alongside Lee, there was friction between militia officers and their Continental counterparts once Williams came into the picture, despite the fact that the latter was a capable officer. On March 2, a combined force of elements of Pickens's militia, Lee's dragoons, and Williams's men advanced south of Alamance Creek and collided with a substantial British force at Clapp's Mill. Pickens did not accompany the movement, leaving the command to Williams. The American force was not routed, but it was repulsed.

Pickens now had to work harder than ever to hold the militia together. He had informed Greene on February 19 of the poor discipline among the Salisbury troops and the desire of the more southern-based men to fight closer to home. Greene had responded sympathetically that desertion was "the practice of all Militia." All he asked of Pickens was to "make the most of those remaining to you."[37] For more than two more weeks Pickens certainly made the most of what he had. As the Salisbury men continued to melt away, he had been joined by nearly 300 men under Virginian William Preston on February 25. The expected Virginia reinforcements under Colonel William Campbell did not arrive until March 2, and when they did they consisted of 60 men rather than the 1,000 Greene had anticipated. Pickens had also expected contingents under Isaac Shelby and John Sevier, but they never arrived at all.[38]

On March 2, the enlistments of the North Carolina men of the Salisbury Brigade expired, and their officers pointed this out to Pickens the next day. Pickens asked the officers to persuade their men to stay a few days longer as he thought that a general engagement was coming soon and that since the men had "been so well tried, [they] might be the means of giving General Greene the advantage."[39] By now there were scarcely 120 Salisbury men from the several hundred that had begun the campaign. Preston's 300 Virginians had dwindled to 179; there were 158 South Carolinians and Georgians under James McCall, still impatient to be sent home. Altogether, Pickens's returns on March 4 showed a total of 453, though that did not include 80 men from Surry County under Colonel James Williams, who joined him that day.[40] In fairness to the militiamen, their service had indeed been hard. They had lived in the cold and the rain without tents or other camp equipment for at least two months and had no regular supplies of food or forage. Each man had little more than a blanket and a pair of saddlebags with one change of clothes. As Joseph Graham recalled, the currency was so devalued that a month's pay for a private "would not purchase half a pint of whiskey." The men "without shelter [were] frequently wet, sometimes sleeping in wet clothes, marching whole nights without sleep, irregularly supplied with provisions, sometimes bordering on starvation."[41]

Continental officers did not help with the militia's morale. Otho Williams and Lee asked Pickens and Preston to assemble the militia officers and then made a proposition to them—the militiamen should give up their horses. The regular officers, based on the experience of the Clapp's Mill engagement, judged that the availability of horses made the militia less effective in a conventional battle. Horses contributed to the "celerity of their movements," but in battle, when told to withdraw or move from their initial position, every man sprang to his horse, and it was difficult to bring them back under firm control.[42] The Continental officers suggested therefore that every third man be detached to remove the horses to a place of safekeeping where they could be guarded by men who were old or in bad health. The militia would become standard infantry rather than "mounted" infantry. The militia officers responded unanimously that their men would never accept this proposal. In fact, Pickens reported to Greene, the idea "has proved a bone of contention for them."[43]

By March 5, Pickens was convinced that it was time to abandon his command in North Carolina and return home. Though part of him wanted to see the issue through with Cornwallis in North Carolina, he understood that he could be more effective closer to home. Pickens told Greene that within a few days there would be "hardly a man left belonging to the Salisbury district." Meanwhile the South Carolinians and Georgians were in a "miserable plight, not one to be met with a second shirt." Moreover, he informed Greene, these men had been in the field since the fall of Charleston. Much of that time they had been serving without pay or provisions, and Pickens said that he could no longer ask them to stay. Then he made his own wishes known: "If it was possible and agreeable to you, I could wish likewise to return, altho I would serve my Country in any part, but [as] I look on it I am capable of doing more good there than here; I am better known and perhaps another Officer might suit these parts better. I confess I want to see what becomes of Cornwallis; but should it be thought more advisable by you I again repeat I had rather return."[44]

On the same day that Pickens announced his desire to return to South Carolina, the remaining Salisbury officers under his command wrote Greene and asked for a new commander, their own Colonel Thomas Polk. Pickens was summoned to meet with Greene and South Carolina governor-in-exile John Rutledge the next day, March 6, and the decision was made that Pickens would return to the south.[45] As if to confirm the decision, yet another incident occurred that same day that thoroughly disgusted Pickens's militia. A battle occurred at Wetzell's Mill on Reedy Fork Creek; Pickens was at Greene's headquarters, and his men were temporarily serving under Colonel Otho Williams. The Americans performed respectably in the engagement, but Williams and Lee were forced to give ground. When they did so, they used the militia as a rearguard while the Continentals escaped across the creek, which resulted in the militia suffering the bulk of the casualties. Pickens arrived on the field that evening and found his troops "much displeased. . . . They thought they were not treated fairly & were improperly exposed, being ordered to cover the retreat of the regulars— . . . they told me they were determined to stay no longer."[46] The militia may have been justified in reading a lack of concern in Otho Williams's handling of the affair. After the battle, Williams reported to Greene that his loss was "very inconsiderable."[47] It turned out that while Williams had lost only two Continentals killed and three wounded, casualties among the militia amounted to twenty or twenty-five. Militia officer Joseph Graham remarked that the Continental officers were unwilling to admit that their actions at Wetzell's Mill were based on a cold-blooded logic: the loss of three of four militiamen whose enlistment would expire in a week was equal to that of one "regular."[48]

The rationale of the decision to send Pickens southward was clear. Greene was thoroughly frustrated with desertions among the militia, but he still had great confidence in Pickens. Sending Pickens and his men back into western South Carolina was an option that had been on the table ever since the days immediately following Cowpens. Pickens's return, and his cooperation with Thomas Sumter, could galvanize resistance in South Carolina, making Cornwallis's rear more insecure than ever and perhaps forcing his retreat from North Carolina. The frontier partisan had proven that he could operate independently and sustain himself logistically when operating far

　　　　　　　　　　　　　　　　The North Carolina Campaign

from home; clearly he could do at least as well in more familiar territory. As much as Pickens had proved that he could fight with a national outlook rather than simply a local one, everyone understood that the Ninety Six District of South Carolina and the upper regions of Georgia were Pickens's natural theater of operations. He would be better able to recruit and keep men in the ranks when operating on his own turf, and he might seriously undercut Cornwallis's control there. On March 8, Greene formally ordered him to "immediately return with the S Carolina and Georgia troops now under your command to the district under your immediate direction."[49] Pickens would once again be fighting for his own home.

EIGHT

Fighting His Way Back Home

When the way was opened and [Greene] determined to return
[to South Carolina], he wrote me to harass the [enemy] foraging
parties at Ninety Six and Augusta, and as much as possible
encourage the desponding inhabitants.

Andrew Pickens to Henry Lee, August 28, 1811

Near the end of March 1781, Brigadier General Thomas Sumter informed
the "Swamp Fox," Brigadier General Francis Marion, that "Gen. Pickens
has gone to take command of his brigade."[1] Sumter was acknowledging the
same fact that Nathanael Greene was when the latter had ordered Pickens to
return with his men to "the district under your immediate direction."[2] At this
point in the war, Andrew Pickens was nothing if not a local warlord to whom
belonged a particular pool of manpower and a wide swath of territory. But as
a local chieftain, Pickens knew his task was not only to wage war but also to
provide a semblance of civil order and protection. The British still controlled
all the major posts in South Carolina, but in the vast hinterlands between
them, partisan warfare and banditry often prevailed. "When I returned to
S. Carolina," he later recalled, "the scenes were awful. When partisan opposition met, quarters were seldom given." He reported to Greene at the time
that the region was "in the greatest distress" due to the "Enemy's marauding and plundering parties."[3] Moreover, rumors abounded that the British
were arming slaves and that some bands of Cherokees had returned to the
warpath. Pickens was concerned about the latter threat but decided the more
immediate one for the time being was nearby Tories and British troops.[4]

On March 15, Greene's U.S. troops and the militia with him finally met Cornwallis in open battle at Guilford Court House, North Carolina. Attempting to utilize the militia much as Morgan had at Cowpens, the American army made a respectable showing against Cornwallis's regulars but ultimately had to abandon the field. Though the battle was at best a draw on the tactical level for the Americans, in strategic terms it was a victory. Cornwallis's army was exhausted and bloodied and lacked the supplies and the strength to continue to pursue Greene or even to sustain itself in the hinterland of the North Carolina piedmont. Cornwallis did not even have sufficient wagons to evacuate his own wounded after the battle, leaving them on the field as he withdrew southeastward to the port city of Wilmington.

Greene followed Cornwallis as far as Ramsey's Plantation on the Deep River. Then he made his next fateful decision of the southern campaign, one that has further cemented his place in history as an excellent strategist. Greene decided that, rather than shadow Cornwallis and allow him to gather strength for another fight, he would return to South Carolina. If Cornwallis followed him, it would mean that the British general had been forced to abandon his northward campaign. Additionally, if Cornwallis chose to spar with Greene in South Carolina, the superior ability of Sumter, Marion, and Pickens to keep troops in the field would ensure that the patriots still had a numerical advantage in the state. If, on the other hand, Cornwallis chose not to chase Greene or fight him in South Carolina, the British would soon lose all of the posts they had captured in the South Carolina interior. Greene informed Sumter of his decision and asked him to "give orders to Genls. Pickens and Marion to collect all the militia they can to co-operate with us."[5]

By March 20, when Pickens wrote to Thomas Sumter, he was at the Catawba River on the North Carolina–South Carolina border. Pickens had traveled 125 miles in twelve days, a rather slow pace, suggesting that he may have taken time to collect his family or at least make arrangements for their return to South Carolina. Pickens knew that Georgia militia colonel Elijah Clarke, his comrade from the Florida and Kettle Creek campaigns, was operating in the Ninety Six area and may have anticipated Long Cane soon being safe for Whig families. Pickens probably met personally with Sumter a few days later. This was about the time (March 23) that Clarke inflicted a stinging defeat on the despised Major James Dunlap at Long Cane, killing thirty-four loyalists and capturing forty-two. Pickens sent orders for Clarke to join him on the Broad River.[6]

After joining forces with Clarke, Pickens learned that Cruger was marching north toward him from Ninety Six with a force of about

300 regulars and 200 Tory militia. Pickens, "determined to risque an action," collected the small number of South Carolinians and Georgians with him and advanced toward Cruger, crossing the Tyger and then reaching the Enoree. Cruger, however, withdrew. Everywhere Pickens went, he found "the Country . . . in the greatest distress chiefly broken up for want of assistance by the Enemy's marauding and plundering parties." He believed that if he had not arrived on the Tyger when he did, "the whole Country would have been evacuated by our Friends." The lack of Whig or neutral inhabitants apparently impeded Pickens's ability to provision his troops, which in turn made it difficult for him to keep a large body of men in the field. Pickens asked Sumter for help and reported to Greene that he would keep pressure on Cruger as much as he could but was hampered by lack of provisions.[7]

By the time Pickens reached the Enoree River, he learned of an atrocity committed by his own side. The Tories whom Clarke had captured in Long Cane had been sent northward under guard toward Virginia via Gilbert Town, North Carolina. When the prisoners reached Gilbert Town, Dunlap, the man Whigs accused of mistreatment of the McCall and Pickens families as well as of other crimes, had been murdered. Pickens related what he knew to Greene:

> I am exceedingly sorry to inform you of the inhuman action committed on Major Dunlap after his being delivered by Colonel Clark[e] into the hands of a Guard, prepared for that purpose at Gilbert Town in North Carolina. A set of men chiefly unknown except one Cobb an over Mountain man forced the Guard and shot him. I have issued a Proclamation offering reward of ten thousand Dollars for apprehending him and do not despair of yet getting him and sending him to you. I sent a Flag to Colonel Cruger intimating the matter to him and informed him with what horror and detestation American Officers looked on the act, intimating however; that the many barbarous massacres committed by those calling themselves their Officers on our own people after their capture, particularly the murder of Captain Watson a valuable young Officer under the sanction of their own Flag might have actuated those persons to that mode of redress.[8]

Cruger responded to Pickens on April 3, saying that Pickens's "abhorrence and detestation" of Dunlap's murder did honor to Pickens's "feelings as [a] Man and a Soldier."[9] Perhaps Cruger understood even better than

Fighting His Way Back Home

Pickens that wartime passions and human nature made such barbarity unpreventable. In any event, Cruger seems not to have lost his respect for Pickens despite his "betrayal" of the British and his parole agreement four months before.

By the first week of August, Pickens had reestablished patriot control over most of the area north of the Saluda but was not confident in his ability to maintain it or to push any farther without reinforcements. Greene wanted Pickens to isolate the posts at Augusta and Ninety Six, but Pickens could not do so without drawing forces from Sumter and weakening him.[10] Sumter eventually ordered four regiments west of the Broad to join Pickens. Sumter was perhaps unaware of Greene's instructions to Pickens to operate against Ninety Six and Augusta, for he sent orders for him instead to stay nearby, close to the confluence of the Tyger and the Broad, near Fish Dam Ford. Pickens, however, took his reinforcements to the south, where he organized more Whig militia detachments, harassed Tory detachments, and endeavored to cut off supplies and communications to Ninety Six and Augusta. From early April to early May, Pickens had detachments operating throughout the upper Georgia and the Ninety Six area. Their leaders were Colonel James McCall (who died of smallpox in mid-April), Colonel Elijah Clarke (who contacted smallpox and was out of action for some time), Colonel Robert Anderson, Colonel Micajah Williamson, Colonel James Baker, Lieutenant Colonel Samuel Hammond, and Colonel Le Roy Hammond. Later a regiment of lowcountry militia that normally reported to Marion came under the command of Colonel William Harden. By early May they had almost completely cut off supplies and communications to the British-held posts at Augusta under Colonel Thomas Brown and Ninety Six under Cruger.[11]

While Pickens and his men were operating in the Ninety Six–Augusta area, Greene had been attempting to capture the key British post at Camden. These efforts led to the battle of Hobkirk's Hill on April 25, in which British troops under Colonel Lord Francis Rawdon defeated Greene. Greene, as well as Pickens in later years, was apt to fault Sumter for not physically joining Greene before that battle. The criticism is perhaps unfair. Greene had made arrangements to receive wagons of supplies from North Carolina. He had also sent the bulk of the men available to him to Pickens, even after it was clear that Pickens was to operate in the Ninety Six–Augusta area rather than closer to Sumter. Sumter had moved quite slowly to join Greene, but it does seem that he was attempting to be a team player in this situation.[12]

At the end of April, both Greene and the British were discouraged, and militia leaders like Pickens were unsure that they could hold on to the gains they had made. Pickens had informed Greene on May 3 that in his area there was "an almost general disposition among the People to Join us, but there is a great want of Arms."[13] Greene sent Pickens a modest supply of flints, powder, and lead. He told Pickens to seize the arms that had been captured at Cowpens and stored at Gilbert Town, despite the fact that they had found their way into the hands of local men in the area. He also told him to confiscate weapons from the aged and infirm and put them into the hands of younger men who were willing and able to fight.[14]

Despite their difficulties, it is clear in hindsight that the tide was now flowing the Americans' way. Lord Rawdon was contemplating a withdrawal from the key British port at Camden to the area around Charleston; the major British posts in the upcountry—Ninety Six and Augusta—were nearly cut off and greatly outnumbered.[15] The war continued in its barbarous vein, with Pickens reporting to Greene on May 8 about a confused skirmish in which his men captured a few horses but lost three men captured, who were "most Barbarously cut to pieces." Pickens indicated that such behavior was not unusual: "This seems to be [the enemy's] determination with every one who falls into their hands."[16]

On May 10, another key event suggested that the tide had turned in South Carolina. Rawdon finally evacuated Camden, site of the devastating American defeat only nine months before. As late as mid-March, the Whig presence in South Carolina had been confined to Sumter's toehold on the Catawba in the far north, Marion's annoying presence between the Santee and the Pee Dee, and small roving bands of militia west of Ninety Six. In early May, though, Greene's main army as well as Pickens had returned. Sumter was advancing down the Broad; Pickens had driven organized Tory resistance south of the Saluda and was threatening Augusta; and Greene was threatening Camden. When Marion captured Fort Watson, astride the British supply route from Charleston to Camden, Rawdon had little choice.[17] His withdrawal further emboldened Whig recruiting efforts and discouraged the Tories, many of whom fled toward Charleston in the wake of the British army. The fall of Camden was followed by that of Orangeburg, Fort Motte, and Fort Granby to Sumter, Marion, and Lieutenant Colonel Henry Lee respectively, and within days the entire northern half of the state was under Whig control. Greene now anticipated the easy capture of the only remaining major base outside Charleston—Ninety Six—as well as Augusta. The American commander therefore sent Lee to assist Pickens in

Fighting His Way Back Home

capturing Augusta and made preparations for the bulk of his own army to besiege Ninety Six.[18]

Before Pickens even received these instructions, he wrote eagerly to Greene as soon as he heard of the fall of Camden. Pickens predicted that Cruger would withdraw from Ninety Six to join Thomas Brown's garrison in Augusta, and from there both would retreat toward Savannah. Pickens feared that Cruger would be able to accomplish this without his being able to cut him off and attack him, due to Pickens's lack of arms. "The situation of this Country," reported Pickens, was "almost unanimously in our favour, but the greatest Want of Arms to make them useful." Pickens therefore asked Greene to send regulars his way immediately. If Greene did so, Pickens felt sure that "the whole force of the enemy will soon fall into our hands."[19] Days before, Pickens had already left Robert Anderson to keep an eye on Cruger at Ninety Six while taking the bulk of his own command toward Augusta. There he took command of the various Georgia and South Carolina militia formations in that area. Upon receiving Greene's orders on May 16 to join Pickens, Lee marched quickly for Augusta. The Virginian's orders were to report his arrival to Pickens, cooperate with him in the capture of the town, and safeguard from plundering any stores that may be captured.[20]

Pickens and Lee were thus thrown again into close coordination. This time, despite each man's respect for the other, their joint operations would bring yet another test to the Continentals-militia relationship. When Pickens and Lee joined forces, they decided the first task would be to reduce Fort Dreadnought, a simple stockade on the property of wealthy Indian merchant George Galphin. The fort was twelve miles downstream from Augusta and thus vital to any British attempts to reinforce the town from their main base in Savannah. On the twenty-first, troops under Captain John Rudolph of Lee's legion, along with some of Pickens's militia belonging to Le Roy Hammond's regiment, assaulted the fort. The position was held by nearly 190 loyalists, including 61 "Armed Negroes."[21] The day was "sultry beyond measure," Lee reported, resulting in the death of one American soldier from heat stroke.[22] Otherwise, the attack was a complete success, resulting in the capture of virtually the entire garrison, as well as of clothing and a large quantity of ammunition.[23]

Lee moved upstream a few hours later to unite with Pickens, but disagreement erupted over the distribution of the captured supplies, with Lee apparently meaning to keep all of it for Lee's legion or other Continental troops. Pickens, of course, had been dealing with severe ammunition shortages almost constantly for months. At times he had received some from Greene, while at other times Greene had received supplies such as food or horses from the militia. Four days after the capture of the supplies at Galphin's, Pickens informed Greene that he still had not been able to acquire a list of what was taken and that many of his militiamen, especially the Georgians, had been in the field a long time and were "almost Naked."[24] Fortunately no open feud erupted between Lee and Pickens personally, and Greene was determined not to allow it. He intervened on the twenty-ninth, giving Pickens the authority to distribute captured stores as he thought best among the militia. Greene told Lee that he hoped he had not appropriated any of the supplies for his own legion, but if he had he must "let the things received be part of the continental proportion." Greene judged that a solid relationship between Pickens and Lee was more important to the American cause than clothes or ammunition: "I am happy to hear that you and General Pickens are upon a perfect good footing; and I beg you will cultivate it by every means in your power. He is a worthy good Man and merits great respect and attention; and no Man in this Country has half the influence that he has."[25]

British defenses at Augusta actually consisted of two forts—Fort Cornwallis and Fort Grierson. The town itself was bordered on the east side by the Savannah River and on the west by woods. In the center of the town stood Fort Cornwallis, held by the redoubtable Tory Thomas Brown. Altogether Brown had commanded some 300 men, including Indians, though some of his troops had been captured days earlier at Fort Dreadnought. North of the town was a large open area that extended 700 or 800 yards, with "a lagoon or swamp with a rivulet passing through it." To the northwest was the smaller Fort Grierson, held by 80 Georgia loyalists under Colonel James Grierson.[26] Both Pickens and Lee had several times as many men.[27]

Pickens and Lee decided to take Fort Grierson first. On May 24, Pickens's militia attacked the north and west of the fort, with many of the men carrying axes to hack it apart if necessary. Lee sent Major Pinkerton Eaton with a battalion of North Carolina Continental infantry to attack the south. Meanwhile, Lee positioned the rest of his force so as to defeat any attempt by Brown to send a relief force to Grierson from Fort Cornwallis. As Pickens's men advanced across the plain, Grierson and his garrison shut themselves in the fort. Brown moved forward as if to reinforce Grierson, but Lee prevented it. Finally Grierson attempted to evacuate and escape across the field and lagoon to the main fort inside the town. That decision was a disaster for the loyalists. Pickens's and Eaton's men destroyed Grierson's

Fighting His Way Back Home

command, killing thirty and capturing over forty men and two field pieces. Only a handful of Grierson's men escaped to the woods or with Grierson himself to Fort Cornwallis. Whig casualties were extremely light, but they included the death of the gallant Major Eaton. One story is that after he was shot in the thigh, loyalists seized his own sword and killed him with it. After the capture of the fort, a troop of Lee's dragoons took possession of the rest of the town so that Brown now held only Fort Cornwallis.[28]

The two patriot commanders now focused on the defeat and capture of Brown himself, hated by local Whigs but grudgingly respected by their officers. The "active and sagacious" Brown, as Lee described him, improved his defenses. Beginning on the banks of the Savannah north and east of the city, Lee's infantry began digging siege works (trenches) by which to approach Fort Cornwallis. Below the town Pickens's men also dug trenches and then began work on a "Maham tower." This structure drew its name from Major Hezekiah Maham, a South Carolinian and former Continental army officer. During General Marion's seizure of Fort Watson, at which Lee was present, Maham had devised a tower that allowed Whig militiamen to fire down into the British fort. At Augusta, the goal was to mount a field piece in the tower that could fire down into Fort Cornwallis. On the nights of May 28 and 29, Brown vigorously attacked Lee's siege works near the riverbank but was driven back. By that time the tower was nearly finished, and Lee and Pickens suspected, correctly, that on the third night Brown would attack in that sector. Pickens was ready for the attack, and Lee reinforced him with Maryland Continentals under Captain Samuel Handy. After fierce fighting with heavy losses on both sides, Brown was driven back to his fort once again.[29]

By June 3, Lee's trenches that began at the river had advanced to within a few feet of the walls of the fort. Pickens had been able to mount a six-pounder in the Maham tower, which had fired over the walls into the fort itself and disabled Brown's cannon. Fortunately for Brown's garrison and for the Whig prisoners with him, his men could hide in caves that were dug into the side of the fortress and suffered few casualties. Still, this latest development must have taken a toll on the Tories' morale as well as on their firepower. Pickens had also placed sharpshooters in an old house close to the fort's wall. With no artillery available to destroy the Maham tower or the sharpshooters' outpost, the wily Brown had two more tricks up his sleeve. On June 2 he sent a spy, pretending to be a deserter, to set fire to the tower. The man eventually aroused suspicions and was arrested. Then, at 3:00 A.M. on the fourth, a massive explosion obliterated the house in which

Pickens had posted sharpshooters. Brown's men had tunneled from the fort to the house and emplaced explosives. Fortunately, the sharpshooters had been withdrawn from the house previously and no one was hurt.[30]

Clearly, events were going Pickens and Lee's way, but the siege was not without suspense until the last day. The two Whig commanders had made plans for a 9:00 A.M. assault on June 4. Their overwhelming numbers, the closeness of their trenches, Brown's isolation, and Pickens's ability to provide covering fire for Lee's assaulting infantrymen from the tower indicated that Brown's only logical choice was to surrender. Since May 31, Pickens and Lee had kept up a polite and regular correspondence with Brown in which they attempted to persuade him to give up. Brown had respectfully but firmly refused each offer. On June 1, before the completion of the siege lines or the tower, Pickens had feared that the reduction of the fort would take longer than expected. Brown had more provisions than previously assumed and clearly intended to make "an obstinate defence." The fort was strong and the arms that the Whigs had captured at Galphin's, being intended for trade with the Indians, were of inferior quality. Pickens's scouts had informed him that a British relief effort was on the way from Savannah, though one of his officers said that the force was too small to break the siege. Most of all, however, as a militia commander, Pickens was sensitive to the fact that "the Season of the year [makes] it so very necessary that as many of the Militia as possible Should be at their farms." If there was no one to put a crop in the ground, starvation and ruin would result just as surely as if the British controlled the country. Therefore, Pickens had asked if Greene might be able to provide 200 regular troops to speed the end of the siege.[31]

The immediate tactical situation had improved by the morning of June 4, and Lee was eager to carry out the assault as planned. Pickens, however, wished to delay it.[32] He seems to have had several reasons. A few of them revolved around indications that within a few days, Brown would be weaker and the besiegers considerably stronger, guaranteeing success and minimizing friendly casualties. Pickens expected by that night to have two more redoubts established for his riflemen "within fifty yards of their Ditch." A number of deserters and "half starved Negroes" had recently abandoned the fort, indicating that Brown's force was losing manpower and morale.[33] The previous day, Greene had stated in a letter to Lee that the reinforcements Pickens had requested on the first should arrive in a few days. Moreover, Greene had explicitly warned against making an assault without a "force adequate to the purpose."[34] The more impatient Lee deferred to the older Pickens, who technically was the senior officer. Instead of an

Fighting His Way Back Home

assault on the morning of the fourth, the American commanders instead gave Brown another chance to surrender, which the latter refused.[35]

The next day, however, Brown sent a flag of truce. Brown suggested giving up the fort under terms identical to those offered the American forces at the surrender of Charleston the previous year. A series of notes ensued in which Pickens and Lee granted some but not all of Brown's requests. The American commanders claimed that had Brown surrendered earlier they would have acceded to all of them and that now they were justified in demanding unconditional surrender. In the interest of humanity, however, they did grant several of the terms desired by Brown. Notably, Pickens and Lee conceded that, as the besieged garrison had conducted a "judicious and gallant defence," the men were entitled to march out with their arms shouldered and drums beating and deposit their arms. Officers and citizens would be allowed to keep, but not wear, their sidearms, and humane arrangements were made for the sick and wounded.[36] Brown's losses at Augusta comprised 52 killed and 334 prisoners, which included the wounded, against 23 killed and 35 wounded among the Continental and Whig militia forces.[37]

The recapture of Augusta by the combined patriot forces was a significant victory for the American cause, but it revealed the continued tension in the regular-militia relationship. Lee repeatedly showed contempt for the militia in his private letters to Greene, though he continued to get along well enough with Pickens himself.[38] On May 24, as Pickens's men and Lee's dragoons (not infantry) prepared to storm Fort Grierson, Lee sniffed that "none but the Legion Infantry . . . are in any sort calculated for operations of this sort." Though he conceded that the "distresses and exertions (at least some of them)" of the militia entitled them to a share of the stores captured at Galphin's, he minimized the role of the militia in that post's capture.[39] More than once he explained to Greene that the small number of Continentals in the besieging force and the unreliability of the militia promised to delay the capture of Fort Cornwallis. On June 4 he claimed to hope for victory the following day but stated that one could not predict "the conduct of the Militia, which may disappoint again."[40] Given the string of successes to which the militia had contributed recently and the Continental army's dismal record so far in siege operations in the South, Lee's disparaging comments were unjust.

Lee was on solid ground, however, when he pointed to the brutality of the militia and the local Whig population toward their foes. Chivalrous, polite letters between commanders and civilized surrender ceremonies could not hide the fact that the real war was one in which murder and mayhem were the norm. Lee warned Greene that unless he imposed martial law in Georgia, he would "loose [*sic*] all the benefit from it. . . . They [ex]ceed the Goths & Vandals in their schemes of plunder murder & inequ[ity]. All this under pretence of supporting the virtuous cause of America."[41] Now that the Whigs were regaining control over the Carolina-Georgia backcountry, vengeance was the order of the day, and Whig officers were nearly powerless to restrain it. Greene complained to Pickens in a letter of June 5 about men from Colonel LeRoy Hammond's regiment. Some of Hammond's men were marauding through the Saluda River area, a previous stronghold of loyalism, murdering and plundering "the defenceless people just [as] private peak [pique] prejudice or personal resentments shall dictate." The behavior was not only inhumane but also prevented peace and unity in the future. Greene urged the use of capital punishment against such mayhem.[42]

Pickens, of course, had little hope of immediately curbing the behavior of men nominally under his control but currently more than fifty miles away. And probably before he even received Greene's letter, he had another atrocity to address right where he was in Augusta. On June 6, the captured Tory officer Colonel James Grierson, formerly commander of Fort Grierson, was murdered. He was confined in a guardhouse when a man rode up on horseback, asked where Grierson was, and, without dismounting, shot him through the doorway. The killer was pursued but escaped. Another Tory officer, Major Williams, was wounded in the shoulder the same day.[43]

Pickens dutifully reported the incident to Greene as "a very disagreeable and Melancholly affair" and did what he could to redress it. He ordered that Grierson be buried with military honors and expressed the hope that the killer would be caught. Originally, Pickens had thought that the thoroughly hated Thomas Brown was in greater danger of assassination and had taken more precautions in his case, not realizing that Grierson, too, was a target of vengeance. When a guard "insulted" Brown, Pickens had the offender confined. But he was "fully perswaded" that neither Brown nor the other Tories with him would be safe if marched toward the British lines near Savannah as the surrender terms specified.[44] Georgia Whigs would have their revenge.

Rather than have the prisoners exchanged for captured Whigs at Savannah, therefore, Pickens placed most of them under a heavy guard and sent them over the Savannah River to Greene's protection near Ninety Six, after which they could be exchanged in Charleston. Meanwhile, Brown and the British regulars (not Tory militia) with him obtained permission

Fighting His Way Back Home

from Greene to have their captors take them directly to Savannah after all. Pickens complied. One Whig captain, Tarleton Brown, was determined to kill Thomas Brown but "had no chance to do so" while he was in custody in Augusta. Tarleton Brown related years later that when he learned of the plan to send the Tory colonel south along the Savannah, he and a small group of men tried to ambush and assassinate him, but their prey escaped "through the shades of the night, in a small canoe." Tarleton Brown had his reasons. The Georgia captain considered Thomas Brown to be a horrible villain, guilty of the same crimes as the roving Tory gangs that had murdered his little brother and then his father.[45] Meanwhile, Grierson's assassin was never arrested, despite Greene posting a reward of one hundred guineas for his capture. One account states that the culprit was Captain Samuel Alexander, whose father Grierson had deliberately placed in an exposed position on a bastion at Fort Cornwallis and apparently mistreated in other ways as well. The old man had survived, but the son demanded vengeance. Upper Georgia and South Carolina were full of Whigs who felt no guilt in murdering Tories; Pickens and Green found that no one would betray a fellow Tory-hater, even for one hundred guineas.[46]

When Pickens had warned Greene on May 11 that Colonel Cruger would probably evacuate Ninety Six soon, he had read British intentions correctly. Both Lord Rawdon and Colonel Nisbet Balfour at Charleston had sent messages to Cruger ordering or urging him to withdraw toward Augusta. However, Pickens's men had so thoroughly cut off British communications to Ninety Six that Cruger never got them. Greene therefore commenced a siege of the key remaining British post in the South Carolina upcountry about the time that Pickens and Lee besieged Augusta. Thus, in the previous weeks Pickens had succeeded too well in isolating Cruger, resulting in a bloody siege of Ninety Six rather than a chance to crush Cruger as he attempted to flee toward Augusta.[47]

After the reconquest of Augusta, Lee rejoined Greene to aid in the siege of Ninety Six. Greene asked Pickens to handle the prisoners and to stay in Georgia a few days to "regulate matters in some way" and to restrain the "confusion and [dis]order which prevails in Georgia by private murders and plundering parties."[48] Greene, Pickens, and other American as well as British officers were deeply disturbed by the private murders occurring in Georgia and both Carolinas. Men of both sides were ambushed and horribly murdered, stripped, and left unburied along roadsides. Men, women, and children were murdered in their beds at night, sometimes as their neighbors fired into their cabins through gaps in the logs. No life or property was safe.[49]

The meanness of the war was not simply an abstraction that Pickens had a duty as an officer to restrain but also a matter of personal heartbreak. As Pickens was tidying up details from the siege of Augusta, his brother Joseph, at Ninety Six, was singled out and killed by the enemy. In the early days of the siege, a Tory neighbor named McGuire recognized Joseph standing near the edge of some woods a few hundred yards away from the fort and exclaimed, "Yonder is Captain Pickens, and by —— I'll kill him!"[50] McGuire picked up a large rifle that was known throughout the neighborhood for its long range, put it to his shoulder, and fired. Initially it was assumed that Joseph would survive the wound, but he died a few days later, on June 17, from internal bleeding. The real cause of his death, though, was pure personal vindictiveness—like so many deaths in this war, it crossed the boundary from legitimate warfare to murder. Joseph had been not only a brother and a comrade but also a friend. Often when Pickens had been away on campaigns, it was Joseph who had stayed with Becky and the children as an adult male protector. Joseph left behind his widow, Eleanor, and eight children.[51]

Pickens joined Greene near Ninety Six by June 17, the day Joseph died, and probably got to see him one last time. But the pace of events did not allow much time for grieving. Greene had been patiently besieging Cruger's strong, star-shaped fort and extending his trench lines for weeks, but now reports that a British relief force was on the way gave Greene a new sense of urgency. Lord Rawdon had received reinforcements of British regulars in Charleston and set out on June 7 with 1,700 men to relieve Cruger's garrison at Ninety Six.[52] Greene had heard word of this from Sumter on June 9 and immediately ordered Sumter, with Marion's help, to do all in his power to delay Rawdon's approach in order to give the American army time to capture Ninety Six.[53] Inexcusably, Sumter failed to place himself between Rawdon and Ninety Six. Pickens, once he arrived on the seventeenth, was tasked with gathering more militia that he might aid Sumter and Marion. Before he could do so, the near approach of Rawdon forced Greene to storm the works at Ninety Six on the eighteenth, and his Continental army soldiers from North Carolina, Virginia, and Maryland bravely assaulted the "Star Fort." Just as courageous was the fierce resistance of loyalist provincials under the capable leadership of Cruger. The American troops could not take the fort. Greene called off the assault after suffering losses of 185 killed or wounded; the loyalists' losses were 85.[54]

Fighting His Way Back Home

Profoundly disappointed, Greene confided to friends his anger at Governor Thomas Jefferson, who had reneged on a promise of troops from Virginia, and at Thomas Sumter for failing to delay Rawdon's approach by even a few days. One of those to whom he confided was Pickens. Pickens recalled the conversation in a letter to Henry Lee thirty years later and generally agreed with Greene's criticism:

> What I thought more inexcusable in [Sumter] and Marion, was their not harassing Lord Rawdon on his march from Charleston to raise the siege of Ninety Six, they had a number of men in the lowcountry, and knew every defile on the way, and I believe not the least attempt was made by them—the night the siege was raised at Ninety six, I asked Genrl Green, if he knew the cause of their not harassing the enemy, or their not, joining the army, he was much irritated, and expressed himself, in a manner, I had not heard him before or after.

Pickens had more to say about Sumter. Pickens excused Sumter himself for not joining Morgan before the battle of Cowpens due to his recent wound but thought he should have at least sent his troops there. Overall, Pickens had much the same opinion of Sumter as Greene did: "he was self important, and not communicative, I had little connection with him during the war."[55]

Greene knew that the failure of his siege and Rawdon's imminent arrival meant that he would have to withdraw, at least temporarily. The decision had immediate importance for the Whig inhabitants of the area. Many of them had reoccupied their homes since the return of Greene and Pickens to the state. It is unclear at what point Pickens's own wife and children had returned, but probably they would have felt safe to do so at the time that Pickens himself crossed to the south side of the Saluda in April; small bands of Whig militia had asserted their presence in Long Cane even before that. On June 19, though, families were convinced it was time to flee once again. A column of wagons was already loaded and traveling northward in the wake of Greene's army when Pickens received a letter from Greene. The army commander clearly intended for Pickens to make its contents known. Greene explained that he would not be able to meet Rawdon in the field for "a day or two." He wanted Pickens to "give the Inhabitants the strongest assurances that it is my intention to maintain our footing in this State." Greene knew, of course, that the flight of the Whig population would make it far more difficult for the patriot army to feed itself in that area.

He therefore claimed he was convinced that if the people remained in arms the British would not be able to hold Ninety Six. His own cavalry, he promised, "will be continually hovering round the enemy during their stay in this Neighbourhood and prevent their plundering the Country."[56]

Greene was asking the people to stay, to trust him even as he withdrew from the immediate area. Every family had to make a decision, and clearly Greene was counting on Pickens's influence. Pickens played the role that Greene expected, though he knew that even he himself would be temporarily withdrawing. As usual with Pickens, he made no grandiose speech and published no bold proclamation. What was different this time was that instead of simply leading by his own example, he also had to persuade Becky to do the same. When a column of refugee wagons came into the American camp, Pickens found Becky and the children. Quietly he asked her to turn around and go back home. He could not ask other men to leave their families unprotected unless he was willing to do the same. Now it was Becky's turn to make a courageous statement by a single public act. With her brother-in-law Joseph dead and many of the local men riding in Pickens's ranks, she was unprotected, save for the proven loyalty of their slave Old Dick. With the quiet grace and courage she had become known for, Becky agreed and herded the children and slaves back to the homestead. Noting the example set by the Pickenses, other families followed suit. Contemporaries asserted that the course pursued by General and Mrs. Pickens prevented mass desertions from the militia ranks and the dispersal of the Whig population in the area.[57]

The decision by Andrew and Becky that the Pickenses would stay, and the decision of many others to do the same, was strong proof that Greene's failure to capture the fort at Ninety Six was only a temporary setback. By sending his family home, Pickens made it clear that not only Greene but also Pickens himself felt that their return was imminent and that for now the Tories would not be strong or confident enough to exact vengeance on the Whigs who remained. The "Inhabitants," as Whig officers called their civilian supporters, could tend their crops and animals, which in turn would ensure provisions for patriot forces. Soon, perhaps, with a bit more determination and martial sacrifice, they would even be able to move about with relative safety to visit friends, attend church, and tend to business. Good crops would therefore contribute to security, which in turn would lead to even more prosperity, liberty, and honorable and peaceful pursuits. That, after all, was what the war was all about.

NINE

Ninety Six and Eutaw

You know whether I did my duty.

Andrew Pickens to Henry Lee, August 28, 1811

The failure of the siege of Ninety Six meant that much more fighting lay ahead before that longed-for day of peace and prosperity could arrive. As Greene and Pickens withdrew northward, the army commander had them split up. Greene left his army's baggage train in Pickens's custody and withdrew north of the Saluda and then east of the Broad to recruit. Pickens, slowed by the wagons, withdrew into the hilly terrain west of the Saluda, perhaps into North Carolina, also intending to recruit more men and hopefully gather supplies. For about a week and a half, the two American commanders lost track of each other. On June 23, 1781, just four days after their parting, Greene wrote Pickens that he wished him to gather his force and join him at Fish Dam Ford on the Broad River, several days' march east of where Pickens was. The army commander sent the same order to Sumter, as he learned that Lord Rawdon had crossed the Saluda and believed the British commander was pursuing him. It took several days for the message to Pickens to make its way through the hinterland of northwestern South Carolina and reach him. Nevertheless, Greene was angry that he did not get an immediate reply from him. On the twenty-fourth, he complained to Henry Lee that Sumter was determined to operate instead against Moncks Corner in the lowcountry and that "Pickens I can get no account of."[1] It seems likely that Greene had written Pickens earlier at some point between the nineteenth and twenty-third, yet he was unwilling to make allowance for the amount of time it might take to communicate with him in his remote location. Moreover, on the very day that Greene complained that he despaired of being able to consolidate with Pickens and Sumter, he actually left Fish Dam Ford, where he had told the militia generals to join him, and marched east for the Catawba, apparently without informing them. On June 28, Greene, still out of contact with Pickens, wrote to him that "I have been impatiently waiting to hear from you and the Waggons in your quarter. Not a line have I receivd since we parted at Ninty Six. The enemy made push after us, and we retird at our ease."[2]

When Pickens wrote to Greene on the thirtieth, he had not received this scolding of the twenty-eighth but had finally received Greene's earlier letter of the twenty-third. His reply indicated that he had been faithfully doing what Greene had asked him to do. Pickens informed the army commander that he was "so far on my mark to join you with Between four and five hundred Men" belonging to the regiments of Samuel Hammond and Robert Anderson. He was forced to leave the wagons behind but would bring all the horses. Pickens asked Greene where he wished him to join him. Pickens was then at Grindal Shoals on the Pacolet River, about ten miles west and upstream of the point where the Pacolet emptied into the Broad.[3]

By the time Greene received this note and dictated a reply the next day, momentum seemed to be flowing once again in the patriots' favor. Rawdon had abandoned Ninety Six, leaving a reduced force under Cruger. As Rawdon withdrew down the Saluda and Congaree, Greene followed him while also trying to get Sumter to harass him and hastening Pickens's return to the army. As Greene pursued Rawdon in the steamy July climate of the South Carolina midlands, Pickens pursued Greene. Pickens finally reached the main army at Friday's Ferry (modern-day Columbia) on the morning of July 6, having just completed an eighty-mile march from Turkey Creek in just over two days. Greene himself was not with the army at that time. By the time Pickens arrived, Greene no longer wanted Pickens to be physically with him but rather operating in the area around Ninety Six to discover the enemy's movements there. Pickens had to report that the long march in oppressive weather with little forage along the way had left most of his horses so exhausted that "they are intirely unfit to perform the service of discovering the enemys movements or even to get out of their way should they prove too powerful for us." Pickens intended to rest the horses and feed them on grain "for a day or two." Even so, Pickens did send a small detachment toward Ninety Six to gather intelligence and in fact had already anticipated Greene's orders by sending out others. Pickens informed Greene that he had also left nearly 100 men selected from Robert Anderson's regiment in the Ninety Six area when they had departed in mid-June "for the purpose of covering that country and harassing our foes." By anticipating Greene's orders over a period of two and a half weeks, Pickens demonstrated that he understood the real value of militia better than Greene did. Moreover, Pickens had already made several attempts to contact Georgia's Lieutenant Colonel Elijah Clarke to ask him to cooperate with Pickens's "picked men" on the Carolina side of the Savannah River. A day and a half after sending this letter, Pickens, true to his word, saddled up his recovering horses and crossed the Saluda en route to Ninety Six.[4]

RESTORING ORDER IN NINETY SIX

It became clear to Pickens that his most important mission would soon be to restore Whig control and some semblance of lawful order in the Ninety Six area, and Greene belatedly concurred. Pickens received word of Cruger's abandonment of Ninety Six on July 10, the same day that it occurred.[5] This was a momentous event—Ninety Six had anchored the British presence in the South Carolina backcountry for more than a year and was its last remaining base there. Greene initially focused on the hope that Pickens could pursue and damage Cruger as he withdrew toward the southwest. Pickens made some effort along that line. He was able to capture three British soldiers, "some Tories," and a number of fleeing Tory women, children, and old men whom he sent back into British lines. Pickens was far more concerned, however, with tamping down chaos in his home district. He had received intelligence from his scouts that Cruger had promised to burn everything between Ninety Six and Orangeburg as he withdrew and that parties of Tories had been burning houses and attacking the Whig population. Undoubtedly most distressing to Pickens was the report "from the uper settlements of Long Cain . . . very strong parties of Indians and Tories was Murdering the Frontier Inhabiters, which gave the people much uneasiness, on account of their Families." No doubt Pickens fretted over the fate of Becky and the children. In light of those reports, he explained to Greene, "haveing but a Dull prospect of doing Cruger much Dammage . . . I marched to the Relief of them settlements."[6]

Upon his homecoming, Pickens was glad to find that reports of damage in the area had been exaggerated and that no women or children had been murdered. Still, the area was far from secure, and there was much to do. The Whig population was alarmed by the fact that a number of Tories had "gone into the Indian Contry," presaging Indian-Tory raids in the near future. One of these gangs of Tories was led by the brutal William "Bloody Bill" Cunningham, who indeed conducted raids on Whig settlements along the Saluda and the Enoree. A Whig force under Major Fields Purdue repulsed Cunningham, killing five of his men and recapturing some stolen slaves and horses. Pickens ordered Anderson to organize 100 men in the northwestern part of his territory to guard against other incursions and posted another 100 men under Samuel Hammond in the east to guard against loyalists or Tories under Cruger sallying out from Orangeburg. The rest of Pickens's brigade stood ready to reinforce either Anderson or Hammond or to march anywhere else that Greene ordered. Pickens also gathered government wagons that had been expropriated by Tory residents, ordered the manufacture of swords and horseshoes, rested the horses, and attempted to suppress looting. By July 25, so many Tories were "giving up" that Pickens considered the last task to be the most pressing one:

> That spirit of plunder, so general among our own people, seems to be the greatest Difficulty we labour under at present. I almost Dispair of totally suppressing it notwithstanding my best Endeavours. . . . People who have removed their Families to the remote parts of N. Carolina and Virginia, at least many of them seem to make a Trade of carrying off every thing valuable out of the Contry, either the property of friend or enemy, the loss of our Horses distress us in a particular manner.[7]

For Pickens, once again the defeat of political and military enemies did not mean that all was well. Instead it led to another struggle against the sinful tendencies of "our own people."

Policies of militia officers, including Pickens, actually contributed to the "spirit of plunder." In April, Thomas Sumter issued orders for the recruitment of state troops by promising them payment in slaves confiscated from Tory estates. Francis Marion refused to follow this policy, but for a time it had tacit, reluctant approval from Greene and Governor John Rutledge. Greene urged that certificates be given when loyalists' property was seized, so that they could be reimbursed after the war, but Greene also felt that he had little legal authority in state domestic matters. With the legislature disbanded and Rutledge still absent, Sumter was perhaps the closest thing there was to legal authority in the state, and the practice of paying troops with confiscated slaves became known as "Sumter's Law." Pickens himself participated in the practice, albeit on a smaller scale. In August, Rutledge returned to the state and issued a proclamation that effectively repealed Sumter's Law. In the meantime, however, it had given semi-official sanction and encouragement to plundering, which was already out of control.[8]

Greene may not have fully appreciated the need for restoring order in the Ninety Six area, as he remained eager for Pickens to move eastward and join in the pursuit of Cruger and Rawdon. At the same time, the army commander's humane instincts led him to suggest another task for Pickens. Hearing that "many of the Inhabitants are reduced to beggary and want from the late ravages of the enemy," Greene wanted Pickens to be not only warlord but also social worker. Greene urged Pickens to appoint individuals who would appropriate goods from citizens who had plenty and distribute them to those who were suffering, keeping "an account of the things/when from whom and to whom given. These matters may be finally adjusted by government hereafter."[9] Thus, in the absence of civil government, Pickens was to engage in forced property redistribution. There is no evidence that Pickens followed through on Greene's recommendation. He probably felt he was doing all he could to prevent suffering by suppressing looting and returning stolen property.

As if Pickens did not have enough to do, Greene subsequently asked him to begin recruiting men for the Continental army. Frustrated with the difficulty of keeping militia units embodied and in the field for an extended period, Greene hoped that Pickens could recruit 400 to 500 men to serve in Lieutenant Colonel William Henderson's regiment of South Carolina Continentals for a full year. If that were impossible, he wanted Pickens to mobilize one-third of his brigade with a service obligation of four months. Pickens probably made this unrealistic request his last priority. With several hundred men in the field, manpower in his district was largely mobilized already, and it is safe to guess that almost none of these men were more interested in joining the Continental ranks than in protecting their homes near Ninety Six and Long Cane.[10]

While Pickens struggled throughout July to restore order on the southern and western side of the Saluda, Thomas Sumter operated against small British posts along the Santee and south to Moncks Corner. Several contemporaries bitterly criticized Sumter's bungling in what became known as the "Dog Days Expedition." By July 16, however, with the help of Marion and Lee, the "Gamecock" had scored several modest successes and forced the British out of Moncks Corner, just twenty-five miles above Charleston.[11]

Greene was still determined to bring the British to bear in a large, decisive battle that would cover his "Southern Army" in glory. Throughout the Carolinas campaign, there had been plenty of local successes as well as tactical defeats and draws that nevertheless became strategic victories in the long run as the British were forced to withdraw. But there had been no Saratoga, no Yorktown (still in the future) in which Greene himself led his entire army as it delivered a crushing, irreversible blow. His last opportunity for such a climactic battle would come in early September.

Sometime by August 13, Pickens had received orders to move downstate and join Greene's army.[12] With him were about 280 men, indicating that a significant portion of the men in his brigade had stayed home in preparation of the harvest and to resettle their families in Ninety Six District. At the Congarees he united with a 200-man contingent of South Carolina State Troops under Colonel Henderson. Henderson had just taken command of these troops from Thomas Sumter. The "Gamecock," physically unwell and stung by conflicts with Greene and Governor Rutledge and criticisms of other officers, had gone home in mid-August.[13] Greene placed Pickens temporarily in command of the state troops until they joined Greene's army, after which the two South Carolina contingents again separated.[14]

By September 7, Greene had assembled the forces of Marion, Pickens, and Henderson and about 1,000 Continental infantry and other small contingents—just over 2,000 men in all—at Burdell's Plantation just south of the Santee and a day's march east of Orangeburg. He had finally closed within seven miles of the main British force at Eutaw Springs under Lieutenant Colonel Alexander Stewart, with the latter unaware of his presence. Greene put his army on the move at 4:00 A.M. on the eighth and advanced directly toward Eutaw as quickly as possible. Henry Lee's legion and Henderson's state troops were at the head of the column, followed by the militia contingents of the Carolinas and then the Continental infantry and cavalry. Though two American deserters had come into Stewart's camp on the night of the sixth and warned him of Greene's proximity, the British commander had dismissed the men's report and placed them under guard. He may have had second thoughts, however, for later that morning he sent an advance party westward in the direction of Greene's army. Lee's and Henderson's men sparred with this British advance party of skirmishers and drove them back into the main line. The American army also encountered a British "rooting party" of forty or fifty men and captured them. The mission of the rooting party was to dig up sweet potatoes, which Stewart needed for his hungry force.

Now fully aware of Greene's presence, Stewart put his little army into line of battle. Stewart had roughly 2,300 men at Eutaw Springs. He had only recently become the senior British field commander, having replaced Lord Rawdon. (The health of His Lordship, at age twenty-seven, had been wrecked by the brutal South Carolina summer, and he had obtained leave to return to England.) The British line was deployed entirely in wooded terrain. Its right flank was anchored by the steep banks of Eutaw Creek and held by the Third Foot (The Buffs) and other regulars belonging to the Sixty-Third and Sixty-Fourth Regiments, led by the gallant Major John Majoribanks. In the center were Cruger's veteran loyalist troops of New Jersey and New York, lately the occupants of Ninety Six, as well as Stewart's two artillery pieces placed in the main road that would bisect the lines of both armies. Behind this tree-covered line was a large field, at the rear of which was a two-story brick house with smaller outbuildings.

After the initial skirmish four miles from the British position, Greene formed his army into line. The militia made up the front line. On the right were Marion's 360 men. The center was manned by the 180 North Carolina militiamen and the left by Pickens's force of 280 troops. The weakest part of this line was that held by the North Carolina contingent, a recently formed unit led by a French officer, Colonel Francis Malmedy, whom the Tar Heels had not known long enough to trust. As usual, the militia, having ridden to the battlefield, were dismounted and ready to fight on foot. The extreme left flank of this line was held by Henderson's state troops and the far right by Lee's legion. Behind the militia was a line of Continental troops. From right to left they consisted of troops from North Carolina, Virginia, and Maryland. Lieutenant Colonel William Washington's Continental dragoons were in the rear in reserve, along with a regiment of South Carolina cavalry under Lieutenant Colonel Wade Hampton.

Greene's decision to put the militia in the front rank had now become standard American practice whenever patriot militia and Continentals fought together. At Cowpens and Guilford Court House, part of the thinking had been that the militia could deliver a few volleys into advancing enemy troops before withdrawing, causing casualties and disorder that would help the Continentals defeat and rout them. This time, however, the militiamen were leading in the advance, not the defense, and would have to maintain order and discipline as they advanced into British volleys. This was a much more difficult task, and it is unclear how successful Greene

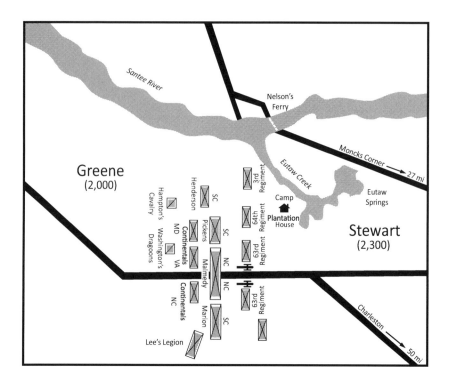

Battle of Eutaw *(Map by Chris Cartledge)*

thought that his veteran militia officers, Marion and Pickens, would be in accomplishing it.

If Greene thought that Pickens's, Marion's, and Malmedy's men would simply fire a few volleys and then retire, they far exceeded his expectations. First they advanced on foot, in line formation, for roughly four miles through lightly wooded terrain. To keep the ranks aligned, they advanced slowly. Pickens was on horseback. As the Carolinians approached the British line, Pickens's troops were probably facing elements of the Third Foot and their old foes among Cruger's loyalists, as well artillery fire from the center of the British line. In the style of frontier fighting, they paused occasionally to load and fire, then resumed the advance.

Despite withering musket, rifle, and cannon fire, the militia and state troops continued doggedly forward, with men shouting orders and encouragement to each other. This front half of Greene's army was facing nearly all of the British force and thus charging into odds of two to one. Regular officers observing the attack were astounded by the militia's steadiness. Colonel Otho Williams of the Maryland Line, just behind Pickens's troops,

Ninety Six and Eutaw

claimed that the veteran Continentals were astonished to observe Pickens's militia, "steadily and without faltering, advanc[ing] with shouts and exhortations into the hottest of the enemy's fire, unaffected by the continual fall of their comrades."[15]

Eventually, though, the volume of British fire slowed the militia's advance. Seeing disorder beginning to develop in the ranks, elements of Cruger's corps and the Sixty-Fourth Regiment counterattacked. The brunt of the counterattack fell on the less cohesive North Carolina militia in the center, who held briefly but then began to fall back in disorder. This exposed Pickens's and Marion's interior flanks, forcing them to pull back as well, though the retreat was a fighting one—measured and orderly, not a disorganized flight. Soon almost all of the militiamen were out of ammunition, having been issued seventeen rounds per man. As they withdrew from the field, Greene ordered the Continentals forward. At this point in the battle, Pickens was struck by a bullet in the chest. The impact knocked him from his horse and into the arms of an officer from the Maryland Line. He was presumed dead and his body dragged away. Fortunately, the bullet had struck the buckle of Pickens's sword belt. It had driven part of the buckle deep into his breast bone, leaving a permanent indentation that would cause Pickens pain for the rest of his life.[16]

As the Continentals swept forward, a fierce hand-to-hand struggle ensued. The British were driven back in disorder through the field and their own camp. On the British right, Major Majoribanks, who would soon give his life in his king's service, manned a stout defense centered on the brick house, allowing Stewart to rally the rest of his disorganized force. As the Continentals advanced through the British camp, the temptation to loot the tents of the enemy proved too much, particularly when rum was found. This breakdown of discipline, along with Majoribanks's skillful defense, cost Greene a dramatic victory. The British counterattacked once again, and the Continentals fell back. Greene was forced to reorganize his forces and pull back to Burdell's Plantation, leaving Stewart in control of the battlefield.

Once again, Greene had fought what was at best a tactical draw that would become a strategic victory—Stewart knew his battered force could not maintain its position long and withdrew toward Charleston two days later. Casualties on both sides were high—about one-fourth of the American army and one-fifth of the British. At times the Americans, both militiamen and Continentals, had fought brilliantly. Ironically, the most serious and costly lapse in discipline had occurred among the Continentals.

Eutaw went down in South Carolina lore as one of the great battles for American independence, ranking close to Cowpens and the 1776 defense of Charleston in its contribution to state pride. It further solidified the martial reputations of Marion, Lee, and Pickens, as well as William Henderson, who was badly wounded. It also helped build the reputations and fortunes of men with whom Pickens would connect later in life. When Henderson fell, his South Carolina State Troops were rallied by Lieutenant Colonel Wade Hampton, who received statewide praise for his leadership. Hampton, a frontier merchant like Pickens, would later build on his martial reputation with a series of advantageous marriages and successful investments in land, sugar, and cotton and become one of the wealthiest men in the South. Although Pickens could have barely known Hampton during the war, the two would serve together in the state's General Assembly afterward.[17] Another postwar connection involved Major Reading Blount, commander of the Second North Carolina Regiment of the North Carolina Continental Brigade at Eutaw. Blount's older brother was William Blount, who would become the first provisional governor of the Tennessee territory and a bitter foe of Pickens in the postwar years.

Greene gave tremendous praise to all his troops after the battle, including the militia. In his report to the Continental Congress, Greene reported that "General Marion, Colo. Malmady [sic], and General Pickens conducted the Troops with great gallantry and good conduct, and the Militia fought with a degree of spirit and firmness that reflects the highest honor upon this class of Soldiers."[18]

Pickens himself never said much publicly about the battle to anyone. His silence was typical for him but still surprising in light of what he had experienced. Eutaw had rivaled Cowpens and Kettle Creek for its fierceness and casualty ratio, and Pickens had been in the thick of the fight. Moreover, he experienced his only serious wound of the war there and perhaps his closest brush with death. He related nothing of what it was like to feel the sudden, stunning blow to his chest and find himself unhorsed, perhaps semiconscious, and in extreme pain. Did he assume at one point that the bullet had killed him? What was it like to know that he had been presumed dead? Pickens's contemporaries would have eagerly consumed a full account of his personal experiences at Eutaw. In his 1811 letter to Henry Lee, Pickens supplied them with only half a sentence: "[At] the battle of the Eutaw . . . you know whether I did my duty."[19]

TEN

A State of Alarm and Confusion

I am determined to make one more attempt to save the frontiers.

Andrew Pickens to Elijah Clarke, January 25, 1782

Fewer than six weeks after Eutaw, the United States Army and its French allies won an astounding victory over Lord Cornwallis at Yorktown, Virginia. On October 19, 1781, Cornwallis surrendered his entire 8,000-man army, the British leaving respectable garrisons only in the port cities of New York, Charleston, Savannah, and Wilmington, North Carolina. Within weeks the British would evacuate from Wilmington as well. History traditionally has treated the British surrender at Yorktown as the end of the military phase of the American Revolution and focused on diplomatic and civil affairs of the new American nation thereafter. Indeed, for many Americans the fighting was over. Yet this simple chronological divide drawn at the battle of Yorktown is an artificial one for South Carolina and Georgia. After Eutaw and Yorktown, Andrew Pickens and other Americans in the backcountry were still preoccupied with military affairs. For Pickens, there was still plenty of fighting, killing, and personal tragedy ahead.

Moreover, several difficult problems remained to be solved that were both military and political. One was what to do with the Tories who remained in the state after its reconquest by patriot forces. Pickens had confronted this problem head-on ever since he began attempting to reestablish civil society in Ninety Six District in July 1781. When the British evacuated Ninety Six, Cruger had promised protection—and vacant Whig estates—to local Tories if they would leave with the army and remain behind British lines. According to Pickens, Cruger had followed this threat with a warning—those choosing to stay would "be treated as Enemies in future."[1] Many Tories had fled with Cruger, but many others had remained, willing to take their chances in the face of their Whig neighbors' vengeance. Some men had stayed with Cruger but left relatives behind.[2]

Pickens recognized the lingering presence of Tories in the Ninety Six region both as a security threat and as a guarantee that reprisals and lawlessness would continue. In a July 19 letter to Greene, he advised that family members of Tories who had already left should be forced to leave and take protection from the British. Pickens's awkward sentence structure somewhat obscures his logic and motivations, but with enough historical context both can be clarified:

> I am induced to think it Politick by the following Reasons; first
> it was Brittish orders; secondly while their friends & Family
> Connexions are amongst us; they will be harbour'd, & get every
> Intelligence that is known in the Contry, to our Prejudice—thirdly,
> as they set us the precedent formerly with Respect of our Families,
> & it's their Desire to have them there, we heap Coals of Burning
> fires on our Enemies by Rewarding them with good for Evil. And
> Lastly, it's impossible for us and them to Inhabit one Contry, and
> Live together in peace, at one time. Many of them are lying out,
> some of which have given up. . . . The settlements are much allarm'd
> as a number of Tories have lately gone into the Indian Contry.[3]

To Pickens, banishing the Tories from his district was both a practical necessity and ultimately more humane. It was actually "Brittish orders" for them to leave, he explained, and of course those who remained could provide intelligence to the enemy. When Pickens said that the British "set us the precedent," he referred to the fate of many Whigs who had been captured when Charleston fell to the British the previous year. In a modern-day Babylonian exile, many of them, and later their families, had been forced to leave their homes and live in captivity in St. Augustine, Florida, and later Philadelphia. The patriots, however, by driving their enemies into the arms of their protectors rather than into foreign lands, would actually be returning good for evil, following the biblical injunction to treat one's enemies with kindness: "If thine enemy be . . . thirsty, give him water to drink: For thou shalt heap coals of fire upon his head, and the LORD shall reward thee."[4] This would be more merciful than leaving them in Whig-controlled territory, where Pickens and other officers still had minimal ability to protect them from the vengeance of the Whig population. As he said, Whig and Tory still could not "Live together in peace, at one time."[5]

Greene made no direct reply to Pickens's proposal. After another letter in which Pickens despaired of being able to control plundering by Whigs, Greene simply urged leniency and mercy toward loyalists. But Greene's definition of mercy toward the Tories was that they be encouraged to return home, a suggestion that not only contradicted Pickens's preferred course but also ignored the difficulty he was having in preventing violence.[6] Undoubtedly Pickens considered this course unrealistic for the time being. In August, Colonel Robert Anderson ordered elements of his regiment in Pickens's brigade to "order off the families and dangerous connections" of Tories who were within British lines or "lying out" in the countryside.[7]

The problem of what to do with Tories still living in the vast liberated portions of the state concerned civil leaders as well. Governor Rutledge, who had only recently been able to return to the state himself, tried to tackle the problem in September. After the battle of Eutaw, Rutledge consulted with Generals Pickens, Sumter, and Marion on a plan for reorganizing the militia, and probably also on the state's policy toward Tories and others who had remained under British protection. Pickens stayed with Rutledge on the Congaree River rather than returning immediately to Long Cane until these decisions were sorted out. On September 27, Rutledge issued a proclamation offering pardon to Tories and their families if the head of household would turn himself over to one of the brigadier generals of the state militia— Sumter, Marion, or Pickens—and enlist for a term of six months. Those who failed to take this course would have their families banished to British lines. The proclamation was full of exclusions and exceptions, however. Some considered it harsh, and it was rife with possibilities for confusion and deliberate misinterpretation. The issue of whether and how much to allow loyalists to reclaim their citizenship and their property would remain a thorny one for more than a decade.[8]

Anxious to show the British and recalcitrant loyalists that South Carolina's sovereignty was restored, Rutledge sent out writs of election for the re-formation of the legislature. The writs for election went out in late November, the elections were complete in December, and the General Assembly was to convene for the first time in nearly two years in January 1782. Greene persuaded Rutledge to have the legislature convene in Jacksonborough, only thirty miles from Charleston, to illustrate how little of the state still remained in British hands. There was another reason, however, for convening at Jacksonborough rather than at Camden, the first suggested location: Greene believed his army could better protect the governor and the legislators at Jacksonborough; at Camden, they would be in more danger from attempts by backcountry Tories to kidnap them.[9]

Pickens was elected to the House of Representatives from Ninety Six District. He was not able to attend in January, however, because Greene was right: the upcountry was still far from safe. In fact, the entire northwest quadrant of the state west of the Broad River was descending once again into murder and mayhem. With British encouragement, Tories who had been uprooted by recent Whig successes in the South joined with Indians in new attacks on Whig settlements.[10] (Over the course of 1781, several Cherokee chiefs had sought peace with the new American states. Others bitterly rejected this course.)[11]

In other cases, Tories acted on their own. The most infamous among them was William "Bloody Bill" Cunningham. Bloody Bill was the cousin of Patrick and Robert Cunningham, backcountry men who had been prominent in the Tory cause at the beginning of the war. His neighbors remembered his disposition before the war as "lively, jovial . . . , open-hearted and generous, priding himself upon keeping his word, but of a quick and fiery temper." William initially served the Whig cause, participating as a junior officer in Andrew Williamson's 1776 campaign against the Cherokees. His early service, however, led to friction with his superiors, and he later declared that his opinions had changed. His name may not have become a byword for savagery had it not been for a feud with a neighbor, Whig captain William Ritchie. According to local Tories, Ritchie killed William's lame brother by whipping him to death and later killed his father as well. Because he had no horse at the time, William walked all the way from Savannah to Ninety Six for the express purpose of killing Ritchie, whom he shot down in Ritchie's own yard.[12]

This act was only the beginning of Bloody Bill's career of vengeance. He served as a Tory militia officer during the British occupation of Ninety Six, eagerly punishing Whigs who violated their parole and occasionally mistreating their female relatives. Cunningham's most notorious acts occurred after the British withdrawal from Ninety Six. In early August, Cunningham set out from British lines with 150 riders to punish Whigs in Ninety Six who had mistreated the wives and children of some of his men. They killed eight men. On November 7, Cunningham's large force surprised a thirty-man force of Whigs at Cloud's Creek, a tributary of the Little Saluda. After the Whigs surrendered unconditionally, they were massacred, with only two men escaping to tell the tale. The bodies were left on the ground, so mutilated that the men's mothers and sisters who came to bury them had trouble identifying them. Cunningham continued to blaze a trail of arson and bloodshed until, later in the month, he fell upon a post of sixteen men at Hayes' Station under the command of Colonel Joseph Hayes of Pickens's brigade. After a fight of several hours, the Whigs were forced to surrender. Hayes and another man were hung on the pole of a fodder stack. When the pole broke, Cunningham "slew the half-strangled men with his own hand."[13] Cunningham then allowed his men to single out particular foes and hack each of them to pieces until all the Whigs were dead.[14]

Meanwhile, in late October, a Tory known only as "Bloody Bates" led a band of Cherokees and white men who painted their face like Indians in an attack on Gowen's Fort on the Pacolet River. The Whigs defending the fort eventually surrendered. Bates then went back on his word to protect the occupants and killed all but a few who managed to escape—men, women, and children.[15]

The entire territory of Pickens's brigade was awash in blood. No wonder he had left detachments behind when he had marched east to join Greene at Eutaw. Now Pickens himself went in pursuit of Bates's Tories and their Cherokee allies with two regiments of mounted men. In an eleven-day raid, Pickens's men killed about thirty Indians, captured thirty more, and destroyed several villages.[16] Pickens returned to find that several formations from his brigade and from Sumter's were in pursuit of Cunningham as well as his confederate who often operated alongside him, Hezekiah Williams. Pickens himself took charge of the pursuit.

Hezekiah Williams separated from Cunningham and intercepted a convoy of wagons that Pickens had sent from Long Cane to Augusta to get corn for the brigade. One member of the wagon train was John Pickens, the general's younger brother. After capturing the wagons, Williams split his column to escape converging columns of his Whig pursuers. Williams himself rejoined Cunningham farther east while sending the wagon train and the prisoners across the Savannah. The Tories delivered their Whig captives to the Cherokees in mid-December. There two or three of the captives were spared when Cherokee women intervened on their behalf. The Cherokees killed the rest. While some accounts say they were shot in "cold blood," other reports circulated that John Pickens and his fellow prisoners were placed on a pile of lightwood and burned to death. Andrew Shellito, a nephew of one of the men who was killed, wrote that when Pickens heard about his brother's death, "he wept like a child."[17]

The statement by Pickens's neighbor that he "wept like a child" is a rare glimpse into the emotional life of a man with a stern exterior. John was Pickens's last surviving brother, the "baby" of the family whose future had been entrusted to him in his father's will. Pickens's grief is also a reminder that his desire to restore moral and social order in the backcountry was not an abstract goal; it was intertwined with the need to come to grips with personal loss.

It was often difficult to separate vengeance from political necessity and sound military policy. Contemporaries stated that Pickens launched his next series of Cherokee expeditions in retaliation for John's death. This was a natural assumption and unremarkable in a place and time awash with bloody acts of vengeance—the Cherokees themselves would have been surprised if Pickens had not retaliated. Indeed, there is little doubt that John's death made those campaigns even more personal. Pickens, however, who demanded "courage and action" of himself and others, would have launched them even without John's murder. Moreover, defeat of the Cherokees was important, if not vital, to the final defeat of the Tories. The Indian settlements in the mountains were a base to which Tories could flee and regroup for renewed raids. Pickens and other Whigs were correct in assuming that Tories such as Thomas Brown and Thomas Waters were encouraging and organizing further Indian attacks. In late 1781, the Indians and Tories were still an intolerable threat to liberty and order, and Pickens was the man his neighbors looked to most to protect them. He therefore spent much of January 1782 trying to organize a large expedition "against the Cherokees and Tories that are harboured in [their] nation."[18] The backcountry brigadier apparently argued to Governor Rutledge that a large, coordinated expedition of troops from the two Carolinas and Georgia could secure the frontier and allow patriot forces then to concentrate against the British. Moreover, such an expedition was necessary to "save this Country from total ruin." Rutledge approved of the plan and Pickens tried to get several North Carolina militia commanders and Colonel Elijah Clarke of Georgia to join him. To Clarke he wrote, "I am determined to make one more attempt to save the frontiers."[19]

For some reason, the expedition did not come off in February as Pickens had hoped, but he did launch it in mid-March.[20] The campaign was a disappointment. The North Carolina detachments did not arrive, and Pickens was also unhappy with the "lukewarmness" of several South Carolina officers.[21] He did capture and hang a Tory spy named Crittenden, but the Indians themselves stayed out of Pickens's path. Pickens sent

A State of Alarm and Confusion

another Tory who had been captured with Crittenden to tell the Indians that he had heard they wanted a fight and that he had come many miles to give them one. The Indians refused to give battle, so Pickens marched through the villages looking for corn to destroy or consume, finding only forty bushels and four small cattle. Meanwhile, his troops struggled against rain, heavy snow, and dwindling provisions. Nineteen days later, Pickens was back, forced to admit that his expedition had "not been as successful as I could have wished." Despite his disgust with those who had not participated, he was proud of the officers and men who did so in the face of great hardship: they had "done their duty with more cheerfulness and less complaint or murmuring, than I ever saw amongst militia."[22] In what had by now become the standard way to recruit militia, Pickens paid his men with cattle confiscated from Tories.[23]

Shortly after Pickens's return in April, Greene ordered his brigade to join him in the area around Charleston, where he was still harassing the British garrison. Pickens obeyed. He saw no action, but he did speak with the new governor, John Mathews, about another multistate campaign against the Cherokees. Mathews in turn wrote the governors of Virginia, North Carolina, and Georgia and asked them to have their commanders coordinate with Pickens. When Pickens returned to Long Cane on June 20, he found that there had been more trouble with the Indians while he was gone. It was clear that, with British encouragement and Tory support, the Indians were trying to establish a base from which they could raid settlements in Georgia and South Carolina. Some of his men under Robert Anderson and some Georgians under Elijah Clarke had broken up a band of Indians who were planning a major assault. Before Pickens could make much headway in organizing a new expedition, however, Greene ordered him to the lowcountry once again in late July. Due to the current harvest and more Tory raids, including recent ones by Cunningham, Pickens did not bring his entire brigade. Again there was no major action around Charleston, and Pickens returned to Long Cane in mid-August 1782.[24]

Because the North Carolinians were not ready, Pickens delayed his Cherokee expedition once again, to September 16. In the meantime he tried to address the civil disorder that raged throughout Ninety Six. What the district needed most now, he told Greene and Governor Mathews, was "the quick & timely establishment of Courts of Justice." Without them, the people continued to take "unlawfull liberties" in avenging themselves and recovering lost property. Greene himself had frequently bemoaned the killing of Tories by Whig citizens, and Pickens certainly agreed in principle.

But Greene's recommendation that former Tories be invited to return to their homes was utterly unrealistic in Pickens's eyes. Pickens explained that since he had returned from Greene's headquarters several weeks ago, there had been more incursions by Tory gangs. For the time being, they had been "chiefly killed or drove from amongst us," but their periodic return was a serious problem: "I regret that so very considerable a number of the disaffected, who justly bear infamous characters, are returned into this Contry, the people have, with some difficulty, been restrained from Acts of Violence." In other words, until Tories could be pursued in the courts, it would be utterly impossible for Pickens and his officers to prevent violence against them.[25]

Pickens was not exaggerating, for even after the war was over, the spirit of vengeance was alive and nearly irresistible. The Tory who had delivered John Pickens's captured wagon train into the hands of the Cherokees was a planter named John Crawford. Later reports reached Whigs that Crawford had refused some of the condemned men's pleas for mercy. Crawford did not return to Ninety Six but instead moved to British-held territory in East Florida. After the end of the war he did send his wife, Peggy, to see to his property. Peggy's former neighbors believed that it was she who had provided her husband intelligence on the approach of the wagon train in November 1781. Unfortunately for her, they also knew that she was now staying in the house of her sister. Andrew Shellito related that "when the Whig women of the neighborhood heard of her presence, they went in a body to the house where she was.... They drew Peggy by the heels from the house, took her out, tied her, & gave her a terrible whipping, each taking their turn."[26] Another victim of Whig vengeance was Matthew Love, who had ridden with Bloody Bill Cunningham and allegedly thrust his sword through several dying men at Hayes' Station. Early in 1784, Love returned to Ninety Six, apparently hoping that the peace treaty would protect him from acts committed during the war. Judge Aedanus Burke agreed and had the man released. However, without communicating any disrespect to the judge, several respectable and upright citizens seized Love and calmly but firmly took him to some woods. When Love tried to protest the injustice of killing a man without a trial, his former neighbors replied that "he should have thought of that when he was slaughtering their kinsmen."[27] They then hung him from a tree.

The Whigs' hatred of the Indians was no less intense when Pickens, Clarke, and their men set out for Cherokee country in mid-September 1782. But while hatred and vengeance drove many of his men, Pickens focused on the military considerations. In his thinking, the threat would be reduced or even eliminated if the Cherokee nation could be emptied of renegade Tories who instigated and led Indian raids. The most dangerous was Thomas Waters, a Tory colonel who had formed a group of loyalist Indian traders into a military company. Pickens was unhappy that waiting on the North Carolinians under Colonel John Sevier and Brigadier General Charles McDowell had forced a delay of at least a month. As it happened, he never would form a junction with the North Carolina troops—and it was not the first time Sevier had failed to give him the promised support. As Pickens explained to Greene, the delay of four to six weeks meant that by the time American patriot forces reached the Cherokee nation, the Indians would have had time to harvest their corn and take their families and food supplies deep into the mountains: "They are a people who only can be brought to measure by fear or Necessity & as they can have the Mountains for shelter, & their corn can be hid there for their support, I fear it will be difficult to reduce them to measures, but we must do what rests in our power, to disconcert their plans."[28] On September 18, Pickens's force of more than 300 men met Clarke's 100-plus Georgians at Long Creek in Georgia.[29] As was usually the case for patriot forces in the South, there was a shortage of ammunition, sufficient for only four or five rounds per man. Pickens had therefore ordered local blacksmiths to produce a large supply of swords. Later he admitted that "it may be thought rash to have gone, with so little ammunition, against a powerful tribe of Indians, aided by a banditti of desperadoes."[30]

A third strike against the expedition occurred when a Tory spy deserted the column and informed Waters and the Indians. The latter posted scouts along the route that Pickens had used in the past, between the upper reaches of the Chattahoochee and Tugaloo Rivers. Pickens, however, used a more southerly and westerly route, a heavily wooded one that none of his men had ever traveled. He was aided by two Indians they had captured along the way who agreed to lead them to the village where Waters was staying—probably "Long Swamp" on the north shore of the Etowah River in modern Cherokee County, Georgia.[31] On the last segment of the march, Pickens moved by night until he arrived within a half mile of the settlement. He gave strict orders forbidding fires and directing each man to hold his horse by the bridle, so that no stray horses would alert the enemy. By daylight, he was ready to charge into the upper end of the town while Clarke's men charged into the lower. To save ammunition, the men were to use their swords first and their pistols only if necessary.[32]

Pickens was seeking to deliver a decisive, crushing blow, but he was also determined to maintain basic standards of humanity—a difficult balance to achieve in such a war as this. The task was to toe the line between acceptable and necessary acts of retribution and unlawful acts of vengeance. The problem was more difficult than recognized today because of the absence of written guidelines such as the Uniform Code of Military Justice or Geneva Convention. Pickens gave strict orders that no women, children, or old men were to be killed. Any soldier violating this command was to be executed. On the other hand, they were positively to kill "all who had the appearance of warriors." As the white militiamen charged into the town, the terror among the Indians was complete. Some dashed into cabins to retrieve weapons, while others fled for their lives. Few escaped, for the town was surrounded by much open ground. Pickens and Clarke's troops pursued the men in every direction, cutting them down. Private Andrew Pickens, the general's cousin, recalled that "if one blow failed of the object, a second or a third from some of the others, did up the work." One powerful man named William Greene had a very large sword and "cleft [open] the heads of flying Indians like so many pumpkins."[33]

As the carnage continued, one Cherokee fled with his gun into a deep ravine, with Pickens and twelve or fifteen men pursuing. The ravine was too steep for horses, so a soldier named Parata dismounted and went after him alone. As Parata advanced, the Indian "kept up a dancing, like a defying turkey." After a series of taunts, advances, retreats, and missed shots, the two finally came to blows. When the Indian's bullet merely grazed Parata's shoulder, the latter exclaimed, "Now, by G——d, it's my turn." As the Indian tried to club Parata with his gun, Parata sliced his throat with his sword so that the Indian's head slumped onto his chest and his body to the ground. In a fit of bloodlust, Parata then chopped his enemy's head to pieces, exclaiming with each blow, "G——d damn you." Pickens was not impressed. Private Andrew Pickens reported that "Gen. Pickens, who was always as humane as brave, remarked, 'Parata acts like a fool'; & when the Indian killer, with the gun & shot pouch for his plunder, came up, he said to Gen. Pickens—'General, you like to have lost the best soldier you have'— Pickens, with a grunt of disapprobation for his fool hardy conduct, turned away without saying a word."[34]

While Pickens had little patience for "fools" who blasphemed and who mutilated their foes in fits of rage, he also had no regard for traitors. Sometime after the battle, his men caught up with David Pickens, a cousin who had been living with the Indians and was able to flee on horseback and

A State of Alarm and Confusion

escape the initial slaughter. David was young and had been enticed into joining the Tories and settling in the Indian country by his older brother John. Nevertheless, he was, in Pickens's eyes, associating with the enemies of his people. One Major Taylor wanted to kill David, but Captain Robert Maxwell, who knew him well, interposed, with the two officers nearly coming to blows. When they met Pickens, Maxwell said, "Here, General, is a person of whom you know something." Pickens replied, "Yes, but why do you bring him to me?" Maxwell said that he thought Pickens might have something to say to his cousin. Pickens answered, "I have nothing to say to him," and turned away. After the war, David Pickens would be forgiven by his neighbors and allowed to resettle among his own people and would serve as a spy on the frontier. His older brother John would spend the rest of his life among the Indians. Several other Tories were tried for crimes and sentenced to hang. Clarke intervened on behalf of four of them, but at least one was executed and another assassinated by a militiaman while in Clarke's custody.[35]

The Tory colonel Waters was able to escape, but otherwise Pickens's victory was impressive. Somewhere between 40 and 79 men were killed and 50 women or children were taken prisoner along with a few men, though another participant says the number of prisoners approached 100.[36] Pickens sent detachments along the upper Chattahoochee and Coosa Rivers to raid more villages. More prisoners were taken; corn, beans, and cattle were seized or destroyed. Stolen horses and slaves were recaptured. With the Cherokees reeling from his successful campaign, Pickens was determined to force them to come to terms. As his detachments scoured the nearby villages in upper Georgia, he sent three Cherokee men he had captured at Long Swamp as emissaries to those who were in hiding. They were to inform the chiefs that "I did not blame the Indians so much as the white men that were amongst them who encouraged or assisted them in the war against us." Pickens promised to end his campaign and release all his Indian captives if the Cherokees would turn over all the white men they had, both Tories and Whig prisoners, as well as captured slaves. He said he would wait for them for two days; if they did not comply, "I would proceed as far as I could & would destroy as many of their towns & as much of their provisions as possible & if they wished to fight they knew where to find me."[37]

Severely beaten and facing a long winter ahead with scant provisions and destroyed villages, the chiefs were eager to settle. They sent a flag of truce the next day and asked for more time to comply, so Pickens gave them three more days. In a few days, The Terrapin and some ten warriors came into Pickens's camp with six of Waters's Tories, and Pickens soon collected more. (Interestingly, Pickens's brother Joseph had captured The Terrapin during the 1779 campaign.) On October 17, a dozen chiefs and 200 warriors made a treaty with Pickens. They ceded to Georgia a large tract of land east of the Chattahoochee River and agreed to meet with Georgia officials in Augusta later to confirm the treaty. They also swore to remain at peace with the white settlements and to no longer tolerate the presence of Tories in their territory.[38]

By October 22, Pickens had returned to his home state and discharged his men; he had not lost a single one. Pickens had waged his last military campaign, and his victory was indeed decisive. If the British had had any idea of continuing the war or improving their position at the peace table by using the Cherokees to harbor Tories and harass the southern backcountry settlements, that plan was defeated. Additionally, never again would there be full-scale war between the Cherokees and the state of South Carolina. Occasional murders and depredations on both sides would continue, but large raids on South Carolina ceased. At the cost of massive suffering among the Cherokees, Pickens and the men under him had finally brought an acceptable level of order and security to their neighborhoods. No longer would the Tories have safe havens from which to launch or instigate raids. Finally, in Pickens's eyes, he had achieved all this while still keeping his humanity and virtue intact. Later historians would be understandably horrified at the carnage and suffering that Pickens had inflicted. At the time, however, no American patriot east or west of the Savannah would have shared that feeling.

A State of Alarm and Confusion

ELEVEN

Rebuilding Civil Society

Freedom and Happiness . . . are the Great Objects
of all good Government.

Andrew Pickens to South Carolina
House of Representatives, March 21, 1786

Andrew Pickens was forty-three years old when he returned home from his victory over the Cherokees in the fall of 1782. He and Becky now had six surviving children. The oldest four (Mary, sixteen; Ezekiel, fourteen; Ann, twelve; and Jane, nearly eight) had come of age or lived their entire childhoods in the midst of war. As children, they had experienced the enemy's destruction of their home, wartime shortages, and often hiding out fearfully in the woods or fleeing the Long Cane area altogether when the tide of the war swung against their father's side. During one of these forced exiles in the forest, they had seen a baby brother die of smallpox.[1] Meanwhile, Margaret, 5, and Andrew, nearly 3, had been born during the war itself and at times had seen very little of their father. Pickens had been away from home for nearly all of 1781; in 1782 he had left his family repeatedly to march to Charleston, campaign against the Cherokees, and lead the pursuit of Tory marauders.[2]

Pickens's peacetime duties began at home. Throughout the backcountry and most of the state, families had to rebuild depleted herds of livestock as well as fences, barns, and houses. Undoubtedly he also felt some responsibility for the families of his deceased brothers. Joseph's widow, Eleanor, was also his first cousin. She had eight children and never remarried. When Pickens and Becky later moved northwest from Long Cane to present-day Pendleton, South Carolina, Eleanor settled nearby about the same time. John, recently killed by the Indians, had left a widow named Mary.[3] Pickens also hoped to reestablish his trading business as a middleman between the Indians and lowcountry merchants. Unlike many of his neighbors, he could afford to concentrate on public duties as well. With a teenage son and a handful of slaves as a labor force and Mary, Ann, and Jane to help Becky in the house and with the little ones, the Pickenses were better off than many families. The simple fact that Pickens had survived was critical; there were perhaps 1,200 widows in Ninety Six District.[4]

Thus Pickens expanded his public leadership role after the war. He was still an elder in the Upper Long Cane congregation and a justice of the peace. Moreover, he was a war hero, one of the most respected soldiers in the Carolinas. His neighbors expected him to lead. Unlike the situation just eight or ten years before, however, Pickens' leadership was no longer confined to just the local level. Lowcountry and national elites would soon entrust Pickens with great responsibility at the state and national levels as a state legislator, congressman, federal treaty negotiator, and military adviser to presidents and secretaries of war. It is easy to forget how revolutionary this was. Before the Revolution, authority and leadership at those levels were entrusted only to elites. Eighteenth-century Americans had understood that higher offices were reserved for gentlemen of rank. Backcountry farmers with a few hundred acres and perhaps half a dozen slaves—men with no pedigree or formal education—simply did not get elected or appointed to such positions. Even when they did obtain greater wealth, they often had to learn to demonstrate other traits that were supposed to characterize the gentry—polish and personal refinements, ease of carriage, witty and urbane conversation, and literary knowledge—skills and traits that Pickens never acquired.[5]

Thus the fact that Pickens was admitted to the ranks of the gentry requires explanation. Some of the reasons were practical. It was natural for governors to consult a frontier Indian merchant and Indian fighter for advice on dealing with the Cherokees and Creeks. Pickens quickly gained a reputation in his own state and in the nation at large as the South Carolina citizen with the most knowledge of Indian affairs. Lowcountry politicians also turned to Pickens as the most respected man in the expanding backcountry when they needed to establish districts and counties, resolve northwestern border disputes with North Carolina and Georgia, and organize military defenses in that part of the state.

Lowcountry elites also sought alliances with Pickens for economic gain. Some wished to become partners with him in his trading activities. Ex-governor John Rutledge, attorney John Lewis Gervais, John Owen, and Pickens formed "Andrew Pickens & Company" in 1784, with Gervais and Owen attending to the company's affairs in Charleston and Pickens doing the same in Ninety Six. Pickens benefited from their capital investment and they from his knowledge of the Indian trade and the Indians' familiarity with him.[6] Others who wished to buy, lease out, and sell land in the backcountry asked for Pickens's advice and assistance. These included prominent lowcountry planters Arnoldus Vanderhorst and Felix Warley and Governors Thomas Pinckney and Charles Cotesworth Pinckney. Letters from these men to Pickens show that they trusted his knowledge, prudence, and honesty. If one wanted to do business in the most westerly portions of the state, Andrew Pickens was a good man to know.[7]

The most fundamental reason for the amount of public trust placed in Pickens, however, had to do with his generation's understanding of virtue and what was required to make a republic work. American elites of the 1780s were not just trying to rebuild a society shattered by war. They were also trying to construct an entirely new political order without kings or hereditary lords—a republic where liberty and order were protected by men selected to lead because of their "virtue" rather than their lineage. They had no illusions about the difficulty of their task. The evangelical tradition told them that men were naturally prone to sin and to violate the rights of their fellow men. Yet the Revolutionary generation had also inherited a classical republican tradition that said that republics, and therefore liberty, were impossible unless some men could be counted on to rise above their own selfish interests. The state must find virtuous men who devoted themselves to the welfare and liberties of their fellow citizens.[8]

This was the selfless public virtue of the new model republican citizen—a new ideal for political and social leadership in the public sphere. Neither before nor after the Revolution did others seriously question Pickens's private virtue—he was not an adulterer, a drunkard, or a thief. He was a pious Christian and was "proverbial for his honesty," as one contemporary said.[9] But what added to Pickens's reputation was his contemporaries' sense that he was not seeking to enhance his own fortune through public service.

The war had made this concept of republican virtue only more powerful, and it had also emphasized its militaristic strands. No one could deny that the saviors of the state in the dark days of 1780–81 had been its soldiers;

they had become recognized as the epitome of self-sacrificing virtue, and this especially applied to the militia commanders: first to Sumter, then to Marion and Pickens and their key subordinates. The war had done much to militarize the concept of republican virtue.[10]

It had also democratized it. Seven years of military conflict had refashioned republican virtue so that it could be attributed to men from society's middling and lower ranks. When South Carolina's elites took on the king's army in 1775 and 1776, the state's Provincial Congress had appointed men of property, prestige, and usually aristocratic origins to the command of regiments and then brigades—men with names like Moultrie, Pinckney, and Gadsden. By the time the war ended, the leading warrior chieftains in the state—Sumter, Marion, and Pickens—were all men from humbler backgrounds. Sumter was born into a poor family in Virginia, had little formal education, and had once escaped from a debtors' prison. Marion's family was relatively prosperous in comparison but did not have the wealth or lineage of the men who led the state in the early days of the conflict. Pickens was a backcountry merchant and farmer with little more than functional literacy. These three men owed their military rank not to the Charleston elites in the General Assembly but rather to the simple fact that other men had chosen to follow them in the darkest days of the war. The partisans in York District had literally elected Sumter as their general, and Rutledge's promotion of him to that rank simply recognized the fact he had become the focus of Whig resistance in mid-1780. Pickens's promotions, including his last one to brigadier general, had been completely due to his performance and local reputation, not to wealth or previous social status. The new state of South Carolina would turn not only to its aristocrats for leadership but also to its heroes. It was no longer necessary to be the former to be considered one of the latter.[11]

Pickens's neighbors in Ninety Six District elected him to the state house of representatives for the third time in November 1782. He had never served on the previous occasions because of his military duties. In January 1783, however, Pickens finally took his seat in the General Assembly. Other members elected from Ninety Six District included two of his regimental commanders, Colonels Robert Anderson and Le Roy Hammond.

Pickens had no legislative experience. He did, however, have deep knowledge of military affairs and issues relating to the Indians and conditions in the backcountry. For more than a year and a half he had been not only the senior military commander in the western third of the state but also the closest thing to civil authority that then existed in the war-ravaged countryside. Partly because of this knowledge and experience, he won seats on several important committees. Pickens worked hard on these committees but rarely spoke in house debates. His articulation was not clear, and he lacked the ability to make classical references or engage in witty repartee. Though he often chaired committees, he would sometimes allow a more articulate member to deliver the committee's report to the house. This was not always the case, however, and "on great occasions he would modestly give his opinion which always had weight."[12] As Clyde Ferguson explains, "He seldom dodged a voice vote, even when he stood with a hopeless minority" or against the majority of his backcountry colleagues.[13]

Much of the work of the General Assembly over the next few years involved cleaning up unfinished business from the war: what to do with the Tories, how to compensate soldiers who had not been properly paid, and how to resolve legal complaints resulting from Sumter's Law. The Jacksonborough assembly of January 1782 had taken legal action against several hundred of the 12,000–15,000 South Carolinians who had aided the British. Pickens, busy organizing a campaign against the Cherokees, had not attended this session, but he would have wholeheartedly supported these measures. One statute identified 283 notorious Tories who were to be banished from the state and have their estates confiscated. There was a thin thread of humanity in this measure: the commission established to oversee the confiscations could allow a portion of the estate to be used for the temporary support of the banished families who needed it. Forty-seven other individuals were punished by amercement, meaning that they were to pay the state 12 percent of the assessed value of their estates. Finally, lesser traitors could be granted amnesty and pardon after paying a fine amounting to 10 percent of their estates' value.

There were several problems with the confiscation and amercement acts. Those punished by them were not given trials. The laws were rather blunt instruments that could not take into account the specific predicaments faced by many South Carolinians when they had fallen into British hands in 1780. The acts actually singled out a small proportion of South Carolina loyalists, overwhelmingly in the lowcountry. Some had been guilty of little more than accepting British protection in 1780, as Pickens and many other patriots had done; unlike Pickens, they had neither the opportunity nor the courage to break their parole later. In the backcountry and interior of the state, where the conflict between Whig and Tory neighbors had often become meaner and bloodier than in the British-controlled lowcountry, there was overwhelming support for the acts. Almost as soon as they were passed, however, numerous efforts emerged from the lowcountry to lessen the punishment for certain individuals or have them forgiven entirely. By 1784, the General Assembly had already passed an act of clemency that allowed most loyalists on the confiscation list to be moved to the far less onerous amercement list. These efforts to alleviate the punishment of former Tories continued through the remainder of the decade.[14]

Pickens almost always opposed leniency in the confiscation and amercement cases. He may have felt that the acts themselves were adequately merciful and respectful of the rule of law. They did not allow outright executions, for one. And the reason more lowcountry loyalists were subject to the acts is that only wealthier individuals who had held officer-level positions were singled out. The punishment of those more affluent Tories was more orderly and arguably more humane than that suffered by non-elite Tories in the backcountry. Pickens certainly knew of the lynching of Matthew Love, the whipping of Peggy Crawford, and the practice of gangs of men physically attacking former Tories in their own homes and dismantling their houses. Pickens abhorred lawlessness and had never excused the murder of Tory prisoners of war, but unlike many in the lowcountry, he had no enthusiasm for carte-blanche forgiveness. He repeatedly voted against the repeal of the acts and usually opposed individual petitions for relief from them.[15]

Pickens seems to have felt a particular vindictiveness toward his old commander Andrew Williamson. It is difficult to understand exactly why. Pickens later charged that Williamson's defection to the British had begun as early as February 1779, around the time of Pickens's victory at Kettle Creek, Georgia. As Pickens recalled in his letter to Henry Lee more than three decades later, Williamson had done nothing aggressive to support Pickens's maneuvers at this time and had not pursued the British as they withdrew from Augusta: "There was not a gun fired between [the British] and Williamson, all this time opposite each other at Augusta—Here I believe Williamson was corrupted."[16]

Pickens's allegation seems incorrect if not unfair. Williamson somehow continued to serve the patriot cause, at least outwardly, for another full year. In May 1780, when patriot resistance had collapsed in South Carolina, Williamson had pled with Pickens's men to continue the fight. Pickens had said nothing in support and, like Williamson, subsequently surrendered his forces and signed his parole. During the British occupation of Ninety Six, Williamson had openly cooperated with British officers. Pickens had been more circumspect but had been in regular contact with him. Williamson had convinced the British of Pickens's importance and abilities and told them he was very hopeful that Pickens would soon fight in the king's service.

Whatever alliance that still remained between Pickens and Williamson had collapsed in December 1780. It was then that Pickens angrily renounced his parole and soon became an American hero at the battle of Cowpens. Williamson, on the other hand, removed to Charleston where the British could better protect him. Some Whigs believed that he accepted a British commission, though there has never been any evidence of that. Very late in the war, when it was clear that the British cause in South Carolina was doomed, he turned on the British and provided intelligence to Nathanael Greene. Learning in December 1782 that Pickens had been elected to the General Assembly, he lamented to Greene that Pickens was one of "my most violent Enemies." He claimed to believe that Pickens feared Williamson reassuming command and making Pickens his subordinate once again, though it "would be quite needless to say" how silly such a notion was: "Genl. Pickens should always command my voluntary Services, and chearfully recieve my advice whenever he thought proper to consult me."[17] Williamson hoped Greene would intercede for him with Pickens and others, but Pickens was unmoved.[18]

By the time of Williamson's death in 1786, many South Carolinians had forgiven him, partially because of Greene's testimony that Williamson had acted as a double agent for the American cause. They regarded his defection more as poor judgment and temporary cowardice rather than outright treason, an act that had unfortunately ruined his earlier reputation as a patriot. Pickens apparently did not agree. Williamson made several appeals for mercy to the General Assembly and was eventually able to avoid confiscation of his estate but not amercement. And although his beloved White Hall plantation in Ninety Six was saved, he wisely recognized that he would never be able to resettle there peacefully, selling it in 1785. Just after concluding the 1785 Hopewell treaty with the Cherokees, Pickens informed Governor William Moultrie that the latter complained of Williamson allegedly keeping several Indian child captives as slaves. A committee of the General Assembly conducted an investigation the following year, determined to demand the release of the Indian children if the allegation turned out to be true.[19] (The allegation was probably true, and Pickens at the time was striving for better Indian-white relations on the frontier.) Pickens pursued his former commander after the grave when he still opposed removing the amercement on his estate in 1787. Finally, in 1791, as a state senator, Pickens apparently decided it was inhumane to continue his vendetta.

Appointed to the senate committee on petitions regarding amercement and banishment, he heard the request of Williamson's heirs, his minor sons Andrew and William. The petition was brought by Ephraim Ramsay and Charles Goodwin for their wives, Mary Ann Ramsay and Eliza Goodwin, on behalf of the two boys. Rejecting the petition would place the committee in the unchivalrous position of spurning the request of two ladies on behalf of two unoffending children. Pickens had probably met the two lads at some point during the war years. Pickens's committee gave the petition a favorable recommendation, and it seems that the attorney general's office ceased its actions against the Williamson estate.[20]

Other unresolved business from the war involved compensation for troops who had not been paid and untangling the mess created by Sumter's Law. When the General Assembly met in January 1784, there were still state troops who had not been paid for their services. Under Sumter's Law, they had been promised payment in "negroes" seized from the Tory estates. At the time, Governor Rutledge, Nathanael Greene, and others had been forced to admit tacitly that this measure was a necessity. In fact, it only formalized the widespread plundering and robbery committed by both sides. After the military emergency faded, however, and Rutledge had disallowed the practice, military officers found themselves threatened with lawsuits, and many citizens petitioned the legislature for the return of their property. Most vulnerable to these suits was Sumter himself, as he and the officers in his brigade had recruited the most under Sumter's Law. Pickens had too, however, and the legislature was caught between the just claims of its soldiers, the respect of its citizens' property rights, and the honor of its most respected military officers. The state, meanwhile, had custody over a number of slaves who had been confiscated from Tories.

In March 1784, the General Assembly decided to return slaves to masters who could prove their ownership. The remainder were sold and the proceeds used to compensate troops who had not been paid. Pickens had served on the joint committee assigned to tackle this particular problem. Thus the legislature did what it could to honor the rights and liberties of its citizens and its soldiers, though no one publicly acknowledged the sordidness of a republican state trafficking in human flesh.[21]

Legislators also sought justice in the case of the state's military officers, several of whom were asked to submit their accounts for examination by the General Assembly. The outcome was different for Marion, Pickens, and Sumter. When it was proposed that Marion be protected from lawsuits resulting from confiscations, Marion himself hotly objected. The "Swamp

Fox" had never agreed with Sumter's Law and had stubbornly refused to apply it during the war. He now insisted that if he had done anything improper, he must be held to account.[22]

Pickens had often allowed confiscations of Tory property in order to recruit, though not to the same extent as Sumter. He submitted his papers to the house on January 31, and they were examined by a committee chaired by Charleston's Charles Cotesworth Pinckney, a former brigadier general of the Continental army. On March 5, the committee reported that it had carefully investigated Pickens's case, finding that Pickens "was under the necessity of taking and disposing of Nine Negroes belonging to Persons then with the enemy and to barter or dispose of them for such Public Services as appears by the paper marked No. 1" and that "such Disposition was proper and warranted by the necessity of the Service, and the Situation of the State." The committee also looked into the use of all the public property that had come under Pickens's control and could find no discrepancies except for four horses that were in the general's hands and one currently in the possession of Colonel Robert Anderson. Pinckney's committee recommended that those horses be left where they were and their value applied against state payments that were still due to Pickens and Anderson. Additionally, at various times Pickens had been forced to enlist troops for periods of six months by promising them "a Cow and Calf per Month" seized from Tories. These, too, the committee judged "necessary in the Situation of public Affairs at that period." Finally, the committee reported that while invading Cherokee country in the autumn of 1782, Pickens had captured "Twenty two Negroes belonging to our friends." Pickens had returned each of them to their owners. He had also seized nine slaves belonging to Tories during that expedition, sold them, and used the money to pay his troops.[23]

Pinckney and the other committee members found that "General Pickens has acted in every Matter that has come to the Knowledge of your Committee as an Excellent Officer and good Citizen, anxious to free his Country from British Tyranny and at the same time attending as far as Circumstances would permit to preserve their private property to the Citizens of this State, and they are of opinion the orders and Proceedings above referred to were beneficial to the Country." Furthermore, the committee recommended that Pickens and officers acting under him be indemnified "from all manner of Suits and Damages on Account of the above Orders and Transactions."[24] The legislature agreed and passed a statute saying as much on March 21. Clearly, Pickens had acted repeatedly under the understanding that slaves were property to be either returned or plundered; their welfare and basic humanity were secondary considerations. To Pickens's white contemporaries, however, his claims to republican virtue were vindicated—though some of his acts were not in accord with "strict forms of law," he had done all he could, honestly and zealously, for the cause of liberty.[25]

Sumter, too, submitted his accounts for examination. However, the outcome for the "Gamecock" was slightly more ambiguous. Sumter had been particularly sensitive to criticism of his confiscation policy. Perhaps because he had been responsible for so many applications of Sumter's Law, the legislature did not attempt a point-by-point defense of each instance of it as it did in Pickens's case. Instead, the General Assembly decreed that any citizens seeking redress had to bring their case to the legislature rather than bring indictments or suits against Sumter or his officers. Thus, the protection was a "blanket" one that potentially covered more cases. However, it was not absolute: "nothing herein . . . shall be construed . . . to preclude the General Assembly from demanding an account and enquiring into the appropriation of all such property of and from the said Thomas Sumpter [sic]."[26] The state's defense of Sumter, then, was more equivocal, and it would be many more years before he achieved the complete public vindication he craved.[27]

The legislature also acted to ensure that veterans and their families were compensated in other ways. Militiamen had to receive their back pay, pensions had to be awarded to those who were wounded, and the state had to honor its previous promises of land grants to those who had enlisted. Pickens served on most of the committees dealing with these military issues.[28]

Meanwhile, Pickens used the vast amounts owed to him by the state for his services to expand his own landholdings. The governor's privy council examined the general's accounts in September 1784 and determined that Pickens was owed just over £1,193 for back pay going back to 1780 and for compensation "for Sundrys for Militia use" as far back as 1779.[29] Pickens had already borrowed against that account to purchase a tract of roughly 600 acres owned by the state on the Savannah River opposite Augusta. South Carolina had previously confiscated this land from the Chickasaw Indians for their support of the British at the siege of Augusta.[30] Additionally, the state of Georgia, apparently in appreciation for his services, granted him 500 acres of land abutting the Creek Indian boundary in 1784.[31]

While farming in Long Cane, establishing Andrew Pickens & Company, and converting his back pay into landholdings, Pickens also devoted himself to reestablishing lawful order and peaceful government in Ninety Six. In an attempt to address long-standing grievances in the backcountry and the demands of local leaders like Pickens, the General Assembly moved rather quickly to establish courts and jails, as well as to create new counties to allow more efficient local government and representation in the legislature.[32] Those efforts fell far short of satisfying legitimate backcountry complaints, but they were a start. In 1783 Pickens was once again appointed a justice of the peace in Ninety Six District, along with Patrick Calhoun, Colonel Robert Anderson, Major John Bowie, Major Andrew Hamilton, and Reverend John Harris.[33] The legislature gave these judges authority to select a location for a courthouse and jail and contract for their construction. Pickens was also appointed as a commissioner to divide the sprawling Ninety Six District into counties. His and the other justices' efforts eventually resulted in Ninety Six being divided into six counties: Abbeville (containing the Long Cane settlement), Edgefield, Newberry, Laurens, Spartanburg, and Union.[34] County courts were established that had the authority to hear noncorporal criminal cases, while district courts dealt with more serious offenses. The Ninety Six justices took it upon themselves to police the morality of the republic they had founded. At the end of the 1784 Ninety Six District court session, Pickens and two other justices who were Presbyterian church elders fined Isaac Mayfield "for seven profane oaths."[35]

Equally important to the manners and morals of society were churches and schools. As late as 1787, Pickens was still an elder in the Upper Long Cane congregation. His fellow churchgoers selected him as one of five commissioners assigned to establish the boundaries between the four formally organized Presbyterian congregations between the Savannah and the Saluda—Upper Long Cane (Hopewell), Lower Long Cane, Bull Town, and Saluda. The commissioners met at Pickens's house on August 20, 1783, to complete their work.[36] Such formal organization was necessary in order to apply to the presbytery for full-time ministers and to discipline and encourage members whose lives had become openly sinful. Pickens was not alone in regarding religion as vital to a civil and virtuous society. The Revolutionary generation in South Carolina had disestablished the Anglican Church, and Protestant dissenters like Pickens had supported that move.[37] This did not mean, however, that the state should not support religious institutions. The legislature allowed any group of fifteen or more male Protestants to seek incorporation of their church; in 1791 the General Assembly passed statutes allowing Roman Catholic and Jewish congregations in Charleston to enjoy the legal benefits of incorporation, which Pickens supported. He also supported a bill that allowed Presbyterian churches in Charleston to incorporate that they might hold and manage property by which they could support the widows and children of deceased Presbyterian ministers. This, according to the statute, would "tend greatly to the promoting of religion and virtue among [the congregations], by encouraging pious and able men to devote themselves to the ministry of the Gospel."[38] Always painfully aware of his own lack of education, Pickens continued his interest in making it available for others. He had joined other Protestants in the Mount Zion Society in 1780 to encourage public education in the backcountry. In August 1783, the legislature appointed him and six others, all Presbyterians, as trustees for a public school to be established in Ninety Six.[39]

Even as Pickens tended to public affairs in Ninety Six, he was contemplating a move. He had his eye on land along the Keowee River near the spot where he and Andrew Williamson had defeated the Cherokees in 1776 at the village of Esseneca. The area was north of the old boundary line that had separated Cherokee territory from the district of Ninety Six below it and near the northwestern edge of South Carolina's claims. This would be the fourth time in his life that Pickens had moved from a more settled area to a more remote one; in fact, as of 1785 there was virtually no white settlement north of the old Cherokee boundary line.[40] An earlier biographer has claimed that Pickens was "essentially a frontiersman" who "liked the challenge of unsettled, untouched land."[41] Pickens's tendency to stay near the advancing edge of white settlement also had to do with the opportunity to acquire, improve, and perhaps resell land. Still, Pickens seemed to be seeking a degree of permanence with this move. On July 16, 1784, he was granted 573 acres on the east bank of the Keowee. He named his new plantation "Hopewell," the name often also given to his previous congregation in Long Cane.[42] Records indicate that in the following year, Andrew Pickens Jr., "son of Genl. Pickens," received 560 acres adjacent to his father's tract for a sum of fifty pounds and twelve shillings. As Andrew Jr. was not yet six years old, clearly his father had obtained it for him. On the same day, seventeen-year-old Ezekiel Pickens received 523 acres in the same area. Earlier in 1785, 300 acres had been granted nearby to Pickens's widowed cousin and sister-in-law Eleanor Pickens for a sum of thirty pounds. Like earlier Pickens settlements, the general intended this move to be a family migration. However, Pickens did not immediately move his family into the new house at Hopewell. His military subordinate and old friend Robert Anderson later moved as well and settled on a tract adjacent to Pickens's on the western side of the Keowee.[43]

Rebuilding Civil Society

Pickens set out to recreate the moral and social order he had defended in Long Cane and that his father had defended in the Waxhaws. By 1788 or 1789 he and Robert Anderson established a new Presbyterian congregation very near to Pickens's new home. They named it Hopewell, after their old church in Long Cane, served as elders, and set about acquiring a permanent minister; Pickens supplied the log structure with its pews. On occasion they received visits and sermons from Reverend John Simpson, one of the fighting parsons of the backcountry who had preached and even taken up arms against the British. In 1792, the congregants obtained the services of the learned Reverend Dr. Thomas Reese, who ministered at Hopewell as well as at the "Carmel" congregation, some ten or twelve miles away. Reese reported that the Hopewell congregation was "better united, more catholic in their principles, and *disposition*, and liberal in its sentiments. A few of their number are wealthy and very forward to support the gospel; among whom are General Pickens and Colonel Robert Anderson."[44]

The entire northwestern corner of the state north of the pre-1777 Cherokee boundary and west of the Saluda was filling up quickly. In 1785, the nearest courts for the new settlers were in Abbeville County some sixty miles away. Petitions to the General Assembly resulted in the creation of Greenville County in 1786 and Pendleton County in 1789. The town of Pendleton was established in 1790, just two miles east of Pickens's plantation. Pickens, of course, became one of the original county justices in the county he had helped create and was elected Pendleton County's first state senator that spring. Thereafter, the legislature appointed Pickens and seven other men to purchase a tract of land in Pendleton County and contract for the construction of a courthouse and jail. In 1792, the settlement was officially named "Pickensville." Pickensville did not thrive, however, and later local elites moved the seat of Pendleton County to the town of Pendleton itself.[45]

Courthouses, jails, and an increasing population brought a growing sense of permanence to the new community, but so did the maintenance of the church. Hopewell Church burned down in 1799. Fortunately the congregation had already begun construction of a stone structure to replace the old log building. Completed in 1802, it became known as the "Stone Meeting House." Pickens and other leading men of the community were once again the main contributors.[46] By 1808, the town of Pendleton had five stores, a blacksmith shop, two beef markets, two taverns, a boarding-house, a Presbyterian-led and Pickens-supported "Hopewell Academy," and a newspaper.[47]

Local tradition emphasizes the rough equality and simple virtues of early Pendleton. Within a few decades, large-scale cotton cultivation and the growth of slavery would make its culture seem more similar to the plantation districts in the lowcountry. But early accounts portrayed the settlers much like they did Pickens himself: sober, pious, and with simple tastes and virtues. Reverend Reese, having moved to the area from the lowcountry, was certainly pleased with the character of his new flock. "Those who make a profession of religion," he wrote in 1793,

> are well-informed, considering the opportunities they have had. They are attentive to the instruction of their children in the principles of religion, and many of them appear to be truly pious. . . .
>
> The people who compose [the Hopewell and Carmel] congregations are, in general, remarkable for the great simplicity of their manners, the plainness of their dress, and their frugal manner of living. At the distance of 250 miles from the Capital, they are strangers to luxury and refinement. . . . There is a quiet degree of equality among them. . . . None are very rich, few extremely poor. There are few slaves among them, and these are treated with great kindness and humanity. They enjoy all that liberty which is compatible with their situation. . . . These are all circumstances favorable to virtue and religion, and give ground to hope that these will flourish long here, when they shall have been in a great measure banished from those parts of the country where slavery, luxury, and wealth have taken possession.

Reverend Reese was deeply gratified when he reflected that Christian churches, public worship of the Creator and Redeemer, and the proclamation of the gospel flourished in "these wide-extended forests where the cruel savage lately roamed."[48]

The flaws and inherent inequalities in the community will be discussed later. Modern Americans would disapprove of the dependent role it fixed for women and of the presence of slavery. Pickens himself and even Reese were too indoctrinated as stern Calvinists to overlook the human sinful tendencies that constantly threatened to corrupt their community, their neighbors, and even themselves. The "principles of religion" and the favor of God were vital to avert that corruption. Reese's assessment, however, is a revealing description of the ideal of republican virtue and its connections to evangelical religion.[49]

Though it seems that Reese did not consider Pickens "rich," at least by lowcountry standards, he did consider him "wealthy." It was good for

Pickens's family that he was acquiring wealth, because his brood had grown rapidly. By 1791, he and Becky had nine surviving children. (The eldest, Mary, would soon marry John Harris, a stalwart young veteran of the Revolution who had lost an eye from the impact of a Tory bullet.) Another daughter had arrived in January 1784, named "Becky" after her mother. In 1786 Catherine was born, named after her great-grandmother Catherine Calhoun, scalped by the Indians near Long Cane in 1760. At the age of forty-six, Becky delivered her twelfth and last child, Joseph, named for his uncle who was killed at the siege of Ninety Six. Pickens was determined to give his children a better education than he had. He hired a private tutor, a Scot named James Alexander Douglas, to teach them and to prepare the older boys for college. Soon he would send Ezekiel, his eldest son, to Princeton and Andrew Jr. to Brown.

Nearly all local histories of Pendleton allude, if only indirectly, to the impact that Pickens's own personality had on the culture of the community.[50] His very appearance suggested inflexible moral rectitude. When he entered the courtroom, litigants and defendants beheld a man of middle age, tall and slender. His clean-shaven face highlighted his angular features, hawklike nose, high forehead, and generally stern appearance. In the fashion of the day, he wore a frilled white shirt, knee pants, and white hose covered by a swallowtail coat or military "undress" uniform coat. When outdoors, a tricornered hat and a sword or a brace of pistols completed the martial appearance. When he rode into Pendleton, "he would move slowly," recalled William Martin, "every one giving way & addressing him respectfully."[51] He rarely smiled; when he spoke, his words were simple and direct. By now everyone in western South Carolina knew of the general's reputation for implacable determination. But while he conversed little, few perceived him as arrogant, and he had a reputation as a fair and understanding judge.[52]

While Pickens led at the local level, there were several other urgent issues that could be addressed only by the state legislature. As a representative of the backcountry, Pickens generally supported his section's demands for better representation in the General Assembly and the removal of the state capital from Charleston to the state's interior. He did not always vote with his fellow backcountry colleagues, however. He sometimes joined with lowcountry planters and merchants, and he always supported what he considered duly constituted authority in the maintenance of law and order. In South Carolina politics, the "Republican" and "Federalist" factions had not yet crystallized, or were at least not fully developed. Later, the backcountry would emerge as a stronghold of Republican Party support, while Federalism was stronger in the lowcountry. As early as the 1780s, however, one can detect a subtle pattern in Pickens's voting behavior and political philosophy. He shared the nascent Federalist faction's concerns with establishing order and protecting virtue in the new Republic and, later in his career, with their emphasis on national unity. Yet as a product of the more egalitarian society on the frontier, he did not join Federalists in championing traditions of hierarchy and deference nor share their fear of "democracy." Because he did not consistently align with any voting bloc—backcountry, tidewater, Federalist, or Republican—one might consider his voting pattern erratic. His contemporaries, however, as well as later biographers, were more likely to attribute it to his independence of mind and hatred of "party spirit."[53]

One long-standing grievance that had to be addressed for the unity of the state was the backcountry's gross underrepresentation in the General Assembly. Pickens, of course, supported more representation for his own section, but the new state constitution in 1790 granted the interior districts only minor concessions. Lowcountry elites stubbornly resisted reform at least until 1808. Another long-standing complaint was the distance that backcountry people had to travel to the state capital in Charleston. Pickens generally supported the establishment of a new capital in the center of the state and served on a committee that would help determine a location. In 1786 the legislature narrowly voted to build a new permanent capital city named "Columbia" near the confluence of the Saluda, Broad, and Congaree Rivers. After the legislature's vote, however, Governor Thomas Pinckney appointed a committee of six to consider a compromise plan.[54] The committee consisted of two backcountry delegates (Pickens and Anderson), two from the lowcountry, the governor, and the governor's brother Charles Cotesworth Pinckney, both of the latter having Charleston roots. The committee unanimously reached an awkward compromise in which there would be two state treasurers, one residing in Columbia and the other in Charleston. The secretary of state and surveyor-general would maintain offices in both cities. The governor could choose to reside in either city except when the legislature was in session, when he was required to stay in Columbia. Clyde Ferguson suggests that Pickens's agreement to this compromise was a matter of bending to political reality and an effort to secure the Pinckneys' support on other issues, especially his proposed policy toward the Indians.[55]

While Pickens appeared to be a backcountry democrat on issues of representation and the relocation of the capital, he steered a different course on another issue that had class overtones as well as moral implications. The postwar economy of South Carolina was crippled by debt and a shortage of currency. Tidewater elites were in debt to British merchants. Elsewhere throughout the state, ordinary citizens were debtors to more wealthy creditors. Credit had been too easy to obtain, and the situation was exacerbated by many citizens increasing their debt by purchasing slaves from slave importers. In fact, it was clear that many citizens were taking advantage of easy credit and the depreciating currency to make a fortune by less-than-honest means. Some citizens went deeply into debt to buy land and slaves on the gamble that they could make a profit, even if they already owed debts to others. Too many South Carolinians sought to rebuild their wealth through speculation, says one historian, rather than through "patient labor." Perhaps even more immoral was the fact that "men refusing to pay their suffering creditors sported the finest clothes, furniture, and equipages."[56] Thousands of other debtors were simply honest victims of wartime anarchy, the lack of currency, and larger economic forces, and three years of crop failures from 1783 to 1785 made the situation even worse. Conditions were similar in other states, resulting in the famous rebellion led by Daniel Shays in Massachusetts in 1786–87.[57]

There was so much fear and anger among debtors that it threatened to undermine law, order, and public decency. In Cheraw County, debtors banded together to prevent sheriffs or constables from conducting sales of foreclosed property. In Winton County, a mob destroyed posted notices of sale and then returned to vandalize and set fire to the courthouse. Judges were insulted, robbed, or pelted with cow dung or mud as they traveled their circuits. Sometimes even gentlemen who might be expected to uphold law and order did not, such as Hezekiah Maham, a former Continental officer and hero from the war. When the sheriff in Camden attempted to serve a writ to Maham, the colonel literally forced him to eat it, as well as three others.

In South Carolina, there were several efforts, some successful, to ease the burdens on debtors and inflate the currency. Pickens the backcountry merchant was probably a creditor to at least as many people as he was a debtor to. But also his legalistic mind abhorred a scenario in which contracts and legal obligations meant nothing. He opposed a plan to issue a paper currency backed by unsold lots in the new capital city. He also voted against a pro-debtor initiative that his fellow Ninety Six delegates largely supported. In 1783 the legislature had approved a depreciation table that prevented debtors from paying off loans with worthless paper money.[58] When there was an attempt to repeal that safeguard for creditors in 1787, Pickens opposed it. He did support giving debtors additional time, however. He also supported giving planters more time to recover from the crop failures and backed the Installment Act, which gave debtors three years to repay debts contracted before January 1, 1787. However, he opposed this measure until it was amended to ban the importation of slaves for three years. In this vote, Pickens was aligned with lowcountry legislators who felt the slave trade needed to be temporarily closed to prevent worsening the debt crisis. In contrast, Pickens's upcountry colleagues, many of them aspiring planters, hoped to keep it open. Pickens did not wish to be an enabler to irresponsible debtors seeking to delay payment of their obligations so that they could incur more.[59]

Soon many of Pickens's fellow citizens began coming around to his more conservative views and worrying that overprotection of debtors could become unhealthy. In February 1787, seventy-eight "Freeholders and Inhabitants" from Ninety Six District petitioned the legislature to cease interfering in the creditor-debtor relationship. The Sheriff's Sale Act, in particular, they complained, "Affords . . . Easy Means for dishonest men to defraud their Just Creditors."[60] A year later, there was a proposal in the General Assembly to extend the terms of the Installment Act so that debtors now had seven years, rather than three, to pay off their loans. Pickens led the Ninety Six delegation in opposing the scheme.[61]

The struggles between creditors and debtors pointed to one of the greatest underlying fears of the Revolutionary generation: that a republic devoted to individual liberty might not also be able to ensure order. Without the respect for lawful authority that allowed civil society to function, liberty itself could not long survive. Pickens fought against efforts to weaken the jurisdiction and powers of tax collectors.[62] In the January 1786 session, Governor William Moultrie reported to the legislature that threats and violence had been offered to the sheriff's deputy in Charleston as he had attempted to perform his duties. The house appointed Pickens chair of a committee to study the problem and make recommendations. This was one case in which Pickens stood and announced his committee's report himself, and he made his own position abundantly clear: "It is the opinion of your Committee that Resistance to the Execution of the Laws tends to the Subversion of all Order in the Community and to the Total Annihilation of that mutual Support, Freedom and Happiness, which are the Great Objects of all good Government, That it is therefore a Crime against the State of a most Atrocious and alarming nature." Pickens recommended that the governor be authorized to spend any funds necessary to help the sheriff overcome all violent opposition. Moreover, the legislature should "strongly recommend to the good Citizens of this State to perform their Obligations to the Community by lending all possible Assistance to the Civil Officers whenever it shall be found necessary to call upon them for it."[63]

When Pickens had first taken his seat in the General Assembly in January 1783, most of his fellow citizens knew only his reputation as a military officer. Tidewater aristocrats who did not know him well would have perceived him as one of the rough backcountry men who had clawed his way to prominence due to native ability and hard fighting. Within a few years, though, he was known also as a businessman, religious and educational leader, and practical legislator. He was an important player in the 1780s as South Carolinians attempted to reestablish social order in the wake of civil war, Tory-Whig bitterness, sectional rivalries, and economic chaos. But while war-weary legislators and governors attempted to solidify the internal structure of the state, there were still very real threats that could be met only with military readiness and external diplomacy. Beyond the Keowee and Savannah Rivers lay the Cherokees—defeated, sullen, but still capable of retaliation—and the Creeks, who were as formidable as they had been before the war. Throughout the decade, reports of Indian-white murders and massacres and rumors of impending war disturbed the new state. Besides tensions with the Indians, there were border disputes with the neighboring states of North Carolina and Georgia, and the Confederation government in Philadelphia lacked the power to solve these problems alone. Pickens's fellow citizens needed him to be a legislator, judge, and church elder. But they still might need him to be a soldier as well.

TWELVE

General Pickens, Indian Treaty Commissioner

The Hatchet shall be forever buried.

Hopewell treaty, November 23, 1785

On February 26, 1783, the General Assembly voted to award Andrew Pickens a gold medal for his "great, glorious, and meritorious conduct in the service of this country."[1] This was certainly a grand honor for a functionally literate man from the backcountry with no aristocratic pedigree. It was not, however, a "good-bye" token of thanks for someone retiring from military service. The same session of the legislature turned to Pickens's military expertise to put down gangs of Tory bandits. Although Pickens had resigned his commission as a brigadier general of South Carolina militia shortly after the end of the war, the state's governors and the General Assembly continued to rely on him throughout the 1780s for military advice and for recruiting and organizing the regiments in the western part of the state. He was retired in name only and remained one of the most trusted military authorities in South Carolina. As a general, though, he would be expected to master diplomacy as well as he had war. Even as Pickens's contemporaries trusted him to oversee military readiness on the frontier, the legislature also turned over management of Indian affairs to him in the hopes that he could reestablish commercial ties with the tribes and, most of all, preserve the peace. Thus, Pickens the general was to become the state's leading Indian diplomat; yet Pickens the diplomat was never to cease being a general.[2]

Military victory over Britain did not magically usher in an age of peace and stability. British troops evacuated Charleston on December 14, 1782.

Months and even years later, backcountry residents still complained of roaming gangs of bandits (usually identified as Tories) who robbed travelers and homesteads. Much like the aftermath of the Cherokee War, military victory left social chaos in its wake—"it was the 1760s all over again," says historian Walter Edgar. As Ninety Six District judge Aedanus Burke complained, "No man has security for even a worthless plow horse. . . . As to Trade and commerce it is at an end in that District unless the Government take some measures for extirpating the outlyers."[3] There is much evidence that diehard Tories were the cause of much of the crime and that prominent Revolutionary leaders were special targets. Pickens himself would not escape damage. In 1786, he lost four wagonloads of goods to a gang of six highway robbers.[4]

While the 1783 legislature was still in session, word arrived that William "Bloody Bill" Cunningham had gone on another rampage through the interior of the state. The General Assembly authorized Pickens to raise a company of rangers that would serve an enlistment of six months in an effort to track Cunningham down.[5] This was not an isolated incident. Throughout the decade, governors and general assemblies in South Carolina would turn to Pickens to mobilize militia companies, organize companies into regiments, procure supplies and ordnance, and be ready to quell disturbances.

The defeat of Britain obviously established the independence of the United States, but it left most of the key issues on the southern frontier unsettled. In fact, the removal of British authority and the end of the war left a power vacuum that the Confederation Congress was too weak to fill, creating a situation that was more complex than ever. One problem was boundary disputes among the newly independent states. In the spring of 1784, it became clear that both Georgia and South Carolina claimed the area between the Keowee and Tugaloo Rivers in the upper reaches of the Savannah River system. Imprecise wording in Georgia's colonial charter was partly to blame, but Georgia's determination to begin making land grants in the area deeply concerned Pickens. Pickens was then in the process of acquiring his Hopewell tract on the eastern bank of the Keowee, just outside the boundary of what Georgia claimed. The area claimed by Georgia had been previously reserved by South Carolina for its Continental army veterans and was part of what South Carolina had acquired from the Cherokees in the Treaty of Dewitt's Corner in 1777. After hearing rumors of Georgia's intentions, Pickens traveled to Augusta to speak personally with Georgia officials and learned that they were determined to go through with granting the lands.

Meanwhile, a number of Cherokee headmen had come to Pickens that spring and complained to him of the behavior of white settlers and traders in the region. With no British (or Congress-appointed) superintendent of Indian affairs to regulate Indian-white relations, friction was building. Pickens informed South Carolina governor Benjamin Guerard in April that unscrupulous traders and violent white men from the Carolinas and Georgia were going among the Cherokees and causing disturbances and disputes. The Cherokees disliked the sight of whites settling in their old towns in far northwestern South Carolina. Most conceded that they had given up this land in the 1777 treaty, but some Cherokee leaders claimed they had not been consulted in that decision, and besides, white settlements were appearing on land that the Cherokees had not ceded. Specifically, the Cherokees warned Pickens that Colonel Benjamin Cleveland had taken possession of a tract of land on the Tugaloo River, west of the Keowee. Nearly 100 families from North Carolina, under the auspices of the state of Georgia, had come with him and settled in this disputed Keowee-Tugaloo area.[6]

Pickens himself was satisfied that South Carolina had legal authority by right of conquest and treaty to settle the land but that North Carolina and Georgia did not—nor did any whites have the right to encroach upon Indian land that had not been granted by treaty. This legalistic approach typified his approach to Indian-white relations throughout his career. Pickens's letter to Governor Guerard suggests that the Cherokees were as disturbed as Pickens by the growing anarchy; they were, he said, "very uneasey and much alarmed." He urged that South Carolina take action immediately: "Unless some Measures are fell on to settle the boundary between Georgia and this state—I fear Carolina will Repent the Delay—their are a grait many Disorderly persons goes up amongst the Indians and Creates uneasiness amongst those people." Pickens urged new regulations forbidding anyone to travel or trade among the Cherokees without obtaining a license and giving security for himself and his "hirelings." Such regulations would "graitly add to the security and safety of the Frounteers of this state."[7]

With the legislature not in session, Governor Guerard showed the letter to his privy council and asked what action should be taken. With regard to Georgia, the officials in Charleston were fairly proactive. Pickens was to "warn off" Cleveland and the other settlers from South Carolina's land until the boundary dispute with Georgia could be resolved.[8] Meanwhile, Robert Anderson, the state's "commissioner of location," was to begin granting lands to South Carolina veterans and others as provided for by the legislature. Over the next few years, Georgia and South Carolina issued a series

General Pickens, Indian Treaty Commissioner

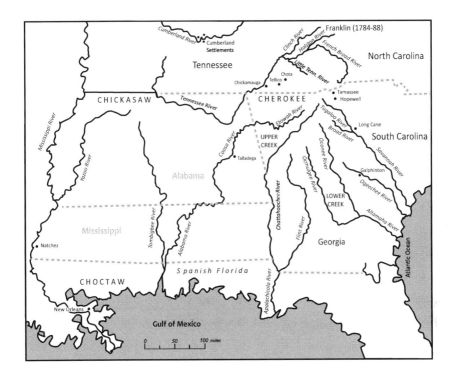

Indian Country *(Map by Chris Cartledge)*

of protests, proclamations, and caveats against each other. South Carolina petitioned Congress in 1785 for help in resolving the dispute, but the national body did not act.[9] In the end, both states appointed commissioners to resolve the dispute, and Pickens was a member of the South Carolina delegation. The commission met in Beaufort, South Carolina, in April 1787 and reached a compromise: South Carolina retained control over the region between the Tugaloo and the Keowee, while Georgia retained control over another chunk of land south of the Altamaha River, to which South Carolina had made a specious claim. It seems that it was shortly after this conference that Pickens finally moved his family to the Hopewell tract on the Keowee, and the settlement of the Pendleton area began in earnest. The following August, Congress ratified the agreement reached between the two states.[10]

While South Carolina leaders acted decisively enough in the border dispute with Georgia, Governor Guerard and his council had punted on the parts of Pickens's letter that dealt with the Cherokees, deciding that only Congress had jurisdiction in matters concerning the Indians. This position was logical enough. The Articles of Confederation gave Congress "exclusive right and power" in "managing all affairs with the Indians." However, this "exclusive power" was contradicted with an important caveat—"provided that the legislative right of any State within its own limits be not infringed or violated."[11] Otherwise, the Articles generally gave Congress authority to handle matters of war and diplomacy. Moreover, by the Treaty of Paris, Britain ceded the land east of the Mississippi to the United States as a whole, not to individual states—the land unsettled by whites was, arguably, the collective domain of the nation.[12]

Yet the Treaty of Paris also created profound contradictions that bedeviled relations between the Indians and the new American republic for decades to come. The Indians understandably questioned Britain's right to cede their tribal lands to anyone. The tribes, especially those that had fought and suffered in the British cause, felt deeply betrayed. Chief Little Turkey of the Cherokees denounced the Treaty of Paris with the claim that "the peacemakers and our Enemies have talked away our Lands at a Rum Drinking."[13] The powerful Creek leader Alexander McGillivray complained that his people had done nothing to justify King George giving away their territory "unless . . . Spilling our best blood in the Service of his Nation can be deemed so."[14] The Cherokees, of course, and to a much lesser extent the Creeks, might reasonably be said to have shared in Britain's military defeat. The Choctaws of modern-day Mississippi and lower Louisiana, however, had played no direct role in the fighting. They too rejected the concept of American sovereignty over their lands and proudly asserted that they had not been defeated by anyone.[15] The same could be said of the Chickasaws of present-day northern Mississippi and western Tennessee.[16]

Well before the ink on the Treaty of Paris was dry, the situation on the southern frontier was becoming explosive. Many white frontiersmen believed they had won a great victory against the twin evils of Indian savagery and British tyranny. The fruit of their victory was, or should be, liberty and freedom from restraint—the right to claim western lands, build homes and farms, and seek profit. The American victory stimulated a voracious appetite for land among Georgia legislators, speculators, and ordinary settlers leading to perpetual conflict with the Cherokees and more so with the Creeks. Farther north, as early as 1781, settlers from North Carolina and Virginia began flooding into the upper Tennessee valley. Some North Carolinians proclaimed the establishment of the autonomous state of Franklin in 1784 in what is now northeastern Tennessee. They proceeded to conclude their own treaty with several Cherokee chiefs—a treaty that they quickly broke and that many Cherokees and other white leaders did not consider valid anyway.[17]

Pickens's concerns over this situation were driven by pragmatism, legality, and morality. Pickens himself, as a backcountry merchant who traded with Indians, stood to profit from peace and stability. His family's and his neighbors' homes were safer without Indian-white misunderstandings. Moreover, South Carolina as a whole could derive no practical benefit from war with the Indians. While Georgians, North Carolinians, and Virginians had hopes of acquiring vast territories to the west, South Carolina could not reasonably expect much more territory than it had acquired in the 1777 treaty at Dewitt's Corner. In the 1780s and 1790s, most South Carolinians' hunger for land seemed to be satisfied by the ability to finally settle the land acquired in 1777. Though there were notable exceptions, wealthy and up-and-coming South Carolinians proved generally more likely to invest in slaves and plantation agriculture than in vast land speculation schemes west of the mountains. Pickens himself was typical of this trend, buying and selling tracts that consisted of hundreds of acres of land rather than tens or hundreds of thousands, and virtually all of his holdings were located within South Carolina itself.[18]

Legally, Pickens and other leading South Carolinians quickly concluded that binding agreements with the Indians could be made only under the auspices of the national Congress. In time, some educated elites would philosophize about the need to "civilize" Indians according to white ways, while others asserted the necessity of destroying the "savages." Both points of view could be used to justify national expansion and the seizure of Indian lands.[19] Pickens, predictably, left no philosophical musings or sophisticated statements supporting either position. However, the entire course of his career illustrated his belief that no whites had the right to cultivate, settle on, or claim Indian land prior to a treaty concluded by legitimate authorities.

This legalistic position was informed both by practicality and ethics. Obviously, a situation in which states, entities like Franklin that claimed to be states, and individual settlers purchased land from chiefs who may or may not have represented the interests of their entire tribe was a recipe for chaos. That was a practical difficulty, but there was also the moral problem of unrestrained human greed. Again and again Pickens's generation of South Carolinians had seen how unscrupulous trading practices and white rapacity had been factors leading to war with the Indians. Pickens expressed few sentimental notions about Indian virtue or innocence. He had seen them commit brutal acts against his own men and family members and believed many of them just as capable of treachery and murder as white men were. There was a moral and practical obligation, however, to treat them with justice and humanity.[20]

Pickens quickly emerged as South Carolina's foremost authority on Indian affairs. Ironically, it was an act of compassion that helped establish the fierce Indian fighter in that role. In the aftermath of the war, the situation of the Cherokees was dire. Though they had been forced to give up millions of acres of land in treaties with the Revolutionary state regimes, their most pressing problem was dire poverty. With villages and food supplies destroyed (some of them by Pickens), they were being devastated by famine and disease, and some bands were almost literally naked. William Christian, a Virginia militia officer who, like Pickens, had wreaked devastation on the Cherokees, found their situation in December 1782 appalling: "The miseries of these people from what I see and hear seem to exceed description; here are men, women & children almost naked; I see very little to cover either sex but some old bear skins . . . their crops this year have been worse than ever was known . . . many are already out [of food supplies], particularly widows and fatherless children, who have no men nearly connected with them."[21]

About this time, Cherokees sent delegations to southern state leaders to plead for emergency relief. Several Cherokee leaders came to Charleston to beg Governor John Mathews for peace and for supplies. Apparently they asked Pickens to intercede as well, and Pickens persuaded the governor and the privy council to provide them with goods at the state's expense. The Indians could pay back later in deerskins. Pickens bought goods worth £200 sterling and had them delivered to the Cherokees, for which he was reimbursed by the state more than a year later. Altogether the state eventually supplied the Cherokees with goods worth over £1,100 sterling.[22] Probably Pickens's contribution was partially a bid to build his own future trading relationships with the Indians. In any event, the Cherokees came to see Pickens in a new light. Since his miraculous escape from them in the legendary 1776 "Ring Fight," the Cherokees had paid respect to Pickens's martial prowess by calling him "Sky-a-gun-sta," often translated either as "Great Warrior" or "Wizard Owl." But his intercession on their behalf in the winter of 1782–83, just a few months after he had destroyed many of their villages, suggested another translation for "Sky-a-gun-sta." In Cherokee lore, "Sky-a-gun-sta" was also a great Indian peacemaker. Pickens had begun his reputation among the Cherokees as a white warrior who could also be reasonable and humane.[23]

South Carolina's lowcountry aristocracy likewise turned to Pickens as an emissary to the Indians. The recommendation of mercy by the state's most respected Indian fighter must have carried weight, as the General Assembly readily approved Mathews's action, and his successor Governor Guerard endorsed it. At the same time that Mathews informed the General Assembly of this decision in late January 1783, he also asked legislators to appoint state commissioners to establish peace and regulate the trade of South Carolinians with the Indians. The legislature appointed a committee to recommend suitable names. Pickens was on the committee, which in turn named Pickens, Robert Anderson, and Simon Berwicke as the commissioners. In August of that year, Governor Guerard asked the legislature to appoint a temporary state superintendent of Indian affairs while it waited for Congress to appoint one. Guerard strongly hinted that Pickens was the right man for the job: "A Person well known by [the Indians], and wou'd be agreeable to the nation, a man of business and honesty withal, wou'd be the most proper." Guerard made the hint unmistakable by then reporting that one of the Cherokee headmen had shown his respect for Pickens by surrendering to him a medal originally given to him by the British so that it could be recast into one symbolizing his new alliance with South Carolina.[24]

As the leading South Carolinian with whom the Indians had to do business, Pickens was well positioned to resume his trading business, now in the form of Andrew Pickens & Company, with new investors, as well as to struggle for long-desired order and stability on the frontier. Attracting investors was easy—John Rutledge, John Lewis Gervais, and John Owen entered into partnership with him in March 1784. Achieving stability was an entirely different matter. As the state's lead Indian negotiator, Pickens initially hoped for a temporary settlement between South Carolina and the Indians that would suffice until Congress fulfilled its responsibility for a more permanent one.

However, it became more apparent than ever in 1784 and 1785 that little could be accomplished until the national government took the initiative. Cherokee chiefs were complaining to Pickens about white traders and settlers' intrusions; North Carolinians were settling on South Carolina land claiming to own Georgia-issued patents to it—and if South Carolina could not even establish its own claim to the land, how could it regulate the activities of those who settled on it? The establishment of the state of Franklin in December 1784, which embarked on its own Indian policy, only exacerbated the chaos.

Even more ominous was the mounting conflict between Georgia and the Creeks. When Pickens had defeated the Cherokees in the autumn of 1782, they had signed the Treaty of Long Swamp and ceded their claim to land east of the Oconee River in Georgia and west of the Tugaloo branch of the Savannah. Georgia had later confirmed this treaty with the Cherokees. The problem was that the Creeks also claimed this land. At the Treaty of Augusta in November 1783, Georgia persuaded two Creek chiefs to cede the Creek claim to this land. This greatly angered the thirty or so other Creek chiefs, who refused to recognize the treaty. Nevertheless, white settlers began moving into the territory.

Confronting the Creeks brought white negotiators into contact with Alexander McGillivray, who styled himself the leading Creek chief of a Creek "nation." McGillivray, born in 1750, was the son of a Creek woman and a Scottish merchant in Georgia, Lachlan McGillivray. He had spent much of his childhood among his mother's people, but his father had also seen to it that he obtained a thorough education. When the Revolutionary War began, Lachlan McGillivray retired to Scotland, leaving his American possessions in the hands of his twenty-five-year-old son, though the state of Georgia confiscated much of his property. Though claiming to be Creek, Alexander McGillivray lived like a white planter and slave owner and built his wealth through trade. He was closely connected with the English trading firm Panton, Leslie, & Company, the primary vehicle through which Spain tried to monopolize Indian commerce in the Old Southwest. Though McGillivray had great wealth and influence, other Creeks did not recognize him as their leader as fully as he declared; his claim to represent a unified Creek nation-state was untrue. Still, he put himself forward to American leaders as the Creek chief with whom they must deal. He was a wily negotiator and more fluent in written English than many white Americans with whom he sparred, including Pickens.[25]

Though McGillivray was often self-serving, he had a sincere desire to protect Creek interests in the 1780s. The war had left a legacy of bitterness and retaliation between Creeks and white South Carolinians and Georgians, and the latter especially craved Creek lands, squatting on territory that Creeks thought still belonged to them. Creek warriors responded with violence, which brought retaliation in kind. Any general war between Georgia and the Creeks threatened to involve South Carolina, and in fact violence between the two races occasionally spilled over into that state as well. More concerning to the national government was the fact that the situation could easily lead to a war with Spain—still

General Pickens, Indian Treaty Commissioner

the master of Florida and the Gulf Coast—and this was a conflict that the infant United States certainly could not afford.

By 1785, Congress was finally ready to act. In March, the national body appointed commissioners to negotiate a treaty with the Cherokees and other southern Indian tribes. The treaty commission as finally constituted consisted of Pickens from South Carolina, Benjamin Hawkins of North Carolina, Joseph Martin of Virginia, and Lachlan McIntosh of Georgia.

Benjamin Hawkins was the son of a prosperous tobacco planter and had served in his state's legislature and the Confederation Congress. Educated at Princeton, he conversed well in French and was a fluent writer in English. He had also studied Indian languages at Princeton and was taken with the idea of assisting the Indians' "progress" in white ways of agriculture and manufacturing. He was probably responsible for the final composition of most of the letters that the commissioners wrote collectively to the Indians or to white officials. Humane and dedicated to the welfare of the Indians as he saw it, he would later settle and live for two decades among the Creeks as the U.S. agent to them. Around the time of the Hopewell treaties he informed McGillivray that he hoped to settle among the Creeks one day as a friend and asked the Creek chief to help him find a Creek wife, "a young damsel, out of one of your most reputable families . . . handsome and agreeable, skilled in the customs of her own Country."[26] Hawkins and Pickens came to share a mutual respect; for seventeen years, they would remain partners in their efforts to maintain peace with the Indians.[27]

Joseph Martin was the son of a Virginia planter, but most of his life had been one of adventure on the frontier. During the war he had fought the Indians as a Virginia militia officer but had also engaged in important negotiations with them that had temporarily neutralized the Cherokees' strategic threat to the Carolinas and Virginia in 1780. He was heavily involved in speculating in western lands but would show enough consideration of the Indians during his career to earn the enmity of many whites who were more eager for the Indians to be pushed aside. Several letters from Cherokee chiefs indicate that they saw him as a friend. Pickens would work alongside Martin in Indian diplomacy for several years. The two men seemed to get along well, though Pickens probably disapproved of much of his behavior. While Martin seemed committed to peace and justice on the frontier, he had a reputation as a gambler and a brawler. He was also a bigamist, having taken a Cherokee wife. Several years previously, Martin had married Betsy Ward, the mixed-race grandniece of the powerful chief Attakullakulla. This strategic marriage undoubtedly assisted Martin in his diplomacy and may

Benjamin Hawkins
(Courtesy Georgia Archives, Vanishing Georgia Collection, bib026)

well have saved his life during times of white-Indian tension when he was among the Cherokees. Martin's first and second legal wives both knew of this adulterous relationship (which produced a son) but accepted it. Such relationships between Indian women and white frontiersmen, particularly traders, were not uncommon but almost certainly would not have met approval from the moralistic Pickens. Martin's white son William Martin would later become a close friend of Pickens.[28]

Georgia rice planter and Revolutionary War general Lachlan McIntosh was the fourth member of the commission. McIntosh's views were somewhat closer to the extreme states' rights position of his own state.[29] However, McIntosh's role seems to have been relatively uncontroversial, and in any event he played the least prominent part in the negotiations. Overall, as Clyde Ferguson points out, "a body of men, better aware of frontier interests combined with a predilection to give the Indian justice, did not exist in America."[30] It was clear that, as a group, they believed that bad white men were just as responsible for insecurity on the frontier as the Indians were. In June 1785 they would inform North Carolina governor Richard Caswell that the Creeks had offered to help the Cherokees "repel any attempt that may be made by the disorderly Citizens of the United States on their property." They also warned Caswell that former Tories, white men who were still enemies of America, were fomenting much of the trouble: "the disaffected, disorderly white people among them, who have been inimical to us during the last war, are now industrious in their endeavors to prevail on the Indians to commence hostilities against us."[31] Thus, the frontiersmen moving onto the Indians' lands were not freedom-loving and patriotic, they argued, but rather "disorderly," "disaffected," and tainted with treason.

The commissioners' charge from Congress was to conclude a treaty or treaties with the southern Indians to "make peace with them and receiv[e] them into our favour and protection and removing as far as may be all causes of future contention or quarrels."[32] The commissioners were to assemble in Charleston on May 16 and fix a place and time for the treaty negotiations. In inviting the tribes to meet with them, their tone was to be that of magnanimous victors. Congress directed the commissioners to officially inform the Indians of America's victory in the Revolution and of the fact that Britain had granted the United States the land east of the Mississippi and to demand the return of all persons and property they had taken during the war. They were also to inform the states of Virginia, North Carolina, South Carolina, and Georgia of the time and place of the treaty so that they could send their own state-appointed representatives if they wished.[33]

Congress then directed the southern commissioners to strike a triumphant pose with the Indians south of the Ohio River. Congress's instructions, however, left room for a far more magnanimous treaty than the earlier ones recently concluded with the northern Indians. The first treaties between the new United States and Indian tribes took place at Fort Stanwix, New York, in October 1784 and Fort McIntosh, Pennsylvania, in January 1785, and they reflected the view that the Indians were conquered peoples who had little right to refuse American demands for land. During the negotiations, U.S. treaty commissioners insisted on large swaths of territory in what is now Ohio and western Pennsylvania. When Iroquois, Delaware, Chippewa, and Wyandot Indians objected, the white negotiators arrogantly and "in a high tone" reminded them that they were defeated peoples.[34] Further emphasizing white superiority, the commissioners demanded and received Indian hostages as a guarantee that white and black prisoners of the Indians would be returned.

So far that approach had not worked well. The treaties provoked great resentment among the Indians, including many who were not present and refused to recognize them. The Confederation government, meanwhile, had scarce military resources with which to enforce them. In the South, such an approach was even less promising. The southern tribes—Cherokees, Creeks, Choctaws, and Chickasaws—were larger and more unified than the northern ones. Aside from the Cherokees, they had suffered few losses from the war and had no reason to concede that they had been "defeated." Moreover, state land claims complicated the situation in the South. Virginia and the northern states had ceded their western land claims north of the Ohio River to the national government. The southern states, however, had not ceded their claims south of the Ohio, complicating any provisions whereby the Indians might cede land to Congress—land that Georgia, North Carolina, or Virginia still claimed for themselves. And, in appointing Pickens, Hawkins, and Martin as negotiators, Congress had selected men who were not inclined to demand large concessions from the Indians anyway, as long as peace and order could be restored on the frontier.

The clumsiest part of Congress's plan for the southern treaty was that the four southern states were asked to contribute funds for it. Traditionally, holding treaties with the Indians meant that the whites were to serve both as hosts and gift-givers. The chiefs and their retinues had to be fed, and they expected gifts of food, alcohol, guns, ammunition, and other goods. The Indians would bring less expensive gifts as well, but everyone

General Pickens, Indian Treaty Commissioner

understood that gifts were necessary to grease the wheels of diplomacy. The entire treaty enterprise in the South in 1785 nearly failed due to the states' reluctance to contribute. Pickens's own state initially supplied only £200 of the amount requested of her; not until October did the legislature reluctantly and belatedly approve the remainder of its quota, making a total contribution equivalent to $3,000. North Carolina and Virginia supplied nothing until August; Georgia, angry that Congress was usurping its role in settling with the Creeks, provided no funds at all. Even as Georgia officials stubbornly refused to contribute, Creek raiding parties were attacking Georgia settlers.[35]

Clearly the most urgent task was to bring the Creeks to terms. On June 10, 1785, Hawkins, Pickens, and Martin wrote a letter to the "Kings Headmen and Warriors of the Creeks." They invited Creek leaders to meet with them at Galphinton, Georgia, on the Ogeechee River. The United States, they asserted, "are a great and wise Nation they have a great many Warriors, and have Conquered all their Enemys, and are now desirous of peace with all the World. They remember you were once their friends and they intend to forget that you were their enemies in the Last War. But you must forget it also, and we will take you by the hand."[36] On the same day, the commissioners wrote to the state governors as well, informing them of the Galphinton location and repeating their request for funds.[37] (The commissioners also began making plans to meet later with the Cherokees, Choctaws, and Chickasaws at Pickens's Hopewell plantation.)

Neither the Creeks nor the state of Georgia responded enthusiastically. Governor Samuel Elbert of Georgia was busy trying to get a few Creek leaders to confirm the 1783 cession east of the Oconee River, providing it with a few more shreds of legality, and feared that the new commission sent by Congress would interfere. He delayed answering the commissioners until July 20 and dishonestly claimed that he did not receive their letter until July 5. Though Georgia was asked to provide the smallest contribution for the treaty, $2,000, he claimed that the legislature would not approve it.[38]

For his part, McGillivray, the Creek leader, assumed that the pushy Georgians were in cahoots with Congress's commissioners—that the latter intended to support Georgia's claims. On July 24, Pickens wrote McGillivray personally. The general tried to assure McGillivray of Congress's benign intentions. He also had to apologize, though, for not being able to set a date yet for the Galphinton conference. Shamefacedly he had to admit that the states had not yet provided or promised enough funds to make the meeting possible.[39]

McGillivray did not respond until September 5. His response, though, showed that he was a master negotiator. McGillivray had already begun playing a double game with the Spanish and the Americans. He kept Spanish officials informed of Congress's overtures, hinting that the Creeks might accommodate the Americans unless they could be sure of Spanish support. With the possibility of American support, McGillivray tried to persuade Spain that it must offer better trade terms and lower taxes, or else the Creeks might ally with the Americans instead.[40] To Pickens, however, McGillivray emphasized that the Creeks could count on Spanish support if they were pushed too hard by the Americans. In fact he expressed surprise that the Americans, especially the Georgians, had not gone out of their way to placate the Creeks immediately after the Treaty of Paris. As for the information in the commissioners' letter that the treaty had given the United States all the land east of the Mississippi, he indignantly asserted that no British or American diplomats in Paris had the right to sign away Creek hunting grounds, "which have been ours since the beginning of time." Though the Creeks had sent raiding parties to remove white settlers from the disputed lands "in the most peaceable manner possible," he promised to suspend these raids as an indicator of good faith. The Creeks, he said, "want nothing from you but justice," and he was confident that with Spanish help, they could defend their lands "against every attempt to take them from us." Despite the defiant tone, McGillivray indicated that he and his chiefs would be glad to meet with Congress's commissioners anytime "in expectation that every Matter of Difference will be made up and settled, with that Liberality and Justice, worthy [of] the Men who have so gloriously asserted the Cause of Liberty and Independency, and that we shall in future consider them as Brethren and Defenders of the Land."[41]

The letter was a masterpiece. Besides illustrating the ability to employ American Revolutionary rhetoric (such as "Liberty and Independency"), McGillivray portrayed himself as a man equally dedicated to peace and the just claims of "his" people. Parts of it contained a frankness and self-assertion that sounded much like Pickens himself. On the other hand, Pickens might have wondered about McGillivray's statement that he had not received the letter until recently; and the Creek leader's claim that the recent raids had been as "peaceable" as possible sounded less than sincere. Most of all, though, Pickens and the other American leaders had come to see McGillivray as the Creek with whom they must deal, and that was convenient since he was so fluent in the language of white diplomacy.

Meanwhile, Pickens also continued to communicate with Georgia's Governor Elbert, and the two of them agreed that Georgia would provide a mounted guard of twenty men and one officer. In all other respects Elbert deliberately worked to sabotage the treaty efforts. He sent messages to Creek leaders with false claims that Congress was seeking to confirm the cessions that Georgia claimed it had received in 1783. His efforts were well calculated to undermine Creek support for negotiations with the federal Congress.[42]

By the time Pickens and the other delegates assembled at Galphinton between October 24 and 28, they had overcome numerous financial and logistical obstacles. Even after finally being able to purchase supplies and gifts for the treaty, Pickens had had great difficulty procuring wagons to transport them.[43] Another potential complication had arrived in Georgia in the form of William Blount, the state agent appointed by North Carolina. Blount was a prominent tidewater planter and politician and currently North Carolina's representative in the Confederation Congress. His younger brother, Major Reading Blount, had served with the North Carolina Continentals at the battle of Eutaw.

Under William Blount's leadership, he and his brothers had invested heavily in land west of the North Carolina mountains. Some of this land had been formally claimed by North Carolina, and some of it had been purchased in private deals between land speculators like Blount and individual Indians. Blount was naturally very concerned that any federal treaty with the Indians might prevent white settlement of this land and his ability to profit from his investment. Moreover, Blount was charged by his own state to ensure that no federal treaty violated North Carolina's Land Act of 1783, by which it legally opened much of its Tennessee territory to settlement. For the time being, Blount was far more interested in the Cherokees, while the commissioners' most pressing concern was the Creeks. North Carolina had provided funds for Blount to conclude a separate state treaty later with the Cherokees, though Blount's supplies for doing so had not yet arrived.[44]

Pickens and Hawkins's goals were directly opposed to Blount's and the Georgians'. The federal agents told Blount that they would not try to prevent him making a separate treaty with the Cherokees, but they stood their ground on key points. First, the Indians, they believed, were "free and Independent People and the sole Proprietors of the soil" until they chose to relinquish it.[45] Second, now that the British king was no longer the protector and guardian of Indian rights, that role was now vested in Congress. While waiting for the Creeks to assemble, the treaty commissioners began drafting a document that would confirm those principles. If concluded, a treaty based on those principles would be a blow to the states' rights claims of Georgia and North Carolina and a personal disaster for many land speculators, including Blount. Georgia's state Indian commissioners penned a formal protest before negotiations could even begin. Blount, confronted with Hawkins's articulate logic, Pickens's taciturn firmness, and the authority vested in them by Congress, could do little for the time being but stay in Georgia to observe the proceedings with the Creeks—and hope that his supplies arrived at Hopewell soon so that he could deal with the Cherokees before the federal agents could.[46]

The attempt to conclude a treaty at Galphinton was a disaster from Pickens's point of view. Only about eighty Creeks from two towns showed up, leaving the rest of the towns—the commissioners believed about a hundred—unrepresented. McGillivray was also notably absent. At first the Creeks present informed the commissioners that messengers were summoning the other Creeks and that they could be expected shortly. Soon, though, the commissioners learned that someone—they suspected both McGillivray and the Spanish—had sent "false reports . . . through the nation, which had created jealousies among them, and discouraged them from coming to meet us."[47] McGillivray would later claim that he had not received final word on the place and date of the meeting with the commissioners. In reality, McGillivray had extracted a promise of Spanish support in case the United States attacked the Creeks; in return, he promised the Spanish not to meet the American commissioners at Galphinton.[48] The federal commissioners had been thwarted by the treachery and obstinacy of almost everyone involved. Profoundly disappointed, they gave gifts to the few Creeks who were present, told them they could not conclude a meaningful treaty with such a small part of the nation, and departed. The very next day, a state delegation from Georgia concluded a treaty with this minority faction, giving them gifts for another large cession of land that the rest of the Creeks had no intention of honoring. Now there was another phony treaty that would lead to more recriminations and bloodshed. Thus, despite all of Pickens's efforts, the situation with the Creeks was, if anything, more dangerous than before. In fact, the commissioners now had information that convinced them that McGillivray was "forming a dangerous confederacy between the several Indian nations, the Spaniards, and British agents, with whom he is connected."[49]

With such a conspiracy to unite the Indians supposedly brewing, it was all the more important to conclude a treaty with the Cherokees,

General Pickens, Indian Treaty Commissioner

Chickasaws, and Choctaws, who so far seemed willing to talk. The commissioners therefore repaired to the designated place to meet them—Pickens's new Hopewell tract on the Keowee. (The place was also known as Seneca because of its being adjacent to the old Cherokee village of Esseneca, one of the places where Pickens had fought the Cherokees in 1776.) Blount followed the federal commissioners, still hoping his supplies would arrive at Seneca in time for him to first make his own state treaty with the Cherokees. Unfortunately for him, they did not.

Pickens, Hawkins, Martin, and McIntosh arrived at Hopewell on November 18 and Blount soon after. On the twenty-first, they were joined by a vast throng of more than 900 Cherokees, far more than they had planned for. The commissioners had invited only the chiefs of Cherokee towns. Many of the chiefs, however, had brought young warriors as well as wives and children with them, fearing that "disorderly people" from the state of Franklin would attack them in their absence.[50]

The next day, the commissioners delivered their opening address to the Cherokees, with Hawkins apparently doing most of the actual speaking. The white commissioners and the Cherokee chiefs who met at Hopewell had much more at stake than the establishment of boundaries and the cessation of hostilities. Both sides wished their counterparts to see them as worthy of leadership. For their part, the white commissioners believed that their status as gentlemen, the legitimacy of their leadership, and the honor of the new Republic they represented rested largely on their ability to persuade the Indians that they were men of justice and humanity. They were the victors, of course, in the late war, a war in which the Cherokees had chosen a "bad" cause when they had sided with the king of Great Britain, and they claimed the authority entrusted in them by a great nation. The Indians were now dependents, or wards, of the United States, as Congress now had "sovereignty over this land." But they took pains to show the Indians that they were worthy of that authority. The commissioners themselves were men of self-control and goodwill rather than brutality and vindictiveness. And Congress, they said, would receive the Cherokees into its "favor and protection." To demonstrate their benevolence, they invited the Indians to present any grievances they had and to "speak their minds freely," so that they could take proper measures to redress them "as may be proper." It was an attempt, as historian Andrew Cayton has documented concerning other early treaty negotiations, to combine "power" with "civility." Expressing a desire for peace, they hoped to receive them "into the favor and protection of the United States." Now that the United States had replaced the British king as the new sovereign power in the region, the commissioners asserted that "we sincerely wish you to live as happily as we do ourselves, and to promote that happiness as far as is in our power, regardless of any distinction of color, or of any difference in our customs, our manners, or particular situation." Most stunning to the Cherokees, the commissioners did not demand any new land cessions: "Congress . . . want none of your lands, or any thing else which belongs to you." At the end of this address, the commissioners invited the Cherokees to reflect on what they had told them and meet with them the next day.[51]

The journal kept by the commissioners suggests that the remainder of the negotiations proceeded at the same measured pace. Most whites considered Cherokees to be grave, deliberate, and thoughtful in their speech.[52] Indeed, after the commissioners and chiefs assembled on November 23, everyone waited for a highly respected chief named The Tassel of Chota, also known as Corn Tassel or Old Tassel, to speak first. "After sitting some time in silence," The Tassel addressed the commissioners in what apparently was the longest speech by any Indian at the treaty. His speech, as well as those of other chiefs later, indicated that Cherokee leaders also wanted to be seen as sincere and trustworthy, as men (and women) who desired peace and who would do everything within reason to preserve it.[53] At the same time, as the original occupants of the land, they had a right to be treated with respect and consideration. As The Tassel asserted, "the red people are the aborigines of this land," and the "great man above" had made it "for us to subsist on."[54] The Cherokees were willing to acknowledge the leadership role that the commissioners claimed for themselves and for the Congress of the new United States. But that meant that they also had the right to enjoy the protection that such leadership entailed. Like Old Tassel, the chiefs Unsuckanail, Chescoenwhee, Tuskegatahee, Oonanootee, and Nowota clearly stated that they looked forward to the new government providing them with justice and assistance when cheated by traders or encroached upon by white settlers. As Tuskegatahee said in his last speech, "As I am within the limits of the United States, I shall always expect their protection and assistance."[55]

Meanwhile, the Indians also attempted to mobilize the metaphor, or even the reality, of kinship to smooth Indian-white relations. The second Cherokee leader to speak on the twenty-third was the War Woman of Chota, who brought out a pipe and some tobacco to share with the commissioners. Also known as Nanye-hi or Nancy Ward, the War Woman had received this honored title from her tribe in 1755, when she had distinguished herself in a

General Pickens, Indian Treaty Commissioner

battle against the Creeks, a battle in which her Cherokee husband had died. She had later married a white trader, Bryant Ward, taken his name, learned English, and borne a mixed-race daughter named Betsy. It was this Betsy who was the Cherokee wife of Joseph Martin. Nancy Ward had the rank of "beloved woman," giving her the authority to participate in tribal councils and treaty negotiations, and she had long been an advocate of finding ways to live peaceably with the white people. She expressed her pleasure that the commissioners wanted peace: "I have seen much trouble during the late war. I am old, but hope yet to bear children, who will grow up and people our nation, as we are now under the protection of Congress, and shall have no more disturbance."[56] The War Woman was forty-seven years old when she spoke at Hopewell. She probably was not hoping for more biological children of her own but rather envisioning a "more encompassing conception of kinship" between whites and Indians.[57] Besides, she had something of an actual kinship tie with one of the commissioners to whom she was speaking, Joseph Martin. The other chiefs at times appeared to be capitalizing on this connection, as when The Tassel and Tuskegatahee asked that Martin be specifically empowered to find and return several Cherokee captives.[58]

Along with the broad principles of civility, authority and protection, and kinship, there were specific details to iron out. Like the chiefs who spoke later, The Tassel was pleasantly surprised that the commissioners did not come to ask for more land: "I was very much pleased at the talk you gave us yesterday; it is very different from what I expected when I left home." Given the chance to complain of grievances, however, The Tassel had several. They mostly centered on white encroachments in modern-day Tennessee and Kentucky, on lands the Cherokees had not ceded in any treaty. Probably in Blount's hearing, he stated that "they, the people of North Carolina, have taken our lands for no consideration, and are now making their fortunes out of them." The Tassel said his people would be satisfied with payment for those lands that had already been settled, "but we will not, nor cannot, give up any more."[59]

Over the course of the next several days other chiefs spoke as well, but the core of the Cherokee position emerged in the speeches of Old Tassel. He disputed the legitimacy of a past purchase that encompassed large parts of Kentucky and north-central Tennessee in the area of Nashville. In 1775, Richard Henderson and a group of North Carolina speculators had purchased this tract of some 27,000 square miles. Ever since that purchase, Cherokee leaders had claimed that they were deceived as to what they were

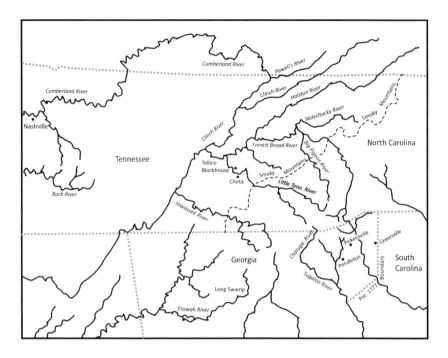

The U.S.-Cherokee Frontier *(Map by Chris Cartledge)*

signing. At Hopewell, The Tassel said that Richard Henderson was "a rogue and a liar, and if he was here I would tell him so."[60] The commissioners insisted there was nothing they could do about the matter. Both Henderson and the Cherokee chiefs who had signed the agreement were dead, and the deeds clearly gave the lands in question to the purchasers. Moreover, thousands of whites had already settled on the land, and the commissioners knew it would be politically and practically impossible to remove them. The Tassel eventually was forced to concede and to promise that the Cherokees would accept the white settlers' presence.

The Tassel also strongly protested the presence of some "three thousand souls" living between the forks of the French Broad and Holston Rivers, part of the state of Franklin. The Cherokees considered that land very valuable and too close to their own towns. The commissioners responded that those people were "too numerous to engage to remove." The Tassel then asked, "Are Congress, who conquered the King of Great Britain, unable to remove those people?"[61] The old chief's challenge pointed out an uncomfortable reality. Despite the commissioners' claims about Congress's authority, the Confederation government really did not have the political legitimacy or even the military capability to evict 3,000 determined frontiersmen from their homes. Ultimately, it was agreed that the situation of the French Broad–Holstein settlers would be referred to Congress. The commissioners admitted to Richard Henry Lee, president of Congress, that they were at a loss as to how to handle that situation: "[We] see that justice, humanity, and good policy, require that some compensation should be made to the Indians for these lands; but the manner of doing it would probably be difficult." They suggested, however, that Congress could compensate the Indians by raising revenue from those lands and using it to teach the Indians some "useful branches of mechanics. . . . Some of the women have lately learnt to spin, and many of them are desirous that some method should be fallen on to teach them to raise flax, cotton, and wool, as well as to spin and weave it."[62]

Finally, on November 28, the commissioners wrote out a treaty and carefully explained each article, making sure that the Cherokees did not misunderstand any of it. The treaty stated that the Cherokees were now under the protection of the United States, which had the sole right to regulate trade between the two peoples. The new boundaries were described, and the treaty declared, remarkably, that any whites who trespassed those bounds forfeited the protection of the United States—the Indians could punish them as they wished. Moreover, the same applied to any whites who had already settled beyond those boundaries and did not vacate within six months (excluding the settlers between the French Broad and the Holston). All prisoners and property, including "negroes," still held from the late war were to be returned. The Cherokees were to turn over to the United States any of their own people who had committed robbery or a capital crime. Those prisoners would be tried and punished according to American law, and no punishment would be given beyond what would be given a citizen of the United States. If any U.S. citizens committed such crimes, they also would be tried and punished by white authorities, and Cherokees were welcome to witness the punishment being carried out. Both sides condemned retaliation against innocent parties. The Cherokees could send a deputation to Congress whenever they thought necessary. Finally, and most hopefully, the treaty proclaimed, "The Hatchet shall be forever buried . . ."[63]

The Hopewell treaty with the Cherokees was the first formal treaty made between the new United States and any Native American tribe south of the Ohio River. Unlike the preceding treaties of Fort Stanwix and Fort McIntosh north of the Ohio, it demanded no new land cessions, nor did it require the Indians to supply hostages to ensure their good behavior. While much fairer to the Indians, the treaty provoked howls of protest from North

Carolina and Georgia, principally among western settlers, land speculators, and state legislators who decried it as an attack on individual liberties and states' rights. As one twentieth-century historian remarked, it was "an admirable example of how generous a government can be with Indians when lands in question do not belong to that government."[64] Georgia's and North Carolina's legislatures would soon reject the treaties. Blount immediately delivered a formal protest to Pickens and the other commissioners and indeed had warned them in writing even before the treaty was signed not to give away any lands claimed by North Carolina.[65]

Pickens and the other commissioners were fully confident in their authority to conclude the terms they had in the name of Congress. They were aware, however, that the treaty would be impossible to enforce without the cooperation of the states. The commissioners formally acknowledged Blount's protest on the day they received it. Without bothering to address his grievances, they rather insultingly suggested that he, as North Carolina's Indian agent, attempt to enforce the articles dealing with the return of captives. Both to Blount and to Congress, however, the commissioners admitted that the treaty would be ineffective without Georgia's and North Carolina's support.[66]

Nor were Pickens and Hawkins confident about their immediate situation in December. Feeding and providing suitable gifts for 918 Cherokee Indians had used up much of their supplies. McIntosh and Martin went home on December 4, leaving Pickens and Hawkins to conclude any remaining business. The commissioners had expected the Choctaws and Chickasaws to come to Hopewell too and did not know why they had not yet arrived; perhaps the Creeks or Spanish had conspired to keep them away. If the Choctaws and Chickasaws did appear, they would find Pickens and Hawkins low on supplies as well as cash to pay for their military guard. As an economy measure, Pickens and Hawkins dismissed the guard, leaving themselves relatively unprotected. On December 9, however, the two men got word that the Choctaws were on the way and would arrive before the end of the month. Martin received the news and returned to Hopewell; McIntosh was already too far away and would not return.[67]

Eighteen starving, thinly clad Choctaw Indians arrived at Hopewell on December 27. They had been traveling for seventy-seven days. Along the way, the Creeks had misdirected them and tried to steal their horses; they were determined, however, to cement a friendship with the United States. They told the American commissioners that they disliked the Creeks and the Spanish. They had been impressed with the power of the British, and the fact that the United States had defeated the soldiers of the British king

General Pickens, Indian Treaty Commissioner

proved to them that the Americans would be their best protectors. Before negotiations could begin, however, they needed food and clothing. The commissioners gave them U.S. Army coats and other apparel. In fact, they reported, the Choctaws may not even have arrived had the commissioners not sent provisions to them while they were still on the road. About that time, a handful of Chickasaws arrived to announce that the full Chickasaw delegation was on the way as well.

Pickens was relatively familiar with Cherokees and Creeks but had never dealt with Choctaws or Chickasaws. He and his fellow commissioners now had a chance to form their own opinions and biases. They were gratified at how eager the Choctaws were to form an alliance with the United States and judged them to be "honest" and "simple." They reported, however, that that tribe consisted of the "greatest beggars, and the most indolent creatures we ever saw, and yet honest, simple, and regardless of any distress. Their passion for gambling and drinking is very great; we have had instances of them selling blankets at a pint of rum each, and gambling them away, when they had no prospect of replacing them, and knew they must return this winter five hundred miles to their nation with a shirt only."[68]

The Chickasaws made a very different impression. Pickens and his fellow commissioners found them "the most honest and well informed, as well as the most orderly and well governed of any [Indians] we have seen." They were particularly impressed with the sincerity and intelligence one of the chiefs, Piomingo.[69] The treaty commissioners concluded their treaty with the Choctaws on January 3, 1786, and with the Chickasaws on January 10. The terms were very similar to those reached with the Cherokees, and the Indians seemed pleased. The Chickasaws also agreed to allow the United States to establish a trading post at Muscle Shoals on the Tennessee River.[70]

As Hawkins, Martin, and Pickens concluded their business and finally returned to their homes, they must have had a sense of accomplishment. After almost an entire year of effort against great obstacles, they had rendered what they thought was a just settlement between the United States and three of the four major southern tribes. The treaties were faithful to assumptions that they considered the basis of any meaningful agreement: the Indians had the right to land they did not willfully cede in a fair sale or honest treaty; the national government must have ultimate authority over the course of Indian diplomacy; federal treaties with Indians had the force of law among all American citizens; and law must trump the self-aggrandizing desires of individuals and states. Unfortunately, these assumptions did not faithfully describe the real world in which Pickens lived.

THIRTEEN

The Struggle for Peace

I agree there is rogues among us. . . . I am obliged to say there is
some also amongst the Whites, which is the reason that we cant
live as Brotherly as I wish.

Corn Tassel and Hanging Maw to Andrew Pickens,
September 24, 1787

The Treaty of Hopewell with the Cherokees was a respectable accomplishment, but as Andrew Pickens returned home to Long Cane in the spring
of 1786, it was already breaking down. Many whites never acknowledged
its legitimacy and violated it with impunity. The Cherokees had hoped
that regular communication between themselves and white officials would
prevent minor violations and misunderstandings from escalating. Instead,
white encroachment and bad behavior by traders kept tensions high, and
the Cherokees claimed that Congress was neglecting them. In a missive to
Congress, they complained that the treaty was not being honored as "bad
people" were not being removed from their lands and horses were being
stolen. Cherokee chiefs grumbled that "we find your people settle much
faster on our Lands after a treaty than before."[1] Over the summer, war broke
out between several bands of Cherokees and the state of Franklin. A series
of raids and skirmishes finally resulted in a Franklinite victory and Franklin officials forcing a number of Cherokees to sign a "Treaty of Coyatee"
on August 3. In brazen violation of the Treaty of Hopewell, Franklin now
claimed all the lands north of the Little Tennessee River and opened a land
office the following spring. Then, early in 1787, a party of Kentucky militia

killed six men from an unoffending band of the Cherokee tribe's "beloved town" of Chota, with whom Pickens traded.[2]

Desperately trying to stay ahead of the situation, Congress passed an act four days after the Treaty of Coyatee that established two Indian districts, one north and one south of the Ohio River. Each district would have a superintendent who regulated Indian-white interaction and reported to Congress. There would be a fine of $500 for anyone attempting to trade with the Indians without first obtaining a license from the appropriate superintendent of Indian affairs.[3] Dr. James White, a congressman from North Carolina, was eventually appointed superintendent for the southern district, but he had little contact with the Creeks until early 1787. As late as September 1787, the Cherokees complained that they still had no relationship with him. The Cherokees noted that while White was probably a good man and had visited the Creeks, "he has never thought it worth his while as yet to call on our Nation—and we think it is the first place he ought to have called on."[4]

While federal oversight was still far from established, Cherokee and Creek leaders kept in contact with state leaders such as Pickens and Joseph Martin. After the Hopewell treaty, Pickens's formal role at the national level mainly consisted of looking for an opportunity to finally make a treaty with the Creeks. But since he was also South Carolina's state Indian agent and a businessman who traded with the Cherokees as well as the Creeks, he corresponded with leaders of both tribes. In August 1787, Pickens sent a message to the Cherokees demanding an explanation for the murder of a white trader in Cherokee territory, Tom Kades.

Several weeks later Pickens received a joint reply from Corn Tassel, or "The Tassel" or "Old Tassel," and Hanging Maw written in the first person singular, "I." The chiefs' answer reassured Pickens that the Cherokees did not want war, though it warned him that "the Creeks are not for peace." More important, The Tassel and Hanging Maw pointed out how difficult it was going to be for honest leaders like themselves and Pickens and Martin to keep the peace. They pled that they did not know of Kades's murder until recently. They had since learned, though, that Kades was killed because he was a horse thief. Along with several other white men, he had stolen horses from Indians during the previous winter—"Kades was certainly a bad man," the chiefs asserted. They also complained to Pickens of the murders committed by the Kentucky militia. They admitted that an Indian named James Golohorn had stolen horses, "for which agreeable to our agreement we had him killed." In fact, they pointed out, "there is rogues among us & I am sorry I am obliged to say that there is some also amongst the Whites, which is the reason that we cant live as Brotherly as I wish." For this reason, Corn Tassel (or perhaps Hanging Maw) asserted, "I have had new Laws made throughout my Land to punish Rogues very severely, so as to keep peace with you all. I will endeavor to keep my people in order & therefore I hope you also try to keep yours so, that we may live in peace." It seems that the Cherokee headmen saw the problem much as Pickens did—it was a simple matter of man's depravity, or that of some of them. The solution was that good men must make good laws and enforce them.[5]

Pickens kept Governor Thomas Pinckney informed of his diplomacy with the Cherokees. Between August and October, messages went back and forth between the Indian leaders and Pickens and between Pickens and the governor. Several Cherokee headmen visited Hopewell in October, and Pickens reported that "they all profess great friendship, and say they will use their utmost Influence to prevent the Creeks coming this way." Pickens did not believe he could rely fully on that promise, but it was encouraging. "Every thing in my power," he assured Pinckney, "will be done to prevent a War, and to keep the Cherokees and our own Frontiers quiet."[6]

PREVENTING A "GENERAL WAR" WITH THE CREEKS

While Pickens was hopeful he could prevent war with the Cherokees, the Creeks were another matter. Pickens had continued to keep up a correspondence with Alexander McGillivray after the Hopewell treaty. He and Benjamin Hawkins demanded to know why the Creek leader had failed to show up at Galphinton, and then they pretended to accept his excuse. In October 1786, Pickens wrote a very friendly letter to McGillivray. He assured him that Congress's intentions toward the Creeks were still "equal, just, and liberal" but stated that he doubted the sincerity of the Georgians. Pickens also frankly admitted to McGillivray that he believed the latter's claims against Georgia resulting from Georgia's confiscation of his father's estate were "just."[7]

Still, relations between the state of Georgia and the Creeks continued to deteriorate through 1786 and 1787. Robberies, murders, and raids by both sides were frequent. Virtually everyone of both races expected war to break out between Georgia and the Creeks in 1787, despite Superintendent James White's visit to the Creeks in April.[8] Pickens and his neighbors became particularly alarmed when, on September 3, 1787, a small band of Indians believed to be Creeks attacked the home of Samuel Isaacs, a settler on the

Georgia side of the Tugaloo River. Isaacs's thirteen-year-old son was killed and scalped and a woman, a white child, and a black child were taken prisoner. Pickens was in Long Cane at the time, a day's ride to the south. Robert Anderson, though, was near Hopewell and prevented the wholesale flight of settlers on the South Carolina side of the Tugaloo by organizing a number of volunteers and establishing a guard. Anderson immediately informed Pickens, who in turn asked the governor to replace the unpaid volunteers by authorizing a "company of men with a careful officer" and to supply powder and lead. (Later it turned out that Pickens's neighbors on the Keowee pledged to pay the volunteers if the state did not.) He also asked the governor to appoint militia officers and raise two regiments, one north of the Saluda and one to the south, the latter commanded by Anderson. Pickens explained that the danger was great. Tension between Georgia and the Creeks was so high that "I am of opinion an open war must shortly take place between them, so that the frounteers of this State will be very much exposed."[9]

Governor Pinckney immediately authorized Pickens to raise a company of militia and select its captain and appointed him and Anderson as commissioners to "lay off and divide" the new Greenville County into districts for raising companies and organizing a regiment. In the event of a serious attack on the state, the governor authorized Pickens to mobilize any of the militia in his district "without waiting for further instructions." Finally, Pinckney directed Pickens to "demand satisfaction" of the tribe that had committed the murder—he had misunderstood Pickens's report to say that the murder had occurred on the South Carolina side of the river.[10]

Pickens and Anderson mobilized an "Independent Company" under Captain John Norwood, called out the Upper Ninety Six regiment, and organized a new one from Greenville. The regiments were "to hold themselves in readiness on the shortest notice—This I presume will give spirit to the Inhabitants and show the Indians that we are in some measure prepared for them in case they should make an attack on the Inhabitants of our State." Even as Pickens mobilized the troops, he also informed the governor of his talks with the Cherokees and of his hopes that he could prevent war. Having no absolute proof that it was Creeks who committed the murder, he wrote to McGillivray "pointing out to him the impolicy of Indians killing or taking prisoners innocent women and children." He also politely corrected the governor's impression that the attack on the Isaacs family had occurred in South Carolina. Finally, he respectfully reminded the governor that while he was honored to follow his instructions, he was not actually a general anymore and did not want to command the troops:

What your Excellency has intrusted me with in the present instance I will attend to with chearfulness, but I presumed your Excellency had known that I had resigned my command of the Ninety Six Brigade some years past, and my determination never again to assume any command whatever—it is not essential to know my reasons, the[y] are many and with me conclusive. It is vain for me to contend with men whom I have every reason to believe are my real friends; it is useless to say more on the subject, but let me earnestly intreat you to appoint some other person to the command, and not expect it from one who has often declared he never would—I am Dear Sir with real regard and esteem your Excellencys most obedient and very humble servt. Andw. Pickens.[11]

Pickens's plea not to be asked to command the militia was clearly heartfelt. His desire not to "contend" with "friends" suggests that he had profound regard for the Cherokee chiefs whom he had now met several times, traded with, and entertained in his home. Despite the sincerity of his request, Governor Pinckney had no desire to honor it. In his reply of October 31, Pinckney assured Pickens that "I will not give you pain by again urging what seems so incompatible with your determination." In the very next sentence, however, he ordered Pickens to arrange the governor's inspections of each regiment in the brigade.[12] For the next two months, Pickens continued to arrange the inspections and report on military affairs. Pinckney began addressing Pickens as "The Honorable Brigadier General Pickens" and continued to authorize him "to order out such detachments of the militia as may be necessary for the defence of the State, [and] be pleased to inform me frequently of the State of affairs on the Frontiers."[13]

Goaded by the threat of war between Georgia and the Creeks and Spain and between the Cherokees and North Carolina, Congress took action in late October 1787. The states of North Carolina, South Carolina, and Georgia were each to appoint a new treaty commissioner who would work with the superintendent of Indian affairs for the southern tribes to conclude new treaties, with obvious emphasis on the Creeks. Sometime in mid-December, Pickens learned that Governor Pinckney had appointed him to be South Carolina's representative.[14] Long before this commission's work could even begin, Pickens had another reason to write McGillivray. On the night of December 17, seven or eight Indians, again thought to be Creeks, crossed the Tugaloo River into South Carolina. There they killed a man, woman, and child. Another child three months old was wounded

The Struggle for Peace

when the bullet that killed its mother passed through her and struck the child. Men from Captain Norwood's company immediately informed Pickens and went in pursuit. Pickens wrote McGillivray and demanded that the Indians who committed the "barbarous murder" be put to death in the presence of white men appointed by Pickens: "You may rest assured the State will not suffer such unprovoked insults without ample satisfaction."[15]

In the same letter, Pickens informed McGillivray of Congress's establishment of a new treaty commission and the desire for a new treaty the following spring. Thus, with this message, Pickens once again took on the tedious and complex business of trying to arrange a treaty. A key factor in the equation, of course, was McGillivray. Sometime in January or February 1788, Pickens received McGillivray's friendly answer to his October 1787 letter. (The Creek chief apparently had not yet received Pickens's letter about the murders in December.) McGillivray expressed his devotion to principles of humanity, his orders to "his" warriors not to attack South Carolina but only Georgia, and his appreciation to Pickens for acknowledging the justice of his private claim against the state of Georgia.[16]

On February 15, McGillivray finally answered Pickens's letter of December 24. Pickens must have studied the letter closely in an attempt to judge the trustworthiness of his Creek counterpart. McGillivray suggested, first, that Pickens must have been misinformed about the December murders on the South Carolina side of the Tugaloo—the perpetrators must have been Cherokees. The Creek leader testified that he had told his people that they must not attack South Carolina, and "I have no reason to think that I've been disobeyed." Pickens found this alibi possible but not likely. In May, Pickens confided to Governor Pinckney that he still thought the Creeks were the culprits in the murders of December.[17] McGillivray further asserted the generally humane way in which the Creeks had prosecuted the war with Georgia, as opposed to the barbarity of the Georgians, who

> killed an old man and woman whom they flayed . . . partly alive . . .
> at Crooked Creek on the Oconee. A party fell upon a camp of the
> Tallasses a-hunting, of them they kill'd eleven men women &
> children, the pregnant women were ripped open the men's privates
> cut off & put in the women's mouths with other enormities of the
> like nature. . . . It is such abominable actions as these that has stimu-
> lated the Indians to so many cruel but just retalliations.[18]

Pickens, who had been personally affected by Indian cruelty, probably did not accept McGillivray's claims to their superior humanity. On the other hand, he did not doubt his charges about the cruelty of white Georgians, being well aware of the depths of savagery to which white men could sink when fighting Indians. As he wrote Governor Pinckney, there was "two much truth" in McGillivray's charges of white brutality.[19] Thus, Pickens still could not make a conclusive judgment about McGillivray's sincerity. Pickens could not forget McGillivray's behavior during the Galphinton episode, and McGillivray mixed questionable statements of fact with others that could not be denied. As usual, the chief closed his letter with language that sounded honorable and sincere. Expressing a deep desire for peace, he also confidently predicted that the Creeks would fight well and win if they did not receive fair terms. In case war did come, "we should stand justified by the almighty Ruler of the World & all just men for the part we shall then take." As a soldier and a religious man, these were words that Pickens could understand.[20]

In late March, Pickens and Georgia's treaty commission appointee, George Matthews, sent messages to the Creeks by way of George Whitefield. Whitefield was a Creek trader who enjoyed the confidence of both Pickens and McGillivray. They informed the Creeks that Georgia had ceded some of its western claims to Congress, a fact that might influence the negotiations. The two commissioners hinted at the offer of U.S. citizenship to key Creek chiefs such as McGillivray and the principals in the Panton trading firm. They expressed Congress's earnest desire for a just and reasonable peace but also informed the Creeks that Congress was sending "Arms Ammunition and field pieces" to be ready to protect Georgia in case the Indians refused to sign a treaty.[21]

The year 1788 dragged on with little progress toward a Creek treaty, and the obstacles the commissioners faced were similar to those preceding the meetings at Galphinton and Hopewell. North Carolina and Georgia were slow to provide funds, a situation that South Carolina governor Thomas Pinckney found "incomprehensible."[22] North Carolina did not even appoint a commissioner until December 1.[23] White Georgians were as adamant as ever that the land gained by the Augusta and Galphinton treaties was now theirs, while McGillivray steadfastly insisted that negotiations could not even begin until the pre-1783 boundaries were agreed upon. Pickens, Matthews, and General Richard Winn, the new superintendent of Indian affairs who replaced James White, doggedly continued their efforts, and there was real anxiety on the white side for a resolution. Georgia continued to lose lives and property and did not have the resources to prosecute a war on its own. The new secretary of war, Henry Knox, warned the Confederation Congress that an effective war with the Creeks would require no less than 2,800 troops and $450,000.[24]

The Struggle for Peace

Despite his efforts, Pickens was not optimistic. He confided to Governor Pinckney that he and George Matthews thought their best hope was to "evade a general war," a war for which South Carolina must prudently prepare nonetheless.[25] Pickens saw three fundamental obstacles to a treaty, one practical, one constitutional, and one moral—the same barriers that would complicate Indian-white negotiations throughout his career. First, as he explained to Pinckney, both Georgia and the Creeks refused to budge on their land claims. Congress officially instructed the treaty commissioners that "no cession of land is to be demanded from the Indian tribes." However, Congress also ordered the commissioners to ensure that "the States may not conceive their legislative rights in any manner infringed."[26] Georgia had just passed a statute reserving lands between the Oconee and Chattahoochee Rivers for its Revolutionary War veterans, and these lands were in the heart of what the Creeks still considered their territory. Thus, the commissioners' task was impossible without the unlikely event of one side giving up its claims.[27]

But there was also a larger constitutional question, which in turn involved the moral issue of man's depravity. Despite Congress's concession to the states' "legislative rights," the national body still professed its right to "constitutionally fix the bounds between any State and an independent tribe of Indians." Pickens wholeheartedly agreed. Not only did Congress have this right, but no state, Pickens believed, had the right to take land belonging to the Indians without going through the "medium of Congress, and then only by Treaty . . . tho they are within the chartered limits of the State." Pickens was well aware that many disagreed with him on these points, which made his duty of rendering a fair treaty a "disagreeable business." Of course, if the Indians and the states could abandon greed and vengeance and embrace magnanimity, the national government would not need to play this strong hand. But that was exactly the problem. "Virtue is wanting," Pickens declared. Therefore, "till we have strength and energy in government a permanent peace between us and our Red Brethren can hardly be expected."[28]

THE CHEROKEES

While Pickens and others sought a long-term understanding with the Creeks in 1788, he also had to address a series of crises with the Cherokees. In February, a white trader named Peterkin who lived among the Cherokees was killed. Pickens demanded that the Cherokees, in accordance with the Hopewell treaty, put the murderers to death. Until that was done, he warned, he would not allow any ammunition to be sold to the Cherokees. This threat had teeth in it, as the Indians needed lead and shot for hunting and for self-defense. Initially, Pickens reported, the chiefs tried to "evade" the question. They sent white beads and professions of peace. Rather than denying the murder took place, they said they did not wish to execute the perpetrator but instead would ensure "that the like shall not happen again." Pickens, having accepted the Cherokees' explanation for the killing of Tom Kades and unable to prove the Creeks' guilt in the Norwood's Station murders, was determined to exact justice this time. He told the Cherokees he was ready to compel their compliance "in a manner I shall be sorry to see" and recommended to Pinckney that a military expedition be sent out. This was necessary, Pickens told the governor, "as it will show them that the lives of men are not to be trifled with."[29]

This was a difficult matter for the Cherokees, not least because the murderer was a relative of one of their leading headmen—Black Dog, the prince of Notaly. In the end, the chiefs, including Black Dog, agreed to put the murderer to death. They informed Pickens so that he might "let ammunition & Goods come to us as usual, for want of it prevents us from hunting."[30]

This affair was not quite resolved when a much greater atrocity was committed, this time by white men upon Cherokees. In mid-May, a supposedly nonhostile band of Cherokees from the village of Chilhowee killed several members of the Kirk family in the upper Tennessee valley. John Sevier was determined to lead a large group of Franklin men to avenge the murders. To prevent this, Joseph Martin had stayed for several weeks in the town of Chota, the most influential Cherokee town, close to Chilhowee. Martin had successfully turned back several Franklinite expeditions, but he left in late May, and Sevier resumed his march toward the Little Tennessee River.

The vengeance of the Franklinites was savage. They destroyed the village of Hiwassee and killed seven Indians who were tilling their corn and nine more at Chilhowee. Cherokee Indians began fleeing the Little Tennessee area into what is now upper Georgia. After they fled Chota, Sevier lured several of their leaders back under a white flag. One of them was Pickens's friend, the respected chief Corn Tassel or "Old Tassel." The Tassel had been the leading Cherokee spokesman at the Hopewell treaty; ever since, he had been a partner with Pickens in seeking peace. In a message, white officers informed the Indians that it was against the law of nations to kill an enemy under a white flag. Reassured by this, Old Tassel and three other headmen entered Chota carrying a white flag. According to the Cherokees,

The Struggle for Peace

the white troops "immediately fell upon them without speaking a word & killed them all." The troops cut off Old Tassel's head and impaled it on a stick erected in the town.[31] One of the killers was John Kirk, a survivor of the murdered white family. Altogether, Sevier and his troops destroyed perhaps nine villages and killed as many as ninety Indians. Hundreds of others fled without being able to harvest their corn and were in danger of starvation. In desperation, Hanging Maw, Black Dog, the Jobber's Son, and John Watts appealed to Pickens for help and for justice.[32]

Pickens was ashamed and outraged. He stirred up a hornet's nest of indignation in an attempt to provide justice for the Cherokees and notified southern Indian superintendent Richard Winn of the atrocities. He also wrote to Governor Pinckney and to Joseph Martin, who was now the U.S. agent to the Cherokees and Winn's subordinate. Winn, equally outraged, notified Secretary of War Knox, and Martin wrote North Carolina governor Samuel Johnston suggesting that he take action against Sevier. The South Carolina privy council, too, voted to forward Pickens's letters and those of the Cherokee chiefs to Congress and to Governor Johnston. Pickens also convened a meeting of the justices of Abbeville County to write a scathing public letter to the settlers along the Nolichucky, Holston, and French Broad Rivers from whence the expedition had come, appealing to their sense of honor and decency to condemn Sevier. The Abbeville justices particularly denounced the treachery of luring peaceful Cherokees out under a flag of truce, "Sacred by the Law of Nations," and then killing them, disregarding a "protection inviolable even among the most barbarous people."[33]

Pickens was only one of the eleven Abbeville justices who signed the letter, and probably he did not compose its final draft. But as he was the most prominent member of the court and the leading authority on Indian affairs, it is equally certain that he convened the meeting and that the letter reflected his feelings. It was by far the most angry and passionate letter to which he ever signed his name. The last two-thirds of it clearly illustrate the old general's conceptions of international justice and honorable warfare:

> The objects of these murders & massacres were an harmless
> peaceable and almost defenceless people—circumstances which
> give them a just claim to the compassion of every humane & noble
> mind, & it is unworthy of American Valor which bled in the cause of
> Liberty & defended it when attacked by the most formidable power
> on Earth to kill & plunder a few naked and unarmed Savages, who
> wish for nothing but to possess their lands & kill their Venison in

peace—They are also a free & independent Nation to whom the protection of the United States has been granted for their freedom of possession by the most Solemn Treaties. . . . These people have also constantly testifyed the most friendly dispositions towards your Settlements & when attacks have been meditated or expeditions set on foot against you by the Creeks, have given you timely warning of the danger.

Pickens and the other justices assumed, or pretended to believe, that a large number of the Franklin settlers were as horrified and indignant as they were. It was up to that noble part of the community to reassert the rule of law and punish wickedness:

All people have bad men among them & it is highly incumbent on the virtuous & considerate part of the community to watch over the actions of the undeserving to prevent them from involving their Country in Calamities to gratify their own base & unworthy passions—By a strict Search you may find out the persons who come under the above description & you are bound by every Tie of Justice, Honor, Duty, & Policy to restrain such as they are, from a similar conduct in future.

We therefore being Citizens of the United States with yourselves anticipate the evils that must necessarily flow from the impropriety of passing unnoticed such a misconduct in a few Individuals, acting from the meanest & basest motives.[34]

Pickens and other white leaders were able to stir up enough outrage over Sevier's actions to produce an official response from Congress. On September 1, Congress issued a proclamation condemning the "many unprovoked outrages" by "disorderly Persons" and the violations of the Treaty of Hopewell that were "highly injurious and disrespectful to the authority of the Union."[35] On the same day, Congress ordered its secretary of war, Henry Knox, to have troops ready to march if necessary from the Ohio to Chota to protect the Cherokees and order whites off their hunting grounds. North Carolina authorities would soon apprehend Sevier and imprison him for a short time. By the terms of the treaty, the Cherokees should have been able to expect that Sevier and a few others would be executed. Of course, this did not happen, but Pickens and others had been able to provoke federal authorities and the state of North Carolina into uncharacteristic decisiveness.[36]

This mediation probably also limited the fallout. Before the Cherokees learned of Congress's proclamations, an army of 600 Cherokees led by John Watts of the more warlike faction of Cherokees called the Chickamaugas, along with 400 Creeks and a handful of white men, attacked a fort on the Holston River and overwhelmed it; ten whites were killed and twenty-seven women and children taken prisoner. John Watts made it known that the white prisoners would be treated humanely. As soon as he heard of the attack, Pickens began corresponding with Cherokee leaders and Joseph Martin about his proposed plan to have the white prisoners brought to Hopewell and released.[37]

POSTPONEMENT OF THE CREEK TREATY

Pickens had feared that the outbreak of white-Cherokee violence would upset the negotiations with the Creeks. Depredations by both sides continued in Georgia. The Creeks and the treaty commissioners agreed to meet on September 15, 1788, but it became clear by late summer that this date would be too soon. Georgia was not prepared for all-out war with the Creeks, but neither did the legislature convene in time to appropriate funds for a treaty. North Carolina balked as well, and Congress itself had delayed providing additional funds that Pickens reported were necessary. McGillivray remained suspicious and cagy as always, and Superintendent Richard Winn probably gave the Creek chief unnecessary, if unintended, offense when he proposed a site for the negotiations—within the state of Georgia—that Pickens knew would be unacceptable to the Creeks. Pickens himself may have unwittingly encouraged McGillivray's stubborn stance when he earlier confided to him that he saw the justice in McGillivray's personal claim against the state of Georgia. He had also repeatedly assured McGillivray that Congress was determined to give the Creeks "justice." Pickens had meant to appear sincere and conciliatory, but the remarks alerted McGillivray to the possibility that there was at least one key negotiator on the white side who might favor the return of Creek lands settled on since 1783—as a result, McGillivray never budged on his stance that that requirement had to be agreed upon before a meeting could take place. Finally, of course, Congress's instructions to the commissioners were virtually impossible to fulfill.

On August 28, 1788, the commissioners wrote McGillivray urging postponement of the treaty to the following spring. All sides seemed to agree that this outcome was second-best to a favorable treaty but far preferable to outright war. The commissioners hinted to McGillivray that once a newly constructed federal government went into operation under the new Constitution, there would be greater potential for a more permanent settlement. Pickens himself may have been optimistic about this, as he had previously asserted that "more strength and energy in government" was necessary before a stable peace could be achieved.[38] For his part, McGillivray seems to have thought that the new federal government under the Constitution could give the Creeks a better deal. McGillivray promised to honor and extend the official truce as long as the Georgians did as well. As Pickens had predicted, it had proven impossible to conclude a treaty given the parameters of 1787 and 1788. His efforts, however, had helped all sides "evade a general war," the wish he had ardently expressed to Governor Pinckney back in March.[39]

THE CHEROKEE PRISONER EXCHANGE

In December 1788, the Hopewell treaty was three years old. South Carolina was the only state in which it had been honored, with no South Carolinians settling past the state's western boundary with the Cherokees and with Pickens and key Cherokee headmen resolving the handful of murders that had occurred in the area. Still, in the wake of the Franklinite raids of the previous summer and John Watts's retaliatory strike against the white settlement on the Holston, a "general war" between Cherokees and North Carolina or Franklin could erupt at any time. Pickens thought that a new treaty could be made "unless the people over the Mountains should continue to prosecute their hostile intentions." He also believed that "a number of bad [white] Militia-men" living among the Indians were responsible for most of the "Robberies" taking place along the Georgia and South Carolina frontiers. That, he thought, would not cease until a new treaty was signed. Finally, Pickens and others believed North Carolina must appoint someone to the treaty commission, something the Tar Heel State had not done since Congress had formed the latest commission in 1787.[40]

—By the end of 1788, North Carolina leaders showed signs of seeking a new settlement with the Cherokees. Not only was Sevier arrested but also Governor Johnston signed a proclamation in November ordering all citizens to refrain from hostilities against the Indians until after new negotiations had taken place. The legislature finally appointed North Carolina's federal treaty commissioner, the twenty-four-year-old planter and state legislator John Steele of Salisbury. Steele's home state, however, gave him

The Struggle for Peace

difficult instructions. He was to insist that the Cherokees cede much of the disputed land in modern east Tennessee, still claimed by North Carolina, and this was the very thing that Congress's instructions forbade him to do. William Blount also tried to influence Steele. Blount pointed out, logically, that North Carolina's "only object" in complying with Congress's recommendation to appoint a treaty commissioner "was to have a Treaty with the Cherokees, the only Indians that are troublesome to her." Blount warned Steele that he would be judged by his fellow North Carolinians on how successful he was in obtaining Cherokee land. Therefore, when he met with the other commissioners, he should persuade them to treat with the Cherokees first. The wily Blount advised Steele on how he might accomplish North Carolina's (and Blount's) purposes:

> When you meet with your brother Commissioners . . . your grand Object will be to get them to hold the treaty with the Cherokees first. . . . Pickens trades much more with the Cherokees than with the Creeks consequently Peace with [the Cherokees] will be most advantageous [to him] . . . hence I suppose you will have his Interest. Pickens is a cunning artful Man. [George] Matthews, I am told . . . is not so much so. I think you may manage him to your purposes by talking much to him privately about the interest of North Carolina and Georgia being the same both having vacant Western Territory on which the United States have an Eye for this has ever been the Language of the delegates of Georgia to those of North Carolina.

In a postscript, Blount added, "Please present my Compliments to my friend, General Pickens."[41]

Just as these early arrangements for a new treaty began, however, news of another hostile act almost wrecked them. John Sevier, released from his arrest and back in the former territory of Franklin (the breakaway republic collapsed in 1788), was back on the warpath. The Cherokees, with assurances from Richard Winn that they need fear no more attacks, sent out hunting parties in December, leaving women and children alone in the villages. Late that month or in early January, Sevier plundered one of those villages and captured twenty-nine women and children. Martin complained to Secretary of War Knox that this action "made great confusion again, but by the early imposition of General Pickens and others, that affront was allayed."[42] Pickens interceded by telling the Cherokee leaders that Sevier had taken the prisoners only so that they could be exchanged for the similar number of white prisoners taken by Cherokee chief John Watts. Martin wrote Governor Johnston of North Carolina that "had not Genl. Pickens exerted himself as well as some others," he believed that Sevier's action would have resulted in a "General War."[43]

Despite Blount's warnings to Steele, the young North Carolinian soon established a good rapport with Pickens and the rest of the treaty commission. Richard Winn assembled the commissioners and Joseph Martin at Ninety Six in mid-February 1789. The five men got to work planning for a treaty with the Cherokees, followed by one with the Creeks, as well as for a separate prisoner exchange suggested by Pickens. The commissioners decided to ask the Cherokees to meet them at the War Ford on the French Broad River on May 25. Additionally, Pickens wrote to Sevier, asking him to bring the Indian prisoners on March 23 to Cowee (near modern-day Franklin, North Carolina, and about seventy miles northwest of Hopewell). Steele assisted by asking the North Carolina governor for the commissioners' power to order the state militia to seize the captives and deliver them to Cowee if Sevier did not cooperate.[44] Pickens also wrote to the Cherokees about the exchange but received no answers. Belatedly, the Cherokees replied that they would bring the captives on April 6. Sevier finally sent Pickens a reply but did not directly answer whether he would bring his captives or not.[45]

Unknown to Pickens, Winn, and the rest of the commissioners, Sevier was working to hijack the prisoner exchange planned by Pickens and to derail the larger treaty altogether. His principal lieutenant in these activities was "an amazing scoundrel," one Bennet Ballew.[46] To McGillivray, Ballew offered to serve as the Creeks' agent to the Cherokees. To Congress, he represented himself as a delegate from the Cherokees. A few years later, he would be in the service of Spain, stirring up conflict between the pro- and anti-American factions among the Chickasaws. Most important in the first few months of 1789, he persuaded the Cherokees, or at least some of them, that he was a representative of Congress, that he opposed white expansion into their lands, and that he would represent them to Congress and protect them from the evil designs of the treaty commissioners. He even forged a letter from the Cherokees to Congress in which the Indians had supposedly appointed him as their agent to Congress and asked legislators to stop negotiating through the treaty commissioners.[47]

On April 4, Pickens set out from Hopewell for Cowee, still uncertain whether or not Sevier would show up with his captives. Meanwhile, Ballew set out with Sevier's captives. Pickens arrived at Cowee on the sixth; Ballew arrived at Hiwassee, about sixty miles to the west, about the same time. There Ballew released the Indian captives. The Cherokees, seeing the captives released, turned over the white captives at Hiwassee as well. Pickens, mystified at the failure of either Sevier or the Indians to show up at Cowee, waited for several days until he learned what had happened. He returned to Hopewell on the twelfth.[48]

Sevier's latest shenanigan was an annoyance, but Pickens had reason for consolation. He soon received a letter from The Badger that indicated that at least some of the Cherokees still trusted Pickens far more than they did Ballew. Disapproving of how Ballew had handled the prisoner exchange, The Badger and others complained that "this was contrary to the desire of our . . . friend General Pickens, for we was happy he would be present at the Exchange."[49] The Cherokees also discovered that Ballew had forwarded letters from Sevier to the Chickasaws, but the Cherokees intercepted these and forwarded them to Pickens. The signers of the letter to Pickens stated that they hoped Ballew would not come into their territory again: "In Short we have no Opinion of Such Men."[50]

This April 15 letter by The Badger and other headmen also indicated that the Cherokees were still interested in peace. They were willing to meet the commissioners on May 25 as proposed but wanted to do so at Hopewell rather than at the War Ford on the French Broad, which they saw as too close to their late Franklinite enemies. Additionally they delivered three white child captives to Pickens.[51]

Despite Pickens's optimism, several factors were working against the Cherokee negotiations. First, Pickens probably erred by ignoring the Cherokees' request to move the meeting place, confident that they would still treat even without a last-minute change of venue. Second, Steele had great difficulty in getting his own state to appropriate adequate funds. The North Carolina legislature had provided funds, but only in rapidly depreciating paper currency. It was not enough, and Steele did everything he could to rectify the shortfall. He asked if he could borrow from South Carolina's account. Pickens explained that half of his state's funds were already expended for the Cherokee treaty and he had to save the rest for the negotiations with the Creeks, since Georgia had once again failed to provide anything. Pickens did what he could to help Steele, who ended up transporting goods to the French Broad at his own expense. Third, McGillivray boasted that he had played a role in preventing cooperation between his most dangerous enemy, the Americans, and his northern neighbors the Cherokees. To his business partner William Panton he wrote, "Pickens returned for the Cherokee Treaty, but in that I took measures to disappoint him, for those Chiefs would not meet."[52]

Most damaging, though, was probably the continued interference of Sevier and Ballew. Pickens, his fellow commissioners, Winn, and Martin arrived at the War Ford on May 27. Not a single Cherokee was in sight other than Pickens's friend The Terrapin. Pickens and this Cherokee chieftain had probably first met when Captain Joseph Pickens had captured The Terrapin in 1779. If Pickens had taken care to spare and release The Terrapin, the chief had returned that favor in 1782 when he had brought a number of Tory captives into Pickens's camp, which helped bring an end to Pickens's campaign against the Cherokees in upper Georgia in the autumn of 1782. At the War Ford, the white diplomats and The Terrapin waited for twelve days. Pickens could not afford to wait for the Cherokees any longer; he was convinced there would be a "general war" between the Creeks and Georgia if there was no treaty soon.[53] Reluctantly they decided that they must hurry away and begin negotiations with the latter tribe as soon as possible.[54]

As they left, the commissioners dispatched a letter to the Cherokees explaining that they could wait no longer because they had to meet with the Creeks.[55] While the timing and details are murky, it seems clear that Sevier and Ballew worked to undermine a treaty between the United States and the Cherokees, probably so that Sevier could arrange his own land purchase for himself or others. Over a period of several days, the commissioners received more evidence that Sevier and Ballew had warned the Indians not to meet with the commissioners because the latter were attempting to cheat them.[56] As the federal commissioners traveled south to meet with the Creeks, a delegation of Cherokees intercepted them at Hopewell and confirmed that Ballew had been working mischief. The Cherokees assured their friend Skyagunsta that they still wanted peace but that Ballew had given "bad talks" to them. According to the Cherokee delegation, Ballew had charged that the commissioners would have the Cherokee headmen put to death if they did not give up their land. The commissioners had stocked a large amount of goods in order to "steal" the Indians' land, said Ballew, and he was the one who would see justice done to them.[57]

Pickens responded on June 15, acknowledging that the Cherokees' absence from the treaty ground was due to "bad talks given out in your nation by bad desining white men who wish to be the distruction of your people—I mean a certain Bennet Balowe . . . he is a rogue and a liar." Pickens asserted that The Terrapin could testify to the honesty of the commissioners' intentions. He promised that the new president had the authority to force obedience to treaties and finally asked them not to listen again to anyone not appointed and sent to them directly by Congress or by the president—only they could ensure that the Indians received justice. In the hope that violence could be averted before new treaty arrangements were made, Pickens asked the chiefs to prevent their warriors from "molesting any of the inhabitants" and concluded with the hope that soon "our women and children may live as one people on one land and never more be made afraid by the alarm of war."[58]

Pickens also asked that Little Turkey meet with him at Hopewell after the Creek talks. Little Turkey had been one of the Cherokee leaders who had angrily denounced the British for giving away Indian lands at a "Rum Drinking"; since then, Pickens had conferred several times with him and asked him to serve as an emissary to the Creeks. After sending the invitation to Little Turkey, Pickens and the other white negotiators continued their journey south.[59]

THE ROCK LANDING DEBACLE AND THE TREATY OF NEW YORK

Sometime in the spring of 1789, the Creeks received a letter from Pickens and Henry Osborne, Georgia's replacement for George Matthews on the federal treaty commission. This time the commissioners bypassed McGillivray and addressed their letter to the "Head-men, Chiefs, and Warriors of the Creek Nation." They asked to meet with the Creeks on June 20 at Rock Landing on the Creek side of the Oconee River, paying respect to the Creeks' aversion to meeting in Georgia territory:

> We have changed the place of meeting from that of the last year; so that none of you should have reason to complain; it is your own ground, and on that land we wish to renew our former trade and friendships, and to remove every thing that has blinded the path between us.
>
> We are now governed by a President, who is like the old King over the great water; he commands all the warriors of the thirteen great Fires. He will have regard to the welfare of all the Indians; and, when peace shall be established, he will be your father and you will be his children, so that none shall dare to do you harm.
>
> We know that lands have been the cause of dispute between you and the white people; but we now tell you that we want no new grants; our object is to make peace, and to unite us all under our great chief warrior and President, who is the father and protector of the white people. Attend to what we say: Our traders are very rich, and have houses full of such goods as you used to get in former days; it is our wish that you should trade with them, and they with you, in strict friendship.[60]

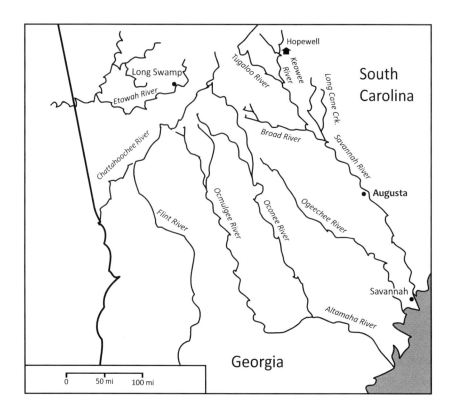

The Creek Frontier (*Map by Chris Cartledge*)

Thus renewing the pledge that the United States was not seeking new land cessions from the Creeks, Pickens began his third great campaign to conclude a treaty with the proud Creek nation. The task was as urgent as ever, for once again war between the Creeks and Georgia seemed imminent. McGillivray had spoken at a Creek council in the town of Cussitah on May 13 just days before the letter arrived. There he had explained to them the treaty commissioners' letter of November 28, when the commissioners had asserted that it was impossible to remove white citizens from the disputed lands as a prerequisite to a treaty—that could be done only by means of a treaty itself. The Creek headmen then determined for war, and war parties were already moving toward the frontiers when the letter arrived. The Creeks were able to recall their war parties, but not before some white settlers were killed by their attacks.[61] McGillivray signaled to other Creek leaders that he would join the meeting at Rock Landing if they were determined to negotiate with the white men. A letter composed by the Lower Creek chiefs on June 1 was even more positive: "We now hope all will be forgot, and we now come to

The Struggle for Peace

make our talks firm again, as we did when we first took white people by the hand. As we were all made by one master of breath, although put in different parts of the earth, he did not make us to be at variance against each other; but it has happened, by the bad doings of our mad people, on both sides."[62] Both sides, however, soon concluded that the meeting would need to be postponed until September. The Creeks' reasoning was that with a number of white Georgians recently killed, time was needed for passions to cool—a "meeting" between Creek warriors and white men backed by a guard of Georgia militia could easily turn into a battle or ambush. Pickens and Osborne's given reason was the "great scarcity of corn" within an eighty-mile radius of Rock Landing; they doubted they could feed everyone at the treaty site.[63]

With the postponement of the treaty, Pickens finally had several weeks to spend at home. Stopping near Augusta, he paused to write Governor Pinckney about the latest events. Pickens once again pointed out how difficult it was for the commissioners to obtain a "lasting peace" when "in one claus of our instructions, it says that we shall not infringe the Legislative right of any state, in another that no demand of land shall be made from the Indians." Pickens hoped that the formation of the new federal government under the Constitution would solve that dilemma, that "the President of the united states with the Senet will so arrange the business respecting the indians . . . that it will put it out of the power of the individual states having a pretense of holding treaties or purchasing lands from the indians without the concert of Congress."[64]

Pickens was not the only one who hoped that the new national government could facilitate more productive diplomacy and lasting peace. Secretary of War Henry Knox had been studying all the correspondence dealing with Indian affairs that had been submitted to the Confederation Congress and preparing reports for President George Washington. To Knox, the negotiations with the tribes in the Southern Department seemed to be in disarray. Writing to the president on July 6 and 7, Knox knew that Superintendent Winn and the treaty commissioners had failed to conclude a treaty with the Cherokees. He also was aware that the Creeks had been invited to talk at Rock Landing, but he did not know that they had sent any replies. According to the information he had, no talks were occurring, but instead the Creeks had recently sent warriors to attack white settlements in Georgia— and the Creeks had been warned previously that the United States would defend Georgia if the Indians refused to sign a treaty. Was there any reason, he therefore asked, why the United States should not "raise an army?"[65]

Knox was not advocating a total abandonment of diplomacy, but he did want a fresh start. The commissions issued by the old Confederation Congress to Winn and Martin as superintendent and deputy superintendent for the Southern Department had expired with the Confederation, as had those of the treaty commissioners, Pickens and Osborne. Moreover, many of the Cherokees had now joined the Creeks, he believed. And even if Winn was soon able to render a treaty with the Cherokees, the commissioners would not have the power to restore them to their lands that they were entitled to by the Treaty of Hopewell.[66]

By July 28, Knox had received the commissioners' letter of June 30 reporting that both the Cherokees and Creeks were disposed toward peace. Knox now envisioned a new national policy of "civilizing" the Indians—teaching them to engage in settled agriculture and industrial pursuits.[67] First, though, a new treaty commission had to be established and new treaties concluded that protected them in their current lands. President Washington incorporated Knox's thinking in messages to Congress. The United States had the need and the duty to establish relations with the Indians based on "justice and humanity."[68] One step toward that goal would be made by appointing new treaty "commissioners whose local situations may free them from the imputation of prejudice on this subject."[69] In other words, treaties with Creeks or Cherokees would not be negotiated by men from Georgia or the Carolinas. Congress complied.

Pickens journeyed to Rock Landing once again in September without knowing that he was no longer an official representative of the federal government. He and Osborne had been relieved by men of higher rank and prestige. One was Major General Benjamin Lincoln of Massachusetts, former commander of American troops at the siege of Charleston; another was Cyrus Griffin of Virginia, the last president of the Confederation Congress; and the third was David Humphreys of Connecticut, personal friend and former aide-de-camp to General Washington. There is some evidence that leaders in New York (the temporary national capital) felt that a more ostentatious delegation would "impress the Southern Indians with an idea that trifling is at an end."[70]

Even the instructions that the new commissioners received suggested a lack of confidence in men like Pickens who had been managing Indian relations in the South for the last several years. Washington and Knox ordered that if the new commissioners arrived after Pickens and Osborne had already concluded a treaty, they were to study the agreement. If they concluded that an inadequate number of Creek leaders had been present or

The Struggle for Peace

that the treaty was inconsistent with the "justice and dignity" of the United States, they were to disapprove it.[71]

Pickens and Osborne arrived at Rock Landing in mid-September; a large Creek delegation had been there since about September 2. Both sides seemed optimistic that a deal could be reached. This was Pickens's first face-to-face meeting with McGillivray, that enigmatic character who always seemed to American leaders as both the necessary link and the greatest obstacle to a lasting settlement with the Creeks. Pickens did not record his initial impression, but McGillivray did. "Pickens," he wrote, "I take to be a worthy moderate man."[72] Before business could begin in earnest, however, Pickens and Osborne received word on the sixteenth from Lincoln, Griffin, and Humphreys that they had been replaced. The new commissioners said they would depart Savannah for Rock Landing as soon as possible. Pickens and Osborne took the news gracefully; the Creeks less so. With growing impatience, the chiefs threatened that if the new commissioners did not arrive by "Friday next" (September 25), they would depart. Meanwhile, Pickens and Osborne promised to do all they could to "keep the Indians together, and in good humor."[73]

Fortunately, Lincoln and Humphreys arrived on the twentieth, and Pickens and Osborne had worked hard to keep the Creeks from leaving. Unfortunately, however, the new commissioners had an incomplete understanding of the situation—especially Humphreys, who assumed the role as lead negotiator. By the time they arrived at Rock Landing, they had met and corresponded with state officials and been exposed only to the Georgians' point of view—the Treaties of Augusta, Galphinton, and Shoulderbone were valid and the Creeks had repeatedly violated them.[74]

Humphreys and the other new commissioners had relatively detailed instructions from Secretary Knox. They were to inquire into the validity of the previous disputed treaties. If the treaties were not fully legitimate but Georgia citizens were already settled on the disputed territory east of the Oconee, they were to promise monetary compensation for it. Further, they were to promise the Creeks the protection of the United States and persuade them to give up their alliance with Spain for one with the Americans. They could be promised a port of entry on the Altamaha River and the protection of a permanent garrison of U.S. troops at that location if they wanted it. In private talks with McGillivray, the commissioners could offer the Creek leader "pecuniary awards" as well as the rank of colonel or brigadier general in the U.S. Army.[75]

The white American and Creek representatives negotiated for several days, but antagonism between Humphreys and McGillivray kept the situation tense. Humphreys saw McGillivray as shrewd and "cunning" but also "slovenly" and "addicted to debauchery."[76] McGillivray described Humphreys as "a great boaster" who alternated between flattery and intimidation. He was deeply insulted when Humphreys tactlessly questioned McGillivray's authority to conclude a treaty that the entire Creek nation would accept as binding.[77] Humphreys reported that he did have some confidential discussions with McGillivray but did not reveal their content. Probably he offered personal concessions to the Creek chief as suggested in his official instructions. If so, McGillivray was not sufficiently impressed with them to sacrifice his comfortable relationship with the Spanish. The latter had just sent arms and ammunition to the Creeks and also granted more lucrative trade arrangements.[78]

After a few days, the commissioners drew up a treaty and presented it to the Creeks. Some articles mimicked the Hopewell treaties in providing for the punishment of whites and Indians who committed crimes on the other; in requiring the return of captives; and in renouncing the principle of blind retaliation. The United States promised to protect the Creeks' claim to land west of the Oconee River and granted them the right to punish whites who settled west of it. There would be a port on the Altamaha, and the United States would grant duty-free trade rights to the Creeks. The sticking points were the alliance with Spain and the lands in dispute since the previous treaties. The Creeks would accept "the protection of the supreme authority of the United States" and no one else, and they would not be allowed to make treaties with other states or nations.[79] McGillivray had recently confided to his business partner William Panton that if the Americans made such a demand he would break off negotiations immediately. Throughout much of the rest of the letter, however, McGillivray made it clear that his continued loyalty to Spain was contingent on that nation's strong support and that he was very interested in hints that the Americans might reimburse him for his father's confiscated estate. Events of the following year would prove that McGillivray's loyalty could be bought—Humphreys simply failed to make that purchase in 1789. The other problem with the terms offered by the new commissioners was that they not only insisted on the land cessions in the previous treaties—always a deal-breaker with the Creeks—but even failed to offer the Creeks reimbursement for those lands. Pickens was well aware how important the lands east of the Oconee were to the Creeks. He adamantly tried to persuade the commissioners to amend that article, but his advice was ignored.[80]

The next morning, the entire white delegation was stunned to learn that the Creeks had packed up and headed for home. McGillivray sent a short note explaining that they objected to the proposed boundary. It was now hunting season, he said; the Indians were done negotiating for the current year, but they would maintain the existing truce throughout the winter. For his part, McGillivray continued to dissemble in a series of messages to the commissioners. He first promised that he would cross the Oconee and speak personally with them; later that day he explained that he needed forage for his horses, so he would temporarily have to move about five miles away. In consternation, the commissioners dispatched Pickens and several other men to catch up with McGillivray and deliver a note in which they asked for more clarification and further talks. Pickens rode after McGillivray and found him not five miles away but more than thirty and already west of the Ocmulgee. During a long conversation, Pickens tried to convince McGillivray to return. However, the commissioners had not authorized him to promise the Creek leader that they would offer reimbursement for the lands east of the Oconee. "This they could not do," McGillivray later wrote, "so I remained obstinate to my purpose." McGillivray and Pickens parted on friendly terms, but the negotiations had failed.[81]

The Rock Landing talks had miscarried badly for numerous reasons. Both McGillivray and the commissioners blamed the other. Humphreys charged that McGillivray refused to explain the Creeks' objections to the treaty in writing (which was not true), while McGillivray claimed that he did.[82] McGillivray's caginess had once again played a role in the diplomatic failure, but so had the new commissioners' inexperience and incompetence. Unknown to Pickens or the new commissioners, the Creek leader had received promises of stronger Spanish support just before the Rock Landing talks began. McGillivray may have pretended that the Creeks saw the treaty draft as a final ultimatum when in reality he saw that the Americans were still not likely to offer him a better deal than the Spanish had. Humphreys later claimed that the proposed articles were only a draft intended as a basis for future discussion, but he had overplayed his hand throughout the negotiations and not offered enough up front. Federal officials, too, had shown poor judgment and worse timing in replacing men like Winn, Martin, and Pickens, who were the most familiar with the situation. Federal authority, it seemed, was a two-edged sword—while promising order, it also brought unwelcome, clumsy interference.

There were two silver linings in this debacle. One was that McGillivray was thoroughly impressed with the trustworthiness of Pickens. He would later compare him to another white diplomat with the compliment "I find him just as Genl. Pickens a Candid and Benevolent Character, possessing abilitys but without Show or parade."[83] "We got well acquainted," McGillivray said of Pickens, "and I am sure if he had remained in his appointment, we should have come to some agreement."[84] It seemed likely that McGillivray's goodwill toward Pickens might smooth the road to peace in the future. As Pickens returned home, the commissioners sent a message with him for the Cherokees asking that they maintain the truce.[85] McGillivray aided Pickens's efforts by urging the Cherokees "to take the advice of Gen. Pickens how they should behave; that the General was good and honest, and, if he promised them any thing they might depend on his word."[86]

More important for the American side, U.S. officials were more impressed than ever with the possibility of buying off McGillivray with payments and flattery. President Washington sent Colonel Marinus Willet of New York to McGillivray to invite him and other Creek chiefs to New York to discuss a new treaty. Willet was far more successful than Humphreys in wooing and flattering McGillivray, especially when armed with Washington's permission to promise him certain personal and financial "lures."[87] Willet also had a letter for McGillivray from Benjamin Hawkins, now a U.S. senator from North Carolina. Hawkins professed his continued friendship but warned him that the failure to conclude a treaty with the United States now would bring disaster to the Creeks. Hawkins, too, dropped the revealing hint that "the U. States have the means of estimating properly the value of your character."[88] With these blandishments, Willet was able to persuade McGillivray and more than two dozen other Creek chiefs that summer to make an overland journey to New York, stopping at Pickens's Hopewell house along the way.

In New York, the Creek delegation was lavishly entertained by Washington himself, and the two sides signed the Treaty of New York in August 1790. The treaty did not give the United States full sovereignty over the Creeks or complete control over their trade, but it did break Spain's monopoly. The Creeks refused to give up their prized hunting lands below the Ocmulgee stretching southward to the St. Marys; thus the federal government annulled the Treaties of Galphinton and Shoulderbone. However, it did confirm the Treaty of Augusta by recognizing the United States' title to the more agriculturally valuable tract east of the Oconee in exchange for an annual payment to the Creeks of $1,500 in goods. Later, leaders throughout the Creek nation learned that McGillivray had personally profited from

The Struggle for Peace

the treaty. The white fathers had given him the title of brigadier general with a handsome annual salary of $1,200. Even without that knowledge, many Creek leaders opposed the treaty.[89]

Pickens played no direct role in the 1790 negotiations. Most of his public service in that year involved work in the South Carolina state senate and local affairs around Pendleton. However, in some ways the Treaty of New York was the product and culmination of his personal efforts. The treaty finally established the federal government's authority to make treaties with the Indians and establish national boundaries—the era of separate state treaties was over. Pickens had always advocated this principle of federal control over Indian negotiations as logical and as vital for peace. Ultimately, the agreement satisfied neither most Creeks nor Georgians. However, the very fact that a treaty was concluded without a "general war" was due largely to the efforts of Pickens, who had dealt personally with McGillivray and labored for peace with the Creeks for more than five years.

FOURTEEN

The Strong Hand of Government, 1789–1793

It appears essential that something at this critical Period should
be done to satisfy them temporarily, that is, until the Strong
Hand of Government is exercised over the Creeks.

*Andrew Pickens and William Blount to Secretary of War
Henry Knox, August 6, 1793*

When Andrew Pickens returned to Hopewell following the Rock Landing
debacle with the Creeks, he temporarily abandoned his direct role in Indian
affairs, at least at the federal level. In 1790 and 1791, he would influence federal Indian diplomacy through informal advice rather than as an appointed
federal official, and even then his influence was minimal. At the local level,
however, the general's role as soldier, legislator, merchant, and judge in the
newly organizing Pendleton area was just as important as ever. The same
was true for his role in state affairs. Pickens was one of several backcountry elites who served as a link between lowcountry Federalists and backcountry Republicans—leaders who were critical in the unification of South
Carolina. During 1792 and 1793, however, he would once again be a key voice
at the federal level on Indian affairs—a voice that advocated the federal
government taking a decisive role for the sake of justice and national honor.

Pickens was elected the first state senator from the recently organized
Pendleton County in May 1789. That summer he was a delegate to the
convention that met in Columbia to revise the state's constitution now
that the Palmetto State had joined the new federal union. As a representative of the backcountry, Pickens fought for more representation for his

section in the legislature and had earlier supported moving the capital from Charleston to a more central location. Like most of his constituents and fellow backcountry leaders, Pickens favored frugal government and shared the outlook of the Presbyterian and Baptist evangelicals who were so prominent in the region. As a state senator, he sponsored a successful bill to provide state aid to the orphans and widows of deceased Presbyterian ministers.[1]

Yet lowcountry elites had much in common with him and other back-country leaders such as Robert Anderson, Patrick Calhoun, and John E. Colhoun. Though far less wealthy than most of the coastal aristocracy, Pickens was a fellow landowner, slaveholder, and merchant who supported the development of the state's economic infrastructure. He favored state support for the building of roads, ferries, bridges, and tobacco inspection warehouses.[2] Federalists also shared Pickens's concern for maintaining law and order. And, as would become increasingly clear during the 1790s, Pickens was a nationalist at a time when such a stance was primarily associated with the Federalist faction in national politics. He not only supported federal control of Indian diplomacy but also tended to favor a strong military (by 1790s standards) that could stand up to the insults and intimidation of the European powers.

Even Pickens's family life illustrated the rise of the backcountry elites and their growing connections with the lowcountry. In 1790, his son Ezekiel graduated as valedictorian at Princeton. Pickens, who always regretted his own lack of education, was extremely proud of his eldest son's accomplishment. Ezekiel took a seat in the state house of representatives in December 1791 as his father served in the senate. Less than two years later, Ezekiel married a daughter of the lowcountry aristocracy, Elizabeth Bonneau. Elizabeth's father, Samuel Bonneau, was a wealthy rice planter and perhaps a relative of Pickens's great-grandmother Jane Bonneau. Though Ezekiel kept the land his father obtained for him in Pendleton, he chose to settle in Charleston and become a lawyer. After Elizabeth Bonneau Pickens died in 1803, Ezekiel would marry another lowcountry heiress, Elizabeth Barksdale.[3]

By 1792, Pickens was emerging once again as a leader on the national stage. The first sign that the Washington administration might not distrust his abilities after all was his appointment as federal inspector of whiskey distilleries for western South Carolina on March 15, 1791. Pickens was responsible for the eight uppermost counties of South Carolina and received an annual salary of $450 and a commission of 1 percent of the duties collected.[4]

Not surprisingly, however, the real catalyst pushing Pickens back to the national stage was continued friction with the Indians on the nation's western frontiers. Secretary of War Henry Knox and President George Washington soon came to admire Pickens and sought to take advantage of his talents—both military and diplomatic—in dealing with Indians. It helped that Pickens's philosophy in Indian affairs was compatible with the approach of Knox, who had impressed his views on Washington. Knox's beliefs clashed with those who defended the states' rights to control Indian policy within their borders. To Knox and other Federalists, the ad hoc local approach had been a recipe for chaos and for dishonorable treatment of the Indians. Knox believed that decisive leadership by the federal government would lessen conflict between frontier whites and Indians and prevent the annihilation or extinction of the latter. Knox argued that "the obligations of policy, humanity, and justice, together with that respect which every nation sacredly owes to its own reputation, unite in requiring a noble, liberal, and disinterested administration of Indian affairs." This required, first, that federal military power be used to retard encroachment on Indian lands. Knox conceded that it would be impossible to halt the "disposition" of white settlers to move into Indian territory; however, the federal government could restrain and regulate that impulse: "It may be restrained, by postponing new purchases of Indian territory, and by prohibiting the citizens from intruding on Indian lands. It may be regulated, by forming colonies, under the direction of Government, and by posting a body of troops to execute their orders."[5]

While federal troops and territorial "colonies" slowed the tide of white expansion, federal officials would meanwhile attempt to "civilize" the Indians. The government would provide schools and agricultural tools for Indians, teach them to farm instead of hunt, and instruct them in "industry" and "useful branches of mechanics" so that they could provide themselves with goods instead of rely on gifts. Indians who began to live more like whites would need less land and be more willing to sell it. This cultural assimilation was the only way that Knox and others believed that the Indians could be protected from ultimate extinction. The Knoxian civilization program would also, in a way, civilize whites—the "disorderly people" on the frontier—by forcing them to comply with treaties and the rule of law. As Leonard J. Sadosky has explained, "Knox and other Federalists saw this as the height of humanitarianism. . . . The new order would be one where the 'obligations of Policy, humanity, and justice' were respected."[6] Anything less would reflect dishonor on the new nation.[7]

The Strong Hand of Government, 1789–1793

Thus, there was a strong moral component in the Federalist policy, one shared by Washington himself. During his tour of the southern states in 1791, Washington reflected in his diary on the "manners of the people" in Georgia and the Carolinas. He believed they were "orderly and civil" and generally contented with the federal government. The exceptions to this rule were often greedy men who wished to cheat the Indians: "In Georgia the dissatisfied part of them at the late treaty with the C[ree]k Indians were evidently Land Jobbers, who, maugre [that is, in spite of] every principle of Justice to the Indians & policy to their Country would, for their own immediate emolument, strip the Indns. of all their territory if they could obtain the least countenance to the measure. But it is to be hoped the good sense of the State will set its face against such diabolical attempts."[8]

Pickens thoroughly agreed with the general thrust of Knox's plan. He had been advocating a stronger role for the national government in Indian affairs since 1783 for many of the same reasons. There were two elements in Knox's approach, however, in which Pickens showed less interest. First, Pickens seemed less concerned with the desirability of teaching Indians to farm and learn the trades of white men. He was, of course, a member of several negotiating teams that offered the Indians agricultural tools, blacksmithing equipment, and schools. In his own correspondence, however, he rarely discussed the presumed merits of this policy. If Pickens sought "civilization" for the Indians, he defined the civilization project for them much as he did for whites: instilling respect for laws and treaties, disapproval of personal vengeance and blind retaliation, and a commitment to peace and self-restraint. A second way in which Pickens's concerns varied from Knox's is that he always showed more interest in achieving a stable and honorable peace than in acquiring land. Occasionally, as a commissioner, he did convey his countrymen's desire for Indian land. At other times he expressed adamant opposition to whites' attempts to seize Indian land, both to his fellow countrymen and to the Indians themselves. Like Knox and other federal leaders, however, he never wavered from his belief that such land must be acquired by open and fair treaties between the legitimate leaders of the Indian nations and the national government, not states or individuals.

While Pickens had spent most of his time from 1790 to 1792 immersed in legislative and local affairs, tension had continued to build between the Cherokees and white settlers in the Tennessee and Cumberland valleys. William Blount was now governor of the Southwest Territory as well as superintendent of Indian affairs south of the Ohio. For his own benefit and for that of his white constituents, he wished to obtain title to more Cherokee land. It seemed clear to whites that the old Hopewell treaty boundary could not be restored. There were simply too many white settlers already on the southern or western side of the line. In 1791, Blount invited the Cherokee chiefs to meet him at White's Fort (now Knoxville) on the Holston River under the pretense of discussing ways to better enforce the Hopewell treaty. When they arrived, the forty-one Cherokee leaders were stunned when Blount instead demanded more land in western North Carolina and eastern Tennessee. John Watts, kinsman of the murdered Corn Tassel, became so emotional that he walked away from the meeting, fearing he would burst into tears and embarrass himself. Sullenly, even angrily, most of the chiefs agreed to a new line. This Treaty of Holston River on July 2, 1791, promised that the United States would provide the Cherokees an annuity of $1,000 in goods, though Chief Bloody Fellow later claimed that such a paltry sum "would not buy a breach clout for each of my nation." By the end of the year, whites were already trespassing over the new boundary.[9]

The Holston River treaty was so unpopular among the Cherokees that the tribe split into two factions. One group, led by Doublehead (a brother of Corn Tassel) and his nephew Captain Bench, and later by John Watts, was so angry that it went to war. Another, led by Bloody Fellow and Jobber's Son, sought better terms through further negotiations. This more moderate faction contacted Pickens, who had warned the Cherokees against treating with Blount. They now sought an audience with President Washington, and Pickens and Governor Charles Pinckney wrote letters on their behalf. The delegation of six chiefs, a woman, and an interpreter arrived at the federal capital in Philadelphia on December 28, 1791. In meetings with Knox, Bloody Fellow demanded an increase in the annuity to $1,500 and that the goods be delivered to Pickens and distributed through him. Knox, Washington, and the U.S. Senate readily agreed.[10] Knox also ordered Blount to use a "greater degree of delicacy" in surveying the new line in order to avoid war.[11]

Even as the Philadelphia agreement was reached, relations between Indians and whites on the frontier were approaching the boiling point. Throughout 1792 and 1793, the threat of war against a vast Indian confederation including the southern tribes was greater than it had been since the Revolutionary War. In November 1791, warriors from several northwestern tribes had combined and soundly thrashed an army of U.S. troops under Major General Arthur St. Clair. In the wake of this disastrous defeat to American arms, the prestige of the United States was at low ebb in the west. More warlike factions of Indians were encouraged to take up the red tomahawk. Militant parties of Cherokees mobilized for war and made

The Strong Hand of Government, 1789–1793

limited attacks. Referred to by contemporaries as the "Chickamaugas" or as the warriors of the "five lower towns," they came under the leadership of Chief John Watts. Throughout 1792, tension continued to build. Murders and raids by both sides grew more frequent. Friendlier Cherokees warned Blount and Pickens that John Watts and other warriors, as well as large numbers of Creeks, were planning a great attack on the Cumberland settlements. The problem spread far beyond the Cherokees. The governor of Spanish Louisiana and West Florida, with the assistance of Alexander McGillivray, was attempting to unite all the southern Indian tribes in resistance against the United States. English adventurer William Bowles was also among the Creeks. Though he was a rival to McGillivray, he too sought to incite the southern tribes against the United States. The Shawnees were also seeking Indian unity and provoking resistance to white Americans.[12]

Washington and Knox's new strategy, initially, was to replace St. Clair with a new general and reorganize war preparations in the Northwest Territory while avoiding war with the southern tribes. Early in 1792, Washington and Knox were still unaware of just how tense the situation in the Southwest Territory was becoming. They even thought that they might be able to enlist hundreds of southern Indians to join them against the Miamis, Shawnees, and Delawares north of the Ohio. Was there any experienced Indian fighter who also might have enough influence with the Cherokees and other southern Indians to convince them to fight alongside him?

To Washington, the answer to that question was clear enough by April. South Carolina governor Charles Pinckney may have been the first to formally recommend Pickens to the president. Pinckney strongly urged that if the Indian war should spread "to the southward," Pickens should be asked to lead the war effort. Pinckney asserted that Pickens was "a man at least as well qualified to manage a contest with the Indians as any in the Union." Pickens had great influence with the Indians and great "knowledge of their affairs." However, Pinckney, explained, "his modesty is so great, that he . . . will never solicit or offer himself."[13]

Washington replied on March 17 that he was taking Pinckney's suggestion seriously and acknowledged Pickens's "talent, knowledge, and influence."[14] In fact, Washington had already given serious thought to whom he should appoint as generals for the upcoming Indian war. In an extensive memo to himself, the commander in chief worked through several scenarios in which there would be a major general and two brigadiers. He wrote several sentences critiquing the strengths and weaknesses, including drinking habits, of sixteen officers from the old Continental army and several militia officers. Pickens was one of the few former militia officers he considered. Washington had never met Pickens, however, and he made no substantive comments beside Pickens's name. In one scenario, though, Henry Lee would be appointed major general, with Pickens and James Wilkinson serving as the brigadiers.[15]

As the situation deteriorated, Governor William Blount's position grew increasingly difficult. His superiors in the federal government, including the president, clearly wanted peace in the Southwest Territory, and Blount honestly strived to maintain it. His own constituents, however, were eager for war. Blount mobilized small detachments for defensive purposes only and, like Pickens, tried to make sure peaceful or allied Indians were not attacked because of hostility toward the race in general. Meanwhile, he continually forwarded information to Knox to try to make him understand how serious the situation actually was. Pickens helped in this regard when he wrote Blount that "the Cherokees have stole more horses from the frontiers of this State, these six months past, than they have done for years before." Pickens reported that most Cherokee leaders seemed to favor peace, but because so many "active young men" were "killing people and stealing horses, it is extremely difficult [to know] how to act." Pickens still wanted peace but understood that most of his neighbors preferred war in order to avoid the fatal consequences of mistaking an enemy Cherokee or Creek Indian for an ally. Even those on the most exposed parts of the frontier "would prefer an open war to such a situation. The reason is obvious; a man would then know, when he saw an Indian he saw an enemy, and be prepared and act accordingly." Blount forwarded the letter to Knox.[16]

Thus, early in 1792, Andrew Pickens and William Blount finally found themselves allies after seven years of mutual distrust. For once, the two men shared similar goals. Both were willing to go the extra mile for peace. However, they both led local constituents who were growing more anxious for war, and both were willing to recommend military solutions to the crisis if there was no alternative. Blount proposed making a new treaty with the Chickasaws and Choctaws.[17] The stated purpose of meeting with those tribes would be to establish a trading post at Bear Creek near Muscle Shoals on the Tennessee River, in modern northwestern Alabama. The Treaty of Hopewell had called for such a post six years before, but the U.S. government had been unable to establish it. More urgently, though, Blount hoped that in the event of a larger Indian war, the United States could secure the alliance, or at least the neutrality, of the Chickasaws and Choctaws. The meeting would be scheduled for early June in Nashville.

Knox and Washington approved of Blount's plan and envisioned a key role in it for Pickens. Anthony Wayne had finally been appointed major general and tasked with defeating the tribes in the northwest if they did not sign a treaty. Knox asked Pickens to join Blount and use his influence with the Chickasaws and Choctaws and Cherokee leaders. Knox wanted Pickens to coordinate with Wayne and, once he was at Nashville, persuade up to 500 Indians to join him in an expedition against the northern tribes if Wayne was ready to launch it. Pickens would prepare to take command of some U.S. cavalry and infantry forces as well. Throughout this period of federal service, Pickens would hold the rank of brigadier general in the U.S. Army and be paid accordingly. Knox tried to appeal to Pickens's sense of duty: "The President of the United States, upon mature reflection, has conceived that your influence over the Cherokees particularly, and the Southern Indians generally, would, if exerted at the present time, be peculiarly useful and important to your country. And the reputation you possess will not permit him to doubt, that, if possible, you will not hesitate to undertake the object."[18] Pickens reluctantly agreed, though he confided to a friend, "I have two large a family and getting two old for such active service." Revealing only the diplomatic part of his mission, Pickens explained that the journey to Nashville would be arduous: "This is a jorney of upwards of 400 miles, grait part of the way through mountains, and a dangerous wilderness, this my friend, for my Country."[19]

Pickens left home on June 5 and joined Blount in Knoxville on the tenth. The supplies and gifts for the treaty were delayed, so the two men did not depart for Nashville until July 5. Even then, a serious drought kept water on the Cumberland River so low that the goods could not be transported immediately, and negotiations could not begin until August. While the goods traveled by river, Blount and Pickens and a small guard of militia made a difficult and dangerous journey through war-infested territory. Pickens reported that more than twenty whites were killed by bands of Creeks, Cherokees, and Shawnees while he was on his mission, and Secretary Knox feared for Pickens's and Blount's safety. During the negotiations in Nashville, the Choctaws and Chickasaws refused to allow the trading post to be set up at Bear Creek. Moreover, Pickens never received any word from General Wayne, so he did not formally ask the Indians to join him in an expedition. He was probably relieved, as he clearly had no wish to command troops again. But the Chickasaw and Choctaw chiefs were so agreeable in private conferences that Pickens believed they would have joined American troops if asked. They also warned Pickens and Blount about the hostile intentions of the Creeks and confirmed that the Spanish were trying to unite the southern tribes against the United States.[20]

Pickens left the negotiations more convinced than ever that it was time to punish the Creeks. In his view, the Cherokee situation was morally ambiguous, as whites had consistently violated the Treaty of Hopewell of 1785 and there were still many Cherokees who earnestly desired peace. The Creeks were another matter. McGillivray, it seemed, had made absolutely no effort to honor the long-sought-for Treaty of New York of 1790. Having promised to maintain the peace and having accepted a general's commission in the U.S. Army, he had almost immediately returned to conspiring with the Spanish. (Unknown to the Americans, Spain began paying McGillivray $2,000 a year in 1791, $800 more than he was receiving from the United States. In 1792, the Spanish increased his annual stipend to $3,500.) Creek warriors were regularly ranging far from their homes to steal horses and kill white settlers in Tennessee. Pickens told Knox that it was just as well that arrangements could not be made to get the Chickasaws and Choctaws to fight the northern Indians; they should be used instead against the Creeks. The latter tribe, he asserted, "would never desist from murdering and robbing the defenceless frontier citizens . . . until they are chastized and restrained by the hands of Government."[21] Pickens made the same recommendation to South Carolina governor Charles Pinckney. Convinced that the "Creeks are on the eve of going to war with us," he urged that it was time to rearm the state's frontiers and *carry a vigorous campaign into the Creek country; this would convince the Southern Indians, in general, that we are able and determined to protect ourselves, and would chastise their insolence. This might prevent the junction of more tribes against* [us] *than perhaps is now expected*" (emphasis in original). When it came to some enemies, diplomacy was impossible without war, and only a strong and determined government could wage such a war: "It is vain to attempt treaties with the Creeks, or to make any offers to them, until they are chastised by the arm of Government."[22]

With Pickens away from home in mid-1792, Robert Anderson had been the ranking officer in the South Carolina backcountry, and he too recommended war against the Creeks. Anderson explained what all leaders on the frontier knew about waging war with Indians. It was impossible to defeat them by means of a passive defense, allowing the Indians to strike where and when they wished. One must destroy their villages and food supplies, forcing them to come out in the open and fight or else sue for peace.[23] Governor Pinckney complied with Anderson's and Pickens's requests to ready troops, arms, and ammunition on the frontier but decided not to send an expedition without federal approval, and Secretary Knox was still not

The Strong Hand of Government, 1789–1793

convinced that it was time to take on the Creeks. Everyone agreed, however, that when war came, Pickens must be placed in command. Anderson insisted on it, saying that he was the most capable man for the job and that the respect for him was so great that the militia would undoubtedly turn out to serve under him. Blount, Pickens's former enemy, agreed, "most heartily" recommending Pickens to command any troops raised from the Carolinas: "He unquestionably is a brave, prudent, experienced officer in Indian warfare."[24] There was no need to convince Knox. In August, he had informed Pickens that the president still wanted him to lead troops if a campaign was launched the following year.[25] The only one who seemed to disagree was Pickens himself. Pickens protested that he was "too far advanced in life to engage again in the trouble and difficulty of military affairs, especially with the militia; and have, perhaps too long neglected the interest of a large family." Pickens was content to suggest to the governor what orders he should give to Anderson.[26]

Pickens returned to his "large family" after an absence of three months. Less than three months after that, he was off again to Columbia for the fall session of the state senate. A great deal of his work in the senate was devoted to military affairs and readiness along the frontier. Near the close of the session, he was chosen as a presidential and vice-presidential elector and would soon cast his vote for the reelection of George Washington and John Adams.[27] The General Assembly also addressed the need to elect another congressman. After the census of 1790, South Carolina rated a sixth congressman. Pickens served on a joint senate-house committee that wrote a new statute redrawing congressional districts and establishing times of election. South Carolina would now have a district encompassing the court districts of Washington and Pinckney, essentially the northern tier of the state west of the Catawba River.[28] When the legislators from these districts met, they asked Pickens to accept the candidacy. Initially he refused, so the nomination was given to Captain Samuel Earle, who had served under Pickens during the Revolution. After Pickens later regretted his decision, Earle immediately withdrew his candidacy.[29] When the election took place on Monday, February 4, 1793, Pickens was chosen as the upper backcountry's next congressman and would take his seat the following autumn. It was a momentous week for the Pickens family—the day before the election, Ezekiel Pickens married Elizabeth Bonneau in Charleston. Elizabeth was the sister of Floride Bonneau, who had married Andrew Pickens's brother-in-law John Ewing Colhoun.[30]

The situation along the southwestern frontier remained volatile throughout 1793. One of the few pieces of good news was that the threat from the Chickamaugas—the militant faction of Cherokees—had been partially blunted the preceding fall. In September, John Watts had led several hundred Cherokees and Creeks, perhaps more than 700 in all, against the settlement of Nashville. Before attacking Nashville itself, the Indians had to overwhelm nearby Buchanan's Station, consisting of two stone blockhouses surrounded by a stockade. Sixteen white men and several women and children defended the stockade when the Indians attacked on the night of September 30. According to Tennessee lore, the women reloaded the guns so that the men could keep up a continual fire as they aimed through the portholes. "Mrs. Buchanan," says one account, "went around from bastion to bastion, with a bottle of whiskey in one hand, and with the other distributing bullets from her apron, and thus aiding and encouraging all." The well-fortified white defenders inflicted a bloody repulse on the Indians, and Watts himself was wounded and unable to control his force.[31]

Thus outright war with the entire Cherokee nation was averted for the time being. The Creek situation, however, was more dangerous than ever when President Washington invited Pickens and Blount to Philadelphia in the summer of 1793 for meetings with him and Knox. Pickens's invitation indicated that the Washington administration was still seriously considering war on the southern tribes, especially the Creeks. Upon receiving the summons, Pickens hurried to Charleston in early July to confer with Governor William Moultrie.

Both of these Revolutionary War veterans—Pickens and Moultrie—were convinced that "nothing else can be done" but to raise an army of 5,000 men from the southern states and launch an expedition against the Creeks. They calculated that the army could be ready by October 1.[32] Pickens had received word in April, probably from Cherokee traders, that the bulk of the Creek nation had declared war on the United States.[33] Though McGillivray had proven himself elusive and untrustworthy, Pickens and others had perceived him as one whose influence had kept the Creeks from launching all-out war on the American states. But McGillivray, his body wracked by sloth and heavy drinking, had died in February. By that time, the Creeks were officially at war with the Chickasaws, with whom Pickens and Blount had had friendly talks six months previously. In August, Pickens had personally promised the Chickasaws and Choctaws that "your enemies are our enemies, and ours, yours."[34] In February 1793, the Chickasaws challenged and begged American leaders, including Pickens, to honor that promise.[35]

The Strong Hand of Government, 1789–1793

From Charleston, Pickens sailed to Philadelphia, arriving before July 24 and immediately meeting with Knox and Blount. Pickens carried with him Moultrie's letter to Governor Knox expressing the governor's support for a military campaign. Moultrie's letter also enthusiastically recommended Pickens as the man who should command the expedition. Pickens delivered the letter, which lacked earlier statements that Pickens was reluctant to take the field—showing that he was now willing to do so. Pickens, as usual, allows us no personal insight to explain his change of heart. However, Robert Anderson, who was perhaps his closest friend, had predicted back in September that that change would occur. Though he had not broached the subject with him, Anderson thought that Pickens would eventually consent to lead troops again for "self-defence, or more properly, the defence of the country in which he lives."[36] This makes sense when one remembers that Pickens had grown more and more convinced throughout 1792 that the Creeks were "on the eve" of attacking the frontiers of Georgia and South Carolina.[37] Pickens had also grown convinced, like so many others, that he was the best man for the job.[38]

As soon as Pickens arrived in Philadelphia, Knox began plying him with detailed questions from himself and Washington, seeking advice on how to conduct a war against the southern Indians if necessary. Pickens provided estimates of the fighting strength of the various tribes; information on terrain and the feasibility of crossing troops over rivers at various times of year in the South; the number of militia that should be mobilized from each state; estimates of how long it would take to mobilize them; distances from various departure points to key Creek settlements; and supply needs and costs, including, for example, how expensive it would be to obtain pack horses on the southern frontier. Pickens reemphasized that "only a demonstration of the power of the United States" would stop the Creeks' depredations. Knox prepared a long memorandum with Pickens's information and delivered it to Washington on July 25.[39] The next day, the president sent eight further queries to Pickens. Among other things, the commander in chief wanted to know if the 5,000-man force Pickens recommended was meant to deal with the Cherokees also, and if not, how many more men would be needed to fight them if the need arose. Finally, what would be the best way to easily distinguish and protect factions of those tribes who desired peace—might the peaceful Indians be ordered to stay in designated places where they would not be molested? Pickens responded with another detailed memorandum. Though he still did not believe war with the Cherokees was necessary, he answered Washington's questions in case the latter decided that it was. He also did not believe that Washington's proposed plan for protecting Indians who were not warring with whites would be effective—Washington would have to trust to the experience and good judgment of the commander. Though Pickens agreed that "humanity and justice points out everything . . . should be done to preserve those unfortunate people from harm," the best course would be to "leave it to the prudence and humanity of the commanding Officer of the Southern armies."[40]

By the time Pickens arrived in Philadelphia, there had been indications that the Cherokee lower towns had been ready to bury the hatchet. This promising development was upset by the renegade actions of a Tennessee militia officer, Captain John Beard. Blount had sent diplomats to the village of the peace-seeking chief Hanging Maw to confer with him. Hanging Maw had fought the Americans during the Revolution and had refused to participate in the Treaty of Dewitt's Corner in 1777. After the Cherokees suffered devastating attacks from Virginia militia led by John Sevier and Arthur Campbell in the summer of 1780, Hanging Maw changed course. He declared himself for peace in a tribal council in early 1781 and then sent messages to Colonel Joseph Martin asking for peace and denouncing the British. Since that time, he had consistently been a partner for peace with Pickens and communicated often with him. While the white diplomats were conferring with Hanging Maw, however, Captain Beard's company burst into the village and killed eight or nine peaceful Indians. One of them was Hanging Maw's wife, and the chief himself was shot through the arm. Daniel Smith, acting governor of the territory while Blount was away, was mortified, as were Blount, Knox, Pickens, and Washington when they heard about the atrocity. Beard was court-martialed and ordered to disband his men, but the damage was done.[41] Now no one, including Pickens, could predict whether even the larger faction of peaceful Cherokees would remain peaceful for long.[42] Hanging Maw angrily told Smith that he no longer trusted the whites and refused Smith's suggestion that he go to Philadelphia.[43]

With this added factor of uncertainty to consider, Knox asked Pickens and Blount to provide detailed recommendations on how to handle Indian affairs in the Southwest. Blount was elated to find that he and Pickens were in total agreement—the federal government must act decisively. Blount and Pickens stressed that the United States should finally establish the long-planned trading post at the mouth of Bear Creek near the Tennessee, in the Chickasaw territory. Though some Chickasaws had objected to this

The Strong Hand of Government, 1789–1793

in the summer of 1792, lately they had pled for supplies from American traders.[44] It would take a battalion of troops to establish the post and half that amount to maintain it, and it would accomplish several goals. First, Pickens and Blount explained that if the Chickasaws could not get goods from American traders, they would have to get them from Spain. They would be forced to make peace with the Creeks and ally themselves with Spain. On the other hand, if the Americans could supply the goods needed by the Chickasaws and Choctaws, those tribes would certainly adhere to the United States and have no need to cooperate with the Spanish or with their hated enemies, the Creeks. A post on Bear Creek could also disrupt communications between the northern and southern tribes, making a grand Indian confederation against the United States less likely. The Creeks might object to the post, but they could not be any more hostile toward American intentions than they already were at that time and had no legitimate claim to the area anyway. The Cherokees also claimed the territory belonged to them, but as the Chickasaws actually occupied it, the Cherokees' claim was weak.[45]

Knox followed Pickens and Blount's first report with two additional questions: what could be done to delay war with the Creeks, and how could the government assuage the anger of the Cherokees after the recent murders by lawless whites?[46] The two frontier leaders responded immediately, and all their answers suggested that war with the Creeks was unavoidable. The only possible way to delay war with the Creeks, they said, was to send "some Person of Address and knowledge of Indian Affairs" to the Creeks, ostensibly as a trader. That person could distribute gifts to the chiefs and probably "induce the Creeks to commit fewer Murders and Robberies than they otherwise would." Meanwhile the white agent could "collect much Information that would be useful in the War with that Nation."[47] The situation with the Cherokees ironically also pointed to war with the Creeks. Blount and Pickens concluded that unfortunately no jury in the Southwest Territory would convict Beard and put the white murderers to death, because the "Frontier People" did not believe the government had done anything to avenge the murder of their own people by Indians. However, execution of the white murderers was the only result that would permanently satisfy the Cherokees. A large number of gifts would satisfy them temporarily, and thus postpone war, but eventually the Cherokees would demand blood vengeance and take it themselves if necessary. "Yet to us," wrote Pickens and Blount, "it appears essential that something at this critical Period should be done to satisfy them temporarily, that is, until the Strong Hand of Government is exercised over the Creeks and then Fear may restrain them permanently." Thus, even peace with the Cherokees depended on war with the Creeks. Until the war was begun, the Americans should invite "the [Cherokee] Chiefs generally and the Friends of the deceased to a Conference."[48]

Discussions continued nearly until the end of August, and Pickens was eager to return home. By the middle of the month, Washington and Knox were backing away from war again. As for the Cherokees, Knox doubted the nation could honorably attack the Cherokees after the largely unpunished atrocities by Beard and other whites. And the federal agent to the Creeks, James Seagrove, persuaded Knox that most of the Creeks were not eager for war. Meanwhile Washington feared that war with the Creeks might also mean war with Spain. Secretary of State Thomas Jefferson had just begun talks with the Spanish in regard to their relationship with the Creeks, and the president was hopeful that the latter would produce positive results. Until Congress reconvened later in the year, war could not be officially declared anyway. On August 27, Washington invited Pickens and Blount to dine with him and announced the conclusion to postpone a decision on war until Congress met. Pickens was thanked for his services and dismissed. Washington informed Governor Moultrie that he was "satisfied with the information of General Pickens, and if the time shall arrive [for an expedition], I shall be greatly gratified by his taking an eminent part therein."[49]

Pickens's attitude toward the Creeks from 1792 to 1794 was fundamentally different from that of 1783–90. This change of outlook was due to external events, not changes in his basic beliefs. Pickens had assumed the role of a peacemaker ever since the Long Swamp treaty of 1782. Beneath this diplomatic garb, however, the old warrior was still there. The world was violent and treacherous, and peace was not possible without strength. Even more important, Pickens believed treaties carried the force of both law and morality. Americans should restrain and punish their own countrymen who would violate them and be ready to punish the Indians for doing the same. The turn in Pickens's attitude toward the Creeks was due to his perception that they had flagrantly violated the Treaty of New York. Moreover, Creek hostility was a key linchpin in the dreaded threat of a multitribal alliance that could devastate white settlements on the frontier and produce national humiliation. Until the national government acted decisively, it would have to endure more depredations, tolerate more Spanish meddling, and sacrifice self-respect. The United States had a duty to punish the Creeks. Law, order, national honor, and the safety of the nation's citizens demanded it.

FIFTEEN

War, Peace, and Corruption, 1793–1797

[Congress should adopt] wise and vigorous laws [for the]
preservation of the national character.

George Washington to Congress, January 30, 1794

When Andrew Pickens went home in September 1793, he knew he would be returning to Philadelphia in three months as a congressman. He would have an even greater opportunity to educate others on the realities of the frontier and to push for decisive and humane action. Pickens the frontier patriot, the advocate for law and order, the man who valued "courage and action," took his nationalism to Congress.

During Pickens's service in the Third Congress (1793–95), the philosophical differences between Federalists and Republicans were more clearly defined than ever and were producing distinct and increasingly bitter factions. Like most political leaders of the day, Pickens abhorred the growing factionalism and "party spirit," but he voted more often with Federalists. Federalists such as Alexander Hamilton, Henry Knox, and the president himself tended to favor a stronger, more energetic national government, while Republicans feared that such a government would threaten the autonomy of states and the rights of individuals. Federalists favored Hamilton's economic program with taxes, tariffs, and a national bank, designed to restore the nation's credit and currency, while Republicans objected that these measures were unconstitutional. In foreign affairs, the fledgling United States was caught in the midst of the economic rivalry and intermittent war between Britain and France. Federalists tended to curry favor with Britain at the expense of France, while Republicans were anti-British and admired—at least initially—the radicals in the French Revolution who were overthrowing the monarchy and attempting to establish a French republic. The core of Federalist support came from New England, while Republicans tended to predominate in the South and West.

Pickens's views made him into something of a unique hybrid of Federalist and Republican. In the late 1780s and early 1790s, Federalism represented nationalism, national unity, and the need for the "strong hand of government" to establish legal and moral order in the new Republic. Violence and vice had to be restrained. Pickens agreed, but the assumptions that brought him to this viewpoint were not identical with those of other Federalists. To Pickens, only decisive leadership at the federal level could provide some measure of justice for the Indians and therefore preserve peace and order on the frontier. However, the frontier fighter of yeoman origins did not share the strands of Federalism that emphasized hierarchy and deference to one's social betters. And while lawful authority must be obeyed, it did not have the right to restrict freedom of speech and conscience. When Federalism moved too far in this direction at the end of the 1790s, Pickens broke with it.

As a southerner and westerner who usually voted with Federalists, Pickens was relatively rare. Most westerners and frontier citizens resented a federal government that drew treaty lines that voided their personal claims and territorial ambitions and that allegedly attempted to protect Indians but did not do enough to protect its own citizens. When they did ask for federal military support, they rarely found it to be adequate or timely and would have been content for the federal government to leave them alone to make their own treaties, make their own land purchases, and prosecute war against the "savages" as they saw fit. Pickens, of course, disagreed, but he tried to convince easterners that the government must act to protect the frontier people.

Pickens was also fairly unique as a Federalist in that he was vehemently anti-British. This was not simply because of bitter wartime memories but because more often it was Britain, rather than France, that appeared as the primary threat to American national honor from the 1780s to the 1810s. Pickens did not object to Frenchmen overthrowing a king and establishing a republic. Like many Americans, however, his approval turned to disgust when the French Revolution, growing ever more radical, spiraled into anarchy and murder. When King Louis XVI was executed in 1793, Pickens wrote his kinsman John Ewing Colhoun, "The manner in which the late King of France lost his life, I am sorry for."[1] Once the liberty ship began drifting into license and murder, Pickens was no longer on board.

War, Peace, and Corruption, 1793–1797

Perhaps the primary reason Pickens had become a candidate for Congress was because he saw the opportunity to shape federal policy on the frontier. By the time he took his seat in December, the Creek situation had improved greatly. Constant Freeman, a War Department official in Georgia, was extremely hopeful that there would soon be peace between the Creeks and Georgians. Then in the last week of December 1793, an event occurred that epitomized the inability of the federal government to maintain the peace. Four white men led by a Captain Jonathan Adams treacherously attacked nine unsuspecting Creeks led by the White Bird-Tail King. The Creeks were hunting well within their own boundaries and had entertained the white men in their camp earlier in the day. When the whites attacked later, two Creeks were killed and the remainder fled to the safety of a small federal garrison at Fort Fidius. There the White Bird-Tail King demanded an explanation. Embarrassed white officials at the fort promised safety for him and his band, which they knew they could not provide as soon as the Indians left the fort; and they promised to seek justice, well knowing that no white jury in Georgia would convict white men for killing Indians.[2]

President Washington laid this information before Congress and asked it to pass "wise and vigorous laws" for the "preservation of the national character." Because of the actions of "some lawless white men," he argued, it was clear that "existing legal provisions are entirely inadequate."[3] Pickens was one of five congressmen appointed to study the matter and make a report. Pickens, a junior congressman, was not the chair of the committee, but the report it composed revealed his influence. Pickens almost never spoke on the floor of Congress, but in this case he actually delivered the report. In order to prevent "depredations of the hostile Indians, as [well as] to prevent unauthorized attacks, by the lawless white inhabitants," the committee made several key recommendations. First, the president should be authorized to call out the militia of various states when necessary to protect white settlers and enforce the Indians' compliance with treaties. He should also be authorized to establish military posts and garrison them with locally recruited troops and to have mounted companies patrolling between the posts. These troops would prevent depredations by both sides and encroachments on Indian hunting grounds. Finally, any state militia officer or enlisted soldier who committed murder or other crimes upon Indians without federal authorization would be subject to a military court-martial—if the crime was murder, they could be executed if convicted.[4]

This last provision would take justice out of the hands of biased local juries and make it possible for white murderers of Indians to be actually punished. This was the measure most likely to restrain white depredations and Indian retaliation. When the bill was finally presented, however, that provision was stripped out of it. Debate over the frontier defense bill continued for the rest of the session. The House of Representatives eventually approved the other measures proposed by Pickens's committee and sent the bill to the Senate. The Senate, however, approved its own greatly altered version. Dominated by northeastern Federalists less familiar with the southwestern frontier, the Senate version rejected the provisions for calling out the militia and establishing military posts. Instead of allowing the president to mobilize up to 10,000 militiamen, it simply provided for the raising of a new regiment of regulars (1,140 men) to protect the frontier. House Republicans from western districts exploded with anger at this drastic change to the bill. They asserted that local militiamen were far more capable and knowledgeable than regular troops when it came to fighting Indians, and their constituents would find a standing army obnoxious. Legislators from more settled eastern districts, they charged, were too ignorant of frontier affairs, and they were unsympathetic to white victims of Indian attacks. Pickens voted for the new Senate version, apparently feeling that some new military measure was better than none at all. He had little choice, for the Senate and House Republicans were unable to come up with a meaningful compromise. Republican James Madison of Virginia, meanwhile, objected to language that had appeared in the bill allowing governors to authorize retaliatory attacks against Indians who attacked whites, a tool designed to help the governors compel the Indians' adherence to treaties. Madison's legalistic argument was that once hostilities commenced, treaties were no longer in operation and therefore could not be enforced. The hostilities could lead only to new treaties, not to the enforcement of old ones. Madison's objection resulted in more unproductive debate. Whether or not his argument was unnecessarily pedantic, it was certainly unhelpful. Ultimately, Pickens's (and Washington's) effort to bring order to the frontier was stymied. The bill failed, a victim of northeastern Federalists' ignorance of frontier realities and Republicans' refusal to compromise.[5]

Pickens's fierce nationalism was not always obvious during the first session of the Third Congress. In April he was assigned to a committee to examine a petition by western citizens regarding the navigation of the Mississippi River. The westerners wanted Congress to take measures to ensure their free navigation of the river and to prevent interference of that right by Spain and other powers. The Washington administration, however, asked Congress to delay taking action, since it was already involved with negotiations with Spain. Pickens's committee acceded to the president's wishes and recommended that the House delay consideration of the matter at least until the next session.[6]

At first Pickens seemed reluctant to support the administration's desire for more naval vessels to protect overseas commerce. In early February, the House had debated the request for authorization to build six small warships in response to the attacks on merchant shipping by pirates off the Algerian coast. The House finally approved the measure, but only after adding the stipulation (supported by Pickens) that a committee be appointed to study ways to minimize the expense. Even as this debate was taking place, however, the threat of another war with Britain was looming. Now at war with revolutionary France, Britain began seizing American merchant ships doing business with French colonies. His Majesty's government also asserted its intention to retain control of forts in American western territories. An angry anti-British backlash followed, and Pickens was part of it. He voted several times to cut off all trade with Britain until Britain abandoned military posts on American soil, compensated American citizens for all shipping losses and damages, and returned slaves taken during the evacuation of Charleston.[7] While he had earlier shown some reluctance to support the building of new warships, he now supported the navy's plan to build ten galleys.[8] He also served on a committee that recommended raising a corps of artillerists and engineers to strengthen the nation's coastal fortifications; authorizing the president to call out 80,000 militiamen ready to march "at a moment's warning"; and increasing the size of the regular army as soon as war was actually declared.[9]

Pickens's generally nationalist, pro-military stance continued into the Third Congress's second session (November 1794–March 1795). While other congressmen feared a "large" standing army, Pickens thought it necessary. When some Republicans led an attempt to reduce the size of the regular army, or "legion," of the United States from 4,000 men to 2,500, Pickens opposed it.[10] Republicans, however, probably approved of his frugality in other areas. When the threat of war with Britain faded in late 1794, Pickens supported reducing the appropriations for harbor fortifications—improvements he had supported in the previous session. His nationalism and suspicion of Britain reemerged the following year, when he was out of Congress, with his reaction to the treaty concluded between Secretary of State John Jay and Britain. The Jay Treaty strengthened trading ties with Britain but greatly compromised American neutral trading rights and other grievances that the Republic had against its former mother country. Many Americans were outraged, and Pickens was one of them. In a public meeting in Pendleton, citizens denounced the treaty and warned against close association with the "monarchical and unregenerated" nation of Britain. The leaders of the meeting were Pickens, his friend Robert Anderson, his brother-in-law John E. Colhoun, and his pastor, Reverend Dr. Thomas Reese.[11]

Congress and the president in 1794 faced not only the threat of war with foreign powers but also domestic rebellion. The "Whiskey Rebellion" resulted from frontier farmers' hatred of the "Whiskey Tax," passed in 1791. Treasury secretary Alexander Hamilton had successfully proposed the law as part of his fiscal plan to restore the nation's economic health. Whiskey, however, was vital to the economy of many frontier districts and even served as an unofficial form of currency. In fact many farmers could not get their corn to market and profit from it unless they first distilled it into whiskey, which was much cheaper to transport. In the summer of 1794, frontier anger finally exploded into outright rebellion and attacks on revenue officers in the four western counties of Pennsylvania. Since Congress was not in session, President Washington acted on his own to mobilize an army and put down the rebellion, then officially reported his actions to Congress when it reconvened. Pickens, as a frontier farmer, no doubt understood the frustration of the frontiersmen. But the stern law-and-order man had no sympathy for those who insulted and attacked law enforcement officers. He voted with the majority of Congress to sanction Washington's actions and to seek reimbursement for those who had property damaged in the insurrection. But Pickens drew the line on attempts to curb free speech and free association. Part of Washington's message to Congress condemned "self-created societies," which had allegedly flamed the rebellion.[12] The president was referring to groups called "democratic societies" or "republican societies" that generally opposed the federal government and the growth of federal authority. When Federalists in the House proposed congressional censure or "reprobation" of these societies, Republicans objected. The debate raged on the House floor for four days. Republicans argued that Congress had no right to condemn private associations of citizens. Pickens agreed. He insisted on law and order and respected property rights, but government had no right to condemn citizens who formed associations and expressed dissent.[13]

Pickens generally supported Hamilton's Federalist program of taxes designed to eliminate the federal budget deficit and restore the nation's credit. He supported a controversial "stamp tax," excise taxes on sugar and snuff produced in the United States, and tariff duties on a host of imported products.[14] He also joined a majority of the House in imposing a tax, which some considered unconstitutional, on the use of carriages.[15] At other times Pickens voted with the interests of his home state on matters of finance or in support of the petitions of South Carolina citizens. One example of his state and regional loyalty appeared after he left Congress and served again as a presidential elector in the election of 1796. Pickens and the rest of the South Carolina delegation voted for the southerner, Thomas Jefferson, a Republican, over the Federalist John Adams of Massachusetts. For vice president, they voted for South Carolina native son Thomas Pinckney rather than Aaron Burr of New York.[16] By the time Pickens left Congress for good in the spring of 1795, he had established a record as an independent with Federalist leanings. While typically supporting a strong central government and vigorous national defense, he was sympathetic to the concerns of the South and West, and he opposed the administration's pro-British stance. Despite these occasional departures from Federalist policy, he still had the confidence of Washington and Knox's Federalist administration.

While he was in Congress, the leaders of his own state continued to look to Pickens for military leadership. In May 1794, the General Assembly geographically reorganized the state militia into an upper and a lower division. Pickens was promoted to major general and made commander of the upper division. More than ever before, Pickens's fellow South Carolinians left the defense of the state's western border to him. When he returned home from Congress in the spring of 1795, he found that the legislature had weakened defenses on the frontier by reducing the size of the frontier guard. This was an economy measure, and Governor Arnoldus Vanderhorst tried to further the legislature's intent by asking the federal government to assume some of the costs. The timing for such retrenchment was not good—the Creeks were threatening new attacks and actually stole some horses at Oconee Station in the northwestern corner of the state. Partially on his own initiative, Brigadier General Robert Anderson had slightly increased the size of the guard to fifty-seven men. Vanderhorst apparently agreed that this measure was necessary, but he felt it his duty to report it to the legislature. Rather than continue to micromanage the defense of the frontier and haggle over costs, both houses passed resolutions implicitly trusting Pickens's judgment on how to defend the frontier, "that such Guard may be in future maintained at Oconee Station, as may appear to Major General Pickens necessary."[17]

For a brief time between 1792 and 1794, Pickens had begun to sound more hawkish in his policy toward the Indians. Even then, however, he never abandoned his role as a would-be peacemaker and Indian protector. In the summer of 1794, just after his return to Hopewell and the first session of the Third Congress, Pickens received a request from Secretary of War Knox. Knox had just concluded the Treaty of Philadelphia with several Cherokee chiefs, including the previously pro-war chief Doublehead. The Cherokees confirmed their cessions made in the Treaty of Hopewell and to the marking of the new boundary; in return their annuity was increased from $1,500 in goods to $5,000.[18] Knox feared that the Cherokee delegation, laden with supplies and gifts, might be ambushed by "lawless whites" on the way home, with disastrous consequences for Indian-white relations.[19] Knox therefore sent them home by way of Pickens's territory in upper South Carolina. He wrote Pickens on June 27, 1794, and asked him to increase the guard at Oconee Station and ensure that the Cherokees arrived safely in their own territory. Oconee Station was about thirty miles northwest of Hopewell and Pendleton Courthouse, in the extreme northwest corner of the state near where it abutted Cherokee territory. Pickens did not receive Knox's letter until August 10 but acted quickly and decisively to carry out his request, ordering Anderson to mobilize 200 men from his brigade for a period of two months. Pickens received intelligence that a "Captn. McCluskey from Georgia, who is famous for such business," was raising men and planning to attack and rob the Cherokees before they reached Pendleton. He therefore sent a company to meet the Indians and escort them to Pendleton. From there, they would be escorted to Oconee Station and then into the Cherokee nation. Pickens placed the entire operation under the leadership of Major Edward Taylor, a former Continental officer with an excellent record—Pickens called him a "man of confidence and respect." These forceful measures resulted in a safe journey through hostile territory for the Cherokees.[20]

By the time Pickens left Congress, several other events brought him out of the war camp and reinvigorated his attempts to protect the Indians—not only the Cherokees but the Creeks as well. In August 1794, an unauthorized expedition against the Cherokees launched from the Cumberland settlement had resulted in the destruction of the Indian villages of Nickajack and Running Water and the death of between 50 and 100 Cherokees.[21] This had occurred while Doublehead and other Cherokee leaders were under Pickens's protection at Pendleton. A few months earlier, in May 1794, 150 Georgia militiamen had attacked another group of Creek Indians while they were camped near U.S. troops for protection. At the time, five of their chiefs were in Augusta negotiating with the governor of Georgia.[22] That same month, another lawless act was committed by Pickens's former Revolutionary comrade Elijah Clarke. Clarke and other settlers had established an illegal settlement on the southwest side of the Oconee River, clearly in Creek territory. It took five months of warnings and finally a military expedition to force Clarke and his followers to abandon their adventure.[23]

As had happened before, Pickens found himself disapproving not only his countrymen's lawless aggression but also their greed. During the second session of Pickens's congressional service, William Blount and his associates made several attempts to protect their western land investments. One of Blount's younger brothers, Thomas, was a congressman from North Carolina. He supported efforts of speculators to receive federal reimbursement for lands they had purchased that had later been recognized as Indian territory by federal treaties. To Pickens and most other congressmen, those purchases were illegal, and they blocked the Blounts' efforts.[24] Thus, the issue that had divided Pickens and William Blount at the Hopewell treaty in 1785 reappeared, as did the acrimony between the two men. Pickens was also appointed to a committee to resolve a boundary dispute between Virginia and Blount's Southwest Territory. His committee presented a bill favoring Virginia settlers' claims at the expense of Blount's, though the bill was tabled and the dispute left unresolved for several more years.[25]

Blount's dealings, however, paled in comparison to the massive "Yazoo Land Fraud" that occupied headlines in 1795. In December 1794, the Georgia legislature passed a bill granting 35 million acres to four land speculation companies for a total of $500,000—a cost of less than two cents per acre. Most of the land was territory still claimed by the state of Georgia as a result of its own treaties with the Indians at Augusta, Shoulderbone, and Galphinton but preserved for the Creeks in the Treaty of New York. When Governor George Mathews vetoed the bill—called the "Yazoo bill"—its sponsors crafted a devious strategy. They passed a new bill that was much less objectionable. It provided the means by which the land would be opened to the state's Revolutionary veterans; appropriated money to purchase it from the Creeks; instructed the state's congressmen and U.S. senators to ask the federal government to conclude a treaty with the Creeks by which the land could be purchased; and called for three Georgians to be appointed as state treaty commissioners. Then, the previously vetoed bill was attached to the new, more benign one as a "supplementary" bill. Governor Mathews signed it on January 7, 1795.

The passage of the bill created popular outrage in Georgia. There was undeniable evidence of massive bribery and intimidation in the passage of the law, with many legislators standing to profit, including one of Georgia's U.S. senators, James Gunn. The measure was a windfall to wealthy investors at the expense of ordinary citizens. In Philadelphia, Congress at first seemed unaware of the size of the fraud that had been perpetrated. On March 2, the day before adjournment, Pickens and a majority of the House voted in favor of a resolution that would allow the president to negotiate for the territory in question (so that it could be transferred to the four Yazoo land speculation companies).

Some congressmen, however, perceived that they were dealing with an issue of great legal complexity. The Senate chose to ignore Georgia's request that the president be allowed to negotiate for the land. Instead, that body resolved that the attorney general should investigate the legality of the Yazoo Act and report to Congress at the next session. The next day, March 3, the House agreed with the Senate's course. As time passed, the whole affair became known as the "Yazoo Land Fraud." The scandal represented just the type of chaos and corruption that horrified Federalist proponents of moral and legal order on the frontier; meanwhile, the way in which it promised to enrich lawmakers and wealthy speculators at the expense of common Georgia citizens offended many Republicans as well.[26]

A year later, Georgia would repeal the obnoxious portion of the act— the "supplementary bill" that was a boondoggle for speculators. However, the rest of the law was still intact, leaving the state committed to asserting its land claims for the sake of its veterans. The territorial issue was not just a legal question of whether the Creeks had title to the lands or whether they belonged to Georgia as per the treaties of Galphinton and Shoulderbone. President Washington recognized, as did Pickens and many others, that nothing was more likely to incite the Creeks to war than an attempt to acquire more land from them. Secretary of War Thomas Pickering explained to Governor Mathews that the government had worked hard to keep the Creeks peaceful, "and it is well known, that no measures excite so much jealousy among them, as those which affect their lands."[27]

Washington decided on a course almost diametrically opposed to Georgia's. He decided to accede to Georgia's request to seek a new treaty with the Creeks. The treaty would provide an opportunity to investigate the

"causes of the dissatisfaction of the Creeks" and their recent attacks. However, he stipulated that the treaty would be "made in the general terms of the
treaty of New York." Additionally, it would not "be considered as affecting
any question which may arise, upon the supplementary act, passed by the
Legislature of the State of Georgia."[28] In other words, the next treaty would
not be a massive land grab for the sake of speculators and corrupt politicians.
As if to emphasize this point, in June Washington announced his nomi-
nees for the new treaty commission: George Clymer, Benjamin Hawkins,
and Andrew Pickens. Clymer was a reliable Federalist from Pennsylvania;
Hawkins, of course, was Pickens's former colleague on the Hopewell treaty
commission. Both Hawkins and Pickens had been recognized, sometimes
criticized, as too protective of Indian rights; none of the three were likely
to cave in to the demands of frontier speculators or the state of Georgia.[29]

Pickens left Congress for good on March 3, 1795, perhaps not yet
knowing that Washington would appoint him to yet another treaty commission. As the negotiations with the Creeks would not begin for another
fifteen months, he had a longer period than usual to tend to his own affairs.
Andrew Pickens & Company sold lots, traded with Indians and merchants,
and attempted to collect debts. Pickens devoted attention to the state's frontier defenses, Hopewell Church, local government in Pendleton, and his
own plantation.

Pickens did not receive official word of his appointment to the treaty
commission until May 2, 1796, the year after he left Congress. The new
secretary of war, James McHenry, informed him that he was to meet the
Creeks in mid-May at Coleraine on the St. Marys River in extreme southern
Georgia—territory claimed by both the Creeks and the state of Georgia.[30]
A garrison of federal troops under Lieutenant Colonel Henry Gaither was
there. Washington's specific instructions to the federal commissioners—
Hawkins, Pickens, and Clymer—are not extant; from other correspondence, however, it is fairly clear what they were. The Georgians would be
allowed to try to persuade the Creeks to give up land between the Oconee
and Ocmulgee Rivers in middle Georgia and between the Altamaha and
St. Marys in the south. However, the federal commissioners were to use the
Treaty of New York as a guide. They would seek the establishment of one
or more trading posts garrisoned by federal troops and a school in Creek
territory for the education of Creek youth.

At least two elements of the instructions foreshadowed tensions that
would burst forth at the treaty grounds. First, the commissioners were to
stringently prevent all contact between Georgia traders, speculators, and

militiamen with the Creeks during the negotiations. There was to be no interference, no side deals, no sabotaging the negotiations by supplying the Indians with wild rumors or liquor. Second, Washington and Secretary McHenry were determined to get to the bottom of the murders and reprisals on the Georgia and Cumberland frontiers. In his March 1796 letter to Governor Jared Irwin, McHenry complained that nothing had been done to investigate recent white murders of Indians. Washington had asked the previous governor, George Mathews, to probe and try these crimes in November 1795 but had received no response. McHenry lectured Irwin that failure to try these crimes would hinder the negotiations and bring shame to the American government: "It would indeed be an awkward situation for the Commissioners to find themselves in, were nothing to be done.—How could they censure murders committed by Indians, or call upon them to punish such crimes, whilst recent and glaring murders remain unnoticed by your Government, or unpunished by its laws? Let me, Sir, press your reflexions to this subject, so interesting to the character of Georgia, to justice, humanity, and peace." McHenry's prophecy would prove true—when the Creeks brought up the recent murders during the course of negotiations, the federal commissioners could give them little satisfaction.[31]

Upon receiving his instructions, Pickens hurried to Savannah. There he caught a ride on a schooner traveling up the St. Marys River with Georgia's three state commissioners—James Hendricks, James Simms, and James Jackson. Jackson was an old acquaintance, having served as Pickens's brigade major at Cowpens. Later in his career he claimed that he, not Pickens, had captured the commander of the Seventy-First Highlanders in that battle and that Pickens had not given him proper credit. Pickens did not know that Jackson made this claim and in fact would later defend Jackson against those who tried to minimize his Revolutionary service. Thus, Jackson and Pickens were on amiable terms, no doubt enhanced by Pickens's admiration of Jackson's course during the Yazoo scandal. Jackson had been one of Georgia's U.S. senators when the Yazoo bill passed and had been offered bribes if he would support it. Instead, Jackson denounced the bill and gave up his Senate seat so that he could come home to Georgia to fight against it. Disgusted by the corruption and preferential treatment given to wealthy investors, Jackson led the campaign to repeal the act. This did not mean, though, that Jackson saw the upcoming negotiations in the same light as the federal commissioners.[32] Jackson shared the point of view of most Georgians—the Treaties of Augusta, Galphinton, and Shoulderbone were still valid, the disputed lands should belong to Georgia, and the federal government in Philadelphia had treated Georgia shabbily. Indeed, Georgians of all socioeconomic classes resented federal opposition to the state's efforts to settle land to the west. Ordinary settlers saw land as critical to their economic security and status as autonomous citizens; wealthy speculators craved the opportunity for profit, which in turn might allow them to discharge personal debts. Additionally, Georgians had long eyed western land as the solution to the state's economic troubles. Like neighboring South Carolina, a lack of currency and indebtedness had plagued the state in the years after the Revolution.[33]

The clash between the federal and Georgia treaty commissioners erupted as soon as the latter arrived on May 30. Hawkins and Clymer had been at Coleraine for some time and had posted regulations strictly prohibiting any Georgians' contact with the Creeks without their permission, the rules to be enforced by Lieutenant Colonel Gaither's U.S. Army garrison. The Georgia commissioners saw the rules as an insult to themselves and to the state of Georgia. There was no power on earth, they declared, that had the right to restrict citizens of Georgia from going wherever they wished on Georgia soil. Additionally, Georgia sent a small contingent of state militia with Jackson, Simms, and Hendricks. This move surprised Hawkins and Clymer, since Washington had made it clear to Governor Irwin that federal troops, not militia, would constitute the guard for the treaty negotiations. They agreed to supply provisions for the Georgia troops but refused to allow them to debark from the schooner and asserted that they came under the articles of war and the commands of Lieutenant Colonel Gaither. A tense exchange of notes continued over the next six days, with the Georgians feeling insulted and asserting their place as equal partners in the Creek negotiations and the federal commissioners adamantly maintaining their authority. Jackson would later remember that Pickens was more apt to sympathize with Georgia than were Hawkins and Clymer. Within days of the two commissions meeting, however, Pickens was decidedly in the same camp with Hawkins and Clymer. It does seem that Pickens initially tried to conciliate Jackson and the two other Georgia commissioners whom he had recently got to know on the journey to Coleraine. However, he signed every stern reply by the federal commissioners, and it is not hard to imagine him being the one to insert the clause about the Georgia militia being under the legal authority of Gaither. By June 5, both sides had made conciliatory gestures and could stop bickering with each other long enough to deal with the Creeks.[34]

The negotiations formally began on June 16. Nearly 400 kings, head-men, and warriors processed toward the commissioners, a leader bearing the flag of the United States. Then they danced the "eagle tail dance," which began by having an eagle tail waved over the heads of the commissioners. Six kings or headmen approached the commissioners, one after the other. As each Creek leader did so, there was an eagle tail dance, then handshakes between the Creek headman and the commissioners, and then the smoking of a peace pipe, until the entire ritual had been performed six times. On the seventeenth, negotiations began in earnest. On the eighteenth, the federal commissioners agreed to allow the Georgia commissioners to make their address to the Creeks. Jackson demanded that the Creeks honor the Treaties of Augusta, Galphinton, and Shoulderbone, which neither the Creeks nor the federal government considered valid. (Later it would become clear that Georgia was eager to purchase the land, assuming the Creeks and the federal commissioners maintained that stance.) He also read a long list of grievances and claims for damages. Hawkins reported that the Creeks listened attentively until the Georgia commissioners listed the number of white settlers' hogs the Creeks had killed, "when they all laughed."[35] Big Warrior told the federal commissioners that evening that the Creeks had lost hogs, too, but thought that too trivial a matter to bring up. Besides, he said, if he could be furnished with a piece of paper longer than what the Georgians had, he could fill it up with Creek claims against them. In any event, Hawkins undercut the Georgia commissioners by telling the Creeks they did not have to accept the Georgians' demands or requests for land.[36]

Before the negotiations were over, the Georgia commissioners realized that they would fail in acquiring any significant land cession for their state. They went home but not before writing a formal protest against the conduct of the federal commissioners. Georgia got very little of what it wanted from the Treaty of Coleraine. The Creeks steadfastly refused to relinquish the region between the Oconee and the Ocmulgee, or that below the Altamaha, and the federal commissioners did not press them. In fact, they assured the Creeks, Georgia could not take that land from them unless they chose to sell it, because the Treaty of New York recognized it as theirs. This firm stand behind the Treaty of New York did lead to friction over a disputed strip of land along the upper reaches of the Oconee. The New York treaty stipulated that the border ran along the southern, or western, fork of the Oconee, a tributary known as the Apalachee. The Creeks thought that the border was actually the northern fork, the Little Oconee. Over the last six years, Georgia settlers had poured into the area between the two streams,

War, Peace, and Corruption, 1793–1797

established farms, and paid taxes on the lands. The Creeks insisted that the land was valuable to them and that Alexander McGillivray, while alive, had told them that the border was the Little Oconee. Both sides agreed that McGillivray had deceived his countrymen, but Pickens and the other commissioners would not budge—both sides had to honor the letter of the treaty. The Creeks reluctantly agreed.

Besides confirming Georgia's title to the disputed strip of land, the federal commissioners achieved much of what the Washington administration wanted. The border would be actually marked, with Creek chiefs assisting. The Creeks would also aid the Spanish and Americans in marking the recently agreed border between those nations. The United States would be allowed a five-square-mile tract on the south bank of the Altamaha on which to build a trading post and keep a garrison. This would hopefully force most trading contact to occur where it could be monitored by federal troops. All prisoners and hostages, including slaves, were to be returned, and the Creeks would receive a one-time gift of $6,000 worth of goods. Two requests by the commissioners reflected the administration's "civilizing" mission to the Indians. The treaty stipulated that the United States would provide two blacksmiths with their tools to the Creeks. More important, the commissioners wanted Creek permission to establish a school in their territory for the education of Creek youth. The Indian leaders responded that all their sons who had been sent to white schools had been corrupted into bad young men. The commissioners countered that was because they had come under evil influences. Under the current plan, they would still be in Creek territory and have the moral guidance of their parents. The provision for schools, however, did not appear in the final treaty.[37]

The final document was calculated to achieve Federalist goals for the frontier—a relatively stable boundary and a significant federal presence that could enforce order and justice for both races. Georgians, however, bitterly resented the results. Once again, it seemed, the national government was infringing on the rights of Georgia and the liberties of frontier citizens. Liberty meant the right to buy, sell, and clear land, to prosper and provide better for one's family. The "savages" were an intolerable hindrance to those goals. If the federal government would not help eliminate that obstacle, it should step aside and allow Georgians to do so themselves. To Pickens, the quest for prosperity was laudable as long as it did not violate lawful statutes, treaties, and constitutions. When it did, liberty crossed the line into license and immorality.[38]

Pickens went home in July 1796 after the Treaty of Coleraine and served in the South Carolina house of representatives during the winter of 1796–97. By March 1797, there was a new cast of characters managing Indian policy on the southern frontier. Tennessee had obtained statehood. William Blount had left the governor's office to serve as U.S. senator from Tennessee, and his place was taken by John Sevier, the old Indian fighter whose arrest Pickens had helped bring about several years before. Blount, of course, was also no longer superintendent of Indian affairs south of the Ohio. That role was now filled by Pickens's old friend Benjamin Hawkins, who decided actually to live among the Creeks. John Adams succeeded Washington as president in March 1797. Silas Dinmoor served as federal agent to the Cherokees.

The thrust of federal policy toward the Indians changed little, however. and neither did the desire of westerners to obtain Indian lands. Just a few weeks before the Treat of Coleraine was concluded, Congress had passed the Indian Trade and Intercourse Act. It was yet another example of the Federalists' attempt to have the federal government codify, regulate, and control Americans' relationship with the Indian tribes. Borrowing language from the most current existing treaties, the act described the entire boundary between the United States and the native tribes, from Lake Erie to southern Georgia. The law provided stiff penalties for white citizens who trespassed on Indian territory without a passport signed by a federal official; prescribed the death penalty for any citizen who murdered an Indian; placed tight restrictions on fur traders; authorized U.S. Army officers to apprehend white trespassers on Indian lands; and gave jurisdiction over all such violations to federal courts. The right and duty to punish Indian criminals, meanwhile, belonged to government officials, not to individuals seeking private vengeance. The intent was clear—respect for laws and treaties would drive Indian-white relations, and the federal government would be the enforcer. Land entrepreneurs seeking profit and ordinary settlers seeking land and opportunity would have to succumb to the laws. Liberty was a laudable goal, but it was not true liberty if it transgressed the bounds of law and order.[39]

Now that the western boundaries were defined by various treaties and an act of Congress, it was time to mark them; in fact, section 20 of the Trade and Intercourse Act called for that task, as most of the boundaries had not been actually surveyed and marked. Pickens, Hawkins, and others on the frontier knew that the lack of a clearly marked boundary in Tennessee and

Georgia contributed to misunderstanding and made a lasting peace impossible. President Washington had concurred, but he had instructed Secretary of War McHenry that the project would have to be postponed until 1797 so that commissioners for marking the line could be nominated and approved by the Senate. The president also told McHenry that he hoped Pickens would agree to serve on the commission. Thus, in February 1797, Hawkins, Pickens, and General James Winchester of Tennessee were appointed to mark the Indian boundaries from the Oconee River in Georgia north to the Ohio River.[40]

By the time Hawkins, Pickens, and a small team of surveyors got to work, Hawkins had decided that the Cherokee line would have to be run first, then the Creek. For the moment, the greatest threat to peace was along the Cherokee frontier in Tennessee. The Cherokee line was deemed more urgent because, in Hawkins's words, "every day adds to the number of intruders on their land."[41] As Hawkins and Pickens conferred on these matters at Pickens's home in Hopewell, Winchester was in Tennessee. At Hawkins's request, Pickens had already dispatched local Cherokee friends to Silas Dinsmoor to inform him, and presumably other Cherokees, of their plans and to ask for assistance. Hawkins and Pickens, along with two surveyors and a military escort of fourteen soldiers, set out from Pickens's house at Hopewell on March 23. They proceeded west to Pickens's newly acquired Tamassee property, which bordered Cherokee territory and encompassed the site of the old Ring Fight of 1776, where Pickens had miraculously escaped death more than two decades before. From there, the small party traveled to the Tellico Blockhouse on the Tennessee River in southeastern Tennessee. There they met and conferred with several leading settlers and Cherokee chiefs.[42]

Secretary McHenry feared that the main problem the commissioners would face would be the Indians because of confusion over where the Treaties of Holston and Philadelphia had established the boundaries. In reality, they faced far more opposition, and even danger, from their own countrymen. The trouble began within the commission itself. James Winchester was heavily invested in western lands and feared the running of the line would jeopardize his prospects. He delayed the survey as long as possible, pretending to misunderstand in a series of letters where he was supposed to meet Hawkins and Pickens. Governor Sevier claimed to have heard a rumor that 300 Indians were gathering at Tellico and that such a large threat required him to mobilize his troops and respond in kind—clearly Sevier meant to disrupt the commissioners' mission. Sevier also demanded to know on what authority Hawkins and Pickens intended to run the line. Ordinary settlers who knew that the commissioners would mark the line north or east of where they had already made claims attempted to intimidate or otherwise delay the boundary team, which often had to travel with a detail of U.S. troops for protection. Meanwhile, Senator Blount pressured U.S. Army captain Richard Sparks, commander of U.S. troops in the area, and soon to be Sevier's son-in-law, not to cooperate with the commissioners; he also asked Secretary McHenry to delay the survey. Captain Sparks in turn ordered Ensign George Strother, commanding U.S. troops at the Tellico Blockhouse, not to obey the commissioners' orders. He also sent a letter to the commissioners that they considered "very unbecoming an officer and a gentleman."[43]

The commissioners dealt with each of these threats aggressively. They easily saw through Winchester's deception and asked Secretary McHenry to modify their instructions so that they could proceed without him. Pickens and his colleague received confidential reports that a "postponement of the runing of the line by some means or other was in contemplation by some persons interested in intrusions on Indian rights."[44] Pickens and Hawkins informed McHenry that they were "well aware" of Winchester's "speculative pursuits." "He knows we are at Tellico," they explained, "and he affects ignorance of every thing, offers his services to get an additional escort, surveyors, assistants, &c, to go to Duck River to save time. There are no troops in his neighbourhood and he knows we are not going to Duck River."[45] The two friends began running part of the line without Winchester. They took white settlers with them to show them that they were strictly adhering to the Treaty of Holston; the white men conceded that the line was being run accurately and that they had been the "dupes of misinformation."[46] Later, Indian representatives would accompany the survey team as well.[47]

Hawkins and Pickens also dealt with the threats of military resistance by U.S. and Tennessee officials. They sent a two-sentence reply to Captain Sparks's disrespectful letter, refusing to address its content other than to "submit the propriety of your conduct to your own reflections." Meanwhile, through an intermediary, they threatened to see that he was court-martialed. Four days later, when they ordered Sparks to furnish them a platoon-sized escort, Sparks readily complied and soon visited the two commissioners' camp to apologize for his behavior.[48] The commissioners also responded immediately to Sevier's letter, restating their legal authority. Additionally, they disproved the rumors of an impending Indian attack and showed instead that the natives were peaceful and cooperative.[49]

Yet another threat to peace in late 1796 and 1797 was an effort by the adventurer Zachariah Cox to establish a settlement at Muscle Shoals under the authority of the now defunct Yazoo Act. Cox had invested heavily in the scheme, and he asked Hawkins for a license to establish a trading post there. The commissioners learned that the Indians strongly opposed the project and that Cox intended to raise a body of armed men to "secure" the territory around Muscle Shoals. Once Hawkins could see that Cox's scheme was more of an invasion than an innocent attempt to establish a trading post with the Indians' permission, he refused to approve it. Cox was soon forced into bankruptcy.[50]

The treatment the boundary commission received from ordinary white settlers vacillated from respectful and compliant to hostile and threatening. In April, just as the work was beginning, a group of settlers in the Little River area north of Tellico had dutifully approached Pickens and Hawkins and admitted that some of their lands and crops apparently lay on the Cherokee side of the boundary. They asked if anything might be done to save their crops. Pickens and Hawkins responded that they could delay the final "closing" of the line in that sector until the farmers could harvest their "small grain and fruit" but that the line must be run strictly according to the treaty.[51] These harmonious relations between the boundary commission and Tennessee settlers did not last. Dinsmoor eventually wrote Secretary McHenry on June 4 that he felt safer residing among the Cherokees than among the settlers observing the survey.[52]

Of all the schemes and intrigues swirling about the southwestern territories in 1797, one in particular shocked politicians in Philadelphia and rose to the level of national scandal. At the center of it was Pickens's old nemesis Senator William Blount. The details of the plot are still not entirely clear, but Blount's friends later claimed that he and his co-conspirators simply wished to gain free navigation of the Mississippi River for the citizens of Tennessee, a worthy and patriotic goal. It seems that achieving that goal, however, involved getting high-ranking British, French, and Spanish officials to speculate in American western lands. It also envisioned expeditions by British forces and American frontiersmen against Spanish possessions in Florida and the Gulf Coast. The plan would also certainly complicate and undermine federal attempts to establish a firm boundary behind which the Indians were secure in their lands. The reverse was also true—clearly recognized Indian boundaries would hinder the plans of Blount and his fellow schemers—which was one reason Blount had done all he could to frustrate Hawkins and Pickens's efforts. Though the scheme became known as the "Blount conspiracy," the senator from Tennessee was only one of the highly placed participants, who also included his brothers, the British foreign secretary, the British minister to the United States, the royal governor of Canada, the Spanish ambassador to Britain, the former French minister to the United States, a trustee of Columbia College, at least three other members of Congress, future president Andrew Jackson, numerous officials in frontier land offices and surveyors, Governor John Sevier, and several U.S. Army officers. One of the latter group even included General Winchester, the third member of Pickens and Hawkins's boundary commission.[53]

It was two of the lower-ranking players in the scheme, however, who were Blount's undoing. Frontier adventurer John Chisolm, one of Blount's land agents, was a linchpin in the scheme. In attempts to interest others, he became more and more talkative until rumors of a vast conspiracy were circulating throughout the southwestern frontier and reached Hawkins and Pickens. Hawkins later recalled that he and Pickens "had not been two days on the frontiers of Tennessee before I suspected there was some thing in train of execution injurious to the United States. Colonel [David] Henley, Mr. Dinsmoor, Gen'l Pickens and myself spoke freely to each other on the subject, and we were induced to exert all our vigilance."[54]

These four agents of the government probably did not know the extent of Blount's involvement, however, until June 4. Just before Blount departed Knoxville in April for the next session of the U.S. Senate, he sent a confidential letter to James Carey. Carey was a Cherokee interpreter and another low-ranking Blount confederate. He also comes across as one of the least clever of the conspirators, and his fondness for the bottle often addled his thinking. Blount, however, trusted Carey with detailed instructions.

Carey received the letter on May 20. Parts of it confused him, and in fact he needed help reading the more difficult words. He held on to it for a few days; then, perhaps under the influence of whiskey, or perhaps afraid that he was now involved in more than he bargained for, he showed the letter to James Byers. Byers was a U.S. government factor at Tellico and a supporter of Hawkins and the commission. Byers showed the letter to Colonel Henley, who sent a copy to Hawkins. Receiving the letter on June 4, Hawkins immediately dispatched Byers with the letter to President John Adams, who received it on June 20.[55]

The arrival of the letter in Philadelphia created a sensation. Though it was still vague exactly what Blount was up to, it seemed to involve treasonous collusion with foreign powers; deliberate obstruction of federal officials such as Hawkins, Byers, and Dinsmoor; and an unpatriotic desire to discredit the former president, George Washington. In several passages, Blount demanded secrecy: "You must take care in whatever you say to Rogers or anybody else, not to let the plan be discovered by Hawkins, Dinsmoor, Byers or any other person in the interest of the United States or Spain. . . . I have now to tell you to take care of me . . . for a discovery of the plan would prevent the success, and much injure all parties concerned." Further darkening the letter's sinister appearance, Blount ordered Carey to burn the letter after he had read it three times.[56]

Blount was blissfully unaware that anyone had seen his letter until July 3, his day of reckoning. On that day, he had briefly strolled out of the Senate chamber during a debate that he found rather dull when President Adams's secretary delivered the letter to the Senate. When Blount walked back into the chamber a short while later, he was mortified to hear his letter to Carey being read aloud to the entire body. The vice president asked Blount whether it was his letter. Pale-faced and shaken, Blount replied that he could not recall and would have to refer to his papers and answer the next day. Blount stalled for as long as he could, but four days later the House drafted impeachment charges and sent them to the Senate. A senatorial committee seized his clothes, trunks, and papers, and the Senate voted to expel Blount. Blount fled the capital for Tennessee, just ahead of several creditors and attempts to have him prosecuted for crimes. His impeachment charges would later be dismissed as senators doubted whether they could try charges against a man they had already expelled.[57]

Blount left federal office in disgrace, but it should be noted that he was only one member of the conspiracy that felled him and the most prominent scapegoat. Blount was far from being the only white American trying to profit from western lands. He represented the speculative spirit of the age. Pickens himself sought profit from buying and selling land, albeit on a smaller scale and only in territory to which the Indians had no legal claim. The stern, moralistic Washington, as well as other Federalists, had also invested heavily in western lands. Blount had crossed a hazy line separating honest enterprise from greed and treason, but so had hundreds of others. In fact, Blount faced no disgrace back home in Tennessee. Westerners sympathized with and even admired him, and he soon returned to prominence.[58] Indeed, it would be unfair to dismiss Blount as the bad guy in a simple morality play. At times Blount had joined Pickens in the struggle for peace on the frontier. He had been a determined patriot in the American Revolution and a signer of the Constitution. The Blounts had served the American cause bravely; so had Sevier, Winchester, and many others whose goals were now opposed to Pickens's. Blount's brother Reading, a partner in Blount's land jobbing schemes, had fought alongside Pickens at Eutaw. Pickens probably did not ponder these moral ambiguities, and Pickens the Calvinist was probably not shocked when Blount's machinations were discovered; but with his legalistic approach to morality, he certainly did not approve of them. He never recorded his thoughts on the matter, but his like-minded partner Hawkins did, celebrating the "exposure of those dirty intriguers and their villainous attempts."[59]

The fifty-seven-year-old Pickens labored throughout the summer marking the line. He and his fellow commissioners did not quite complete it. Working their way back east from the Cumberland, they reached the mountain settlement of Gallatin, Tennessee, in late August. They could not continue the trek without packhorses, and the mountain terrain was too rugged for the latter. At that point the heat and drought of late summer had become severe. Hawkins noted that the journey could not be attempted "with rum only."[60] Planning to complete the line at a later time, the party broke up around August 28, 1797.[61]

When Pickens returned to his family at Hopewell in September, he was thoroughly exhausted after six months in the wilderness battling heat, humidity, and the bad tempers and schemes of other men. He himself had been sick and bedridden during part of the expedition. Fifteen years later he remembered the running of the Cherokee line as a "Laborious Service."[62] Still, a few weeks after his return, working without Hawkins, Pickens went back to the forest to mark the shorter line between South Carolina and the Cherokees. When Hawkins set out in January 1798 to run the Creek line in Georgia, Pickens assisted him by dispatching a team of surveyors but did not join him.[63]

Pickens and Hawkins's grueling labors of 1797 and 1798—formalizing the boundaries defined at Hopewell and Holston—were supposed to bring stability and peace to the frontier. The completion, or near-completion, of the project was a massive achievement by a handful of government officials, surveyors, and soldiers. They had hoped to prevent war, establish federal authority, and preserve Indian land rights. Their efforts had achieved the former, but they had stirred up outrage among white Tennesseans and only slightly delayed the inexorable tide of settlers flooding Indian lands. Tennesseans denounced the line that the commissioners had marked out. U.S. Army troops under Lieutenant Colonel Thomas Butler removed some settlers that autumn who had settled on the Cherokee side of the line, further inflaming white citizens. Blount returned from Philadelphia with his reputation undamaged among his fellow Tennesseans, who were far more likely to denounce Hawkins, Pickens, and Butler. The Tennessee state legislature appointed in the fall of 1797 its own boundary commissioners, who rejected the line and charged that Hawkins had made false official statements to the secretary of war. The Tennessee legislature then protested the line in a formal petition to Congress. Blount wrote to his brother John Gray Blount that "never was man more execrated in any Country than Hawkins in this and as to Pickens he has no character but that of being his humble Follower"—a far cry from Blount's assessment of Pickens a few years before.[64]

Even before the line was completely drawn, it was erased by ambitious speculators and angry, land-hungry settlers determined to carve out their own share of liberty and prosperity on the southern frontier. On October 2, 1798, a new treaty with the Cherokees—the Treaty of Tellico—erased many of the lines that Hawkins and Pickens had marked and made it unnecessary for them to complete the line east of Gatlinburg. Political maneuvering resulted in pro-Tennessee men being appointed to the commission. Remarkably, those excluded from the Tellico treaty commission included Hawkins, the regional superintendent of Indian affairs, and Pickens, perhaps the most experienced Indian negotiator in the southern states. The two men may have won their battles for federal authority and stable boundaries in the summer of 1797, but they were losing the war.[65]

SIXTEEN

Every Thing That Was Possible
for Men of Honor to Do

[I am] much pleased with the cool, sensible, firm, and Manly
conduct of our Envoys, who have certainly done every thing that
was possable for men of Honour to doe.

Andrew Pickens to Jacob Read, August 4, 1798

Andrew Pickens turned sixty years old on September 19, 1799. Even before
reaching this milestone, he had expressed weariness with public service.
Considering the endurance, physical hardship, and extensive travels
required by his duties, his fatigue was understandable. There had only been
a single year between 1778 and 1799 in which Pickens had not been away
from home for at least several months.[1] He had spent thousands of days in
the saddle and nearly as many nights sleeping in tents or beside campfires
in every type of weather, in war and peace, in terrain varying from swamps
and meadows to forested mountains. Meanwhile, his wound from the battle of Eutaw continued to cause discomfort. In his fifties he had begun to
reveal to friends that he considered the wilderness journeys and long family
separations a sacrifice. In the seventh and eighth decades of his life, Pickens
clearly sought retirement yet was continually called back to duty. As biographer Clyde Ferguson has noted, "The remainder of [Pickens's] life falls into
a pattern of successive retirements from public affairs, retirements which
he repeatedly renounced whenever he thought the nation needed his services."[2] Pickens returned to public service at the state or national level three
times between 1798 and 1812. Each time he responded to requests to serve,

either the nation was facing the threat of war or he perceived a real opportunity to bring about peace and justice on the frontier.

Pickens's first return to public service occurred as war clouds appeared on the horizon in 1798. For several years, the fledgling United States had been caught in the rivalry between two economic and military superpowers, Britain and France. The Federalist administrations of George Washington and John Adams had generally followed a pro-British policy, to the disgust of the Republican faction led by Thomas Jefferson. In 1793, the U.S. Senate had ratified the Jay Treaty, establishing closer economic ties with Britain and angering the radical republican regime in France. Supposedly an ally, France had stepped up its policy of seizing American merchant ships caught trading with Britain and even announced that American sailors who had been impressed into the British Royal Navy would be hanged if subsequently captured by France.

The tense diplomatic situation eventually exploded into American national outrage. In 1797 the new president, John Adams, tried to ease Franco-American tension by sending three peace commissioners to France—one of them Pickens's wealthy friend and patriot from the South Carolina lowcountry, Charles Cotesworth Pinckney. But the three American diplomats received a hostile reception in France and made little progress. In the spring of 1798, Pinckney and another commissioner, John Marshall, returned and reported to President Adams, who in turn eventually laid their entire story before Congress. One particular sequence of events became known as the "XYZ Affair." During the preceding autumn, three French agents of the French foreign minister, Charles Maurice de Talleyrand, had met with the American commissioners. The Frenchmen angered the Americans by demanding a bribe of $250,000 before negotiations could begin, along with a $12 million loan to France and apologies for an anti-French speech made by President Adams months before. Bribes commonly served to grease the wheels of European diplomacy, but Talleyrand's price just to negotiate was extraordinarily high and only one of the many insults the American commissioners had endured. Pinckney's response to the demand was "No, no, not a sixpence." Republicans and newspapers would later rephrase the American response as "Millions for defense, but not one cent for tribute." As this rallying cry suggested, France's high-handed treatment finally provoked an angry defense of American national honor and calls for war. Both Federalists and Republicans in Congress agreed to vastly expand the army, commission new warships, and suspend commerce with France. War fever raged in South Carolina as hotly as anywhere in the Union.[3]

Pickens's response was what one might expect from an elderly patriot who had seen more than enough war in his lifetime. Writing to South Carolina's U.S. senator Jacob Read, Pickens confessed that it pained him to think that his country would soon experience the "calamity" of war, "which was my earnest wish, never to see again in my day." He asserted, though, that he was "much pleased with the cool, sensible, firm, and Manly conduct of our Envoys, who have certainly done every thing that was possable for men of Honour to doe." As a man who felt he had striven to act honorably in many difficult or impossible situations, Pickens's words were revealing. The three commissioners had shown due regard for their country's "Honour"— its external reputation and status on the international scene—after first enduring a series of slights and rebuffs. But they had also been attentive to their duty and to their instructions to seek peace. Pickens himself had often been frustrated when pursuing similar goals. He had unsuccessfully tried to prevent and punish atrocities in war; and his attempts to prevent injustice to the Indians often seemed in vain. Men might act with honesty and conviction and still be unable to prevent injustice and bloodshed. The aging veteran of the Revolution was also optimistic, though, that in the coming conflict his country could avoid two problems that had made the previous war with Britain especially tragic. First, Pickens could not foresee "devition among the people" in the conflict with France, and second, he was optimistic that this time "prudent management" would prevent the Indians from joining the enemy.[4] Pickens the veteran disliked the prospect of another war; Pickens the nationalist was devoted to defending his nation's prestige and already thinking of the most "prudent" ways to conduct that war.

As Pickens wrote these words in the summer of 1798, the South Carolina General Assembly was appropriating more than £7,000 for the anticipated war and Governor Charles Pinckney was mobilizing portions of the state militia. With fellow citizens calling on Pickens for military advice and political leadership, he agreed to stand for election once again to the state house of representatives. His neighbors elected him on October 10. Joining the General Assembly in late November, the old general was immediately appointed to the Judiciary, Ways and Means, and Privileges and Elections Committees, as well as to a committee formed to report on what military preparations were necessary in case of war. The latter group persuaded the house to fund the purchase of 5,000 stands of arms and the construction of magazines and other military facilities in Camden, Beaufort, and Georgetown.[5]

Every Thing That Was Possible for Men of Honor to Do

When Pickens returned to the General Assembly for the November 1799 session, he found that his fellow legislators no longer shared his determination to prepare for war. The efforts Pickens had begun in the previous session to put the state on a stronger war footing bore little fruit in 1799. By that time, fewer Americans seemed to think war was likely. Meanwhile, Pickens was active in other efforts that had been typical of his career as a state legislator: further strengthening and standardizing the state court system and promoting education. He helped write a law that allowed the South Carolina Agricultural Society to sell property to acquire funds for the establishment of a school "for the education and support of orphans, or the children of poor people."[6] On December 21, 1799, he was appointed to help oversee repairs to Pendleton's courthouse and jail. This was on the final day of the session, after which Pickens returned home in time for Christmas, once again thinking that his public service at the state level was finished.[7] By the time Pickens departed from his "final" legislative session, his attachment to the Federalist faction in national and state politics was probably weakening. As late as November 1798, Federalists in the state had been sure enough of his loyalty to nominate him for U.S. Senate. This was a bid to defeat the Republican candidate and sitting governor, Charles Pinckney. Pinckney was a cousin of Charles Cotesworth Pinckney and, like his kinsman, friendly with Pickens. Unlike his cousin, Governor Pinckney was hated by South Carolina elites for being a "democrat" and a traitor to his own class, though he was popular among less affluent South Carolinians. Apparently, Federalists recruited Pickens to run against Pinckney, probably hoping that he could draw some support among backcountry legislators when the vote was taken in the General Assembly. Pickens lost by a vote of seventy-nine to sixty-three. As Pickens never commented on this episode, it is unclear why he accepted the nomination unless he felt that no patriot could decline the call to national service when war threatened. There is no record of a quarrel between him and Pinckney. Several days after the election, in fact, Pickens voted to defend Pinckney's decision earlier in the year to bolster the state's military defenses when the legislature was not in session.[8]

Though identified with the Federalists, Pickens was no "party man." By the time of the election of 1800, he was disgusted enough with the Federalists to support the Republican leader, Thomas Jefferson, for president. Partly the switch was due to Pickens's belief that the Adams administration had been guilty of "arbitrary Government."[9] During the period of hostility with France, the Federalists had passed several controversial laws.

Ostensibly, the Naturalization Act, Sedition Act, and two Alien Acts signed by President Adams were supposed to guard against treason in a time of war or near-war; they also seemed a convenient means by which to crush the Republican opposition, which traditionally had been pro-French. Generally the laws were no harsher than those passed against loyalists during the American Revolution. Pickens, however, was not the only American who thought they were vindictive and went too far in suppressing liberty. The new laws generated a backlash against the Federalists and proved decisive in the Republican victory of 1800.

Just as important in Pickens's shift to the Republicans was his disgust with "party spirit." Newspapers and politicians from both parties had unleashed vicious and slanderous attacks against each other through most of the 1790s. Back home in South Carolina, though, Pickens had become convinced that the Federalists were far more guilty. Their leader was Robert Goodloe Harper, a staunch Federalist congressman who hailed from Ninety Six. After losing his congressional seat in the Republican landslide of 1800, Harper sent circular letters to his constituents that lauded the Federalists and criticized the Republicans strongly enough that Pickens considered the remarks indecent. Pickens was so disgusted with the tone of the letters that he soon became part of a bitter partisan controversy himself. Hoping that "some person would give [Harper] what he deserved," Pickens forwarded the letters to Robert Anderson. A rebuttal by Anderson to Harper appeared in the newspapers, which in turn received a rude reply from former governor John Rutledge, who had become a mentally unstable man. Rutledge's letter, which Pickens called an "indecent piece," was answered in turn by a Republican, after which Rutledge wrote another letter. Relating the entire affair to his son Andrew, Pickens charged that Rutledge's second letter was written in the "Same unhansom Stile as the first."[10] Nine months after the election, Pickens complained that the Federalists still maintained a violent spirit of opposition against "the present administration."[11]

Pickens played no role in politics in 1800 and 1801 besides these private expressions of disgust with Federalist leaders. He had great hopes, however, for moderation and wisdom in government under the new Republican administration of Thomas Jefferson. Writing to his brother-in-law John E. Colhoun, now a U.S. senator, Pickens expressed his approval of Jefferson's 1802 state of the union address and the fiscal policy announced by the secretary of the treasury. Pickens hoped that Jefferson's recommendations and the treasury report "may be acted on with prudence, not taking the extreme, in any point." He was uncomfortable, though, with Jefferson's proposed cuts to the military. The old general believed that not only was the army too small to govern and protect the nation's extended frontier but also that "expence and extravagance" had "got into our little army." The only things that could eliminate those weaknesses were "time and strict disciplin."[12]

Pickens's next return to public service resulted from his being called, once again, to treat with the southern Indians. The veteran negotiator told a friend that he was surprised at this appointment; at nearly sixty-two years of age, he considered himself in "the decline of life."[13] Nevertheless, Pickens accepted and in fact was perhaps the least important member of the new treaty commission. One of the other members was Pickens's old colleague Benjamin Hawkins, who fundamentally shared Pickens's sense of justice when it came to dealing with the Indians. Hawkins was now agent to the Creeks and federal superintendent of Indian affairs south of the Ohio. The leader of the commission was Brigadier General James Wilkinson, commanding general of the U.S. Army. Wilkinson had never proved himself a particularly talented soldier. He was, however, a charismatic and clever schemer. Presidents Washington and Adams and senior members of their administrations had privately confided to each other their doubts about Wilkinson's character. Only later, however, would Wilkinson cement his reputation as one of the most devious and unscrupulous adventurers in American history.[14]

As Pickens answered the summons to serve in the summer of 1801, the Indian policy of the new Jefferson administration had not yet fully taken shape. So far, it was clear that Jefferson approved of the "civilization plan" espoused by his Federalist predecessors—the Indians must be encouraged to embrace concepts of private property, to farm, to read, and to develop manufacturing enterprises such as the spinning and weaving of cotton and blacksmithing. If anything, Jefferson would prove to be even more aggressive than Washington and Adams in following this approach. Hawkins himself had thoroughly embraced it since he had become the government's agent to the Creeks several years before. Eventually Jefferson would also follow a policy of acquiring as much Indian land as possible and as quickly as it could be done without instigating wars. The new president envisioned a democratic republic of sturdy, independent yeoman farmers. The acquisition of western land for the growing white population was vital to this vision—land that was currently occupied by the Indians was the key to vitality, equality, freedom, and economic growth in the new nation.

Jefferson's land-hungry policy did not become fully clear, however, until 1803. In the summer of 1801, he was still "tying up loose ends left by his predecessors while formulating a mature policy of his own."[15] Congress had passed laws in 1799 and 1800 providing for further negotiations with the Indians south of the Ohio, but those negotiations had not taken place when the nation was still preoccupied with the threat of war with France. There was great need for a road connecting the settlements in middle Tennessee around Nashville with the settlement of Natchez on the Mississippi River. To build that road through Indian territory, the United States would have to win the permission of the Cherokees, Chickasaws, and Choctaws. Jefferson also wanted to establish more trading posts and government-run "factories" where Indians could trade for manufactured products. Additionally, there were areas where boundaries were not clearly defined and where thefts, murders, and encroachments on Indian land had been particularly serious, in turn leading to retaliations and the threat of general war. This was true in various areas of Tennessee and even more so in Georgia. Jefferson's constituents in Georgia had long been angry about the federal government's lack of support for white expansion in their state. Since the founding of the Republic, no other state had acquired less land from the Indians. Pickens's diplomacy had been one reason for that, as he and the Washington administration—at Rock Landing, New York, and Coleraine—had long refused to press the Creeks to give up any land west or south of the Oconee and Altamaha Rivers. Finally, there were tracts of Indian land, especially in Tennessee, that divided areas of white settlement and made trade and communications more difficult.[16]

Jefferson's more limited initial goals were generally reflected in the official instructions that Secretary of War Henry Dearborn sent to Wilkinson, Hawkins, and Pickens in the summer of 1801. Especially when dealing with the Cherokees, Chickasaws, and Choctaws, Dearborn stressed that the commissioners must take a gentle approach. The commissioners were to see if the Cherokees were willing to cede a tract of land in the Duck River area west of Nashville, as well as land west of the Cumberland mountains. If the Cherokees were unwilling to sell these lands, the commissioners were to ask for all the land north of the road that connected Knoxville and Nashville; and if the Cherokees refused that, the commissioners were to seek control of a one- to five-mile strip of land along that road as it passed through Cherokee territory. Most of all, whether the Cherokees ceded any land or not, the commissioners were to seek permission to build the road to Natchez. The commissioners were directed to take great care not to antagonize the Cherokees, Chickasaws, or Choctaws: "You will state none of [the government's objects] in the tone of demands."[17] Only nine days after

Every Thing That Was Possible for Men of Honor to Do

Dearborn wrote these instructions, he sent another letter to the commissioners. A delegation of Cherokees was in Washington at the time. They had heard rumors that soon a treaty commission of Tennesseans was to demand more land from them, and they had protested vigorously. The Cherokees were relieved to hear that the commissioners actually included Hawkins and Pickens but were still indignant at the thought of giving up more territory. Dearborn therefore told the commissioners that "it is the wish of the President that you should treat the subject with great tenderness, and that you should not *press* them on any other subjects than those which relate to roads."[18]

After meeting with the Cherokees, the commissioners were to proceed to Chickasaw Bluffs (modern-day Memphis) and negotiate with the Chickasaws. From the Chickasaws, they were to ask nothing more than permission to build the road and settle "two or more families" on it to maintain lodgments or taverns. Then the three federal agents would travel down the Mississippi to conclude a treaty with the Choctaws. The main object of this meeting was, once again, to secure permission for the road to Natchez. Additionally, Jefferson and Dearborn wanted the commissioners to mention a tract of land that had had an ambiguous status and "endeavor, indirectly," and politely, to clarify the United States' claim to it. The Choctaws had ceded a long, narrow tract of land to the British that was bounded on the west by the Mississippi River, on the east by the ninety-first meridian, on the north by the Yazoo River, and on the south by the thirty-first parallel. Rights to this land had passed to the United States after the end of the Revolutionary War, but the boundaries had never been marked.[19]

After concluding business with the Choctaws, the commissioners were to meet with the Creeks. Dearborn did not send his instructions on dealing with the Creeks until after Pickens had accepted his appointment. The goals of the Creek negotiations were far more ambitious. The Jefferson administration wanted the commissioners to acquire the land between the Oconee and Ocmulgee Rivers, the tract that had caused so much contention throughout the negotiations at Coleraine, Rock Landing, and earlier. Pickens and Hawkins, perhaps more than anyone, had been responsible for preventing Georgia's acquisition of that area that the Creeks had been so determined to keep. Also, the commissioners were to acquire possession of another chunk of territory that the Georgia legislature had designated "Tallassee County." For this land, the commissioners could offer the Creeks $12,000, a rather larger sum in comparison with earlier treaties, and an additional annual payment of $2,000 on top of the Creeks' current annuity. Finally, the commissioners had to address the problem of the Wofford settlement. Colonel William Wofford and others had illegally settled on a twenty-three-by-four-mile strip of land on the western side of the Creek boundary in northern Georgia. Wofford claimed that if Hawkins had run the line properly in 1799, his land would be on the right side of the line. Dearborn ordered the commissioners to investigate this claim as well as the claim of the Cherokees that the land actually belonged to them, not to the Creeks. (Pickens and Hawkins knew the tract was actually in Cherokee territory.)

With the Creeks, then, the administration wanted the commissioners to be far more assertive in seeking land, partly in an effort to conciliate politicians and voters in Georgia. Even the Creeks, though, Jefferson was keen not to antagonize—"every assurance of the protection and friendship of the president, which you were authorized to make to the other Indian nations, should be tendered to the Creeks also. . . . The Creeks being a powerful and proud nation, and great jealousies having at different times arisen between them and the frontier inhabitants, all prudent means in your power should be exerted to reconcile them, and to remove every obstacle to their mutual friendship."[20]

Pickens began his westward journey in August, joining Wilkinson and Hawkins at South West Point on the Tennessee around September 1. The commission did not get off to a great start. The Cherokees were not in a generous mood. A Cherokee woman had been recently murdered near Knoxville, several Indian prisoners from previous hostilities were still being held by Tennessee authorities, and the subject of land cessions was a sore one. Noting that there was great rejoicing in Tennessee upon the recent election of Jefferson, the Cherokees assumed this meant that the new president was a man who would aggressively seek to take their land. The chiefs flatly rejected all the government's requests, and the commissioners, obedient to their instructions, did not press them. By September 5, the conference was over and the commissioners departed to meet with the Chickasaws.[21]

The journey was a difficult one lasting more than five weeks, even though it was mostly by water. After floating down the "pellucid Tennessee, opaque Ohio and muddy Mississippi" in the heat of summer, Hawkins recorded that "we have all had the fever of the climate."[22] Even as the commissioners struggled with illness, however, they managed to conduct a much more successful conference with the Chickasaws. This tribe had always valued its good relations with the United States, boasting that it "ha[d] never spilt the blood of a white man."[23] Originally fearing that the United States would ask

Every Thing That Was Possible for Men of Honor to Do

them for land, the Chickasaws were happy to grant the building of the road to Natchez through their territory. The Chickasaws would provide guides, paid by the United States, to assist in laying out the road but would retain ownership of any ferries crossing streams and rivers. In return, the commissioners left $700 worth of goods, fifty gallons of whiskey, and a quantity of tobacco for the Chickasaws before they departed the Chickasaw Bluffs on October 28.[24]

Besides their success in obtaining permission for the road, the Chickasaw conference pleased the commissioners for several reasons. Though the Chickasaws would not allow white families to build "licensed establishments" along the road, the commissioners did not press the point, as they believed that the Chickasaws and white people living among them would soon build such facilities themselves.[25] The conference also served to ease the commissioners' minds about the overlapping claims of the Chickasaws and Cherokees to the northern section of the road itself. It was good, the federal agents reported, that the Cherokees had not granted access to the road, since the Chickasaws convinced them that the territory in question was actually theirs. The chiefs themselves produced a copy of a declaration of President Washington dated July 1, 1794, which persuaded the commissioners of Chickasaw ownership. Just as Piomingo had shown facility with maps at the Hopewell conference in 1786, the Chickasaws once again demonstrated their knowledge and skill in the ways of white diplomacy. Spending time with the Chickasaws confirmed Hawkins's and Pickens's opinion of them not only as intelligent but also as "amicable and orderly." The three white men, perhaps Hawkins in particular, were also encouraged by the Chickasaws' progress in the "habits of civilization," although they were not as "advanced" as the Cherokees.[26] The Chickasaws were beginning to embrace private property, "setting out from their old towns and fencing their farms."[27] Some families were beginning to plant cotton, and the women were learning to spin and weave it. The commissioners urged the federal government to assist the Chickasaws in their progress for the "civilization, and consequent salvation, of a devoted race of human beings."[28]

Sometime in mid- to late November, Pickens and his colleagues arrived at Fort Adams on the Mississippi (forty miles south of Natchez) to prepare for their meeting with the Choctaws. Once again they were successful, and again Pickens and Hawkins were confirmed in their initial impressions. At Hopewell they had seen the Choctaws as honest and peace-loving but "indolent," "simple," and lacking self-control.[29] Fifteen years later, their report described the Choctaws as "this humble, friendly, tranquil, peaceful people" who nevertheless previously had been buried in "sloth and ignorance."[30] The Choctaws, too, readily agreed to allow the white men to build the road to Natchez once they were reassured that the latter were not seeking land. Discussions on the tract along the Mississippi previously ceded to the British went well also. Dearborn had instructed the commissioners to handle that subject delicately, so it must have been a relief when the Choctaws themselves insisted on marking the boundary. Chief after chief came forward to acknowledge the cession that had been made to the "white people," but they wanted the line marked to avoid future conflict and wanted white settlers who had settled east of the line to be moved back toward the Mississippi.[31] This desire to recognize treaties, mark lines, clarify boundaries, and prevent conflict had been the thrust of Pickens's Indian diplomacy since 1782, and the commissioners readily agreed to the Choctaws' request in the subsequent treaty. The Choctaws also showed common sense and a desire for peace in their objection to allowing "houses of entertainment" along the Natchez route. They pointed out that this would only increase the likelihood of thefts and violence between Indians and whites and destroy the peace. The commissioners conceded that the Choctaws were right and did not press the issue. To Dearborn they explained that it would be nearly impossible "to give protection to such solitary, sequestered settlements . . . against the rapacity and abuse of vicious, mischievous individuals, to be found in every community, civil and savage."[32] Indirectly, then, the commissioners acknowledged the wisdom and foresight of this supposedly "simple" people.

Moreover, the American officials reported encouragingly that the Choctaws were abandoning their "sloth" and advancing rapidly in absorbing the white man's ways. They were beginning to cultivate small amounts of cotton and requested a cotton gin, cotton cards and spinning wheels, and blacksmiths' tools, as well as instructors to teach their women how to spin. Just as impressive to the commissioners was the Choctaws' refusal to accept any gifts of whiskey.[33] Mingo Hom-Massatubley told the white diplomats that "we came here sober, to do business, and wish to return so, and request, therefore, that the liquor which we are informed our friends had provided for us, may be trained in store, as it might be productive of evil."[34] Interestingly, certain Cherokee leaders were making the same request. Little Turtle wrote personally to President Jefferson himself asking that the "great council of the Sixteen Fires" (Congress) prohibit white traders from selling liquor, "this fatal poison," to Cherokees.[35]

Every Thing That Was Possible for Men of Honor to Do

Pickens and his colleagues departed Fort Adams on December 22, leaving $2,000 in goods for the Choctaws and promising the delivery of three sets of blacksmiths' tools. Hawkins declared that it was useless to attempt to meet with the Creeks until the following spring, since the latter hunted during the winter. General Wilkinson, therefore, went to oversee preparations for Indians and soldiers building the Natchez road. Hawkins and Pickens set out for Hawkins's home at the Creek agency, after which Pickens continued on to Hopewell. For Pickens this trek homeward from Fort Adams would be a "long and fateaguing journey" of nearly 800 miles, which the sixty-two-year-old frontiersman completed in forty-nine days.[36]

Pickens had about two and a half months at home before he needed to leave again to conduct business with the Creeks. So far, he was generally happy with the Jefferson administration as a whole and with his and his fellow commissioners' success in the latest round of treaty negotiations. From his letter to his brother-in-law John E. Colhoun, the U.S. senator, it seems that he had wholeheartedly adopted the government's civilizing mission to the Indians: "The natives were friendly, and well disposed towards the United States, many in all the nations are desirous to be instructed in farming and to be assisted with emplements of husbandry. Many of the wemen and girls spin cotton well, particularly among the creeks and cherokees and some weave." If the government continued to support these efforts, he thought, the four southern tribes could be made a happy and "useful people." The main obstacle to this outcome, Pickens charged, was "flagrant encroachments" by the "neighbouring white people." The veteran diplomat was particularly upset by Wofford's settlement and by the fact that so far the administration had done nothing to break it up: "If those encroachments, are not . . . prevented, and those who are now setled on their land, removed, it will weaken the confidence of the indians, in our government, which now apears to be well secured, and has been a prinsaple object with the commissioners, at the late treaties."[37] Obviously Pickens shared other Americans' relatively condescending, or paternalistic, attitude toward the Indians. He did not think his own government, however, deserved authority or respect unless it could see that justice was done to them.

Despite Pickens's satisfaction with the course of the Indian negotiations so far, tension had developed between Pickens and Hawkins on the one hand and Wilkinson on the other. Despite Hawkins's obvious expertise on Creek customs, Wilkinson wrote privately to Secretary Dearborn that he was "perplexed" by the former's assertion that attempts to meet with the Creeks would be fruitless until the spring.[38] Pickens, also an experienced

Creek negotiator, would have concurred with Hawkins. For his part, Hawkins was exasperated with Wilkinson's officers and troops interfering with the Creeks—issuing rations to the more "idle" Indians without his knowledge and "certificates" for drawing rations to certain chiefs of "worthless and . . . doubtful characters." It was upsetting the government's plan of civilization. Hawkins spoke several times to Wilkinson about it and received assurances from Wilkinson that the practices would stop. In December 1801, though, Hawkins was still upset enough about the problem to go over Wilkinson's head to the secretary of war.[39] Pickens himself indirectly criticized Wilkinson, the army's senior commander, in his complaint to Senator Colhoun that the army was rife with "extravagance" and in need of more "strict disciplin."[40]

By the time negotiations with the Creeks were concluded in the summer of 1802, the division between Wilkinson on the one hand and Pickens and Hawkins on the other had grown deeper. The Creek talks began promisingly enough. Pickens joined Hawkins at Fort Wilkinson on the Oconee River on May 2; Wilkinson did not arrive until the eighth. While arrangements were made to procure provisions for the treaty and the white men waited for the Creeks to arrive, Pickens and Hawkins were able to dispose of one of their assigned tasks from the government. The commissioners were supposed to acquire more land from the Creeks between the Apalachee and Tugaloo Rivers in northeastern Georgia, land that included the illegal Wofford settlement. Pickens and Hawkins believed the land actually belonged to the Cherokees. To settle the matter, they traveled with a delegation of Creek leaders towards the disputed territory. When the Creek headmen saw the land in question, they readily confirmed that it belonged to the Cherokees. Thus Pickens and Hawkins were relieved of one unpleasant or difficult task for the upcoming negotiations. Cherokee and Creek leaders actually met and clarified the boundary between them in the presence of Hawkins and Pickens.[41]

Unknown to Hawkins and Pickens, Congress and the Jefferson administration had just taken action that, in principle, contradicted any previous efforts to restrict the size of land grabs in Georgia. The commissioners did not know this when Wilkinson made a quick trip sometime after May 12 to the Georgia capital to confer with Governor Josiah Tatnall Jr. The immediate object was to learn when the Georgia legislature would finally meet and send representatives to the treaty grounds. (The federal commissioners ultimately decided they would have to proceed without the presence of Georgia officials.) While meeting with Tatnall, Wilkinson also learned that on April 24, Congress had agreed to accept a large land cession from the state of Georgia. The cession, once formally approved by the Georgia legislature, would include all of Georgia's land west of its modern boundary. In return, Congress would pay Georgia $1,250,000 and immediately seek to extinguish Creek claims to all the lands east of that line—in other words, over half of the modern state of Georgia. The document gave special mention to the "Tallasee country" and to the coveted tract between the Oconee and Ocmulgee Rivers that Georgia had sought to wrest from the Creeks for the last two decades. Pickens and Hawkins learned of this official act on May 23 when Wilkinson returned to the treaty grounds.[42] The commissioners had certainly been aware that negotiations between Georgia and the federal government had been taking place, and the lands in question had been mentioned in the commissioners' instructions from Dearborn the previous July. The recent agreement, however, provided new momentum for the effort to acquire land, despite Dearborn's earlier orders to "reconcile" the "powerful and proud" Creeks.[43] Moreover, it cut against the grain of all of Pickens's previous promises as a commissioner to the Creeks. Wilkinson, it seems, seized this momentum, while Pickens and Hawkins apparently tried to restrain it.

Thus, by the time formal talks began on May 24, the white negotiators were under considerable pressure from their superiors in the federal government to acquire sizable land cessions. It was a different situation from that faced by Pickens and Hawkins at Hopewell back in 1785. At Hopewell, the federal commissioners were well aware of land hunger on the part of local whites and some state leaders but felt confident in their authority to ask for no more land cessions from the Cherokees. At Fort Wilkinson in 1802, it was clear that pressure was coming both from the state of Georgia and the Jefferson administration to acquire more land.

The formal talks began with the Creeks performing the eagle tail dance, symbolically burying the weapons of war and covering the commissioners with white deerskins to symbolize peace. As the Cherokees and other tribes had done at Hopewell, the Creek leaders swore that they were committed to peace and that they were men of sincerity who could be trusted. The main Creek speaker, Efau Haujo, asserted that all sides were there to negotiate honestly with "straight hearts."[44] Wilkinson responded with traditional expressions of goodwill, but as the negotiations proceeded over the next several weeks he would become more and more adamant that the Creeks must sell much of their land.

In hopes that Georgia's representatives would soon arrive, both sides suspended talks on May 25 for several days. When they resumed on the twenty-ninth, Wilkinson politely suggested to the Creeks that it would benefit them to sell much of their land. It would allow them to satisfy their trading debts and provide better for their people, especially now that hunting was no longer as profitable to them. Wilkinson also asked the chiefs why they were unable to fulfill their treaty obligations by punishing their "own people" who had committed crimes.[45] The official report the commissioners submitted to Dearborn shows that the commission, as a whole, followed a strategy of pointing out the Creeks' failures to them in order to convince them to give up land and "to excite a strong sense of humiliation and dependence: for these points have proved a fruitful source of discussion to the superintendent, and are well understood by the Indians, who attach due importance to them."[46] Hawkins himself took some advantage of the chiefs' sense of shame at being unable to apprehend the murderer of a white man. He also listed a number of killings, thefts, and kidnappings of slaves for which the Creeks had provided no "satisfaction" to white settlers.[47]

The heavy pressure on the Creeks was not applied, however, until June 13, and it was Wilkinson who did the talking. The Creeks had responded to Wilkinson's original requests for large land cessions by offering only a small strip of the Tallassee territory at the price of two dollars per acre. As for the request for land to the south between the Altamaha and St. Marys River, the Creeks explained that they could not discuss that territory because the chiefs from that area were not present.[48] In fact, many of the latter had aligned themselves with the adventurer William Bowles, who had been troublesome to both American and Spanish authorities in the region for some time.[49] Wilkinson's response on the thirteenth was an insulting scolding full of condescension, ridicule, and threats. Wilkinson mocked the Creeks' inability to provide for themselves by pointing out how long it had taken them finally to learn to fence their fields and to use "the plough, the wheel, and the loom." He also blasted them for allowing the chiefs below the Altamaha to refuse to come to the treaty grounds and to dictate their own response. The result was an insult to the president of the United States that he would not take lightly: "We call on you, chiefs, head-men, and warriors, to say, whether your Father [Jefferson] should look with kindness on such bad children." By failing to compel their kinsmen to negotiate, the chiefs had acted foolishly and proven their inability to lead: "Should you be afraid to exercise your own judgment, because of the fools and mischief-makers, who run after the lying vagabond Bowles . . . or, because boys and mad young men, may differ from you in opinion[?]" Wilkinson recommended that if the Creek leaders were unable to control

Every Thing That Was Possible for Men of Honor to Do

their own people, they should ask President Jefferson to do so for them, for "his arm is as strong as a whirlwind, and, if it is raised, will level to the earth all . . . who may oppose your will."[50]

The tone of Wilkinson's address of June 13, 1802, was a far cry from that of Hawkins, Pickens, and the other white commissioners at Hopewell in 1785 or at Coleraine in 1796. Rather than ratify the Creeks' claims to be men with "straight hearts," Wilkinson had ridiculed them as "bad children," and rather than promise justice and protection, he had threatened the use of military force to punish the president's enemies.

Undoubtedly considering this veiled threat of force, several Creek leaders went to Hawkins that evening and agreed on a somewhat larger cession. In the end, the Creeks sold a strip of land on the western side of the Oconee about 110 miles long and 20 miles wide at its widest point. This was still only about a quarter of the coveted land between the Oconee and the Ocmulgee—the new boundary still did not extend as far west as the latter river. Even at the time, though, both sides saw that it was an unreliable boundary because there was no body of water that clearly marked it; white settlers and their livestock were bound to trespass, leading to more friction and violence. Additionally the Creeks ceded another narrow strip in the south stretching from the south bank of the Altamaha to the northern head-water of the St. Marys. In return, the Creeks received an annuity of $3,000, a ten-year annuity of $1,000 to the chiefs of the Creek national council, and $25,000 worth of goods. (Only $10,000 worth of those goods were actual presents; the rest went to satisfy debts to the United States and served as restitution for stolen property). The commissioners conceded to Secretary Dearborn that they had offered more compensation than their instructions allowed but explained that the tract they had obtained was very valuable and that the Creeks had resisted strongly because a surrender of territory threatened to cause dissension and unrest within the Creek nation.[51]

The commissioners had indeed pledged about twice what they were authorized to offer the Creeks. It seems, though, that Pickens was at best unenthusiastic about the role he was playing in wresting land from them. The treaty journal did not record him speaking at all. Pickens left for home the day after the treaty was signed, leaving Wilkinson and Hawkins to distribute presents and conclude business.[52] This was so unlike his behavior in previous treaty negotiations that it suggests he was disgusted or embarrassed by the outcome. White Georgians, meanwhile, were unhappy with how little the treaty commissioners had acquired. Rumors soon spread that Wilkinson claimed he could have acquired more land of the Creeks had it not been for Pickens and Hawkins's opposition.[53] In his memoirs, Wilkinson claimed credit for what land had been gained. He pointed out that Hawkins and Pickens had been with him when he had gained only a small amount of land from the Creeks with treaty expenses of more than $33,000. Implying that Pickens and Hawkins were the reasons that the Creeks were paid too much, he pointed out that the following autumn he was the sole negotiator in another treaty with the Choctaws that obtained a much larger cession for only $2,388.10.[54]

Previous historians have concluded with good reason that Pickens was disgusted and that this was why he refused to accept any more appointments from the Jefferson administration.[55] Pickens went into the treaty negotiations knowing, of course, that the Jefferson administration wanted land from the Creeks, since this was written into his instructions. It does seem likely, however, that the man who had done so much in the past to honor the Creeks' desire to hold on to their lands was eager to see them fairly compensated.[56] Pickens went home as a man who had done his duty to his country but who wanted no more of such work. In 1804 and 1805 he would watch from the sidelines as the United States acquired the rest of the Creeks' land east of the Ocmulgee as well as the Cherokees' land that Wofford and his neighbors had illegally settled.[57] In his 1811 letter to Henry Lee, Pickens said little about his treaty work in 1801–2, other than "after attending those treaties, I declined excepting any more appointments."[58] Pickens would never again participate in formal Indian diplomacy.

Every Thing That Was Possible for Men of Honor to Do

SEVENTEEN

Retirement and Looking Back

And to see the homage paid to Virtue!
What a strong incentive to imitate it!

William Martin on Andrew Pickens, January 1, 1843

The negroes . . . have been a means, under Providence,
to procure many of the comforts of life, which myself and others
have enjoyed. I request that they may be used with justice,
and humanity.

Andrew Pickens's will, 1809

In the spring of 1805, Pickens made his final migration, once again moving
west, yet again closer to the frontier. For at least four years he had been
planning and building his new estate at Tamassee.[1] About twenty-three
miles northwest of Hopewell, Tamassee was at the foot of the Blue Ridge
Mountains and only a few miles from the boundary separating the northwestern corner of South Carolina from the Cherokee nation. The house was
situated on a small hill from which Pickens could see the mountains that
formed that boundary. It was adjacent to the abandoned Cherokee village
of Tamassee and only a few minutes' walk from the site of the Ring Fight
where, nearly three decades before, a much younger Andrew Pickens had
miraculously survived and defeated a Cherokee ambush.[2]

The new abode reflected the sturdiness and simplicity of its builder;
it was comfortable for its day but not ostentatious. The structure was one

and a half stories tall and made of hewn logs. About fifty feet long, it had ten-foot-wide porches and a rock stack chimney in the center and featured small glass windows with plain solid shutters. It was ceiled inside with planks, and perhaps in deference to Becky's tastes, the bedrooms were painted in colors. In addition, Pickens painted the exterior of the house red and the shutters green. It became known in the area as the "Red House," and the long winding path that led up the hill to it was called "the General's Road."[3] As one traveled up the General's Road to the Red House, he or she would notice two large cedar trees standing directly in front of the house. Pickens moved Becky into the house in the spring, along with their younger children: Rebecca, now twenty-one; Catherine, eighteen; and Joseph, fourteen. A couple of grandchildren may have been present during the move, as Ezekiel's children often stayed with their grandparents at Tamassee for months at a time. Probably the family was accompanied by at least ten slaves. Judging from Pickens's will written just four years later, those slaves likely included Old Dick; Lucy; Pompey and his wife, Fillis; Jame and his wife, Seala; Rob and his wife, Clarasey; July; and Sambo. Though we do have a description of the Red House, there is no contemporary mention of the slave quarters.[4]

There is little doubt that Pickens considered the move part of a "retirement" from public life; his contemporaries certainly deemed it so. Perhaps the fullest personal description of Pickens in the 1790s and early 1800s was penned years later by William Martin, son of Joseph Martin, who had served alongside Pickens as a treaty commissioner at Hopewell. The younger Martin lived near Pendleton, sometimes stayed at Pickens's house, and believed that the general was fond of him. "In after life," wrote Martin,

> he became much retired—seldom went from home. He lived four
> miles from the court house. He would commonly go to court
> one day of the term, as if to see his old friends. I have seen him
> come, with his broad beaver [hat], his other dress corresponding
> all remarkably neat, and with as much solemnity as if at church.
> He would move slowly about, every one giving way & addressing
> him respectfully, and he once in a while, touching his beaver—
> occasionally meeting with, and taking by the hand, an old friend,
> with a little commonplace conversation, & then pass on. Thus
> would he spend two or three hours, and then mount & away. At that
> day I envied no man so much as I did him. And to see the homage
> paid to Virtue! What a strong incentive to imitate it![5]

Another contemporary who met Pickens after his move to Tamassee was William Ancrum, a young gentleman with Charleston roots who made a tour of the upcountry in 1810. Upon reaching Pendleton on July 7, Ancrum spent four days at Robert Anderson's house. Ancrum found Anderson to be a congenial and gentle old man, "now grown very infirm and inactive." On the eleventh, eighteen-year-old Joseph Pickens who lived with his older brother Andrew, politely waited on Ancrum and escorted him on the twenty-three-mile journey to his father's plantation at Tamassee. Upon arriving, Ancrum presented a letter of introduction from a Mr. Montgomery to the master of the estate. Ancrum recorded that after perusing the letter, Pickens "gave me a hearty wellcome, if I can put up with his plain fares." Ancrum found Pickens, however,

> to be a very different man to what Genl Anderson is; he is a thin spare man, a few years younger [actually Anderson was two years younger than Pickens], and still an active man, and more serious and distant in his manners than [the] other. He and his Old Lady lives a very retired life at the very foot of the mountains, at the boundry of the state. . . . The Genl has regular morning and Evening family prayers; he first delivers a short preparatory prayer, then reads a portion of the Scripture, then a more lengthy prayer.

Ancrum was taken with the rustic beauty of Pickens's surroundings. Later that day Joseph took him to Tamassee Knob just beyond Pickens's property line, "a mountain of considerable heighth." Joseph and Ancrum had to dismount to reach the summit and Ancrum "nearly gave out with fatigue." After breakfast the next day, Pickens took the younger man south on a ride across Tamassee Creek, through a "fine open wood," and up to the peak of Oconee Mountain. He showed Ancrum one of his wolf traps and told him that he had often caught wolves in them. Ancrum marveled at the "delightful ranges for Cattle" and the beauty of the mountain flora.[6]

Andrew and Becky Pickens, then, lived a "very retired life," and the general's visits to the courthouse probably became even less common after his move to Tamassee. He did not cut his ties with Pendleton, however. He had divided his lands along the Keowee there between Ezekiel and Andrew, and he and Becky visited often. Though he helped found a new congregation, Bethel Presbyterian Church in the mountains, he maintained his ties with Hopewell Church in Pendleton.[7] He was not so far removed from Pendleton's affairs that its citizens no longer turned to him for leadership at critical or exciting moments. War fever swept large parts of the nation again in 1807. A public meeting of the "Inhabitants of Pendleton District" met on August 12 to condemn the deadly attack of the HMS *Leopard* on the USS *Chesapeake* earlier in the summer. "General Pickens," of course, was elected chairman of the meeting. The citizens announced their readiness to assume any duty the nation's authorities deemed necessary and insisted that the U.S. government should enact whatever measures were necessary to satisfy the insult to national honor. In the preface of the committee's resolutions, Pickens's neighbors paid homage to his generation's virtue a quarter century before: "When . . . our connection with Great Britain was severed by a combination of valour and patriotism, and political wisdom unparalleled in the annals of Nations, it became the duty of every Citizen of our Republic . . . to support the dignity of our Government, and promote the best interest of our common country."[8] Pickens and his contemporaries, then, had defined patriotism and virtue, and their example placed obligations on succeeding generations. The crisis soon passed, however, and Pickens returned to his plantation at the foot of the mountains.

While seeing to his crops and cattle at Tamassee, Pickens had much time to reflect on the nature of the new republican society he had helped build. In America's first two decades of independence, liberty had thrived, though its health was always threatened by its citizens' selfish ambition and greed. Pickens was disappointed that Thomas Jefferson's election had not led to a new period of national unity. Now that they were in power, the Republicans, as he had feared, were not all "cool and dispassionate." Instead, he remarked to his brother-in-law John E. Colhoun, "party Spirit . . . still continues high in congress."[9]

Unprincipled behavior had affected Pickens's business enterprises as well. Andrew Pickens & Company had profited for several years in its trade with the Indians, but the company dissolved in 1798. The supply of skins was dwindling as the frontier moved away from Pickens. Moreover, the firm had fallen deeply into debt because of its inability to collect debts owed it from a number of traders.[10] Former governor John Rutledge, who had been mentally incompetent for several years, had failed to supply his share of capital. The principals of the firm met in Charleston and on June 9 empowered William Steele to collect as many of their debts as possible and reimburse their creditors. Any amount left over would be divided four ways and the company dissolved. John Owen, however, asserted that Pickens was responsible for most of the amount owed by Rutledge. In the days that followed, Pickens stewed over the arrangements that had been made and

Retirement and Looking Back

concluded that he had been cheated. Writing his attorney son, Ezekiel, in Charleston, Pickens confessed, "The more I think of the statement, I dislike it the worse—the large sum which they charge for interest is a mistery to me and the method of stating my account with the concern, I do not see the justice of it. I wish you to look as carefully into the matter as you can before you leave it to Owen . . . one thing more, the adding 75 per cent on the goods in the statement I do not see the propriety of."[11] For several years afterward, Pickens continued to be plagued and perhaps gouged by his former partners and current agents. In 1800, Pickens wrote his son Andrew that he had just had to pay $1,500 "on account of [John Lewis] Gervais and Owen which has taken all the money I could get at the present and that my staff fed Steers sold for. I had lodged double that Sum in the hands of —— to pay that debt, but it was put to other [uses]."[12] As late as 1805, Pickens had an agent endeavoring to collect debts worth more than £732 from twenty Cherokee traders, a majority of them Indians or of partial Indian descent but several of them white men as well.[13]

Despite this major setback, Pickens and his family had prospered over-all in the new Republic. Pickens was grateful to be able to provide his eldest two sons with the college education he had never had. Several letters that he wrote to Andrew at Brown survive. They show Pickens to be an attentive father who nevertheless expected his sons to be thrifty and studious. One letter also sheds more light on Pickens's theology. He believed in a God who would one day bring fire and judgment to the earth. In the meantime, God used storms and other trying ordeals to improve the character of those who had come to appreciate his mercy. Just after his arrival at college for the spring 1800 term, young Andrew related that during the journey he had survived a terrible storm at sea. Pickens expressed thanks that his son was well but urged Andrew to appreciate God's sovereign power and mercy: "I have heard you had a very hard Storm at Sea—there, often the preserving providence of God, is plainly to be Seen, if those things are remembered and improved, for the purposes they are Sent, it will be an advantage, when worlds are on fire."[14] Pickens was also pleased with his sons' academic per-formance but did not believe that it necessarily translated into solid charac-ter or worldly success. Ezekiel had been valedictorian of his class at Yale but so far had been slow to fulfill the expectations of him. Writing to Andrew at Brown, the general told his second son that he was pleased that he had earned the good opinion of the faculty, "but you must remember, that many, under tutors and Governors, perform well, but after they come to act for themselves, doe not act so well[. T]he improvement of those advantages you have receivd, will under the devine guidance, be an advantage to your Self, and Satisfaction to your friends."[15]

Pickens had been able to provide sufficiently for his sons, and by the time he moved to Tamassee they were doing well enough. After settling in his mountain home, he split the remainder of his Hopewell estate between Ezekiel and Andrew; in his will he specified that young Joseph would inherit the scenic but perhaps less valuable Tamassee tract.[16] Pickens's eldest son continued to reside mostly in Charleston. Unlike his father, Ezekiel was educated and sophisticated and moved easily among the circles of the low-country aristocracy. Ezekiel disliked his profession, however, and Pickens tried to help. The doting father asked Marinus Willet to intercede with the latter's friend, Vice President Aaron Burr, to try to find a position in the federal government for Ezekiel. Asking for special favors did not come easily for Pickens: "Pardon me, dr sir, for those requests it is the first kind I ever made for myself or any relation."[17]

Overall, though, Ezekiel gave his father no reason to be ashamed of him. He was deemed an honest, affable gentleman and served as South Carolina's lieutenant governor from 1802 to 1804. (His successor was Thomas Sumter Jr.) Ezekiel's marriage to the wealthy Elizabeth Bonneau lasted ten years and produced four children.[18] After Elizabeth's death in 1803, Ezekiel allowed his sons Ezekiel Jr. and Samuel to spend long periods of time with their grandparents at Tamassee. In an 1806 letter, Ezekiel discussed bringing five-year-old Samuel down from Tamassee "if his Grandfather & Grandmother will consent[;] they love him better I believe than one of their own. My Father cannot be without him."[19] In 1807, Ezekiel married Elizabeth Barksdale, who gave Pickens three more grandchildren.[20]

Andrew Pickens Jr. seemed more "his father's son."[21] Young Andrew became a local leader in Pendleton and took over the general's place as a trustee of Pendleton's Hopewell Academy.[22] Like his father, Andrew pursued military service. During the War of 1812, he served as the senior colonel in South Carolina's brigade of state troops. Less than a year before Pickens died, he would see Andrew Jr. inaugurated as governor of South Carolina, the first governor of the state who did not hail from the lowcountry aristocracy.[23] There might be no better proof of the Revolution's impact than frontiersmen of the yeoman class, or at least their children, entering the ranks of the elite. Meanwhile his nephew John C. Calhoun had become a congressman and was on his way to becoming one of the most prominent statesmen of the antebellum era.

If a family's happiness was measured by the respectability of its daughters' husbands, then Andrew and Becky Pickens succeeded in that area as well. Their oldest child, Mary, was already sixteen when her father returned from his last military campaign in the autumn of 1782. She married a young war veteran from the Long Cane area, John Harris. John served in the campaigns of 1778 and 1779 and lost his eye in an engagement with Colonel James Boyd's forces a few days before the battle of Kettle Creek. He later returned to service and fought under Pickens at Cowpens. John, unlike most of Pickens's sons-in-law, settled reasonably near his wife's family and was buried near modern-day Anderson.[24] The other Pickens girls married doctors, a lawyer, and the sons of clergymen and Revolutionary War militia officers who had fought with Pickens—the up-and-coming professional and landowning class. Ann married John Simpson, son of the Reverend John Simpson, a veteran of the war with Britain. The elder Simpson preached twice a month at Pickens's Hopewell church for several years until the congregation was able to hire a full-time pastor.[25] Jane married her cousin Dr. John Henry Miller, son of the Reverend Robert Miller and her aunt Jane Pickens Miller. Margaret married Major John Bowie, a prominent lawyer and citizen of Abbeville. Rebecca, or "Becky," married William Noble, the son of Major Alexander Noble, another wartime comrade of her father's. Young William's mother was Catherine Calhoun, his bride's maternal aunt; thus, Becky also married her first cousin. Catherine, the youngest Pickens daughter, married Dr. John Hunter.

Like his father before him, Pickens divided his lands fairly equally among his sons while giving his daughters modest dowries and marrying them off to respectable young men. The general and his wife did not enjoy the benefit of their daughters and their daughters' children living close by. With Ezekiel and Andrew assuming the bulk of their father's estate and political prestige around Pendleton, the sons-in-laws generally chose to settle elsewhere. Thus, most of Pickens's daughters eventually settled with their husbands in Alabama or Mississippi.[26]

Though Pickens never spent time publicly recounting his exploits, he took some time in 1811 to reminisce and reflect. The reason for this self-assessment was a request from his former comrade Henry Lee, who was writing a book on the Revolution. Lee asked Pickens to relate his life story and particularly his experiences in the war. The old general responded with two letters, which are the closest things we have to an autobiography of Pickens, though even in these letters he showed little introspection or self-absorption. His coverage of his own life was sparse, condensing more than seven decades of war and adventure into eight handwritten pages. When relating events with which he knew Lee was unfamiliar, such as the Kettle Creek campaign or the anarchy following the British evacuation of Ninety Six, Pickens went into more detail. But he virtually skipped discussing altogether those campaigns at which Lee was present: "The siege of Augusta, of Ninety Six, the battle of the Eutaw & in other services with the army you know whether I did my duty." The fact that Pickens had been shot in the chest at Eutaw and still carried the pain from that wound received no mention. Toward the end of the letter, he apologized for writing as much as he did. For Pickens it was enough to say that he knew he had done his best: "I leave it to my Country to say, whether in my public transactions, I have discharged the duties assigned me with honesty & fidelity & whether I have been an humble instrument in the hand of Providence, to its advantage— But whatever the public sentiment may be I have a witness within myself that my public life & conduct have been moved & actuated by an ardent zeal for the welfare & happiness of my beloved Country."[27] Lee wrote back less than a month later asking for more details, especially concerning Pickens's family, legislative service, and Indian negotiations. Pickens responded with a three-page missive but still did not bring up the sad topic of the wartime deaths of his two brothers or of his infant son. Recounting his numerous campaigns and journeys into the wilderness perhaps led Pickens to a renewed sense of amazement that he was still healthy. He ended the second letter abruptly: "But kind Providence has favoured me with much health after being so much exposed to so much inclement weather, and fatigue."[28]

Pickens, then, could look out over his rolling pastures and fields at Tamassee and be relatively pleased. He was confident that he had no reason to be ashamed of his own conduct. He had survived two-thirds of a century of war and upheaval, and much had been achieved in the way of liberty, order, and prosperity. The upper portion of the state was now dotted with courthouses, jails, and churches. The forests were giving way to cleared fields, and profits were growing from the rapid spread of short-staple cotton. Rivers that Pickens and his tired, drenched soldiers had swum their horses across were now spanned by bridges and ferries. Old battlefields were plowed over or grazed by cattle and horses, including at Pickens's own Tamassee. Moreover, his children were prospering and enjoying the blessings of liberty in the Republic he had helped create.

Much of this prosperity, however, resulted from the forced labor of African Americans. Pickens almost certainly spent time wrestling with the issue of slavery in the latter decades of his life. Since he wrote little on the topic, however, and since nothing he may have said about it is recorded, it is difficult to determine exactly how his views evolved. The best way to ascertain his views is to extrapolate from his own acquisition of slaves, from the way slavery functioned in his community, from the way it was debated in his church, and from his will written in 1809.

Slave labor had assisted Pickens in his own rise as a backcountry merchant and planter. It is impossible to trace precisely the growth of his slave population, but by 1773 he owned two slaves, Dick and July. By the latter years of the Revolutionary War he owned several, as Pickens family tradition included stories of the slaves loyally scavenging food for Becky and the children as they hid in the woods from roving bands of Tories. His slaveholdings grew rapidly during or after the war. Like other militia officers and enlisted troops, part of his pay from the state of South Carolina may have come in the form of enslaved people confiscated from Tory estates, and he may have acquired others from customers or traders who were indebted to Andrew Pickens & Company. By the time of the 1790 census, Pickens owned thirty-three slaves. Though such a slave population was well below average in comparison with state legislators from the lowcountry or middle districts, it made him the largest slaveholder in Pendleton County. Pickens's black labor force provided manual labor in his fields, barns, pastures, and trading business, as well as household help for Becky and the Pickens daughters. His neighbor, friend, and fellow militia officer Robert Anderson had the second-largest holding with twenty-eight, and Generals Pickens and Anderson were the only two citizens in the county who owned more than twenty. Altogether, only 251 of the 1,418 households (18 percent) in Pendleton County owned any slaves, with the vast majority of those owning five or less. Still, slavery was becoming more economically important to the upcountry than it had ever been. Pickens's own holdings increased from thirty-three in 1790 to thirty-eight in 1800.[29]

During the war, few white people in South Carolina saw slave ownership as a moral issue. Contemporaries judged Pickens's character not by his ownership of human beings but by how trustworthy he had been in handling other citizens' human property. In those cases in which South Carolinians questioned what military officers had done under Sumter's Law, the questions were whether officers or troops had seized slaves unlawfully from good patriots rather than from Tories; whether officers had returned slaves captured from patriot citizens to their original owners instead of keeping them for themselves; or whether they had cheated their troops by keeping more than their share. As related in chapter 11, the General Assembly attempted to resolve these questions by examining the accounts of senior officers in 1784 and finally concluded that Pickens had acted properly in every case.[30]

The South Carolina General Assembly wrestled with the issue of the slave trade, both domestic and transatlantic, between the establishment of independence and 1808. Again, the debate centered primarily on economics, not on the morality of buying and selling human beings or of transporting them across the ocean in ships under wretched conditions. For much of the period, backcountry representatives tended to favor more slaves coming into the state from other states and from overseas, which would lower prices and speed the growth of plantation agriculture. Lowcountry planters who already owned large numbers of slaves preferred for prices to remain high. As related in chapter 11, Pickens had opposed the importation of slaves in 1787 as a means to ease the state's debt crisis and prevent the unethical practice of citizens going more deeply into debt when they already owed large amounts to creditors. For Pickens, then, the question was partly a moral one, but not because he questioned the inhumanity of slavery itself. The issue resurfaced in 1803 when, in the wake of the Louisiana Purchase, lowcountry representatives managed to reopen the slave trade in South Carolina in order to capitalize on the expected spike in demand from western settlers. By that time, of course, Pickens was out of the legislature and rarely commenting on public affairs.[31]

South Carolinians, then, were loath to debate the morality of slavery within the confines of courthouses and the General Assembly. By the late 1780s, this was emphatically not true in the case of the evangelical denominations, including the Presbyterians. Evangelical Christianity inspired much of the attack on slavery in America, as well as much of its defense. As a devout believer, Pickens could no longer avoid considering the moral implications of slavery, as they were hotly debated within his own denomination, within his own presbytery and synod, and within the walls of Hopewell Church itself.

Southern Presbyterians openly wrestled with slavery as early as 1787, when Reverend Henry Patillo of the North Carolina piedmont (and a member of Pickens's Synod of the Carolinas) published a pamphlet arguing that "the Negro" and whites were born with the same abilities and the same tendencies to sin. People of both races were equally prone to laziness, thievery, and other wickedness. The only physical differences lay in the Negro's "black skin, and curled head," and blacks and whites were even "more alike in their souls, than in their bodies." Patillo, however, did not go so far as to advocate immediate manumission, trusting to God's providence rather

Retirement and Looking Back

than man's ability to manage the social and economic disruption that would result from mass emancipation. He did not oppose enslaved persons fleeing cruel masters but did not think that benign masters should be pressured to free their servants. Ultimately, he thought, God would show "how to provide for them, and what to do with them."[32]

It might be easier to understand how many evangelicals, particularly literal-minded Calvinists, could be deeply ambivalent on the issue when one considers their emphasis on the inerrancy of God's word. The Bible, on the one hand, was as adamant as any known text in the Western world on the fundamental moral equality of all people before God. Paul's letter to the Galatians reminded the early church that, in God's eyes, "there is neither Jew nor Greek, there is neither bond nor free, there is neither male nor female: for ye are all one in Christ Jesus."[33] Similarly, Paul warned masters in Ephesus to be kind to their slaves and not to threaten them, "knowing that your Master also is in heaven; neither is there respect of persons with him."[34] These very passages, though, as well as many others in both the Old and New Testaments, implicitly recognized the existence of slavery and never called for its abolition. Just a few verses before Paul's injunction to masters, in fact, he had ordered slaves to "be obedient to them that are your masters according to the flesh, with fear and trembling, in singleness of your heart, as unto Christ."[35] Christians who were troubled by the implications of freeing all of America's slaves might easily conclude that while the Bible insisted on slaves' and masters' intrinsic moral equality before God, it also sanctioned social inequality. Indeed, there was plenty of room in Calvinist doctrine for the idea that God placed people in different social standings. Conversely, though, Calvinism's emphasis on human depravity made it possible that some human institutions were the result of man's sin and not approved by God. This was the opinion of Charleston's Dr. David Ramsay, who, like Pickens, was a South Carolinian, a Presbyterian, and a native of Lancaster County, Pennsylvania. "White pride and avarice," he wrote in 1780, "are great obstacles in the way of black liberty."[36]

Several Presbyterians in the Synod of the Carolinas refused to accept the notion that God approved of slavery and made their point more forcefully than Patillo did. In 1794, Reverend William C. Davis preached a sermon before the Presbytery of South Carolina in which "he denounced all his fellow-Christians who owned slaves."[37] Reverend Dr. Thomas Reese, the pastor of Pickens's congregation at Hopewell, refuted Davis with an address that "met the entire approbation of the presbytery."[38] The result of the exchange evidently greatly "mortified" Davis.[39]

Another anti-slavery Presbyterian minister, James Gilliland Sr., was perhaps more careful and yet more effective than Davis. Gilliland was the pastor of the Bradaway congregation, just twenty-five miles from Pendleton. He had often preached at Hopewell and Carmel churches near Pendleton before being called to a full-time position at Bradaway in 1796. Quite possibly Gilliland had preached against slavery in Pickens's presence, as the young minister was already somewhat controversial by the time he assumed leadership of the Bradaway congregation. Three months before Gilliland was scheduled to be formally ordained as the pastor at Bradaway, some members of that church remonstrated to the presbytery against his appointment because of his antislavery views. The Presbytery of South Carolina ordered Gilliland to be silent on the issue "without previously consulting [the] presbytery."[40] Gilliland initially agreed but months later returned to the presbytery and "laid his conscientious scruples on [slavery] before them as still existing & requested advice whether he should continue to conceal or to declare his sentiments from the pulpit."[41] The presbytery referred his appeal to the next higher body, the Synod of the Carolinas, which met the next month in the mountain town of Morganton, North Carolina. "After deliberation upon the matter," the synod concurred with the presbytery "in advising Mr. Gilleland [sic] to content himself with using his utmost endeavors in private to open the way for emancipation, so as to secure our happiness as a people, preserve the peace of the Church, and render them capable of enjoying the blessings of liberty." The synod opined that publicly charging believers that it was their duty to free their slaves "in present circumstances . . . would lead to disorder and open the way to great confusion." Pickens might have approved of this move to safeguard public order, and it is possible that he was one of those who initially complained to the presbytery about Gilliland's abolitionist sermons. But Pickens probably approved of the synod's next injunction as well. All slaveholding members of the church, it ordered, were "to teach the children [of slaves] to read the Scriptures so as to receive instruction from them."[42]

The issue, however, did not go away; Gilliland continued to serve at Bradaway and probably was responsible for the "overture" introduced at Hopewell Church in 1799. In fact, he continued to preach periodically at Hopewell from 1796 until at least 1802.[43] The overture, or proposal, recommended that the synod cooperate with other denominations to bring petitions to state legislatures "in favor of Emancipation, in order to have it on the footing which has obtained in some of the Northern States: that is— that all children of slaves born after the passage of such an act shall be free at such an age."[44] The Committee of Overtures voted to forward the proposal to the synod. Rather than rejecting the proposal out of hand, the synod agreed to refer it to a committee of several of the most respected clergymen in the region. Ultimately, however, the synod could not bring itself to take the proposed step. The committee members reported the following year that while it was their "ardent wish" that emancipation would one day occur, "it appears to us that matters are not yet matured for carrying it forward, especially in the southern parts of our States." As hesitant as that statement sounds, the committee went on to recommend that every member of the synod be "enjoined ... to use his influence to carry into effect the directions and recommendations of the Synod of New York and Philadelphia and ... the General Assembly."[45] The latter Presbyterian bodies had condemned slavery and recommended that all Presbyterians do all that was prudent and consistent "with the interest and the state of civil society in which they live, to procure eventually, the final abolition of Slavery in America."[46] Part of these efforts toward gradual emancipation should include "the instruction of those who are in a state of slavery to prepare them the better for a state of freedom."[47]

The Synod of the Carolinas, then, did not attempt to shut down the debate in its 1800 ruling. James Gilliland apparently continued to make cautious antislavery comments at Bradaway, and conflict between him and local believers continued. Moreover, as a "Great Revival" swept over the upcountry in 1802, some slaveholders feared the radical abolitionism of wild-eyed Methodists and Quakers.[48]

While Presbyterians and other denominations debated the morality of slavery, secular authorities in Columbia continued to be more attuned to slavery's economic value and its contribution to maintaining social order. In 1800, lowcountry planters concerned with the rising number of manumissions and evangelical Christianity's supposed threat to slavery took action on both scores. A new statute passed that year required masters seeking to free their slaves to appear before a jury of five freeholders and a justice of the peace. The master had to present the enslaved persons at the hearing and persuade his fellow citizens that they could support themselves and had good character. The law also forbade locked-door, daylight gatherings at which slaves or free blacks were present "for the purpose of mental instruction or religious worship" and forbade all mixed-race religious meetings after sundown as well.[49] The intent was clearly to prevent evangelizing of slaves in a way that promoted antislavery doctrines. This section of the law prompted a strong backlash from Baptists, Presbyterians, and Methodists throughout the state. Over a period of three years, Protestant clergymen and their congregations continually petitioned the legislature to revise the law, insisting that religious instruction strengthened social order rather than threatened it. In 1803 the legislature revised the law, and restrictions on mixed-race religious gatherings eased.[50]

Arguments over slavery's legitimacy continued to roil the Carolina piedmont, at least in the churches, through the first decade of the new century. By that time, however, the southern presbyteries seemed to have settled on their position: the abolition of slavery itself was desirable in the abstract but threatened so much civil disorder that the church should not pressure the state to act; instead, it should allow emancipation to remain primarily a civil issue. The internal operation of slavery, however, was a moral and religious issue, and the church had the right and duty to instruct its members on how to treat their slaves.[51]

Historians point to the efforts of southern evangelicals to reconcile slavery with Christianity as the most important source of the tradition of paternalism. Paternalism began with the assumption that some people owed deference or obedience to others. Its most benign features were the injunctions that while slaves should obey their masters, the latter should in turn recognize the humanity of their slaves, treat them humanely, systematically teach them Christianity, and see to their moral instruction. And yet paternalism would also develop as a means for slave owners to defend slavery by thinking of it as a humane institution. The most recent extensive work on southern slavery finds paternalism beginning to flourish in the early nineteenth century, its growth heavily dependent on the "Great Revival" that swept through the South in 1801 and 1802.[52]

The attitudes of Pickens and other leaders in Pendleton appear to have aligned almost exactly with the paternalistic approach of the evangelical leaders of the early nineteenth century. In fact, Pendleton court records of the 1790s indicate that they were on the leading edge of paternalism. Pickens and the other major landowners in Pendleton often intervened to see that local blacks were treated humanely, black families were kept together, and they were taught to read the Scriptures.

Pickens and his fellow local elites clearly had no problem with individual cases of manumission. In 1804, Pickens served as an executor of William Hallum's will. Six of Hallum's slaves were distributed among his widow, Mary; his daughter; and his brother. A seventh, Peter, was to go free once Mary died or remarried. In the words of Hallum, Peter was "to go free to be his own master. . . . On his becoming free he is to have 50 acres of land, a cow and calf and a gun."[53] When Mary Hallum subsequently married James Barr, Peter was officially freed on November 15, 1804.[54] Another case of manumission involved "a certain Mullatto mail child named Isaac Williams, now three years old." In 1790, Pickens, "in his official capacity" as justice of the peace, bound little Isaac to William Sloan until he reached the age of twenty-five. After that point Isaac was to be free. In the meantime, he was to "obey the lawful command of his Master, to be diligent and attentive to his Master's interest." Pickens ordered Sloan, meanwhile, to properly feed, clothe, and house Isaac and "learn him to spell and read the Holy Scriptures." The deed was recorded in the presence of Colonel Benjamin Cleveland, a war veteran and Pendleton County justice.[55]

Clearly, early leaders of Pendleton were beginning to recognize that slaves deserved formal legal protections and even emancipation in certain cases. This acknowledgment of slaves' humanity also extended informally to masters' treatment of their slaves on their own plantations. As previously mentioned, Pickens seems to have had a special affinity for Old Dick, perhaps the first slave he ever acquired in the 1770s. Old Dick had proven his worth as a man to Pickens on the battlefield and in his loyalty to the Pickens family in the darkest days of the Revolution when they were in hiding from the Tories. He had served alongside Pickens in battle against both the British and the Cherokees, and Pickens praised his bravery to his sons. On at least one occasion, according to Pickens's grandson Francis Pickens, a future South Carolina governor, "Dick swam the Broad River *twice* one cold night, in the dead of winter, to get to the camp of his master—the first time he swam it, he got into a camp of the enemy by mistake, & the second time he reached his master. He was with Gen. Pickens through the war."[56] Pickens allowed Old Dick to go wherever he wished on his estate with a large knife, and no white man, including Pickens's sons, was allowed to rebuke him. Pickens could have recognized Dick's dignity far better, of course, by freeing him, but the story suggests that Pickens had advanced beyond simply viewing his slaves as chattel property. There are few other comments about Pickens's characteristics as a master, but those few indicate that he took the biblical command to be kind to his servants seriously. His younger friend William Martin, who knew Pickens in the 1790s, remembered that the general "was remarkably mild and gentle in his family, and to his servants."[57]

At times the paternalistic slaveholders of Pendleton intervened to keep slave families together. Even when they did so, however, they implicitly asserted their right not to take such action or even to split black families apart. Pickens's friend and neighbor Robert Anderson noted in his will that he had bought the slave "Jeffe, the Husband of Hannah, at a considerable disadvantage, on account of his great attachment to his Wife and Children." By the time Anderson wrote his will in 1810, however, Jeffe and Hannah had "differed" and lived apart. Anderson bequeathed Jeffe to his son Robert and Hannah to Henry Dobson Reese, a son of his deceased wife by her previous marriage. Anderson stipulated, however, that if Jeffe and Hannah "should compromise their differences, and desire to be together; It is my Will that Mr. Reese buy Jeffe from Robert; or Robert buy Hannah and her two [remaining] Children from Mr. Reese, as they may agree themselves." In the same document, however, Anderson was willing enough to see slave families split up. His large slave population was divided among his children, grandchildren, and other relatives—in some cases a parent and child were deliberately willed to the same white heir, while in others this was not the case. In several instances, Anderson specified that the slave in question was "not to be sold out of the family," meaning, of course, his white family. One of these was the old slave woman Rose, who had been the personal maid to his deceased wife. Anderson took special care to see that he did not violate the special relationship between Rose and his wife: "I will not have her sold in her old age, as she was always a faithful Servant to her old Mistress: they were raised together, and near of an age."[58]

By the time Anderson—Pickens's friend and fellow Presbyterian elder—wrote this will, he had dismissed any doubts he may have had about the legitimacy of slavery itself as an institution. In the same year that Anderson wrote the will, he was visited by young William Ancrum as the latter toured the upcountry. Ancrum recorded that "the Old General [Anderson] is at present studiously employed in writing a Piece in Vindication of Slavery; he tells me it will consist of about 600 pages, which when he is done writing, he will have it critically examined, and if then thought worth publishing, he will have it published by Subscription."[59] Pickens, of course, wrote no learned treatises on slavery or anything else. We can only infer his thoughts from his actions and from the way the debate played out around him. Pickens acquired slaves, profited from their labor, and apparently did not free them in his lifetime. He and his fellow members of the backcountry gentry balanced the gentler side of paternalism against stern punishment for slaves who threatened their masters. Paternalism, in fact, valued social order, and that is one of the reasons Pickens embraced it. In 1798 he participated in the trial of several slaves who tried to poison his brother-in-law and their master, John E. Colhoun. A slave named Will, who acquired the poison, was hanged. The others—Suky, Hazard, Sue, and Jack—were punished by whipping and branding. In 1787, a slave belonging to Pendleton's sheriff Robert Maxwell was executed for destroying his master's property, probably by arson.[60]

By the time Pickens was fifty years old, his denomination was in the midst of a soul-searching debate over the scriptural and moral legitimacy of slavery. He may have given a hostile reception to James Gilliland, William Davis, and other liberal preachers who advocated immediate abolition. On the other hand, he was probably willing to give serious consideration to the prospect of gradual emancipation. One such proposal had been debated within the walls of his own church, of which he was the most prominent member, and had been forwarded from there to the synod. He apparently was considered a kind master, at least by his white neighbors, and prone to give special consideration and respect to certain slaves such as Old Dick.

The fact that Pickens's mind was not closed to manumission or gradual emancipation comes from the most useful piece of evidence on this question—Pickens's own will. His 1809 will, in fact, reveals several of his beliefs about slavery and freedom by that time. First, scripture permitted slavery, and God in his providence had appointed some human beings to be slaves and others to be free. In fact, he thought, God in his inscrutable wisdom had ordained that the "negroes" would be a means by which Pickens and his family could enjoy prosperity. Second, masters were morally obligated to treat their slaves humanely. Third, while God had put some individuals in bondage to others, he had not necessarily made their condition permanent; providence might dictate their freedom at some future date. Finally, freedom meant little unless a "free" man had property and the means to sustain himself and his family. Republicanism regarded the individual freeholder as the backbone of a healthy, virtuous society, and without property no man, black or white, could ever be truly independent.

Pickens began his will by making sure that Becky would be able to live comfortably at Tamassee, with $500, use of the house, two feather beds, a horse, a chair, produce from the plantation, and anything else "my executors may think necessary for her comfort," including "a negro girl named Lucy." The remainder of the Tamassee estate went to Joseph, then eighteen and legally underage, as his older children "have [already] got their proportion of the property which God in his providence has given me." This phrase indicates that the reason Pickens now owned ten slaves instead of more than thirty is that he had given many of them to Ezekiel and Andrew, along with his land near Pendleton, and others to his daughters as part of their dowries.[61]

Having provided for Becky and for Joseph, Pickens now turned to the remaining nine slaves, not counting the girl Lucy. So that Becky might be "freed from more care and trouble," Pickens directed that a "careful industrious man, should be got as an overseer, that will be humain and careful, and have plenty raised or procured, for the women to spin, that comfortable warm clothing, may be had at all times for the negroes, as they have been a means, under Providence, to procure many of the comforts of life, which myself and others have enjoyed. I request that they may be used with justice, and humanity."

Next Pickens considered what would happen to the slaves if Joseph died before he came of age, married, or wrote a will. In that case, the slaves would be free. Not only were they to be emancipated, but Pickens's heirs and executors also were to ensure that they had the means to provide for themselves. Old Dick; Pompey and his wife, Fillis; Jame and his wife, Seala; Rob and his wife, Clarasey; July; and Sambo were

> to be free from Slavery, and that one hundred and fifty acres of
> Land be reserved for them to live upon, and to cultivate for their
> support, the land laid of[f] for them on the north east side of Little
> River, begining on the river at the indian boundary and along that
> boundary, and down the river so as to include the cleared land
> and houses on that side of the river, where Rob now lives to live on
> during their lives, my executors are hereby directed to give them
> two young work horses with two plows, with Gears and tackling,
> each of them to be given a good weeding hoe, the man each an
> ax, with pair of iron wedges the women each a cotton wheel and
> cards, likeweis to be given them five young cows and calves, six
> head of sheep, and four Breeding sows, and to be supplied, with
> provition for themselves and creatures out of the provition, from
> the provition of the plantation, and likeweis with three bushels
> of salt for the first year, and doe appoint and nominate William
> Beatty John McWhorter, who lives near Mr. Beatty, and Alexander
> Keion to be gaurdians, for the above mentioned negroes, and
> have justice done them, and to give direction as to their work and
> conduct.

Finally Pickens addressed the unlikely event that Becky would outlive Joseph. In that case, she would be attended not only by Lucy but also by Jame and his wife, Seala, until Becky died. Then Jame and Seala would be freed and live with the other freed slaves as described earlier.[62]

Pickens's will was not an antislavery statement. First, Joseph Pickens did not die young, and it is unlikely that the enslaved people at Tamassee were ever freed. Moreover, Pickens was more concerned with providing for Becky and Joseph than he was with his slaves' opportunity to be free. But the conditional manumission clause was relatively unusual for its time and place. By the time Pickens wrote the will, the wave of manumissions that had swept through the Upper South after the Revolution was waning, and his own state's General Assembly had taken steps to limit its impact in South Carolina. The vast majority of manumissions that did take place in South Carolina were in the lowcountry, particularly Charleston, and typically involved a master freeing a particularly favored slave such as his black mistress or her children.[63] This was obviously not the case with Pickens.

Most of all Pickens's will showed that he had been wrestling with the moral implications and ethical dimensions of the peculiar institution. He was not unaware of the economic advantages slavery had brought him. He did not hide the fact that his prosperity and his family's "comforts of life" owed much to the labor of the "negroes." But he was keen to convince himself and others that he was driven by considerations of right and wrong, not by greed. He undoubtedly considered it unethical and irresponsible to send ten lifelong slaves out into the world with no means of support and no white sponsors, or "guardians," or without the means to provide for themselves, such as land, tools, and work animals. Such an act would actually be a dereliction of his duty to his slaves. It could also introduce a measure of the social disorder that many of his generation feared when they contemplated emancipation schemes. And he considered it very important to try to make sure the slaves had a "humain and careful" overseer. Ultimately Pickens's course of action fell short of the standard that modern Americans would approve, but it illuminates much about his internal struggle to reconcile slavery with his religion and morality.

In 1812 Pickens was called to public service one more time. As the nation went to war with Britain, his neighbors again turned to the general for leadership—the nationalist who was attuned to military affairs. He was elected to the state house that autumn. He and Becky came down from their mountain home weeks before the session began and stayed with Frances, the wife of their son Andrew, in Pendleton. Andrew was then stationed in Salisbury, North Carolina, serving as colonel in the South Carolina brigade of state troops. After two weeks, Becky insisted on returning to Tamassee, while Pickens traveled downstate to the capital. Fellow lawmakers were surprised at the seventy-three-year-old's return to Columbia but treated him with great respect. He was immediately appointed to several import-ant committees, including chair of the Military Committee. He was quite ill when he first arrived and for a while did not go to committee meetings at night. Chairmen of the committees he served on scheduled the more important meetings in the morning so that Pickens could attend. Despite his infirmity at the beginning of the session, his colleagues selected him to serve as a presidential elector. Some also wanted him to serve as governor in this time of war. Pickens wrote to his son Andrew that "I am much pressed from all parts of the State to be a candidate for the Gov's place my present impression is not to except."[64] Pickens eventually refused to be a candidate, explaining that the post should go to a younger man.[65]

Pickens was extremely active, both in 1812 and 1813, in military affairs. His strenuous efforts to improve the state's military readiness had mixed results. He failed to persuade his fellow legislators to increase the appro-priation for new military equipment or to build a warship that would be given to the federal government but succeeded in convincing them to raise a battalion of volunteers to defend "the Maritime Frontier of this State."[66]

In 1813, Pickens worked hard to reform the state's militia system. Throughout that year British ships had sailed into South Carolina's coastal inlets and captured private vessels and looted plantations. The militia had proven completely inadequate and at times had openly defied the author-ity of Governor Joseph Alston.[67] In the regular session of 1813, Pickens convinced his colleagues to reduce the size of the unwieldy Military Committee to five members, with himself as chair. He then crafted a bill by which the state's militia would be organized into five divisions rather than two. Pickens explained that the current system was unlike that of any neighboring state or of European armies, in that it produced divisions that were too large and unwieldy. Additionally, South Carolina major generals never ended up serving in the field. This meant that South Carolina troops, when serving with troops from other states, were never commanded by a South Carolinian. The legislature agreed to this reform. Even more vital for military efficiency, however, was Pickens's recommendation to elimi-nate elections for all officers above the rank of captain. Field-grade officers should be promoted strictly on the basis of seniority, he argued, and general officers appointed by the legislature. This would prevent promotions being the result of popularity contests and result in better discipline and more effective officers. After several votes on the issue, opponents were able to defeat this reform measure, to Pickens's disgust.[68] He was probably just as

Retirement and Looking Back

irritated when the legislature refused to support the city of Charleston's efforts to fortify its harbor. When the city sought reimbursement for the artillery pieces it had emplaced at its own expense, the house refused the request by the astounding vote of seventy-four to twenty, with Pickens of course voting in the minority.[69]

Pickens had always been a supporter of military readiness and efficiency, and his votes on other matters reflected his earlier record as well. He voted for law and order by supporting an anti-dueling bill and for education by opposing an effort to eliminate the state system of free schools that had just been established in 1811.[70] He also helped secure a measure by which the town of Pendleton was authorized to sell part of its public square in order to fund a circulating library for the use of its citizens. Pickens also favored public support for economic development, particularly in his vote for a $10,000 state appropriation to build a "cotton manufactory" in Greenville.[71]

Pickens's public service in 1812 and 1813 increased the immense respect that contemporaries had for his patriotism and selflessness. Coming as it did roughly a decade after his "retirement," it was easy for them to conclude that his willingness to return to Columbia had nothing to do with ambition and everything to do with patriotism in time of war. "Determined to enjoy the serenity and tranquility which he had so greatly contributed to establishing," they reported, he returned to Tamassee.[72]

Epilogue

I leave it to my Country to say.

Andrew Pickens to Henry Lee, August 28, 1811

Pickens still had a few more years to enjoy his retirement at Tamassee after his legislative service in 1813. He was still remarkably fit for his age, and those who knew him said he had lost none of his mental powers or alertness. The Red House often had visitors who had traveled far from the beaten path to see him. Traditional accounts state that many of them were Cherokee Indians, some of whom still lived in the mountain fastness of north Georgia and western North Carolina, not far from Pickens's home. One story relates a small contingent of them visiting Tamassee and playfully marching in a circle around Pickens's house while holding one of his infant grandsons, to the great alarm of the child's mother. Pickens assured her there was no need for alarm.[1]

Despite these frequent visits, Pickens's home was gradually becoming a lonelier place. Joseph now spent much of his time with his brother Andrew Jr. in Pendleton rather than at the Tamassee estate he was soon to inherit. Ezekiel died in May 1813 at the age of forty-five, a few months before Pickens's last stint in the state legislature. Pickens surely mourned his eldest son, but it is likely that Becky's death a year and a half later was an even harder blow. Her cheerful playfulness had always enlivened the Pickens household, even in the couple's old age. It provided balance to Pickens's sterner demeanor, and theirs had been a happy union, perhaps for that very reason. Like her husband, Becky's life story reflected that of the Revolutionary generation on the frontier. As a girl she had watched in horror as her grandmother was

308

scalped, and she had been, in effect, a single mother with a large brood of children during Pickens's long absences as well as a refugee in time of war. She later shared in her husband's prosperity and social status as the mistress of a large plantation over dozens of slaves. She was remembered also for her faith. Pickens buried her next to Hopewell Church, inscribing on her headstone, "She was through life religious and charitable and died humbly relying on the mercy of her Redeemer."[2]

Perhaps he was thinking of her two and a half years later when he walked outside into his yard the last time. It was August 11, 1817. Pickens sat in a chair beneath some cedar trees, facing the mountains, with a packet of mail. As he read, he suffered a stroke and died quietly, in his seventy-eighth year. As there were so few white residents at Tamassee, it may have been one of the black servants who found him, perhaps Old Dick or July, one of the old-timers who had been with him for nearly half a century. Days later, family members and friends followed his casket down the "General's Road" to the stone church at Hopewell, where he was buried beside Becky.

By the time Pickens was buried, the graveyard beside the stone church had already become a family cemetery for the Pickenses and other Presbyterian families, and the church building itself was on the verge of becoming a historical landmark. Only seven years after Pickens's funeral, the Hopewell congregation would build another structure within the town of Pendleton itself that was more convenient for most of the worshippers. The Stone Meeting House, as local residents referred to it, soon became known as the "Old Stone Church" and was used mainly for funerals or other special occasions. Though they rarely worshipped there after 1824, the old sacred ground remained the place where Pendleton's Presbyterians buried their loved ones. The Old Stone Church soon became less a place of worship than it was a shrine to northwestern South Carolina's early pioneers and to the virtues their descendants attributed to them. To this day the building and cemetery are carefully preserved and maintained. Like Pickens himself, the old edifice has served as a nostalgic reminder of the simple faith, conviction, and sturdiness of the area's earliest settlers.[3]

Pickens's obituary described him exactly as his contemporaries had long since come to see him—as an embodiment of the patriotism and virtue that had established their new Republic. They remembered, of course, that he had been skilled and courageous in war. But also he seemed uncorrupted by greed or ambition, unlike scores of his contemporaries who had converted, or tried to convert, their military fame into financial profit through shady land deals.

A eulogy in *Niles' Register*, a national newspaper, suggested that Pickens's example showed that one could prosper by honest effort and enjoy the fruits of one's labor without being greedy. "In his domestic circumstances," the paper reported, "he was fortunate. By industry and attention he soon acquired a competency, and never desired more." His material prosperity corresponded with a happy family life: "He married early in life, has left a numerous and prosperous offspring, and his consort, the sister of John E. Colhoun, formerly a Senator in Congress, died but a few years before him." Most of all, he was a man of virtue, or at least of the virtues his generation professed to admire: "Of the private character of the deceased little need be said; for among its strongest features was simplicity without contrariety or change; from his youth to age he was ever distinguished for the punctual performance of all the duties of life. He was from early life a firm believer in the Christian religion, and an influential member of the Presbyterian Church. The strong points of his character were decision and prudence, accompanied, especially in youth, with remarkable taciturnity."[4]

It is increasingly rare for heroes of an earlier age to enjoy the same respect they did more than two centuries after their death. More and more the leading lights of the founding generation have been criticized for their racism, greed, or even hypocrisy. Somehow, though, while Pickens is slightly less well known than he was in his own time, his image has suffered little tarnish. His own generation and the immediately succeeding ones admired him for his readiness to thrash their Indian enemies. Ironically, twentieth-century Americans, more attuned to the injustices suffered by the Indians but perhaps still somewhat condescending toward the "red men," noted how much the Indians supposedly admired Pickens.[5] More cynical observers today might conclude that the Indians knew a moderate white leader when they saw one and cultivated relations with him for the sake of their people's survival. Meanwhile, though, a new wave of scholarship recognizes that while the wholesale removal and near-disintegration of the native tribes was a national disgrace, there were white leaders who aimed for a more just and humane outcome, and Pickens was one of them. He transformed himself after 1782 from an Indian fighter to a peacemaker and even at times to an "advocate for the Cherokees."[6] Likewise, American patriots of his own day appreciated his fierce fight against their British and Tory enemies in a brutal civil war. A more dispassionate observer today might be equally impressed by his attempts to protect the lives of prisoners and to spare the lives of Indian women and children in his raids on Cherokee villages. Thus Pickens has managed to appear as a "good man" to different generations for different—and sometimes conflicting—reasons.

Pickens's life, in fact, remains relevant for Americans of all political persuasions who still dream that public policy might be driven by moral considerations. Liberals of a more secular mindset might be uncomfortable with Pickens's deep religiosity but approve of his strong support for public education and of his outrage (at least occasional) at injustices inflicted on the Indians. Conservatives of a libertarian bent might flinch at his support for state taxation and greater federal authority, though this support was never absolute and the power he imagined for the central government was far inferior to what it enjoys today. He certainly objected to government attempts to restrict freedom of speech and conscience, and this concern helped lead to his break with the Federalist Party. Modern evangelicals would certainly appreciate his devout spirituality and stern morality though perhaps be puzzled at his rejection of the open display of emotion in worship. Americans today of all political stripes cannot escape the fact that Pickens was a slaveholder—but it is also difficult to avoid the impression that Pickens at least made an attempt, perhaps unsuccessfully, to wrestle with the most difficult issue of his later years in terms of morality and divine will rather than of personal interest alone.

Perhaps that note of ambiguity is the most appropriate way to sum up the relevance of Pickens's life in the larger American story. Right or wrong, for good or ill, Pickens's life represents that part of American history, that part of Americans' understanding of themselves, that still insists on putting God, or at least morality—in some way—at the heart of their story. More principled than most, Andrew Pickens was nonetheless a product of the culture in which he lived—of that frontier Revolutionary ethic of faith, courage, and violence; of individual freedom and opportunity growing alongside racism and inequality—that made the new American Republic what it was. Striving to act virtuously in the midst of sin and injustice, he did not completely succeed by the standards of our day. It was lives like his, however, that helped future generations of Americans define some of the very standards by which they have judged the founding one—physical courage and selfless patriotism, often softened by a desire for justice, magnanimity toward defeated foes, and even a recognition, perhaps belated and sometimes incomplete, of the humanity of individuals of other races. Though better known as a warrior than anything else, he spent his life seeking order and peace in the midst of rapid change and turbulence. Andrew

Pickens's story, then, was profoundly American. His children and friends were perhaps more eloquent than they knew when they composed the epitaph on his headstone at the Old Stone Church:

> A Christian A Patriot and A Soldier, His Deeds and Character Are Incorporated With the History of His Country

Acknowledgments

I am deeply grateful for the support and professional advice I have received while working on this biography. Sometime in 2009, Joel Collins of Columbia, South Carolina, wondered aloud in a conversation with my then-department chair Tom Kuehn why there had not been a recent biography of his ancestor, Andrew Pickens. He thought that perhaps a graduate student at Clemson University might be interested in writing a master's thesis on him. As the department's graduate coordinator at the time, I knew that we had no students currently studying the Revolutionary era. But I also realized that Joel was right—it was time for a more up-to-date, scholarly study of this fascinating leader of the Revolutionary War in the southern backcountry. I deeply appreciate Joel's moral support and enthusiasm for this project. At the other end of the pipeline, I thank the staff of the University of North Carolina Press, and I particularly appreciate the outstanding support and assistance of editorial director Mark Simpson-Vos.

I have also received encouragement and valuable advice from several colleagues in my department and from others who are connected with Clemson University in various ways: Tom Kuehn, Vernon Burton, Jim Jeffries, Paul Anderson, Steve Marks, and Peter Eisenstadt—and in fact all of my departmental colleagues who attended my sabbatical lecture early in 2015 and offered valuable suggestions and critiques. Will Hiott, director of Clemson University's Historic Properties, deserves particular mention for granting me access to Pickens's Hopewell House and the "Old Stone Church," which are located on Clemson's campus, and for providing other useful information and assistance. The generosity and skill of my friend Chris Cartledge of Promark Art made the maps in this book possible.

Historians John "Bill" Gordon, David Calhoon, Erskine Clarke, and Turk McClesky have also provided help and advice along the way.

The South Carolina upcountry is blessed with a host of local historians who have an astounding, even encyclopedic, knowledge of the area's history. I appreciate the support of Charles Baxley of the group Southern Campaigns of the American Revolution and that of two of its members in particular: Ms. Nancy Lindroth, who provided me with useful research material she had compiled; and the late Ms. Barbara Abernethy, who was kind enough to drive my wife and me into the mountains and point out the former location of Pickens's Tamassee home and the most likely spot of the "Ring Fight." The greatest service was rendered by Mr. Frederick C. Holder, an expert on the area's history. In an act of incredible generosity, Fred carefully read an entire draft of the manuscript and offered useful advice on how to clarify the narrative and avoid several errors or misleading statements of fact. There are many other knowledgeable individuals in whose presence I know I am the amateur, and I hope they will forgive any remaining errors for which I, of course, am solely responsible.

And finally, I want to acknowledge the love and support of my wonderful family. My daughters, Jessica, Lydia, and Marina, have inspired and supported their dad as much as I have them. No words can convey how much I owe my best friend and partner in this world, Karmin Heather Andrew, to whom this work, and much more, is lovingly dedicated.

Soli Deo gloria.

Notes

ABBREVIATIONS

Collections

APCLS   Andrew Pickens Papers, Charleston Library Society, Charleston, S.C.

APCU   Andrew Pickens Papers, Clemson University Library, Clemson, S.C.

APHL   Andrew Pickens Papers, Huntington Library, San Marino, Calif.

APSCL   Andrew Pickens Papers, South Caroliniana Library, University of South Carolina, Columbia

ASP, IA   *American State Papers, Indian Affairs*, vols. 1–2 (Washington, D.C.: Gales and Seaton, 1832, 1834)

Draper CUL   Lyman C. Draper Collection (microfilm), Clemson University Library, Clemson, S.C.

PCC   *Papers of the Continental Congress*, National Archives, Washington, D.C., and Atlanta, Ga.

Libraries and Archives

CLS   Charleston Library Society, Charleston, S.C.

SCDAH   South Carolina Department of Archives and History, Columbia

PREFACE

1. William Martin to Lyman Draper, Jan. 1, 1843, Draper CUL 5DD11514. I have adapted William Martin's description of Pickens's occasional visits to Pendleton as if he were describing a visit on one particular day.

2. Ibid.

3. My understanding of these themes owes much to the following works: Appleby, *Capitalism*; Bailyn, *Ideological Origins*; Bushman, *From Puritan to Yankee*; Bullock, *Revolutionary Brotherhood*, esp. 2–4, 137–50; Calhoon, *Evangelicals and Conservatives*; Clarke, *Our Southern Zion*; Hatch, *Sacred Cause of Liberty*; Kelly, *Emergence of Liberty*;

Kidd, *God of Liberty*; Noll, *Christians in the American Revolution*; Weir, *"The Last of American Freemen"*; Wood, *The Creation of the American Republic*; and Greene, *"'Virtus et Libertas.'"*

4. Both quotes from Andrew Pickens to Henry Lee, Aug. 28, 1811, Draper 1VV108 (hereafter Pickens to Lee, Aug. 28, 1811). This letter can also be found in a printed form in Skelton, *General Andrew Pickens*, 9–21.

5. Wyatt-Brown, *Southern Honor*; Greenberg, *Honor and Slavery*; Appleby, *Inheriting the Revolution*, 41–45, 244.

6. Freeman, *Affairs of Honor*, xx (first three quotes), 247 (fourth quote). Appleby's *Capitalism* perceives a contradiction between Revolutionary understandings of "private" and "public" virtue (14–15). See also Bloch, "The Gendered Meanings of Virtue in Revolutionary America," in *Gender and Morality*, 136–53. This biography, like Wood's *Creation of the American Republic*, sees much more overlap between the two (Wood, *Creation of the American Republic*, 68–69).

7. Andrew Pickens to Henry Lee, Aug. 28, 1811, Draper CUL 1VV108 (hereafter Pickens to Lee, Aug. 28, 1811).

8. William Martin to Lyman Draper, Jan. 1, 1843, Draper CUL 5DD11514.

9. The colonial port of Charles Town changed its name to Charleston in 1783. This book uses the modern name for the city throughout.

10. R. Brown, *South Carolina Regulators*; Klein, *Unification of a Slave State*.

11. Previous biographies of Pickens include Ferguson, "General Andrew Pickens"; Waring, *Fighting Elder*; Reynolds, *Andrew Pickens*; and A. Pickens, *Skyagunsta*.

12. Noll, *Christians in the American Revolution*, 52. See also Kidd, *God of Liberty*; Hatch, *Sacred Cause of Liberty*; and Bloch, *Visionary Republic*, xiv, 3–4, 14–15, 47–56, 61–62. Michael Winship's *Godly Republicanism* studies the relationship between sixteenth- and seventeenth-century puritanism and republicanism.

13. An excellent summary of Calvinism's impact on political theory and history in early modern Europe and the American colonies is Kelly, *Emergence of Liberty*. See also Leyburn, *Scotch-Irish*, esp. 145–49. Other works that emphasize, or at least discuss, the ties between Presbyterianism or Congregationalism and the American Revolutionary cause include Gardiner, "Presbyterian Rebellion"; Calhoon, *Evangelicals and Conservatives*, 76, 80–81, and passim; Clarke, *Our Southern Zion*, 92–102; Kramer, "Muskets in the Pulpit, Part II," passim; Kramer, "Muskets in the Pulpit, Part I," 230; Smylie, "Presbyterian Clergy"; Barnes and Calhoon, "Moral Allegiance"; Balmer and Fitzmer, *Presbyterians*, 34–37; Isaac, *Transformation of Virginia*, esp. 243–69; and White, *Southern Presbyterian Leaders*, 158, 161–62. See also Humphrey, *Nationalism and Religion in America*, 67; and Noll, *Christians in the American Revolution*, 52. Some sources (W. Brown, *King's Friends*, 213–28; McCrady, *South Carolina in the Revolution, 1775–1780*, 32–52; and R. Barnwell, "Loyalism in South Carolina," 131–34) state that South Carolina Presbyterians were divided during the American Revolution. Most others adamantly insist on firm Presbyterian support for the patriot cause: see Clarke, *Our Southern Zion*, 90–97; Kramer, "Muskets in the Pulpit," (both parts); "Contributions to the Ecclesiastical History," 82–87; Hatch, *Sacred Cause of Liberty*, 6–7, 19; White, *Southern Presbyterian Leaders*, 144–47, 149, 151, 159–62; Howe, *Presbyterian Church*, 1:454; Gardiner, "Presbyterian Rebellion";

and Stokes, "Presbyterian Clergy," esp. 275–82. A nuanced view is found in Leyburn, "Presbyterian Immigrants," 24–26, 29.

14. Bushman, *Refinement of America*; Taylor, *William Cooper's Town*; Wood, *Americanization of Benjamin Franklin*.

15. Bushman highlights the conflict and accommodation between aristocratic gentility and egalitarianism in *Refinement of America*.

16. Klein, *Unification of a Slave State*.

17. William Blount and Andrew Pickens to Henry Knox, Aug. 6, 1793, in *Territorial Papers of the United States*, 205.

18. Hawkins, Pickens, Martin, and McIntosh to Richard Henry Lee, President of Congress, Dec. 2, 1785, *ASP, IA*, 1:38.

19. Nichols, *Red Gentlemen*; Andrew R. L. Cayton, "'Noble Actors,'" in Cayton and Teute, *Contact Points*, 243–45, 269; Cayton, *Frontier Republic*; Sadosky, *Revolutionary Negotiations*, 156–59; A. Wallace, *Jefferson and the Indians*, 166–69; W. Dennis, "American Revolutionaries." Ethridge contrasts the attitudes of white land speculators and many southern state leaders with other national leaders, especially Benjamin Hawkins, in *Creek Country*, 10–20, 196–97, 211.

20. Francis W. Pickens to J. H. Marshall, Nov. 4, 1847, in Draper CUL 16VV360, 16VV361–62.

21. Will of Gen. Andrew Pickens, June 2, 1809, Probate Judge Estate Papers, Anderson County, roll #547, SCDAH.

22. Egerton, *Death or Liberty*; Taylor, *Slavery and War in Virginia*. Piecuch's *Three Peoples, One King* has relatively more information on slaves from the southern backcountry, but their individual stories are still virtually impossible to document.

23. For more thorough discussion of these matters, one may start with McCoy, *Elusive Republic*; and Sloan, *Principle and Interest*.

24. Perdue, *Cherokee Women*; Perdue, *Slavery and the Evolution of Cherokee Society*; Dowd, *Spirited Resistance*; Dowd, "Spinning Wheel Revolution"; Calloway, *American Revolution in Indian Country*; Saunt, *New Order of Things*; Cumfer, *Separate Peoples*; Hudson, *Creek Paths*; Tortora, *Carolina in Crisis*; Ethridge, *Creek Country*; Hatley, *Dividing Paths*; Braund, *Deerskins and Duffels*; Boulware, *Deconstructing the Cherokee Nation*. See also Cayton, "'Noble Actors,'" and other essays in Cayton and Teute, *Contact Points*.

25. Quote from Barnes and Calhoon, "Moral Allegiance," 282. A great deal of scholarship emphasizes the profound impact of evangelical religion and Calvinist doctrine on emerging concepts of republicanism and republican virtue. A small sample includes Calhoon, *Evangelicals and Conservatives*; Kidd, *God of Liberty*; Hatch, *Sacred Cause of Liberty*; Noll, *Christians in the American Revolution*; and Bloch, *Visionary Republic*.

CHAPTER 1

1. Pickens to Lee, Aug. 28, 1811; Ferguson, "General Andrew Pickens," 1; Phifer, "Notes," 1; Sharp, *Pickens Families*, 1; E. B. Pickens, *Life of General Pickens*, 131.

2. Day, *Pickens Family*, 20.

3. Clarke, *Our Southern Zion*, 30–31; White, *Southern Presbyterian Leaders*, 22–23, 28–30; Howe, "Early Presbyterian Immigration," 25–26, 28–29, 31–33.

4. Vann, *In Search of Ulster-Scots Land*, 62–64; Balmer and Fitzmer, *Presbyterians*, 29–30; Fischer, *Albion's Seed*, 606–8; Leyburn, *Scotch-Irish*, 180.

5. Day, *Pickens Family*, 23; Sharp, *Pickens Families*, 2–3.

6. Sharp, *Pickens Families*, 3, 35, 65; White, *Southern Presbyterian Leaders*, 32–35; Day, *Pickens Family*, 24–25.

7. Vann, *In Search of Ulster-Scots Land*, 91; Leyburn, *Scotch-Irish*, 157–75.

8. Miller et al., *Irish Immigrants*, 140–42.

9. Clarke, *Our Southern Zion*, 3.

10. Ibid., 15–17 (quote on 17).

11. Ibid., 66–67; Posey, *Religious Strife*, 27; Leyburn, *Scotch-Irish*, 149–50; Vann, *In Search of Ulster-Scots Land*, 59–60.

12. For passages describing what was valued in a pastor, see Reese, "Memoir of the Late Rev'd. Thomas Reese," 116–20; and Howe, *Presbyterian Church*, 1:292, 440–43, 638, 2:49, 51, 73–74, 76–77. For examples of militant, or militaristic, leadership by eighteenth-century pastors, see Kramer, "Muskets in the Pulpit, Part I," 242; Kramer, "Muskets in the Pulpit, Part II," 38, 42–46; White, *Southern Presbyterian Leaders*, 144–47, 149, 151, 160–62; Fischer, *Albion's Seed*, 618; and Leyburn, *Scotch-Irish*, 229.

13. White, *Southern Presbyterian Leaders*, 33; Leyburn, *Scotch-Irish*, 288–95.

14. White, *Southern Presbyterian Leaders*, 34.

15. Ibid., 35; Leyburn, *Scotch-Irish*, 288–95.

16. Quoted in White, *Southern Presbyterian Leaders*, 34.

17. Ibid., 35.

18. McCleskey, "Rich Land, Poor Prospects."

19. Moore, *World of Toil*, 20.

20. Leyburn, *Scotch-Irish*, 206, 208–13; Pickens to Lee, Aug. 28, 1811; Sharp, *Pickens Families*, 12, 31, 33; Day, *Pickens Family*, 38, 79. For the likelihood of elders being men of property and status, see Leyburn, *Scotch-Irish*, 261–62.

21. *Colonial Records of North Carolina*, 4:1250; Ferguson, "General Andrew Pickens," 5.

22. *Colony of North Carolina, 1753–1764*, 1:6; Howe, *Presbyterian Church*, 1:285, 289; *State Records of North Carolina*, 22:381–82; Ferguson, "General Andrew Pickens," 5–7; Waring, *Fighting Elder*, 2.

23. *Colony of North Carolina, 1753–1764*, 1:59, 325, 339; preceding two quotes from Moore, *World of Toil*, 2.

24. Moore, *World of Toil*, 2. The first minister, Robert Miller, was hired in 1756 but lasted only a short time. He was replaced by William Richardson.

25. Ibid., 2, 16–17, 19–20, 29; Meriwether, *Expansion of South Carolina*, 13. The best study of the Catawbas is Merrell's *Indians' New World*.

26. Quoted in Ferguson, "General Andrew Pickens," 7.

27. Moore, *World of Toil*, 55.

28. Ibid., 54–55; Meriwether, *Expansion of South Carolina*, 138–39.

29. Howe, *Presbyterian Church*, 1:289.

30. Ibid., 289–90; *Anson County Record of Deeds*, 121–22; Sharp, *Pickens Families*, 31; White, *Southern Presbyterian Leaders*, 91; Meriwether, *Expansion of South Carolina*, 143–44.

31. Howe, *Presbyterian Church*, 1:289–90.

32. Ibid.

33. Will of Andrew Pickens, *North Carolina Original Wills, 1763–1790*.

34. *Anson County Record of Deeds*, 121–22; Pickens to Lee, Aug. 28, 1811.

35. Pickens to Lee, Aug. 28, 1811.

36. Leyburn, *Scotch-Irish*, 264.

37. Ibid.

38. Ibid., 265. For other descriptions of rowdy frontier customs, see Fischer, *Albion's Seed*, 669–75; and Meriwether, *Expansion of South Carolina*, 176–77.

39. Waring, *Fighting Elder*, 5.

CHAPTER 2

1. Meriwether, *Expansion of South Carolina*, 200–201, 209.

2. Oliphant, *Anglo-Cherokee Frontier*, 20, 41–60 passim; Meriwether, *Expansion of South Carolina*, 215–18; Tortora, *Carolina in Crisis*, 23–54 passim.

3. Meriwether, *Expansion of South Carolina*, 218; Oliphant, *Anglo-Cherokee Frontier*, 79–112.

4. Meriwether, *Expansion of South Carolina*, 117–18, 124, 134; Salley, *Calhoun Family*, 1, 3–4.

5. Salley, *Calhoun Family*, 5–11; Waring, *Fighting Elder*, 3; Meriwether, *Expansion of South Carolina*, 222; *South Carolina Gazette*, Feb. 9, 23, 1760.

6. Edgar, *South Carolina*, 206; Tortora, *Carolina in Crisis*, 105–10, 113–15.

7. Howe, *Presbyterian Church*, 1:307.

8. Waring, *Fighting Elder*, 4.

9. McCrady, *South Carolina under the Royal Government*, 346–47; Meriwether, *Expansion of South Carolina*, 226–34; Edgar, *South Carolina*, 206–7. Some sources claim that Pickens served in the 1760 campaign. It is possible to imagine that Pickens served in 1760, as his future uncle-in-law Patrick Calhoun was an officer in the provincial regiment in that campaign (Meriwether, *Expansion of South Carolina*, 228) and several dozen Catawba Indians from the Waxhaws region served as well. Pickens's autobiographical account written in 1811 is cryptic and unclear enough to leave the possibility open. Pickens referred to the Cherokee war of "1761 and 2," when the actual dates of the war were 1760–61: "During the War with the Cherokees in 1761 & 2 I was young, fond of a gun & an active life and was much out in that war, was intrusted for some time with a small detatchment of men on the frontiers where the Inhabitants had been driven from their newly settled plantations—I served as a volunteer in Grant's Expedition against the Cherokees in the year 1762" (Pickens to Lee, Aug. 28, 1811). (This expedition actually took place in 1761, and Pickens definitely participated in it.) The wording of Pickens's account, while making it obvious that he served under Grant in 1761, does not exclude the possibility that he served in 1760 as well. The campaign was over by August, in time for Pickens to be one of the buyers of James McCorkall's estate in October.

10. Meriwether, *Expansion of South Carolina*, 236–39; Bass, *Ninety Six*, 51; Edgar, *South Carolina*, 207; *South Carolina Gazette*, July 18, 1761.

11. Quoted in Oliphant, *Anglo-Cherokee Frontier*, 163.

12. Pickens to Lee, Aug. 28, 1811.

13. Bass, *Ninety Six*, 52.

14. Day, *Pickens Family*, 38–39.

15. *Colonial Plat Books*, 7:369; Sharp, *Pickens Families*, 25.

16. *Colonial Plat Books*, 9:244.

17. For family-driven economic behavior, see Moore, *World of Toil*, 2, 22, 25. Rachel Klein discusses the economic goals of backcountry planters in the colonial period in chapter 1 of *Unification of a Slave State*.

18. *Conveyance Books*, volume 03FO: 501–5.

19. Sharp, *Pickens Families*, 151.

20. *Colonial Plat Books*, 8:30; Sharp, *Pickens Families*, 12.

21. *Colonial Plat Books*, 14:285, 18:133, 10:54.

22. R. Brown, *South Carolina Regulators*, 6–7, 10–12.

23. Howe, *Presbyterian Church*, 1:341–44.

24. Ibid., 342.

25. Waring, *Fighting Elder*, 5.

26. Ferguson, "General Andrew Pickens," 14; Meriwether, *Expansion of South Carolina*, 179; "Contributions to the Ecclesiastical History," 81–82 and 82n; Klein, *Unification of a Slave State*, 44.

27. "Contributions to the Ecclesiastical History," 80; Howe, *Presbyterian Church*, 1:354–55; Edgar, *South Carolina*, 182–83; Klein, *Unification of a Slave State*, 42–44; R. Brown, *South Carolina Regulators*, 21, 27–30.

28. Klein, *Unification of a Slave State*, 9–15 (quote on 9).

29. R. Brown, *South Carolina Regulators*, 25–26; Klein, first quote, in *Unification of a Slave State*; second quote in Klein, "Frontier Planters," 45.

30. Leyburn, *Scotch-Irish*, 14–17, 33–34, 70, 261–62.

31. Klein, *Unification of a Slave State*, 28–29, 35–36.

32. Quoted terms are found in Klein, *Unification of a Slave State*, 51–56; and R. Brown, *South Carolina Regulators*, 27–28.

33. R. Brown, *South Carolina Regulators*, 27–31; Klein, *Unification of a Slave State*, 51–64.

34. R. Brown, *South Carolina Regulators*, 31–35, quote from 34.

35. Ibid. This quote is from Brown, not a primary source. See also Edgar, *South Carolina*, 212.

36. Klein, *Unification of a Slave State*, 9, 45; R. Brown, *South Carolina Regulators*, 15, 18.

37. R. Brown, *South Carolina Regulators*, 17–18.

38. Ibid., 16; Moore, *World of Toil*, 54; Edgar, *South Carolina*, 205.

39. R. Brown, *South Carolina Regulators*, 38; Edgar, *South Carolina*, 212.

40. R. Brown, *South Carolina Regulators*, 39.

41. Quoted in ibid.

42. Quoted in ibid.

43. Quoted in ibid., 42.

44. Quoted in ibid., 39.

45. Klein, *Unification of a Slave State*, 51, 61; Sharp, *Pickens Families*, 25.

46. R. Brown, *South Carolina Regulators*, 41–95; Edgar, *South Carolina*, 213–15.

47. R. Brown, *South Carolina Regulators*, 97–104 (quote on 104).

48. Ferguson, "General Andrew Pickens," 15.

49. Sharp, *Pickens Families*, 25–27.

CHAPTER 3

1. Edgar, *South Carolina*, 218–23; Weir, *Colonial South Carolina*, 314–16.

2. Weir, *Colonial South Carolina*, 322–23.

3. R. Brown, *South Carolina Regulators*, 43, 65–82; Weir, *Colonial South Carolina*, 278–81.

4. Leyburn, "Presbyterian Immigrants," 17.

5. Leyburn, *Scotch-Irish*, 293.

6. An excellent summary of Calvinism's impact on political theory and history in early modern Europe and the American colonies is Kelly, *Emergence of Liberty*; see also Leyburn, *Scotch-Irish*, esp. 145–49; Gardiner, "Presbyterian Rebellion"; Calhoon, *Evangelicals and Conservatives*, 76, 80–81; Clarke, *Our Southern Zion*, 92–102; Kramer, "Muskets in the Pulpit, Part II"; Smylie, "Presbyterian Clergy"; Barnes and Calhoon, "Moral Allegiance"; Balmer and Fitzmer, *Presbyterians*, 34–37; White, *Southern Presbyterian Leaders*, 158, 161–62; and Hatch, *Sacred Cause of Liberty*, 3, 19, 22. A thorough treatment of evangelical religion's impact on Revolutionary thought is Kidd, *God of Liberty*.

7. Quoted in Leyburn, *Scotch-Irish*, 305.

8. Quoted in Kramer, "Muskets in the Pulpit, Part I," 230; see also Humphrey, *Nationalism and Religion in America*, 67.

9. Noll, *Christians in the American Revolution*, 52.

10. For citations and discussion on the issue of Presbyterian support for the American Revolution, see note 12 in the preface.

11. Pickens to Capt. John Irvin, Aug. 29, 1778, in Gibbes, *Documentary History*, 2:96; Ferguson, "General Andrew Pickens," 40–41; Waring, *Fighting Elder*, 23; Clower, "Notes on the Calhoun-Noble-Davis and Thomas Family," 51; Howe, *Presbyterian Church*, 1:441, 454.

12. Klein, "Frontier Planters," 66, 69. A number of historians focus on the maintenance of order as a central concern in the Revolutionary era and a key consideration determining whether southern colonists chose the Tory or Whig side (see R. Brown, *South Carolina Regulators*, vii–1, 115, 124; essays by A. Roger Ekirch, Jeffrey J. Crow, and Robert M. Weir in Hoffman, Tate, and Albert, *Uncivil War*; and Mercantini, *Who Shall Rule at Home?*, 13–14).

13. R. Brown, *South Carolina Regulators*, 124.

14. Edgar, *South Carolina*, 221–22.

15. Ibid.; Weir, *Colonial South Carolina*, 314–16; Moultrie, *Memoirs*, 1:41, 44–45.

16. Gibbes, *Documentary History*, 1:103.

17. Quote from Olson, "Loyalists and the American Revolution," 203; Weir, *Colonial South Carolina*, 319; McCrady, *South Carolina in the Revolution, 1775–1780*, 4; Bass, *Ninety Six*, 78–79.

18. Gibbes, *Documentary History*, 1:107–8.

19. Pickens to Lee, Aug. 28, 1811; *Extracts from the Journals of the Provincial Congresses*, June 6, 7, 9, 12, 1775, 39–48.

20. *Extracts from the Journals of the Provincial Congresses*, June 3, 1775, 36.

21. Moultrie, *Memoirs*, 1:14, 44–45; Weir, *Colonial South Carolina*, 321; Edgar, *South Carolina*, 223.

22. Olson, "Loyalists and the American Revolution," 204.

23. Quoted in Bass, *Ninety Six*, 87; Jones, *South Carolina Civil War*, 32.

24. Bass, *Ninety Six*, 55.

25. Quoted in Clarke, *Our Southern Zion*, 93.

26. Quoted in ibid., 94.

27. Bass, *Ninety Six*, 88–97; Edgar, *South Carolina*, 223; Drayton, *Memoirs*, 1:383–84; Tennent, "Fragment of a Journal," 304.

28. Ferguson, "General Andrew Pickens," 20.

29. Tennent to the Council of Safety, Sept. 1, 1775, in Gibbes, *Documentary History*, 1:165; Ferguson, "General Andrew Pickens," 20.

30. Drayton, *Memoirs*, 1:389.

31. Bass, *Ninety Six*, 98–99, 101.

32. Drayton, *Memoirs*, 1:400 (first quote), 402 (second quote).

33. *South Carolina Gazette*, Dec. 8, 1775, in Draper CUL 3VV9.

34. Moultrie, *Memoirs*, 1:96; Drayton, *Memoirs*, 1:407; Bass, *Ninety Six*, 111–12.

35. "Agreement for a Cessation of Arms," in Gibbes, *Documentary History*, 1:214; Major Mayson to Colonel Thomson in ibid., 215–16; Major Williamson to Mr. Drayton in ibid., 216–19; "A Report of the Militia and Volunteers on Duty in the Fortified Camp at Ninety-Six," in ibid., 221; "Extract of a Letter from an Officer at Ninety Six, dated November 29th," in *South Carolina Gazette*, Jan. 19, 1776; *South Carolina Gazette*, Dec. 8, 1775, in Draper CUL 3VV9–12. Contemporary estimates of Tory losses found in these sources vary greatly. The highest estimate is fifty-two killed and "many" wounded (*South Carolina Gazette*, Jan. 19, 1776), while the Tories told Major Mayson that their losses were nearly identical to the Whigs'. Mayson doubted this, as he claimed that from "the best information they have buried at least twenty-seven men, and have as many wounded" (Mayson to Thomson).

36. Richard Richardson to Henry Laurens, Dec. 12, 16, 22, 1775, Jan. 2, 1776, in Gibbes, *Documentary History*, 1:239–44, 246–48; Ferguson, "General Andrew Pickens," 26–27, 27n68; Draper CUL 3VV241.

37. *Extracts from the Journals of the Provincial Congresses*, Mar. 26, 1776, 255.

38. Ibid., 257.

39. Ibid., 265.

40. Draper CUL 3VV17; *Extracts from the Journals of the Provincial Congresses*, Feb. 10, 1776, 182–83.

41. Gordon, *South Carolina*, 46–47.

42. Rev. James Creswell to W. H. Drayton, July 27, 1776, in Gibbes, *Documentary History*, 2:30.

43. Ferguson, "General Andrew Pickens," 28; Col. William Christian to the Commander of the South Carolina Troops, Aug. 15, 1776, in *Colonial Records of North Carolina*, 10:748.

44. The use of these titles probably reflects the fact that Williamson later held both these ranks and how widely his authority and leadership was recognized unofficially, if not in his actual rank.

45. Andrew Pickens (cousin of this book's subject), "Williamson's Campaign of 1776," in Draper CUL 3VV135.

46. Draper CUL 3VV136.

47. William Drayton to Francis Salvador, July 24, 1776, in Gibbes, *Documentary History*, 2:29.

48. Pickens to Lee, Aug. 28, 1811.

49. Gordon, *South Carolina*, 45–46. Recently John Grenier has argued that an American "first way of war" that emphasized destroying villages and killing Indian prisoners as well as women and children was colonial Americans' usual and preferred mode of fighting. Despite the excellent insights in his study, Grenier gives little recognition that destroying villages and food supplies was the only way to defeat the Indians. Also, as will be seen later, there were leaders such as Pickens who exchanged Indian prisoners, forbade the killing of women and children, and were outraged at killings of Indians that took place under flags of truce (Grenier, *First Way of War*).

50. Andrew Williamson to—, July 22, 1776, in Gibbes, *Documentary History*, 2:27; Andrew Williamson to William Drayton, Aug. 4, 1776, in Drayton, *Memoirs*, 2:369–70; "Colonel Williamson's Campaign," *South Carolina Gazette*, Aug. 14, 1776, in Draper CUL 3VV18; Cousin Andrew Pickens's account, Draper CUL 3VV135–36. Today, this section of the waterway is known as the Seneca River rather than the Keowee.

51. "Colonel Williamson's Campaign," in Draper CUL 3VV19–20; Cousin Andrew Pickens's account, Draper CUL 3VV136–37.

52. Cousin Andrew Pickens's account, Draper CUL 3VV137.

53. Gordon, *South Carolina*, 51.

54. Quotes from Capt. John Swelling's statement, Draper CUL 16VV379–80. See also Cousin Andrew Pickens's account, Draper CUL 3VV140; and Andrew Williamson to Gen. Griffith Rutherford, Aug. 14, 1776, in *Colonial Records of North Carolina*, 10:746–48. Williamson's letter mentions sending "a party" about half a mile upstream to find a crossing point but does not mention Pickens's crossing. Instead his letter gives the impression that the "party" could not find an unopposed crossing point and therefore Williamson sent about 220 men directly across in Indian canoes (Williamson to Rutherford, 747).

55. Williamson to Rutherford, Aug. 14, 1776, 747. An alternate reading of the quoted phrase is "their own knives and tomahawks," meaning that Pickens's men wrested the Cherokees' weapons from them and used those weapons against them. This is how it was rendered in an article in the *Pennsylvania Evening Post*, Oct. 15, 1776, which reprinted Williamson's letter to Rutherford. This article can be found in Draper CUL 16VV134. Either reading of Williamson's handwriting makes it clear that much of the fighting was hand-to-hand.

56. Francis W. Pickens to J. H. Marshall, Nov. 4, 1847, in Draper CUL 16VV363. This particular account is somewhat romantic and obviously based on oral tradition, but I have accepted the statement that Pickens's men were covered with blood and smoke as completely or at least mostly true because (1) other testimony makes it clear that there were numerous white and Indian casualties within a very small area and that several of them were caused by hand-to-hand combat, and (2) Williamson stated that the firing continued for an hour and a quarter. Under these circumstances, all of Pickens's men would have faces blackened from powder smoke, and most if not all of them would have been spattered with the blood of their comrades and enemies, if not their own.

57. There are several slightly conflicting accounts of the Ring Fight, with some more reliable than others. I have favored the accounts in Williamson's August 14, 1776, letter to Rutherford and Cousin Andrew Pickens's second-hand account (Draper CUL 3VV140–41). More romantic accounts include that of Francis W. Pickens, grandson of Pickens (Draper CUL 16VV362–63). Some sources describe Pickens's Indian guide as a Catawba called "Monday," while Francis W. Pickens referred to him as "Cornels" and Cousin Andrew Pickens called him "Branan." All sources agree that he remained loyal to the Whig cause (Draper CUL 16VV253, 16VV262, 3VV140–41).

58. Francis W. Pickens to J. H. Marshall, Nov. 4, 1847, in Draper CUL 16VV364.

59. Williamson to Rutherford, Aug. 14, 1776; Ferguson, "General Andrew Pickens," 33–35; Ferguson, "Functions of the Partisan-Militia," 251.

60. Pickens to Lee, Aug. 28, 1811.

61. Francis W. Pickens to J. H. Marshall, Nov. 4, 1847.

62. Edgar, *South Carolina*, 229.

63. Ferguson, "Functions of the Partisan-Militia," 241.

CHAPTER 4

1. Ferguson, "Functions of the Partisan-Militia."

2. *Journals of the General Assembly and House of Representatives, 1776–1780*, 14, 322, 324 (hereafter *S.C. Journals, 1776–1780*). John Ewing Colhoun was Becky Pickens's brother. For most of his life, he chose to spell his name differently from the rest of the Calhouns (Salley, *Calhoun Family*, 18–19).

3. Edgar, *South Carolina*, 230; McCrady, *South Carolina under the Royal Government*, 760.

4. Edgar, *South Carolina*, 230.

5. Ibid.

6. Ferguson, "General Andrew Pickens," 35–36; McCrady, *South Carolina under the Royal Government*, 502.

7. *Statutes at Large of South Carolina*, 1:147 (hereafter *S.C. Statutes*).

8. Ibid., 4:410.

9. Ibid., 411.

10. Ibid., 411–12.

11. Ibid., 9:667.

12. Ibid., 666–79.

13. Ibid., 677.

14. Ibid., 681.

15. Ferguson, "General Andrew Pickens," 36.

16. Williamson "hinted" that his troops would be unwilling to serve under Continental officers, or indeed under any command other than his own. Meanwhile Houstoun flatly refused to take orders from Howe (Col. C. C. Pinckney to Brig. Gen. William Moultrie, July 10, 1778, in Moultrie, *Memoirs*, 1:230).

17. Waring, *Fighting Elder*, 22.

18. Pension statement of Robert Long, Draper CUL 16VV144–45.

19. Pension statement of Robert McCreight, Draper CUL 11VV400–40.

20. Waring, *Fighting Elder*, 21–23; Ferguson, "General Andrew Pickens," 36–39; Olson, "Thomas Brown (Part I)," 9–10; excerpts from *South Carolina Gazette*, July 15 and 24, 1778, in Draper CUL 3VV33–35; Gibbes, *Documentary History*, 2:94–95; Draper CUL 16VV144–45, 11VV400–401.

21. Pickens to Capt. John Irvin, Aug. 29, 1778, in Gibbes, *Documentary History*, 2:96; Ferguson, "General Andrew Pickens," 40–41; Waring, *Fighting Elder*, 23; Clower, "Notes on the Calhoun-Noble-Davis and Thomas Family," 51; Howe, *Presbyterian Church*, 1:439–43. The young John Harris who became Pickens's son-in-law was not the Presbyterian minister who led the congregation at Long Cane but probably the latter's son. He was born in December 1762 and married Pickens's eldest daughter, Mary (pension statement of John Harris, Draper CUL 11VV394; Phifer, "Notes," 3).

22. Ferguson, "General Andrew Pickens," 41.

23. A. Pickens, *Skyagunsta*, 39.

24. Ferguson, "General Andrew Pickens," 42.

25. Davis and Thomas, *Kettle Creek*, 17–22; Ferguson, "General Andrew Pickens," 43–49; McCrady, *South Carolina in the Revolution, 1775–1780*, 327.

26. Pickens to Lee, Aug. 28, 1811.

27. Ibid.

28. Ibid.

29. Ibid.; Waring, *Fighting Elder*, 24.

30. All quotes from Pickens to Lee, Aug. 28, 1811.

31. Ibid.

32. Ibid.; Davis and Thomas, *Kettle Creek*, 27–28.

33. Pickens to Lee, Aug. 28, 1811; Davis and Thomas, *Kettle Creek*, 28; A. Pickens, *Skyagunsta*, 41, McCall, *History of Georgia*, 2:393.

34. Pickens to Lee, Aug. 28, 1811.

35. Ibid.; A. Pickens, *Skyagunsta*, 34.

36. Pickens to Lee, Aug. 28, 1811; Ferguson, "General Andrew Pickens," 52.

37. Davis and Thomas, *Kettle Creek*, 30.

38. Ibid., 30–31; Ferguson, "General Andrew Pickens," 46–48, 46n9, 53; Pickens to Lee, Aug. 28, 1811.

39. Pickens to Lee, Aug. 28, 1811.

40. Davis and Thomas, *Kettle Creek*, 32–33; Ferguson, "General Andrew Pickens," 53–54; deposition of Joseph Cartwright, Sept. [?], 1779, Draper CUL 3VV250.

41. Pickens to Lee, Aug. 28, 1811; Ferguson, "General Andrew Pickens," 54–56; McCall, *History of Georgia*, 2:395.

42. Pickens to Lee, Aug. 28, 1811.

43. Ibid.; Davis and Thomas, *Kettle Creek*, 37; McCall, *History of Georgia*, 2:395–96.

44. Pickens to Lee, Aug. 28, 1811; Davis and Thomas, *Kettle Creek*, 37; McCall, *History of Georgia*, 2:396.

45. Pickens to Lee, Aug. 28, 1811.

46. Ibid.

47. Ibid.

48. Ibid.; Davis and Thomas, *Kettle Creek*, 38–39; McCall, *History of Georgia*, 2:397–99.

49. Pickens to Lee, Aug. 28, 1811; Davis and Thomas, *Kettle Creek*, 39–40, 40–43. Davis and Thomas provide a helpful chart in *Kettle Creek*, 40, with various reports of casualty numbers according to various sources and a detailed explanation of what happened to these prisoners.

50. Pickens to Lee, Aug. 28, 1811.

51. McCall, *History of Georgia*, 2:398.

52. A. Pickens, *Skyagunsta*, 45.

53. Copy of Francis W. Pickens to J. H. Marshall, Nov. 4, 1847, Draper CUL 16VV358–59. Another contemporary source supports the general outline of this story, though not all the details. Major Andrew Hamilton stated after the war that he was with Pickens at Kettle Creek and witnessed the death of Boyd. Hamilton did not mention what Pickens said to Boyd but quoted Boyd as saying "'that he had this consolation, that he died a true friend to his Majesty, King George the Third.' Boyd then gave something to Col. Pickens to forward to his wife, & then expired." Hamilton did not mention whether Pickens actually forwarded or personally delivered the item to Mrs. Boyd (Statement of Maj. Andrew Hamilton, Draper CUL 11VV355).

54. Pickens to Lee, Aug. 28, 1811.

55. Ferguson, "General Andrew Pickens," 89.

56. Pickens to Lee, Aug. 28, 1811.

57. Davis and Thomas, *Kettle Creek*, 154; Ferguson, "General Andrew Pickens," 88; quote from Dawson, *Battles of the United States*, 487; Olson, "Thomas Brown (Part I)," 13; Pancake, *This Destructive War*, 33.

58. Pickens to Lee, Aug. 28, 1811; pension statement of Robert Long, Draper CUL 3VV43–45.

59. D. Wilson, *Southern Strategy*, 91–99.

60. Ibid., 97–98.

61. Pickens to Lee, Aug. 28, 1811; extract from *South Carolina Gazette*, Apr. 9, 1779, in Draper CUL 3VV46; Pickens to Capt. John Irvin, Mar. 14, 1779, in Gibbes, *Documentary History*, 2:113.

62. D. Wilson, *Southern Strategy*, 101.

63. Ibid., 101–31. Wilson convincingly disputes lower estimates of Lincoln's strength in ibid., 123, 270–71.

64. Benjamin Lincoln to William Moultrie, June 20, 1779, in Moultrie, *Memoirs*, 1:490–92; Pickens to Lee, Aug. 28, 1811; Ferguson, "General Andrew Pickens," 78; Dawson, *Battles of the United States*, 500; C. Ward, *War of the Revolution*, 2:685–87.

65. According to the militia law of February 13, 1778, the governor could call the militia out for a period not exceeding three months in response to an alarm in a neighboring state. The only exception to the three-month limit was that if a relieving force was on the way to replace another but had not arrived yet, the men were required to stay until it did. Since many of Pickens's men had originally mustered in January because of the British invasion of Georgia and there was no relief for them in sight, there must have been some present who had already done more than the law required (*S.C. Statutes*, 4:466; Moultrie to Rutledge, July 3, 1770, in Moultrie, *Memoirs*, 2:7).

66. See correspondence between Moultrie, Lincoln, and Rutledge, July 3, 5, and 7, 1779, in Moultrie, *Memoirs*, 2:7–8, 11, 15–17; Ferguson, "General Andrew Pickens," 80; and D. Wilson, *Southern Strategy*, 130.

67. Extract from *South Carolina Gazette*, Sept. 24, 1779, Draper CUL 3VV53–56; pension statement of Robert Long, Draper CUL 16VV146.

68. Extract from *South Carolina Gazette*, Sept. 24, 1779, Draper CUL 3VV56.

69. Ferguson, "General Andrew Pickens," 85–86.

70. Ferguson, "Functions of the Partisan-Militia."

CHAPTER 5

1. McCrady, *South Carolina in the Revolution, 1775–1780*, 310–11, 372.

2. D. Wilson, *Southern Strategy*, 196, 238–41; Edgar, *South Carolina*, 232–33.

3. Ferguson, "General Andrew Pickens," 91, 96; *S.C. Journals, 1776–1780*, 256, 264, 275, 282.

4. Ferguson, "General Andrew Pickens," 92–93 (quote on 93).

5. Deposition of Andrew Pickens, July 3, 1798, Draper CUL 11VV542–43; excerpt from *Maryland Journal*, May 30, 1780, in Draper CUL 5VV250, ibid.; Ferguson, "General Andrew Pickens," 93–94.

6. Ferguson, "General Andrew Pickens," 97–98; Draper CUL 2DD307, 16VV146–47.

7. Edgar, *South Carolina*, 233; Edgar, *Partisans and Redcoats*, 50; Gordon, "Age-of-Sail Expeditionary Warfare."

8. Pancake, *This Destructive War*, 91; Saberton, *Cornwallis Papers*, 1:32, 262, 2:29 (hereafter, *Cornwallis Papers*).

9. Samuel Hammond's narrative, in Draper CUL 1DD5–7; Johnson, *Traditions*, 149–52.

10. D. Wilson, *Southern Strategy*, 264.

11. Rauch, "Southern (Dis)Comfort," 43; Willcox, *Portrait of a General*, 321.

12. Rawdon to Cornwallis, July 7, 1780, *Cornwallis Papers*, 1:193.

13. D. Wilson, *Southern Strategy*, 265.

14. See Andrew Hamilton's pension statement in Draper CUL 11VV346.

15. Extract of a letter from a "gentleman at Bullsborough . . . dated the 17th [of July]" in *South Carolina Gazette*, July 26, 1780, in Draper CUL 3VV57.

16. Cornwallis to Clinton, June 30, 1780, *Cornwallis Papers*, 1:160.

17. Quote from Gordon, *South Carolina*, 104; Edgar, *Partisans and Redcoats*, 60.

18. Edgar, *South Carolina*, 234; Pancake, *This Destructive War*, 81–82; Edgar, *Partisans and Redcoats*, 61.

19. Draper CUL 9VV392; Gordon, *South Carolina*, 86; Edgar, *Partisans and Redcoats*, 55–57. Sources generally date the destruction of Sumter's plantation on May 28 and the defeat of Buford's force on May 29, despite commenting on Tarleton's legion's remarkable *two*-day ride from Nelson's Ferry to the Waxhaws Creek area. It is not easy to resolve this discrepancy, but it is clear that the two events occurred within a couple of days of each other (Gordon, *South Carolina*, 86; Edgar, *Partisans and Redcoats*, 55–57; Morrill, *Southern Campaigns*, 77–79; Tarleton, *Campaigns*, 27–32, 77, 82–84).

20. A few modern historians have questioned whether Tarleton's massacre of surrendering American troops at the Waxhaws actually occurred (see, for example,

Piecuch, *Blood Be upon Your Head*). There is no doubt, however, that many Carolinians were convinced that it did occur and in the end that it was the most important fact (Rider, "Massacre or Myth"; Sciotti, *Brutal Virtue*).

21. Edgar, *Partisans and Redcoats*, 62.

22. Quoted in Leyburn, *Scotch-Irish*, 305.

23. Weigley, *Partisan War*, 13; Edgar, *Partisans and Redcoats*, 61–62, 65.

24. Salley, *Col. William Hill's Memoirs*, 9; "Memoir of Major Joseph McJunkin," from *The Magnolia* (Charleston, no. 1, vol. 2, n.s., Jan. 1843), in Draper CUL 23VV18–19; also Edgar, *Partisans and Redcoats*, 73–74.

25. Kramer, "Muskets in the Pulpit, Part II," 45–46; Howe, *Presbyterian Church*, 1:441–42.

26. White, *Southern Presbyterian Leaders*, 144–45, 173; Howe, *Presbyterian Church*, 1:510–12.

27. White, *Southern Presbyterian Leaders*, 161–62; Kramer, "Muskets in the Pulpit, Part II," 45–46. Works that emphasize, or at least discuss, ties between Presbyterianism or Congregationalism and the American Revolutionary cause include Leyburn, *Scotch-Irish*; Calhoon, *Evangelicals and Conservatives*, 76, 80–81; Balmer and Fitzmer, *Presbyterians*, 34–37; Kelly, *Emergence of Liberty*; as well as sources cited earlier in the preface, note 12.

28. Several modern works and contemporary Whig sources express respect for Cruger. For example, see Draper CUL 21VV74; and Bass, *Ninety Six*, 276. On Balfour's attempts to prevent plundering, see Pancake, *This Destructive War*, 94.

29. Ferguson, "General Andrew Pickens," 108–10. See also McCrady, *South Carolina in the Revolution, 1775–1780*, 834. No extant sources identify Ker's first name, but apparently the reference is to a Captain George Ker. Orderly books of DeLancey's Brigade refer to a Captain or Captain-Lieutenant George Ker several times. In one of the six places mentioned, his name is spelled "Kerr" (Kelby, *Orderly Book*). See also online information about DeLancey's Brigade at http://www.royalprovincial.com/military/rhist/delancey/delist.htm, accessed June 6, 2012; and Dornfest, *Military Loyalists*, 183.

30. Balfour to Cornwallis, June 24, 1780, *Cornwallis Papers*, 1:239, 240.

31. *Cornwallis Papers*, 1:152.

32. Balfour to Cornwallis, June 24, 1780, *Cornwallis Papers*, 1:240. In referring to "Hammond," Balfour probably meant Colonel Le Roy Hammond, a former regimental commander under Williamson, though Le Roy Hammond's son Captain Samuel Hammond also became an important figure.

33. Lambert, *South Carolina Loyalists*, 134, 160–62; Bass, *Ninety Six*, 291–92.

34. For example, see Cruger to Cornwallis, Aug. 27, 1780, *Cornwallis Papers*, 2:173, and Cornwallis to Germain, Sept. 21, 1780, ibid., 39.

35. Allen to Cornwallis, Dec. 29, 1780, ibid., 3:288.

36. This can be inferred from Balfour to Cornwallis, June 27, 1780, *Cornwallis Papers*, 1:243; Cruger to Cornwallis, Sept. 1, 1780, ibid., 2:175; and Williamson to Balfour, Sept. 21, 1780, ibid., 2:104.

37. Cruger to Cornwallis, Nov. 14, 1780, ibid., 3:270.

38. Ibid., Nov. 27, 1780, 274–75.

39. Cornwallis to Cruger, Aug. 27, 1780, ibid., 2:172.

40. Cornwallis to Balfour, Sept. 27, 1780, ibid., 100.

41. Cornwallis to Cruger, Nov. 30, 1780, ibid., 3:277.

42. Andrew Hamilton's pension statement, Draper CUL 11VV356. Hamilton was a friend and former subordinate of Pickens.

43. Balfour to Cornwallis, June 24, 1780, *Cornwallis Papers*, 1:239–40.

44. Ibid., June 27, 1780, 243.

45. Patrick Ferguson to Captain Ross, July 19, 1780, Charles Cornwallis Papers, reel 44, frames 1–2, Library of Congress.

46. Sumter to Brig. Gen. Sumner, Sept. 23, 1780, Draper CUL 7VV81.

47. McCall, *History of Georgia*, 2:482.

48. Cornwallis to Lord Germain, Sept. 21, 1780, *Cornwallis Papers*, 2:39.

49. Cruger to Cornwallis, Sept. 28, 1780, ibid., 194; Bass, *Ninety Six*, 251.

50. Quote from Williamson to Balfour, Sept. 21, 1780, *Cornwallis Papers*, 2:104. See also Cruger to Cornwallis, Sept. 13, 1780, Charles Cornwallis Papers, Library of Congress, reel 44, folios 52–53; Cruger to Balfour, Sept. 19, 1780, *Cornwallis Papers*, 2:103; and Balfour to Cornwallis, Sept. 20, 1780, *Cornwallis Papers*, 2:91.

51. William Campbell to William Preston, Dec. 12, 1780, in "Preston Papers," 315. Although Campbell's letter to Preston does not make clear when it was that the interview between him and Pickens occurred, Ferguson is probably correct to place it before the battle of Kings Mountain and not after. Campbell said the meeting occurred at Gilbert Town, and the patriot militia had assembled there a few days before the battle (Ferguson, "General Andrew Pickens," 107).

52. Lambert, *South Carolina Loyalists*, 143–44; Bass, *Ninety Six*, 276–77. For correspondence regarding the fate of British and Tory prisoners taken at King's Mountain, see *Cornwallis Papers*, 3:401–8 passim.

53. Malcolm Brown to Maj. John Bowie, Nov. 26, 1780, John Bowie Papers, SCDAH.

54. Waring, *Fighting Elder*, 40; see also Samuel Hammond's account in Johnson, *Traditions*, 531. Governor Rutledge, reporting second- or thirdhand, gave a somewhat different account of the discussions of Williamson in his letter to South Carolina's delegates to Congress (see Draper CUL 16VV108).

55. Waring, *Fighting Elder*, 40; see also A. Pickens, *Skyagunsta*, 61.

56. McCall, *History of Georgia*, 2:503–4.

57. A. Pickens, *Skyagunsta*, 62; Waring, *Fighting Elder*, 41.

58. Dunlap departed Ninety Six in time to arrive in Charleston at least by November 24 (Cruger to Cornwallis, Nov. 14, 1780, *Cornwallis Papers*, 3:270; Balfour to Cornwallis, Nov. 24, 1780, ibid., 93). Other correspondence suggests that as late as January, Dunlap was still in Charleston attempting to procure equipment for his troop of dragoons (see *Cornwallis Papers*, vol. 3).

59. Cruger to Cornwallis, Nov. 28, Dec. 3, 1780, ibid., 3:276, 278.

60. Cruger to Cornwallis, Dec. 9, Dec. 15, 1780, ibid., 280–83; McCall, *History of Georgia*, 2:502–3; Draper CUL 3VV28–29.

61. Pickens to Nathanael Greene, Dec. 8, 1780, in Conrad, *Papers of General Nathanael Greene*, 6:557–58 (hereafter *Greene Papers*); Ferguson, "General Andrew Pickens," 112; Moss, *Roster of South Carolina Patriots*, 88.

62. Cruger to Cornwallis, Dec. 15, 1780, *Cornwallis Papers*, 3:282–83.

63. Allen to Cornwallis, Dec. 29, 1780, ibid., 288; Clower, "Notes on the Calhoun-Noble-Davis and Thomas Family," 51; Ferguson, "General Andrew Pickens," 113.

64. Gordon, *South Carolina*, 89–95.

65. See, for example, D. Wallace, *History of South Carolina*, 2:245; and McCrady, *South Carolina in the Revolution, 1775–1780*, 834.

66. McCall, *History of Georgia*, 2:504; A. Pickens, *Skyagunsta*, 63.

67. A. Pickens, *Skyagunsta*, 63.

68. Quoted in ibid. The quote closely follows the wording in McCall, *History of Georgia*, 2:504. See also Waring, *Fighting Elder*, 41–42.

69. Quote in A. Pickens, *Skyagunsta*, 63. See also McCall, *History of Georgia*, 2:504; Waring, *Fighting Elder*, 42.

70. Waring, *Fighting Elder*, 42. My account agrees with sources that place the destruction of Pickens's property in late November. It is possible, however, that it actually occurred directly on the heels of the British victory at Long Cane on December 11. There are several advantages to that interpretation. It gives an alternate explanation of why Clarke, Few, and McCall felt the need to "compel" Pickens to consult with them and persuade him to join them as late as December 4; it would also make it easier to explain why Cruger seemed confident as late as December 15 of Pickens's loyalty. Cruger left Ninety Six on either December 10 or 11. However, the works that support that interpretation are secondary accounts, such as Robert Bass's *Ninety Six* and A. L. Pickens's *Skyagunsta*, which do not cite any primary sources. And if the raid occurred on the eleventh or twelfth, then it is seems clear from Pickens's letter to Greene on December 8 that Pickens had decided to rejoin the patriot cause *before* the raid, and one can no longer state that the raid is what caused him to do so. My version of events more closely parallels Ferguson's "General Andrew Pickens"; both Ferguson and I give more weight to contemporary sources such as McCall, *History of Georgia*, and Pickens's letter to Greene.

71. There may have been some delay in other officers besides Ker learning of Pickens's defection. Cruger informed Cornwallis at one point that British intelligence of the situation in Long Cane was "very bad" (Cruger to Cornwallis, Dec. 9, 1780, *Cornwallis Papers*, 3:281).

72. Allen to Cornwallis, Dec. 29, 1780, ibid., 288.

73. Cornwallis to Cruger or officer commanding at Ninety Six, Jan. 16, 1781, ibid., 291.

CHAPTER 6

1. Francis W. Pickens to Charles Allen, Draper CUL 16VV345; Francis W. Pickens account, Nov. 4, 1847, in Draper CUL 16VV361. Genealogical sources indicate that a young son of Andrew and Rebecca Pickens "died in infancy." His birth order indicates he would have been very young in the 1770s (Day, *Pickens Family*, 40).

2. Piecuch, *Three Peoples, One King*, 160–63; Edgar, *South Carolina*, 240, Egerton, *Death or Liberty*, 85–87.

3. Phifer, "Notes," 3–6.

4. Scoggins, "South Carolina's Backcountry Rangers," 160–73; Gordon, *South Carolina*, 6–7.

5. Pickens to Lee, Aug. 28, 1811, 1.

6. Thayer, *Nathanael Greene*, 33.

7. Ibid., 87.

8. Ibid., 15–17, 20–24, 32, 40, 44–46; Tucker, *Rise and Fight Again*, ix–x, 3, 5–6; Golway, *Washington's General*, 14; Carbone, *Nathanael Greene*, 11. More commentary on Greene's moral and ethical sense, particularly in regard to the conduct of warfare, can be found in the essays by Conrad, Buchanan, Moseley and Calhoon, and Maass in Massey and Piecuch, *General Nathanael Greene*.

9. Thayer, *Nathanael Greene*, 291; Carbone, *Nathanael Greene*, 156.

10. Golway, *Washington's General*, 231–33, 237, 239; Greene to Washington, Oct. 31, 1780, *Greene Papers*, 6:448. Several authors correctly point out that Greene's reliance on the militia was based on necessity, not preference; for example, see essays by D. Wilson, Buchanan, and McIntyre in Massey and Piecuch, *General Nathanael Greene*.

11. Thayer, *Nathanael Greene*, 283, 285.

12. Carbone, *Nathanael Greene*, 158.

13. Golway, *Washington's General*, 241–42; Thayer, *Nathanael Greene*, 296–98.

14. Thayer, *Nathanael Greene*, 299; Weigley, *American Way of War*, 30–31.

15. Morgan to Greene, Dec. 31, 1780, *Greene Papers*, 7:31. Pickens was definitely with Morgan by December 31, though at least one account claims he joined him on the Pacolet on the twenty-fifth (see Ferguson, "General Andrew Pickens," 120n79). Some secondary accounts assert that Pickens joined Morgan on December 29. The wording of Morgan's letter to Greene makes that possible but far from certain. In any event, those works do not cite the letter or any other primary source (for example, see Reynolds, *Andrew Pickens*, 205–6).

16. Ferguson, "General Andrew Pickens," 124–25; Babits, *"Devil of a Whipping,"* 28; O'Kelley, *Blood and Slaughter*, 3:27–30. While Pickens commanded the bulk of the South Carolina militia at Cowpens, including men from the Fair Forest, Little River, and Spartanburg regiments, many of his own men from Long Cane were temporarily attached with Major James McCall to William Washington's dragoons or to South Carolina state troops under Samuel Hammond.

17. Tarleton, *Campaigns*, 210–12, 244–45; O'Kelley, *Blood and Slaughter*, 3:30–32.

18. Morgan to Greene, Dec. 31, 1780, *Greene Papers*, 7:31.

19. Ibid., Jan. 4, 1781, *Greene Papers*, 7:51.

20. Babits, *"Devil of a Whipping,"* 49.

21. Morgan to Greene, Jan. 15, 1781, *Greene Papers*, 7:128.

22. Pension statement of Robert Long, Draper CUL 16VV150–51.

23. Morgan to Greene, Jan. 15, 1781, *Greene Papers*, 7:128.

24. Babits, *"Devil of a Whipping,"* 53–54.

25. Ferguson, "General Andrew Pickens," 126; Greene to Morgan, Jan. 13, 1781, *Greene Papers*, 7:106.

26. Ferguson, "General Andrew Pickens," 124–26; Babits, *"Devil of a Whipping,"* 51–53; Morgan to Greene, Jan. 19, 1781, 7:153.

27. John Eager Howard, the commander of the Maryland Continentals, wrote that militiamen entered Morgan's camp throughout "most of the night" of January 16–17 (H. Lee, *Memoirs*, 226n). Joseph McJunkin, a South Carolina militia officer, wrote that Pickens's militia came into the camp "in the course of that day [the sixteenth]." It seems likely that both statements could be correct and that Pickens himself would have been among the first to reach Morgan's headquarters so that he could consult with the latter and advise him (Joseph McJunkin's memoir, Draper CUL 23VV37).

28. Quoted in Babits, *"Devil of a Whipping,"* 54.

29. Quoted in H. Lee, *Memoirs*, 226n.

30. Quoted in Piechuch and Beakes, *"Cool Deliberate Courage,"* 59.

31. Ibid.

32. The most careful and detailed description of the terrain and disposition of the patriot units is in Babits, *"Devil of a Whipping,"* 60–81.

33. Ibid., 11, 13–15, 18, 60–81; Gordon, *South Carolina*, 132; Stephenson, *Patriot Battles*, xvi, 15, 130–32.

34. Joseph McJunkin's memoir, Draper CUL 23VV38.

35. Quoted in Johnson, *Traditions*, 449–50.

36. Babits, *"Devil of a Whipping,"* 60.

37. Pension statement of Robert Long, Draper CUL 16VV151; Babits, *"Devil of a Whipping,"* 73–76.

38. Babits, *"Devil of a Whipping,"* 80; Gordon, *South Carolina*, 133.

39. Babits, *"Devil of a Whipping,"* 89.

40. Ibid., 91–93 (quote on 93).

41. Ibid., 93–97 (quote on 95).

42. Ibid., 140.

43. Ibid., 97–99 (quote on 98).

44. Ibid., 99.

45. Ibid., 100–123, 128–29.

46. Pickens to Lee, Aug. 28, 1811, 7.

47. Ibid. Pickens's letter written in Jackson's support appears in Charlton, *Life of Major General James Jackson*, 25–27. See also Ferguson, "General Andrew Pickens," 139–40n138.

48. Babits, *"Devil of a Whipping,"* 137.

49. Pickens to Lee, Aug. 28, 1811, 7; Babits, *"Devil of a Whipping,"* 129–36. Pickens recalled that he and Washington pursued Tarleton for twenty-two miles.

50. Account of Francis W. Pickens to J. H. Marshall, Nov. 4, 1847, Draper CUL 16VV361.

51. Babits, *"Devil of a Whipping,"* 138–39.

52. Pickens to Lee, Aug. 28, 1811, 7; pension statement of Robert Long, Draper CUL 16VV152; Morgan to Greene, Jan. 19 and Jan. 23, 1781, in *Greene Papers*, 7:154, 178; Greene to Washington, Jan. 24, 1781, *Greene Papers*, 7:183.

53. In reporting losses of twelve killed and sixty wounded, Morgan did not count those of the militia but instead only those belonging to his own original force of regulars. Babits, *"Devil of a Whipping,"* 151–52.

54. Morgan to Greene, Jan. 19, 1781, *Greene Papers*, 7:153.

55. Greene to Gen. James M. Varnum, Jan. 24, 1781, ibid., 188.

56. Greene to Henry Lee, Jan. 26, 1781, ibid., 202–3. Congress's resolution appears in Ramsay, *History of the Revolution of South Carolina*, 2:470–71.

57. Ferguson, "General Andrew Pickens," 143–44.

CHAPTER 7

1. Pickens to Lee, Aug. 28, 1811; Ferguson, "General Andrew Pickens," 147; Morgan to Greene, Jan. 23, 1781, *Greene Papers*, 7:178.

2. Samuel Hammond to Greene, Jan. 31, 1781, *Greene Papers*, 7:229.

3. Morgan to Greene, Jan. 24, 1781, ibid., 192.

4. Ibid., 178.

5. Morgan to Greene, Jan. 25, 1781, ibid., 199, 201; Morgan to Greene, Jan. 28, 1781, ibid., 211.

6. Quoted in Thane, *Fighting Quaker*, 206.

7. Ferguson, "General Andrew Pickens," 152–54.

8. Greene to the Officers Commanding the Militia in the Salisbury District of North Carolina, Jan. 31, 1781, *Greene Papers*, 7:227.

9. Forty-six years later, Captain (later General) Joseph Graham of North Carolina stated that Pickens had "twenty or thirty" South Carolina men with him during the retreat from the Catawba to the Yadkin in February. Elsewhere, he stated that Pickens had "not more than 40" South Carolinians at that time, as opposed to 600 or 700 North Carolinians who joined him. This statement was made in the context of Graham's general complaint that South Carolina got too much credit for the success of the campaign at the expense of North Carolina (Gen. Joseph Graham to Archibald D. Murphey, Dec. 20, 1827, in Hoyt, *Papers of Archibald D. Murphey*, 1:370, and "General Joseph Graham's Narrative of the Revolutionary War in North Carolina in 1780 and 1781," ibid., 2:214 [hereafter "Graham's Narrative"]).

10. Morgan to Greene, Jan. 24, 1781, *Greene Papers*, 7:190–92; Greene to George Washington, Feb. 9, 1781, ibid., 267. By February 6, Morgan was also complaining of severe piles (hemorrhoids) (Morgan to Greene, Feb. 6, 1781, ibid., 254).

11. Greene to Col. Francis Lock and Others in the Rear of the Enemy, Feb. 9, 1781, ibid., 262.

12. Ferguson, "General Andrew Pickens," 151. Joseph Graham remembered that the vote by the North Carolina officers occurred around February 11 (Graham to Murphy, Dec. 20, 1827, in Hoyt, *Papers of Archibald D. Murphey*, 1:370).

13. Greene to Pickens, Feb. 3, 1781, box 1, APCU. In a letter of the same day to Thomas Sumter, Greene informed Sumter that Pickens had orders to operate in the Ninety Six–Augusta area. It is possible that Greene had verbally communicated this to Pickens when they met in Salisbury, but his written orders simply specified "on the other side of the Catawba." The distance from Augusta to the area of North Carolina where Pickens actually did much of his recruiting in February was some two hundred miles. The context of the letter suggests that Greene was trying to encourage Sumter to retake the field and to soothe his prickly ego by promising that Pickens, while operating in South Carolina, would come under Sumter's command (Greene to Sumter, Feb. 3, 1781, *Greene Papers*, 7:245–46).

14. Ferguson, "General Andrew Pickens," 158–60; Pickens to Greene, Feb. 19, 1781, *Greene Papers*, 7:320. Cornwallis had followed Greene to the Dan. Unable to overtake him, he moved south back to Hillsborough, which he reached on the twentieth, two days after Pickens's arrival at Guilford Court House.

15. Greene to Pickens, Feb. 19, 1781, *Greene Papers*, 7:316; Greene to Pickens, Feb. 20, 1781, ibid., 318; Pancake, *This Destructive War*, 167–71.

16. Pickens to Greene, Feb. 20, 21, 23, *Greene Papers*, 7:325–41 passim; a fuller version of Pickens's February 23 letter to Greene is in box 1, APCU; see also Ferguson, "General Andrew Pickens," 163–68; and "Graham's Narrative," 2:279.

17. "Graham's Narrative," 2:270.

18. Ibid., 271.

19. Pickens to Greene, Feb. 23, 1781, box 1, APCU. Captains Joseph Graham and Richard Simmons of North Carolina led the mounted Whig detachments that made up this forty-man force. Years later, Graham denied recalling any substantial role played by McCall and doubted he was even there. The latter seems unlikely given the wording of Pickens's letter to Greene (Graham to Murphey, Dec. 20, 1827, in Hoyt, *Papers of Archibald D. Murphey*, 1:372). See also "Graham's Narrative," 2:270.

20. "Graham's Narrative," 2:271–72; Ferguson, "General Andrew Pickens," 168.

21. Pickens to Greene, Feb. 20, 1781, *Greene Papers*, 7:325.

22. Ibid., Feb. 19, 1781, 320. It seems that between the first days of February, when Pickens supposedly had only 30 or 40 men, and the date of this letter, more Georgians and South Carolinians had actually rejoined Pickens. Despite the desertions Pickens complained of here, he had 158 Georgia and South Carolina men with him on March 5 (Pickens to Greene, Mar. 5, 1781, box 1, APCU).

23. Pickens to Greene, Feb. 19, 1781, *Greene Papers*, 7:320.

24. Ibid., Feb. 23, 1781, 341.

25. Ibid., Feb. 21, 1781, 331.

26. "Graham's Narrative," 2:269.

27. Pickens to Greene, Feb. 19, 1781, box 1, APCU.

28. "Graham's Narrative," 2:269.

29. Lee to Greene, Feb. 25, 1781, *Greene Papers*, 7:347–48; H. Lee, *Memoirs*, 253–58. Lee states in his memoirs that upon meeting the two Tory sentries, he sent a message back to Pickens asking him to keep his militia hidden in the woods and not follow his column. Pickens did so, but the Tories supposedly noticed Pickens's men and began firing at them. Pickens does not mention these events in his letter to Greene, and Graham contradicts them. I consider that Pickens and Graham were in better positions to know what happened in that part of the battlefield (Pickens to Greene, Feb. 26, 1781, *Greene Papers*, 7:358; "Graham's Narrative," 2:273; Graham to Murphey, Dec. 20, 1827, Hoyt, *Papers of Archibald D. Murphey*, 1:374).

30. "Graham's Narrative," 2:273.

31. Ibid., 274–76; Pickens to Greene, Feb. 26, 1781, *Greene Papers*, 7:355; Lee to Greene, Feb. 25, 1781, *Greene Papers*, 7:347–48; H. Lee, *Memoirs*, 258.

32. "Graham's Narrative," 2:275.

33. O'Kelley, *Blood and Slaughter*, 3:99. The small, weakened Catawba tribe had decided by the 1750s to pursue a policy of accommodation with South Carolina's

white leaders. When the majority of those leaders broke with the British crown, the Catawbas readily declared their support for the Whig cause, and Catawba men served in a number of campaigns, including the expedition against the Cherokees in 1776 (Piecuch, *Three Peoples, One King*, 26, 63–64, 71, 115, 153, 154, 209, 260–61, 289).

34. Pickens to Greene, Feb. 26, 1781, *Greene Papers*, 7:358; see also Lee to Greene, Feb. 25, 1781, ibid., 348.

35. Pancake, *This Destructive War*, 173–74.

36. "Graham's Narrative," 2:279; *Cornwallis Papers*, 4:6; Ferguson, "General Andrew Pickens," 178–82.

37. Greene to Pickens, Feb. 21, 1781, *Greene Papers*, 7:327; Pickens to Greene, Feb. 19, 1781, ibid., 320.

38. *Greene Papers*, 7:331n2, 325n2, 380–81n1; William Campbell to Greene, Mar. 2, 1781, ibid., 380.

39. "Graham's Narrative," 2:288.

40. Pickens to Greene, Mar. 5, 1781, box 1, APCU.

41. "Graham's Narrative," 2:294.

42. Ibid., 283n1.

43. Pickens to Greene, Mar. 5, 1781, *Greene Papers*, 2:399. For more on the reasons and tactical implications of dismounting the militia, see Buchanan, "'We Must Endeavor to Keep Up a Partizan War,'" 128–30.

44. Pickens to Greene, Mar. 5, 1781, *Greene Papers*, 2:399..

45. Greene informed Thomas Sumter of the decision that very day, March 6 (Greene to Sumter, Mar. 6, 1781, *Greene Papers*, 7:401; a fuller version is found in Draper CUL 7VV210).

46. Pickens to Lee, Aug. 28, 1811.

47. Williams to Greene, Mar. 7, 1781, *Greene Papers*, 7:408.

48. "Graham's Narrative," 2:292.

49. Greene to Pickens, Mar. 8, 1781, box 1, APCU.

CHAPTER 8

1. Sumter to Marion, Mar. 28, 1781, Draper CUL 6VV21.

2. Greene to Pickens, Mar. 8, 1781, box 1, APCU.

3. Pickens to Greene, Apr. 8, 1781, ibid.

4. Ferguson, "General Andrew Pickens," 195.

5. Greene to Sumter, Mar. 30, 1781, *Greene Papers*, 8:12; H. Lee, *Memoirs*, 320–22.

6. Pickens to Sumter, Mar. 20, 1781, Draper CUL 7VV222; Pickens to Greene, Apr. 8, 1781, box 1, APCU.

7. Pickens to Greene, Apr. 8, 1781, box 1, APCU; Sumter to Greene, Apr. 13, 1781, *Greene Papers*, 8:91.

8. Pickens to Greene, Apr. 8, 1781, box 1, APCU.

9. *Greene Papers*, 8:72n6.

10. Ferguson, "General Andrew Pickens," 198–99.

11. Ibid., 199–202; Sumter to Greene, Apr. 13, 1781, Draper CUL 7VV240–41; Ferguson, "General Andrew Pickens," 197–202.

12. Sumter to Greene, Apr. 13, 1781, Draper CUL 7VV240–241; Sumter to Greene, Apr. 25, 1781, Draper CUL 7VV254–57, and ibid. (second letter), 258–59; Greene to Lee, Apr. 29, 1781, *Greene Papers*, 8:173 and 8:173n7); Pickens to Lee, Nov. 25, 1811, Draper CUL 1VV109 (hereafter Pickens to Lee, Nov. 25, 1811). For evidence of Sumter supplying Greene even after April 25, see Sumter to Greene, May 2, 1781, Draper CUL 7VV261–262.

13. Pickens to Greene, May 3, 1781, *Greene Papers*, 8:197–98.

14. Greene to Pickens, May 9, 1781, box 1, APCU.

15. Tarleton, *Campaigns*, 484–85.

16. Pickens to Greene, May 8, 1781, *Greene Papers*, 8:223.

17. Landrum, *Upper South Carolina*, 317.

18. Nathaniel Pendleton (Greene's aide) to Sumter (copy to Pickens), May 10, 1781, Draper CUL 7VV290; Greene to Lee, May 16, 1781, *Greene Papers*, 8:272.

19. Pickens to Greene, May 11 (or 12), 1781, box 1, APCU.

20. Ferguson, "General Andrew Pickens," 207; Greene to Lee, May 16, 1781, *Greene Papers*, 8:272; Greene to Pickens, *Greene Papers*, May 16, 1781, 8:272.

21. O'Kelley, *Blood and Slaughter*, 3:243. O'Kelley identifies the Continental officer as Major Michael Rudolph.

22. H. Lee, *Memoirs*, 354.

23. Ibid.; Lee to Greene, May 22, 1781, *Greene Papers*, 8:293; Pickens to Greene, May 25, 1781, *Greene Papers*, 8:310–11.

24. Pickens to Greene, May 25, 1781, *Greene Papers*, 8:312.

25. Greene to Lee, May 29, 1781, ibid., 326; Ferguson, "General Andrew Pickens," 210–11; Greene to Pickens, May 29, 1781, *Greene Papers*, 8:328. In his letter to Pickens, Greene suggested that the supplies should be divided evenly between the militia and the Continentals but that ultimately he "submit[ted] the whole matter to your discretion" (Greene to Pickens, May 29, 1781, *Greene Papers*, 8:328). Meanwhile, his letter to Lee stressed the importance of Lee deferring to Pickens. In the end, Pickens allotted one-third of the captured stores to the Georgia militia, one-third to the South Carolinians, and one-third to the Continentals, which Greene said he found "perfectly satisfactory" (Pickens to Greene, June 1, 1781, *Greene Papers*, 8:335; quote from Greene to Pickens, June 3, 1781, *Greene Papers*, 8:341).

26. H. Lee, *Memoirs*, 356; O'Kelley, *Blood and Slaughter*, 3:260.

27. Olson, "Thomas Brown (Part II)," 193. Though it is clear Pickens and Lee each commanded a few hundred men, there are no known precise and reliable figures.

28. Pickens to Greene, May 25, 1781, *Greene Papers*, 8:310–11; H. Lee, *Memoirs*, 356–57; O'Kelley, *Blood and Slaughter*, 3:261.

29. H. Lee, *Memoirs*, 357–58, 361–63; Bass, *Ninety Six*, 362–63.

30. H. Lee, *Memoirs*, 363–70.

31. Quotes from Pickens to Greene, June 1, 1781, *Greene Papers*, 8:335; see also ibid., June 2, 1781, 339.

32. Ferguson, "General Andrew Pickens," 220.

33. Pickens to Greene, June 4, 1781, *Greene Papers*, 8:347.

34. Greene to Lee, June 3, 1781, *Greene Papers*. 8:340.

35. H. Lee, *Memoirs*, 366.

36. Ibid., 367–69 (quote from surrender terms on 369).

37. McCrady, *South Carolina in the Revolution, 1780–1783*, 273.

38. Greene wrote Pickens that, after rejoining Greene at Ninety Six, Lee paid Pickens "the highest compliments for your extraordinary exertions" (Greene to Pickens, June 7, 1781 *Greene Papers*, 8:357).

39. Lee to Greene, May 24, 1781, ibid., 8:309.

40. Ibid., June 4, 1781, 346.

41. Ibid.

42. Greene to Pickens, June 5, 1781, ibid., 350.

43. Pickens to Greene, June 7, 1781, ibid., 359.

44. Ibid.; McCrady, *South Carolina in the Revolution, 1780–1783*, 274.

45. Olson, "Thomas Brown (Part II)," 194; T. Brown, *Memoirs of Tarleton Brown*, 25; Greene to Pickens, June 7, 1781, *Greene Papers*, 8:357.

46. T. Brown, *Memoirs of Tarleton Brown*, 24, McCrady, *South Carolina in the Revolution, 1780–1783*, 270, 277; McCall, *History of Georgia*, 2:519.

47. Tarleton, *Campaigns*, 484; H. Lee, *Memoirs*, 344; Rawdon to Cornwallis, *Cornwallis Papers*, 5:291; Ferguson, "General Andrew Pickens," 207.

48. Greene to Pickens, June 7, 1781, *Greene Papers*, 8:357.

49. A few of the many letters that express this concern are Wade Hampton to Greene, June 10, 1781, ibid., 377; Greene to Elijah Clarke, June 7, 1781, ibid., 356; and Cornwallis to Rawdon, May 20, 1781, *Cornwallis Papers*, 5:287. For numerous examples of murders and revenge killings, see T. Brown, *Memoirs of Tarleton Brown*, 8–28 passim.

50. Draper CUL 3VV136.

51. A. Pickens, *Skyagunsta*, 102; Sharp, *Pickens Families*, 12.

52. Rawdon to Lee, June 24, 1813, in H. Lee, *Memoirs*, 618.

53. Marion to Greene, June 6, 1781, *Greene Papers*, 8:374; Greene to the Marquis de Lafayette, June 9, 1781, ibid., 367; Greene to Marion, June 10, 1781, ibid., 374; Greene to Sumter, June 10, 1781, ibid., 375; Greene to Sumter, June 10, 1781 (second letter), 376.

54. Greene to Samuel Huntington, June 20, 1781, ibid., 419–22. Casualty figures come from H. Lee, *Memoirs*, 377. In *This Destructive War* (214), Pancake, citing a secondary source, gives figures of 127 killed and wounded and 20 missing for the patriots and 85 killed and wounded for the loyalists.

55. Pickens to Lee, Nov. 25, 1811.

56. Greene to Pickens, June 19, 1781, *Greene Papers*, 8:415.

57. Francis W. Pickens to Charles H. Allen, Mar. 26, 1848, Draper CUL 16VV346; A. Pickens, *Skyagunsta*, 103; see also Ellet, *Women of the American Revolution*, 3:306–7; and Ramsay, *History of the Revolution of South Carolina*, 2:246.

CHAPTER 9

1. Quote from Greene to Lee, June 24, 1781, *Greene Papers*, 8:452; see also Greene to Pickens, June 23, 1781, and Greene to Sumter, June 23, 1781, ibid., 448, 449.

2. Greene to Pickens, June 28, 1781, ibid., 470; see also Greene to Lee, June 24, 1781, ibid., 452.

3. Pickens to Greene, June 30, 1781, box 1, APCU.

4. Quotes from Pickens to Greene, July 6, 1781, ibid. See also Isaac Huger to Greene, July 6, 1781, 8:502; Pickens to Greene, July 3, 1781, 8:488; and Otho Williams to Greene, July 8, 1781, *Greene Papers*, 8:512.

5. On July 15, Greene ordered Pickens to move to Friday's Ferry after pursuing Cruger. Pickens explained on the nineteenth that it was necessary to restore order and rest his horses in the Ninety Six–Long Cane area, at least for several more days. Greene neither countermanded nor confirmed Pickens's decision, but he did suggest that Pickens take time to see that citizens in his area suffering from want be given humanitarian relief (Greene to Pickens, July 15, 1781 [two letters], *Greene Papers*, 9:10–12; Pickens to Greene, July 19, 1781, ibid., 48–50).

6. Greene to Pickens, July 19, 1781, ibid., 48–49. See also Capt. Josiah Towles to Pickens, July 7, 1781, and Pickens to Greene, July 10, 1781, in box 1, APCU.

7. Pickens to Greene, July 25, 1781, box 1, APCU; see also Pickens to Greene, July 19, 1781, *Greene Papers*, 9:48–50 and 50n4. On the manufacture of swords and horseshoes, see Ferguson, "General Andrew Pickens," 237–38.

8. Bass, *Gamecock*, 145–46, 203–4; Pancake, *This Destructive War*, 206–7; Gregorie, *Thomas Sumter*, 148–50; Buchanan, "'We Must Endeavor to Keep Up a Partizan War,'" 135.

9. Greene to Pickens, July 15, 1781, *Greene Papers*, 9:11–12.

10. Ibid., July 22, 1781 (second letter), 61.

11. *Greene Papers*, 9:13–17; Gordon, *South Carolina*, 159–62.

12. Abstract of Pickens to Samuel Hammond, Aug. 13, 1781, Draper CUL 1DD20.

13. Bass, *Gamecock*, 200–205.

14. The following account of the Eutaw campaign relies on the following primary sources: Greene to Thomas McKean, Sept. 11, 1781, *Greene Papers*, 9:328–33; Alexander Stewart to Charles Cornwallis, Sept. 9, 1781, in Gibbes, *Documentary History*, 3:136–39; account by Otho Williams et al. in Gibbes, *Documentary History*, 3:144–58; Gov. John Rutledge to delegates of South Carolina in Congress, Feb. 9, 1781, Draper CUL 16VV110–111; and H. Lee, *Memoirs*, 464–74. Useful secondary accounts include McCrady, *History of South Carolina in the Revolution, 1780–1783*, 441–63; Lumpkin, *From Savannah to Yorktown*, 212–21; Gordon, *South Carolina*, 164–67; Pancake, *This Destructive War*, 216–20; Weigley, *Partisan War*, 63–68; and Ferguson, "General Andrew Pickens," 240–48.

15. Otho Williams et al. in Gibbes, *Documentary History*, 3:148.

16. F. W. Pickens to J. H. Marshall, Nov. 4, 1857, Draper CUL 16VV366.

17. Bridwell, "South's Wealthiest Planter."

18. Greene to McKean, Sept. 11, 1781, *Greene Papers*, 9:329.

19. Pickens to Lee, Aug. 28, 1811.

CHAPTER 10

1. Pickens to Greene, July 19, 1781, *Greene Papers*, 9:49.

2. Piecuch, *Three Peoples, One King*, 251.

3. Pickens to Greene, July 19, 1781, *Greene Papers*, 9:49.

4. Proverbs 25:21b–22; Romans 12:20 (King James Version, used throughout).

5. Pickens to Greene, July 19, 1781, *Greene Papers*, 9:49; on the exile of 65 leading Charleston Whigs and their families, eventually totaling some 500 people, see D. Wallace, *South Carolina: A Short History*, 304–5.

6. Greene to Pickens, July 30, 1781, *Greene Papers*, 9:109.

7. *Greene Papers*, 9:50n3. The exact phrase "lying out" was not used in this quote.

8. Proclamation by His Excellency John Rutledge, in Gibbes, *Documentary History*, 3:175–78; McCrady, *History of South Carolina in the Revolution, 1780–1783*, 521–27; Ferguson, "General Andrew Pickens," 252.

9. McCrady, *History of South Carolina in the Revolution, 1780–1783*, 495–96.

10. Piecuch, *Three Peoples, One King*, 303–4.

11. Calloway, *American Revolution in Indian Country*, 205–7; McCrady, *South Carolina in the Revolution, 1780–1783*, 477. For more on the split between Cherokees who wanted peace and a militant faction called the Chickamaugas who wished to continue to fight the United States, see Dowd, *Spirited Resistance*, esp. 48, 63.

12. McCrady, *South Carolina in the Revolution, 1780–1783*, 467–70.

13. Ibid., 474.

14. Ibid., 470–75; "Biographical Sketch of William Cunningham."

15. McCrady, *South Carolina in the Revolution, 1780–1783*, 477–78.

16. Ferguson, "General Andrew Pickens," 253–54.

17. Andrew Shellito's Traditions, Draper CUL 16VV309. Shellito stated that the Whig captives were shot; one example of those who asserted that they were burned alive was Pickens's grandson Francis W. Pickens (F. W. Pickens to J. H. Marshall, Nov. 4, 1847, Draper CUL 16VV365; and F. W. Pickens to Benjamin F. Perry, Apr. 24, 1859, Draper CUL 11VV258). See also Draper CUL 3VV148; Ferguson, "General Andrew Pickens," 256–57; and A. Pickens, *Skyagunsta*, 109–10. For correspondence on the pursuit of Cunningham and Williams, see Draper CUL 7VV522, 539, 541; 16VV90–91, 93, 434–35; and 12VV225.

18. Pickens to Elijah Clarke, Jan. 25, 1782, box 1, APCU.

19. Ibid.; Piecuch, *Three Peoples, One King*, 303–4.

20. Pickens to Samuel Hammond, Mar. 8 and 12, 1782, Draper CUL 1DD20–1.

21. Quoted in Ferguson, "General Andrew Pickens," 262.

22. Ibid.

23. Ibid., 261–63.

24. Ibid., 263–64; Francis Marion to Col. Peter Horry, May 3, 1782, in Gibbes, *Documentary History*, 2:173; William Pierce to Pickens, July 23, 1782, *Greene Papers*, 11:452 ; Pickens to Greene, July 23, 1782, *Greene Papers*, 11:452; Pickens to Greene, Aug. 9, 1782, *Greene Papers*, 11:512; McCrady, *South Carolina in the Revolution, 1780–1783*, 528–31.

25. Pickens to Greene, Sept. 7, 1782, box 1, APCU.

26. Andrew Shellito's Traditions, Draper CUL 16VV310.

27. Justice Aedanus Burke to His Excellency Governor Guerard, Dec. 14, 1784, in Draper CUL 20VV120.

28. Pickens to Greene, Sept. 7, 1782, box 1, APCU.

29. McCall, *History of Georgia*, 2:585–86.

30. Quote from Pickens to Lee, Aug. 28, 1811; Ferguson, "General Andrew Pickens," 268.

31. There is much confusion as to the name and location of this attack. Pickens's cousin Private Andrew Pickens called it "Saita" and said it was less than a mile from Chota. Andrew Logan said the village was actually Chota. Ferguson, citing other accounts, calls it "Long Swamp." Given the geography cited in the sources and the fact that archaeological sources confirm the presence of a Cherokee settlement at Long Swamp, this seems the most likely location (Draper CUL 3VV142, 11VV446; McCall, *History of Georgia*, 2:546–47; Ferguson, "General Andrew Pickens," 272; Waring, *Fighting Elder*, 115).

32. Pickens to Lee, Aug. 28, 1811; account of Pickens's cousin Private Andrew Pickens in Draper CUL 3VV142.

33. Account of Private Andrew Pickens, Draper CUL 3VV142–43.

34. Ibid.

35. Ibid., 3VV146.

36. Compare figures given in the accounts of Private Andrew Pickens (Draper CUL 16VV145), Andrew Logan (Draper CUL 11VV446–7), and General Andrew Pickens (Pickens to Lee, Aug. 28, 1811).

37. Pickens to Lee, Aug. 28, 1811.

38. McCall, *History of Georgia*, 2:546–47; Ferguson, "General Andrew Pickens," 275.

CHAPTER 11

1. F. W. Pickens to J. H. Marshall, Nov. 4, 1847, Draper CUL 16VV361.

2. Phifer, "Notes," 3–4.

3. Sharp, *Pickens Families*, 12, 33.

4. Edgar, *South Carolina*, 244.

5. Taylor, *William Cooper's Town*, 13–14; Bushman, *Refinement of America*, xii–xiv, 31–60, 83–84, 90–92; Wood, *Americanization of Benjamin Franklin*, 17–60.

6. Memorandum of Agreement, Mar. 19, 1784 (John Rutledge, John Lewis Gervais, John Owen, and Andrew Pickens), John Rutledge Letters, #140, CLS.

7. Maj. Felix Warley to Pickens, July 27, 1788, APCLS; Memorandum of Agreement between John Marsh and Andrew Pickens in trust for Arnoldus Vanderhorst, Feb. 21, 1805, Arnoldus Vanderhorst Papers, #177, CLS; Charles Cotesworth Pinckney to Pickens, Dec. 1, 1809, Charles Cotesworth Pinckney Papers, #125, CLS; Thomas Pinckney to Pickens, Aug. 30, 1788, box 1, APCU.

8. Appleby, *Capitalism*, 8–9, 14–15; Bailyn, *Ideological Origins*; Wood, *Creation of the American Republic*, 34, 64–70; Weir, *"The Last of American Freemen,"* 3–5; Hatch, *Sacred Cause of Liberty*, 105.

9. William Martin to Lyman Draper, Jan. 1, 1843, Draper CUL 5DD11514.

10. Bloch, "The Gendered Meanings of Virtue in Revolutionary America," in *Gender and Morality*, 142.

11. Bass, *Gamecock*, 5–6, 19, 56; Bass, *Swamp Fox*, 5–6, 10; Rankin, *Francis Marion*, 3–4.

12. William Martin to Lyman Draper, Jan. 1, 1843, Draper CUL 5DD11513.

13. Ferguson, "General Andrew Pickens," 280.

14. Edgar, *South Carolina*, 239; Brannon, "Reconciling the Revolution," 8–9.

15. Ferguson, "General Andrew Pickens," 367–68; *Journal of the House of Representatives of the State of South Carolina* (hereafter *S.C. House Journal*), Feb. 21, 1787, 124–25; Piecuch, *Three Peoples, One King*, 291.

16. Pickens to Lee, Aug. 28, 1811.

17. Andrew Williamson to Nathanael Greene, Dec. 22, 1782, *Greene Papers*, 12:340.

18. See ibid.; Anthony Wayne to Greene, Dec. 12, 1782, ibid., 288–89; Greene to John Mathews, Dec. 22, 1782, ibid., 331–32; and Williamson to Greene, Jan. 28, 1783, ibid., 395. A more thorough explanation of the general animosity toward Williamson and the reasons for it are found in Toulmin, "Backcountry Warrior," 1–46.

19. Pickens to Moultrie, Jan. 6, 1786, folder 1, APCU; General Assembly, *Committee Reports*, S165005, item 173, Mar. 7, 1786.

20. General Assembly, *Committee Reports*, S165005, item 253, Jan. 21, 1791; *S.C. House Journal*, Mar. 18, 1784, 569–70; *Journal of the Senate of the State of South Carolina* (hereafter *S.C. Senate Journal*), Jan. 21, 1791, 50; Toulmin, "Brigadier General Andrew Williamson and White Hall." A glowing obituary of Williamson appeared in the *Charleston Morning Post* shortly after his death (Draper CUL 8VV32–33).

21. Ferguson, "General Andrew Pickens," 304. In the Confiscation Act of 1782, the General Assembly forbade the separation of parents from their children when Tory estates were confiscated and auctioned (*S.C. Statutes*, 4:522).

22. Bass, *Swamp Fox*, 241.

23. Quotes from *S.C. House Journal*, Mar. 5, 1784, 523–24; see also ibid., Jan. 31, 1784, 397; and Ferguson, "General Andrew Pickens," 301n59.

24. *S.C. House Journal*, Mar. 5, 1784, 524.

25. *S.C. Statutes*, 4:598–99 (quote on 599).

26. Ibid., 600.

27. Bass, *Gamecock*.

28. *S.C. House Journal*, Aug. 8, 1783, 337; Aug. 9, 1784, 342; Feb. 21, 1783, 175.

29. Ferguson, "General Andrew Pickens," 312; *Journals of the Privy Council*, Sept. 8, 1784, 137.

30. Ferguson, "General Andrew Pickens," 291.

31. Ibid., 313.

32. D. Wallace, *South Carolina: A Short History*, 337; Edgar, *South Carolina*, 285.

33. *S.C. House Journal*, Mar. 12, 1783, 308.

34. *S.C. Statutes*, 4:661; *S.C. House Journal*, Feb. 27, 1784, 502.

35. Waring, *Fighting Elder*, 127; *Abstracts of General Sessions Court Rolls*, i.

36. Howe, *Presbyterian Church*, 1:548.

37. Nadelhaft, *Disorders of War*, 285–86.

38. *S.C. Statutes*, 8:158–60; *S.C. Senate Journal*, Jan. 18–19, 1790, 33, 35.

39. *S.C. Statutes*, 4:574–75. The other trustees were Rev. John Harris, Robert Anderson, John Bowie, John Ewing Colhoun, Patrick Calhoun, and William Moore (ibid.)

40. Mills, "Early Religious Efforts in Old Pendleton District," folder 27, box 2, William Hayne Mills Collection, 26, Clemson University Library, Clemson, S.C.; Mills, "The Old Stone Church," folder 4, box 4, ibid.

41. Waring, *Fighting Elder*, 129.

42. Howe, *Presbyterian Church*, 1:548; A. Pickens, *Skyagunsta*, 128–29.

43. *Mortgages*, S218157; *Land Grants*, 1:6, 6:309, 8:464; *Index of Land Grants*, s.v. "Pickens, Ezekiel"; *Plats*, S213192, 42:48. Quote is from *Land Grants*, 6:309. On Pickens's actually settling at Hopewell in 1787, see Ferguson, "General Andrew Pickens," 372 and 372n45.

44. Quote from Howe, *Presbyterian Church*, 1:599; see also ibid., 636; White, *Southern Presbyterian Leaders*, 173–74, 248; and Mills, "Old Stone Church."

45. *S.C. House Journal*, Mar. 10, 1789, 256, and Mar. 13, 1789, 285; Simpson, *History of Old Pendleton District*, 11–13; *S.C. Statutes*, 4:561, 661, 7:252, 5:105, 210.

46. Brackett, *Old Stone Church*, 42, 88.

47. Friend, "Frontier and Plantation," xxi. It is often claimed that Pickens was a trustee of Hopewell Academy, with authors citing articles in *Miller's Weekly Messenger*, Pendleton's newspaper. The newspaper articles cited, however, list Andrew Pickens Jr. as a trustee, which almost certainly refers to Pickens's son. However, given Pickens's deep interest in education, Presbyterian roots, close relationship to the other trustees (Robert Anderson, Colonel Elias Earle, and the original headmaster, Reverend Thomas Reese), and central leadership role in Pendleton, it is almost inconceivable that he did not provide leadership and financial support to Hopewell Academy—which, after all, took the same name as his plantation and the church that he helped establish (see, for example, Klein, *Unification of a Slave State*, 244; and *Miller's Weekly Messenger*, Oct. 1, 1807).

48. Quoted in Howe, *Presbyterian Church*, 1:637.

49. For more on the early development of Pendleton District, see Megginson, *African American Life*, esp. chapters 1–7 passim.

50. See, for example, Mrs. John N. Hook, "Old Pendleton District—A Sketch," 3–4; and Mills, "The People and their Homes about Pendleton," both in folder 24, box 2, Mills Collection.

51. William Martin to Lyman Draper, Jan. 1, 1843, Draper CUL 5DD115 (13–14).

52. Waring, *Fighting Elder*, 127; Rebecca Pickens Bacon, "General Andrew Pickens," [1904], folder 3, box 4, Mills Collection. It is difficult to find criticism of Pickens's conduct as a judge, military officer, or legislator. One exception might be Colonel Samuel Hammond, who seems to have complained around 1782 or 1783 that Pickens's recent treatment of him had been unfair. A committee of the state house of representatives investigated the claims and fully vindicated Pickens (*S.C. House Journal*, Mar. 13, 1783, 270).

53. Ferguson, "General Andrew Pickens," 280–81, 366, 584, 629–30; quote from ibid., 584, and Pickens to John E. Colhoun, Apr. 7, 1804, folder 8, APSCL; see also Appleby, *Capitalism*, 3. Pickens did not move solidly into the Republican fold until the late 1790s. Rachel Klein ably describes the emerging alliance of lowcountry and backcountry Republicans in South Carolina (*Unification of a Slave State*, especially 203–37 passim).

54. D. Wallace, *History of South Carolina*, 2:349–50.

55. Ibid., Edgar, *South Carolina*, 245–63; Ferguson, "General Andrew Pickens," 475–77.

56. D. Wallace, *History of South Carolina*, 2:327; Edgar, *South Carolina*, 246.

57. Nadelhaft, *Disorders of War*, 192–200. For more discussion of political economy and the problem of debt in the early Republic, as well as the thoughts of more educated

and articulate statesmen such as Jefferson, Franklin, Madison, and others, see McCoy, *Elusive Republic*; and Sloan, *Principle and Interest*. As in some other areas, Pickens's lack of writings or speeches on the subject does not permit deeper discussion than what is offered here.

58. *S.C. Statutes*, 4:563–64, 5:3–38; Edgar, *South Carolina*, 247; Ferguson, "General Andrew Pickens," 366–67.

59. D. Wallace, *History of South Carolina*, 2:326–27; *S.C. House Journal*, Mar. 9, 1787, 199; Ferguson, "General Andrew Pickens," 366.

60. Quote from Petition No. 72, 1787, General Assembly, *Petitions*. See also *S.C. House Journal*, Feb. 9, 1787, 76–78.

61. *S.C. House Journal*, Feb. 20, 1788, 469–71.

62. Ibid., Feb. 16, 1788, 450–51; *S.C. Statutes*, 5:50–57.

63. Quote from *S.C. House Journal*, Mar. 21, 1786, 584; see also Mar. 20, 1786, 581.

CHAPTER 12

1. *S.C. House Journal*, Feb. 26, 1783, 227–28.

2. In 1787, after handling several military matters at the request of Governor Thomas Pinckney, Pickens reminded him that he had "resigned my command of the Ninety Six Brigade some years past." As will be seen, this had absolutely no effect on Pinckney continuing to rely on Pickens to fill the role as commander of the state's military forces in the western part of the state (Pickens to Thomas Pinckney, Oct. 6, 1787, box 1, APCU).

3. Edgar, *South Carolina*, 246.

4. Klein, *Unification of a Slave State*, 117.

5. *S.C. House Journal*, Mar. 4, 1783, 214–15.

6. *Journals of the Privy Council*, May 1, 1784, 102.

7. These quotes appear in Ferguson and retain the wording and spelling probably used in Pickens's original letter. A copy of the letter is also in the *Journals of the Privy Council* but was almost certainly revised by the editors to correct Pickens's grammar and spelling (Ferguson, "General Andrew Pickens," 306; *Journals of the Privy Council*, May 1, 1784, 102).

8. *Journals of the Privy Council*, May 1, 1784, 102.

9. Petition of the Legislature of South Carolina to Congress, Mar. 24, 1785, M247, roll 86, item 72, pp. 576–77, PCC.

10. Ferguson, "Andrew Pickens," 310–11, 370–71; *S.C. House Journal*, Mar. 22, 1786, 590–91; *Journals of the Continental Congress, 1774–1789* 33:467–75.

11. Articles of Confederation, Article IX.

12. Leonard J. Sadosky recognizes the Articles of Confederation's ambiguity on this issue but argues that the document leaned far more heavily toward preserving state sovereignty in handling Indian affairs (Sadosky, *Revolutionary Negotiations*, 85–89).

13. Quoted in Calloway, *American Revolution in Indian Country*, 273.

14. Quoted in Dowd, *Spirited Resistance*, 93.

15. O'Brien, "Conqueror Meets the Unconquered."

16. Calloway, *American Revolution in Indian Country*, 213–17.

17. Downes, "Creek-American Relations," 144; Calloway, *American Revolution in Indian Country*, 205, 207.

18. Prominent South Carolinians who did invest heavily in western lands included Thomas Sumter, William Moultrie, and John Rutledge, all of whom were in financial distress by the turn of the century (W. Dennis, "American Revolutionaries," 157).

19. A. Wallace, *Jefferson and the Indians*; Griffin, *American Leviathan*, 125–278 passim.

20. For more on Pickens's more moderate or "conservative" policy vis-à-vis the Indians and those whose views resembled or opposed his, see W. Dennis, "American Revolutionaries," esp. chapters 1 and 6.

21. Quoted in Calloway, *American Revolution in Indian Country*, 58. Like Pickens, Christian had been prone to show unusual restraint in his prosecution of war against the Cherokees (W. Dennis, "American Revolutionaries," 214).

22. *S.C. House Journal*, Jan. 27, 1783, 45; Mar. 14, 1783, 277; Mar. 25, 1784, 614; Aug. 9, 1783, 341. According to one source, £1,100 British in 1782 would equal approximately $178,524 (U.S.) in 2014. Pickens's initial personal donation was worth $38,442 (Nye, "Pounds Sterling to Dollars").

23. W. Dennis, "American Revolutionaries," 272–73; Nichols, *Red Gentlemen*, 45.

24. *S.C. House Journal*, Aug. 9, 1783, 341.

25. The most recent scholarly works on the Creeks, their cultural transformation, and the role of McGillivray include Saunt, *New Order of Things*, with pp. 67–89 paying special attention to McGillivray; Hudson, *Creek Paths*; and Ethridge, *Creek Country*.

26. Hawkins to McGillivray, Jan. 8, 1786, in Caughey, *McGillivray*, 102.

27. Henri, *Benjamin Hawkins*; Grant, *Writings of Benjamin Hawkins*, 1:ix–xxvii; Ethridge, *Creek Country*, 10–20; Nichols, *Red Gentlemen*, 45–46.

28. Morrison, *Joseph Martin*; Nichols, *Red Gentlemen*, 45.

29. H. Jackson, *Lachlan McIntosh*, 138–40.

30. Ferguson, "General Andrew Pickens," 318. Ferguson provides the most comprehensive account of the negotiations of 1785, particularly from Pickens's point of view, on pp. 314–49. A shorter but still useful account is in W. Dennis, "American Revolutionaries," 283–86.

31. Hawkins, Pickens, and Martin to Richard Caswell, June 19, 1785, in *State Records of North Carolina*, 17:475.

32. Commission from Congress, M247, roll 63, item 49, p. 273, *PCC*; see also commission of Mar. 1, 1785, ibid., 283–84.

33. Charles Thomson (secretary of Congress) to Treaty Commissioners, Mar. 24, 1785, M247, roll 25, item 18A, p. 71, ibid.

34. Calloway, *American Revolution in Indian Country*, 282–83 (quote on 283); texts of the treaties of Fort Stanwix and Fort McIntosh are found in *ASP, IA*, 1:10–11.

35. *Journals of the Privy Council*, June 8, 9, 1785, 165–66; *S.C. House Journal*, Oct. 7, 1785, 336–37; H. Jackson, *Lachlan McIntosh*, 138.

36. Letter found in Caughey, *McGillivray*, 96.

37. Hawkins, Pickens, and Martin to Gov. Richard Caswell (North Carolina), June 10, 1785, APHL; ibid., June 19, 1785, in *State Records of North Carolina*, 17:473–75.

38. Ferguson, "General Andrew Pickens," 322–23; H. Jackson, *Lachlan McIntosh*, 138.

39. Pickens to McGillivray, July 24, 1785, in Caughey, *McGillivray*, 96–97.

40. See McGillivray to Arturo O'Neill, Spanish governor of West Florida, in Caughey, *McGillivray*, 97–98 and 98n46.

41. Alexander McGillivray to Pickens, Sept. 6[?], 1785, M247, roll 99, item 178, 16:467–71, *PCC*.

42. Pickens to Samuel Elbert, Sept. 14, 1785, folder 1, APSCL; Ferguson, "General Andrew Pickens," 322.

43. Hawkins to Caswell, Sept. 26, 1785, *State Records of North Carolina*, 17:524.

44. Masterson, *William Blount*, esp. 70–73, 99–104.

45. The quoted material comes from a formal message delivered by the federal commissioners to Blount and to the Indian treaty agent appointed by the state of Georgia. Blount extracted the federal commissioners' statement and included it in a letter to Governor Caswell of North Carolina. (William Blount to Richard Caswell, Nov. 11, 1785, *State Records of North Carolina*, 17:567.)

46. Masterson, *William Blount*, 103.

47. Hawkins, Pickens, Martin, and McIntosh to Charles Thomson, secretary of Congress, Nov. 17, 1785, *ASP, IA*, 1:16.

48. Caughey, *McGillivray*, 98n46; McGillivray to Gov. Thomas Pinckney, Feb. 26, 1789, *ASP, IA*, 1:20.

49. Hawkins, Pickens, Martin, and McIntosh to Charles Thomson, secretary of Congress, Nov. 17, 1785, *ASP, IA*, 1:16; see also Hawkins and Pickens to Thomson, Dec. 30, 1785, ibid., 49. Another useful summary of the Galphinton negotiations is in Downes, "Creek-American Relations," 147–52.

50. Hawkins, Pickens, Martin, and McIntosh to Richard Henry Lee, president of Congress, Dec. 2, 1785, *ASP, IA*, 1:38.

51. All commissioners' quotes from *ASP, IA*, 1:40–41; Cayton, "'Noble Actors,'" in Cayton and Teute, *Contact Points*.

52. Henri, *Benjamin Hawkins*, 17.

53. Cayton, "'Noble Actors.'"

54. *ASP, IA*, 1:41.

55. Ibid., 41–43 (Tuskegatahee's quote on 43).

56. Ibid.

57. Perdue, *Cherokee Women*.

58. *ASP, IA*, 1:43; McClary, "Nancy Ward."

59. *ASP, IA*, 1:41.

60. Ibid., 42.

61. Ibid., 43.

62. Hawkins, Pickens, Martin, and McIntosh to Richard Henry Lee, Dec. 2, 1785, *ASP, IA*, 1:39.

63. "Articles of a Treaty, concluded at Hopewell on the Keowee River [with Cherokees]," Nov. 28, 1785, M247, roll 194, item 174, pp. 10–17 (quote on 15), *PCC*.

64. Quote by Randolph C. Downes in Ferguson, "General Andrew Pickens," 339.

65. Extract of minutes from Georgia General Assembly, Feb. 11, 1786, *ASP, IA*, 1:17; North Carolina House of Commons to North Carolina Delegates to Congress, Jan. 6, 1787, M247, roll 86, item 72, pp. 289–90, *PCC*; Blount to Commissioners for Treating with the Southern Indians, Nov. 22 and Nov. 28, 1785, *ASP, IA*, 1:44..

66. "A Copy of the Commissioners' Answer to Colonel Blount's Letters and Protest," Nov. 28, 1785, *ASP, IA*, 1:44.; Hawkins, Pickens, Martin, and McIntosh to Richard Henry Lee, Dec. 2, 1785, ibid., 39.

67. Hawkins and Pickens to Charles Thomson, Dec. 30, 1786, ibid.

68. Hawkins, Pickens, and Martin to John Hancock, president of Congress, Jan. 4, 1786, *ASP, IA*, 50.

69. Ibid., Jan. 14, 1786.

70. Hopewell treaties with Chickasaws and Choctaws, M247, roll 194, item 174, pp. 17–22 and 23–29, *PCC*.

CHAPTER 13

1. Representation of the Cherokees to Congress, Sept. 5, 1786, M247, roll 69, item 56, p. 417, *PCC*.

2. Ferguson, "General Andrew Pickens," 372–73; Kentawa or Corn Tassel and Scolacutta or Hanging Maw to Pickens, Sept. 24, 1787, box 1, APCU.

3. "An Ordinance for the Regulation of Indian Affairs," Aug. 7, 1786, *ASP, IA*, 1:14.

4. Cherokee Indians' talk, Sept. 8, 1787, M247, roll 69, item 56, p. 422, *PCC*.

5. Kentawa or Corn Tassel and Scolacutta or Hanging Maw to Pickens, Sept. 24, 1787, box 1, APCU.

6. Pickens to Thomas Pinckney, Oct. 15, 1787, ibid.

7. Pickens to McGillivray, Oct. 20, 1786, ibid.

8. In November 1786, Georgia leaders, backed by 1,500 troops, pressured some Creeks into signing the Treaty of Shoulderbone, another treaty that most Creeks rejected and that did not lessen hostilities (Downes, "Creek-American Relations," 154–58).

9. Pickens to Pinckney, Sept. 12, 1787, folder 8, APSCL. See also Pickens to Pinckney, Oct. 6, 1787, box 1, APCU.

10. Pinckney to Pickens, Sept. 28, 1787, "Extract of Minutes of Council," Sept. 27, 1787, box 1, APCU.

11. Pickens to Pinckney, Oct. 6, 1787, ibid.; on Captain Norwood's company, see Pickens to Capt. John Norwood, Oct. 10, 1787, folder 8, APSCL.

12. Pinckney to Pickens, Oct. 31, 1787, box 1, APCU.

13. Ibid., Dec. 19, 1787; see also Pickens to Pinckney, Oct. 15 and Dec. 18, 1787, ibid.; and Pickens to Pinckney, Nov. 9 and Nov. 12, 1787, APCLS.

14. Resolve of Congress, Oct. 26, 1787, APHL; Ferguson, "General Andrew Pickens," 388.

15. Pickens to McGillivray, Dec. 24, 1787, box 1, APCU; Pickens to Pinckney, Dec. 18, 1787, ibid.

16. McGillivray to Pickens, Jan. 2, 1788, ibid.

17. Quote from McGillivray to Pickens, Feb. 15, 1788, ibid.; Pickens to Pinckney, May 29, 1788, ibid.

18. McGillivray to Pickens, Feb. 15, 1788, ibid.

19. Pickens to Pinckney, May 29, 1788, ibid.

20. McGillivray to Pickens, Feb. 15, 1788, ibid.

21. Pickens and George Matthews to McGillivray and the Creeks, Mar. 29, 1788, ibid.; Pickens and Matthews to George Whitefield, Mar. 29, 1788, ibid. (quote from latter).

22. Pinckney to Pickens, Aug. 30, 1788, ibid.

23. *State Records of North Carolina*, 21:127.

24. Downes, "Creek-American Relations," 168; Knox to Congress, July 26, 1788, *ASP, IA*, 1:25.

25. Pickens to Pinckney, Mar. 26, 1788, APCLS.

26. "Instructions to the Commissioners," Oct. 26, 1787, *ASP, IA*, 1:26.

27. Pickens to Pinckney, Mar. 26, 1788, APCLS.

28. Pickens to Pinckney, May 2, 1788, box 1, APCU.

29. Pickens to Pinckney, May 29, 1788, APHL.

30. "Head men & warriors from several Towns" to Pickens, June 20, 1788, M247, roll 69, item 46, p. 429, *PCC*; Jobber's Son to Pickens, June 30, 1788, 435, ibid.; Pickens to Pinckney, July 10, 1788, 441, ibid.

31. Joseph Martin to Henry Knox, Aug. 23, 1788, roll 165, item 150, 361, ibid.

32. "Talk from the Hanging Maw & John Watts . . . also from the Black Dog . . . to General Pickens," June 25, 1788, roll 69, item 56, pp. 431–33, ibid.; Ferguson, "General Andrew Pickens," 411–13.

33. "From the Justices of Abbeville County now Sitting to the People living on Nolichuckie French Broad & Holston," July 9, 1788, M247, roll 69, item 56, p. 488, *PCC*; Pickens to Thomas Pinckney, July 10, 1788, box 1, APCU; Pickens to Richard Winn, June 30, 1788, M247, roll 165, item 150, 461–62, *PCC*; Richard Winn to Henry Knox, Aug. 5, 1788, M247, roll 165, item 150, 369–70; Felix Warley to Pickens, July 27, 1788, APCLS; Ferguson, "General Andrew Pickens," 417.

34. "From the Justices of Abbeville County," July 9, 1788, 438–40.

35. Proclamation of Congress, Sept. 1, 1788, APHL.

36. Ibid., and Resolution of Congress (directing the secretary of war to organize an expedition), Sept. 1, 1788, APHL; Samuel Johnston to Judge Campbell, July 29, 1788, *State Records of North Carolina*, 21:484.

37. Pickens to Martin, Nov. 10, 1788, box 1, APCU; Pickens to Thomas Pinckney, Dec. 8, 1788, ibid.

38. Pickens to Pinckney, May 2, 1788, ibid.

39. Pickens to Pinckney, Mar. 26, 1788, APCLS. Helpful, detailed summaries of Creek–treaty commissioner negotiations between May and the end of 1788 appear in Ferguson, "General Andrew Pickens," 418–27, 434–36; and Downes, "Creek-American Relations," 169–74.

40. Pickens to Thomas Pinckney, Dec. 8, 1788, APCU.

41. William Blount to John Steele, Jan. 17, 1789, in Wagstaff, *Papers of John Steele*, 1:28–30.

42. Martin to Henry Knox, Jan. 15, 1789, *ASP, IA*, 1:47.

43. Martin to Samuel Johnston, Feb. 5, 1789, in Morrison, *Joseph Martin*, 67.

44. Steele to Samuel Johnston, Feb. 19, 1789, *State Records of North Carolina*, 21:528.

45. Pickens to Winn, May 16, 1789, APCLS.

46. Ferguson, "General Andrew Pickens," 442n30.

47. Ibid.; *ASP, IA*, 1:56–57.

48. Pickens to Winn, May 16, 1789, APCLS; Ferguson, "General Andrew Pickens," 444.

49. The Badger and other Headmen & Warriors of the Cherokee to Richard Winn and Andrew Pickens, Apr. 15, 1789, APCLS.

50. Ibid.

51. Ibid.; Pickens to Winn, May 16, 1789, APCLS.

52. Pickens to Winn, May 16, 1789, APCLS; McGillivray to Panton, Aug. 10, 1789, in Caughey, *McGillivray*, 245.

53. Pickens to Winn, May 16, 1789, APCLS; John Steele to James Carey, June 8, 1789, in Wagstaff, *Papers of John Steele*, 1:51.

54. Ferguson, "General Andrew Pickens," 446–53; Pickens and Henry Osborne to George Washington, June 30, 1789, *ASP, IA*, 1:34.

55. Pickens, Steele, and Osborne to the Head-men, Chiefs, and Warriors of the Cherokee Nation, June 7, 1789, *ASP, IA*, 1:34.

56. For example, see deposition of Anthony Forman, June 15, 1789, in Wagstaff, *Papers of John Steele*, 1:52–54.

57. Pickens to Little Turkey and other Headmen of the Cherokees, June 15, 1789, APCLS.

58. Ibid.

59. Ibid.; AP to Thomas Pinckney, Oct. 15, 1788, APCU; quote from Calloway, *American Revolution in Indian Country*, 273.

60. Pickens and Henry Osborne to the Head-men, Chiefs, and Warriors of the Creek Nation, Apr. 20, 1789, *ASP, IA*, 1:31.

61. Talks from Headmen and Chiefs of the Lower Creeks, May 23 and June 1, 1789, ibid., 1:34–35; McGillivray to George Galphin, May 18, 1789, ibid., 35; McGillivray to John Galphin, June 16, 1789, ibid., 37.

62. Talk from the Chiefs, Head-men, and Warriors of the Lower Creeks, June 1, 1789, ibid.

63. Quote from Pickens and Osborne to Washington, June 30, 1789; see also Talks from Headmen and Chiefs of the Lower Creeks, May 23 and June 1, 1789; McGillivray to George Galphin, May 18, 1789; and McGillivray to John Galphin, June 16, 1789, all in ibid.

64. Pickens to Pinckney, July 4, 1789, APHL.

65. Henry Knox to George Washington, July 6, 1789, *ASP, IA*, 1:16; Knox to Washington, "The Cherokees," July 7, 1789, ibid., 38.

66. Knox to Washington, July 28, 1789, ibid., 33–34.

67. A. Wallace, *Jefferson and the Indians*, 166–69.

68. President Washington to the Senate, Aug. 7, 1789, *ASP, IA*, 12.

69. Report of President Washington to the Senate, Aug. 22, 1789, ibid., 55.

70. Ferguson, "General Andrew Pickens," 461–62, quote found on 462n69.

71. Henry Knox, "Instructions to the Commissioners," Aug. 29, 1789, *ASP, IA*, 1:66.

72. McGillivray to William Panton, Oct. 8, 1789, in Caughey, *McGillivray*, 253.

73. Quotes from Pickens and Osborne to Lincoln, Griffin, and Humphreys, Sept. 16, 1789, *ASP, IA*, 1:71; Lincoln, Griffin, and Humphreys to Pickens and Osborne, Sept. 11, 1789, ibid., 68.

74. Downes, "Creek-American Relations," 177–79; Whitaker, "Alexander McGillivray, 1789–1793," 292.

75. Henry Knox, "Instructions to the Commissioners," *ASP, IA*, 1:65–66 (quote on 66).

76. Whitaker, "Alexander McGillivray, 1789–1793," 291.

77. McGillivray to Panton, Oct. 8, 1789, in Caughey, *McGillivray*, 253.

78. Whitaker, "Alexander McGillivray, 1789–1793," 291.

79. "Articles of Peace and Amity" (proposed treaty), *ASP, IA*, 1:73.

80. Ibid.; McGillivray to Panton, Oct. 8, 1789, in Caughey, *McGillivray*, 253; Pickett, *History of Alabama*, 397.

81. McGillivray to Panton, Oct. 8, 1789, in Caughey, *McGillivray*, 253; see also ibid., 253n225.

82. Journal and correspondence of commissioners, *ASP, IA*, 1:74, 76–79; McGillivray to Commissioners, Sept. 27, 1789, in Pickett, *History of Alabama*, 398. This last letter, in which McGillivray clearly explained his objection to the Oconee land cession, was not included in the papers Humphreys submitted to Knox; however, it is true that McGillivray did not make these explanations until he and the Creeks had already cut off negotiations and headed for home.

83. McGillivray to Panton, May 8, 1790, in Caughey, *McGillivray*, 260.

84. Ibid., Oct. 8, 1789, 253.

85. *ASP, IA*, 1:77.

86. Quoted in Ferguson, "General Andrew Pickens," 469.

87. Whittaker, "Alexander McGillivray, 1789–1793," 294.

88. Hawkins to McGillivray, Mar. 6, 1790, in Caughey, *McGillivray*, 258.

89. Treaty of New York, *ASP, IA*, 1:81–82; Whitaker, "Alexander McGillivray, 1789–1793," 296–301; Hudson, *Creek Paths*, 32–33; Downes, "Creek-American Relations," 182–84. McGillivray deceived his fellow Creek leaders about the actual terms of the Ocmulgee–St. Marys cession, leading them to believe that they had ceded less of that land than the written treaty stipulated (Saunt, *New Order of Things*, 192–94).

CHAPTER 14

1. D. Wallace, *History of South Carolina*, 2:345–49; Schaper, *Sectionalism*, 376–79. In *Unification of a Slave State*, Rachel Klein documents the growth of an "interregional Republican political coalition" in the 1790s based on shared interests between backcountry and lowcountry landowners and slaveholders like Pickens. I accept this argument and agree that Pickens had close ties to many lowcountry Republicans; however, Pickens voted more often than not as a Federalist through most of the 1790s (Klein, *Unification of a Slave State*, esp. 135–268 passim and 304–5).

2. General Assembly, *Committee Reports*, S165005, item 86, Jan. 25, 1789; *S.C. Senate Journal*, Jan. 17, 25, 26, 27, 28, 1791, 27, 64–65, 75, 79, 85.

3. Nix and Snell, *Thomas Boone Pickens*, 83–85. Elizabeth's older sister, Floride, married Ezekiel's uncle (and Andrew Pickens's brother-in-law) John Ewing Colhoun (ibid., 84).

4. Fitzpatrick, *Writings of George Washington*, 31:233–38.

5. Knox to Washington, July 7, 1789, *ASP, IA*, 1:53.

6. Sadosky, *Revolutionary Negotiations*, 158.

7. Ibid., 157–63; A. Wallace, *Jefferson and the Indians*, 166–69, 286, 290; Nichols, *Red Gentlemen*, 99, 134, 136; Horsman, *Expansion*, 53–65.

8. Jackson and Twohig, *Diaries of George Washington*, 6:158.

9. Quote from *ASP, IA*, 1:204; Symonds, "America's Indian Policy," 30–31.

10. *ASP, IA*, 1:203–6; Ferguson, "General Andrew Pickens," 492–94; W. Dennis, "American Revolutionaries," 302; Symonds, "America's Indian Policy," 31–32.

11. Knox to Blount, Jan. 31, 1792, *ASP, IA*, 1:245; ibid., May 5, 1792, 265.

12. Symonds, "America's Indian Policy," 32–35; Masterson, *William Blount*, 214–16; Dowd, *Spirited Resistance*, 104–6.

13. Charles Pinckney to Washington, Jan. 8, 1792, in W. Ford, *Writings of George Washington*, 12:114n.

14. Washington to Charles Pinckney, Mar. 17, 1792, ibid., 32:7.

15. Washington, "Opinion of the General Officers," Mar. 9, 1792, ibid., 31:509–15.

16. Pickens to Blount, Apr. 28, 1792, *ASP, IA*, 1:267; Masterson, *William Blount*, 216–18, 221–24; Symonds, "America's Indian Policy," 32–35; Grenier, *First Way of War*, 176–78.

17. Masterson, *William Blount*, 216.

18. Knox to Pickens, Apr. 21, 1792, *ASP, IA*, 1:251.

19. Pickens to William Hart, May 29, 1792, Draper CUL 1VV20.

20. Correspondence in *ASP, IA*, 1:258, 267, 270, 284–87, 316; Washington to the Secretary of State, Aug. 23, 1792, in Fitzpatrick, *Writings of George Washington*, 32:129; Knox to Blount, Aug. 15, 1792, in *Territorial Papers of the United States*, 163.

21. Pickens to Knox, Aug. 22, 1792, box 1, APCU.

22. Pickens to His Excellency the Governor of South Carolina, Sept. 13, 1792, *ASP, IA*, 1:316; Saunt, *New Order of Things*, 78–79; Whitaker, "Alexander McGillivray, 1789–1793," 300.

23. Anderson to Charles Pinckney, Sept. 20, 1792, *ASP, IA*, 1:317.

24. Blount to Knox, Sept. 26, 1792, ibid., 288.

25. Anderson to Charles Pinckney, Sept. 20, 1792, ibid., 316; Knox to Pickens, Aug. 15, 1792, ibid., 258; Pinckney to Knox, Sept. 30, 1792, ibid., 316.

26. Pickens to Charles Pinckney, Sept. 13, 1792, ibid., 316.

27. *S.C. Senate Journal*, Dec. 4, 1792, 47. The other electors were General Charles Cotesworth Pinckney, General Robert Anderson, General Robert Barnwell, Captain John Chesnutt, and Captain John Hunter (ibid.).

28. Ibid., Dec. 15, 17, 21, 1792, pp. 129–30, 137, 206.

29. *S.C. Statutes*, 5:212–14; Samuel Earle to L. C. Draper, June 18, 1873, Draper CUL 12VV176.

30. Sharp, "Pickens Families," 26; Salley, *Calhoun Family*, 18, 20.

31. Symonds, "America's Indian Policy," 35–36 (quote on 36); Dowd, *Spirited Resistance*, 110.

32. Moultrie to Knox, July 11, 1793, in Sparks, *Correspondence of the American Revolution*, 4:434.

33. Pickens to Elijah Clarke, Apr. 28, 1793, *ASP, IA*, 1:369.

34. *ASP, IA*, 1:286.

35. Chickasaw Chiefs to General James Robertson, Feb. 13, 1793, ibid., 442; ibid., Apr. 29, 1793, 456; see also letters of William Glover, William Colbert, Piomingo, and Thomas Brown, in ibid., 456–57.

36. Anderson to Charles Pinckney, Sept. 20, 1792, ibid., 318.

37. Pickens to Charles Pinckney, Sept. 13, 1792, ibid., 316.

38. In May, James Seagrove, the federal agent to the Creeks, had suggested a two-prong invasion, with Pickens commanding one wing and perhaps John Sevier the other. Pickens undoubtedly considered Sevier to be a bloodthirsty murderer of peaceful Cherokees after his 1788 murder of The Tassel and other depredations, and he had never had satisfactory cooperation with him during the war (James Seagrove to Knox, May 24, 1793, ibid., 388). General James Jackson of Georgia had suggested a three-prong operation with either Pickens or Sumter commanding the middle prong; Pickens's opinion of Sumter was ambivalent at best, and the latter had played little role in military affairs since 1781 (Ferguson, "General Andrew Pickens," 527–28).

39. "Memorandum from the Secretary of War and Andrew Pickens," July 24, 1793, in *Territorial Papers of the United States*, 4:283–86 (quote on 284); also Secretary of War to the President, July 25, 1793, ibid., 286–87.

40. Memorandum from Andrew Pickens, July [n.d.], 1793, ibid., 288–89 (quote on 289); memorandum from the President, July 26, 1793, ibid., 287.

41. Daniel Smith to Capt. John Beard, July 17, 1793, *ASP, IA*, 1:464; Calloway, *American Revolution in Indian Country*, 200–201, 204–5, 209.

42. Acting Governor Smith to the Secretary of War, June 13, 1793, in *Territorial Papers of the United States*, 4:271; ibid., June 17, 1793, 273–74; Smith to James Robertson, June 19, 1793, ibid., 275–76; Smith to Knox, July 27, 1793, ibid., 290; see also correspondence in *ASP, IA*, 1:363, 430, 431, 459, 460; and Grenier, *First Way of War*, 178.

43. Beard escaped punishment in his court-martial (Nichols, *Red Gentlemen*, 156).

44. See correspondence of Chickasaws to white leaders, *ASP, IA*, 1:442–43, 456–57.

45. Gov. Blount and Andrew Pickens to the Secretary of War, Aug. 1, 1793, in *Territorial Papers of the United States*, 4:291–93; Gov. Blount to Judges Campbell, McNairy, and Anderson, Aug. 28, 1793, ibid., 302.

46. Two notes from the Secretary of War to Gov. Blount and Andrew Pickens, Aug. 5, 1793, ibid., 294, 295.

47. Blount and Pickens to Knox, Aug. 6, 1793, ibid., 205.

48. Ibid., 206.

49. Washington to Moultrie, Aug. 28, 1793, in Fitzpatrick, *Writings of George Washington*, 33:73–74 (quote on 74); Ferguson, "General Andrew Pickens," 538.

CHAPTER 15

1. Pickens to John Ewing Colhoun, Apr. 17, 1793, folder 8, APSCL.

2. Correspondence of Jan. 1 and 2, 1794, in *ASP, IA*, 1:472–74.

3. Washington to Congress, Jan. 30, 1794, ibid., 472.

4. Report read by Pickens, Feb. 19, 1794, ibid., 475–76 (quotes on 475).

5. *Journal of the House of Representatives of the United States* (hereafter *U.S. House Journal*) Jan. 30, Feb. 19, and June 7, 1794, 51, 66, and 213–14; *Debates and Proceedings in the Congress of the United States*, 3rd Cong. (hereafter *Annals of Congress*), Apr. 4, Apr. 8, May 16, June 4, June 6, and June 7, 1794, 560, 565, 696–97, 764, 774–79, and 781–82.

6. *U.S. House Journal*, Apr. 15, June 5, 1794, 120 and 206; *Annals of Congress*, Apr. 15, 1794, 594–95.

7. *U.S. House Journal*, Apr. 21, 1794, 126; *Annals of Congress*, Apr. 16, 18, 21, 1794, 596, 600–601, and 603.

8. *Annals of Congress*, June 4, 1794, 765.

9. Ibid., Mar. 24, 27, 1794, 527–28, 534–35 (quote from 534).

10. Ibid., Feb. 13, 1795, 1220–23.

11. Ibid., Jan. 23, 1795, 1129–31; *U.S. House Journal*, Jan. 23, 28, Feb. 6, 23, 24, 1795, 302, 307, 314, 338, 341; Klein, *Unification of a Slave State*, 220 (quote).

12. Washington's Message to Congress, *U.S. House Journal*, Nov. 19, 1794, 234.

13. *Annals of Congress*, Nov. 24–27, 1794, 898–945. The terms "democratic societies" and "republican societies" were used throughout the debate.

14. *U.S. House Journal*, May 8, 10, 19, 27, 1794, 143–46, 150–52, 167–68, 181–83.

15. Ibid., May 7, 8, 19, 29, 1784, 139–46, 167–68, 184–85; *Annals of Congress*, May 29, 1794, 729–30.

16. *S.C. House Journal*, Dec. 6, 1796, 76; D. Wallace, *History of South Carolina*, 2:353–54, 356–57.

17. *Governor's Messages*, S165009, Message 649, Nov. 24, 1795; General Assembly, *Committee Reports*, S165005, item 12, Dec. 18, 1795.

18. Treaty of Philadelphia, June 28, 1794, *ASP, IA*, 1:543.

19. Knox to Pickens, June 27, 1794, box 1, APCU.

20. Quotes from Pickens to Knox, Sept. 6, 1794, ibid.; see also Pickens to Maj. Edward Taylor, Sept. 22, 1794, APHL.

21. *ASP, IA*, 1:529–30; Masterson, *William Blount*, 267–68.

22. *ASP, IA*, 1:483–84.

23. Ibid., 495, 498–99.

24. *U.S. House Journal*, Jan. 29–30, 309–10; *Annals of Congress*, Jan. 28–30, 1147–62 passim.

25. *U.S. House Journal*, Dec. 1, 8, 11, 24, 1794, 248, 259, 263, 274; Ferguson, "General Andrew Pickens," 561 and 561n102.

26. The most thorough study of the Yazoo scandal appears in Lamplugh, *Politics on the Periphery*, esp. 64–138; see also W. Stevens, *History of Georgia*, 2:466–96; and *Annals of Congress*, Mar. 2, 3, 1796, 1278–80, 1282–83.

27. Secretary of War to Governor of Georgia, Mar. 20, 1795, *ASP, IA*, 1:561.

28. George Washington to the Senate, June 25, 1795, ibid., 560.

29. Ibid.

30. James McHenry to Pickens, Mar. 13, 1796, box 1, APCU; *ASP, IA*, 1:590.

31. McHenry to Jared Irwin, Mar. 3, 1796, box 1, APCU. The thrust of the commissioners' instructions can be inferred from this letter; from the commissioners' journal of the Coleraine negotiations in *ASP, IA*, 1:583–613 passim; from Washington's

communication to the Senate of June 25, 1795, *ASP, IA,* 1:560; and from Pickering's letter to Mathews on Mar. 20, 1795, *ASP, IA,* 1:561.

32. Charlton, *Life of Major General James Jackson,* 25–27. See also Ferguson, "General Andrew Pickens," 139–140n138; Pickens to Lee, Aug. 28, 1811; and W. Stevens, *History of Georgia,* 2:479–80, 485–90.

33. Lamplugh, *Politics on the Periphery,* 12, 28–37, 64–65, 98.

34. *ASP, IA,* 1:587–94; Ferguson, "General Andrew Pickens," 569–71; Sadosky, *Revolutionary Negotiations,* 168–71.

35. *ASP, IA,* 1:597–98 (quote on 598).

36. Ibid., 598, 695.

37. Treaty of Coleraine (in ibid., 586–87) and Coleraine Journal (ibid., 603, 604–6, 608, 612, 613–14).

38. Nichols, *Red Gentlemen,* 182–84; Sadosky, *Revolutionary Negotiations,* 165–75.

39. *Statutes at Large of the United States,* 4th Cong., 1st sess., May, 19, 1796, 469–74.

40. Washington to McHenry, July 18, 1796, in Fitzpatrick, *Writings of George Washington,* 35:146–48; McHenry to Pickens, Feb. 2, 1797, APHL. James Seagrove had briefly replaced Blount as superintendent of Indian Affairs south of the Ohio. Neither the Creeks nor Georgians fully trusted Seagrove; Pickens and Hawkins considered him honest but ineffective.

41. Hawkins to Pickens, Mar. 7, 1797, in Foster, *Collected Works of Benjamin Hawkins* (hereafter *Hawkins Letters*), 94.

42. *Hawkins Letters,* 142–44, 148.

43. Ibid., 152.

44. Ibid., 146.

45. Ibid., 159.

46. Ibid., 151–52 (quote on 152).

47. Ibid., 160.

48. Ibid., 130–31, 152–53 (quote on 152).

49. Hawkins and Pickens to Sevier, Apr. 16, 1797, ibid., 157–58.

50. *Hawkins Letters,* 189–90 (quote on 189); Masterson, *William Blount,* 315; Ferguson, "General Andrew Pickens," 600; Pickett, *History of Alabama,* 447.

51. *Hawkins Letters,* 153–54.

52. Ferguson, "General Andrew Pickens," 603.

53. Henri, *Benjamin Hawkins,* 200–201; Masterson, *William Blount,* 307.

54. Henri, *Benjamin Hawkins,* 198.

55. Ibid., 202–3; Melton, *First Impeachment,* 101–3; Masterson, *William Blount,* 316.

56. William Blount to James Carey, Apr. 21, 1797, *Annals of Congress,* 5th Cong., appendix, 3152–54.

57. Masterson, *William Blount,* 315–23; Henri, *Benjamin Hawkins,* 204–5.

58. Melton, *First Impeachment,* 4.

59. Hawkins to McHenry, June 4, 1797, *Hawkins Letters,* 177.

60. Hawkins to Dinsmoor, Sept. 20, 1797, ibid., 196; Hawkins to James Winchester, Nov. 9, 1797, ibid., 225.

61. Ferguson, "General Andrew Pickens," 607.

62. Pickens to Lee, Nov. 25, 1811.

63. Ferguson, "General Andrew Pickens," 609; *Hawkins Letters*, 242, 243, 267, 286.

64. Masterson, *William Blount*, 331; Ferguson, "General Andrew Pickens," 607–8n195; *Annals of Congress*, Dec. 4, 1797, 476.

65. Treaty of Tellico, *ASP, IA*, 1:637–38; Henri, *Benjamin Hawkins*, 204–5.

CHAPTER 16

1. By my reckoning, 1787 was the only year in which Pickens may not have been away from home for more than a few consecutive weeks. Even during that year, however, he was very busy with military affairs in the western portion of the state.

2. Ferguson, "General Andrew Pickens," 615.

3. J. Miller, *Federalist Era*, 164–67, 205–7, 210, 214–19; D. Wallace, *History of South Carolina*, 2:354–55.

4. Pickens to Jacob Read, Aug. 4, 1798, in Ferguson, "General Andrew Pickens," 615.

5. *S.C. House Journal*, Nov. 28, 29, Dec. 14, 15, 17, 1798, 10–12, 42, 56, 162, 166–70, 178–81; General Assembly, *Committee Reports*, S165005, item 61, Dec. 14, 1798, item 110, Dec. 15, 1798.

6. *S.C. Statutes*, 5:359–60 (quote on 359).

7. *S.C. House Journal*, Nov. 26, Dec. 4, 6, 10, 12, 17, 18, 21, 1799, 12–13, 47, 55–57, 74–75, 88–89, 120–21, 139, 198–99. Pickens had been active in similar work on the state's court system in the 1798 session (Ferguson, "General Andrew Pickens," 617).

8. D. Wallace, *History of South Carolina*, 2:357–58; Ferguson, "General Andrew Pickens," 617; *S.C. House Journal*, Dec. 6, 15, 1798, 103–4, 166–72.

9. Pickens to Marinus Willet, Aug. 15, 1801, box 1, APCU.

10. Pickens to Andrew Pickens Jr., June 15, 1801, folder 8, APSCL; Ferguson, "General Andrew Pickens," 628–29.

11. Pickens to Marinus Willet, Aug. 15, 1801, box 1, APCU.

12. Pickens to John Ewing Colhoun, Feb. 13, 1802, folder 8, APSCL

13. Pickens to Marinus Willett, Aug. 15, 1801, APHL.

14. Some of the works on Wilkinson include Jacobs, *Tarnished Warrior*; Linklater, *Artist in Treason*; Narrett, "Geopolitics and Intrigue"; Clark, *Proofs of the Corruption of Gen. James Wilkinson*; and Green, *Spanish Conspiracy*.

15. A. Wallace, *Jefferson and the Indians*, 218.

16. Ibid., 218–20; Hudson, *Creek Paths*, 61; *Statutes at Large of the United States*, 5th Cong., 3rd sess., Feb. 19, 1799, 618, and 6th Cong., 1st sess., May 13, 1800, 82.

17. Henry Dearborn, "Instructions to William R. Davie, James Wilkinson, and Benjamin Hawkins," June 24, 1801, *ASP, IA*, 1:649–50 (quote on 650). Davie was originally appointed to the commission but declined, and Pickens was appointed in his place.

18. Ibid., 650.

19. Ibid., 649–50.

20. Dearborn to Wilkinson, Hawkins, and Pickens, July 17, 1801, ibid., 651.

21. *Hawkins Letters*, 369–85.

22. Hawkins to Dearborn, Nov. 14, 1801, ibid., 395.

23. Wilkinson, Hawkins, and Pickens to Dearborn, Oct. 25, 1801, *ASP, IA*, 1:651.

24. *ASP, IA*, 1:648–49, 642–53.

25. Wilkinson, Hawkins, and Pickens to Dearborn, Oct. 25, 1801, ibid., 651.

26. Ibid.

27. Hawkins to Dearborn, Oct. 28, 1801, *Hawkins Letters*, 393.

28. Wilkinson, Hawkins, and Pickens to Dearborn, Oct. 25, 1801, *ASP, IA*, 1:651.

29. *ASP, IA*, 1:50.

30. Wilkinson, Hawkins, and Pickens to Dearborn, Dec. 18, 1801, ibid., 658.

31. See, for example, the comments of Tuskonohapia and Puck-shum-ubee in ibid., 661. The Choctaws said that the British had never paid them for the land, and one of them, Puck-shum-ubee, asked that the United States give them some compensation. The commissioners did not address this request for compensation directly.

32. Wilkinson, Hawkins, and Pickens to Dearborn, Dec. 18, 1801, ibid., 658.

33. *ASP, IA*, 1:659, 661–62.

34. Ibid., 662.

35. Extract of a talk from Little Turtle to the President of the United States, Jan. 4, 1802, ibid., 1:655.

36. Pickens to John E. Colhoun, Feb. 13, 1802, folder 8, APSCL; Hawkins to Dearborn, Nov. 14, Dec. 21, 1801, *Hawkins Letters*, 396, 412–13.

37. Pickens to John E. Colhoun, Feb. 13, 1802, folder 8, APSCL.

38. Wilkinson to Dearborn, Oct. 27, 1801, *ASP, IA*, 1:653.

39. Hawkins to Dearborn, Dec. 21, 1801, *Hawkins Letters*, 413.

40. Pickens to Colhoun, Feb. 13, 1802, folder 8, APSCL.

41. Wilkinson included his signature on the commissioners' letter to Dearborn explaining this situation. The letter was dated May 10, but the commissioners' journal suggests it was written on the eighth. Since Wilkinson did not arrive until the eighth, it seems likely that Pickens and Hawkins made the journey with the Creek representatives up the Oconee to inspect the disputed territory and returned before Wilkinson's arrival (*ASP, IA*, 1:669–71).

42. Ibid., 671; *Hawkins Letters*, 423, 426; "The Articles of Agreement and Cession," Apr. 24, 1802, in *American State Papers, Public Lands*, 1:125–26.

43. *ASP, IA*, 1:651.

44. Ibid., 672.

45. Ibid., 673.

46. Wilkinson, Hawkins, and Pickens to Dearborn, May 30, 1802, ibid.

47. *ASP, IA*, 1:677; see also Hawkins's discussions with Creek leaders on May 19–20 in *Hawkins Letters*, 424–26.

48. *ASP, IA*, 1:675.

49. Henri, *Benjamin Hawkins*, 228, 230.

50. *ASP, IA*, 1:678.

51. Ibid., 669, 680.

52. Wilkinson and Hawkins to Dearborn, July 15, 1802, ibid., 669.

53. Pound, *Benjamin Hawkins*, 179–80.

54. Ferguson, "General Andrew Pickens," 650n78; Wilkinson, *Memoirs*, 2:561–62, appendix cxxii.

55. Ferguson, "General Andrew Pickens," 650; W. Dennis, "American Revolutionaries," 317.

56. Ferguson makes this argument in "General Andrew Pickens," 650 and 650n78.

57. Coleman, *History of Georgia*, 100; the TNGenWeb Project's website Indian Land Cessions in the American Southeast, http://www.tngenweb.org/cessions (accessed Aug. 19, 2014); *Indian Affairs: Laws and Treaties*, 73–74, 85–86.

58. Pickens to Henry Lee, Nov. 25, 1811.

CHAPTER 17

1. In June 1801, Pickens wrote his son Andrew, "I have no white person at Tamassee, therefore, am most of my time there." Obviously Pickens had slaves working on the Tamassee estate at that date (Pickens to Andrew Pickens Jr., June 15, 1801, folder 8, APSCL).

2. Waring, *Fighting Elder*, 199; Journal of William Ancrum, July 11, 12, 1810, William Ancrum Papers, SCL.

3. A. Pickens, *Skyagunsta*, 155; Skelton, *General Andrew Pickens*, 33.

4. Skelton, *General Andrew Pickens*, 33; Sharp, *Pickens Families*, 29; Ezekiel Pickens to Floride Calhoun, Sept. 27, 1805, July 17, 1806, Apr. 18, 1808, unnumbered folder, APCU; will of Gen. Andrew Pickens, 1809, Probate Judge Estate Papers, Anderson County, roll #547, SCDAH. Though Pickens's will certainly reads as if he formally owned ten slaves, the 1810 federal census states that there were twenty-two slaves actually living on his plantation (United States, Third Census, 1810).

5. William Martin to Lyman Draper, Jan. 1, 1843, Draper CUL 5DD11514

6. Journal of William Ancrum's travels, 4 July–5 Aug. 1810, entries of July 7–12, Ancrum Papers, SCL.

7. Waring, *Fighting Elder*, 202.

8. *Miller's Weekly Messenger*, Aug. 13, 1807.

9. Pickens to John E. Colhoun, Apr. 7, 1804, folder 8, APPSCL.

10. For example, Pickens and his partners sued "Major Persons" in 1788 for £300 sterling for failing to pay as promised for merchandise delivered to him. In 1793, a jury finally awarded the plaintiffs the much smaller amount of £55 9 s. (*Judgment Rolls*, Charleston District, series L10018, year 1793, item 200A).

11. Quoted in Waring, *Fighting Elder*, 189.

12. Pickens to Andrew Pickens Jr., Apr. 12, 1800, folder 8, APPSCL.

13. Agreement of Pickens, Gervais, Rutledge, and Owen, June 9, 1798, APCU; List of Debts due to Andw. Pickens & Company from Traders of the Cherokee country . . . , Feb. 8, 1805, APCU.

14. Pickens to Andrew Pickens Jr., Apr. 12, 1800, folder 8, APPSCL.

15. Pickens to Andrew Pickens Jr., June 15, 1801, ibid.

16. Will of Gen. Andrew Pickens, 1809, Probate Judge Estate Papers, Anderson County, roll #547, SCDAH.

17. Pickens to Marinus Willet, Aug. 15, 1801, APCU.

18. Tragically, one of these children, Andrew, died of an accidental gunshot before the age of two (Sharp, "Pickens Families," 26).

19. Ezekiel Pickens to Floride Colhoun, July 17, 1806, unnumbered folder, APCU.

20. Sharp, "Pickens Families," 26–27.

21. Ferguson, "General Andrew Pickens," 665–66.

22. *Miller's Weekly Messenger*, Oct. 1, 1807.

23. Klein, *Unification of a Slave State*, 267.

24. Sharp, "Pickens Families," 25; "Visit to Old Cemetery," *Anderson Independent*, June 26, 1972; Moss, *Roster of South Carolina Patriots*, 419.

25. "Reverend John Simpson," p. 5, folder 27, box 2, William Hayne Mills Collection, Clemson University Library, Clemson, S.C.

26. Sharp, "Pickens Families," 27–29; Day, *Pickens Family*, 55, 57, 72–73, 75, 77.

27. Pickens to Lee, Aug. 28, 1811.

28. Ibid., Nov. 25, 1811.

29. United States, First Census, 1790; United States, Second Census, 1800; Klein, *Unification of a Slave State*, 155, 247–51. In 1790, blacks made up 8.7 percent of the population in Pendleton County; in 1800 they accounted for 12.4 percent of individuals in Pendleton District (Friend, "Frontier and Plantation," 29).

30. Pickens had to submit another deposition in 1798 relating to his handling of two or three of the nine slaves he captured from the Cherokees in 1782 and sold to pay the Georgia troops that were with him. Holman Freeman of South Carolina maintained that the slaves had belonged to him, and a complex legal case developed involving Freeman, the state of Georgia, and the state of South Carolina (*S.C. House Journal*, Dec. 19, 1798, 199–200; General Assembly, *Committee Reports*, S165005, item 62, Dec. 15, 1798, S165015, item 130, 1798; Deposition of Andrew Pickens, July 3, 1798, Draper CUL 11VV542–43).

31. L. Ford, *Deliver Us from Evil*, 79–83, 94–102.

32. Quoted in Deschamps, "Antislavery Presbyterians," 6–7.

33. Galatians 3:28.

34. Ephesians 6:9.

35. Ephesians 6:5.

36. Calhoon, *Evangelicals and Conservatives*, 128. Orville Vernon Burton discusses this deep ambivalence over slavery among South Carolina upcountry Baptists in *In My Father's House*, 23–28.

37. Brackett, *Old Stone Church*, 91; Howe, *Presbyterian Church*, 1:638.

38. Brackett, *Old Stone Church*, 91.

39. Howe, *Presbyterian Church*, 1:638.

40. John B. Davis, Transcription of Minutes of the Presbytery of South Carolina, 1785–1799, July 20, 21, 1796 (quote from July 21), Columbia Theological Seminary; Mills, "South Carolina's Contribution to Our Presbyterian Heritage," p. 3, box 2, folder 26, Mills Collection, Clemson University Library, Clemson, S.C. See also extracts from the synod's minutes in Foote, *Sketches of North Carolina*, 294.

41. Davis, Transcription of Minutes of the Presbytery of South Carolina, 1785–1799, Oct. 31, 1796.

42. Mills, "South Carolina's Contribution to Our Presbyterian Heritage," 4.

43. Howe, *Presbyterian Church*, 1:635, 640, 2:149.

44. Mills, "South Carolina's Contribution to Our Presbyterian Heritage," 4–5.

45. Quoted in Foote, *Sketches of North Carolina*, 304.

46. Quoted in Mills, "South Carolina's Contribution to Our Presbyterian Heritage," 7.

47. Quoted in Foote, *Sketches of North Carolina*, 304.

48. L. Ford, *Deliver Us from Evil*, 86–87; Mills, "The Historical Background of the Presbyterian Church in the United States," p. 1, box 2, folder 27, Mills Collection, Clemson University Library, Clemson, S.C. Several sources claim that Gilliland never reconciled himself to living in a slave state, obtained permission from the presbytery in 1805 to leave, and became a well-known abolitionist in Ohio. However, presbytery minutes indicate that Gilliland continued to serve as a pastor in South Carolina until at least 1814 (Sprague, *Annals of the American Pulpit*, 4:137–38; Deschamps, "Antislavery Presbyterians," 8; Howe, *Presbyterian Church*, 1:635, 2:146–47; Mills, "South Carolina's Contribution to Our Presbyterian Heritage," 4; for proof that Gilliland remained in South Carolina, see Minutes of the Second Presbytery of South Carolina, 1800–1810, Apr. 4, 1804, Apr. 2, 1805, Sept. 30, 1809; and Minutes of the Presbytery of South Carolina, 1811–1814, Apr. 1, 1814, Columbia Theological Seminary).

49. *S.C. Statutes*, 7:441.

50. L. Ford, *Deliver Us from Evil*, 88–89, 92–93.

51. For more on the denominations' internal wrangling over slavery in the 1780s and 1790s, see Irons, *Proslavery Christianity*, esp. 55–56; and Calhoon, *Evangelicals and Conservatives*, 125–27.

52. L. Ford, *Deliver Us from Evil*, 143–49; for more on proslavery Christian paternalism in the South Carolina upcountry, see Klein, *Unification of a Slave State*, ch. 9.

53. *Pendleton District and Anderson County Wills*, 30.

54. Ibid., *Pendleton District Deeds*, 345.

55. *Pendleton District Deeds*, 90.

56. Francis W. Pickens to J. H. Marshall, Nov. 4, 1847, in Draper CUL 16VV361.

57. William Martin to Lyman Draper, Jan. 1, 1843, in Draper CUL 5DD11514.

58. Will of Gen. Robert Anderson, S108093, SCDAH.

59. Journal of William Ancrum, July 4–Aug. 5, 1810, Ancrum Papers, SCL.

60. Megginson, *African American Life*, 27, 28, 78; John Ewing Colhoun Papers, folder 16, SCL. There is no record of Pickens's slaves rebelling against him or attempting to escape, although of course it is possible it occurred.

61. The 1810 census indicates that Pickens's son Andrew owned thirty-five slaves near Pendleton, while Ezekiel may have owned a total of eighty-eight on his plantations at St. Thomas and Christ Church near Charleston. Almost certainly Ezekiel acquired many of his slaves through marriage (United States, Third Census, 1810).

62. Will of Gen. Andrew Pickens, June 2, 1809, Probate Judge Estate Papers, Anderson County, Roll #547, SCDAH.

63. Johnson and Roark, *Black Masters*, 31–33; Berlin, *Many Thousands Gone*, 319–21.

64. Pickens to Col. Andrew Pickens Jr., Dec. 2, 1812, folder 8, APPSCL. Pickens and his fellow electors unanimously voted to reelect James Madison for president and supported Elbridge Gerry for vice president (ibid.)

65. Obituary of Andrew Pickens, *Niles' Register*, Sept. 27, 1817.

66. *S.C. House Journal*, Dec. 10, 11, 14, 1812, 109, 127, 142–43 (quote on 142).

67. D. Wallace, *History of South Carolina*, 2:390–91.

68. *S.C. House Journal*, Nov. 24, Dec. 2, 3, 10, 11, 14, 18, 1813, 15, 61, 67–68, 95–96, 107, 122–23, 166; *S.C. Statutes*, 8:523–24.

69. *S.C. House Journal*, Dec. 16, 1813, 140–41.

70. Ibid., Dec. 11, 12, 1812, 124–27, 133–34.

71. Ibid., Dec. 7, 19, 1812, 92, 224. Pickens's work in the legislative sessions of 1812 and 1813 is also summarized in Ferguson, "General Andrew Pickens," 658–65.

72. Obituary of Andrew Pickens, *Niles' Register*, Sept. 27, 1817.

EPILOGUE

1. Obituary of Andrew Pickens, *Niles' Register*, Sept. 27, 1817; Journal of William Ancrum, July 11, 1810, Ancrum Papers, SCL; A. Pickens, *Skyagunsta*, 158; Waring, *Fighting Elder*, 202.

2. Waring, *Fighting Elder*, 203, 207–8 (quote on 208); for a fuller, though idealized, description of Becky, see Ellet, *Women of the American Revolution*, 303–9.

3. Mills, "The Old Stone Church," folder 4, box 4, Mills Collection, Clemson University Library, Clemson, S.C.

4. Obituary of Andrew Pickens, *Niles' Register*, Sept. 27, 1817.

5. Ferguson, "General Andrew Pickens," uses the term "red men" often.

6. Nichols, *Red Gentlemen* (quote on 45); Henri, *Benjamin Hawkins*; Dennis, "American Revolutionaries"; A. Wallace, *Jefferson and the Indians*; Hatley, *Dividing Paths*, 231.

Bibliography

MANUSCRIPT COLLECTIONS

Charleston Library Society, Charleston, S.C.
    John Lewis Gervais Letters
    Andrew Pickens Papers
    Charles Cotesworth Pinckney Papers
    John Rutledge Letters
    Arnoldus Vanderhorst Papers
Clemson University Library, Clemson, S.C.
    Lyman C. Draper Collection. Microfilm.
    William Hayne Mills Collection
    Mills, William Hayne. "The Life of General Andrew Pickens." Bound manuscript.
    Andrew Pickens Papers
Columbia Theological Seminary, Decatur, Ga.
    John B. Davis, Transcription of Minutes of the Presbytery of South Carolina, 1785–1799
    Minutes of the Presbytery of South Carolina, 1811–1814
    Minutes of the Second Presbytery of South Carolina, 1800–1810
Huntington Library, San Marino, Calif.
    Andrew Pickens Papers
Library of Congress, Washington, D.C.
    Charles Cornwallis Papers
South Carolina Department of Archives and History, Columbia, S.C.
    John Bowie Papers
South Caroliniana Library, University of South Carolina, Columbia
    William Ancrum Papers
    Nisbet Balfour Letters
    Pierce Butler Papers
    John Ewing Colhoun Papers
    Andrew Pickens Papers
    Andrew Williamson Militia Reports

NEWSPAPERS AND MAGAZINES

Anderson Independent (Anderson, S.C.). South Caroliniana Library, University of South Carolina, Columbia.

Miller's Weekly Messenger (Pendleton, S.C.). South Caroliniana Library, University of South Carolina, Columbia.

South Carolina and American General Gazette (Charleston, S.C.). South Caroliniana Library, University of South Carolina, Columbia.

South Carolina Gazette (Charleston, S.C.). South Caroliniana Library, University of South Carolina, Columbia.

PUBLISHED LETTERS AND MEMOIRS

Barnwell, Joseph W., ed. "Letters of John Rutledge." *South Carolina Historical and Genealogical Magazine* 17, no. 4 (October 1916): 131–46.

Brown, Tarleton. *Memoirs of Tarleton Brown, a Captain in the Revolutionary Army.* Barnwell, S.C.: People's Press, 1894.

Campbell, Archibald. *Journal of an Expedition against the Rebels of Georgia in North America under the Orders of Archibald Campbell Esquire Lieut. Col. of His Majesty's 71st Regiment.* 1778. South Caroliniana Library, University of South Carolina, Columbia.

Conrad, Dennis L., ed. *The Papers of General Nathanael Greene.* 13 vols. Chapel Hill: University of North Carolina Press, 1991–2002.

Drayton, John. *Memoirs of the American Revolution.* 2 vols. Charleston, S.C.: E. A. Miller, 1821.

Fitzpatrick, John C., ed. *The Writings of George Washington from the Original Manuscript Sources, 1745–1799.* 39 vols. Washington, D.C.: Government Printing Office, 1931–44.

Ford, Worthington C., ed. *The Writings of George Washington.* 14 vols. New York: G. P. Putnam's Sons, 1891.

Foster, Thomas, ed. *The Collected Works of Benjamin Hawkins, 1796–1810.* Tuscaloosa: University of Alabama Press, 2003.

Fry, Rose W., ed. "Recollections of John McElhenney." Richmond, 1893.

Garden, Alexander. *Anecdotes of the Revolutionary War in America, with Sketches of Character of Persons the Most Distinguished, in the Southern States, for Civil and Military Services.* Charleston, 1822. Spartanburg, S.C.: Reprint Company, 1972.

Gervais, John Lewis. "Letters of John Lewis Gervais to Henry Laurens, 1777–1778." Edited by Raymond Starr. *South Carolina Historical Magazine* 66, no. 1 (January 1965): 15–37.

Gibbes, R. W. *Documentary History of the American Revolution.* 3 vols. Spartanburg, S.C.: Reprint Company, 1972. Originally published as *Documentary History of the American Revolution, Consisting of Letters and Papers Relating to the Contest for Liberty, Chiefly in South Carolina.* New York: D. Appleton and Company, 1853–57.

Grant, C. L., ed. *Letters, Journals, and Writings of Benjamin Hawkins.* 2 vols. Savannah: Beehive Press, 1980.

Hill, William. *Colonel William Hill's Memoirs of the Revolution.* Edited by A. S. Salley. Columbia: University of South Carolina Press, 1921.

Hoyt, William Henry, ed. *The Papers of Archibald D. Murphey.* 2 vols. Raleigh, N.C., 1911.

Jackson, Donald, and Dorothy Twohig, eds. *The Diaries of George Washington.* 6 vols. Charlottesville: University of Virginia Press, 1976.

Jameson, J. Franklin, ed. "Diary of Edward Hooker, 1805–1808." *American Historical Association Annual Report*, 1896. Washington, D.C., 1897.

Johnson, Joseph. *Traditions and Reminiscences, Chiefly of the American Revolution in the South*. N.p., 1851. Spartanburg, S.C.: Reprint Company, 1972.

Jones, Newton B., ed. "Writings of the Reverend William Tennent, 1740–1777." *South Carolina Historical Magazine* 61, no. 3 (July 1960): 129–45.

Kelby, William, ed. *Orderly Book, 1776–1778, of the Three Battalions of Loyalists Commanded by Brigadier General Oliver DeLancey. List of New York Loyalists, 1775–1783*. New York, 1917. Published as an e-book and found at http://www.ebooksread.com/authors-eng/de-lanceys-brigade-loyalist-1776-1778/orderly-book-of-the-three-battalions-of-loyalists-commanded-by-brigadier-genera-hci/page-7-orderly-book-of-the-three-battalions-of-loyalists-commanded-by-brigadier-genera-hci.shtml, accessed June 6, 2012.

Lee, Henry. *Memoirs of the War in the Southern Department of the United States*. New York, 1869.

Moultrie, William. *Memoirs of the American Revolution, So Far as It Relates to the States of North and South Carolina, and Georgia*. 2 vols. New York, 1802.

Pickens, Elizabeth B. Monroe-Pickens Scrapbook. Pendleton District Commission, Pendleton, S.C.

"Preston Papers, Relating to Western Virginia." *Virginia Magazine of History and Biography* 27, no. 3/4 (1919): 309–25.

Reese, Thomas W. "An Essay on the Influence of Religion in Civil Society." Charleston, S.C., 1788. South Caroliniana Library, University of South Carolina, Columbia.

———. "Memoir of the Late Rev'd. Thomas Reese, D.D., of South Carolina." *Southern Presbyterian Review* (July 1852): 116–20.

Saberton, Ian, ed. *The Cornwallis Papers: The Campaigns of 1780 and 1781 in the Southern Theatre of the American Revolutionary War*. 4 parts. East Sussex, U.K.: Naval and Military Press, 2010.

Skelton, Lynda Worley, ed. *General Andrew Pickens: An Autobiography*. Clemson, S.C.: Pendleton District Historical and Recreational Commission and Andrew Pickens Chapter, Daughters of the American Revolution, 1976.

Sparks, Jared, ed., *Correspondence of the American Revolution; Being Letters of Eminent Men to George Washington*. 4 vols. 1853. Freeport, N.Y.: Books for Libraries Press, 1970.

Tarleton, Lieutenant General Banastre. *A History of the Campaigns of 1780 and 1781; in the Southern Provinces of North America*. Dublin, 1787.

Tennent, William. "Fragment of a Journal Kept by the Rev. William Tennent Describing his Journey, in 1775 to Upper South Carolina." *Year Book City of Charleston*, 1894. South Caroliniana Library, University of South Carolina, Columbia.

Wagstaff, H. M., ed. *Publications of the North Carolina Historical Commission: The Papers of John Steele*. 2 vols. Raleigh: Edwards and Broughton, 1924.

Wilkinson, James. *Memoirs of My Own Times*. Vol. 2. Philadelphia, 1816.

GOVERNMENT DOCUMENTS

Federal Records

American State Papers. Indian Affairs. Vols. 1–2. Washington, D.C.: Gales and Seaton, 1832, 1834.

American State Papers. Public Lands. Vol. 1. Washington, D.C.: Gales and Seaton, 1834.

Debates and Proceedings in the Congress of the United States, 1789–1824. Washington, D.C.: Gales and Seaton, 1855.

Indian Affairs: Laws and Treaties. Vol. 2. Edited by Charles J. Kappler. Washington, D.C.: Government Printing Office, 1904.

Journal of the House of Representatives of the United States.

Journals of the Continental Congress, 1774–1789. 33 vols. Washington, D.C.: Government Printing Office, 1904–1937.

Papers of the Continental Congress. 1776–1788. Record Group 360. Microfilm. National Archives. Washington, D.C., and Atlanta, Ga.

Statutes at Large of the United States. Vol. 1. Washington, D.C., 1845.

The Territorial Papers of the United States. Vol. 4, *The Territory South of the River Ohio, 1790–1796*. Edited by Clarence Edward Carter. Washington, D.C.: Government Printing Office, 1936.

United States. Bureau of the Census. First Census of the United States (1790).

———. Second Census of the United States (1800).

———. Third Census of the United States (1810).

North Carolina State, Colonial, and County Records

Anson County, North Carolina, Abstracts of Early Records. Edited by May Wilson McBee. Greenwood, Miss., 1950.

Anson County Record of Deeds. Vol. 5. State Archives of North Carolina, Raleigh, N.C.

Anson County Record of Wills, 1751–1779. State Archives of North Carolina, Raleigh, N.C.

Colonial Records of North Carolina. Edited by William L. Saunders. 10 vols. Raleigh, 1886–90.

Colony of North Carolina, 1753–1764: Abstracts of Land Patents. 2 vols. Edited by Margaret M. Hofmann. Weldon, N.C.: Roanoke News Co., 1982.

Land Grants. Anson County. State Archives of North Carolina, Raleigh, N.C.

North Carolina Original Wills, 1763–1790. State Archives of North Carolina, Raleigh, N.C.

State Records of North Carolina. Edited by Walter Clark. Vols. 11–25 (continuation of *Colonial Records of North Carolina*). Raleigh, 1896–1907.

South Carolina State, Colonial, District, and County Records

Abstracts of General Sessions Court Rolls: Washington District, South Carolina, 1792–1799; Greenville County, South Carolina, 1787–1799. Edited by Anne K. McCuen, Jane E. Kirkman, and Penelope Forrester. Greenville: Greenville County Historic Preservation Commission, 1994.

Colonial Plat Books. South Carolina Department of Archives and History, Columbia, S.C.

Conveyance Books. South Carolina Department of Archives and History, Columbia, S.C.

County Wills. Anderson County. South Carolina Department of Archives and History, Columbia, S.C.

Extracts from the Journals of the Provincial Congresses of South Carolina, 1775–1776. Edited by William E. Hemphill and Wylma A. Wates. Columbia, S.C.: Department of Archives and History, 1960.

General Assembly. *Committee Reports*. South Carolina Department of Archives and History, Columbia, S.C.

Governor's Messages. South Carolina Department of Archives and History, Columbia, S.C.

Index of Land Grants. South Carolina Department of Archives and History, Columbia, S.C.

Inventories of Estates. South Carolina Department of Archives and History, Columbia, S.C.

Journal of the Convention of South Carolina Which Ratified the Constitution of the United States, May 23, 1788. South Carolina Department of Archives and History, Columbia, S.C.

Journal of the House of Representatives of the State of South Carolina. South Carolina Department of Archives and History, Columbia, S.C. (Journals for 1783–94 are printed. Edited by Theodora Thompson et al. Columbia: University of South Carolina Press, 1977.)

Journal of the Senate of the State of South Carolina. South Carolina Department of Archives and History, Columbia, S.C.

Journals of the General Assembly and House of Representatives, 1776–1780. Edited by William Edward Hemphill, Wylma Anne Wates, and R. Nicholas Goldberg. Columbia: University of South Carolina Press, 1970.

Journals of the Privy Council, 1783–1789. Edited by Adele Edwards Stanton. Columbia: University of South Carolina Press, 1971.

Judgment Rolls. South Carolina Department of Archives and History, Columbia, S.C.

Land Grants. South Carolina Department of Archives and History, Columbia, S.C.

Mortgages. South Carolina Department of Archives and History, Columbia, S.C.

Ninety-Six District, South Carolina: Journal of the Court of Ordinary, 1781–1786. Edited by Brent Holcomb. Easley, S.C.: Southern Historical Press, 1978.

Pendleton District and Anderson County, S.C. Wills, Estates, Inventories, Tax Returns and Census Records. Compiled by Virginia Alexander, Colleen Morse Elliott, and Betty Willie. Easley, S.C.: Southern Historical Press, 1980.

Pendleton District, S.C. Deeds, 1790–1806. Compiled by Betty Willie. Easley, S.C.: Southern Historical Press, 1980.

Petitions. South Carolina Department of Archives and History, Columbia, S.C.

Plats. South Carolina Department of Archives and History, Columbia, S.C.

Probate Judge Estate Papers. Anderson County. South Carolina Department of Archives and History, Columbia, S.C.

The Statutes at Large of South Carolina. Edited by Thomas Cooper and David J. McCord. Columbia: 10 vols. A. S. Johnston, 1836–41.

SECONDARY SOURCES

Ackerman, Robert K. *South Carolina Colonial Land Policies.* Columbia: University of South Carolina Press, 1977.

Anderson, John Logan. "The Presbyterians and Augusta Parish, 1738–1757: A Political and Social Analysis." M.A. thesis, University of Virginia, 1985.

Andrews, Columbus. *Administrative Court Government in South Carolina.* Chapel Hill: University of North Carolina Press, 1933.

Appleby, Joyce. *Capitalism and a New Social Order: The Republican Vision of the 1790s.* New York: New York University Press, 1984.

———. *Inheriting the Revolution: The First Generation of Americans.* Cambridge, Mass.: Harvard University Press, 2000.

Aron, Stephen. *How the West Was Lost: The Transformation of Kentucky from Daniel Boone to Henry Clay*. Baltimore: Johns Hopkins University Press, 1996.

Babits, Lawrence E. *"A Devil of a Whipping": The Battle of Cowpens*. Chapel Hill: University of North Carolina Press, 1998.

Bacot, D. Huger. "The South Carolina Up Country at the End of the Eighteenth Century." *American Historical Review* 28 (1922–23): 693–98.

Bailyn, Bernard. *The Ideological Origins of the American Revolution*. Cambridge, Mass.: Harvard University Press, 1967.

Balmer, Randall, and John R. Fitzmer, *The Presbyterians*. Westport, Conn.: Greenwood Press, 1993.

Banning, Lance. *The Sacred Fire of Liberty: James Madison and the Founding of the Federal Republic*. Ithaca: Cornell University Press, 1995.

Banning, Lance, Todd Estes, and Gordon S. Wood. *Founding Visions: The Ideals, Individuals, and Intersections That Created America*. Lexington: University Press of Kentucky, 2014.

Barnes, Timothy, and Robert M. Calhoon. "Moral Allegiance: John Witherspoon and Loyalist Recantation." *Journal of Presbyterian History* 63 (Fall 1985): 273–83.

Barnwell, Robert W., Jr. "Loyalism in South Carolina, 1765–1785." Ph.D. diss., Duke University, 1941.

Bass, Robert D. *Gamecock: The Life and Campaigns of General Thomas Sumter*. New York: Holt, Rinehart, and Winston, 1961.

———. *Ninety Six: The Struggle for the South Carolina Back Country*. Lexington, S.C.: Sandlapper Store, 1978.

———. *Swamp Fox: The Life and Campaigns of General Francis Marion*. Columbia: Sandlapper Press, 1959.

Beeman, Richard R. *The Evolution of the Southern Backcountry: A Case Study of Lunenburg County, Virginia, 1746–1832*. Philadelphia: University of Pennsylvania Press, 1984.

Berlin, Ira. *Many Thousands Gone: The First Two Centuries of Slavery in North America*. Cambridge, Mass.: Harvard University Press, 1998.

"Biographical Sketch of the Career of Major William Cunningham." *Southern and Western Literary Messenger and Review* 12 (September 1846): 513–24; 12 (October 1846): 577–85.

Bloch, Ruth H. *Gender and Morality in Anglo-American Culture, 1650–1800*. Berkeley: University of California Press, 2003.

———. *Visionary Republic: Millennial Themes in American Thought, 1756–1800*. Cambridge: Cambridge University Press, 1985.

Boulware, Tyler. *Deconstructing the Cherokee Nation: Town, Region, and Nation among Eighteenth-Century Cherokees*. Gainesville: University Press of Florida, 2011.

Brackett, Richard N. *The Old Stone Church*. Columbia, S.C.: R. L. Bryan Co., 1905.

Brannon, Rebecca Nathan. "Reconciling the Revolution: Resolving Conflict and Rebuilding Community in the Wake of Civil War in South Carolina, 1775–1860." Ph.D. diss., University of Michigan, 2007.

Braund, Kathryn E. Holland. *Deerskins and Duffels: The Creek Indian Trade with Anglo-America, 1685–1815*. 2nd ed. Lincoln: University of Nebraska Press, 2008.

Bridwell, Ronald. "The South's Wealthiest Planter: Wade Hampton I of South Carolina, 1754–183." Ph.D. diss., University of South Carolina, 1980.

Brown, Richard M. *The South Carolina Regulators*. Cambridge, Mass.: Harvard University Press, 1963.

Brown, Richard M., and Don E. Fehrenbacker, eds. *Tradition, Conflict, and Modernization: Perspectives on the American Revolution*. New York: Academic Press, 1977.

Brown, Wallace. *The King's Friends: The Composition and Motives of the American Loyalist Claimants*. Providence, R.I.: Brown University Press, 1965.

Buchanan, John. "'We Must Endeavor to Keep Up a Partizan War': Nathanael Greene and the Partisans." In *General Nathanael Greene and the American Revolution in the South*, edited by Gregory D. Massey and Jim Piecuch, 119–46. Columbia: University of South Carolina Press, 2012.

Bullock, Steven C. *Revolutionary Brotherhood: Freemasonry and the Transformation of the American Social Order, 1730–1840*. Chapel Hill: University of North Carolina Press, 1996.

Burton, Orville Vernon. *In My Father's House Are Many Mansions: Family and Community in Edgefield, South Carolina*. Chapel Hill: University of North Carolina Press, 1985.

Bushman, Richard L. *From Puritan to Yankee: Character and the Social Order in Connecticut, 1690–1765*. Cambridge, Mass.: Harvard University Press, 1967.

———. *The Refinement of America: Persons, Houses, Cities*. New York: Knopf, 1992.

Calhoon, Robert M. "The Evangelical Persuasion." In *Religion in a Revolutionary Age*, edited by Ronald Hoffman and Peter J. Albert, 156–83. Charlottesville: University Press of Virginia, 1994.

———. *Evangelicals and Conservatives in the Early South, 1740–1861*. Columbia: University of South Carolina Press, 1988.

Calloway, Colin. *The American Revolution in Indian Country: Crisis and Diversity in Native American Communities*. New York: Cambridge, 1995.

Carbone, Gerald M. *Nathanael Greene: A Biography of the American Revolution*. New York: Palgrave Macmillan, 2008.

Cashin, Edward J. *The King's Ranger: Thomas Brown and American Revolution on the Southern Frontier*. Athens: University of Georgia Press, 1989.

Caughey, John Walton. *McGillivray of the Creeks*. Columbia: University of South Carolina Press, 2007.

Cayton, Andrew R. L. *The Frontier Republic: Ideology and Politics in the Ohio Country, 1780–1825*. Kent: Kent State University Press, 1986.

———. "'When Shall We Cease to Have Judases?' The Blount Conspiracy and the Limits of the 'Extended Republic.'" In *Launching the "Extended Republic": The Federalist Era*, edited by Ronald Hoffman and Peter J. Albert, 156–89 Charlottesville: University of Virginia Press, 1996.

Cayton, Andrew R. L., and Fredrika J. Teute, eds. *Contact Points: American Frontiers from the Mohawk Valley to the Mississippi, 1750–1830*. Chapel Hill: University of North Carolina Press, 1998.

Charlton, Thomas U. P. *The Life of Major General James Jackson*. Augusta, Ga.: George R. Randolph, 1809.

Clark, Daniel. *Proofs of the Corruption of Gen. James Wilkinson*. 1809. New York: Arno Press, 1970.

Clarke, Erskine. *Our Southern Zion: A History of Calvinism in the South Carolina Low Country, 1690–1990*. Tuscaloosa: University of Alabama Press, 1996.

———. *Wrestlin' Jacob: A Portrait of Religion in the Old South.* Atlanta: John Knox Press, 1979.

Clayton, Frederick Van. *Settlement of Pendleton District, 1777–1800.* Easley, S.C.: Southern Historical Press, 1930.

Clower, George Wesley. "Notes on the Calhoun-Noble-Davis and Thomas Family." *South Carolina Historical Magazine* 53, no. 1 (January 1952): 51–53.

Coker, Kathy Roe. "The Punishment of Revolutionary War Loyalists in South Carolina." Ph.D. diss., University of South Carolina, 1987.

Cole, David. "A Brief Outline of the South Carolina Colonial Militia System." *Proceedings of the South Carolina Historical Association* (1954): 14–23.

Coleman, Kenneth, ed. *A History of Georgia.* Athens: University of Georgia Press, 1977.

Conrad, Dennis M. "General Nathanael Greene: An Appraisal." In *General Nathanael Greene and the American Revolution in the South,* edited by Gregory D. Massey and Jim Piecuch, 7–28. Columbia: University of South Carolina Press, 2012.

"Contributions to the Ecclesiastical History of Abbeville District, S.C." *Southern Presbyterian Review* 15 (July 1862): 78–93.

Cooper, Thomas, ed. *Statutes at Large of the State of South Carolina.* 10 vols. Columbia, S.C.: A. S. Johnston, 1836–1841.

Crass, David Colin, Steven D. Smith, Martha A. Zierden, and Richard D. Brooks, eds. *The Southern Colonial Backcountry: Interdisciplinary Perspectives on Frontier Communities.* Knoxville: University of Tennessee Press, 1998.

Cumfer, Cynthia. *Separate Peoples, One Land: The Minds of Cherokees, Blacks, and Whites on the Tennessee Frontier.* Chapel Hill: University of North Carolina Press, 2007.

Davis, Robert S., Jr., and Kenneth H. Thomas Jr. *Kettle Creek: The Battle of the Cane Brakes.* Atlanta: Georgia Department of Natural Resources, 1974.

Dawson, Henry B. *Battles of the United States by Sea and Land.* New York, 1858.

Day, Kate Pickens. *Cousin Monroe's History of the Pickens Family.* Greenville, S.C.: Hiott Press, 1951.

Dennis, Jeff. "Native Americans and the Southern Revolution, Part II." *Southern Campaigns of the American Revolution* 4, no. 3 (2007): 21–27.

———. "Southern Campaigns against the Cherokees: A Brief Compilation." *Southern Campaigns of the American Revolution* 2, no. 10 (2005): 17–22.

Dennis, William Jeffrey. "American Revolutionaries and Native Americans: The South Carolina Experience." Ph.D. diss., University of Notre Dame, 2002.

Deschamps, Margaret B. "Antislavery Presbyterians in the Carolina Piedmont." *Proceedings of the South Carolina Historical Association* (1954): 6–13.

Diggins, John P., and Mark E. Kann. *The Problem of Authority in America.* Philadelphia: Temple University Press, 1981.

Dornfest, Walter T. *Military Loyalists of the American Revolution: Officers and Regiments, 1775–1783.* Jefferson, N.C.: McFarland, 2011.

Dowd, Gregory Evans. "The Spinning Wheel Revolution." In *The Revolution of 1800: Democracy, Race, and the New Republic,* edited by James Horn, Jan Ellen Lewis, and Peter S. Onuf, 267–87. Charlottesville: University of Virginia Press, 2002.

———. *A Spirited Resistance: The North American Indian Struggle for Unity, 1745–1815.* Baltimore: Johns Hopkins University Press, 1992.

Downes, Randolph C. "Creek-American Relations, 1782–1790." *Georgia Historical Quarterly* 21, no. 2 (June 1937): 142–84.

Draper, Lyman. *King's Mountain and Its Heroes.* Cincinnati, 1887.

Edgar, Walter. *Partisans and Redcoats: The Southern Conflict That Turned the Tide of the American Revolution.* New York: HarperCollins, 2001.

———. *South Carolina: A History.* Columbia: University of South Carolina Press, 1998.

Egerton, Douglas R. *Death or Liberty: African Americans and Revolutionary America.* New York: Oxford University Press, 2009.

Ellet, Elizabeth. *Women of the American Revolution.* 3 vols. New York: Charles Scribner, 1861.

Ethridge, Robbie. *Creek Country: The Creek Indians and Their World.* Chapel Hill: University of North Carolina Press, 2003.

Farley, M. Foster. "The South Carolina Negro in the American Revolution, 1775–1783." *South Carolina Historical Magazine* 79, no.2 (April 1978), 75–86.

Farmer, James O. "Southern Presbyterians and Southern Nationalism: A Study in Ambivalence." *Georgia Historical Quarterly* 75, no.2 (Summer 1991): 275–94.

Farr, Jason. "An Errand into the Backcountry: The Denominational Diplomacy of William Tennent and Oliver Hart's Mission to the South Carolina Backcountry, 1775." M.A. thesis, College of Charleston, 2007.

Ferguson, Clyde R. "Carolina and Georgia Patriot and Loyalist Militia in Action, 1778–1783." In *The Southern Experience in the American Revolution,* edited by Jeffrey J. Crow and Larry E. Tise, 174–99. Chapel Hill: University of North Carolina Press, 1978.

———. "Functions of the Partisan-Militia in the South during the American Revolution: An Interpretation." In *The Revolutionary War in the South: Power, Conflict, and Leadership,* edited by W. Robert Higgins, 239–58. Durham: Duke University Press, 1979.

———. "General Andrew Pickens." Ph.D. diss., Duke University, 1960.

Fischer, David Hackett. *Albion's Seed: Four British Folkways in America.* New York: Oxford University Press, 1989.

Foote, William Henry. *Sketches of North Carolina: Historical and Biographical.* New York, 1846.

Ford, Lacy. *Deliver Us from Evil: The Slavery Question in the Old South.* New York: Oxford University Press, 2009.

———. *Origins of Southern Radicalism: The South Carolina Upcountry, 1800–1860.* New York: Oxford University Press, 1988.

Freeman, Joanne B. *Affairs of Honor: National Politics in the New Republic.* New Haven: Yale University Press, 2001.

Friend, Craig Thompson. "Frontier and Plantation: Pendleton, South Carolina, 1780–1930." M.A. thesis, Clemson University, 1990.

Gallay, Alan. *The Formation of a Planter Elite: Jonathan Bryan and the Southern Colonial Frontier.* Athens: University of Georgia Press, 1989.

———. *The Indian Slave Trade.* New Haven: Yale University Press, 2003.

Gardiner, Richard. "The Presbyterian Rebellion: An Analysis of the Perception that the American Revolution Was a Presbyterian War." Ph.D. diss., Marquette University, 2005.

Golway, Terry. *Washington's General: Nathanael Greene and the Triumph of the American Revolution.* New York: Henry Holt, 2005.

Gordon, John W. "Age-of-Sail Expeditionary Warfare Takes On the 'COIN' Mission: The British Pacification Campaign in South Carolina, 1780–1782." Naval History Symposium, Annapolis, Md., September 2007.

———. *South Carolina and the American Revolution: A Battlefield History.* Columbia: University of South Carolina Press, 2003.

Graham, James. *The Life of General Daniel Morgan.* New York, 1856.

Green, Thomas Marshall. *The Spanish Conspiracy.* 1891. Gloucester, Mass.: Peter Smith, 1967.

Greenberg, Kenneth S. *Honor and Slavery.* Princeton, N.J.: Princeton University Press, 1996.

Greene, Jack P. "'*Virtus et Libertas*': Political Culture, Social Change, and the Origins of the American Revolution in Virginia." In *The Southern Experience in the American Revolution,* edited by Jeffrey J. Crow and Larry E. Tise, 55–108. Chapel Hill: University of North Carolina Press, 1978.

Gregorie, Anne King. *Thomas Sumter.* Columbia: University of South Carolina Press, 1931.

Grenier, John. *The First Way of War: American War Making on the Frontier, 1607–1814.* New York: Cambridge University Press, 2005.

Griffin, Patrick. *American Leviathan: Empire, Nation, and Revolutionary Frontier.* New York: Hill and Wang, 2007.

Hatch, Nathan O. *The Sacred Cause of Liberty: Republican Thought and the Millennium in Revolutionary New England.* New Haven: Yale University Press, 1977.

Hatley, M. Thomas. *The Dividing Paths: Cherokees and South Carolinians through the Era of Revolution.* New York: Oxford, 1993.

———. "The Three Lives of Keowee: Loss and Recovery in Eighteenth-Century Cherokee Villages." In *Powhatan's Mantle: Indians in the Colonial Southeast,* edited by Gregory A. Waselkov, Peter H. Wood, and Tom Hatley, 241–60. Lincoln: University of Nebraska Press, 1989.

Henri, Florette. *The Southern Indians and Benjamin Hawkins, 1796–1816.* Norman: University of Oklahoma Press, 1986.

Heyrman, Christine Leigh. *Southern Cross.* New York: Knopf, 1986.

Higginbotham, Don. *The War of American Independence: Military Attitudes, Policies, and Practice, 1763–1789.* New York: Macmillan, 1971.

Hoffman, Ronald, and Peter J. Albert, eds. *Women in the Age of the American Revolution.* Charlottesville: University Press of Virginia, 1989.

Hoffman, Ronald, Thad W. Tate, and Peter J. Albert, eds. *An Uncivil War: The Southern Backcountry during the American Revolution.* Charlottesville: University Press of Virginia, 1985.

Holton, Woody. *Forced Founders: Indians, Debtors, Slaves, and the Making of the American Revolution in Virginia.* Chapel Hill: University of North Carolina Press, 1999.

Hooker, Richard J., ed. *The Carolina Back Country on the Eve of the Revolution: The Journal and Other Writings of Charles Woodmason.* Chapel Hill: University of North Carolina Press, 1953.

Horsman, Reginald. *The Diplomacy of the New Republic, 1776–1815.* Arlington Heights, Ill.: Harlan Davidson, 1985.

———. *Expansion and American Indian Policy, 1783–1812.* East Lansing: Michigan State University Press, 1967.

Howe, George. "The Early Presbyterian Immigration into South Carolina." Address delivered to the General Assembly in New Orleans, May 7, 1858.

———. *History of the Presbyterian Church in South Carolina*. 2 vols. Columbia, S.C.: Duffie and Chapman, 1870.

Hudson, Angela Pulley. *Creek Paths and Federal Roads: Indians, Settlers, and Slaves and the Making of the American South*. Chapel Hill: University of North Carolina Press, 2010.

Humphrey, Edward Frank. *Nationalism and Religion in America, 1774–1789*. New York: Russell & Russell, 1965.

Irons, Charles F. *The Origins of Proslavery Christianity: White and Black Evangelicals in Colonial and Antebellum Virginia*. Chapel Hill: University of North Carolina Press, 2008.

Isaac, Rhys. *The Transformation of Virginia, 1740–1790*. Chapel Hill: University of North Carolina Press, 1989.

Jackson, Harvey H. *Lachlan McIntosh and the Politics of Revolutionary Georgia*. Athens: University of Georgia Press, 1979.

Jacobs, James Ripley. *Tarnished Warrior: Major-General James Wilkinson*. New York: Macmillan, 1938.

Jennings, Matthew. *New Worlds of Violence: Cultures and Conquests in the Early American Southeast*. Knoxville: University of Tennessee Press, 2011.

Jensen, Merrill. *The New Nation: A History of the United States during the Confederation, 1781–1789*. New York: Vintage Books, 1950.

Johnson, Michael P., and James L. Roark. *Black Masters: A Free Family of Color in the Old South*. New York: Norton, 1984.

Jones, Lewis Pinckney. *The South Carolina Civil War of 1775*. Lexington, S.C.: Sandlapper Store, 1975.

Josephy, Alvin M., Jr. *The Indian Heritage of America*. Boston: Houghton Mifflin, 1968.

Kann, Mark E. *A Republic of Men: The American Founders, Gendered Language, and Patriarchal Politics*. New York: New York University Press, 1998.

Kelly, Douglas F. *The Emergence of Liberty in the Modern World: The Influence of Calvin on Five Governments from the 16th through 18th Centuries*. Phillipsburg, N.J.: P & R Publishing, 1992.

Kerber, Linda K. *Women of the Republic: Intellect and Ideology in Revolutionary America*. Chapel Hill: University of North Carolina Press, 1980.

Kettner, James H. *The Development of American Citizenship, 1608–1870*. Chapel Hill: University of North Carolina Press, 1978.

Kidd, Thomas S. *God of Liberty: A Religious History of the American Revolution*. New York: Basic Books, 2010.

Klein, Rachel N. "Frontier Planters and the American Revolution: The South Carolina Backcountry, 1775–1782." In *An Uncivil War: The Southern Backcountry during the American Revolution*, edited by Ronald Hoffman, Thad W. Tate, and Peter J. Albert, 37–69. Charlottesville: University Press of Virginia, 1985.

———. *Unification of a Slave State: The Rise of the Planter Class in the South Carolina Backcountry, 1760–1808*. Chapel Hill: University of North Carolina Press, 1990.

Kloppenberg, James. "The Virtues of Liberalism: Christianity, Republicanism, and Ethics in the Early American Republic." *Journal of American History* 74, no. 1 (June 1987): 9–33.

Kowalski, Gary. *Revolutionary Spirits: The Enlightened Faith of America's Founding Fathers.* New York: Bluebridge, 2008.

Kramer, Leonard J. "Muskets in the Pulpit: 1776–1783. Part I." *Journal of the Presbyterian Historical Society* 31 (December 1953): 229–54.

———. "Muskets in the Pulpit: 1776–1783, Part II." *Journal of the Presbyterian Historical Society* 32 (March 1954): 37–51.

Krawczynski, Keith. *William Henry Drayton: South Carolina Revolutionary Patriot.* Baton Rouge: Louisiana State University Press, 2001.

Lambert, Robert S. *South Carolina Loyalists in the American Revolution.* Columbia: University of South Carolina Press, 1987.

Lamplugh, George R. *Politics on the Periphery: Factions and Parties in Georgia, 1783–1806.* Newark: University of Delaware Press, 1986.

Landrum, J. B. O. *Colonial and Revolutionary History of Upper South Carolina.* Greenville, S.C., 1897.

Leach, Douglas Edward. *Roots of Conflict: British Armed Forces and Colonial Americans, 1677–1763.* Chapel Hill: University of North Carolina Press, 1986.

Lee, Wayne E. *Crowds and Soldiers in Revolutionary North Carolina: The Culture of Violence in Riot and War.* Gainesville: University Press of Florida, 2001.

Leyburn, James G. "Presbyterian Immigrants and the American Revolution." *Journal of Presbyterian History* 54, no. 1 (Spring 1976): 9–32.

———. *The Scotch-Irish: A Social History.* Chapel Hill: University of North Carolina Press, 1962.

Link, Eugene P. *Democratic-Republican Societies, 1790–1800.* New York: Octagon Books, 1965.

Linklater, Andro. *An Artist in Treason: The Extraordinary Double Life of General James Wilkinson.* New York: Walker, 2009.

Logan, John H. *History of the Upper Country of South Carolina.* Vol. 1. Charleston, 1859.

Lumpkin, Henry. *From Savannah to Yorktown: The American Revolution in the South.* Columbia: University of South Carolina Press, 1981.

Maass, John R. "'With Humanity, Justice, and Moderation': Nathanael Greene and the Reconciliation of the Disaffected in the South, 1780–1783." In *General Nathanael Greene and the American Revolution in the South,* edited by Gregory D. Massey and Jim Piecuch, 191–213. Columbia: University of South Carolina Press, 2012.

Maddex, Jack P. "From Theocracy to Spirituality: The Southern Presbyterian Reversal on Church and State." *Journal of Presbyterian History* 56 (Winter 1976): 438–57.

———. "Proslavery Millennialism: Social Eschatology in Antebellum Southern Calvinism." *American Quarterly* 31 (1979): 48–52.

Manget, Luke. "Backcountry Loyalty: How a Forged Letter Turned the Tide of the American Revolution in the South." *Tuckasegee Valley Historical Review* 18 (Spring 2012): 78–101.

Marsden, George M. *The Evangelical Mind and the New School Presbyterian Experience.* New Haven: Yale University Press, 1970.

Massey, Gregory. *John Laurens and the American Revolution.* Columbia: University of South Carolina Press, 2000.

Massey, Gregory D., and Jim Piecuch, eds. *General Nathanael Greene and the American Revolution in the South*. Columbia: University of South Carolina Press, 2012.

Masterson, William H. *William Blount*. New York: Greenwood Press, 1969.

McCall, Hugh. *The History of Georgia: Containing Brief Sketches of the Most Remarkable Events Up to the Present Day (1784)*. 2 vols. 1811, 1816. Atlanta: A. B. Caldwell, 1909.

McClary, Ben Harris. "Nancy Ward: The Last Beloved Woman of the Cherokees." *Tennessee Historical Quarterly* 21 (1962): 352–64.

McCleskey, Turk. "Rich Land, Poor Prospects: Real Estate and the Formation of a Social Elite in Augusta County, Virginia, 1738–1770." *Virginia Magazine of History and Biography* 98, no. 3 (July 1990): 449–86.

McCoy, Drew R. *The Elusive Republic: Political Economy in Jeffersonian America*. Chapel Hill: University of North Carolina Press, 1980.

McCrady, Edward. *The History of South Carolina in the Revolution, 1775–1780*. New York: Macmillan, 1901.

———. *The History of South Carolina in the Revolution, 1780–1783*. New York: Macmillan, 1902.

———. *The History of South Carolina under the Royal Government, 1719–1776*. New York: Macmillan, 1899.

McDonald, Robert M. S. "Was There a Religious Revival of 1800?" In *The Revolution of 1800: Democracy, Race, and the New Republic*, edited by James Horn, Jan Ellen Lewis, and Peter S. Onuf, 173–98. Charlottesville: University of Virginia Press, 2002.

McIntyre, James R. "Nathanael Greene: Soldier-Statesman of the War of Independence in South Carolina." In *General Nathanael Greene and the American Revolution in the South*, edited by Gregory D. Massey and Jim Piecuch, 167–90. Columbia: University of South Carolina Press, 2012.

McKoy, Drew R. *The Elusive Republic: Political Economy in Jeffersonian America*. Chapel Hill: University of North Carolina Press, 1980.

McWhiney, Grady. *Cracker Culture: Celtic Ways in the Old South*. Tuscaloosa: University of Alabama Press, 1988.

Megginson, W. J. *African American Life in South Carolina's Upper Piedmont, 1780–1900*. Columbia: University of South Carolina Press, 2006.

Melton, Buckner F., Jr. *The First Impeachment: The Constitution's Framers and the Case of Senator William Blount*. Macon, Ga.: Mercer University Press, 1998.

Mercantini, Jonathan. *Who Shall Rule at Home? The Evolution of South Carolina Political Culture, 1748–1776*. Columbia: University of South Carolina Press, 2007.

Meriwether, Robert L. *The Expansion of South Carolina, 1729–1765*. Philadelphia: Porcupine Press, 1974.

Merrell, James H. *The Indians' New World: Catawbas and Their Neighbors from European Contact through the Era of Removal*. Chapel Hill: University of North Carolina Press, 1989.

Miller, John C. *The Federalist Era, 1789–1801*. New York: Harper and Brothers, 1960.

Miller, Kerby A., Arnold Schrier, Bruce D. Booking, and David N. Doyle, eds. *Irish Immigrants in the Land of Canaan: Letters and Memoirs from Colonial and Revolutionary America, 1615–1815*. New York: Oxford University Press, 2003.

Miller, Randall M., ed. "A Backcountry Loyalist Plan to Retake Georgia and the Carolinas, 1778." *South Carolina Historical Magazine* 75, no. 4 (October 1974): 207–14.

Milling, Chapman J. *Red Carolinians.* Chapel Hill: University of North Carolina Press, 1940.

Mooney, James. *Myths of the Cherokees.* St. Claire Shoals, Mich.: Scholarly Press, 1970.

Moore, Peter N. *World of Toil and Strife: Community Transformation in Backcountry South Carolina, 1750–1805.* Columbia: University of South Carolina Press, 2007.

Morgan, Edmund. *American Slavery, American Freedom: The Ordeal of Colonial Virginia.* New York: Norton, 1975.

———. *The Challenge of the American Revolution.* New York: Norton, 1976.

Morrill, Dan. *Southern Campaigns of the American Revolution.* Mount Pleasant, S.C.: Nautical and Aviation Publishing Company of America, 1993.

Morrison, Denise Pratt. *Joseph Martin and the Southern Frontier.* Danville, Va.: Womack Press, 1976.

Moseley, John M., and Robert M. Calhoon. "Nathanael Greene and Republican Ethics." In *General Nathanael Greene and the American Revolution in the South*, edited by Gregory D. Massey and Jim Piecuch, 147–66. Columbia: University of South Carolina Press, 2012.

Moss, Bobby Gilmer. *Roster of South Carolina Patriots in the American Revolution.* Baltimore: Genealogical Publishing Co., 1985.

Murphy, Daniel, and Ron Crawley. "The Real Life Exploits of an Unknown Patriot: Lt. Col. James McCall." *Southern Campaigns of the American Revolution* 3, no. 12 (2006): 19–23.

Nadelhaft, Jerome J. *The Disorders of War: The Revolution in South Carolina.* Orono: University of Maine at Orono Press, 1981.

Narrett, David E. "Geopolitics and Intrigue: James Wilkinson, the Spanish Borderlands, and Mexican Independence." *William and Mary Quarterly* 69, no. 1 (January 2012): 101–46.

Nichols, David Andrew. *Red Gentlemen and White Savages: Indians, Federalists, and the Search for Order on the American Frontier.* Charlottesville: University of Virginia Press, 2008.

Nix, Lois K., and Mary Kay Snell. *Thomas Boone Pickens: His Ancestors.* Amarillo and Wolfe City, Tex., 1989.

Nobles, Gregory H. "Breaking into the Backcountry: New Approaches to the Early American Frontier, 1750–1800." *William and Mary Quarterly* 46, no. 4 (October 1989): 641–70.

Noll, Mark A. *Christians in the American Revolution.* Washington, D.C.: Christian University Press, 1977.

Norton, Mary Beth. *Liberty's Daughters and the Revolutionary Experience of American Women, 1750–1800.* Boston: Little, Brown, 1980.

Nye, Eric. "Pounds Sterling to Dollars: Historical Conversion of Currency." http://www.uwyo.edu/numimage/currency.htm, accessed 12 March 2014.

O'Brien, Greg. "The Conqueror Meets the Unconquered: Negotiating Cultural Boundaries on the Post-Revolutionary Southern Frontier." *Journal of Southern History* 42, no. 1 (February 2001): 39–72.

O'Kelley, Patrick. *Nothing but Blood and Slaughter: The Revolutionary War in the Carolinas.* 4 vols. N.p.: Booklocker.com, Inc., 2005.

Oliphant, John. *Peace and War on the Anglo-Cherokee Frontier, 1756–63*. Baton Rouge: Louisiana State University Press, 2001.

Olson, Gary D. "Loyalists and the American Revolution: Thomas Brown and the South Carolina Backcountry, 1775–1776." *South Carolina Historical Magazine* 68, no. 4 (October 1967): 201–19.

———. "Thomas Brown, Loyalist Partisan, and the Revolutionary War in Georgia, 1777–1782 (Part I)." *Georgia Historical Quarterly* 54 (Spring 1970): 1–19.

———. "Thomas Brown, Loyalist Partisan, and the Revolutionary War in Georgia, 1777–1782 (Part II)." *Georgia Historical Quarterly* 54 (Summer 1970): 183–208.

Olwell, Robert A. *Masters, Slaves, and Subjects: The Culture of Power in the South Carolina Low Country, 1740–1790*. Ithaca, N.Y.: Cornell University Press, 1998.

Onuf, Peter S. *Jefferson's Empire: The Language of American Nationhood*. Charlottesville: University Press of Virginia, 2000.

———. "Liberty, Development, and Union: Visions of the West in the 1780s." *William and Mary Quarterly*, 3rd ser., 43 (1986): 179–213.

Owens, Robert M. *Mr. Jefferson's Hammer: William Henry Harrison and the Origins of American Indian Policy*. Norman: University of Oklahoma Press, 2007.

Pancake, John S. *This Destructive War: The British Campaign in the Carolinas, 1780–1782*. Tuscaloosa University of Alabama Press, 1982.

Perdue, Theda. *Cherokee Women: Gender and Culture Change, 1700–1835*. Lincoln: University of Nebraska Press, 1988.

———. *Slavery and the Evolution of Cherokee Society, 1540–1866*. Knoxville: University of Tennessee Press, 1979.

Phifer, Robert S "Notes on the Pickens, Calhoun, Simkins, Wilkinson, Morton, and Middleton Families." South Caroliniana Library, University of South Carolina, Columbia.

Pickens, A. L. *Skyagunsta: The Border Wizard Owl. Major General Andrew Pickens (1739–1817)*. Greenville, S.C.: Observer Printing Co., 1934.

Pickett, Albert J. *History of Alabama*. Birmingham: Webb Book Company, 1900.

Pickens, E. B. *Life of General Pickens*. New Haven, Conn.: n.p., 1924.

Piecuch, Jim. *The Blood Be upon Your Head: Tarleton and the Myth of Buford's Massacre; The Battle of the Waxhaws, May 29, 1780*. Charleson, S.C.: Southern Campaigns of the American Revolution Press, 2010.

———. *Three Peoples, One King: Loyalists, Indians, and Slaves in the Revolutionary South, 1775–1782*. Columbia: University of South Carolina Press, 2008.

———, ed. *Cavalry of the American Revolution*. Yardley, Pa.: Westholme, 2012.

Piecuch, Jim, and John H. Beakes Jr. *"Cool Deliberate Courage": John Eager Howard in the American Revolution*. Charleston, S.C.: Nautical and Aviation Publishing Company of America, 2009.

Posey, Walter Brownlow. *Religious Strife on the Southern Frontier*. Baton Rouge: Louisiana State University Press, 1965.

Pound, Merritt B. *Benjamin Hawkins, Indian Agent*. Athens: University of Georgia Press, 1951.

Powers, Thomas L. "In Defense of General Thomas Sumter." *Southern Campaigns of the American Revolution* 5, no. 2 (2008): 31–34.

"Presbyterians and the American Revolution: A Documentary Account." *Journal of Presbyterian History* 52 (Winter 1974): 299–500.

Ramsay, David. *The History of the Revolution of South Carolina.* 2 vols. Trenton, N.J., 1785.

Rankin, Hugh F. *Francis Marion: The Swamp Fox.* New York: Thomas Y. Crowell Company, 1973.

Rauch, Steven J. "An Ill-Timed and Premature Insurrection: The First Siege at Augusta, Georgia, September 14–18, 1780." *Southern Campaigns of the American Revolution* 2, no. 9 (September 2005): 1–16.

———. "Southern (Dis)Comfort: British Phase IV Operations in South Carolina and Georgia, May–September 1780." In *The U.S. Army and Irregular Warfare, 1775–2007: Selected Papers from the 2007 Conference of Army Historians,* edited by Richard G. Davis. Washington, D.C.: U.S. Army Center of Military History, 2008.

Reynolds, William R., Jr. *Andrew Pickens: South Carolina Patriot in the Revolutionary War.* Jefferson, N.C.: McFarland, 2012.

Rider, Thomas A., II. "Massacre or Myth: No Quarter at the Waxhaws, 29 May 1780." M.A. thesis, University of North Carolina, 2002.

Royster, Charles. *Light-Horse Harry Lee and the Legacy of the American Revolution.* Baton Rouge: Louisiana State University Press, 1981.

———. *A Revolutionary People at War: The Continental Army and American Character, 1775–1783.* Chapel Hill: University of North Carolina Press, 1979.

Saberton, Ian, ed. *The Cornwallis Papers: The Campaigns of 1780 and 1781 in the Southern Theatre of the American Revolutionary War.* 4 vols. East Sussex, U.K.: Naval and Military Press, 2010.

Sadosky, Leonard J. *Revolutionary Negotiations: Indians, Empires, and Diplomats in the Founding of America.* Charlottesville: University of Virginia Press, 2009.

Saler, Bethel. "An Empire for Liberty, a State for Empire: The U.S. National State before and after the Revolution of 1800." In *The Revolution of 1800: Democracy, Race, and the New Republic,* edited by James Horn, Jan Ellen Lewis, and Peter S. Onuf, 360–82. Charlottesville: University of Virginia Press, 2002.

Salley, A. S., Jr., ed. *The Calhoun Family of South Carolina.* Columbia, S.C.: n.p., 1906.

———, ed. *Col. William Hill's Memoirs of the Revolution.* Columbia, S.C., 1921.

Saunt, Claudio. *A New Order of Things: Property, Power, and the Transformation of the Creek Indians, 1733–1816.* New York: Cambridge University Press, 1999.

Schaper, William. *Sectionalism and Representation in South Carolina.* Washington, D.C.: Government Printing Office, 1901.

Scheer, George F., and Hugh F. Rankin. *Rebels and Redcoats.* New York: World Publishing Co., 1957.

Sciotti, Anthony J. *Brutal Virtue: The Myth and Reality of Banastre Tarleton.* Bowie, Md.: Heritage Books, 2002.

Scoggins, Michael C. "South Carolina's Backcountry Rangers in the American Revolution: 'A Splendid Body of Men.'" In *Cavalry of the American Revolution,* edited by Jim Piecuch, 145–81. Yardley, Pa.: Westholme, 2012.

Shaffer, Arthur H. "Between Two Worlds: David Ramsay and the Politics of Slavery." *Journal of Southern History* 50 (April 1984): 175–96.

Sharp, Rev. E. M. *The Pickens Families of the South*. Memphis, Tenn.: Self-published, 1963. South Caroliniana Library, University of South Carolina, Columbia.

Shy, John. "British Strategy for Pacifying the Southern Colonies, 1778–1781." In *The Southern Experience in the American Revolution*, edited by Jeffrey J. Crow and Larry E. Tise, 155–73. Chapel Hill: University of North Carolina Press, 1978.

———. "A New Look at Colonial Militia." *William and Mary Quarterly*, 3rd ser., 20, no. 2 (April 1963): 175–85.

Silver, Peter. *Our Savage Neighbors: How Indian War Transformed Early America*. New York: Norton, 2008.

Simpson, Richard W. *History of Old Pendleton District, with a Genealogy of the Leading Families of the District*. Covington, Tenn.: Bradford, n.d.

Slaughter, Thomas P. *The Whiskey Rebellion: Frontier Epilogue to the American Revolution*. New York: Oxford University Press, 1986.

Sloan, Herbert E. *Principle and Interest: Thomas Jefferson and the Problem of Debt*. New York: Oxford University Press, 1995.

Smylie, James H. "Presbyterian Clergy and Problems of 'Dominion' in the Revolutionary Generation." *Journal of Presbyterian History* 48, no. 2 (Fall 1970): 161–75.

———. "Presbyterians and the American Revolution: An Interpretive Account." *Journal of Presbyterian History* 54, no. 1 (Spring 1976): 9–32.

Snapp, J. Russell. *John Stuart and the Struggle for Empire on the Southern Frontier*. Baton Rouge: Louisiana State University Press, 1996.

———. "William Henry Drayton: The Making of a Conservative Revolutionary." *Journal of Southern History* 57, no. 4 (November 1991): 637–58.

Sprague, William B. *Annals of the American Pulpit*. Vol. 4. New York, 1858.

Stephenson, Michael. *Patriot Battles: How the War of Independence Was Fought*. New York: HarperCollins, 2007.

Stevens, Michael E. "Legislative Privilege in Post-Revolutionary South Carolina." In *State and Local Politics in the New Nation*, edited by Peter S. Onuf, 485–506. New York: Garland, 1991.

Stevens, William Bacon. *A History of Georgia*. 2 vols. 1859. Savannah: Beehive Press, 1972.

Stokes, Durward T. "The Presbyterian Clergy and the American Revolution." *South Carolina Historical Magazine* 71, no. 4 (October 1970): 270–82.

Swager, Christine R. *Heroes of Kettle Creek, 1779–1782*. West Conshohocken, Pa.: Infinity, 2008.

Symonds, Craig L. *A Battlefield Atlas of the American Revolution*. Baltimore: Nautical and Aviation Publishing Company of America, 1986.

———. "The Failure of America's Indian Policy on the Southwestern Frontier, 1785–1793." *Tennessee Historical Quarterly* 35 (1976): 29–45.

Taylor, Alan. *Slavery and War in Virginia, 1772–1832*. New York: Norton, 2013.

———. *William Cooper's Town: Power and Persuasion on the Frontier of the Early American Republic*. New York: Knopf, 1996.

Thane, Elswyth. *The Fighting Quaker: Nathanael Greene*. New York: Hawthorne, 1972.

Thayer, Theodore. *Nathanael Greene: Strategist of the American Revolution*. New York: Twayne, 1960.

Tortora, Daniel J. "The Alarm of War: Religion and the American Revolution in South Carolina, 1774–1783." *Southern Campaigns of the American Revolution* 5, no. 2 (2008): 43–55.

———. *Carolina in Crisis: Cherokees, Colonists, and Slaves in the American Southeast, 1756–1763.* Chapel Hill: University of North Carolina Press, 2015.

Toulmin, Llewellyn M. "Backcountry Warrior: Brig. Gen. Andrew Williamson; The 'Benedict Arnold of South Carolina' and America's First Double Agent." *Journal of Backcountry Studies* 7, no. 1 (Spring 2012): 1–46.

———. "Brigadier General Andrew Williamson and Whitehall." *Journal of Backcountry Studies* 7 (Fall 2012): 58–98.

Tucker, Spencer C. *Rise and Fight Again: The Life of Nathanael Greene.* Wilmington, Del.: ISI Books, 2009.

Turner, D. K. "General Andrew Pickens (1739–1817)." *Bucks County Historical Collections* 3 (1909): 658–59.

Usner, Daniel H., Jr. *Indians, Settlers, and Slaves in a Frontier Exchange Economy: The Lower Mississippi Valley before 1783.* Chapel Hill: University of North Carolina Press, 1992.

Vann, Barry Aron. *In Search of Ulster-Scots Land.* Columbia: University of South Carolina Press, 2008.

Waddell, Joseph A. *Annals of Augusta County, Virginia, from 1726 to 1871.* Bridgewater, Va.: C. J. Carrier, 1958.

Wallace, Anthony F. C. *Jefferson and the Indians: The Tragic Fate of the First Americans.* Cambridge, Mass.: Harvard University Press, 1999.

Wallace, David Duncan. *History of South Carolina.* 4 vols. New York: American Historical Society, 1934.

———. *South Carolina: A Short History.* Columbia: University of South Carolina Press, 1961.

Ward, Christopher. *The War of the Revolution.* 2 vols. New York: Macmillan, 1952.

Ward, Harry M. *The War for Independence and the Transformation of American Society.* London: University College Press, 1999.

Waring, Alice Noble. *The Fighting Elder: Andrew Pickens (1739–1817).* Columbia: University of South Carolina Press, 1962.

Webb, Jim. *Born Fighting: How the Scots-Irish Shaped America.* New York: Broadway Books, 2004.

Weigley, Russell F. *The American Way of War: A History of United States Military Strategy and Policy.* Bloomington: Indiana University Press, 1973.

———. *The Partisan War: The South Carolina Campaign of 1780–1782.* Columbia: University of South Carolina Press, 1970.

Weir, Robert M. *Colonial South Carolina: A History.* New York: KTO Press, 1983.

———, ed. *The Last of American Freemen.* Macon, Ga.: Mercer University Press, 1986.

———. "Rebelliousness: Personality Development and the American Revolution in the Southern Colonies." In *The Southern Experience in the American Revolution,* edited by Jeffrey J. Crow and Larry E. Tise, 25–54. Chapel Hill: University of North Carolina Press, 1978.

———. "'The Violent Spirit': The Reestablishment of Order, and the Continuity of Leadership in Post-Revolutionary South Carolina." In *An Uncivil War: The Southern Backcountry during the American Revolution,* edited by Ronald Hoffman, Thad W. Tate, and Peter J. Albert, 70–98. Charlottesville: University Press of Virginia, 1985.

Whitaker, Arthur Preston. "Alexander McGillivray, 1783–1789." *North Carolina Historical Review* 5, no. 2 (April 1928): 181–203.

———. "Alexander McGillivray, 1789–1793." *North Carolina Historical Review* 5, no. 3 (July 1928): 289–309.

White, Henry A. *Southern Presbyterian Leaders*. New York: Neale, 1911.

Willcox, William B. *Portrait of a General: Sir Henry Clinton in the War of Independence*. New York: Knopf, 1964.

Wilson, David K. "Civil-Military Relations, Provincialism, and the Southern Command in the Revolution." In *General Nathanael Greene and the American Revolution in the South*, edited by Gregory D. Massey and Jim Piecuch, 56–84. Columbia: University of South Carolina Press, 2012.

———. *The Southern Strategy: Britain's Conquest of South Carolina and Georgia, 1775–1780*. Columbia: University of South Carolina Press, 2005.

Wilson, Howard McKnight. *The Tinkling Spring: Headwater of Freedom*. 2nd ed. Fisherville, Va.: Tinkling Spring and Hermitage Presbyterian Churches, 1974.

Winship, Michael P. *Godly Republicanism: Puritans, Pilgrims, and Massachusetts' City on a Hill*. Cambridge, Mass.: Harvard University Press, 2012.

Wood, Gordon S. *The Americanization of Benjamin Franklin*. New York: Penguin Press, 2004.

———. *The Creation of the American Republic, 1776–1787*. Chapel Hill: University of North Carolina Press, 1969.

———. *Empire of Liberty: A History of the Early Republic, 1789–1815*. New York: Oxford University Press, 2009.

———. *The Radicalism of the American Revolution*. New York: Knopf, 1992.

Wyatt-Brown, Bertram. *Southern Honor: Ethics and Behavior in the Old South*. New York: Oxford University Press, 1983.

Index

Page numbers in italics indicate illustrations.

Dearborn, Henry, 276–78, 280, 281, 283–84, 285

Debtors, 22, 179–80

Declaration of Independence, 51

Deep River, 127

DeLancey's Brigade, 77, 82, 328 (n. 29)

Delawares, 44, 194, 237

Dick (slave). *See* Old Dick

Dickson, Henry, 118, 120

Dinmoor, Silas, 262

Doak, Samuel, 82

Dobbs, Arthur, 11

Dooly, John, 61–62, 64–66, 69

Doublehead (Cherokee chief), 236, 254–55

Douglas, James Alexander, 177

Douglas, John, 11

Dowd, Gregory Evans, xxvii

Downs, Jonathan, 49

Drayton, William, 39–41, 44, 45–46

Duck River 264, 276

Dunlap, James, 88–89, 127–28, 329 (n. 58)

Dutch Fork region, S.C., 29, 40

Dutch Reformed Church, 3

Earle, Elias, 342 (n. 47)

Earle, Samuel, 241

East Florida Rangers, 57, 177

Eaton, Pinkerton, 132–33

Edgar, Walter, 23, 183

Edgefield County, 173

Edict of Fontainebleau, 2

Edict of Nantes, 1

Edisto River, 75

Efau Haujo (Creek chief), 283

Eggleston, Joseph, 120

England, x, 22, 45, 147

Enlightenment, xiv

Enoree River, 81, 128, 144

Eno River, 121

Episcopalians, 55. *See also* Anglicans

Esseneca, 46–47, 51, 199

Estatoe, 17, 48

Etchohih, 17

Ethridge, Robbie, xxvii

Etowah River, 159

Evangelicalism and evangelicals, x, xv–xvi, xxv, xxvii–xxviii, 165, 176, 233, 296–300, 311

Fairforest Creek (and area), 31, 37, 100

Fairforest Regiment 105–6

Federalists, xxii, xxiii, 178, 232–34, 247–48, 250, 252, 262, 267, 271, 273–74

Ferguson, Clyde R., xviii, xxii, 59, 68, 167, 178, 193, 270

Ferguson, Patrick, 68, 85, 86

Few, Benjamin, 88

Fillis (slave), 288, 304

Fish Dam Ford, 64, 129, 141–42

Flax, 203

Fletchall, Thomas, 31, 37–41, 43, 68, 100

Florida, 57, 59, 60, 127, 152, 158, 191, 237, 265

Fort Adams, 279, 281

Fort Charlotte, 43

Fort Cornwallis, 132–37

Fort Fidius, 249

Fort Grierson, 132–36

Fort Tonyn, 58

Fort Wilkinson, 282, 283

France, 1–2, 147, 151, 247–48, 251, 265, 266, 271–72, 273–74, 276

Franklin, Benjamin, xxvii, 343 (n. 57)

Freeman, Constant, 249

Freeman, Holman, 357 (n. 30)

Freeman, Joanne B., xvi

French and Indian War, 7, 15, 98–99

French Broad River, 202–3, 215, 220, 221

French Revolution, 248

Friday's Ferry, 142, 338 (n. 5)

Fulsom's Fort 69

Gaither, Henry, 257, 259

Gallatin, Tenn., 268

Galphin, George, 131

Galphin's (on Savannah River), 132, 134–35

Galphinton (on Ogeechee River), 195, 197–98, 208, 212, 227, 230, 255, 256, 258, 260

Gates, Horatio, 91, 95

and background, 191; and Treaties of
  Hopewell, 194, 197–205
Haw River, 116, 119
Haw's Fields, 119
Hayes, Joseph, 105–6, 155
Hazard (slave), 302–3
Henderson, Richard, 201–2
Henderson, William, 43, 145–47, 150
Hendricks, James, 258–60
Henley, David, 266
Henry, Patrick, xxvii
Hessians, 32, 60, 70
High Rock Ford, 116
Hill, William, 81
Hillsborough, N.C., 89, 116–17, 119, 121,
  334 (n. 14)
Hiwassee, 214, 220–21
Holston River, 202–3, 215, 217, 218, 236
"Honor," xv–xvii, xxiii, xxiv, xxviii, 74,
  85, 90–92, 128, 170, 199, 215–16, 232, 234,
  246, 248, 270–72
Hopewell (house and plantation), xxi,
  174, 183, 185, 195, 208, 209, 217, 220,
  221–23, 230, 232, 254, 263, 268, 281, 287,
  292, 313, 342 (n. 43)
Hopewell Academy, 175, 292, 342 (n. 47)
Hopewell congregation (Long Cane), 173,
  174, 175
Hopewell congregation (Pendleton),
  175–76, 257, 289, 293, 296, 297–98, 309
Hopewell Treaty. See Treaty of Hopewell
Horry, David, 71
House of Representatives (S.C.), 54, 154,
  163, 166, 233, 262, 272, 342 (n. 52).
  See also General Assembly
House of Representatives (U.S.), 250.
  See also Congress
Houstoun, John, 57, 324 (n. 16)
Howard, John Eager, 102, 107–8, 110,
  332 (n. 27)
Howe, Robert, 57–58, 60, 74
Howley, Richard, 77
Huck, Christian, 81–81
Hudson, Angela Pulley, xxvii
Huger, Isaac, 17

Hughes, Joseph, 106
Huguenots, 2, 20, 32, 55
Humphreys, David, 226–30, 349 (n. 82)
Hunter, John, 293
Hutton, Robert, 89
Hycootie Creek, 116

Indian Trade and Intercourse Act, 262
Installment Act, 180
Ireland, x, xii, 1–4. See also Ulster
Iroquois, 10, 44, 194
Irvine, John, 59
Irwin, Jared, 258–59
Isaacs, Samuel, 208–9
Island Ford, 113

Jack (slave), 302–3
Jackson, James, 104, 107–8, 118, 258–60,
  332 (n. 47), 351 (n. 38)
Jacksonborough, S.C., 153–54, 167
Jame (slave), 288, 304
James II, (king of Britain) 2
Jay, John, 251
Jay Treaty, 251–52, 271
Jeffe (slave), 302
Jefferson, Thomas, xxvi, 139, 246, 253, 271,
  273, 281, 284–85, 286, 290, 343 (n. 57);
  and Native Americans, 275–78, 280,
  282–83
Jews, 40, 45, 173
Jobber's Son (Cherokee chief), 215, 236
July (slave), 26, 295, 304, 309

Kades, Tom, 207, 214
Kentucky, 201, 206–7
Keowee River, 46, 56, 174, 181, 183, 184–85,
  199, 209, 289, 323 (n. 50), 345 (n. 63)
Ker, George, 82–83, 92, 328 (n. 29),
  330 (n. 71)
Kerr, John, 3
"Killing Time," 2, 4
Kirk, John, 215
Kirk family, 214–15
Kirkland, Moses, 23, 31, 36, 39, 40, 41, 68
Klein, Rachel, xvii, xxi–xxii, 21, 24, 33

McCluskey, Captain, 254
McCorkall, James, 319 (n. 9)
McDowell, Charles, 159
McGillivray, Alexander, 186, 190–91,
    195–96, 198, 208–12, 217–18, 220–21,
    223–24, 227–31, 237, 240, 242, 261,
    344 (n. 25), 349 (nn. 82, 89)
McGillivray, Lachlan, 190
McGirth, Daniel, 75
McGuire (Tory soldier), 138
McHenry, James, 257–58, 263–65
McIntosh, Lachlan, 191, 193–204 passim
McJunkin, Joseph, 82, 104, 332 (n. 27)
McKay, James, 118, 119
Memphis, Tenn., 277.
    See also Chickasaw Bluffs
Methodists, 20, 54, 299
Miamis, 237
Middle Towns, 17, 51
Militia: brutality and excesses of, xiv,
    xxiii, 72, 87, 135–37, 144–45, 160–61,
    206–7, 244, 255; contributions of, xviii,
    xix, 29, 52–53, 68–69, 72–73, 97–98;
    cooperation with Regulars, 58, 70–71,
    94–95, 109–11, 122–23, 131–32, 135;
    discipline and training of, 46, 52, 65,
    73, 108, 122–23; strategic uses of, xx,
    52–53, 61, 70, 72–73, 97–98, 100, 112–13,
    114, 127, 143; tactics of (*see* Battles,
    campaigns, and sieges, *especially under*
    Cowpens, Eutaw, Guilford Court
    House); Tory (*see* Tories)
Militia Act of 1778, 56–57
Miller, John, 63–64
Miller, John Henry (nephew and
    son-in-law), 293
Miller, Robert, 11–12, 13, 19, 20, 293
Mingo Hom-Massatubley
    (Choctaw chief), 280
Mississippi, 293
Mississippi River, xxii, 186, 193, 196, 250,
    265, 276, 277, 278, 279, 280
Mitchell River, 116
Moderators, 25–26
Monck's Corner, S.C., 141, 145

Monday 324 (n. 57). *See also* Branan
Montagu, Charles, 23–24
Montgomery, Archibald, 17
Moore, James, 54
Moore, John, 63
Moore, Peter N., 10
Moore, William, 11
Moravians, 118
Morgan, Daniel, xx, 90, 94, 95, 98–115
    passim, 122, 127, 139, 331 (n. 15),
    332 (nn. 27, 53), 333 (n. 10)
Morganton, N.C., 298
Moultrie, William, 17, 71, 166, 169, 180,
    242–43, 246, 344 (n. 18)
Mount Zion Society, 55
Muscle Shoals, 205, 238, 265

Nanye-Hi. *See* Ward, Nancy
Nashville, Tenn., 201, 238–39, 242, 276
Natchez, Miss., 276, 277, 279–81
Naturalization Act, 274
Neal, Thomas, 44, 47
Nelson's Ferry, S.C., 79, 327 (n. 19)
New Acquisition District, S.C., 39
Newberry, S.C., 67
Newberry County, 173
New England, 59, 74, 95, 248
New Jersey, 51, 77, 74, 147
New Jersey Volunteers, 77, 84
New Testament. *See* Bible and scriptural
    references
New York, N.Y., 51, 77, 78, 226, 230
New York (colony and state), 77, 79, 82,
    147, 253
Nickajack 254
Niles' Register, 310
Ninety Six, S.C., xvii, xviii, 16, 20, 23–26,
    28, 36, 38, 44, 75, 77–92 passim, 99, 101,
    126, 127, 129–31, 137–40, 141–47, 151–55,
    158, 164–74 passim, 179, 180, 220, 274, 294
Ninety Six, siege of. *See* Battles,
    campaigns, and sieges
Ninety Six Brigade, 71, 72, 210
Ninety Six District, S.C., 19, 29, 34, 37, 40,
    45, 54, 56–57, 59, 63, 71, 81, 85, 125, 151

Ninety Six Regiment, 42, 44–51. *See also* Upper Ninety Six Regiment

Noble, Alexander, 58–59, 90, 293

Noble, Mary Calhoun, 16

Nolichucky, 215

North Carolina, 15, 25, 90, 207, 230, 236, 255, 305; and border disputes, 11, 164, 181, 184; colonial settlement in, 3, 8–11, 13; and Native Americans, xxiv, 9–11, 156–59, 186–87, 193–98, 201–4, 210, 212, 215–21, 308; Presbyterians in, 33, 82, 296, 298; in Revolutionary War, xi, xx, 33, 44–45, 51, 63, 68, 72, 77, 80, 82, 86–87, 89, 99, 101–2, 109, 112–29, 141, 147, 151, 156. *See also* Continental army and soldiers and units: from North Carolina

Norwood, John, 209, 211

Notaly, 214

Nowota (Cherokee chief), 200

Ocmulgee River, 229, 230, 257, 260, 277, 283, 285–86

Oconee (Cherokee village in S.C.), 248

Oconee County, S.C., 51

Oconee Creek (S.C.), 46

Oconee Mountain, 289

Oconee River (Ga.), 190, 195, 211, 213, 223, 227–30, 255, 257, 260, 263, 276–77, 282–85, 349 (n. 82), 355 (n. 41)

Oconee Station, S.C., 253–54

Ogeechee River, 69, 75, 76, 195

Ohio, 194, 358 (n. 48)

Ohio River, 194, 203, 207, 216, 235, 237, 262, 263, 275–76, 278

Old Dick (slave), xxv, xxvi, 26, 94 108–9, 140, 288, 301, 303–4, 309

Old Stone Church, 309, 312. *See also* Hopewell congregation (Pendleton); Stone Meeting House

Old Tassel. *See* Tassel, The

Old Testament. *See* Bible and scriptural references

Oonanootee (Cherokee chief), 200

Orangeburg, S.C., 29, 55, 130, 143, 144, 146

Osborne, Henry, 223, 225–27

Owen, John, 165, 189, 290–91

Panton, Leslie, & Company, 190, 212

Panton, William, 221, 228

Parata (Whig soldier), 160

Paternalism, xxv, 281, 300–305

Patillo, Henry, 296–97

Paxton Township, Pa., 3

Pearis, Richard, 78–83

Pee Dee River, 80, 99, 130

Pendleton, S.C., xi, xiii, 46, 164, 185, 231, 233, 252, 254, 257, 288, 289, 292, 293, 303, 305, 307, 308, 309, 315 (n. 1), 342 (n. 47); courthouse, 254, 273; description, ix, 175–76; slavery in, 295, 297–98, 300–302, 357 (n. 29), 358 (n. 61)

Pendleton County, xxv, 175, 232, 295

Pendleton District, 82, 290

Pennsylvania, x, 1, 3, 4, 7–9, 15, 16, 80, 194, 252, 257, 297. *See also* Philadelphia, Pa.

Perdue, Theda, xxvii

Peter (slave), 300–301

Peterkin (white trader), 213

Philadelphia, Pa., xxii, 3, 34, 53, 81, 152, 181, 236, 242, 243–44, 247, 256, 259, 263, 265, 266, 268

Picken, Andrew (great-great grandfather), 2

Picken, Jean Bonneau (great-great grandmother), 2, 233

Picken, Robert, 2–3

Pickens, Andrew (father), 3, 8–9, 10–11, 12, 13, 19, 21

Pickens, Andrew: ancestry, x, 1–3; "autobiography" of, 293–94; and British parole, xi, xx, 77–79, 83–93; character and reputation of, xi, xvi, xvii, xviii, xxi, xxvii, 12–14, 49, 58, 59, 66–67, 73, 83, 84, 91–92, 110, 115, 128, 132, 140, 165–66, 171–72, 176–77, 226, 229–30, 237, 239–41, 288, 307, 309–12, 342 (n. 52); childhood and early life, 1, 3, 7, 9, 12–14, 17; death, 309; descriptions and personality, ix, xi–xii, xvii, xxviii, 40,